ENCYCLOPEDIA OF BRITISH WRITERS

16TH AND 17TH CENTURIES

Dr. Alan Hager

GENERAL EDITOR
Department of English
SUNY Cortland

Dr. Gregory M. Colón Semenza

ADVISER
Department of English
University of Connecticut

Dr. John Huntington

ADVISER
Department of English
University of Illinois at Chicago

Facts On File, Inc.

Encyclopedia of British Writers, 16th and 17th Centuries

Copyright © 2005 by BOOK BUILDERS LLC

Facts On File, Inc.
132 West 31st Street
New York NY 10001

Library of Congress Cataloging-in-Publication Data

Encyclopedia of British writers, 16th to 18th centuries/[written and developed by Book Builders LLC].
p. cm.
Includes bibliographical references and indexes.
ISBN 0-8160-5495-9 (v. 1) – ISBN 0-8160-5132-1 (set)
1. English literature – Early modern, 1500–1700—Bio-bibliography—Dictionaries. 2. Authors, English—Early modern, 1500–1700—Biography—Dictionaries. 3. English literature—18th century—Bio-bibliography—Dictionaries. 4. Authors, English—18th century—Biography —Dictionaries. I. Title: Encyclopedia of British writers, sixteenth to eighteenth centuries. II. Hager, Alan, 1940– III. Krueger, Christine L. IV. Stade, George. V. Karbeiner, Karen. VI. Book Builders LLC.
PR421.E63 2004
820.9'003—dc22

2004047070

Written and developed by Book Builders LLC

Text design by Rachel L. Berlin
Cover illustration by Smart Graphics
Cover design by Cathy Rincon

Printed in the United States of America

VB Hermitage 10 9 8 7 6 5 4 3 2 1

This book is printed on acid-free paper.

CONTENTS

PREFACE

The entries in *Encyclopedia of British Writers, 16th and 17th Centuries* are designed to familiarize general readers and students with a wide array of writers whom the editors find worthy for their contributions to and impact on world culture. We have augmented the list with entries about figures from the Continent and Americas who influenced British writers. We have included synopses of periods or movements, such as the Reformation and Neoplatonism, which affected or defined many writers of the time; descriptions of institutions, such as the Church of England; and discussions of events, such as the Saint Bartholomew's Day Massacre, which so influenced such writers as Sir Philip Sidney and Christopher Marlowe.

Furthermore, we have included entries for artists, musicians, scientists, and other nonfiction authors, sometimes ones who wrote exclusively in Latin (though translations are readily available). Our choices are based on the two central principles that literature is simply the best writing and that an era of culture must be taken as a whole.

Articles on authors range in length from a few hundred to several thousand words, and they typically include a short biography, a description of major works, and accompanying contemporary bibliographies. Some artists, such as William Shakespeare or Ben Jonson, are well known. Some, such as Mary Astell, have only recently been recognized. Still others, such as Thomas Wilson, remain obscure except to experts but are thought important by the editors. Hierarchies, namely, which authors are thought to be the most valued or influential, are always in flux, and thus, perhaps, some day printers, for example, may be seen as central to the age.

Much of the writing discussed herein is readily available. However, many works are out of print and available only in library collections and on the Internet. These works still deserve to endure—if for no other reason than because of their historical importance—and thus one of the volume's functions is preservation. Another is the active promotion of these authors, certain brilliant men and women, whose words continue to entertain and enlighten.

Encyclopedia of British Writers, 16th and 17th Centuries, of course, cannot replace reading and enjoying the works of the writers and artists whose entries follow, but it will help general readers and student researchers become more informed and appreciative of the works discussed herein. We hope that this encyclopedia creates a critical and historical context for one of the world's greatest ages of the arts and sciences. Within the entries, cross-references, indicated in small capital letters, will lead readers to key influences on the authors and artists; lists of works by and about the authors will point out routes to further reading and appreciation. The selection of figures will make our own age look both large and small. As in the ancient image, we are all dwarfs on the shoulders of giants looking backward.

Alan Hager
General Editor

Gregory M. Colón Semenza
Adviser

INTRODUCTION

Between 1520 and 1650, the population of London soared from about 60,000 to almost 400,000 people, making it the largest city in Europe. Thousands of men and women—including the son of a Stratford-upon-Avon leatherworker, William SHAKESPEARE—left their homes in the countryside and poured into the city located on the Thames River. Although they made the long journey for different reasons, all hoped to benefit from the wealth and prosperity that had helped to transform England in such a short period of time into one of the world's most powerful nations. Historians would later call these people the children of the English RENAISSANCE. And before the end of the 17th century, they and their children would witness not only the greatest literary and artistic revolution in England's long history but also the birth and development of modern politics, law, and science.

Because of this cultural revolution, many present-day students of 16th- and 17th-century England prefer the term *Early Modern* to *Renaissance,* although readers are likely to encounter both terms. While Renaissance ("rebirth" in French) considers the period's significance in relation to Europe's medieval past, that is, the Middle Ages, Early Modern conveys the significance of the period for future eras. It is important to remember that medieval England produced its own magnifi-

cent architecture and literature. Still, historians argue that the Renaissance revived the glorious educational and artistic achievements of ancient Greece and Rome, which had been less important in the Middle Ages than religious issues and projects. Thus, the concept of "rebirth" remains useful today for describing the pivotal events that transformed England in the 16th and 17th centuries.

The most important of these events for our purposes are the Protestant REFORMATION and the emergence of HUMANISM. For centuries the English people had worshipped God according to the rules of the Roman Catholic Church. Although Martin LUTHER's famous stand against the church in 1517 occurred in Germany, it appealed to many Europeans everywhere either because they were disgusted by the corruption of church officials or because they sought a more inward and individualistic religious experience. Luther had rebelled against the oppressive rigidity of the church, which had served to impose upon individuals numerous formal guidelines for the accomplishment of salvation. Highly educated Catholic priests had conducted masses in Latin before their mostly illiterate and uneducated audiences. In contrast, Luther favored a religious experience emphasizing each individual's unique relationship with God and believed that services should be conducted in vernacular (i.e., native) languages, not just in Latin, so that individuals could experience the Bible firsthand. For Luther each individual's faith was the only prerequisite for salvation.

It is possible that England would have remained a Catholic nation had it not been for the personal problems of King Henry VIII. Disturbed by the fact that the first of his six wives, Catherine of Aragon, had failed to give birth to a male heir, Henry, an unfaithful husband, fell in love with one of Catherine's ladies-in-waiting, Anne BOLEYN, whom he impregnated while still married to Catherine. When Pope Clement VII refused to grant Henry a divorce from Catherine, the king took matters into his own hands, manipulating Parliament into declaring his marriage null and void and thereby challenging the authority of the Catholic Church. In 1534 Parliament passed the Act of Supremacy, which declared Henry to be the "Supreme head on earth" of the new CHURCH OF ENGLAND.

Ironically, then, the English Reformation can be said to have been a political, as opposed to a religious, event. The Church of England, in fact, differed little from the Catholic Church during its first 12 years of existence. Everything would change, however, upon the death of Henry VIII in 1547. Henry's only male heir, Edward VI, his 10-year-old son with third wife Jane Seymour, was surrounded by powerful Protestant counselors. The most influential of them, the archbishop of Canterbury, Thomas CRANMER, wrote and issued in 1649 the BOOK OF COMMON PRAYER, a collection of 42 points of religion that effectively transformed England into a Protestant nation.

Imagine living through the changes in England during the middle part of the 16th century. After years and even centuries of Roman Catholic instruction in religious matters, English men and women awakened one day to find that the official religion had changed. What confusion and doubt such a change must have provoked! The problem worsened after the premature death of Edward in 1553 and the crowning of his half sister Mary, the daughter of Catherine of Aragon. A staunch Catholic, Mary immediately worked to restore the authority of Rome by resurrecting the Catholic mass. "Bloody Mary" has become famous mainly because of the hundreds of Protestants who were burned at the stake during her reign, each a MARTYR whose death would, ironically, do more to strengthen than weaken Protestantism.

Mary's death in 1558 left the throne open to Henry's only remaining child, ELIZABETH I, his daughter by Anne Boleyn. Elizabeth's issuance of a revised *Book of Common Prayer* announced her intention to continue the religious reformation that her father and younger brother had initiated. In a period of roughly 20 years, then, English men and women witnessed the transformation of England from a Catholic to a Protestant to a Catholic to a Protestant nation all over again. Furthermore, there were no guarantees that Elizabeth—a young, female monarch with little political experience—would be able to suppress the powerful Catholic factions in England.

As history revealed, Elizabeth did more than stifle religious rebellion. By the end of her reign, England had become one of the most powerful nations in the world; London became an international center of commerce, artistic creativity, and scientific experimentation. Elizabeth allowed these developments to occur by practicing a religious and political philosophy known as "moderation and compromise." Having learned from her sister Mary's unpopularity the costs of excessive governance, Elizabeth did not concern herself too much with what her citizens did and felt in their private lives. Backed by two powerful secretaries of state, Sir William Cecil and Sir Francis Walsingham, the shrewd young queen succeeded in appealing to and earning the love of a majority of her citizens. Rather than denying her womanhood, Elizabeth embraced it, celebrating her unmarried, supposedly virgin status in order to emphasize her "marriage" to her nation, and in the process she transformed herself into an almost mythological being. The 1588 victory of the English military over the invading Catholic, Spanish Armada seemed proof of Elizabeth's divine favor, also symbolizing the triumph of Protestantism over

Catholicism in England. Unfortunately Elizabeth's triumph would not end the bloodshed.

England in the 17th century witnessed much religious turmoil as various factions sought to influence the direction of Protestantism. While the causes of the English Civil War (1642–49) were predominantly political—having to do with the struggle for power between the king and Parliament—religious convictions largely determined which side English men and women supported. Defenders of the king (Royalists) tended to advocate a more conservative form of worship, which their enemies in Parliament viewed as "Popish," or too closely resembling Roman Catholicism. These "Parliamentarians" preferred a congregational form of government—as opposed to the hierarchical one of Roman Catholicism—that allowed individuals to worship according to their own consciences. The wars that raged for nearly a decade ended with the capture, sentencing, and beheading of King Charles I at Whitehall in January of 1649.

For 10 years, England would not be ruled by a king. The period between the execution of Charles I and the RESTORATION of the monarchy in 1660 is called the Interregnum, which means the period "between reigns." During the Interregnum, the victorious opponents of Popery imposed their own religious policies on the nation, in the process outlawing many worldly pastimes and pleasures, such as sports, games, and theatergoing. Predictably the English people resisted the strictness of the new government and longed for their old freedoms. In 1660, they welcomed with open arms into London Charles II, the son of the executed king and the newly appointed monarch of England. Charles's Restoration government quickly issued the Book of Common Prayer, reestablishing the supremacy of the Anglican Church and seemingly restoring stability to a country long at war with itself.

The final chapter in the story of England's religious reformation began in 1685 when James II, the openly Roman Catholic brother of Charles II, came to the throne. His obvious intention to restore Catholicism in England was immediately blocked by his enemies at court, who secretly arranged the invasion of London by James's Protestant daughter, Mary, and her Dutch husband, William of Orange. Terrified, James II fled into France without a fight. The successful takeover of England by William and Mary—known as the "Glorious Revolution" because no blood was shed—ended the Roman Catholic threat once and for all. While defenders of James's right to the throne (known as Jacobites) would arise occasionally over the next few decades, the story of reformation effectively ended in 1688.

The influence of humanism in England cannot really be understood apart from these religious developments. Humanism can be described as the cultural and philosophical life based on the classical world. Its origins are usually traced back to the Italian poet Francis PETRARCH, who first characterized the Middle Ages as the "Dark Ages" and called for greater attention to the achievements of ancient Greece and Rome. This renewed interest in largely secular (nonreligious) learning that both influenced and was influenced by the Reformation. The teachings of Luther and other Protestant reformers such as John CALVIN highlighted the validity of non-Catholic forms of knowledge and celebrated the individual worshipper. As the term would suggest, humanism placed less emphasis on the absolute sovereignty of God and greater emphasis on the dignity of human beings. Humanism is not an antireligious or even a nonreligious philosophy, however. Many progressives saw themselves as Christian humanists because they believed that a greater knowledge of the world led to a greater knowledge of God.

The obvious means to such an end was education. The Italian educator Vittorino da Feltre (1378–1446) revolutionized European education for future clergy members by shifting the medieval emphasis on the practical benefits of reading and writing to the essential value of the liberal arts for individuals. In a sense, we are all students of Vittorino because of our continued reliance on his definition of an appropriate education. Following the example of the ancients, he built a curriculum focused on the study of history, moral philosophy,

Greek and Latin, and even physical education. His ideas spread quickly throughout Italy and eventually throughout Europe. The publication in 1531 of Sir Thomas ELYOT's *The Boke Named the Governour* constituted a crucial moment in England's educational history, for it introduced the ideas propounded by Vittorino into the country.

It is important to stress that the students whom most humanists wished to teach were boys and members of the nobility. Because no more than 2 percent of the population constituted nobility in the early 16th century, the vast majority of Englishmen and almost all English women were simply excluded from the educational revolution. The concept of human dignity would have seemed like a twisted joke to the roughly 80 percent of the population that made up the lowest orders of Renaissance society. For many of these unfortunate souls, cut off from the opportunities celebrated by their social superiors, daily life would have been defined by the painful realities of illiteracy, poverty, disease, and hopelessness.

The growth of the merchant class during the Renaissance did allow some potential for greater social mobility. The transformation of England into a bustling center of trade and industry opened numerous opportunities to men who hoped that financial success would translate into educational success for their children. A young boy named William Shakespeare, for example, would have been permitted to attend the Stratford grammar school because his father, John, a successful leatherworker and moneylender, had worked his way into the local government. Shakespeare's successes as a playwright and shareholder in his acting companies eventually allowed him to purchase both one of the largest houses in Stratford and a coat of arms, which made him a gentleman.

As the case of the Shakespeare family demonstrates, money could buy better educational opportunities, which in turn could lead to social advances. One progressive educator who recognized the positive potential of education for the socially disempowered was Richard MULCASTER. When he published *Positions* in 1581, he argued

that all boys and girls should receive the same basic educational training: "What exercises shall they have? The verie same. What maisters? The same. What circumstance else? All one and the same." Although *Positions* was no best seller in 1581, it would eventually prove highly influential.

It is safe to speculate that neither the spread of humanism nor the Reformation would have been possible had not a German named Johannes Gutenberg perfected the movable-type printing press in 1450. The press was introduced into England about 25 years later by printer William CAXTON. By 1500 more than 9 million books were in print throughout Europe, only about half of which could be described as primarily religious texts. Not only did the press help to spread the ideas of contemporary revolutionaries such as Luther, it also made affordable the classical texts that humanists like Petrarch had been advocating. The availability of books helped the spread of literacy; conversely, the expansion of a literate population increased the demand for books.

The printing press would also succeed in transforming the course of English literature by exposing would-be writers to some of the greatest books ever written. This heightened awareness of the achievements of ancient culture, compounded with the national pride cultivated by Elizabeth, produced a generation of writers eager to match the genius of Homer and Virgil. These authors would attempt to do so, moreover, by writing in their own language. As the poet Edmund SPENSER asked in 1580, "Why a God's name may not we, as else the Greeks, have the kingdom of our own language?" Spenser's literary ambition and his faith in the power of the vernacular reveals the impact of both humanism and the Reformation, and it marks a departure from the type of mindset that governed Renaissance writing prior to Elizabeth's reign. The first masterpiece of the English Renaissance, for instance, Sir Thomas MORE's *Utopia* (1516), was written not in English but in Latin. Over the 60 short years between the composition of *Utopia* and the beginning of Spenser's career, much had changed for the English author.

Unsurprisingly, it was Spenser who set out most deliberately to elevate the status of English literature and language through his writings. His early work, *The Shepheardes Calendar* (1579), announced the arrival of the new English poet by means of a conscious imitation of England's beloved medieval poet, Chaucer. A 12-part pastoral poem written in a deliberately rustic style, *The Shepheardes Calendar* makes clear Spenser's intention to compete with Chaucer from the first line: "Goe little booke: thy selfe present." This tag echoes Chaucer's famous line in *Troilus and Criseyde* (written in the 1380s), "Go, litel bok, go litel myn tragedye." Spenser set his sights even higher in his epic *The Faerie Queene* (1590), a massive political and moral allegory, which he dedicated to Queen Elizabeth I. The first line of Spenser's masterpiece begins, "Lo I the man," words that echo the opening lines of the ancient Roman poet Virgil's *Aeneid*, which was revered by Renaissance readers as perhaps the greatest poem ever written. Spenser's bold suggestion that the English poet might successfully compete with Virgil encouraged other writers to be no less ambitious. Had it not been for Spenser's example, John MILTON, who would brag of experimenting with "things unattempted yet in prose or rhyme" in his *Paradise Lost* (1667), could never have written what would come to be regarded as perhaps the most important epic poem in the English language.

Spenser did much to improve the social status of the poet in 16th- and 17th-century England, but the daily life of the poet was made no easier by his achievement. There was little financial incentive for writing poetry in the 16th century. Poets sold to printers the rights to their works for modest fees. Writers such as Spenser depended upon PATRONAGE, the generosity of aristocratic backers to whom the poets would dedicate their works. In practice, patronage often failed to work; the writings of English poets are riddled with complaints about the stinginess of their patrons.

The only money-making opportunity available to the Renaissance poet was to write plays for the public theaters, since it was common for principal actors and writers to hold shares in their own acting companies. Many poets, such as Sir Philip SIDNEY, refused to do so, believing that public plays represented a debased art form. But Sidney died before he could experience the plays of Shakespeare or Ben JONSON, whose work might have changed his mind. Other than Shakespeare, the most significant dramatist was Christopher MARLOWE, who transformed the stilted, rhyming dramatic verse of an older generation of writers into the naturalistic blank verse (or unrhymed iambic pentameter) that stunned audiences in the 1580s. Plays like *Tamburlaine* and *Dr. Faustus* elevated popular entertainment to the level of serious art. When he embarked upon his own dramatic career in the late 1580s, Shakespeare deliberately chose to imitate what Ben Jonson referred to as Marlowe's "mighty line." Shakespeare's perfection of the blank verse form would result in some of the greatest works of literature in the English language, including *Romeo and Juliet, Hamlet,* and *King Lear.*

Shakespeare's most significant contribution, however, was his creation of complex characters with seemingly unique personalities and distinct ways of expressing themselves. As the famous 18th-century literary critic Samuel Johnson remarked, "no poet ever kept his personages more distinct from each other." One might add that no poet before Shakespeare ever created such psychologically intricate and puzzling personages, characters so alive that they even seem to breathe off of the page.

And it is here that we should pause, because, in a sense, the wheel has come full circle. With few exceptions, characters developed before Shakespeare's plays tended to be secondary to plot and form. After Shakespeare, the dramatic plot seemed to grow out of a central character's personality. If one were to insert Beowulf into Odysseus's poem and Odysseus into Beowulf's, the outcome of both poems would likely remain basically the same. Try plugging in another character for Hamlet, however, and the play would no longer exist. When Hamlet declares that "there is nothing either good or bad but thinking makes it so," he reminds us of the central position of the human in Renaissance thought. How could humankind remain inferior after Luther's spiritual reevaluation of the individual or the humanists' philosophical one?

Seventeenth-century English literature is largely characterized by its increasing celebratory depiction of human beings and the worlds they occupy. When the poet John DONNE defies the annoying light of the sun beams that shine through his bedroom window by exclaiming, "I could eclipse and cloud them with a winke," he employs Hamlet's logic that the universe is nothing without the human beings who perceive and thereby construct it. As Donne would claim later, "It is too little to call man a little world; except God, man is a diminutive to nothing." The century's greatest writer, JOHN MILTON, would not only presume, as a lowly human being, to "justifie the wayes of God to men" through his magisterial epic poem, *Paradise Lost,* but he would also have his most complex character, Satan, surmise that the glory of heaven itself is subordinate to the power of the mind: "The mind is its own place, and in it self / Can make a Heav'n of Hell, a Hell of Heav'n." By the end of the 17th century, in other words, even the greatest and most de-

vout of English religious poems reveals the potent influence of humanist thinking.

Between the Renaissance and the 21st century, English literature and philosophy is defined by a gradual turn inward—away from the necessity of comprehending God as a completely sovereign being and toward the god in man (and, eventually, in woman). As men and women continued to embrace the empowering notion that they, too, might be the makers of meaning and the judges of worldly things, they were participating in the development of a new language for describing their world. Indeed, during Shakespeare's lifetime, Francis BACON would defend the virtues of experimental science, and the birth of another scientific genius, Isaac NEWTON, was only a few decades away. Sixteenth- and 17th-century literature serves as a bridge between the ancient and the modern worlds, balancing the tensions that emerge when revolutionary ideas clash with traditional values. As readers we continue to feel the power of this literature because we witness in these remarkable writings the formation of a surprisingly familiar universe.

Gregory M. Colón Semenza
Adviser

Authors' Timeline

❦

Dates	Author
1304–1374	Petrarch, Francis
1313–1375	Boccaccio, Giovanni
ca. 1422–1491	Caxton, William
ca. 1423–1484	Paston, Margaret
ca. 1424–ca. 1506	Henryson, Robert
1440–1493	Blind Harry
1443–1509	Beaufort, Margaret
fl. 1450	Holland, Richard
1452–1519	Leonardo da Vinci
ca. 1460–ca. 1520	Dunbar, William
ca. 1460–1524	Linacre, Thomas
ca. 1460–1529	Skelton, John
ca. 1465–1536	Boece, Hector
1466–1536	Erasmus, Desiderius
1467–1519	Colet, John
1467–1533	Bourchier, John
1468–1523	Lilly, William
1469–1527	Machiavelli, Niccolò
1473–1543	Copernicus, Nicolaus
1474–1533	Ariosto, Ludovico
ca. 1475–1511	Hawes, Stephen
ca. 1475–1522	Douglas, Gavin
ca. 1475–1552	Barclay, Alexander
1478–1529	Castiglione, Baldassare
1478–1535	More, Sir Thomas
1483–1546	Luther, Martin
fl. 1486	Medwall, Henry

Dates	Author
ca. 1486–1555	Lyndsay, David
1488–1568	Coverdale, Miles
1489–1556	Cranmer, Thomas
ca. 1490–1546	Elyot, Sir Thomas
1490–1549	Boorde, Andrew
1492–1549	Marguerite of Navarre
ca. 1492–1555	Latimer, Hugh
ca. 1494–1536	Tyndale, William
1495–1563	Bale, John
1496–1586	Maitland, Sir Richard
ca. 1497–ca. 1580	Heywood, John
ca. 1498–1547	Hall, Edward
ca. 1500–1546	Brinkelow, Henry
ca. 1501–1536	Boleyn, Anne
1503–1542	Wyatt, Thomas
1504–1575	Parker, Matthew
1505–1544	Roper, Margaret
1505–1556	Udall, Nicholas
1506–1552	Leland, John
1506–1582	Buchanan, George
1509–1564	Calvin, John
1510–1556	Vaux, Thomas
ca. 1513–1548	Parr, Katherine
ca. 1513–1572	Knox, John
1515–1568	Ascham, Roger
1515–1572	Ramus, Peter
1516–1587	Foxe, John

Dates	Author	Dates	Author
1517–1547	Surrey, Henry Howard, Earl of	1544–1595	Tasso, Torquato
1519–1562	Grimald, Nicholas	1544–1596	Puckering, John
ca. 1520–1580	Holinshed, Raphael	1544–1603	Gilbert, William
ca. 1520–1604	Churchyard, Thomas	1545–ca. 1608	Bannatyne, George
1521–1546	Askew, Anne	1545–1612	Gerard, John
1521–1576	Eden, Richard	ca. 1545–1626	Breton, Nicholas
ca. 1523–1581	Wilson, Thomas	1546–1611	Fletcher, Giles, Sr.
ca. 1524–1580	Tusser, Thomas	1547–1617	Cervantes Saavedra, Miguel de
1524–1585	Ronsard, Pierre de	1547–1618	Stanihurst, Richard
ca. 1525–1577	Gascoigne, George	ca. 1547–1619	Hilliard, Nicholas
ca. 1525–1595	Painter, William	1548–1589	Pettie, George
ca. 1525–1605	Stow, John	1548–1600	Bruno, Giordano
1526–1589	Cecil, Mildred	1549–1622	Savile, Sir Henry
1527–1608	Dee, John	ca. 1550–1600	Wilson, Robert
1528–1610	Bacon, Anne Cooke	1550–1587	Whetstone, George
ca. 1529–1591	Puttenham, George	b. ca. 1550	Day, Angel
1530–1566	Hoby, Thomas	1550–1605	Oxford, Edward de Vere, Earl of
ca. 1530–1572	Bassett, Mary	ca. 1550–1605	Davis, John
ca. 1530–1584	Best, George	ca. 1550–1610	Knolles, Richard
ca. 1530–1611	Mulcaster, Richard	ca. 1550–1613	Dowriche, Anne
1530–1566	Hoby, Thomas	ca. 1550–1630	Harvey, Gabriel
ca. 1531–1607	Fortescue, John	1551–1623	Camden, William
1532–1584	Norton, Thomas	ca. 1552–1599	Spenser, Edmund
1533–1592	Montaigne, Michel de	ca. 1552–1616	Hakluyt, Richard
1533–1603	Elizabeth I	1552–1618	Raleigh, Sir Walter
ca. 1534–1590	Lock, Anne Vaughan	1552–1620	Mildmay, Grace
ca. 1535–ca. 1601	North, Thomas	1552–1629	Speed, John
1535–1617	Melville, Sir James	1552–1634	Coke, Edward
ca. 1536–ca. 1606	Golding, Arthur	1552–1637	Holland, Philemon
1536–1608	Sackville, Thomas	ca. 1553–1625	Florio, John
ca. 1537–1577	Lumley, Jane	1553–1633	Munday, Anthony
1537–1598	Preston, Thomas	1554–1586	Sidney, Philip
ca. 1538–1599	Scot, Reginald	1554–1600	Hooker, Richard
ca. 1539–1583	Gilbert, Humphrey	ca. 1554–1606	Lyly, John
ca. 1539–1608	Fenton, Geoffrey	1554–1624	Gosson, Stephen
fl. 1540	Lisle, Honor	1554–1628	Greville, Fulke
1540–1594	Googe, Barnabe	ca. 1555–ca. 1610	Stubbes, Philip
ca. 1540–ca. 1610	Turberville, George	1555–1626	Andrews, Lancelot
1542–1587	Stuart, Mary	ca. 1556–1610	Montgomerie, Alexander
1542–1617	Rich, Barnabe	1556–1614	Melville, James
1543–1607	Dyer, Edward	1556–1625	James I of England
1543–1613	Bodley, Thomas	1556–1625	Lodge, Thomas
1543–1623	Byrd, William	ca. 1557–1602	Morley, Thomas

Dates	Author
1557–1592	Watson, Thomas
1557–1625	Gorges, Arthur
1558–1592	Greene, Robert
1558–1594	Kyd, Thomas
1558–1596	Peele, George
ca. 1558–1609	Warner, William
ca. 1558–1633	Fraunce, Abraham
ca. 1559–1634	Chapman, George
fl. 1560	Howell, Thomas
ca. 1560–ca. 1607	Chettle, Henry
1560–1621	Hariot, Thomas
1560–1627	Heywood, John
ca. 1560–ca. 1630	Reynolds, Henry
ca. 1561–1595	Southwell, Robert
1561–1612	Harington, John
1561–1621	Sidney, Mary
1561–1626	Bacon, Francis
1562–1613	Constable, Henry
1562–1619	Daniel, Samuel
1563–1618	Sylvester, Joshua
1563–1626	Dowland, John
1563–1631	Drayton, Michael
1564–1593	Marlowe, Christopher
1564–1616	Shakespeare, William
1564–1622	Roydon, Matthew
ca. 1565–1618	Davies of Hereford, John
1565–1647	Meres, Francis
1566–1625	James I of England
1566–1638	Hoskins, John
fl. 1567	Whitney, Isabella
1567–1601	Nashe, Thomas
1567–1620	Campion, Thomas
1567–1650	Parkinson, John
ca. 1568–1615	Armin, Robert
ca. 1568–1635	Fairfax, Edward
ca. 1568–1637	Markham, Gervase
1568–1639	Wotton, Sir Henry
1568–1640	Alabaster, William
1569–1609	Barnes, Barnabe
1569–1626	Davis, John
1569–1645	Lanyer, Aemelia
ca. 1570–ca. 1624	Rowley, Samuel
ca. 1570–ca. 1630	Rowlands, Samuel

Dates	Author
ca. 1570–1632	Dekker, Thomas
1570–1638	Ayton, Robert
ca. 1570–ca. 1640	Melville, Elizabeth
1571–1631	Cotton, Sir Robert Bruce
1571–1633	Hoby, Margaret
1572–1631	Donne, John
1572–1637	Jonson, Ben
1572–1642	Mabbe, James
ca. 1573–1641	Heywood, Thomas
1574–1596	Willobie, Henry
ca. 1574–ca. 1601	Guilpin, Everard
1574–1627	Barnfield, Richard
ca. 1574–ca. 1640	Day, John
1574–1656	Hall, Joseph
1575–1615	Stuart, Arbella
ca. 1575–1626	Tourneur, Cyril
1575–1629	Hayman, Robert
ca. 1575–1634	Marston, John
ca. 1575–1640	Swetnam, Joseph
1575–1641	Baker, Father Augustine
1576–1632	Weever, John
ca. 1576–ca. 1634	Peacham, Henry
1576–1640	Alexander, William
1577–1617	Coryate, Thomas
ca. 1577–1626	Purchas, Samuel
1577–1640	Burton, Robert
1577–1640	Rubens, Peter Paul
fl. 1578	Tyler, Margaret
1578–1657	Harvey, William
1578–1664	Sandys, George
1579–1625	Fletcher, John
fl. 1580s	Anger, Jane
1580–1627	Middleton, Thomas
1580–1631	Smith, John
ca. 1580–ca. 1634	Webster, John
1580–1653	Taylor, John
1581–1612	Weston, Elizabeth Jane
1581–1613	Overbury, Thomas
1581–1656	Ussher, James
1582–1621	Barclay, John
1582–1635	Corbet, Richard
1582–1650	Fletcher, Phineas
1583–1625	Gibbons, Orlando

Dates	Author
1583–1640	Massinger, Philip
ca. 1583–ca. 1643	Townshend, Aurelian
1583–1648	Herbert, Edward
fl. 1584	Wheathill, Anne
1584–1616	Beaumont, Francis
1584–1656	Hales, Thomas
ca. 1585–1623	Fletcher, Giles, Jr.
ca. 1585–1626	Rowley, William
1585–1639	Carey, Elizabeth, Lady, Viscountess Falkland
1585–1649	Drummond of Hawthornden, William
1586– ca. 1639	Ford, John
1587–1619	Field, Nathan
1587–1642	Kynaston, Francis
1587–1653	Wroth, Mary
1588–1667	Wither, George
1588–1679	Hobbes, Thomas
ca. 1590–1652	Brome, Richard
1590–1652	Davies, Eleanor
1590–1657	Bradford, William
1590–1676	Clifford, Anne
fl. 1590s	University Wits
1591–1643	Hutchinson, Anne
ca. 1591–1645	Browne, William
1591–1674	Herrick, Robert
d. 1592	Ascham, Margaret
1592–1644	Quarles, Francis
1592–1669	King, Henry
1593–1633	Herbert, George
ca. 1593–1666	Howell, James
1593–1683	Walton, Izaak
ca. 1594–1640	Carew, Thomas
1594–1666	Ware, James
1596–1622	Jocelyn, Elizabeth
1596–1650	Descartes, Rene
1596–1662	Stuart, Elizabeth
1596–1666	Shirley, James
ca. 1597–ca. 1630	Speght, Rachel
1598–1645	Harley, Brilliana
1598–1672	Johnson, Edward
1599–1641	Van Dyck, Anthony
1600–1662	Heylyn, Peter

Dates	Author
1600–1669	Prynne, William
1600–1675	Makin, Bathsua
ca. 1600–ca. 1678	Flecknoe, Richard
ca. 1601–1665	Earle, John
1602–1644	Chillingworth, William
d. 1603	Caldwell, Elizabeth
d. 1603	Grymeston, Elizabeth
1603–1629	Lindsay, Christian
1603–1665	Digby, Sir Kenelm
1603–1676	Benlowes, Edward
ca. 1604–1668	Felltham, Owen
1604–1690	Eliot, John
1605–1635	Randolph, Thomas
1605–1654	Habington, William
1605–1660	Hammond, Henry
1605–1682	Browne, Thomas
1605–1686	Dugdale, Sir William
1606–1668	Davenant, William
1606–1687	Waller, Edmund
1608–1661	Fuller, Thomas
1608–1666	Fanshawe, Richard
1608–1674	Milton, John
1609–1642	Suckling, Sir John
1609–1674	Hyde, Edward
1609–1676	Hale, Matthew
1609–1676	Winstanley, Gerrard
1609–1680	Carey, Mary
1611–1643	Cartwright, William
1611–1660	Urquhart, Thomas
1611–1677	Harrington, James
1612–1650	Graham, James
1612-1672	Bradstreet, Anne Dudley
1612–1680	Butler, Samuel
1612–1683	Killigrew, Thomas
ca. 1613–1649	Crashaw, Richard
1613–1658	Cleveland, John
1613–1667	Taylor, Jeremy
1613–1686	Pearson, John
1614– 1687	More, Henry
1614–1702	Fell, Margaret
fl. 1615	Swetnam, Joseph
1615–1657	Lilburne, John
1615–1664	Hutchinson, Lucy
1615–1669	Denham, John

Dates	Author
1615–1691	Baxter, Richard
fl. 1616	Leigh, Dorothy
ca. 1616–1658	Thimelby, Katherine
1616–1703	Wallis, John
1616–1704	L'Estrange, Roger
fl. 1617	Munda, Constantia
fl. 1617	Sowernam, Ester
ca. 1617–1668	Aston, Gertrude
1617–1692	Ashmole, Elias
1617–1688	Cudworth, Ralph
ca. 1617–1692	Ludlow, Edmund
1618–ca. 1657	Lovelace, Richard
1618–1667	Cowley, Abraham
1618–1690	Thimelby, Winefrid
1619–1689	Chamberlayne, William
fl. 1620	Clinton, Elizabeth
1620–1666	Brome, Alexander
1620–1706	Evelyn, John
ca. 1621–1664	Fowler, Constance Aston
1621–1666	Vaughan, Thomas
1621–1669	Cavendish, Jane
1621–1678	Marvell, Andrew
1621–1695	Vaughan, Henry
1622–1673	Molière
ca. 1622–ca. 1680	Trapnel, Anna
1622–1699	Halkett, Anne
1623–1657	Cary, Patrick
1623–1662	Pascal, Blaise
1623–1673	Newcastle, Margaret Cavendish, Duchess of
ca. 1623–ca. 1680	Woolley, Hannah
1623–1704	Lead, Jane
1624–1691	Fox, George
1625–1678	Rich, Mary
1625–1678	Stanley, Thomas
1625–1680	Fanshawe, Ann
1626–1663	Brackley, Elizabeth, Viscountess
1626–1697	Aubrey, John
1626–1698	Howard, Robert
1627–1691	Boyle, Robert
1627–1695	Osborne, Dorothy
1627–1696	Wilson, John
1627–1706	Thornton, Alice

Dates	Author
1628–1687	Buckingham, George Villiers, Duke of
1628–1688	Bunyan, John
1628–1699	Temple, William
1629–1696	Biddle, Hester
fl. 1630	Primrose, Diana
1630–1669	Alleine, Theodosia
ca. 1630–ca. 1679	Wentworth, Anne
1630–1687	Cotton, Charles
1630–1694	Tillotson, John
1631–1664	Philips, Katherine
1631–1678	Conway, Anne
1631–1700	Dryden, John
fl. 1632	Sutcliffe, Alice
1632–1695	Wood, Anthony à
1632–1704	Locke, John
ca. 1633–1685	Dillon, Wentworth
1633–1695	Savile, Sir George
1633–1703	Pepys, Samuel
1634–1680	Wanley, Nathaniel
1634–1716	South, Robert
1635–1713	Sprat, Thomas
1636–1680	Glanvill, Joseph
1636–ca. 1692	Etherege, George
fl. 1637	Fage, Mary
1637–1674	Traherne, Thomas
1637–1686	Head, Richard
1637–1701	Fuller, Francis
1637–1711	Ken, Thomas
1637–1711	Rowlandson, Mary
ca. 1639–1699	Racine, Jean
1639–1701	Sedley, Charles
fl. 1640	Chidley, Katherine
fl. 1640–1660	Turner, Jane
1640–1689	Behn, Aphra
1640–1692	Shadwell, Thomas
1640–1703	Crowne, John
fl. 1641	Weamys, Anna
1641–1707	Sherlock, William
1641–1713	Rymer, Thomas
1641–1716	Wycherley, William
1642–ca. 1673	Carleton, Mary
1642–1727	Newton, Sir Isaac
1642–1729	Taylor, Edward

Dates	Author	Dates	Author
1643–1715	Burnet, Gilbert	1660–1685	Killigrew, Anne
1643–1737	Strype, John	1660–1746	Southerne, Thomas
fl. 1644	Hume, Anna	1661–1719	Garth, Samuel
1645–1712	Godolphin, Sidney	1662–1735	Atterbury, Francis
1645(8)–1721	Sheffield, John	1662–1742	Bentley, Richard
fl. 1647	Wight, Sarah	1663–1704	Brown, Thomas
1647–1680	Rochester, John Wilmot, Earl of	1663–1709	Walsh, William
1648–1708	Blow, John	1663–1718	Motteux, Peter Anthony
1648–1724	Settle, Elkanah	d. 1664	Chevers, Sarah
ca. 1650–1693	Cellier, Elizabeth	1664–1726	Vanbrugh, John
1650–1726	Collier, Jeremy	ca. 1665–1685	Bathurst, Elizabeth
fl. 1651	Weamys, Anna	1665–1685	Evelyn, Mary
1651–1691	Mollineux, Mary	1666–1720	Pix, Mary
1652–1685	Otway, Thomas	1666–1731	Astell, Mary
1652–1715	Dampier, William	1667–1702	Pomfret, John
1652–1715	Tate, Nahum	1667–1731	Ward, Edward
1652–1732	Barker, Jane	fl. 1669	Boothby, Francis
1653–1683	Oldham, John	1670–1722	Toland, John
1653–1692	Lee, Nathaniel	1670–1723	Egerton, Sarah Fyge
1653–1723	D'Urfey, Thomas	1670–1729	Congreve, William
1657–1711	Norris, John	fl. 1679	Ephelia
1657–1732	Luttrell, Narcissus	fl. 1690	Drake, Judith
1659–1685	Wharton, Anne	d. 1692	Evans, Katherine
1659–1733	Dunton, John		

A

Admiral's Men (Lord Howard's Men)
theater troupe

The Admiral's Men was a theater troupe in Elizabethan and Jacobean England. The troupe was originally known as Lord Howard's Men, after their patron, Charles Howard, first Earl of Nottingham. When Howard was made Lord High Admiral of the Navy in 1585, the troupe changed its name.

The Admiral's Men was the chief rival to William SHAKESPEARE's CHAMBERLAIN's MEN, which became known as the KING's MEN when JAMES I OF ENGLAND became their patron in 1603. The Admiral's Men and the Chamberlain's Men were the two most popular troupes in London. The two rival companies sometimes played together at the same theater or alternated with each other. In 1594, for example, records indicate the Admiral's Men and Shakespeare's troupe played at Newington Butts at the same time. The Admiral's Men, whose most famous actor was Edward Alleyn, had several major plays in its repertoire, including Christopher MARLOWE's *Doctor Faustus* (1589) and *Tamburlaine* (1586–87).

Although the company toured and shifted ownership and actors, it spent most of its time attached to a single theater. First, it was connected to The Theatre through 1591 until a dispute with the owner, Richard Burbage, led them to the Rose Theatre, owned by Philip Henslowe. The troupe remained at the Rose until 1600, then moved to The Fortune, also owned by Henslowe, remaining there until 1621, when the theater burned down.

In 1603 Prince Henry, eldest son of James I, became the patron of the company, changing their name to Prince Henry's Men. When he died in 1612, the king's son-in-law, Elector Palatine, became their patron, prompting another name change. With the destruction of The Fortune in 1621, the company lost many of its props and promptbooks. Although the troupe moved to a rebuilt Fortune Theatre, it never regained its former position as a strong rival to Shakespeare's company. The Admiral's Men disbanded in 1631.

Alabaster, William (1568–1640)
theologian, poet, dramatist

William Alabaster was born at Hadleigh, Suffolk, England, and educated at Westminster School and Trinity College Cambridge. His first published work was a tragedy in Latin, *Roxana* (1532), which was performed at Trinity College. The play tells the story of King Moleo, whose ghost returns and exacts revenge upon Oromasdes, who has usurped Moleo's throne and fallen in love with his daughter,

Roxana. Samuel Johnson praised this play—for the beauty of its Latin verse—in his *Life of Milton*, saying, "If we produced anything worthy of note before the [Latin] elegies of Milton, it was perhaps Alabaster's *Roxana*."

Alabaster also wrote an epic poem, in Latin, in praise of ELIZABETH I (*Elisaeis* (ca. 1591)), which describes her difficult life during the reign of her half sister, Queen Mary. Only the first part survives, but it was admired by Edmund SPENSER in his dedication to *Colin Clouts Come Home Againe*.

Alabaster announced his conversion to Roman Catholicism after accompanying the Earl of Essex on a raid of Cadiz, Spain, in 1597. His openness about this conversion was unwise given the anti-Catholic feeling in England at the time, and he was imprisoned in the Tower of London, then placed under house arrest. At least one of his English sonnets, number 51, may date from that time. He ends the poem with a paradox, suggesting that only while in jail was he free to acknowledge his religion:

> Free men are bound: I never knew ere this,
> That so great liberty in prison is.

Alabaster escaped to Europe. While in Rome he was imprisoned by the Inquisition because one of his theological works was perceived as heretical. He escaped again, choosing to return to England and converting to Protestantism in 1613 or 1614.

Alabaster's English poems were not published in full until 1959, and some modern critics believe he deserves more recognition than he has received. His religious passion almost rivals John DONNE's, and as he notes in a sonnet entitled "My Friends, whose kindness doth their judgements blind," his religious devotion cost him greatly:

> This is the bill: dearness, affection,
> Friends, fortune, pleasure, fame, hope, life
>   undone,
> Want, prison, torment, death, shame—
>   what behind?
> Is then my sense transel'mented to steel,

> That neither this, nor that, nor all, can feel,
> Nor can it bend my mind[?]

He asks the questions—has he given up too much? suffered too much?—and in the final lines answers, saying he feels:

> a double grief that for Christ's sake
> I have no more to spend, nor have spent that.

Alabaster is often included among the later metaphysical poets.

Alexander, William (ca. 1576–1640) *poet, dramatist*

William Alexander, a Scottish poet and playwright of the Elizabethan period, had an influential political career. He was born at Menstrie in Clackmannanshire, Scotland, and educated at the Universities of Glasgow and Leiden. He distinguished himself as a poet and was appointed tutor to Prince Henry of Scotland. He served the royal court of King James VI of Scotland and accompanied the king to London upon his ascension to the throne as King JAMES I OF ENGLAND. In 1621 Alexander was granted lands in Canada, which he named Nova Scotia or New Scotland. He was later appointed secretary of state of Nova Scotia. In 1633 he was made Earl of Stirling.

Alexander is best known for his collection of 106 sonnets, as well as some songs and elegies, entitled *Aurora* (1604), which he wrote while at the court of James I. Many of these are courtly love poems, influenced by Italian and French sonneteers. One of the most famous in this collection, number 221, tells the story of the goddess of the dawn, Aurora, and her human lover Tithon. Alexander portrays the goddess driving her chariot across the sky, raining dew "upon the rural plains, / When from thy bed she passionately goes," and says that Tithon is "favour'd by the fates" to be the beloved of "one so worthy." In number 178, Alexander tells his lover not to "bear the burthen of . . . [her] griefs alone," continuing sweetly, "No I would have my share in what were thine: / And whilst we thus should make our sorrows one / This happy harmony would make them none." Unlike other Scottish poets of the era, Alexander wrote in English.

His play *The Monarchicke Tragedies* (1607) is a dramatic tragedy that deals with four monarchs of the ancient world: Croesus, Darius, Alexander, and Julius Caesar.

Alleine, Theodosia (ca. 1630–ca. 1669)
nonfiction writer

Theodosia Alleine was born in Ditcheat, Somerset, the daughter of Richard Alleine, a preacher. In 1659 she married her cousin Joseph Alleine, a Puritan clergyman who was himself a writer. (His main work is *An Alarm to the Unconverted*, otherwise known as *The Sure Guide to Heaven*, published posthumously in 1672 and immensely popular in its day.) Joseph Alleine was the assistant pastor of a church in Taunton, Somerset, and well known for his preaching. The couple maintained a school in their home in Taunton, with Theodosia serving as a teacher. After the RESTORATION of King Charles II Joseph Alleine's Puritan views were no longer in favor; he lost his job, and when he persisted in preaching was twice imprisoned. Although his stays in prison were not long, they broke his health.

After her husband's untimely death in 1668 at the age of 34, Theodosia Alleine wrote a biography, *Life and Death of The Rev. Joseph Alleine* (1672). She describes his piety and zeal reverently:

> All the time of his health he did rise constantly at or before four o'clock, and on the Sabbath sooner, if he did wake; he would be much troubled if he heard any smiths, or shoemakers, at work in their trades before he was at his duties with God; saying to me after, "Oh how this noise troubles me! doth not my master deserve more than theirs?

Her account of his arrest and imprisonment is dramatic and touching. There may be a suggestion of mixed feelings over her twin roles of wife and sup-portive companion when she reports his customary answer to her complaint that he spent too little time with her. He would say, "Ah, my dear, I know thy soul is safe; but how many that are perishing have I to look after! Oh that I could do more for them!" Theodosia Alleine is remembered today as one of the first women to write and publish in the biographical or autobiographical genre.

Andrews, Lancelot (Lancelot Andrewes)
(1555–1626) *nonfiction writer, translator*

Lancelot Andrews was born in London, the son of a merchant. He was educated at Merchants Taylors' School and Pembroke College, Cambridge University, taking holy orders in 1580.

Andrews became bishop of Chichester in 1605, of Ely in 1609, of Winchester in 1618, and dean of the Chapel Royal in 1619. He served as a chaplain to both ELIZABETH I and JAMES I OF ENGLAND.

Andrews spoke 15 languages, and in 1617 he became one of the translators of the King James Bible (*see* BIBLE, KING JAMES VERSION). He directed the group responsible for the first five books, and those of Joshua through II Kings. Adam Nicolson, writing about the translators, shows that Andrews advocated many of the practices of the Roman Catholic Church, such as the use of incense, but did not acknowledge the pope as head of the church on earth. The language of his translations suggests similar ideas. As Nicolson says, Andrews's style was deliberately archaic, reflecting the search for "true meaning in the most ancient and hence the most reliable texts."

Andrews wrote devotional works and prayers. Little was published in his lifetime, but 96 of his sermons were published in 1628, edited by William Laud, archbishop of Canterbury from 1633 to 1645, and John Buckeridge, bishop of Rochester. Andrews was much admired for his style, which included extended comparisons. For example, in this excerpt he compares Jesus Christ to a wounded deer:

> It is well known that Christ and His cross were never parted, but that all His life long was a

continual cross. At the very cratch [manger], His cross began. . . . He was in the psalm of the Passion . . . a morning hart, that is, a hart roused early in the morning; as from His birth He was by Herod, and hunted and chased all His life long, and this day brought to an end, and as the poor deer, stricken and wounded to the heart. This was His last, last and worst; and this we properly call His cross, even this day's suffering.

The English of the King James Bible, penned by men like Andrews, became part of the language used by writers over many generations. The strength, beauty, and clarity of their translation can be seen from the opening chapters of Genesis: "In the beginning God created the Heauen, and the Earth. And the earth was without forme, and voyd, and darkenesse was vpon the face of the deepe: and the Spirit of God mooued vpon the face of the waters." Andrews and the other translators struggled to be as accurate in their translation as possible, but they did much more than remain faithful to the text.

Anger, Jane (fl. 1580s) *pamphleteer*

Jane Anger is the pseudonym of an unknown writer, author of the earliest known feminist writing in English, Anger's pamphlet *Her Protection for Women* (1589) was written as a response to *Boke His Surfeit in Love, with a farwel to the folies of his own phantasie* (1588) by Thomas Orwin, who asserted that women were untrustworthy.

The pamphlet is perhaps the most radical of all the pamphlets written about the nature of woman during this period. While other women writers such as Constantia MUNDA and Ester SOWERNAM argued for equal status of women (at least in the eyes of God), Anger argued for the *superiority* of women. She writes that "the Gods," in order to prevent women from being overproud of their many virtues, "bestowed the supremacy over us to men, that of that Cockscomb [the red comb of a rooster, signifying the male gender, but the word also meant "fool"] he might only boast. And therefore,

for God's sake let them keep it!" She also criticizes the double standard of sexual behavior that allows men to do what they please while women are punished for being openly sexual. She even advocates separation from men as a solution to the problem of being attacked by them.

Anger's pamphlet is very much of its time in its style and method of argumentation. Her style is euphuistic, that is, similar to the elaborate and witty style of John LYLY, in its balanced sentences, and references to natural history as parallel to the human situation. For example, in her indictment of men she notes that "The Tiger is robbed of her young ones, when she is ranging abroad, but men rob women of their honor undeservedly under their noses." She also follows Lyly in her use of alliteration. She says, for example, that women "languish when . . . [men] laugh, we lie sighing when they sit singing, and sit sobbing when they lie slugging and sleeping."

Anger demonstrates that she is a learned person in that she is able to allude to works by many ancient authors. For example, she refers to Plato's work *Euthydemus,* in which, she says, the philosopher said there were "five kinds of women." She also refers to the Bible, ancient history, and mythology, and she peppers her pamphlets with Latin quotations. On the other hand, she is not above mudslinging, if it will support her arguments about the superiority of women. She says, for instance, that men would be lost without women. Women take care of them when they are sick, cook their food, make their clothes, and ensure that they are clean. "Without our care," she says pointedly, "they lie in their beds as dogs in litter." She also uses scholarly argumentation to prove that women are wiser than men:

> There is no wisdom but it comes by grace this is a principle . . . but grace was first given to a woman, because to our lady: which premises conclude and women are wise. . . . and therefore women are wiser than men.

Only one copy of Anger's *Protection* has survived, and it was not reprinted until 1996—as critics and scholars began to reassess the literature of the RENAISSANCE to include women writers.

Works about Jane Anger

O'Malley, Susan Gushee, ed. *Defences of Women: Jane Anger, Rachel Speght, Ester Sowernam, and Constantia Munda.* Brookfield, Vt.: Ashgate Publishing Company, 1996.

Woodbridge, Linda. *Women and the English Renaissance: Literature and the Nature of Womankind.* Urbana: University of Illinois Press, 1984.

Anglican Church

See CHURCH OF ENGLAND.

Arcasia

See BOOTHBY, FRANCES.

Ariosto, Ludovico (1474–1533) *poet, playwright*

Ludovico Ariosto was born in Reggio Emilia, Italy, the eldest of 10 children of Count Niccolò Ariosto. When he was 10, the family moved to Ferrara, and he was educated there, studying law and classical languages. After the death of his father in 1400, Ariosto took care of the family estates for a time, but in 1503 he took a position in the service of Cardinal Ippolito d'Este. Although the cardinal was very demanding, Ariosto's job allowed him enough time to write. He wrote sonnets and *canzoni* (songs) and began composing *Orlando Furioso* (1505), the romantic epic poem for which he is most famous; a version was published in 1516. In 1518 he moved to the employ of the cardinal's brother, Alfonso I, duke of Ferrara. One of his jobs at the Ferrara court was to organize productions of plays by the classical Roman playwrights Plautus and Terence; inspired by this work, Ariosto wrote five comedies, which use devices such as secret marriages and servants arranging marriages for their masters. He also wrote seven verse satires that reveal some of the hardships of court life.

In 1522 the duke sent Ariosto to govern the Garfagnana region of the Alps, a thankless job from which he escaped three years later. Back in Ferrara, he apparently married, secretly, a widow named Alessandra Benucci whom he had first met in 1509. He continued to work on *Orlando Furioso*. The enlarged and definitive edition was published in 1532. He started work on a sequel, *Cinque Canti* ("Five Cantos"), but died without finishing it.

Orlando Furioso is a continuation of *Orlando Innamorato* (Orlando in love) by Matteo Maria Boiardo, which Boiardo had left unfinished at his death in 1494. The setting is war between Christians and Muslims, with Charlemagne, king of France, and Marsilio, king of Spain, leading their forces against Agramante, king of North Africa, who seeks to invade France and impose the Muslim faith. There are two main plot lines, one involving the love of the warrior Orlando for Angelica, which drives Orlando mad ("furioso") because Angelica does not return it. The other involves the love of Ruggiero, one of Agramante's warriors, for the beautiful female warrior Bradamante; the union of Ruggiero and Bradamante is portrayed as the foundation of the d'Este dynasty, the family of Ariosto's patrons. But *Orlando Furioso* is famous for hurling many characters through fantastic adventures at breakneck speed, so that the overall plan is difficult to perceive. Ariosto's declaration of his intentions in the opening lines (quoted in Harington's translation) gives an idea of the work's breadth:

> Of Dames, of Knights, of armes, of loves delight,
> Of courtesies, of high attempts I speake . . .

His knights and ladies encounter duels, monsters, sorcerers, love, betrayal, and deceit, described with humor, pathos, and sympathy in a style that never allows the reader's attention to flag.

Torquato TASSO drew many of the ideas in his *Gerusalemme Liberata* from Ariosto's work. An English translation of *Orlando Furioso* by Sir John HARINGTON was published in 1591. It was a central influence on Edmund SPENSER's *Faerie Queene* and also influenced SHAKESPEARE, MILTON, and later English poets such as Byron.

Works about Ludovico Ariosto

Ascoli, Albert Russell. *Ariosto's Bitter Harmony: Crisis and Evasion in the Italian Renaissance.* Princeton, N.J.: Princeton University Press, 1987.

Beecher, Donald, Massimo Ciavolella, and Roberto Fedi, eds. *Ariosto Today: Contemporary Perspectives.* Toronto: University of Toronto Press, 2003.

Finucci, Valeria, ed. *Renaissance Transactions: Ariosto and Tasso.* Durham, N.C.: Duke University Press, 1999.

Shapiro, Marianne. *The Poetics of Ariosto.* Detroit: Wayne State University Press, 1988.

Armin, Robert (ca. 1568–1615) *nonfiction writer, playwright*

Robert Armin was born in King's Lynn, Norfolk, England, to a tailor named John Armin. He became a goldsmith before he earned his fame as the accomplished clown of the leading dramatic company of his day.

Armin joined the CHAMBERLAIN'S MEN (the acting company for which William SHAKESPEARE was the principal playwright) by 1599. Armin played the clown, a major character in many plays. Prior to his arrival, Shakespeare's clowns were rustic simpletons. The roles associated with Armin, however, include Touchstone of *As You Like It* (1599), Feste of *Twelfth Night* (1600), and the Fool of *King Lear* (1604). All of these characters are professional clowns whose witty jests offer important, if ironic, observations about the world and the main characters of each play. It is likely that Shakespeare wrote these roles with Armin in mind, catering to his talents. Thus, Armin may be seen as a collaborator with Shakespeare in these works.

Also a talented musician, Armin may have created the original melodies for the many songs he was assigned in the plays, and perhaps even some of the words. As Armin biographer Charles S. Felver states, "[t]he anecdotes, jests, and comic turns" that Armin collected in his works and shared with his fellow actors "were drawn upon by Shakespeare in delineating Touchstone, Feste, the Fool in *Lear,* and other comic parts and comic business."

Though this collaboration in the creative process of some of the greatest plays ever written should be regarded as Armin's primary literary achievement, he was also the author of several pamphlets during his days as a goldsmith's apprentice, though most are now lost. *Fool Upon Fool, or Six Sorts of Sots* (1600) catalogues some of Armin's real and supposed encounters with foolish residents of his homeland. *Quips upon Questions,* published the same year, consists of rhymed humorous verses.

Armin's play *The Two Maids of Moreclacke* (1608) suffers from confusing and inadequate plotting, but it is interesting because the two fools in the play both sound like those in Shakespeare's later work. One of the clowns, John, sings snatches of seemingly irrelevant songs, very reminiscent of the Fool in *Lear,* while the other clown, Tutch, recalls the darker humor of Feste and the similarly named Touchstone. When a character asks Tutch whom he waits on, Tutch replies, "On the world, sir."

Armin continued writing and translating shorter humorous works in his later life. As Felver notes, Armin's "interest in words, his delight in ambiguity, his freshness of invention" were evident both in the works he authored and in the characters he created on stage.

A Work about Robert Armin

Felver, Charles S. *Shakespeare's Fool: A Biographical Essay.* Kent, Ohio: Kent State University Press, 1961.

Ascham, Margaret (d. 1592) *nonfiction writer*

Margaret Ascham, née Margaret Howe, was born in South Ockenden in Essex, England, to a middle-class family. When she was about 18, she married Roger ASCHAM, the humanist and educational reformer, who was twice her age and of delicate health.

Roger Ascham was commissioned by a wealthy patron to summarize his educational views in book form, but the patron died before *The Schoolmaster* was finished. The Aschams could not afford to publish the book, and it remained in manuscript until after Roger Ascham's death in 1568. In memory of her husband, Margaret Ascham took it upon herself to put the manuscript in order and raise the money for publication. The book was published in 1570 and has been in print ever since. One of the main contributors may have been Sir William Cecil, Lord Burghley, the powerful adviser to Queen ELIZABETH I, since it is to him that Margaret Ascham dedicates the book in the short preface that she signs herself. It was unusual for a woman in the 16th century to allow her name to appear in print. We can only speculate about Ascham's feelings as she did so: pride in having brought a most appealing book out of obscurity, perhaps, and a desire for recognition of the efforts she had made. She praises Cecil's learning and kindness, recalls his friendship with her late husband, and concludes:

> And so beseeching you, to take on you the defense of this book, to advance the good that may come of it by your allowance and furtherance to public use and benefit, and to accept the thankful recognition of me and my poor children, trusting of the continuance of your good memory of Mr. Ascham and his, and daily commending the prosperous estate of you and yours to God whom you serve and whose you are, I rest to trouble you.
>
> Your humble Margaret Ascham.

Ascham, Roger (1515–1568) *nonfiction writer*

Roger Ascham was born in Kirby Wiske, Yorkshire, England, the third son of John and Margaret Ascham. John Ascham could not afford to spend much on the education of his sons, and Roger was adopted early into the family of Antony Wingfield, who took care of his education until he completed his bachelor's degree at Cambridge University at the age of 18.

Ascham took to the study of classical Greek with enthusiasm, and, with the idea that teaching would help him learn, he began teaching other boys. Soon after his graduation, he was appointed a fellow of his college. His attentive approach to his students won him a reputation as an outstanding teacher.

Ascham never believed in devoting all one's time to study. He was known as a fine musician on several instruments and developed his handwriting into such an art that people came to him for instruction in that as well as in Greek. He was physically delicate, and to make up for this he spent many hours each day on athletic pursuits, especially archery. His first book, *Toxophilus,* is a treatise on archery, explaining how to go about improving one's skill but also discussing in more general terms the importance of physical training in a complete education. Its publication made an impression: King Henry VIII was so pleased with it that he gave Ascham a pension of 10 pounds a year.

In 1545 Ascham was called to court to be tutor in Greek to Princess Elizabeth (the future Queen ELIZABETH I). He only stayed with Elizabeth for two years, returning to Cambridge in 1550; but another royal summons arrived, appointing him secretary to King Edward VI's ambassador to Germany, Sir Richard Morisine. Morisine's mission left in September 1550. Ascham took care of Morisine's official correspondence and at night wrote personal letters and kept a complete diary of what he had seen. He drew on the diary for his second published book, *Report and Discourse of the Affairs in Germany* (1553). He took a short trip into Italy, which resulted in a famous section of his later book *The Schoolmaster,* in which he warns against Italian travel as "marvelous dangerous" for young men. He writes:

> I was once in Italy my self: but I thank God, my abode there, was but ix. days: And yet I saw

in that little time, in one City, more liberty to sin, than ever I heard tell of in our noble City of London in ix. year.

When Edward VI died in 1553, Morisine and Ascham were recalled to England. Edward's successor, Queen Mary I, was a Catholic, soon to be known as "Bloody Mary" for her persecution of Protestants. Ascham escaped scrutiny in spite of his known Protestant beliefs, perhaps because of his personal charm, and Mary appointed him as her Latin secretary, charged with translating the queen's official letters into Latin and writing them out in his beautiful handwriting. In 1554 Ascham married Margaret Howe (see ASCHAM, MARGARET); they had one son, Giles.

When Elizabeth I succeeded Mary in 1558, she retained Ascham as Latin secretary and also took lessons in Greek with him. But his salary remained fixed at 20 pounds a year, which allowed him no luxuries. He is said to have had a weakness for betting on cockfights and dice, which may have contributed to the poverty he complains of in his correspondence.

In 1563 Sir Edward Sackville asked Ascham to write a book about the art of teaching. Sackville died not long after the work had begun, and though Ascham finished it, he did not publish it, lacking the funds to do so. In 1568 Ascham began to suffer an illness whose main symptom was insomnia. He tried to alleviate this by sleeping in a full-length cradle, but the illness progressed, and he died in December. Queen Elizabeth is said to have exclaimed, on learning of his death, "I would rather have cast ten thousand pounds in the sea than parted from my Ascham."

Ascham's widow arranged for the publication of *The Schoolmaster.* Like Thomas ELYOT's *The Book of the Governor,* the book focuses on the education of the ruling classes. Ascham comments on the different types of intelligence (or "wit," as he calls it), and urges the teacher not to favor the precocious or to ignore the slower-developing student, who, properly nurtured, is likely to retain his learning better and to make better use of it:

Quick wits commonly be apt to take, unapt to keep . . . more quick to enter speedily than able to pierce far. . . . Also, for manners and life, quick wits commonly be . . . light to promise anything, ready to forget everything. . . . and, by quickness of wit, very quick and ready to like none so well as themselves.

The book includes details about the best methods for teaching Latin composition, but Ascham never loses sight of his humanist purpose of molding a moral personality through both intellectual and physical pursuits.

Other Work by Roger Ascham

Letters of Roger Ascham. Edited by Alvin Vos. New York: Peter Lang, 1989.

A Work about Roger Ascham

Dees, Jerome Steele. *Sir Thomas Elyot and Roger Ascham, a Reference Guide.* Boston: G. K. Hall, 1981.

Ashmole, Elias (1617–1692) *antiquarian, historian*

Elias Ashmole was born in Staffordshire, England, son of Simon Ashmole, an artisan and soldier. Ashmole was educated at Lichfield grammar school and attended Brasenose College in London (1645), although he received no degree. As the English Civil War broke out, Ashmole, a Royalist, was appointed by Charles I to collect taxes in Staffordshire. This began his career in civil service. He was appointed commissioner, receiver, and tax collector of Worcester in 1645 and controller and assistant master of ordnance, or weaponry, in Worcester, in 1646.

In 1644 Ashmole befriended Captain George Wharton, who introduced him to the study of astrology. Ashmole's interest in astrology increased when he was introduced to William Lilly and John Booker, regarded as the two best astrologers of their day. Although he never published on astrology, Ashmole developed a fascination for it that would continue for the rest of his life. It was this sort of curiosity that led to Ashmole's being dubbed, in the prefatory material to one of his books, "the greatest virtuoso and curioso that ever was known or read of in England before his time."

This formed the basis of what became the Ashmolean Collection of the British Museum at Oxford, the first such public museum in England.

Other Work by Elias Ashmole

Ashmole, Elias, and William Lily. *Lives of Those Eminent Antiquaries Elias Ashmole and Mr. William Lilly, 1774.* Whitefish, Mont.: Kessinger Publishing, 1998.

Askew, Anne (1521–1546) *nonfiction writer*

Anne Askew was born in Lincolnshire, England, to Sir William Askew, a wealthy landowner, and his first wife, Elizabeth. The daughter of landed gentry, she was well educated by tutors. She was known around Lincolnshire for "gospelling," that is, reading and interpreting the Bible to illiterate peasants.

Askew moved to London, where she became an outspoken critic of Catholicism and a member of the Protestant reformist group surrounding Catherine Parr, sixth wife of Henry VIII. Several powerful politicians, among them Henry's lord chancellor Wriothesley and Richard Riche, had her arrested for heresy. Wriothesley and Riche wanted Askew to implicate their enemies' wives, and especially Catherine, who had great influence over Henry.

While in prison, Askew wrote *The Examinations* (1546), a two-part, first-person confessional account of her persecution and torture. Although it was against the law to torture women, Askew was put on the rack in an attempt to force her to renounce her beliefs. However, she did not waver in her faith, nor would she incriminate others. Here is her account of the torture:

> Then they ded [did] put me on the racks, by cause I confessed no ladyes nor gentyllwomen to be of my opynyon, and theron they kepte me

a longe tyme. And because I laye styll and ded not crye my Lord Chauncellor and mastre Ryche, toke peynes [pains] to racke me with their owne handes, tyll I was nygh [nigh] dead.

Additionally, she reports that she bested her inquisitors in her knowledge of the Bible, quoting back to them lines of scripture supporting her reformist position.

Severely crippled from the racking, unable to walk or even stand, Askew was carried out to be burned at the stake at Smithfield, England. After her death, her narrative was smuggled out of England and published in Germany by John BALE and later included in John FOXE's *Acts and Monuments* (1563).

In a time when women were forbidden by law to quote scripture or even to read the Bible, Askew's intelligent writing, ethical stance, and keen understanding of scripture make her a writer of note.

A Work about Anne Askew

Haigh, Christopher. *English Reformations: Religion, Politics and Society under the Tudors.* Oxford: Clarendon Press, 1993.

Astell, Mary (1666–1731) *nonfiction writer*

Mary Astell was born in Newcastle upon Tyne, England, to Peter Astell, a clerk in a coal company, and his wife, Mary. Astell received a thorough education from her clergyman uncle. Her father died when she was 12, leaving the family with many debts. In 1684 Astell moved to London, where she was assisted by the archbishop of Canterbury, to whom she later dedicated a small volume of poetry. In London Astell befriended many female intellectuals, including Elizabeth Elstob and Lady Mary Wortely Montagu.

In her first major work, *A Serious Proposal to the Ladies for the Advancement of their True and Greatest Interest* (1694), published anonymously, Astell protests against teaching women merely to "attract the Eyes of Men" and "value [themselves] on nothing but [their] Clothes." She suggests that such an education teaches women to be "a burden and a nuisance." Believing that women are "as capable of learning as men," Astell proposes establishing a "Religious Retirement" where women could "Retreat from the World" and attend to "the Service of God and improvement of their own Minds." Astell suggests her school will better prepare women to endure their situations. As critic Regina Janes notes, Astell does not propose changing "the external circumstances" of female life, "but the internal relationship of women to those circumstances." Astell's book was widely read, and the princess of Denmark, later Queen Anne of England, wanted to help establish such a school but was dissuaded from doing so by her advisers.

In *Reflections upon Marriage* (1700) Astell again criticizes the ill-treatment of women. She argues against the subjugation of married women, exclaiming, "If all Men are born free, how is it that all Women are born slaves?" However, Astell does not denounce marriage itself, believing it to be an "Institution of Heaven." Rather, Astell suggests that a woman, when she marries, should either choose a husband with "a Virtuous Mind" or "never consent to be a wife" at all.

Some apparent contradictions in Astell's opinions—that wives should "practice Passive Obedience" but that "a Rational mind is too noble . . . for the . . . service of any Creature"—reflect her political beliefs. Astell felt that kingship, like marriage, was a divine institution and thus objected to the removal of James II from the throne in 1688. Likewise, she disapproved of wives disobeying their husbands. Her insistence on wifely obedience does occasionally seem satirical, as when she compares a wife's duty to a "Man's . . . Duty to keep Hogs . . . if he hires himself out to such employment." Nonetheless, as critic Joan Kinnaird suggests, Astell's "feminism was not born of liberal impulses but of conservative values."

In 1704 Astell published several political pamphlets, including two responding to debates surrounding "Occasional Conformity." At this time only Anglicans could hold public office. However,

dissenters (non-Anglican Protestants) sidestepped this law by attending Anglican services occasionally, a practice called Occasional Conformity. Astell condemned this practice, and in *Moderation Truly Stated* she argues against religious toleration, claiming that "To be Moderate in Religion is the same thing as to be Luke-Warm, which God so much abhors, that he has threatened to spew such out of his mouth." In *A Fair Way with the Dissenters,* which denounces dissenter Daniel Defoe, Astell admits to intending "the Total Destruction of Dissenters as a Party." These pamphlets demonstrate Astell's political skills and, as critic Bridget Hill suggests, show "just how totally committed she was to the views of" conservative Anglicans.

Astell's most extensive philosophical text, *The Christian Religion as Professed by a Daughter of the Church* (1705), was largely a response to John LOCKE, an empiricist who rejected abstract arguments in favor of knowledge derived from the senses. Locke also believed that people should be free to choose their own rulers. In *Christian Religion* Astell rejects both these ideas, insisting that all knowledge comes from the mind and that sensory experience is irrelevant. This principle helps her reject Locke's theories of government, for as critic Patricia Springborg suggests, "freedom of the spirit is given religious, rather than political, expression." In other words, Astell understands freedom as internal and spiritual rather than external and governmental, enabling her to support both female liberty and absolute monarchy.

After the appearance of *Bart'lemy Fair* (1709), a religious pamphlet, Astell gradually stopped publishing, although she wrote a preface for Lady Mary Wortely Montagu's *Embassy Letters* (1724). In her own time Astell's ideas were sometimes considered outrageous. She was satirized by Richard Steele in the *Tatler,* and the bishop of Rochester complained that Astell was "a little offensive and shocking in her expressions." However, she also won great respect, and Montagu's granddaughter, Lady Louisa Stuart, later remembered Astell as "a very pious, exemplary woman, and profound scholar." As Bridget Hill notes, Mary Astell remains a contradictory figure, both "a passionate believer in the divine right of kings at a time when few were prepared to expound such an 'old-fashioned doctrine'" and "an early—if not the first—English feminist."

Works about Mary Astell

Perry, Ruth. *The Celebrated Mary Astell: An Early English Feminist.* Chicago: University of Chicago Press, 1986.

Springborg, Patricia, ed. *Astell: Political Writings.* New York: Cambridge University Press, 1996.

Aston, Gertrude (Gertrude Aston Thimelby) (ca. 1617–1668) *poet*

Gertrude Aston, one of 10 children of Walter, Lord Aston, Baron of Forfor, and Gertrude Sadlier, was born at the family estate of Tixall, Staffordshire, England, and married Henry Thimelby around 1645. After the deaths of her husband and their only child in 1655, Aston joined her sister-in-law Winefrid THIMELBY at St. Monica's convent in Louvain, Belgium, where she became a nun in 1658 and lived out her life.

Much of Aston's surviving poetry concerns religious subjects and features witty wordplay in the vein of her father's friend, metaphysical poet John DONNE. In "No Love Like That of the Soul," Aston explores the foolishness of people who prefer outer beauty to the permanence of the soul, "though today like some bright shrine of art / Th'amazed gazers bend to, Death's cold dart / May ere tomorrow so deform." "Death's cold dart" can easily damage the face, but the soul lives on. Some of Aston's more personal poetry, however, lacks common 17th-century poetic devices such as classical allusions and figurative language. She writes starkly of her son's death in "Mrs. Thimelby, on the Death of Her Only Child": "Dear infant, 'twas thy mother's fault / So soon inclos'd thee in a vault." Although she reveals her skill as a poet with the rhyming couplets and strict iambic tetrameter, Aston resists wrapping the horror of her son's death in a soothing metaphor. Comparing Aston's religious and personal works shows how she altered her poetic style depending upon her subject.

Aston, Katherine Thimelby

See THIMELBY, KATHERINE.

Aston Fowler, Constance

See FOWLER, CONSTANCE ASTON.

Atterbury, Francis (1662–1735) *nonfiction writer*

Born at Milton in Buckinghamshire, Francis Atterbury attended Oxford University and was ordained a priest in the Anglican Church. His preaching was highly regarded, and he wrote persuasive essays on issues of the day. In 1713 Queen Anne appointed him bishop of Rochester. Loyal to the monarchy until the ascension of King George I to the throne, Atterbury increasingly took the Jacobite point of view—that is, he supported the claim to the throne of the heirs of James II, who had been overthrown in the Revolution of 1688. In 1722 Atterbury was arrested for plotting against King George I; he was later exiled to France, where he died.

Atterbury's contribution to English literature was twofold. He was a powerful writer of polemic, or written attacks on the positions of others, and his sermons have been justly praised. His most important polemical writings include a series of pamphlets on what might today be called the separation of church and state, including *A Letter to a Convocation Man* (1697) and *The Rights, Powers, and Privileges of an English Convocation* (1701). The English Convocation was a governing body, much like Parliament, established by William III that was supposed to make decisions regarding religious controversies. Eventually, however, William stopped convening this body, and clergymen began to argue about whether the group had the right to convene itself and decide religious questions without the intervention of the king. In *A Letter to a Convocation Man* Atterbury made a strong case for reviving the convocation. In *The Rights, Powers, and Privileges* he adds to his argument by saying that without the convocation the nation was at risk for a return to absolute monarchy, in which the king would hold power over religion. Atterbury believed such power ought to be in the hands of religious authorities and emphasized his belief that the convocation had the legal right to meet without being convened by the king.

A Work about Francis Atterbury

Barrell, Rex A. *Francis Atterbury, 1662–1732: Bishop of Rochester and His French Correspondents* (Studies in British History, vol. 19). Lewiston, N.Y.: Edwin Mellen Press, 1990.

Aubrey, John (1626–1697) *biographer, essayist*

John Aubrey was born near Chippenham in Wiltshire, England, to a landowning family and was educated at Trinity College, Oxford University. A sociable person, he seems to have personally known most of the important people in the England of his day, a fact that gave him plenty of material to write about—and stood in the way of his ever finishing a writing project. While Aubrey was at Oxford, the English Civil War began, and King Charles I removed his court to Oxford for safety; during these years (1643–46) Aubrey made a number of acquaintances in high society. Many of these people remained his friends 20 years later, after the Reformation and the accession of Charles II to the throne. In 1660, the year of Charles's RESTORATION, Aubrey and some friends—who had been meeting regularly for many years to discuss developments in the sciences and to report on their own experiments—obtained permission from the king to incorporate their organization as the Royal Society, today one of the most prestigious scientific organizations in the world. Members in Aubrey's time included the great architect Sir Christopher Wren and the chemist Robert Boyle.

Aubrey's scientific and humanistic interests were intense and various, and he compiled notes on a wide range of topics. The only work of his to be published in his lifetime was *Miscellanies* (1696), a collection of folklore. *A Perambulation of Surrey* was published in 1719, as part of Richard Rawlinson's *The Natural History and Antiquities of Surrey; A Natural History of Wiltshire* appeared in print in 1847. Aubrey's most important work about antiquities, *Monumenta Britannica,* which contains his observations about the archaeological sites at Avebury and Stonehenge, was not published until 1980. He was one of the first to realize the importance of Avebury, and he noticed features of the site at Stonehenge that were not noticed again or explained until the 20th century.

Aubrey's biographical notes about his contemporaries were begun to help his friend Anthony à WOOD with a book about Oxford's history and alumni, but they grew to fill 75 manuscript volumes about all kinds of people in addition to Oxford graduates. Aubrey's method was to begin by jotting whatever basic facts he could remember about a person's life, leaving blanks for things he could not remember at the moment. He would come back later and fill in anecdotes, often using a personal shorthand that is difficult to decipher. He usually did not get as far as filling in the blanks for missing facts. The 75 manuscript volumes remained in manuscript at his death. It was not until 1823 that some of this work was published, under the title *Lives of Eminent Men.* Subsequent selections have come out under the title *Brief Lives.*

Aubrey's biographies are always readable, often insightful, and must be treated carefully. Aubrey gives no sources and makes no distinction between gossip and verifiable fact, but his descriptions of people he knew are invaluable for their vividness and sympathy. The longest of the *Lives* is also one of the best, that of Aubrey's friend Thomas HOBBES. His description of Hobbes's eyes brings a real person vividly to mind:

> He had a good eye, and that of a hazel colour, which was full of life and spirit, even to the last. When he was earnest in discourse, there shone (as it were) a bright live-coal within it. He had

two kinds of looks: when he laughed, was witty and in a merry humour, one could scarce see his eyes; by and by, when he was serious and positive, he opened his eyes round.

Aubrey never married, though he once came close enough to be sued by a former fiancée. This lawsuit and a series of other reversals left him practically penniless at age 47. He did not complain much about his circumstances; in fact, he remarked that having no more property to worry about left him more time for his work. He found that his friends were always happy to have his company; he lived for years on the hospitality of one friend or another. What did bother him was his inability to see any of his projects published. He had seen that unpublished manuscripts were rarely treated with proper respect after their authors' deaths. (He wrote to Anthony à Wood on the topic of the manuscripts that were then in Wood's keeping: "If in your hands when you die your nephews will stop guns with them.") It was a great relief to him when, in 1688, his friend Elias ASHMOLE, who was setting up a museum in Oxford, offered to keep all the manuscripts in his museum. Oxford's Ashmolean Museum remains one of the great museums of the world, but Aubrey's materials were transferred to the Bodleian Library, also in Oxford, where they are to this day.

Other Works by John Aubrey

Aubrey's Brief Lives. Edited by Oliver Lawson-Dick. Boston: David R. Godine, 1999.

Monumenta Britannica: Or, A Miscellany of British Antiquities. Edited by John Fowles. Boston: Little, Brown, 1981.

Works about John Aubrey

Lawson-Dick, Oliver. "The Life and Times of John Aubrey." In *Aubrey's Brief Lives,* edited by Oliver Lawson-Dick. Boston: David R. Godine, 1999.

Powell, Anthony. *John Aubrey and His Friends.* London: Hogarth, 1988.

Tylden-Wright, David. *John Aubrey: A Life.* New York: HarperCollins, 1981.

Ayton, Sir Robert (Robert Aytoun, Robert Aiton) (1570–1638) *poet*

Robert Ayton was born in 1570 near St. Andrews, Fifeshire, Scotland, the son of Andrew Ayton and Mariona Lundie, members of a family of prominent landowners. He attended St. Leonard's College at St. Andrews University, graduating with a master's degree in 1588. Fluent in French, Greek, and Latin, Ayton composed a Latin tribute to King James VI of Scotland upon his accession to the throne as JAMES I OF ENGLAND; nine years later he was knighted by James and later became gentleman of the bedchamber and private secretary to the queen.

Ayton's poetry reflects the development of Scottish and English linguistic styles during the Elizabethan and Jacobean eras, in that his early works were composed in literary Scots (the English language of Scotland), while later works were composed in English. Ayton was influenced to write in Scots by Alexander MONTGOMERIE and other members of the Castalian movement, which was an effort, encouraged by James VI, to revitalize Scottish literature. His later works were influenced by English court music.

In the 1590s, during his early Scottish period, Ayton wrote two out of seven of the so-called Diaphantus poems with Sir William ALEXANDER and Alexander Craig. These were essentially love laments written in literary Scots; Ayton translated them for later publication in England, but no copies of these have survived. Ayton also wrote Latin verse, most of which was published as *Deliatiae Poetarum Scotorum* (1637).

Among Ayton's most significant poems in English is "To an Inconstant Mistress," one version of which begins wittily:

> *I loved thee once, I'll love no more,*
> *Thine be the grief as is the blame.*
> *Thou art not what thou wast before*
> *What reason I should be the same.*
> *He that love unloved again*
> *Hath better store of love than brain.*

This bitter edge is evident throughout the poem, as when Ayton says he could have been faithful to his love even if she did not love him, but when she fell in love with another, he adds, he disdains "A captive's captive to remain." "To His Forsaken Mistress," also written in English, is a poem of lost love, addressed to an unfaithful woman. Ayton compares his lover to a plucked rose, then warns:

> *Such fate ere long will thee betide*
> *When thou hast handled been awhile*

With sere flowers to be thrown aside;
And I shall sigh, while some will smile,
To see they love to every one
Hath brought thee to be loved by none.

Because Ayton began writing in Scots and also wrote in English, he is regarded as an important link between Scottish and English literary cultures of the Renaissance. Later scholars have explored his influence on Robert Burns, who may have drawn on Ayton's poetry for his "Auld Lang Syne" and who also rewrote Ayton's "To His Forsaken Mistress."

B

Bacon, Anne Cooke (1528–1610)
translator

Anne Cooke Bacon was born in Essex, England, the second of five daughters of Sir Anthony Cooke, a tutor to the future Edward VI, and Ann Cawnton Cooke. From an early age she and her sisters were instructed by her father in Latin, Greek, Italian, and French. All the sisters married powerful men, and four of them produced impressive scholarly writings, Bacon is the most impressive of all. In 1556 Anne married Sir Nicholas Bacon. The couple's second son was Francis BACON, who would become one of the foremost politicians and essay writers of the period.

Bacon was only 22 when her English translation of 14 sermons by the Italian Calvinist Bernardino Ochino (1487–1564) was published; an enlarged version was reprinted in 1564. Because it was considered improper for a woman to enter her name into the public circulation of print, it appeared under the author's initials "A.C."

Bacon went on to translate the Latin work *Apologia Ecclesiae Anglicanae* (*Defense of the Church of England,* 1562), by John Jewel, bishop of Salisbury (1522–71). With this translation, which appeared in 1564, Bacon made available to a wide English audience the official explanation of the relationship between the CHURCH OF ENGLAND and the Roman Catholic Church, which justified the separation of the two and set out the Anglican Church's unifying doctrines. Of Bacon's translation, the great critic and theologian C. S. Lewis (1898–1963) commented, "If quality without bulk were enough, Lady Bacon might be put forward as the best of all 16th-century translators." The book proved popular and was printed again in 1600.

Many of Bacon's personal letters also survive. In them her close relationship with her sons Anthony and Francis and her religious devotion to the Protestant cause become clear. This correspondence can be found in J. Spedding's edition of *The Works of Francis Bacon* (London: Longman's, 1862).

The fact that Bacon and her sisters, in spite of their great accomplishments, confined themselves in their writings to the translation of religious works reflects the ambiguous position of educated women at the time. It was highly acceptable for upper-class women to devote themselves to religious pursuits, but since the Anglican Church still forbade women to preach, almost the only way a woman could give written expression to her devotional efforts was by translating the works of men.

A Work about Anne Cooke Bacon
Lamb, Mary Ellen. "Cooke Sisters: Attitudes toward Learned Women." In *Silent but for the Word.*

Edited by Margaret Patterson Hamnay. Kent, Ohio: Kent State University Press, 1985.

Bacon, Francis (1561–1626) *nonfiction writer, essayist*

Francis Bacon was born in London to Sir Nicholas and Lady Ann BACON. Sir Nicholas had risen to the rank of Lord Keeper of the Great Seal and was the most powerful person in the kingdom after Queen ELIZABETH I. Wealthy and influential, he held the position for two decades.

Lady Ann, Sir Nicholas's second wife, was as formidable a woman as he was a man. Pious and well educated, she was a theologian and linguist who, according to historian Will Durant, "thought nothing of corresponding in Greek with bishops." Lady Ann oversaw the education of her sons Anthony and Francis, instructing them in religious matters herself.

Francis Bacon thus grew up in wealth and privilege. The queen addressed him as "my little Lord Keeper" and enjoyed his conversation. At age 12 Bacon went up to Cambridge to begin his university education and to provide company for his brother Anthony, who was always in ill health. The brothers did not take degrees, and plague twice forced them to leave Cambridge. Eventually Bacon became disillusioned with the university's scholasticism, particularly its reliance on the writings of church fathers and on classical texts. As a consequence, to reform education became Bacon's ambition.

After leaving school, Bacon entered the political world when he went to France as an assistant to the English ambassador, Sir Amias Paulet. He now experienced opposing desires: One was to continue with politics, thus doing good for the nation and becoming a man of wealth and influence like his father; the other was to lead a life of contemplation and to write, thus doing good for the whole of humanity. Bacon's attempts to satisfy both desires shaped his life. He needed the influence of high political office to advance his reforms in education and law, but he also required the seclusion and the time that study and writing demand.

His father's unexpected death when Bacon was 18 brought an end to the privileged life the young man had led. Sir Nicholas, intending to provide an inheritance fitting his youngest son's ambitions, had failed to do so in the end. Biographer John Briggs calls this loss "a double disaster" for Bacon, depriving him at once of his presence at court and financial security. Bacon was left with only £300 per year (the equivalent of $15,000 today) and his father's rooms at Gray's Inn, a well-known London law school. This legacy was just enough to live on, but Bacon, used to living well, began running up debt and then asking wealthy relatives for assistance.

For employment Bacon turned to the law, and his admittance to the bar in 1582 was arranged by the queen. It was the only advancement he received from Elizabeth, though he tried to win her PATRONAGE for years at cost to his reputation. However, as biographer Catherine Drinker Bowen notes, "Outside the circle of royal patronage there was no way for an ambitious man to rise in government, no way at all."

Bacon entered Parliament in 1583 and was returned every year thereafter until 1621. He gained a reputation as an eloquent orator. Ben JONSON claimed that listeners regretted the end of Bacon's speeches because "no man ever spoke . . . more weightily, or suffered less emptiness, less idleness in what he uttered." His early years in Parliament taught Bacon the concerns of the nation and the processes of government.

Bacon was also at work on what some contemporaries considered a fool's enterprise and others thought presumptuous. The *Great Instauration,* or renewal, of learning was a plan, he said, "to set philosophy into a more fertile path." His project was, of course, too vast to accomplish in one lifetime. Still, over the years of its development, it came to include models of "new learning," plans for universities, and methods of experimentation and observation. According to Bowen, Bacon "was the prophet who urged men out of sterile scholasticism into the adventurous, experimental future." Today Bacon's ideas about empirically testing hypotheses are routine, but in his day they were revolutionary, and it took courage to suggest them. Contemporaries elsewhere in Europe, such as Galileo, had been imprisoned, forced to recant, and even executed for proposing similar ideas.

Needing an influential patron to speed his advancement in government, Bacon turned to Robert Devereux, second Earl of Essex. In 1593 this handsome, ambitious court favorite tried to persuade Elizabeth to give Bacon the position of attorney general, though Bacon had never argued a case in court. Elizabeth gave the position to a better-qualified man, Edward COKE, Bacon's lifelong rival. Elizabeth was impressed with Bacon, but not enough to appoint him solicitor general. Essex did what he could for Bacon, even giving him an estate. However, their friendship faltered when Essex challenged the queen's power, failed her in battle, and then threatened her life. Essex was arrested and sentenced to death.

Meanwhile, Bacon continued writing and honing his skills as an attorney. He argued for legal reforms that helped to shape English law for two centuries after his death. In 1597 he published *Essays,* dedicating the book to his brother, an indication that he had given up hope of the queen's patronage.

In 1603 Elizabeth I died, and James VI of Scotland became JAMES I OF ENGLAND. Bacon worked very hard to make himself indispensable to the new monarch—and succeeded. To celebrate his ascendancy, James created many new knights, including Bacon, who also received a patent (a paid position) as King's Counsel Extraordinary. In 1606 Bacon was made solicitor general, with the hated Coke his superior. He also bid for a high prize, dedicating his 1605 *Advancement of Learning* to James in the hope that the king would support his ambitious educational reforms. Although James considered himself a man of learning, he found some of Bacon's ideas incomprehensible and others heretical, in defiance of established religious beliefs. As Bowen observes, Bacon's premise was that "This earth is God's creation; to examine it is not impious." Yet this thinking would lead to conflict with church teachings and thus was dangerous.

The year 1606 also saw Bacon's marriage to 14-year-old Alice Barnham. No children were born to the couple, but their marriage seems to have been amicable until Bacon's final year, when he suddenly wrote Alice out of his will, citing "just and great causes."

As powerful men died, Bacon advanced and finally, in 1613, achieved the position that Essex had tried to deliver in 1593: attorney general. In 1617 he attained his political goal, becoming lord keeper, as his father had been. By 1616 Bacon was a member of the King's Privy Council, and from this position of influence he proved that his rival, now Lord Edward Coke, had attempted to abridge the king's power. The bitter Coke was ousted.

Bacon worked furiously, writing 101 reforms for the Court of Chancery, which tried civil cases that could not be settled by common law. His reforms sped up its processes and cleared its dockets in only three months. In quiet moments he worked on his *Plan of Learning* and the famous *Novum Organum* ("New Tool"), in which he proposed radical new methods of scientific study.

For all his achievements, however, Bacon was dissatisfied. Bowen notes, "His colleges and workshops were still unbuilt; place and prestige had not been sufficient to set his scheme at work. Among thinking men, only a handful were in sympathy with his ideas."

In 1621 Bacon fell afoul of Coke, who claimed that gifts Bacon had accepted from those he had aided were in fact bribes. Although the practice of receiving such gifts was common, Coke prevailed, and Bacon had to pay a hefty fine. Additionally, he was sentenced to a short stay in the Tower of London, stripped of public office, and banished from the court.

Bacon's sudden fall from power might have crushed his spirit, but it did not. Instead, it gave him the opportunity to devote the last five years of his life to his studies. By this time the *Novum Organum* was known in learned communities throughout Europe, and Bacon began to receive complimentary letters from foreign scholars. He continued to record his observations of natural phenomena and to put his knowledge to use. Of learning he wrote, in his essay of the same name,

> Crafty men condemn studies, simple men admire them, and wise men use them; for they teach not their own use; but that is a wisdom without them, and above them, won by observation.

The story of Bacon's death famously portrays a man acting on his own advice. In the late winter of 1626 Bacon was riding in a carriage, musing on whether snow might preserve flesh from decay. He ordered the driver to stop, purchased a chicken from a village woman, and had her gut it. While packing the body with snow, he fell ill and was carried to a nearby house, where he died.

Bacon had written his own final bequest during an earlier illness: "my soul to God . . . My body to be buried obscurely. My name to the next ages, and to foreign nations." He was buried at St. Michael's Church in St. Albans.

Critical Analysis

Bacon's many writings cover law, theology, utopian fantasy, education, philosophy, and science. Most were not published during his life, and unpublished papers remain. Two of his most famous works are the *Essays* and *New Atlantis*.

To *essay* means to make a trial of an idea, to weigh it. Michel de MONTAIGNE pioneered this genre in France, and Bacon was the first English writer to use it. By their final publication in 1625 the *Essays* numbered 58. Each treats an important topic, such as the worth of friendship, the price of truth, and the burden of wealth. Through allusion to classical and biblical stories, aphorism, and metaphor, Bacon focuses attention on the topic. Scholar Will Durant praises both the style and content of the *Essays*:

> Bacon abhors padding and disdains to waste a word; he offers us infinite riches in a little phrase; each of these essays gives in a page or two the distilled subtlety of a master mind on a major issue of life.

Bacon's essays are therefore dense. Readers must take them slowly, a few sentences at a time, and think over what Bacon proposes.

"Of Riches" is one example of Bacon's musings on a topic of which he had great experience. He opens with a simile that clearly illustrates the paradox of wealth:

> I cannot call riches better than the baggage of virtue . . . for as baggage is to an army, so is riches to virtue; it cannot be spared nor left behind, yet it hindereth the march. . . .

Bacon argues that wealth for its own sake is a poor goal, "for, certainly, great riches have sold more men than they have bought out." Rather, wealth must be, not an end, but "the means of doing good." Bacon considers the personal cost of riches:

> Riches gotten by service, though it be of the best rise, yet when they are gotten by flattery, feeding humors, and other servile conditions, they may be placed among the worst.

He also counsels against miserliness because "riches have wings, and sometimes they fly away of themselves, sometimes they must be set flying to bring in more."

The *Essays* are words of advice, designed to prompt readers to deal more shrewdly with today's problems. *New Atlantis*, however, looks forward to a world improved by unfettered scientific discovery. The book is a utopian fable in which travelers discover a land called Bensalem, where men work together in universities and workshops in service of "the knowledge of causes and secret motions of things; and the enlarging of the bounds of human empire, to the effecting of all things possible." Here, science is not the mental plaything of scholars but the useful tool of practical men who wish to improve the human condition. Bowen points out that Bacon was "not a scientist but a propagandist of science." He ignored some of the great scientific breakthroughs of his day, such as William GILBERT's work on magnetism, he clung to some occult beliefs, and he made "no single discovery" that added to scientific knowledge. Rather, he looked ahead to a time when better instruments and methods would reveal secrets and avowed that these secrets were the rightful property of humanity.

In 1660, 34 years after Bacon's death, the Royal Society of London for Improving Natural Knowledge was founded under the influence of *New Atlantis, Novum Organum,* and other of Bacon's scientific works. Its founders compared Bacon to Moses, who led the nation of Israel to the promised land and saw it from afar but could not enter. This Renaissance man described himself in these words:

> Being gifted by nature with desire to seek, patience to doubt, fondness to meditate, slowness to assert, readiness to consider, carefulness to dispose and set in order. . . .

It was this combination of gifts that make Bacon, according to biographer Rosalind Davies, "a major figure in the intellectual tradition of Europe . . . and the patron saint of . . . Restoration science."

Works about Francis Bacon

Durant, Will. *The Story of Philosophy. The Lives and Opinions of the World's Greatest Philosophers.* New York: Pocket Books, 1991.

Jardine, Lisa, and Alan Stewart. *Hostage to Fortune: The Troubled Life of Francis Bacon, 1561–1626.* New York: Hill & Wang, 1999.

Baker, Father Augustine (David Baker)
(1575–1641) *theologian, nonfiction writer*

Augustine Baker, originally called David, was born in Abergavenny, Wales, the son of lawyer William Baker and his wife, daughter of the town's vicar. The young Baker studied at Oxford, received a law degree from the Inner Temple in London, and became the recorder of Abergavenny in 1598. Baker was brought up as a Protestant, although his parents were conformists in name only, maintaining their Catholic sympathies while outwardly appearing Protestant because of restrictions against Catholics. As a youth, he was an unbeliever, but he formally converted to Roman Catholicism in 1603 after experiencing what he considered to be a miraculous escape from death while crossing a bridge. Two years later he joined a Roman Catholic monastic order in Padua, Italy, and he was ordained a Benedictine priest at Rheims in 1611.

During the period of intense religious turmoil between Catholics and Protestants known as the English Counterreformation, Father Augustine Baker promoted Roman Catholicism in that country and also wrote theological works in a mystical vein; these remain an important example of English devotional literature. While serving as a missionary in England, Baker collected and published historical documents verifying the Benedictines' role in the establishment of Christianity in England more than a millennium earlier. Although his name does not appear on the title page, Baker was the primary author of *Apostolatus Benedictinorum in Anglia,* a church history based on his research published in 1625.

It was while he was a spiritual adviser to the English Benedictine nuns at Cambrai, France, (1624–33) that Baker began to write many of his most renowned devotional works. He was a prolific writer, committing nearly 2 million words to print. His most esteemed religious work, *Sancta Sophia [Holy Wisdom]: or, Directions for Prayer of Contemplation,* was originally published in Douay, France, in 1657. This study of Catholic mysticism, which discusses famous mystics such as Saint Teresa of Avila as well as meditation practices, was the most important work of its kind during the period. Father Baker typically employed a highly formal, somewhat didactic style in this and other writings, as when he wrote that some Christian souls "seek rather to purify [themselves] and inflame their hearts in the love of God by internal, quiet, and pure actuations in spirit, by a total abstraction from creatures, by solitude," while "others are naturally of a propension to seek God in the obscurity of faith, with a more profound introversion of spirit and with less activity and motion in sensitive nature, and without the use of grosser images."

Father Baker returned to the English mission in 1638 and died of the plague in London on August 9, 1641.

A Work about Father Augustine Baker

Woodward, Michael, ed. *That Mysterious Man: Essays on Augustine Baker.* Abergavenny, U.K.: Three Peaks, 2001.

Bale, John (1495–1563) *historian, playwright*
John Bale was born in Suffolk, England, to Henry and Margaret Bale. At the age of 12 he was sent to a Carmelite friary to study for the priesthood. In 1514 he entered Cambridge University, earning a bachelor of divinity degree in 1529 and a doctor of divinity five years later.

In 1537 Bale left the Carmelites and moved to London, where he fell in love and married, hastening his rift with Catholicism. About his conversion to Protestantism, he wrote: "I was removed from a barren mountain, to the flowery and fertile valley of the gospel, where I found all things built not on the sand but on a solid rock."

Working for John LELAND, Bale compiled and wrote *Anglorum Heliades,* a history of the Carmelites, completing it in 1539. The scholar May McKisack says that Bale was the "most prolific historian of the Carmelites in England" and that his works were "valuable as documents of . . . [this] transitional period."

Bale next began writing plays on biblical subjects, using allegory to teach the gospel and popularizing ideas of the REFORMATION. In *King Johann* (ca. 1548) Bale writes about a king's responsibility for the religious life of his people, a concept promoted by the CHURCH OF ENGLAND.

When Bale's friend Thomas Cromwell, an influential adviser to Henry VIII, fell from favor during the reign of the Catholic Mary I and was executed, Bale fled to the continent. His works, along with those of other popular reformists, were banned in

England in 1542. While in exile, Bale published and wrote commentaries for a manuscript he had smuggled out of England, *The Examinations* by Anne ASKEW, a Protestant MARTYR.

After Mary's death and Edward VI's coronation, Bale was appointed bishop of Ossory, Ireland, in 1552, an event he chronicled in *Vocacyon of John Bale to the Byshopperycke of Ossorie.* However, according to McKisack, "his attempts to purge and protestantize the Irish had made him the best hated man in the country."

Arguably, Bale's principal work was *Summary of the Illustrious Writers of Great Britain* (1557–59), one of the earliest studies of British literary history. It is basically a catalog, arranged in chronological order, of British writers and their works, many of which were destroyed when the monasteries and their libraries were closed down under Henry VIII. In a notebook he kept Bale described how manuscripts were being used as wrapping paper by shopkeepers:

> I have bene also at Norwyche . . . and there all the library monuments are turned to the use of their grossers, candelmakers, sopesellers, and other worldly occupyers . . . As much have I saved there and in certen other places . . . concerning the authors names and titles of their workes, as I could.

Bale wrote over 85 works, many of which are still in print today, and he remains an important voice of the English Reformation movement. The scholar Arthur Kinney states that Bale wrote "works of great power that managed to combine ardent religious belief, historical occurrence and dramatic effectiveness."

A Work about John Bale

Happe, Peter. *John Bale.* New York: Twayne, 1996.

Bannatyne, George (1545–ca. 1608)
collector of Scottish poems
A native of Newtyle, Forfarshire, Scotland, George Bannatyne was born to James Bannatyne, an Edin-

burgh writer, and his wife, Katharine. He became a prosperous Edinburgh merchant and was admitted a burgess, or representative of a town in Parliament, in 1587. In 1568 a plague spread throughout Edinburgh; Bannatyne returned to his native county, where he lived in isolation. It was during this time that he copied poems written by 15th- and 16th-century Scottish poets. He collected these poems into an 800-page anthology of verse known as the Bannatyne Manuscript. The anthology was inherited by his only daughter Janet, and later by her husband's family. It eventually was passed on to the Advocates' Library in Edinburgh, and it remains part of the core collection of the National Library of Scotland, which absorbed the Advocates' Collection when it was formed in 1925.

Bannatyne's manuscript contains many of the most famous poems of the courtly poets known as makaris, or Scottish Chaucerians. Most important, it preserved the work of writers such as lyric poet Alexander Scott, who might otherwise be unknown. The work also includes much anonymous verse as well. The Bannatyne Manuscript was also an important influence in the 18th-century Scottish revival when a number of the poems were reprinted in *Ever Green* by Allan Ramsay.

In his memoir of George Bannatyne, Sir Walter Scott sums up Bannatyne's importance to Scottish literature: "In this dreadful period, when hundreds, finding themselves surrounded by danger and death, renounced all care save that of selfish precaution for their own safety, and all thoughts save apprehensions of infection, George Bannatyne had the courageous energy to form and execute the plan of saving the literature of a whole nation." Scott founded the Bannatyne Club in 1823. It is dedicated to the study of Scottish history and literature.

Barclay, Alexander (ca. 1475–1552) *poet, translator*

Alexander Barclay was a satirical poet of the pre-Elizabethan era. It is not known exactly where he was born or who his parents were, but he may have been of Scottish descent and was probably educated at either Oxford or Cambridge. Barclay was a Catholic priest who, in 1509, translated the German Sebastian Brant's poem *Das Narrenschiff* (1494) into English as *The Ship of Fools*. This translation was his most famous work, and it would be popular throughout much of Europe for the next two centuries. *The Ship of Fools* is a satire.

In the poem a group of "fools,"—characters who represent or personify certain vices, such as gambling, hypocrisy, and adultery—set sail on a ship for Narragonia, a fools' paradise, providing a perfect opportunity for the poet to satirize each character's particular vice. For example, one of Barclay's barbs is directed at the scholar who gathers books he cannot understand: "Styll am I . . . bokes assemblynge . . . but what they mene do I nat understande."

Many scholars consider Barclay's translation to be so loose that it is almost an original work. In addition to using Brant's original, Barclay included parts of previous Latin and French translations of the work and added many references to English life and people. For example, Barclay names himself as among the ship's passengers, and he refers often to the sinfulness of London. He also refers to English institutions, such as the court system, and people, such as Henry VIII.

Ship of Fools was frequently referred to in Elizabethan dramas and served as an example for many writers in the development of characters who were more than mere abstractions. Along with his rival John Skelton, Alexander Barclay is considered one of the two great satirical poets of the early 16th century.

Barclay, John (1582–1621) *prose writer*

John Barclay was born in Pont-à-Mousson, France, to Anne de Malleviller and William Barclay, a Scottish scholar who wrote in favor of the monarchy. In 1603 Barclay moved to London with his father and spent several years of his life traveling between Paris and London before finally settling in Rome.

His most famous work, *Argenis,* written in Latin and published in 1621 after his death, was read by many influential thinkers throughout Europe, including Cardinal Richelieu, Jean-Jacques Rousseau, and Samuel Taylor Coleridge. The story relates the romantic adventures of two lovers, Poliarchus and Argenis, and, in the process, discusses leading political and historical issues of the day. One question debated in intellectual circles of the 16th century was what sort of limitations citizens could impose on monarchs. Writers and philosophers, such as George BUCHANAN, who were in favor of a limited government, argued that laws should limit the authority of the Crown. Those in favor of the rights of the Crown, including John Barclay's father, William, argued that it was better for the country to let a monarch rule without restraint. Through the argument of the story, *Argenis* makes the case for the rights of the Crown. This important and popular work demonstrated to many that the prose romance could be an effective method to discuss serious issues, such as politics, and entertain at the same time.

Thus, Barclay's writing had a powerful influence on the development of prose fiction in the 17th century. In *The Rise of the Novel of Manners,* Charlotte E. Morgan writes, "Barclay extended [the romantic allegory] from the social life of some special group to the political and social life of all Europe."

Barker, Jane (1652–1732) *poet, fiction writer*

Jane Barker was born in Northamptonshire, England, to Thomas Barker, secretary to the lord chancellor, and his wife, Anne. Barker's brother Edward studied medicine at Oxford and tutored her in anatomy. She practiced medicine, although without a license, even prescribing medications and marketing her own popular remedy for gout.

Barker's first book, *Poetical Recreations* (1687), consists of poems she exchanged with male friends at Cambridge who she knew through family connections. "An Invitation to My Friends at Cambridge" compares her acquaintances to the tree of knowledge, describing their "Philosophy" as "Deep as its root" and their "Reason" as "Large as its spreading arms."

Other poems in the volume assert Barker's own place in the masculine world of medicine. The speaker of "On the Apothecaries Filling My Bills Amongst the Doctors" claims that she has a duty to be proud of her intellectual achievements since "one cause of Adam's fall was this,/ He knew not the just worth of Paradise." Although some poems also exhibit Barker's anxiety about overstepping her role as a woman, most of the poems in *Poetical Recreations* function, as critic Kathryn R. King writes, to make a connection to "learned communities that was crucial to [Barker's] self-image as an educated woman engaged, however marginally, in the nation's intellectual life."

In 1688 the Catholic James II was replaced as king of Great Britain by William of Orange. James fled to France, and in 1689 Jane Barker converted to Catholicism and joined the exiled king's court near Paris. In 1701 she gave James's son a volume of poetry entitled *A Collection of Poems Referring to the Times.* Some of these poems describe the conversion of Fidelia, a poetic version of Barker, to Catholicism. Other poems, such as "Fidelia Weeping for the King's Departure at the Revolution," characterize William's supporters as "Traitors, worse than Judas" and England as hell. Political and religious sentiments intersect in these poems. As critic Carol Barash notes, "Barker often uses hell as a place from which to launch political satire."

In 1704 Barker returned to England, and nine years later she published the novel *Love Intrigues: The Amours of Bosvil and Galesia* (1713). In this novel Galesia's excessive attention to conventional feminine modesty, including feigned indifference to Bosvil, whom she loves, leads Bosvil to marry another woman. *Exilius; or, The Banished Roman,* a historical romance about many virtuous couples who marry after great hardship, appeared in 1715.

Conditions worsened for Catholics living in England. Barker, like others, faced government surveillance and higher taxes. In 1718 her translation of the meditations of François de Salignac Fénelon, a Catholic archbishop, was published in

"English, in the Dialect of the Church of England," as Barker states in the preface. As King notes, Barker attempts in this translation to make "Catholic materials palatable to non-Catholic readers."

Barker's next work was *A Patchwork Screen for the Ladies* (1723). This novel details the further adventures of Galesia, who after failing to win Bosvil embraces the life of an unmarried poet despite her mother's complaints that Galesia "frustrate[s] the End of" female "Creation." After her mother's death Galesia meets a lady making a "patchwork," or decoration made of different "Silks, and Silver, and Gold Brocades," to which Galesia is invited to contribute. Having no fabric, Galesia provides "Pieces of Romances, Poems, [and] Love-Letters," telling the story of each as she adds it to the project. These stories, which end with the death of Charles II, attempt to recreate piece by piece the world before the overthrow of James II, which Barker believed was replaced by a world of turmoil and anarchy. As critic Janet Todd observes, the text's "patchwork" form helps Barker "to make meaningful patterned versions of a world that would otherwise threaten chaotically."

In Barker's *Lining of the Patchwork Screen* (1725) Galesia continues telling stories while making the patchwork's lining. Many of the stories are about English subjects who joined James II in exile. The tone of this novel is nostalgic; there is a sense of something lost forever. For example, in one story Galesia dreams she attends the coronation on Parnassus, the home of the Greek gods, of deceased poet Katherine PHILIPS, who Barker admired. When Galesia's presence is detected, she is given a handful of gold and cast off Parnassus. The critic Jane Spencer suggests that this expulsion indicates Barker's feeling that "she has survived into a new uncongenial."

Barker remained committed to the cause of the deceased James II. In 1730, as part of the effort to have James made a saint, she mailed a tumor to a French nun claiming it had been cured by a handkerchief dipped in James's blood. Rarely read after her death, Barker's work reveals, as King writes, the lost world of those "who felt themselves excluded from official constructions of national identity in post-revolutionary Britain."

Works about Jane Barker

Barash, Carol. *English Women's Poetry 1649–1714: Politics, Community, and Linguistic Authority.* New York: Clarendon Press, 1996.

King, Kathryn R. *Jane Barker, Exile.* New York: Clarendon Press, 2000.

Barnes, Barnabe (1569–1609) *poet, dramatist*

Born in Yorkshire, England, Barnabe Barnes was the younger son of Richard Barnes, the bishop of Durham. Little else is known about his life. He is known to have competed with William SHAKESPEARE for the PATRONAGE of Henry Wriothesley, the Earl of Southampton, in 1593. He also seems to have been involved in political intrigue. In 1598 he was accused of poisoning John Brown, Recorder of Berwick, a magistrate who oversaw criminal trials. He was later acquitted of the charge.

Barnes's literary work includes one play, *The Devil's Charter* (1606). The play's plot is based on a story that claimed Rodrigo Borgia sold his soul to become Pope Alexander VI (1492–1503). Barnes alters the story in order to make the Catholic Church seem corrupt. Thus, in the play Borgia becomes pope through bribery and only later sells his soul. Literary critics regard this play as little more than a sensationalist melodrama, akin to a thriller movie about the fall of an evil dictator, but Barnes's contemporaries saw some merit in it. Shakespeare's acting company, for instance, thought it was good enough to perform before JAMES I OF ENGLAND.

Barnes's most important work is the sonnet sequence *Parthenophil and Parthenophe* (1593). A sonnet is a verse form of 14 lines; Renaissance writers would compose larger works out of series of sonnets. Barnes's sonnet sequence centers around a love affair between two imaginary characters, Parthenophil ("virgin lover") and Parthenophe ("virgin"). This sequence has much in common with Philip SIDNEY's *Astrophel and Stella* (1582). Barnes, like Sidney, allows the woman addressed in the sequence to speak, which was somewhat unusual in this poetic genre. Furthermore, many of Barnes's sonnets have a rhyme scheme that Sidney helped develop. Barnes, however, tried to surpass Sidney, and in "Madrigal 14" his speaker asserts that his mistress is superior to Sidney's Stella (and Petrarch's Laura):

> There thou, 'bove Stella placed;
> 'Bove Laura; with ten thousand more
>   installed;
> And now, proud, thinks me graced,
> That am to thee (though merciless!)
>   enthralled.

Moreover, Barnes follows Sidney by scattering songs (a simpler poetic form than the sonnet) throughout his sequence. But unlike Sidney's songs, Barnes's are original. "The lyric forms in which they are cast," the scholar Philip E. Blank observes, "include forms not previously written in English." Barnes here introduced the madrigal, a love poem of one stanza, usually having no more than 13 lines. Indeed, as Barnes scholar Victor D. Doyno observes, *Parthenophil and Parthenophe* contains "the most varied grouping of forms within the sonnet tradition." Barnes wrote one other sonnet sequence, *A Divine Century of Spiritual Sonnets* (1595), a sequence of 100 sonnets on religious themes such as the Holy Trinity, but he is best remembered for his earlier work.

Barnfield, Richard (1574–1627) *poet*

Richard Barnfield was born at Norbury in Staffordshire, England, and educated at Brasenose College, Oxford University. As a poet he is known as an imitator of the lyrical styles of Edmund SPENSER and Michael DRAYTON.

Barnfield's first work was *The Affectionate Shepherd* (1594), a pastoral poem based on the second eclogue (collection of pastorals) of Virgil, written when Barnfield was just 21 years old. Pastoral poetry is a literary form that was popular during the Renaissance, focusing on the corruption of urban living and the simplicity of rural life. In keeping with the style of pastoral poems of his time, Barnfield celebrates the beauty of nature in descriptive six-line stanzas. He describes "the cristall of a pearle-bright brooke, / Paved with dainty pibbles to the brims," and "Sweet-smelling beds of lillies, and of roses, / Which rosemary banks and lavendar incloses."

Barnfield's best-known work, *Cynthia* (1595), is a collection of 20 sonnets. The title poem, in praise of Queen ELIZABETH I, was written in Spenserian stanza and appears to be the first use of this form outside Spenser's own work. The 20 sonnets that follow this poem of praise are considered by scholars to be more like Shakespeare's sonnets than any other work of the era, though written 14 years before Shakespeare's. In "Sometimes I Wish" the poet thinks that bees are foolish to kiss the flowers and that they should

> Kiss him, but sting him not, for if you do,
> His angry voice your flying will pursue:
> But when they hear his tongue, what can
>   control,
> Their back-return? for then they plain may
>   see,
> How honey-combs from his lips dropping be.

This poem, like many others of Barnfield's, is addressed to a male lover. Barnfield's last work, *The Encomion of Lady Pecunia* (1598), is written in praise of the power of money.

In *History of Elizabethan Literature*, George Saintsbury says that "Barnfield has the common attributes of this wonderful time—poetical enthusiasm, fresh and unhackneyed expression, metrical charm, and gorgeous colouring, which does not find itself ill-matched with accurate drawing of nature."

Bassett, Mary (Mary Basset) (ca. 1530–1572) *translator*

Mary Bassett was the granddaughter of Sir Thomas MORE, and like many other Tudor women, such as

Margaret BEAUFORT and Mary's grandmother Margaret More ROPER, Bassett chose translating as the safest and surest route to publication.

Her most noted translations are those of her famous grandfather, including *St. Thomas More's History of the Passion,* which she translated from the Latin. In 1557 Bassett translated More's *De Tristitia.*

Bassett also translated the first five books of *The Ecclesiastical History of Eusebius,* which was not published until 1860. Eusebius wrote in the third century, and his writing is among the earliest works of Christian theology and history.

Because Bassett was Catholic and lived during a time of religious upheaval, the choice of translating a religious work may have seemed to her less dangerous than writing one of her own. There is little doubt that the martyrdom of her grandfather affected her own choices.

A Work about Mary Bassett

Khanna, Lee Cullen. *Early Tudor Translators: Margaret Beaufort, Margaret More Roper, and Mary Basset.* Aldershot, Hants, England; Burlington, Vt.: Ashgate, 2001.

Bathurst, Elizabeth (ca. 1665–1685)
nonfiction writer

Elizabeth Bathurst was the daughter of Frances and Charles Bathurst of London. She was a sickly and sensitive child and did not walk unaided until age four. Bathurst is known as a Quaker polemicist, or a defender of the thinking of the Quaker movement, a religious group that promoted the idea of an "Inner Light" as taught by George Fox. Her adherence to Quakerism dates from 1678, when she and her sister Anne attended a church service, after which Bathurst spontaneously spoke to the congregation, advising them to seek Jesus in their hearts.

After this initial impulse to address the public on religious matters, Elizabeth began her career of preaching and writing. In her first work, *An Expostulary Appeal,* written in 1678 or 1679 perhaps

with her sister Anne, she describes her life and explains her difficulties finding God in scripture and thus her need to seek God within herself. She was known as a moving preacher and a logical and skilled writer. In *Truth's Vindication* (1679) her defense of Quakers combines sound theological knowledge and scriptural interpretation with her personal profession of religious experience. In 1683 she published *Sayings of Women,* in which she considered significant biblical women. Bathurst was imprisoned at least once for expressing her views from the pulpit.

Baxter, Richard (1615–1691) *nonfiction writer*

Richard Baxter was born in Rowton, Shropshire. Baxter later criticized his education. He said his instructors were ignorant, immoral, or drunkards. In 1638 Baxter was ordained a deacon and two years later settled in Bridgnorth. He began to symphatize with the Puritans and agreed with those who thought bishops should be abolished from the Church of England.

He published his first book, *The Saints' Everlasting Rest,* in 1650. It was written while he was ill and certain he was facing death. The subject of the book is heaven, how it is reached, and how to live a "heavenly life on earth." Baxter is careful to keep his focus on eternity: "Every time I decide that I would like to have my Heaven on earth, the Lord pours in the gall." Here Baxter joyfully imagines the second coming of Christ:

> O fellow-Christians, what a day will that be, when we, who have been kept prisoners by sin, by sinners, by the grave, shall be brought out by the Lord himself! It will not be such a coming as his first was, in poverty and contempt, to be spit upon, and buffeted, and crucified again. He will not come, O careless world! to be slighted and neglected by you any more. . . . If a star must lead men from remote parts, to come to worship the child in the manger; how will the glory of his next

appearing constrain all the world to acknowledge his sovereignty!

At the time Baxter was writing, England was involved in a civil war. The Church of England was in disarray as different factions argued about reform. Baxter often tried to work as a peacemaker and addressed reform in his writing, such as in *Gildas Salvianus, the Reformed Pastor* (1656). This work contains detailed advice to clergy on how to manage every aspect of their vocation. Here Baxter even offers advice on obstinate unbelievers:

> as to those that are utterly obstinate, and will not come to you, nor be instructed by you, deal with them as the obstinate despisers of instruction should be dealt with, in regard to sealing and confirming ordinances; which is, to avoid them, and not to hold holy or familiar communion with them in the Lord's supper or other ordinances.

Baxter continued to write many volumes in spite of his failing health.

After Baxter's death his autobiography was edited by J. M. L. Thomas and published with the title *Reliquae Baxterianae* in 1696. In 1875 a Baxter statue was erected in Kidderminster, a town in which Baxter preached. The plaque at the base of the statue finishes its description with: "In a stormy and divided age he advocated unity and comprehension, pointing the way to 'the eternal.'"

Beaufort, Margaret (Countess of Richmond and Derby) (1443–1509)
translator

Margaret Beaufort, a descendant of John of Gaunt and the mother of King Henry VII of England, was the daughter of John Beaufort, the Duke of Somerset, and of Margaret Beauchamp of Bletsoe. Her father died the year after her birth, and she was raised in the home of her uncle Jasper, the Earl of Pembroke, where she came into contact with the court of the House of York, which she disliked. She

encouraged conspiracies and intrigue, and was described by some later historians as sinister for encouraging her nephew, the Duke of Buckingham, to rebel against King Richard III. It is in this context that she appears briefly as a character in William SHAKESPEARE's play about Richard. There is also a reference to her in William Wordsworth's poem "To the Author's Portrait."

Known as Lady Margaret, the Countess of Richmond and Derby, Beaufort became an important patroness of learning in early Renaissance England. Drawing on her considerable resources, she was instrumental in the establishment of Christ's College and St. John's College, and she also endowed professorships in divinity at Cambridge and Oxford Universities. A devout Roman Catholic and book collector who supported Catholic interests, Beaufort underwrote the printing of prayer books and psalters and commissioned a book of hours from the London printer William Abell. A book of hours is a work that includes religious texts for each hour of the day, sometimes also including calendars, prayers, and psalms. Beaufort also supported the work of the printers William CAXTON and Wynkyn de Worde, notably de Worde's *Scala Perfectionis* ("Ladder of Perfection") (1494). A list of her translations appeared in George Ballard's *Memoirs of Learned Ladies* (1752), and she was included in Horace Walpole's *A Catalogue of the Royal and Noble Authors of England* (1758).

Works about Margaret Beaufort
Jones, Michael K., and Malcolm G. Underwood. *The King's Mother: Lady Margaret Beaufort, Countess of Richmond and Derby.* Cambridge, U.K.: Cambridge University Press, 1992.
Simon, Linda. *Of Virtue Rare: Margaret Beaufort, Matriarch of the House of Tudor.* Boston: Houghton Mifflin, 1982.

Beaumont, Francis (ca. 1584–1616)
playwright, poet

Francis Beaumont was born in Leicestershire, England, to Francis Beaumont, who owned a large estate. Beaumont entered Oxford University in 1597; three years later he transferred to Inner Temple and participated in the witty, theater-loving world of the London law crowd. By 1601 Beaumont was writing occasional verse (poems written for specific events or occasions) for his classmates, and in 1602 he produced a long narrative poem, *Salmacis and Hermaphroditus,* an erotic work in the style of the Greek poet Ovid.

Beaumont's first dramatic effort was the comedy *The Woman Hater* (1607). The play features a duke who loves a woman named Oriana and a general named Gondarino who tries to convince the duke that Oriana is immoral. Oriana's chaste behavior convinces the duke otherwise, and in a brilliantly comic ending, Oriana punishes Gondarino by having him tied to a chair and wooed by several ladies. The play's satiric elements and use of characters dominated by humors (bodily fluids believed to affect human behavior) associate it with the works of John MARSTON and Ben JONSON, but it was not successful.

This play marked the beginning of Beaumont's collaboration with John FLETCHER, who had a small hand in its writing. Most of Beaumont's dramatic writing was done in partnership with Fletcher. Works by each man writing alone and by the two working together or with others were published in a 1647 folio and, more completely, in 1679.

Beaumont's next effort, this time entirely on his own, was *The Knight of the Burning Pestle* (1607). Unique among RENAISSANCE plays, *The Knight of the Burning Pestle* combines adventure with hilarious comedy, mostly provided by characters presented as audience members who break into the action on stage.

The years of Beaumont and Fletcher's successful collaboration followed. *Philaster* (1609) tells the story of a prince, the title character, who falls in love with Arathusa, the daughter of the man who has stolen away Philaster's right to the throne. Philaster's conflicted mental state causes him to act erratically when he suspects Arathusa of an affair with his page Bellario, and he stabs her. However,

Philaster is a prime example of the genre of tragicomedy which Beaumont helped his friend Fletcher develop; thus, a happy ending follows after the difficulties and the danger of death are passed.

The Maid's Tragedy (1610) revolves around the central character Amintor, a soldier who marries the courtier Evadne at the king's command, despite the fact that he had long been engaged to another woman, Aspatia. Only on his wedding night, when his bride refuses to have sexual relations, does Amintor discover that his marriage is a sham: Evadne is the king's mistress and Amintor is necessary to "father" any children resulting from the affair. When Evadne's brother Melantius, who is also Amintor's best friend, discovers the situation, he forces Evadne to kill the king, avenging the lost honor of the family and Amintor's shame.

A King and No King (1611) marked a return to tragicomedy. The title character is Arbaces, a flawed king whose many asides and soliloquies (speeches given when no other character is on stage) allow the audience to understand him more than many other Beaumont and Fletcher characters. When he returns from battle, his sister Panthea has grown into a beautiful woman, and he finds he loves her "better than any brother loves his sister," indeed, "better than a brother ought." After struggling with temptation for a while, Arbaces determines to follow his incestuous passion, casting reason and virtue aside. Only a last-minute plot twist relieves the tension.

In 1613 Beaumont wrote a masque (a performance combining poetry, music, and dance) for a royal wedding. That same year Beaumont married a rich heiress and retired from writing. At his death three years later, Francis Beaumont was the third author—after Geoffrey Chaucer and Edmund SPENSER—to be granted a resting place in the poet's corner of Westminster Cathedral.

Critical Analysis

Many of Beaumont's best works emphasize an idealized form of love in preference to impure sexual passion. In works such as *Philaster, The Maid's*

Tragedy, and *A King and No King,* barriers exist to prevent sexual intercourse in several relationships. In *Philaster,* Arathusa is suspected of carrying on a sexual relationship with Bellario, Philaster's page, until a last-minute revelation proves the relationship was innocent affection. In *The Maid's Tragedy,* the sexual affair carried on by the king and Evadne contrasts sharply with the relationship of Amintor and Aspatia, in which any sexual contact is prevented by Amintor's marriage, as well as Aspatia's disguise as a male youth. In *A King and No King,* Panthea finds herself the object of the passion of two men, Arbaces and Tigranes, king of Armenia. In each case there is a strong barrier to prevent the passion from resulting in sexual intimacy: Arbaces is her brother and Tigranes is betrothed to another woman.

Beaumont's serious drama is best exemplified by *The Maid's Tragedy,* of which he is considered the primary author. Late in the play, Amintor summarizes its central irony: "Those have most power to hurt us that we love, / We lay our sleeping lives within their arms." Thus, Evadne ties the sleeping king to the bed; when he wakes in amorous anticipation, she kills him. Amintor's words describe his own action as well, however. His marriage to Evadne and his behavior toward Aspatia hurt his beloved beyond recovery.

Beaumont's reputation as a comic dramatist is secured by the one play attributed entirely to him: *The Knight of the Burning Pestle.* The play utilizes a device that was unique in its time: the blurring of the line between performer and audience. Two of the characters in the play, the Grocer and his wife, are ostensibly members of the audience who interrupt a play called "The London Merchant" during the prologue and demand that a different play, "The Grocer's Honor," be presented. Instead, the actor playing the prologue offers the satiric title "Knight of the Burning Pestle," suggesting a man suffering the symptoms of syphilis. The grocer and his wife continue to make demands of the players, even inserting their apprentice Rafe into the play and commenting on the performance as it unfolds onstage. Thus, as scholar Andrew Gurr points out,

Beaumont uniquely presents "not just a play within a play but a play within a play within a third play."

The Knight of the Burning Pestle contains multiple levels of irony, as it ridicules both noble tales of knights on chivalric quests and plays that poke fun at the rising middle class. Additionally, the need for playwrights to cater to the tastes of the day is sharply criticized. Beaumont seems to be saying that, if playwrights try to meet the ever-changing demands of the public, chaos will follow. Tastes of audience members are fickle: the Wife at first enjoys a song by Master Merrythought, a comical old man, and asks her husband "Is't not a fine old man?" Later, however, she is offended when Merrythought sings a bawdy song. She terms him an "old fornicating fellow" and demands her husband find her a drink of beer to help her recover.

In a prefatory dedication, the play's publisher comments that *The Knight of the Burning Pestle* was "utterly rejected" by the audience when first performed. The writer surmises that the audience had not understood "the privy [private] mark of irony about" the play. On the other hand, it may be that they understood it all too well and were offended by its satire. The play was, however, popular among the learned reading public and was put on with success by several companies later in the 17th century. Today it is almost universally hailed as a masterpiece. As biographer Lee Bliss explains, "Beaumont's control over his apparently clashing plays and players finally allows a complex, richly textured effect to emerge from [the play's] surface chaos."

According to statements of Beaumont and Fletcher's contemporaries, Beaumont's talent gave structure to the plays, while Fletcher provided an abundance of lively, witty dialogue. However, as his solo work *Knight of the Burning Pestle* shows, Beaumont did not lack in that commodity either. In his seven years of involvement with the English theater, Beaumont wrote one masterpiece of comic irony, helped create the new and long-lived genre of tragicomedy, and had a hand in producing several plays of enduring value. Beaumont's name will always be linked to that of his friend and collaborator Fletcher; the 1679 folio included 52 plays attributed jointly to "Francis Beaumont and John Fletcher, Gent." However, Beaumont's modern reputation is enhanced by the fact that, as Bliss points out, of all those plays, "the plays most frequently reprinted and discussed" belong to Beaumont "either all or in part."

Other Work by Francis Beaumont

Bowers, Fredson, gen. ed. *The Dramatic Works in the Beaumont and Fletcher Canon.* New York: Cambridge University Press, 1966.

A Work about Francis Beaumont

Bliss, Lee. *Francis Beaumont.* Boston: Twayne, 1987.

Behn, Aphra (ca. 1640–1689) *playwright, novelist, poet*

Very little is known about the early life of Aphra Behn. She is believed to have spent some time in Suriname in her youth and probably married a man named Behn who died soon after their marriage. The first definite records of her are from 1666, when she served as a spy for the British government in Antwerp. She returned to London the next year and was imprisoned for debt. At some point after that Behn decided to become a writer to support herself. Her first play, *The Forced Marriage,* a tragicomedy inspired by the Jacobean playwrights Francis BEAUMONT and John FLETCHER, was staged in London in 1670. Behn quickly became a part of the vibrant world of RESTORATION theater, making friends with John DRYDEN and John Wilmot, the Earl of ROCHESTER.

For the rest of her life Behn produced plays, poetry, and novels, becoming the first professional woman writer in England and one of the best-known literary figures of the day. Her most successful play was the comedy *The Rover,* staged in 1677. Other notable plays included *Abdelazer* (1676), a romantic tragedy set in Spain; *Sir Patient Fancy* (1678), a comedy adapted from a work by

the French playwright MOLIÈRE; and *The City Heiress* (1682), one of her best comedies.

Many of her plays express her political beliefs. Behn was a strong supporter of the Stuart kings Charles II and James II and opposed the Puritan Parliamentarians. *The Feign'd Curtizans* (1679), for instance, concerns a group of romantic, roving Cavaliers, or supporters of the exiled Stuart kings, in the decade following the English Civil War, the 1650s, while *The Roundheads* (1682) is a political comedy satirizing the Puritan party who opposed the Stuarts.

While Behn was best known as a playwright, she also produced important works of poetry and fiction. *Poems on Several Occasions* (1684) is her most significant collection of verse, exploring both political and romantic topics. *Love-Letters Between a Noble-Man and His Sister* (1684) is one of the earliest English epistolary novels. It consists of a series of letters based on the true story of a nobleman who was found guilty of eloping with his sister-in-law. In the novel they become Philander and Sylvia and speak in the language of passionate love: "What is it, oh my *Sylvia,* can detain a love so violent and raving, and so wild; admit me, sacred maid, admit me again to those soft delights, that I may find, if possible, what divinity (envious of my bliss) checks my eager joys." The novella *Oroonoko* (1688), one of Behn's final works, was probably based on her experiences in Suriname and depicts the cruelties of the slave trade.

Critical Analysis

Many of Behn's best poems explore issues of the role of women in society. "The Disappointment" (1684) is a rewriting of the male "imperfect enjoyment" poem, focusing on female pleasure in sexual experience rather than on male failure: "The Nymph's resentment none but I / Can well imagine or condole." The critic Carol Barash explains, "Behn's erotic poems play different mythic narratives off one another to create the possibility of female desire, a place where the female sexual subject enters the fundamentally male traditions of erotic poetry." Barash's thesis is vividly illustrated in "To the fair Clarinda, who made Love to me, imagined more than Woman," where the conventions of love poetry are used by a female speaker to express her desire for another woman:

> Fair lovely maid, or if that title be
> Too weak, too feminine for nobler thee,
> Permit a name that more approaches truth:
> And let me call thee, lovely charming youth.

Behn's most famous plays use the theater to explore the ways in which traditional gender roles and social conventions are also performances. *The Feign'd Curtizans,* dedicated to Charles II's mistress, the actress Nell Gwyn, follows a group of young men and women in Rome. The play makes extensive use of disguise and mistaken identity. Thus, the noblewomen Marcella and Cornelia disguise themselves as prostitutes, with the play suggesting that all women make use of disguise:

> Morisini: Stay stay, what women are these? Octavio: Whores Sir, and so 'tis ten to one are all the kind, only these differ from the rest in this, they generously own their trade of sin, which others deal by stealth in.

The critic Alison Shell identifies one of the major themes of the play as "feminism because of its mockery of the stereotypes of whoredom."

The Rover features a group of traveling Cavaliers on the Continent. In the play the prostitute Angellica Bianca attracts customers by displaying an advertising sign with a picture of herself on it. Behn scholar Janet Todd notes that this character shares Behn's initials and thus sees her as a figure of the author: "the identification of the two women indicates that Behn's professional literary concern is with the portrait, with the social construction of woman." Angellica suffers the only tragic fate in this comedy, suggesting Behn's anxieties about her role as a public figure:

> In vain I have Consulted all my Charms,
> In vain this Beauty priz'd, in vain believ'd,

> My eyes cou'd kindle any lasting fires;
> I had forgot my Name, my Infamie.

Today Behn is probably best known for *Oroonoko*. Set in Suriname, the tale concerns an African prince who is sold into slavery. Behn presents the work as a true story: "I was my self an Eye-Witness to a great part, of what you will find here set down; and what I cou'd not be Witness of, I receiv'd from the Mouth of the chief Actor in this History." The story belies Behn's claims of veracity, however. Oroonoko is no ordinary slave, but a figure of romance. There was "something so extraordinary in his Face, his Shape, and Mien, a Greatness of Look, and Haughtiness in his Air," and he sometimes possesses supernatural strength: "he desir'd they would give him a Pipe in his Mouth, ready Lighted, which they did; and the Executioner came, and first cut off his Members, and threw them into the Fire; after that, with an ill-favoured Knife, they cut off his Ears, and his Nose, and burn'd them; he still smoak'd on, as if nothing had touch'd him." Recently, critics have explored the treatment of race and gender in the work. According to the scholar Laura Brown, the most important character in the book is Behn the narrator, because the reader is led to compare the slavery depicted in the novel with the status of women in a patriarchal society: "the figure of the woman in the imperialist narrative—a sign of 'what we have made of ourselves'—provides the point of contact through which the violence of colonial history—'what we have made of them'— can be represented."

Behn's novels, plays, and poems have been of great importance for scholars interested in feminism and the feminine literary tradition. One of the pioneers of feminist criticism, Virginia Woolf, eulogized Behn in *A Room of One's Own,* an early-20th-century work of feminist literary history: "All women together ought to let flowers fall upon the tomb of Aphra Behn which is, most scandalously but rather appropriately, in Westminster Abbey, for it was she who earned them the right to speak their minds."

Other Work by Aphra Behn

Oroonoko and Other Writings. Edited by Paul Salzman. New York: Oxford University Press, 1994.

A Work about Aphra Behn

Todd, Janet, ed. *Aphra Behn Studies.* New York: Cambridge University Press, 1996.

Benlowes, Edward (1603–1676) *poet*

Edward Benlowes was born in Essex, England, to Andrew Benlowes, a landowner, and his wife, Philippa. He enjoyed an affluent upbringing and was educated at Cambridge University, where he converted from Catholicism to Protestantism. In 1613 he inherited his father's estate, and the money from this inheritance allowed him to live comfortably for most of his life. In his later years he ran out of money as a result of his extravagant lifestyle and his generous patronage of other artists.

Benlowes is best known as the author of *Theophila* (1652), a poem of 13 cantos, written in both Latin and English, which frequently alludes to the work of earlier poets. The subject matter of the poem traces the journey of the soul, personified by Theophila, from sin to repentance and religion. Along the way, Benlowes employs both conventional and startlingly unconventional similes. Of his heroine he says, conventionally enough, "Her *Hands* are soft as swannie Down, and much/More white," adding that her "*Warmth* is such, / As when ripe *Gold* and quickening *Sun-beams* inly touch." Sometimes, however, his similes are quite odd. Here he describes a courtesan:

> *She'd coach affection of her cheek: but why?*
> *Would Cupid's horses climb so high*
> *Over her alpine nose t'o'erthrow it in her eye?*

His extravagant writing style made him a figure of some ridicule, although it did not detract from the success of *Theophila*. Benlowes was most notably satirized in *Character of a Small Poet*, in which Samuel "Hudibras" BUTLER criticizes Benlowes's style, saying, "Bar him the Imitation of something he has read, and he has no Image in his Thoughts." Despite Butler's harsh words, however, Benlowes was an influential figure, and a friend and patron to many poets of great ability, even if his own was found, by some, to be lacking.

Bentley, Richard (1662–1742) *nonfiction writer*

Richard Bentley was an English classical scholar and clergyman known for his prominence in the field of textual criticism. He was born at Oulton, Yorkshire, England, and educated at Wakefield Grammar School and St. John's College, Cambridge.

Textual criticism is the process of reconstructing the original text of an ancient document with as much accuracy as possible. Ancient texts were handwritten on poor quality paper, and many times there was no spacing between words. Scribes, who were often illiterate, created copies of the ancient texts. Over time this process led to many variations of the original text. Bentley's expertise as a textual critic required not only a keen understanding of classical history but a sensitivity to Greek and Latin language and style.

His *Epistola ad Joannum Millium* (1691) is said to have prompted a new era in classical scholarship. This collection of brilliant miscellaneous observations, dating back to the sixth-century Byzantine Empire, displayed the comprehensive learning that was to enable Bentley to lay the foundations of the critical scholarship of 18th century.

His *Dissertation on the Letters of Phalaris* (1699), an exposure of a 14th-century forgery, was his most celebrated work. It proved that the letters were not written by a Sicilian tyrant of the sixth century B.C., as was previously thought, but were written much later by a Greek sophist or rhetorician, possibly Adrianus of Tyre, in the second century B.C.

Best, George (ca. 1530–1584) *nonfiction writer*

George Best began his career as a navigator with Martin Frobisher as he sought the Northwest

Passage, a route that many explorers hoped could be found to link the Atlantic Ocean with the Pacific. Best was promoted to captain within a year.

In 1578 Best published his account of the journey as *The Three Voyages of Martin Frobisher in Search of a passage to Cathay and India by the North-West*. Frobisher was intent on both spreading Christianity and abducting and enslaving Eskimos. Best wrote of questioning an apprehended native regarding five men of their expedition who were captured:

> And thereupon calling the matter to his remembrance, he gave us plainly to understand by signs that he had knowledge of the taking of our five men the last year, and confessing the manner of each thing, numbered the five men upon his five fingers and pointed unto a boat in our ship which was like unto that wherein our men were betrayed: and when we made him signs that they were slain and eaten, he earnestly denied, and made signs to the contrary.

Best also wrote of another violent encounter with a group of Eskimos who chose death over capture: "[T]hey could by no means escape our hands, finding themselves in this case distressed, chose rather to cast themselves headlong down the rocks into the sea, and so be bruised and drowned, rather than to yield themselves to our men's mercies."

In 1578 Best's *A True Discourse of the Late Voyages of Discovery* was also published. *Discourse* was about a 1553 journey to Guinea and included the author's thoughts on why the skin of African people was darker than that of the English. Best believed climate caused the difference in skin color and theorized that the darker skin was actually an advanced sort of sunburn. He also took a biblical approach and suggested the skin color was God's stamp on the sons of Ham, "proceed[ing] rather of some natural infection of that man," a view that was often advanced as a biblical justification for slavery.

Like many travelers, Best hoped to find gold in the various places to which he traveled. He was also a proponent of colonization, even in the unknown distant northern territories known at the time as Meta Incognita.

Bible, King James Version (1611)

In the Middle Ages the Roman Catholic Church held complete sway over the religious lives of people in Britain, and the Bible was available only in Latin. Very few people could read in any language, and only people who knew Latin—which effectively meant only priests and some aristocrats—were expected to read the Bible. Ordinary people were expected to learn what they needed to know of what was in the Bible from the priests.

In the 16th century the Anglican Church broke away from the Roman Catholic Church. Having previously put to death William Tyndale, who tried to disseminate his own English translation of the gospels, King Henry VIII declared himself head of the CHURCH OF ENGLAND and decided that people should, after all, be able to read and hear the Bible in their own language. Several translations were made in the 16th century from the original Hebrew (Old Testament) and Greek (New Testament), including Thomas CRANMER's "Great Bible." They were printed and circulated widely, and one of them, the Bishops' Bible, became established as the one used in churches. The discrepancies among the different translations caused confusion and dissension, as some versions were favored by Catholics and others by extremists in the Protestant camp.

Soon after his succession to the English throne (1603), King JAMES I, in the hope of easing religious dissension among his subjects, appointed a commission to produce a new, "authorized" translation. There were 47 members of the commission, divided into six companies, two of which met in Oxford, two in Cambridge, and two in Westminster. The king made sure that each company included members of a range of religious factions. Each was given a specific portion of the Bible to work on. They were instructed to start with the Bishops' Bible and correct it by comparing it line by line with the Hebrew or Greek original. They were given a list of other English translations for reference and charged to come up with a version they could all agree on, in spite of their own doctrinal differences.

The commission began its work in 1604. The initial work of translation took four years; after this, a six-member review committee went over all the work that had been done, polishing the language to improve the way it sounded. An example of the kinds of choices is a passage in Ecclesiastes, Chapter 12. In Cranmer's "Great Bible," it reads:

> Or ever the silver lace be taken away, or the gold band be broke, or the pot broke at the well and the wheel upon the cistern, then shall the dust be turned again unto earth from whence it came, and the spirit shall return to God which gave it. All is but vanity saith the preacher, all is but plain vanity.

The King James Version reads:

> Or ever the silver cord be loosed, or the golden bowl be broken, or the pitcher be broken at the fountain, or the wheel broken at the cistern: Then shall the dust return to the earth as it was: and the spirit shall return unto God who gave it. Vanity of vanities, saith the preacher; all is vanity.

There is not much difference in meaning between the two versions, but the King James translators use repetition more effectively and choose words that give the passage greater rhythmic regularity and a more poetic resonance.

The review committee worked for nine months, and the work was published in 1611. It is still known in Britain as the Authorized Version of the Bible; in other English-speaking countries it is called the King James Version.

Many people have expressed amazement that a work that was put together by committee and was essentially a compromise can have so much power and beauty. There is a movement in the United States today that asserts that the committee was directed by God, so that every word was divinely dictated. An-

other explanation offered for the success of the committee's work is that William SHAKESPEARE was brought in to do the finishing touches. In support of this, some (cited, for example, by Anthony Burgess in his autobiography *You've Had Your Time* [1991]) point to Psalm 46 in the King James Version. Shakespeare was 46 years old in 1610, when the King James Version was nearing completion. Count 46 words from the beginning and you will find "shake"; count 46 lines from the end, and you will find "spear." Proponents argue that this is just the kind of word game that might have appealed to a man who delighted in puns as much as Shakespeare did.

The phenomenon is probably just a coincidence. In *The Story of English*, Robert McCrum, William Cran, and Robert MacNeil describe the King James Version as "a work whose impact on the history of English prose has been as fundamental as Shakespeare's," but they point out a crucial difference: Shakespeare used a vocabulary of about 30,000 words, one of the largest of any English writer, while the translators of the King James Version confined themselves to just 8,000 words, keeping their language simple so that any of their contemporaries could understand it.

The King James Version came into general use gradually. It did not replace the Bishops' Bible in churches until 1661, and even then the Bishops' version of the Psalms was retained, because people were so used to singing them the old way that it seemed it would be impossible to change. But its influence spread as more writers grew up hearing it in church, and phrases first found in the King James Version permeate everyday speech to this day: for example, "labour of love," "clear as crystal," "a thorn in the flesh," "the root of all evil," "the fat of the land," and "the valley of the shadow of death." Among writers whose prose is clearly shaped by the phrasing of the King James Bible are Thomas BROWNE, John MILTON, John BUNYAN, Jonathan Swift, and Edmund Burke.

Works about the Bible, King James Version

McCrum, Robert, William Cran, and Robert Mac-Neil. *The Story of English*. New York: Viking, 1986.

McGrath, Alister E. *In the Beginning: The Story of the King James Bible.* New York: Anchor Books, 2002.

Biddle, Hester (Esther Biddle)
(1629–1696) *nonfiction writer*

Hester Biddle grew up in Oxford a practicing Anglican before moving to London and becoming a Quaker. Her writing was religious and prophetic. In her first published essay (1655) she admonished the Universities of Cambridge and Oxford using a technique in which she made her own and God's voices one. "Woe to thee, city of Oxford," she wrote, "lest I consume you in my fierce anger."

Biddle did not stop with the universities. She also turned her attention to the women of London who ignored social issues, such as the state of the poor. In her typical dramatic style Biddle compared these women to the Whore of Babylon and at the same time criticized the fashion of applying artificial beauty marks: "Yet thou canst pass by them in thy gaudy apparel . . . with thy face decked with black spots, which are the marks of the Whore" (1659).

In 1662 Hester Biddle was arrested at a Quaker meeting for preaching, which at the time was against the law for a woman. While in prison she wrote "The Trumpet of the Lord," in which she assails what she sees as the corruption of contemporary life:

> Oh! the blood of the innocent is found in thee, which cryeth aloud for Vengeance unto my Throne, Drunkenness, Whoredom, and Gluttony, and all manner of Ungodliness, Tyranny and Oppression is found in thee; *Thy Priests Preach for hire, and thy People love to have it so; Rioting and ungodly meetings, Stage-Plays, Ballad Singing, Cards and Dice and all manner of Folly* . . . wicked works and actions are not punished by thee . . . Taverns and Alehouses are frequented day and night.

Biddle was arrested again in 1665 for speaking in the street. She was imprisoned at Newgate, where it is thought she gave birth to a son. The second imprisonment put an end to her writing.

A Work about Hester Biddle
Purkiss, Diane. *Producing the Voice, Consuming the Body: Women Prophets of the Seventeenth Century.* London: Batsford, 1992.

Blackfriars

Blackfriars was a private indoor theater located in the Blackfriars section of London. It was originally leased in 1576 for use as a theater by Richard Farrant, master of the Children of Windsor, a boys' acting company. Originally the building served as cloisters for the Black Friars order, hence the name. When Henry VIII dissolved the monasteries (1536–40), the land and buildings associated with the monastery, including the building known primarily as a theater, were sold and went through several owners before Farrant leased it. Farrant used the theater primarily as a rehearsal hall.

Farrant died in 1580, and in 1584 playwright John LYLY acquired an interest in the theater. His plays *Campaspe* (1584) and *Sapho and Phao* (1584) were acted there. These were among the first five-act plays to be performed in England, marking a transition in English drama from more classic conventions and morality plays or hybrids of these to the kind of drama we know through William SHAKESPEARE. Although classical drama had been based on a five-act structure, medieval morality and miracle plays were usually not divided into acts.

In 1596 James Burbage bought one section of the Blackfriars and used it for performances. The neighbors protested having a theater in their residential neighborhood, upset because theaters were considered immoral by many Elizabethans and actors were commonly thought to be low characters. When Burbage died in 1597, the building went out of use until 1600, when his son Richard again began producing plays there. By labeling these performances as public displays in a private house, Burbage avoided the claim that he was running a public theater.

From 1609 to 1642 Burbage's theater became the private venue for Shakespeare's company, The CHAMBERLAIN'S MEN, later known as The KING'S MEN; they alternated between it and the GLOBE THEATRE, thus maximizing their audience. Unlike the Globe, Blackfriars was an indoor theater, and thus the company could perform even in bad weather. Additionally, the company charged more for admission at the Blackfriars, since the theater was located in an affluent neighborhood and was considered private. The audience at Blackfriars was also generally more respectable than public theater audiences. Another attraction at Blackfriars was artificial lighting (candles and candelabras), which created new effects unavailable at daylight performances at the Globe. Some scholars believe that this intimate setting promoted plays with central female roles. Blackfriars closed in 1642 when all the theaters were closed because of the English Civil War.

A Work about Blackfriars

Berry, Herbert. *Shakespeare's Playhouses.* New York: AMS Press, 1987.

Blind Harry (Henry the Minstrel)
(1440–1493) *poet*

That he was blind from birth is nearly all that is known of Blind Harry, who was also called Henry the Minstrel. He was born in Scotland, possibly to a noble family, and may have been trained as a minstrel by the church. Harry was a welcome performer in the court of James IV.

Blind Harry is important to British literature for having composed one of the most popular anti-English works of the time: *The Wallace* (1460). This patriotic, epic story in verse celebrates the life and death of Sir William Wallace: "And hensfurth I will my process hald, / Of Wilyham Wallas yhe haf hard beyne tald."

Scotland's national hero, Wallace fought to free Scotland from the English and to open independent Scottish trade with Europe. Bloody battles, thousands of Englishmen burned alive, and Wallace's gruesome execution appear in the epic, often in graphic detail. The work is only loosely based on historical events and even portrays Wallace as actively battling the English from the time he was 18 until he was 45, an unlikely proposition. Despite its violently anti-English subject matter, William Wordsworth and Lord Byron were inspired by the work.

Scholars have occasionally questioned whether or not Blind Harry was capable of composing *The Wallace* on his own, and Harry himself was rumored to have derived portions of his work from a Latin text that had been translated for him. But if there were ever a Latin version of the text, it was lost long ago. A manuscript version of the story was copied down in 1488 by John Ramsay; today this text is at the National Library of Scotland.

Because the story of Wallace's life and deeds plays upon the hatred that the Scots had for the English, the work was one of the most popular books of its day in Scotland. In fact, it was once said that every cottage in the country, if it had any books at all, had a copy of this violent epic. The story still has its admirers: *The Wallace* served as the basis for the 1995 film *Braveheart,* starring Mel Gibson in the title role.

A Work about Blind Harry

Hamilton, William. *Blind Harry's Wallace.* Edinburgh: Luath Press Ltd, 1999.

Blow, John (1648–1708) *musician*

John Blow was born in Newark, England, to Henry and Katherine Blow. After receiving the foundations of his musical education in his hometown, he became a choirboy at the Chapel Royal in 1660, the year of the Restoration of the monarchy after the English Revolution and Civil War. During his years as one of the Chapel Children, he continued his musical studies and produced his first compositions. In 1668 he became organist of Westminster Abbey, a position he resigned 11 years later in order to make room for pupil and contemporary

Henry Purcell. Blow eventually became Master of the Children of the Chapel Royal in 1674 and received his doctorate degree in 1677. In 1699 he became the first to hold the position of composer to the Chapel Royal.

Blow's earliest compositions were anthems written while he was a chorister in the Chapel Royal. Blow would continue to write full, verse, and symphony anthems set to biblical texts, the earliest known being *Oh Lord I Have Sinned* (1670). Subsequent anthems include *Sing Unto the Lord, O Ye Saints, Bring Unto the Lord, O Ye Mighty, God Spake Sometime in Visions* (1685), and *My God, My God, Look Upon Me* (1697). Blow's anthems constitute the greater part of his sacred music, along with at least 10 church services and nine Latin motets. According to the scholar Ian Spink, "Blow was widely recognized as the leading church composer of his time."

In addition to his sacred music, Blow wrote several secular works, including organ and harpsichord pieces, odes, and secular songs. The setting of poetic odes to music came largely into its own as a genre after 1680, due in part to the developments of Blow and Purcell. Blow also wrote court odes for New Year's celebrations and the king's birthday. Such odes include *Dread Sir, the Prince of Light,* which, according to scholar Martin Adams, "reveals an innovative, courageous musical mind," and *Begin the Song.* Adams states, "Nowhere in their output does mutual influence emerge more profitably than in the court ode."

Blow composed his only theatrical work, the masque *Venus and Adonis,* in 1683, a work that influenced Purcell's *Dido and Aeneas* (1689). In 1700 Blow published *Amphion Anglicus,* a collection of 50 songs including *Mark How the Lark and Linnet Sing (An Ode on the Death of Henry Purcell)* (1696), a moving tribute to Purcell set to the poetry of John DRYDEN.

Blow contributed to nearly all of the musical genres of his day, and his work reflects, according to Spink, "enough originality, imagination, vigor, expressive power, and, indeed, technique, for half a dozen composers."

Works about John Blow

Adams, Martin. "Purcell, Blow and the English Court Ode." In *Purcell Studies.* Edited by Curtis Price. Cambridge: Cambridge University Press, 1995.

Spink, Ian. "Captain Cooke's Boys: Humpfrey, Blow, and Turner." In *Restoration Cathedral Music, 1660–1714.* Oxford: Clarendon Press, 1995.

———. "The Songs of Blow and Some Younger Contemporaries." *English Song, Dowland to Purcell.* London: B. T. Batsford Ltd., 1974.

Wood, Bruce. "Only Purcell E're Shall Equal Blow." In *Purcell Studies.* Edited by Curtis Price. Cambridge: Cambridge University Press, 1995.

Boccaccio, Giovanni (1313–1375) *poet, prose writer, nonfiction writer*

Giovanni Boccaccio, the illegitimate but recognized son of the wealthy merchant Boccaccino di Chellino, was born in Florence. In 1327 Boccaccio accompanied his father on a business trip to Naples, where he remained to pursue his education until about 1340.

Boccaccino had hoped that his son would pursue a business career, but Boccaccio became involved with other pursuits—literature, scholarship, and the glittering life of the Neapolitan court. When his father moved to Paris in 1332, the son felt greater freedom to pursue his interest in literature. He began to read the poetry of Francis PETRARCH, who was to be his friend as well as a literary inspiration. His first poems, among them the *Teseida (Story of Theseus,* 1339–40) and *Filostrato (Struck Down by Love,* the story of Troilus and Cressida, 1340), were composed during his time in Naples.

In Florence, Boccaccio wrote the *Commedia delle Ninfe Fiorentine (Comedy of the Nymphs of Florence,* 1341–42), a light narrative poem set in the beautiful countryside surrounding his native city; and the *Elegia di Madonna Fiammetta* (1343–44), a prose romance about a lady who was unhappy in love, whose character seems to have been based on a woman Boccaccio knew in Naples. He also began to write a biography of Petrarch.

In 1348 an epidemic of bubonic plague, which had come to Italy the previous year, arrived in Florence. The disease, which became known as the Black Death, killed Boccaccio's father, stepmother, and many friends; in fact, it killed about half the city's population and went on to overrun northern Europe. This plague was to provide the backdrop and rationale for Boccaccio's best-known work, *The Decameron* (1349–51). In it, a group of seven young women and three young men retreat to a country villa to escape the infection ravaging Florence. To help pass the time, they decide to take turns telling stories.

The Proem, or introduction, of *The Decameron* sets up this framing story and includes a vivid account of the social effects of the disease—how living with fear and loss has loosened the bonds of family and of convention. The 100 stories—one from each member of the group for each of the 10 days of their retreat—do not refer directly to the plague, but the freedom with which the narrators speak of subjects that were not then usually discussed openly, especially in mixed company, reflects the social changes Boccaccio describes in the Proem. The stories range in mood from the tragic to the bawdy, cover a wide range of human experience, and have always appealed for their sheer entertainment value.

In 1350 Boccaccio first met Petrarch, who was visiting Florence. The two met again several times over the next 20 years and maintained a correspondence, exchanging copies of their writings, until Petrarch's death in 1374. Although today Boccaccio is remembered most of all for *The Decameron,* the works that followed it were more famous in his time. His Latin works *Genealogia deorum gentilium* (*Genealogy of the Noble Gods,* an account of ancient Greek and Roman mythology, begun in 1350 and finished in 1374), *De casibus virorum illustrium* (*About the Fortunes of Illustrious Men,* 1360–63), and *De mulieribus claris* (*About Famous Women,* 1361–62) were particularly admired and imitated, and he was valued for his scholarship and moral insight. Today, however, he is read more for his humor, psychological realism, far-ranging imagination, and ebullient vitality.

Boccaccio moved around Italy a good deal in the last 20 years of his life, in spite of growing health problems and obesity. He was sought after as a diplomat and as a great teacher. In 1373 the city of Florence appointed him to give a series of lectures and readings about the work of Dante, the third member of the great Italian literary triumvirate that includes Petrarch and Boccaccio. Boccaccio died at his villa in Certaldo, near Florence, a year after Petrarch's death.

Boccaccio's influence on British literature is pervasive, even through his minor works. For example, *Teseida* includes a story, the chivalric tale of Arcita and Emilia, that Geoffrey Chaucer (1343–1400) used in the first of his *Canterbury Tales,* "The Knight's Tale." William SHAKESPEARE, with perhaps an assist from John FLETCHER, dramatized the same story in *Two Noble Kinsmen* (1613), and John DRYDEN adapted it again in his verse *Fables, Ancient and Modern* (1700), which also included three stories from *The Decameron.*

Filostrato includes the story of the Trojan prince Troilo and the Trojan lady Griseida, who loves Troilo but who allows herself to be seduced by the cunning warrior Diomede. Chaucer used the story in the tragic verse romance *Troilus and Criseyde* (ca. 1385); Robert HENRYSON wrote a sequel to Chaucer's work, *The Testament of Crisseid,* in the 15th century; and the story was transformed again by Shakespeare in his bitter tragicomedy *Troilus and Cressida* (1602).

Sir Thomas ELYOT, in his *Book Called the Governor* (1531), tells the story of Titus and Gesippus from *The Decameron* as an illustration of the importance of friendship. British dramatists who drew plots from *The Decameron* include Shakespeare again in *All's Well That Ends Well* (1603–4) and *Cymbeline* (1611), Cyril TOURNEUR in *The Atheist's Tragedy* (1611), Ben JONSON in *The Devil Is an Ass* (1616), and Aphra BEHN in *The Rover* (1677–81).

An English translation, probably by John FLORIO, was published in 1620 and grew in popularity throughout the 17th century. Thomas HOBBES capitalized on Boccaccio's fame by titling his book of 10 dialogues on scientific subjects (1678) *Decameron Physiologicum.*

In the early 19th century Boccaccio won a whole new group of enthusiasts among the English Romantic poets. Samuel Taylor Coleridge (1772–1834) wrote a poem called "The Garden of Boccaccio" in which he addressed him affectionately: "O all-enjoying and all-blending sage." As the scholar Herbert Wright remarked in *Boccaccio in England* (London: Athlone Press, 1957), Boccaccio's "rare narrative power, great love of beauty, . . . keen sense of form and . . . intimate knowledge of the human heart . . . speak . . . across the centuries."

Works about Giovanni Boccaccio

Bullough, Vern L., and James A. Brundage, eds. *Handbook of Medieval Sexuality.* New York: Garland, 1996.

Clements, Robert J., and Joseph Gibaldi. *Anatomy of the Novella: The European Tale Collection from Boccaccio and Chaucer to Cervantes.* New York: New York University Press, 1977.

Mazzotta, Giuseppe. *The World at Play in Boccaccio's "Decameron."* Princeton, N.J.: Princeton University Press, 1986.

Bodley, Sir Thomas (1543–1613)
nonfiction writer, library founder

Thomas Bodley was born in Exeter to John and Joan Bodley. During the reign of Mary Tudor (1553–58), the Protestant family was exiled to Germany and Switzerland, and Bodley studied Hebrew, Greek, and divinity in Geneva. When ELIZABETH I ascended the throne in 1558, he returned to Magdalen College, Oxford University, where he received his bachelor's degree in 1563, then went on to Merton College, Oxford, where he received his master's degree in 1566. He then studied Hebrew and from 1576 to 1578 traveled in Italy, France, and Germany, studying those countries' languages.

Bodley was a member of Parliament for Plymouth (1584) and for St. Germans (1586). He went to Denmark and Germany as a diplomat for the queen (1585–88), and was councilor of state at The Hague (1589–96). In 1587 he married Ann Ball, the wealthy widow of a fish merchant. Bodley was knighted in 1604.

Sir Thomas Bodley published nothing during his lifetime, his writings being either letters or official reports and documents. His autobiographical sketch of 1609 was published posthumously (1647). He is chiefly remembered as the founder of the Bodleian Library at Oxford. He began this work after he retired from diplomacy, wishing to keep "out of the throng of court contentions" but believing he had a duty to God to be "a profitable member in the State." The library was largely financed by his wife's money.

A 15th-century room was restored, and Bodley enlisted help from influential friends, such as antiquarian Sir Robert COTTON, who made a donation of about 12 volumes from his personal collection. The project was completed by 1604, when JAMES I opened the library and named it after its founder. The Bodleian's first librarian summed up what made the library so important in its day: "[U]pon consideration of the number of volumes, their languages, subjects, condition, and their use for six hours daily (Sundays and Holy days excepted), we shall find that the like Librarie is no where to be found."

Since Bodley had no children, he made the university his heir, endowing the library with his property, including his books. He was buried at Merton.

Boece, Hector (Hector Boethius)
(ca. 1465–1536) *historian*

Hector Boece was born in Dundee, Scotland, to a landowning family and educated in Dundee, Aberdeen, and Paris. In Paris he met Desiderius ERASMUS, who dedicated a catalogue of his works to Boece and maintained a correspondence with him for many years. Boece was later an adviser to William Elphinstone, bishop of Aberdeen, when Elphinstone founded the University of Aberdeen, and in 1500 he became the university's first principal. When Elphinstone died in 1514, Boece, to honor the bishop's memory, embarked on a book about the lives of the bishops of Aberdeen; written in Latin, this work was published in Paris in 1522.

However, Boece is best remembered for *Scotorum historiae a prima gentis origine* (*The History and Chronicles of Scotland,* 1526), also written in Latin and published in Paris. A notoriously unreliable mixture of fact and legend, the *History,* which covers the subject up until the reign of James III (reigned 1460–88), glorifies Scottish monarchs and heroes. James V of Scotland (reigned 1513–42) rewarded Boece with a lifelong pension, beginning in 1527.

The *History* was much admired for its style. It was widely circulated in Europe in a French translation, was translated into Scots dialect twice during the 16th century, and was highly regarded into the 18th century. It was Raphael HOLINSHED's source for the story of Duncan and Macbeth, which became the basis for William SHAKESPEARE's famous tragedy.

Bohemia, Elizabeth of
See STUART, ELIZABETH.

Boleyn, Anne (Anne Bullen, Anne Bulen)
(ca. 1501–1536) *nonfiction writer*

Anne Boleyn was born in Norfolk, England, probably at Blickling Hall. Her father, Sir Thomas Boleyn, a courtier whose ancestors were merchants, had made an advantageous marriage to Elizabeth Howard, a daughter of the Duke of Norfolk. Through her father's connections, Boleyn spent much of her childhood at the French court, receiving her education with the royal children there. She returned to England in 1521 or 1522 and entered the service of Catherine of Aragon, the first wife of the king of England, Henry VIII.

Boleyn was admired at court for her wit and style; she had a relationship of some sort with Thomas WYATT, two of whose poems about her survive, and seems to have been secretly engaged to Henry Percy, the heir of the Earl of Northumberland. But sometime in the 1520s, probably in 1526,

Anne caught the notice of the king. There is evidence that the king broke up Boleyn's engagement to Percy, but for several years she resisted Henry's campaign to make her the royal mistress. In the meantime the king's disappointment with his wife, Queen Katherine of Aragon, was growing. Aside from her sober personality, Katherine had only succeeded in producing one surviving child, Princess Mary (1516–58; reigned as Queen Mary I, 1553–58), and Henry desperately felt the need for a male heir. But the Catholic Church forbade divorce.

Ultimately Henry's solution was to sever the connection with Rome, pronounce himself the head of the CHURCH OF ENGLAND, and grant himself a divorce. By the time this was accomplished, in 1533, Anne Boleyn was pregnant. The king made haste to marry her in time for the baby to be a legitimate heir. Boleyn was crowned queen in an elaborate and magnificent ceremony. When the child proved to be a girl (the future ELIZABETH I), the king's disappointment was moderated by the promise of the future. But three years and two miscarriages later, Boleyn was no longer in favor. Her biographer, Retha Warnicke, believes that one of Boleyn's miscarriages may have been of a deformed fetus, something that was regarded with superstitious dread at the time and may have led to her being regarded as a witch. It is documented that Boleyn was tried for and convicted of having adultery with no less than five men, including her own brother. All of those men, in addition to Boleyn herself, were executed.

Anne Boleyn is known to have been highly intelligent and to have had friendships with some of the finest minds of her day, but her surviving literary production is limited to a handful of letters and a dignified and moving speech delivered immediately before her execution, in which she speaks well of Henry, praying that "God save the king and send him long to reign over you, for a gentler nor a more merciful prince there was never." Her importance to literature is less as a writer than as a subject of literary inspiration. She is one of the martyrs mourned in John FOXE's *Book of Martyrs,* and is the subject of a play by John

Banks, *Vertue Betray'd, or Anna Bullen, a Tragedy* (1682). In the 19th century she was celebrated in an opera by Gaetano Donizetti, *Anna Bolena.*

Works about Anne Boleyn

Ives, E. W. *Anne Boleyn.* New York: Blackwell, 1986.

Warnicke, Retha M. *The Rise and Fall of Anne Boleyn: Family Politics at the Court of Henry VIII.* New York: Cambridge University Press, 1989.

Book of Common Prayer (1549) *liturgical work*

Until 1534, when Henry VIII broke away from the Roman Catholic Church and set himself up as head of the CHURCH OF ENGLAND, Britain was a Catholic country, with Catholic rites and rules. Even after 1534, changes in the form of worship and in the ways people were expected to conduct their religious lives came slowly. The archbishop of Canterbury, Thomas CRANMER translated the Bible into English, and his version, the "Great Bible," began to be distributed to churches, but people were still not encouraged to think for themselves about what to believe. Cranmer wrote an English version of the Litany, so that part of the service of worship was now conducted in a language the congregation could understand, but most of the service was still in Latin.

After the death of Henry VIII in 1547 and the accession to the throne of the 10-year-old King Edward VI, things changed quickly. Cranmer issued a *Book of Homilies* to help parish priests prepare sermons that lay people could follow; one of the differences Protestants had with the Catholic Church was that church members could go through the forms of worship without ever being asked to think about their relationship with God, and the *Book of Homilies* addressed this problem. Cranmer and the Council of Bishops met to discuss issues such as whether the new Church of England would allow priests to marry, whether churches would continue to be decorated with images of saints, and—a crucial issue at the time— whether it should be church doctrine that Christ's

body is really present in the consecrated host at Communion, a concept known as transubstantiation. Cranmer's own views on these questions changed over the years.

Cranmer had been working for several years on a new English-language liturgy. When he submitted it for approval to the Council of Bishops in 1548, after much discussion on the doctrinal issues—especially on the question of the "real presence"—and some compromise, it was approved and published in 1549. An Act of Uniformity passed that same year established it as the only authorized form of service in churches.

There was a great deal of controversy surrounding the *Book of Common Prayer* before it came to be accepted. Conservatives found the new liturgy far too radical; many Protestants felt that it did not go far enough. Many ordinary lay people resented change and longed for the old Latin service that they knew. A revised version, issued in 1552, distanced the Church of England even further from Catholic doctrine and practice.

Edward VI died in 1553, at age 16, and was succeeded by his half sister Mary, a Catholic who tried to bring England back to the Roman Catholic Church. Cranmer was one of hundreds who died as a heretic at Mary's command. But when Edward and Mary's half sister ELIZABETH I came to the throne in 1559, she reintroduced the 1552 *Book of Common Prayer,* and it began to take hold in the people's affections. Radical Protestants still found it too close to Catholicism, and during the years of the Commonwealth, when the Puritans were in control (1645–60), it was outlawed. The Restoration brought back the prayer book as well as the monarchy.

Cranmer's *Book of Common Prayer* takes the Church through the entire year. It has a regular morning and evening service; a service of Holy Communion; services for funerals, weddings, and baptisms; and a calendar of special prayers and special Bible readings to be added to the services at different seasons. Its prose is rhythmic and grand, yet simple. This sentence from the service of Evening Prayer, or Evensong, is an example:

O God, from whom all holy desires, all good counsels, and all just works do proceed; give unto thy servants that peace which the world cannot give, that both our hearts may be set to obey thy commandments, and also that by thee, we being defended from the fear of our enemies, may pass our time in rest and quietness, through the merits of Jesus Christ, our Saviour.

The collect, or special prayer, for the last Sunday before Advent (the period of waiting for the birth of Christ, in the month before Christmas) begins,

Stir up we beseech thee, O Lord, the wills of thy faithful people, that they, plenteously bringing forth the fruit of good works, may of thee be plenteously rewarded.

That Sunday came to be nicknamed "Stir-up Sunday," and to be thought of as the Sunday when a good housewife would make plans to stir up the cakes for Christmas. This affectionate reinterpretation shows how comfortable people came to be with Cranmer's work. The *Book of Common Prayer* remains in use in the Anglican Church almost unchanged.

As Cranmer's biographer Albert Pollard remarks, Cranmer "borrowed and learnt and adapted from various sources, but whatever he touched he adorned. Under his hands the rudest and simplest of prayers assumed a perfection of form and expression, and grew into one of the finest monuments of sacred literary art."

Works about the *Book of Common Prayer*

Ayris, Paul, and David Selwyn, eds. *Thomas Cranmer: Churchman and Scholar.* Rochester, N.Y.: Boydell Press, 1993.

Haigh, Christopher. *English Reformations: Religion, Politics, and Society under the Tudors.* New York: Oxford University Press, 1993.

Pollard, Albert Frederick. *Thomas Cranmer.* Hamden, Conn.: Archon Books, 1965.

Boorde, Andrew (Andrew Borde)
(1490–1549) *nonfiction writer*

Andrew Boorde was a physician known for his travel writing. Educated at Oxford University, he went on to become a monk in 1521, although he soon left the monastery to travel and study medicine. In his most famous work, *The Fyrste Boke of the Introduction of Knowledge* (1547), each chapter begins with a verse prologue spoken by a resident of the country being described. These figures are often caricatures of each nation's foibles. For example, a naked Englishman stands around wondering what he should wear; a representative of the Flemish people says he is "as drunken as a rat," and so on. After the prologue, which is written in doggerel, a form of poetry that is intended to be humorous, Boorde goes on to discuss the character of the people, the geography of the country, politics, economics, customs, and religion.

While Boorde unquestioningly accepts much fable as truth—he believes that the magician Merlin built Stonehenge, for example—he is also an acute observer and reporter of what he sees. Here, for example, is a passage about Holland:

In Holland is a good town called Amsterdam; and yet right many of the men of the country will quaff till they be drunk. . . . They be gentle people, but they do not like Scottish men. The women in the church be devout, and often are confessed in the church openly, laying their heads in the priest's lap, for priests there do sit when they hear confessions, and so they do in many provinces annexed to [Holland]. The women be modest, and in the towns and the churches they cover themselves and part of their face and head with their mantles.

The Fyrst Boke of the Introduction of Knowledge is regarded as the first English guidebook for traveling the continent of Europe.

Boorde also wrote *A Compendyous Regyment or a Dyetary of Helth* (ca. 1542), a practical health manual. Boorde is known to be one of the first physicians who recognized the importance of sanitation in public health. He also wrote *Breviary of Health* (1547), a popular text on diet and health.

Boothby, Frances (fl. 1669) *dramatist*

Little is known about the life of Frances Boothby. Her only known play, *Marcelia: or the Treacherous Friend,* written under the pseudonym "Arcasia," was performed at the Theatre Royal in London in 1669 and published the following year with the author's name appearing as "Mrs. F. Boothby." The play is a tragicomedy, a play that treats serious themes, like a tragedy, but has a happy ending, like a comedy. The heroine's cousin Melinet tricks Marcelia into believing that her lover, Lotharicus, is unfaithful. Melinet hopes by this stratagem to persuade the devastated Marcelia to consent to marriage to the king, and by doing so to gain favor with the king and to advance his own position. In typical tragicomic style Marcelia recovers her faith in her true love, the bad are punished, and the good live happily ever after.

It was highly unusual in the 17th century for a woman to write, and still more so for her to publish her work with her name on it. Boothby shows in her preface to the play that she anticipated problems as a woman playwright. She dedicates *Marcelia* to her "kinswoman" Lady Yates, who Boothby asks to defend her against "the Censuring world, upon this uncommon action in my Sex." The prologue asks for the audience's kindness for the writer, who (it is suggested) must be a little crazy: "You'l croud her Wit to death in such a Throng . . . With ballading I think she mad is grown." The aristocratic letter-writer Elizabeth Cottington may have been referring to Boothby and *Marcelia* in a letter written around 1670: "Ther is a bowld woman hath oferd one [a play] . . . I will tremble for the poor wooman exposed among the critticks."

Boothby is a forerunner of Aphra BEHN, whose first play appeared the year after *Marcelia*. The play has only recently been rediscovered by scholars; a critical edition is being prepared by the scholar Erika Mae Olbricht.

Bourchier, John (Second Baron, John Berners) (1467–1533) *translator*

John Bourchier was born in Bourchier, Devonshire, England, son of Humphrey Bourchier, a knight, and his wife, Elizabeth. Bourchier's political and military career started at the age of 15 when he participated in a failed effort to help make Henry Tudor, Earl of Richmond (later Henry VII), king. In 1497 he helped quell a Cornish rebellion in support of Perkin Warbeck, a pretender to the English throne. He went on to serve the English Crown in campaigns in France and Scotland. He was an important influence in diplomacy, helping to develop Henry VIII's alliances with France and Spain. In 1520 he was appointed deputy of Calais, a post he held until his death.

Bourchier is best remembered for his innovative translation of *Chroniques* (1523–25), the early 15th-century work of French historian Jean Froissart that recalled the events of the Hundred Years' War between England and France. Bourchier made a fairly free translation of the work and enlivened the history with the spirit of heroic romance. He also gained fame for his translation of the French romance *Huon of Bordeaux* (ca. 1530). Through this translation, Bourchier was the first to introduce the figure of Oberon, the fairy king, into English literature.

Bourchier's most popular work was *The Golden Book of Marcus Aurelius* (1535), a translation from the French version that was itself based on the Spanish manuscript by Antonio de Guevara. This work, in which Guevara attributed a series of reflections and letters he himself had written to the Roman emperor, was immensely popular and went through 14 editions in 50 years. Through this translation, Bourchier introduced to English literature Guevara's ornate prose style that was later imitated by many writers, including John LYLY. At the end of his career, Bourchier also translated the courtesy book *The Castell of Love,* by Diego de San Pedro. (A courtesy book provides guidelines for the education, conduct, and duties of a courtier or prince.)

Boyle, Robert (1627–1691) *nonfiction writer*

Robert Boyle was one of the great scientists of the 17th century, a natural philosopher and theological thinker who was a prominent member of the Royal Society of London. He was born the son of Richard Boyle, the first Earl of Cork, in Lismore, County Waterford, Ireland. At the time of Boyle's birth his father was the richest man in Great Britain. As a boy Robert was sent, together with one of his brothers, to study at Eton College in England in 1635. At this time the school was becoming fashionable as a place where important people sent their sons. While on a tour of the Continent as a young man, Boyle experienced a thunderstorm that frightened him yet caused him to become much stronger in his religious faith. He said he "was suddenly waked in a Fright with such loud Claps of Thunder . . . & every clap . . . both preceded & attended with Flashes of lightning so numerous . . . & so dazzling, that I began to imagine . . . the Day of Judgement's being come." This led him to vow that "all further additions to my life shud be more Religiously & carefully employed." In 1642 he went to Italy, where he read the work of Galileo and was deeply interested in his use of mathematics as an aid to scientific study. After his return to England in 1644, Boyle settled at his estate in Stalbridge in Dorset, where he wrote a number of treatises on ethics and religion. In 1649, however, he turned his attention to science. He set up a laboratory in his house and embarked on the experimentation that was to make him famous.

In 1660 he published his first scientific piece, *New Experiments Physico-Mechanicall, Touching the Spring of the Air and its Effects,* in which he documented various discoveries he made regarding air pressure. In 1662 he published further discoveries he made with fellow scientist Robert Hooke. Boyle's law, an important scientific law, appears in an appendix written in 1662 to his work *New Experiments Physico-Mechanicall.* This law expresses the inverse relationship that exists between the pressure and volume of a gas (that is, as pressure increases, volume decreases), which was determined by measuring the volume occupied by a constant quantity of air when compressed by differing weights of mercury. The 1660 text was the result of three years of experimenting with an air pump. With the device Hooke and Boyle had discovered a whole series of important facts. He showed, among other things, that sound did not travel in a vacuum and that living creatures and candle flames require air. Boyle was the first person to use the term "chemical analysis" as scientists use it today and began the classification of elements into acids, alkalis, and neutrals. Among his other contributions, Boyle was among the first scientists to publish his experiments in detail, including failed experiments, so that other scientists could replicate them. As one of the founders and members of the British Royal Society, Boyle was unswervingly dedicated to its motto, "Nullius in verba," "Nothing in words," meaning that all science must be based on experimentation.

As a philosopher Boyle was in favor of mechanical philosophy, a viewpoint that saw the universe as a huge machine or clock in which all natural phenomena could be accounted for purely by mechanical, clockwork motion. Boyle was also a man of strong religious beliefs who saw his scientific studies as a religious duty. He argued that studying the mechanics of nature illuminates God's omnipresence and goodness, thereby enhancing a scientist's understanding of the divine. He summarized his philosophical views in *The Christian Virtuoso,* which was published in 1690. Boyle, along with fellow members of the Royal Society of London, sought to reconcile Christian faith with scientific inquiry based on reason. On this subject he said that

> a God who could create a mechanical universe—who could create matter in motion, obeying certain laws out of which the universe as we know it could come into being in an orderly fashion—was far more to be admired and worshipped than a God who created a universe without scientific law.

In addition to his scientific pursuits and religious writings, Boyle was also interested in practical improvements that he hoped would make life better for everyone. Along these lines he studied methods of improving agriculture, investigated the possibility of extracting fresh water from the oceans, and examined the possibility of food preservation through vacuum packing.

Other Work by Robert Boyle
Works of the Honorable Robert Boyle, 1744. Kila, Mont.: Kessinger Publishing Company, 2003.

Works about Robert Boyle
Hunter, Michael. *Robert Boyle (1627–1691) Scrupulosity and Science.* Suffolk, U.K.: Boydell & Brewer, 2000.
Wojcik, Jan W. *Robert Boyle and the Limits of Reason.* Cambridge: Cambridge University Press, 2002.

Brackley, Elizabeth, Viscountess
(1626–1663) *poet, playwright*

Elizabeth Brackley was the daughter of William Cavendish, Duke of Newcastle, and Elizabeth Bassett Cavendish. She was probably born at one of the family's two main residences, Welbeck Abbey in Nottinghamshire or Bolsover Castle in Derbyshire, England. After the death of her mother in 1643, Brackley's father married Margaret Lucas, who became a well-known writer as Margaret Cavendish, Duchess of NEWCASTLE. William Cavendish was an important patron of literature, a friend to such writers as Ben JONSON, Sir John SUCKLING, and William DAVENANT, and he encouraged all his children, the girls as well as the boys, to read widely and to express themselves in writing. Neither Brackley nor her sister Jane CAVENDISH published anything in their lifetimes, but like the CAVALIER poets who were their father's friends, they circulated their writings in manuscript. The family members who would have read their work were a sophisticated and discriminating group of people.

In 1641 Brackley married John Egerton, Viscount Brackley, but, partly because she was so young at the time and partly because of the upheavals caused by the English Civil War, she did not go to live with her husband immediately. The manuscript volume *Poems, Songs, a Pastorall and a Play,* which proclaims Elizabeth Brackley and Jane Cavendish as joint authors on the title page, seems to have been compiled during the 1640s, when William Cavendish was most often absent from the family home, engaged in leading the forces of King Charles I against the parliamentary enemy. The poems are not signed individually, so cannot be assigned to one or the other sister. They are mostly celebrations of the virtues of family members and friends. Many of them refer to their father in adoring terms, praising his military accomplishments, his literary skill, and his attractiveness to women:

> My Lord your Picture speaks you this to be,
> A courtier and a soldier each may see.
> And so both love & war you can true tell
> Having on both sides known the trade full
>   well.

The play entitled *The Concealed Fancies,* seems to have been a late addition to the volume. It represents two sisters, Tattiney and Luceny, living in their family home in the absence of their father, courted by the appropriately named lovers Courtly and Presumption. The sisters put their suitors off in order to educate them about how to behave in marriage. Presumption begins by believing that after flattering Tattiney in courtship he will be able to lord it over her in marriage, but he comes to accept the ideal expressed by Luceny: that "man and wife should draw equally in a yoke." The play ends with the return of the absent father and marriages all round.

The Concealed Fancies was published in 1931 in an edition by Nathan Comfort Starr, whose introductory material suggested that the play had no interest except historic. More recent scholars have found much to admire in it. It has been reprinted as part of *Renaissance Drama by Women: Texts and Documents,* edited by S. P. Cerasano and Marion Wynne-Davies (New York: Routledge, 1996).

After she joined her husband, Brackley continued to write, though still not for publication. Following her death, her husband collected her writings and presented manuscript copies under the title of *Loose Papers Left by the Right Honourable Elizabeth, Countess of Bridgewater* to each of their children.

A Work about Elizabeth Brackley

Cerasano, S. P., and Marion Wynne-Davies, eds. *Readings in Renaissance Women's Drama.* New York: Routledge, 1998.

Bradford, William (1590–1657) *historian*

William Bradford was an American colonist who was instrumental in organizing the voyage of the *Mayflower* to North America. His account of the journey and of early settlement life is an important piece of colonial history.

Bradford was born in Austerfield, Yorkshire, England, and as a boy he became involved in the Protestant REFORMATION. As a member of the Separatist movement, which sought to break away from the CHURCH OF ENGLAND, he moved to Holland in 1609 and began organizing a journey to North America. In 1620 he traveled on the *Mayflower* in search of religious freedom with his wife, Dorothy May, who fell overboard and drowned en route.

Although Bradford lacked much formal education, he taught himself Greek, Latin, Dutch, and Hebrew. His best-known work, *History of Plymouth Plantation* (ca. 1650; first published in full in 1898), chronicles the hardships faced by the Puritans both on the way to North America and in establishing Plymouth colony in Massachusetts. His writing was "plain style," with simple and direct language, designed to reveal his devotion to his religion. For example, in describing why the Separatists wanted to go to the New World, he said they had "a great hope and inward zeal . . . of laying some good foundation . . . for the propagation and advancing the gospel of the kingdom of Christ in these remote parts of the world."

Bradford also helped draft the Mayflower Compact, an agreement signed aboard ship before the voyagers disembarked. The signers agreed to unite in forming a new colonial government and to be bound by its laws. Bradford quickly became an important political leader in the new settlement. In 1621 he was elected governor of Plymouth, a post he held until his death in 1657. In *A History of American Literature, 1607–1765* (1878), historian Moses Coit Tyler states that William Bradford "deserves the pre-eminence of being called the father of American history."

Other Work by William Bradford

Bradford, William, and John Kemp, introduction to *Governor William Bradford's Letter Book.* Reprint. Bedford, Mass.: Applewood Books, 2002.

Bradstreet, Anne Dudley (1612–1672)
poet

The place of Anne Dudley Bradstreet's birth is unknown, but she grew up in Lincolnshire, England. Her father, Thomas Dudley, was steward to the Earl of Lincoln. Anne Dudley received an excellent education for a woman of the era. She had private tutors and was allowed to use the earl's very large library.

When she was 16 years old, in 1628, Anne Dudley married Simon Bradstreet. Two years later the couple sailed for New England with Anne's parents; as devout Puritans, they wanted to be able to practice their faith openly and without fear. When Anne Bradstreet first saw America, she was frightened by the wildness of the place. She later came to believe, however, that God had chosen her to live in the New World.

Bradstreet and her husband had eight children. Although they moved around to various settlements in Massachusetts, they finally settled in North Andover. Simon Bradstreet served twice as royal governor of Massachusetts.

Anne Bradstreet wrote poetry for her own enjoyment and that of her family; she never intended her work to be published. However, without her permission, her brother-in-law published a volume of her poems in England in

1650, under the title *The Tenth Muse Lately Sprung up in America.* Bradstreet's early poems are conventional and give little indication that the author lived in the untamed wilderness of America. She is read today for her later work, which was published after her death. These poems, more deeply felt and less conventional, focus on Bradstreet's daily life as a settler and on the feelings and emotions of a woman as she faces life's hardships.

Onc of Bradstreet's most widely read poems, "Verses upon the Burning of Our House, July 8th, 1666," tells of her anguish as she looks at her ruined home:

> Here stood that Trunk, and there that chest,
> There lay that store I counted best,
> My pleasant things in ashes lie
> And them behold no more shall I.

When Bradstreet thinks about childbirth, she writes to her husband about her fear that she may not survive, a genuine possibility in the days when one in eight women died in childbirth.

> How soon, my dear, death may my steps
>   attend.
> How soon't may be thy lot to lose thy friend.

Bradstreet also wrote about her religious beliefs and about her relationship with nature. Although not a "feminist" in the modern sense of the word, she complained about those who felt women were not suited to the literary life:

> I am obnoxious to each carping tongue
> Who says my hand a needle better fits
> A poet's pen all scorn I should thus wrong,
> For such despite they cast on female wits.
> If what I do prove well, it won't advance;
> They'll say it's stol'n, or else it was by
> chance.

Anne Bradstreet died in North Andover, Massachusetts.

Works about Anne Bradstreet

Martin, Wendy. *An American Triptych: Anne Bradstreet, Emily Dickinson, Adrienne Rich.* Chapel Hill: University of North Carolina Press, 1984.
Rosenmeier, Rosamund. *Anne Bradstreet Revisited.* Boston: Twayne, 1981.

Breton, Nicholas (ca. 1545–1626) *poet, nonfiction writer*

Few details are known about Nicholas Breton's early life, except that he was the son of William and Elizabeth Breton. His father died while Nicholas was just a child, and he was a boy when his mother married the poet George GASCOIGNE. It is known that Breton settled in London as a young man and spent most of his life there as a writer. He dedicated the majority of his works to various wealthy patrons, including Mary Herbert, Countess of Pembroke, and King JAMES I.

Although Breton was once considered one of the best lyrical poets of his era, his reputation declined in his later years as he published disappointing and dull satires. Some of his finest lyrical poetry, and most of his well-known lines, are from "Phillida and Coridon." The following passage is an example of Breton's gift for writing about a simple country life in a relaxed and graceful manner:

> In the merry month of May,
> In a morn by break of day,
> Forth I walk'd by the wood-side,
> When as May was in his pride.

Breton's best-known works are his pastoral poems: *The Arbor of Amorous Devices* (1597), *England's Helicon* (1600) and *The Passionate Shepard* (1604). The following excerpt from *The Passionate Shepard* captured Breton's descriptive ability:

> Who can live in heart so glad
> As the merry country lad?
> Who upon a fair green balk
> May at pleasure sit and walk,

And amid the azure skies
See the morning sun arise;
While he hears in every spring
How the birds do chirp and sing.

Breton's style of lyrical verse has also been noted for its versatility and refinement; his work is satirical, religious, romantic, and pastoral at the same time.

Breton's prose work *Fantasticks* (1604) stands out for his skilled and careful descriptions of time, specifically in describing the passage of months and hours. *Fantasticks* also was based, in part, on character books, a genre and style that would soon become fashionable. Modeled on the *Characters* of the Greek philosopher Theophrastus, character books contained short descriptions and examples of a virtue or vice in personalities such as the generous patron or thieving servant. Breton published two such books: *Characters Upon Essaies* (1615) and *The Good and the Badde* (1616). His *Town and Country* is a valuable work of history in which he carefully and sympathetically depicts country life, illustrating local and social customs and describing picturesque rural scenery.

Breton's contribution to English literature was notable for his exceptional lyrical verse as well as his anticipation of the forthcoming popularity of character books. His best work, however, remains his lyrics and pastoral poems, acclaimed for their descriptions of simple country pleasures.

Other Work by Nicholas Breton

Works in Verse and Prose of Nicholas Breton. Alexander B. Grossart, ed. New York: AMS Press, June 1988.

Brinkelow, Henry (ca. 1500–1546)
nonfiction writer

Little is known of the life of Henry Brinkelow, who wrote satires and political commentaries during the English REFORMATION, the period when England broke with the Catholic Church. Brinkelow criticized the Roman Catholic Church and approved of Henry VIII's suppression of monasteries throughout England. His most prominent work, the *Com-*

playnt of Roderyck Mors (1542) was a speech written from the point of view of Mors, "sometyme a Gray fryre" (a member of the Franciscan order of monks) "unto the parliament howse of Irigland his natural cuntry for the redresse [correction] of certen wicked lawes, even customs and cruel decreys [laws]." In this work Brinkelow rails against the Papacy, regretting that "the body . . . of the pope is not banisshed with his name." He also strongly criticizes the fact that the revenues derived from the sale of monastic properties have gone to enrich the nobility at the expense of the country as a whole. Brinkelow also wrote *The Lamentacyon of a Christen Agaynst the Cytye of London* (1545), a religious complaint about the city of London.

Brome, Alexander (1620–1666) poet

Alexander Brome was born in Evershot, England, to John Brome. Little is known about his early life or the path by which he became an attorney. Poetry was an avocation for him, as it was for most poets of the time.

In the English Civil War, which broke out in 1640, pitting the forces of King Charles I against the antimonarchist Parliamentary forces (called the Roundheads because they wore their hair short), Brome allied himself with the Cavaliers who supported the throne. His main contribution to the king's cause seems to have been a series of drinking songs making fun of Parliament and of the whole idea of going to war. In one of them, from 1645, he wrote:

I love the King and the Parliament,
But I love them both together:
And when they by division asunder are rent,
I know 'tis good for neither.

Another song, from 1646, comments on how things were going badly for the king:

Come pass about the bowl to me,
A health to our distressed King; . . .
We do not suffer here alone,

Though we are beggar'd, so's the King;
'Tis sin t' have wealth when he has none,
Tush! poverty's a royal thing!

Songs and Other Poems (1661) contains most of Brome's poems from the 1640s and the 1650s. Brome's poetry is blunt and unadorned, but it is also always lively. It has affinities with the work of the CAVALIER poets, but he avoids the elaborate metaphors and similes, lengthy words, and complicated rhetorical devices they favored. An amusing example is "The Resolve," the first eight lines of which use the conventional words of courtly love poetry only to show how irrelevant they are to actual relationships:

Tell me not of a face that's fair,
Nor lip and cheek that's red,
Nor of the tresses of her hair,
Nor curls in order laid,
Nor of a rare seraphic voice
That like an angel sings;
Though if I were to take my choice
I would have all these things:
But if that thou wilt have me love,
And it must be a she,
The only argument can move
Is that she will love me.

In 1660 Brome celebrated the RESTORATION of the monarchy by writing *A congratulatory poem, on the miraculous, and glorious return of that unparallel'd King Charles the II* in a grand manner. He also wrote this roistering song to celebrate the same event:

We'll eat and we'll drink, we'll dance and
*   we'll sing,*
The Roundheads and Cavs, no more shall
*   be named,*
But all join together to make up the ring,
And rejoice that the many-headed dragon is
*   tamed.*
'Tis friendship and love that can save us
*   and arm us,*

And while we all agree, there is nothing can
*   harm us.*

In 1666 Brome published a volume of poetry by the ancient Roman poet Horace, translated by himself and others. He was very popular in his lifetime for his high spirits and wit; almost forgotten today, he nonetheless merits attention.

Other Work by Alexander Brome

Alexander Brome: Poems. Edited by Roman R. Dubinski. Toronto: University of Toronto Press, 1982.

Brome, Richard (ca. 1590–1652)
playwright

Where Richard Brome was born or who his parents were are unknown. Nothing, in fact, is known about his life before he entered the service of Ben JONSON sometime before 1614. Although Brome's exact duties are unknown, Jonson referred to Brome as his apprentice. Brome left Jonson and became an actor sometime around 1628. Shortly thereafter, he wrote his first play, *The Northern Lasse* (1629), a comedy about a young woman from the rural north of Britain.

Brome is heavily indebted to Jonson. Like the young (if not the mature) Jonson, he builds his plays around character types, or humor characters, as Jonson called them. As with Johnson, at the core of Brome's philosophy is an esteem for the social system of the Middle Ages in which prestige was established by birth and honor rather than wealth. Brome is, for example, horrified by his contemporaries' tendency to admire people simply because they have money.

Perhaps it is unfortunate that Brome owes so much to Jonson, because his achievement is inevitably judged against that of a man whose learning, intelligence, and talent Brome somewhat lacked. Brome was simply not as adept as Jonson at turning his ideas into dramatic situations. For this reason his work often seems less serious than that of his teacher, something Brome biographer R. J. Kaufmann notes: For instance, "Money worship for Jonson was a fundamental perversion—an abuse of reason. Brome understood this, but he usually conceived of it (less fundamentally) as a practice which rendered a man disagreeable, ridiculous, or at worst, a social liability."

The character of Brome's thought and art is quite visible in *The City Wit* (ca. 1630), one of his most noteworthy efforts. This play pits Crasy, the honest man, against a number of dishonest characters. Brome thus asks his audience to consider the value of honesty. The play opens with Crasy in his office, surrounded by empty moneybags. He has recently become bankrupt, and throughout the first act he suffers the consequences of being poor. His wife rejects him, and his in-laws criticize him for being honest, which was the cause of his downfall. Then he confronts each of his debtors, all of whom show pride in their dishonesty and advise him to "be rather a knave than a Fool." Each of these characters regards himself as Crasy's intellectual and social superior because he is wealthy and Crasy is not. From a moral standpoint, Crasy is superior to them all. But having discovered that one cannot be both honest and successful, he follows his enemies' advice in Acts II through V, turning dishonest and duping them out of their money. The intelligent, the play implies, can become wealthy if they put aside their morality.

Other plays by Brome include *The Queen's Exchange* (1632), a tragicomedy; *The Damoiselle* (1638), whose plot centers around the results of a lottery; and *A Jovial Crew* (1641), a comedy about two wealthy women who become beggars. Brome was among the best dramatists writing in the 1630s, and if he failed to live up to the greatness of his mentor Jonson, he made up for his shortcomings through his extraordinary range.

Other Work by Richard Brome

The Antipodes. New York: Theatre Arts Books, 2000.

A Work about Richard Brome

Sanders, Julie. *Caroline Drama: The Plays of Massinger, Ford, Shirley, and Brome.* Plymouth, U.K.: Northcote House, 1999.

Brown, Thomas (1663–1704) *nonfiction writer, translator*

Thomas Brown was born at Shifnal in Shropshire, England. He was educated at a local grammar school and later at Oxford.

Brown's most famous work is a very short one. Legend has it that while at Oxford Brown was hauled before the dean, Dr. John Fell, for wild behavior. Dr. Fell threatened to expel Brown but offered him a reprieve if he could translate on the spot an epigram by the Roman poet Martial (A.D. 43–120). Browne chose no. 33, addressed to an unknown acquaintance of Martial's. Martial's Latin begins, "Non amo te, Sabide" ("I do not love you, Sabidius"); Brown's version is as follows:

> *I do not love thee, Dr. Fell;*
> *The reason why I cannot tell;*
> *But this I know, and know full well,*
> *I do not love thee, Dr. Fell.*

Unfortunately, Dr. Fell's response was not recorded. Brown left Oxford without taking his degree and moved to London, where he earned his living as a translator of Latin and French works and participated in literary life, writing pamphlets, satires, and epigrams. Under the pseudonym of Dudly Tomkinson he wrote three witty and satirical pamphlets making fun of the poet laureate, John DRYDEN, entitled *The Reasons of Mr. Bays Changing his Religion* (1688), *The Late Converts Exposed* (1690), and *The Reasons of Mr. Joseph Hains the Player's Conversion & Reconversion* (1690). His prose work *Amusements Serious and Comical, Calculated for the Meridian of London* (1700) presents a vivid picture of London. He imagines himself guiding a stranger, an Indian, through various areas of the city. There are sections on "The Court"—that is, the surroundings of the king and queen; "The Play-House"; "Gaming-Houses"; "Coffee-Houses," and so on. In each section he lampoons the people found there; in the section on the court he remarks on the untrustworthiness of courtiers (the people who devote themselves to attending on the royal family):

He that holds a Courtier by the Hand, has a
Wet Eel by the Tail. He no sooner thinks he is
sure of him, but he has lost him.

Brown turned out a quantity of work, most of
which is forgotten. He is generally regarded as an
amusing hack writer. The scholar Charles Whibley
comments in *The Cambridge History of English Literature* that Brown was "well fitted by character
and training to do the work of Grub street"—Grub
Street being the London street where most of the
journalists lived. But he goes on to praise Brown's
scholarship and concludes, "with all his faults, Tom
Brown was a real man of letters."

Browne, Thomas (1605–1682) *nonfiction writer*

Thomas Browne was born in London to Thomas
Browne, a mercer or seller of fabrics, and Anne
Garraway Browne. He entered Oxford University
in 1623 and graduated with a B.A. in 1626, earning his M.A. in 1629. He went on to study medicine in France, Italy, and the Netherlands, finally
receiving an M.D. in 1633. In 1637 he settled in
Norwich. In 1671 Charles II knighted Browne for
his contributions to literature.

Browne's first book, *Religio Medici* (*The Religion
of a Physician*), was written in the early 1630s and
published in 1642. It is an account of Browne's
personal religious beliefs. Published at a time of intense religious conflict between the CHURCH OF
ENGLAND and the Puritans, it became immensely
popular. Soon after, Browne found himself a literary star, and he republished a corrected version of
his tract the following year.

In *Religio Medici,* Browne analyzes the doctrines
of the Church of England, accepting certain of the
church's teachings and rejecting others. He explains, "[T]here are two books from whence I collect my Divinity; besides that written one of God,
another of his servant Nature, that universall and
publik Manuscript, that lies expans'd unto the eyes
of all." Thus he uses nature or reason to prove that
certain of the church's policies are not acceptable.

Critical Analysis

Browne's age was a period of intellectual, political,
and social change. The conflict between the Puritans
and the Church of England led to a political conflict and eventually to a civil war in which King
Charles I was executed. Rather than taking one extreme or the other in this conflict, Browne attempted to find a middle ground. He was, as the
scholar Robert Ralston Cawley explains, "concerned to help man look out upon the world with
a saner eye."

Browne's interest in finding a middle ground
through the use of reason is most pronounced
in *Pseudodoxia Epidemica* (1646), a work in
which he sets out to discredit false notions about
nature, medicine, and other matters that had
been accepted as truth for centuries—for example, the belief that chameleons live only on air. As
Browne scholar C. A. Patrides argues, Browne
shares with Francis BACON a commitment to test
the truth of old beliefs and patiently progress
"through prejudice and misconception towards
the truth." In Book V, Chapter V of *Pseudodoxia,*
for instance, he analyzes the belief that Adam
and Eve did not have navels. This was widely believed at the time: Because they were not born
but created by God, they would not have navels.
The chapter begins with a scientific account of
the formation of the navel, explaining that the
navel appears when the umbilical cord, which
connects the baby to its mother, is cut. "Now the
navel being . . . subsequent unto generation, nativity or parturition [childbirth], it cannot be
well imagined" to have existed, Browne concludes, "at the creation or extraordinary formation of Adam . . . nor also that of Eve."

In the end, he concludes that although Adam
lacked a navel, his body contained the power to
produce navels in the children he would beget after
The Fall. Navels, in fact, are evidence of the connection that existed between Adam and God—and
this is perhaps why Browne argues that Adam's
body, instead of Eve's, was endowed with the ability to produce navels:

All the navel therefore and conjunctive part we can suppose in Adam, was his dependency on his Maker, and the connection he must needs have unto heaven . . . ; in the act of his production there may be conceived some connection, and Adam to have been all navel with his Maker.

Just as the navel is a sign of the connection one had with one's mother, Adam himself is a sign of the connection Man had with God. He is, therefore, linked to God by the symbol of the navel in Paradise.

Browne's definition of Adam as "all navel" illustrates the strain of NEOPLATONISM, a revival of the idealistic philosophy of Plato, in his thought, or his attempt to demonstrate how "this visible world is but a picture of the invisible" to cite the *Religio Medici.* Browne's Neoplatonism is perhaps most pronounced in *The Garden of Cyrus* (1658), a work in which he traces the history of gardening down to the garden of the Persian king Cyrus, who planted trees in "quincuncial patterns," to use the term Browne coined to signify trees planted in groups of five. Cyrus's garden had trees planted one in the center and four at the corners, in the shape of a diamond. The pattern for Browne is more than mere decoration. Planting trees in a quincuncial pattern reflects order in nature, which in turn suggests the divine order.

Hydriotaphia, Urne-Burial, or, a Discourse of the Sepulchrall Urnes Lately Found in Norfolk (1658), published in the same volume as *The Garden of Cyrus,* is one of Browne's greatest works. He begins with a discussion of ancient urns, containers for the ashes of a cremated person, that had been recently discovered in a field. From there he moves to a comparison of different ways that societies have dealt with burial, and from there to a broader philosophical discussion of death.

Because the period of the English Civil War was such a turbulent time, much scholarly and readerly attention has been paid to writers who represent one side or another of the conflict, such as Gerrard WINSTANLEY. Browne's complex and eloquent prose represents an often-overlooked middle ground.

Other Work by Thomas Browne
The Major Works. Edited by C. A. Patrides. New York: Penguin, 1977.

A Work about Thomas Browne
Havenstein, Daniela. *Democratizing Sir Thomas Browne:* Religio Medici *and Its Imitations.* New York and Oxford: Oxford University Press, 1999.

Browne, William (ca. 1591–1645) *poet*
William Browne was born at Tavistock, Devonshire, England, and educated at Exeter College, Oxford University. He is best known for writing *Britannia's Pastorals,* a three-volume collection of poems that glorify England. The first book was published in 1613 and the second in 1616. The manuscript for his third book was not published until 1852. With shepherds and rural living as its subject matter, pastoral poetry generally sought to draw a contrast between the simplicity and purity of rustic living and the difficulty and corruption of urban life. Browne's poems, loosely centered around the story of lovers named Marina and Celandine, are written with warm descriptions of the natural world. In one passage he describes how a robin feeds Marina, who is trapped in a cave.

> Here left the bird the cherry, and anon
> Forsook her bosom, and for more is gone,
> Making such speedy flights into the thick
> That she admir'd he went and came so
>   quick.

William Browne was part of a circle of poets who drew inspiration from the poetry of Edmund SPENSER including George WITHER, Michael DRAYTON and John DONNE. He often honored these fellow poets in Spenserian stanzas. In the second book of *Britannia's Pastorals* he writes of Michael Drayton:

> Our second Ovid, the most pleasing Muse
> That heav'n did e're in mortals braine
>   infuse,

All-loved Draiton, in soule-raping straines,
A genuine noate, of all the Nimphish
   traines
Began to tune

In *A History of Elizabethan Literature,* English historian George Saintsbury said, "All this various literary cultivation had the advantage of keeping [Browne] from being a mere mocking-bird, though it did not quite provide him with any prevailing or wholly original pipe of his own." Yet Browne's reputation remains firm.

Bruno, Giordano (1548–1600) *nonfiction writer*

Giordano Bruno was born in Nola, Italy, to Juano Bruno, a soldier, and Fraulissa Savolino Bruno. In 1565 he entered the Dominican monastery of San Domenico in Naples. While studying there, he read works by Desiderius ERASMUS that the church had forbidden; he also became interested in the controversial Arian teachings that denied Christ's divinity. In 1576 the church authorities were preparing to indict him for heresy. Bruno fled, and for the next 16 years he wandered through Europe, not returning to Italy until 1591. Arrested the following year, he was convicted of heresy in 1592. He remained imprisoned for the next seven years and then was burned at the stake in 1600.

Between 1576 and 1591 Bruno wrote a great many works in both Italian and Latin. From 1583 to 1585 he lived in London, where he frequented the court of ELIZABETH I and associated with writers such as Sir Philip SIDNEY and Fulke GREVILLE. During this period he published, in Italian, the most influential of his writings, works of philosophy and scientific studies. *The Expulsion of the Triumphant Beast* (1584), a dialogue about the limitations of Christian morality, is dedicated to Sidney: "Now I do not know how I should esteem myself, excellent sir, if I did not esteem your intellect, did not respect your customs, did not proclaim your merits, through which you revealed yourself to me at the very moment I arrived on the island of Britain."

Bruno's belief system is a mixture of scientific and religious beliefs. In fact, many of his scientific beliefs derive from his notions about God, not his understanding of the physical universe. "Bruno's philosophy and his religion are one in the same," as scholar Frances Yates observes, and indeed, "Bruno uses thought . . . in a semi-magic way, as a mode of reaching intuitive knowledge of the divine."

Bruno insisted that freedom of thought is necessary to advance human knowledge. In works such as *The Ash Wednesday Supper* (1584) and *On the Infinite Universe and Worlds* (1584), he accepts the Copernican thesis that the Earth moves around the Sun, not vice versa, and he proposes that the universe is infinite at a time when most thought differently.

Bruno has always had a reputation for being a radical thinker. His acceptance of Copernicus's thesis and his belief in an infinite universe has made him seem like a scientific philosopher in an age of theological philosophers. However, he was not a scientist. He neither conducted experiments nor arrived at his conclusions by observing the world around him. As the scholars Edward Gosselin and Lawrence Lerner note, Bruno reached conclusions that are "coincidentally and fortuitously correct from the standpoint of modern physics." The reason he arrived at these conclusions, however, are unacceptable to modern physicists. For example, Bruno's belief in an infinite universe, perhaps his most modern idea, was based on his belief in an immanent God, that is, a God who is present throughout the universe. It would be impossible, Bruno reasoned, to think God, an infinite being, could confine Himself to a finite universe.

In addition to his works of scientific speculation, Bruno wrote works of a more explicitly religious nature. *The Heroic Frenzies* (1585) is an analysis of the state of religious ecstasy, yet he uses scientific language to describe this state: "Consequently, the body becomes lean, undernourished, extenuated, deficient in blood and overcome by melancholy humors."

Despite his unscientific methods, Bruno's influence on the scientific literature of his period was profound.

Other Work by Giordano Bruno

Cause, Principle and Unity and Essays on Magic. Translated by Robert D. Lucca and Richard J. Blackwell. New York: Cambridge University Press, 1998.

Works about Giordano Bruno

Gatti, Hilary. *The Renaissance Drama of Knowledge: Giordano Bruno in England.* New York: Routledge, 1989.

White, Michael. *The Pope and the Heretic: The True Story of Giordano Bruno, the Man Who Dared to Defy the Roman Inquisition.* New York: William Morrow, 2002.

Buchanan, George (1506–1582) *nonfiction writer, poet, playwright*

George Buchanan was born to Thomas and Agnes Heriot Buchanan in Killearn, Stirlingshire, Scotland. His family, which included four brothers and three sisters, was considered respectable but suffered through periods of extreme poverty. As a boy, Buchanan showed academic promise, and at age 15, with the help of his uncle, he was sent to study at the University of Paris. He later went on to the University of St. Andrews in Scotland and then returned to Paris to teach at the Collège de Sainte-Barbe. For the next several years, Buchanan's whereabouts are unknown, but it is known that he returned to Scotland in 1537. There in 1539 Buchanan was denounced and jailed as a heretic for writing two satirical poems against the Franciscan monks: *Somnium* (*Dream,* 1535) and *Franciscanus et fratres* (*Franciscans and Brothers,* 1527). These poems, written in Latin, used irony and sarcasm to criticize the Franciscans as being corrupt and lacking devotion to God. Hugh Walker writes in his *English Satire and Satirists* that Buchanan's

satires on the Franciscans, "though written in Latin, . . . are among the most telling satires in any language." Walker goes on to say that this satire "is one of the most unsparing attacks ever directed against a great community." Buchanan escaped from prison and began teaching in Bordeaux, France, where the famous French essayist, Montaigne, was one of his students. There he distinguished himself as a leading humanist.

While the term *humanism* has come to mean a variety of different things, RENAISSANCE humanism refers specifically to a school of thought that developed at the end of the Middle Ages and was concerned with the ability of humans to determine for themselves truth and falsehood through reason. The humanist movement of the Renaissance was founded on a renewed interest in classical Greek and Roman thinkers. For this reason, Buchanan wrote his prose and verse almost exclusively in Latin.

In 1547 Buchanan went to Portugal to teach at the University of Coimbra. While there he was denounced for his religious views and forced to face the Inquisition. He was tried, found guilty, and imprisoned in a Portuguese monastery, where he composed a Latin paraphrase of the Psalms of David. He dedicated this work to MARY STUART, Queen of Scots.

In 1561 Buchanan returned to Scotland and became involved in the Scottish Reformation, writing fervently in favor of Protestantism. Until 1567 he was a tutor to and supporter of Mary Stuart, but after the murder of her second husband, Lord Darnley, he turned against her. Buchanan helped prepare the case against Mary for ELIZABETH I with his recriminatory *Detectio Mariae Regiae* (1568) and his 20-volume *History of Scotland* (1582). In the *History,* Buchanan wrote that "throughout her personal reign Mary had schemed to establish a tyranny, had behaved recklessly and maliciously at all times, and had ultimately devised the murder of her husband at the hand of her paramour." Mary was executed in 1587.

In 1579 Buchanan published his famous political treatise *De Jure Regni apud Scotos,* or *A Discourse*

Concerning the Due Privilege of Government in the Kingdom of Scotland. Considered by many to be his most important work, *Discourse* argued in favor of limited government, saying that rulers could be held accountable for their actions and asserting that kings ought to be restrained by laws that reflect the will of the people: "The law then is paramount to the king, and serves to direct and moderate his passions and actions." Buchanan's ideas would later serve as philosophical underpinnings for many of the ideas that sparked the American Revolution.

Buchanan also wrote several plays attacking tyranny, including *Baptistes* (1534) and *Jepthes* (1578).

Other Work by George Buchanan

The Tyrannous Reign of Mary Stewart. Translated by W. A. Gatherer. 1958. Reprint. Westport, Conn.: Greenwood Press, 1978.

A Work about George Buchanan

MacQueen, John, ed. *Humanism in Renaissance Scotland.* Edinburgh: Edinburgh University Press, 1990.

Buckingham, second Duke of, George Villiers (1628–1687) *dramatist*

Born in London, George Villiers was the son of the first Duke of Buckingham (also named George Villiers). Like his father, the second duke was chiefly a politician, having been brought up in the household of King Charles I after his father's assassination in 1628 by a naval officer. He was educated at Cambridge, and he married Mary, daughter of Lord Fairfax. Buckingham was a close friend of the young Prince Charles, who would become Charles II at the RESTORATION in 1660, and served King Charles II as a privy councilor. Buckingham had a bad reputation socially: He was a brawler and a philanderer.

Along with Arlington, Clifford, Ashley, and Lauderdale, Buckingham was a part of the so-called Cabal ministry and thus a signer of a secret treaty with France in 1672. (The word *cabal,* which means a small group involved in secret intrigue, is formed by arranging the initials of the five ministers' names.) Buckingham appears as a character in John DRYDEN's poem *Absalom and Achitophel,* which uses a story from Hebrew scriptures as an allegory, or symbolic system, for the contemporary dispute over who would succeed Charles II. In the poem the character of King David represents Charles II, and Zimri represents Buckingham in a most unflattering light. Dryden's inclusion of Buckingham in the poem suggests his importance in the government, but Buckingham lost his influence with the king and eventually retired to Yorkshire.

Buckingham is perhaps more important to English history generally than to English literary history, but he did make an important contribution to the latter with his play *The Rehearsal* (1671), a satire on the heroic dramas of such playwrights as Dryden and William DAVENANT. In it a playwright, Bayes (whose name perhaps reflects the bay wreath accorded to Dryden as official poet laureate), takes two friends, Smith and Johnson, to watch a rehearsal of his play. Much of the dialogue consists of Bayes's explanations of the highly implausible action, which includes a representation on the stage of a planetary eclipse. *The Rehearsal* remained popular for many decades and was often performed; it has been mounted in student productions recently with some success.

Alexander POPE in his *Moral Essays* describes Buckingham on his deathbed, contrasting the dying man with the glorious figure he was once: "Alas! How changed from him / That life of pleasure, and that soul of whim!"

A Work about George Villiers, Second Duke of Buckingham

O'Neill, John H. *George Villiers, Second Duke of Buckingham.* Boston: Twayne, 1984.

Bunyan, John (1628–1688) *nonfiction writer*

John Bunyan was born in Elstow, England, to Thomas Bunyan, a tinker, or one who repairs household tools, and his second wife, Margaret Bentley. Bunyan attended a local grammar school and then began to work at his father's profession. In 1644 he joined the Parliamentary side in the English Civil War, which was sparked by conflict between the king and Parliament over religious issues and questions about the rights of the monarchy. When he left the army Bunyan took up his work as a tinker again and married in 1648.

During the 1650s, while Oliver Cromwell temporarily ruled England, a number of radical Protestant sects flourished. Bunyan became caught up in the religious fervor of this period, joining a Congregational church, a Protestant sect that believed in the rights of each congregation to set religious policy, in 1653. Soon after he began preaching and publishing works of religious controversy, such as *Some Gospel-Truths Opened* (1656) and *A Vindication of Some Gospel-Truths* (1657), both of which attacked another Protestant sect, the Quakers, or Society of Friends.

After the RESTORATION of Charles II in 1660, members of such Protestant sects fell out of favor and were often persecuted for their beliefs. Bunyan was arrested that very year for preaching without a license and for failing to attend services of the Church of England. Refusing to stop preaching, he was repeatedly jailed.

While in prison Bunyan composed a number of religious works, beginning with *Profitable Meditations* (1661), a long religious poem. His most famous work of these years is *Grace Abounding to the Chief of Sinners* (1666). This spiritual autobiography, laden with biblical quotations, relates Bunyan's awakening: "as I was sitting by the fire, I suddenly felt this word to sound in my heart, *I must go to Jesus;* at this my former darkness and atheism fled away, and the blessed things of heaven were set within my view."

Bunyan continued to publish works that reflected his religious beliefs. His masterpiece, *The Pilgrim's Progress* (1678–84), was completed during a second brief imprisonment for illegal preaching.

Bunyan published many other works throughout his life, including *The Life and Death of Mr. Badman* (1680), a dialogue about the effects of evil-doing, which is ranked with *The Pilgrim's Progress* as one of Bunyan's most "novelistic" works. It is considered novelistic because it is not merely a religious tract but tells a story that illustrates a religious point, in this case about the life of Mr. Badman.

Critical Analysis

The critic Richard Greaves has summarized Bunyan's career: "Bunyan was a staunch, sometimes vitriolic [especially harsh or burning] critic of his society." This quality is illustrated in Bunyan's masterpiece, *Pilgrim's Progress.* Presented as a dream-vision of the author's, the book follows the journey of Christian from the City of Destruction, which represents the world in its sinfulness, to the Celestial City, representing the state of Christian salvation. Thus, the book describes an actual journey, which represents a spiritual journey to religious awakening.

As he sets out from the City of Destruction, Christian is accompanied by his neighbor Pliable. The first obstacle they encounter is the Slough of Despond: "here therefore they wallowed for a time, being grievously bedaubed [covered] with the dirt, and Christian, because of the burden that was on his back, began to sink in the mire." This obstacle represents the difficulty of the Christian journey, how easy it is to become mired in despair or hopelessness.

They continue on, however. Another obstacle Christian encounters is the fiend Apollyon, who represents Satan. One of the most memorable moments on the journey is Christian's trip through Vanity-Fair, which represents the allure of worldly pleasures. All types of vanity are sold in this town: "Therefore at this Fair are all such merchandise sold, as houses, lands, trades, places, honours, preferments, titles, countries, kingdoms, lusts, pleasures, and delights of all sorts, as whores, bawds, wives, husbands, children, masters, servants, lives, blood, bodies, souls, silver, gold, pearls, precious stones, and what not."

In the end Christian reaches the Celestial City. Bunyan also wrote a second part to *Pilgrim's*

Progress describing a similar journey undertaken by Christian's wife, Christiana. She undertakes her journey with a companion named Mercy, and like her husband, reaches the Celestial City.

Pilgrim's Progress was initially popular among members of Protestant sects such as the Puritans in Britain and America but has since become an all-time best-seller and has been translated into more than 200 languages. Its popularity derives in part from the universality of the story, a simple religious journey, and also the colorfulness of Bunyan's descriptions of the obstacles along the way. As the Bunyan editor Roger Sharrock argues, "It is [the] sheer creative spontaneity of *The Pilgrim's Progress,* drawing on the deepest resources of the popular tradition and the unconscious mind, that makes the book fascinating."

Other Works by John Bunyan

Grace Abounding with Other Autobiographies. John Stachiewski, ed., with Anita Pacheco. New York: Oxford University Press, 1998.

The Miscellaneous Works of John Bunyan. 6 vols. Roger Sharrock, ed. New York: Oxford University Press, 1976.

Works about John Bunyan

Greaves, Richard L. *Glimpses of Glory: John Bunyan and English Dissent.* Stanford, Calif.: Stanford University Press, 2002.

Hill, Christopher. *A Tinker and a Poor Man: John Bunyan and his Church, 1628–1688.* New York: Knopf, 1988.

Burnet, Gilbert (1643–1715) *theologian, educator*

Gilbert Burnet was born in Edinburgh, Scotland, the son of Robert Burnet, a landowner and judge who later became Lord Crimond, and his wife, Rachel Johnston, of a Scottish border clan. From his earliest years Gilbert gravitated to the Anglican faith—his father was a broad-minded member of that church, while his mother was a strict Presby-

terian. Demonstrating a precocious intellect, Gilbert was schooled at home under his father's tutelage. He mastered Latin at 10 and received his master's degree from the College of New Aberdeen at 14.

After the death of Robert Burnet in 1661, Burnet's mother tried to dissuade him from pursuing an ecclesiastical career in favor of the legal profession. The young man went to England, where he made the acquaintance of leading theologians and churchmen as well as of the chemist Robert Boyle. He was elected a fellow of the Royal Society in 1664 and declined an appointment as bishop of Aberdeen on the grounds of his youth. He traveled abroad to Holland, Flanders, and France, studied homiletics, or the art of preaching, with the Jesuits at Port Royal, France, learned Hebrew under a rabbi in Amsterdam, and continued his religious discussions in the more tolerant atmosphere that the Netherlands then offered. It was there that "he became fixed in that strong principle of universal charity," wrote John Clarke, a 20th-century commentator on his work.

Returning to Scotland in 1664 a confirmed latitudinarian (or someone who was liberal and tolerant in matters of doctrine and religious practice), Burnet was installed as the minister at Saltoun, where he began writing his *Thoughts on Education,* a comprehensive and practical guide for the education of a Scottish gentleman. In it he continued his broad-minded approach to things in general by recommending an exposure to classical writers as well as to proponents of Christian duty, reminding his readers to be temperate in all things. Young men should choose their tutors well, he declared, and steep themselves in philosophy, Latin, rhetoric, and foreign languages while allowing time for hobbies and useful recreations. He cautioned against young men traveling abroad until they were at least 21, when they could more easily be "made capable of larger and freer thoughts." His principles can perhaps be summarized in this extract: "There is nothing in the law of nature doth more oblige men to, than carefully to educate and cultivate their children, this being the truest expression of a father's love." Burnet himself had fathered five sons and four daughters through three marriages and is rumored to have married a fourth time after his third wife's death in 1709.

Burnet served from 1669 to 1673 as chair of divinity at the University of Glasgow but was forced to resign that post after disputes with Presbyterian opponents that were often more political than theological. Casting himself "on the providence of God," he was appointed preacher at the Rolls, a prestigious post that gave him access to the royal family and other prominent figures in London. In 1679 Burnet published the first volume of his lengthy *History of the Reformation of the Church of England,* a project that would occupy him for the rest of his life; the second volume appeared in 1681 and the third in 1713, two years before his death. This work was unprecedented in its approach to history, not only because it was more readable than any previous historical work in English but because Burnet set new standards for careful consultation of documents.

In 1680 Burnet published *Some Passages of the Life and Death of John, Earl of Rochester;* he had ministered to ROCHESTER on his deathbed. His memoir, the historically insightful *The History of My Own Time,* was published posthumously according to the directions in his will. In his last years Burnet indulged his interest in chemistry by building and furnishing a laboratory for himself.

With the death of Charles II and the accession of James II to the throne, Burnet removed himself to Europe, where he published a series of letters to scientist Robert Boyle that set out to offer scientific proof of the existence of God. He settled in Holland, where he became chaplain to William of Orange. He accompanied William to London when he became King William III in 1689. Burnet's star rose under the new regime: He preached the coronation sermon for King William and Queen Mary and was appointed tutor to the Duke of Gloucester. He also continued to work for reform within the Anglican Church and to write theological commentaries, such as *An Exposition of the Thirty-Nine Articles* (1699), in which he argued against "pa-

pistry," rule by popes, in other words Roman Catholicism. Not long before Burnet's death in 1715 he preached before the Hanoverian king George I, marking the end of a long ecclesiastical career that allowed him to wield significant influence in the highest circles.

A Work by Gilbert Burnet

The Boyle Lectures. Bristol, U.K.: Thoemmes Press, 2000.

Burton, Robert (1577–1640) *nonfiction writer, playwright*

Robert Burton was born in Leicestershire, England, to Ralph Burton, a country gentleman, and his wife, Dorothy Faunt. He entered Oxford University in 1593 and remained there for the rest of his life. After taking holy orders, he was made vicar of St. Thomas in the western suburbs of Oxford in 1616. "I have lived," he wrote, "a silent, sedentary, private life . . . in the University . . . penned up [for the] most part in my study."

Burton's career began as a playwright with his collaboration on a comedy, *Alba* (1605), which has not survived. A later comedy, *Philosophaster* (1617), which was written in Latin and only performed once, was not published until 1862. Burton is best known for *The Anatomy of Melancholy,* published in 1621 under the pseudonym of Democritus Junior; he borrowed the name from an ancient Greek philosopher. In this massive work, Burton analyzes the RENAISSANCE ailment of melancholy, roughly equivalent to modern depression and a subject of much discussion at the time. William SHAKESPEARE's character Hamlet, for example, suffers from melancholy, which makes him brooding and indecisive. The book was an immediate success and went through many revisions.

Critical Analysis

The Anatomy of Melancholy begins with a long preface, "to the Reader," a discussion of the similarities between Burton's personality and that of Democritus. The most important similarity is that both he and Democritus suffered from melancholy. What is perhaps more significant to Burton is that the book he is introducing is supposedly a continuation of Democritus's final work, since "the subject of his [Democritus's] book was melancholy and madness." Burton seeks "to find out the seat of . . . melancholy, whence it proceeds, and how it was engendered in men's bodies to the intent he might better cure it in himself, and by his writings and observations teach others how to prevent and avoid it. . . . Democritus Junior is therefore bold to imitate . . . to revive again, prosecute, and finish this [lost] treatise."

Burton, however does much more. *The Anatomy of Melancholy* is an encyclopedic work, "a vast mobilization of the notions and expressions of others," as the scholar Holbrook Jackson observes, "yet . . . it is [Burton], not they, who peeps from behind every quotation. The reason is clear. He is an artist of mosaic, using shreds and patches he has torn from the work of others to make a picture emphatically his own." Burton is thus what modern scholars call an appropriator, one who incorporates into his own writing the words and ideas of others, drawing from them in such a way that they become something different from what they were in their original context. He cites more than 1,300 writers, ranging from classical authors such as Virgil and Ovid to the Bible to other medical writers. Consequently, even though about two-thirds of the book uses quotations or paraphrasing, it is a wholly new work.

Indeed, Burton's *Anatomy* is something akin to a sprawling history of the effects of melancholy on a world which is itself, in Burton's view, infected with melancholy: "And this, belike, is that which our fabulous poets have shadowed unto us in the tale of Pandora's box, which, being opened through her curiosity, filled the world full of all manner of diseases."

Burton's goal was, in fact, to create a counterpart to the world through his words. As he points out:

"'Tis not my study or intent to compose neatly . . . So that as a river runs sometimes . . .

swift, then . . . slow; . . . now deep, then shallow; . . . doth my style flow; now serious, then light; now comical, then satirical . . ., as the present subject required, or as that time I was affected. And . . . this treatise . . . shall seem . . . the way to an ordinary traveller, sometimes fair, sometimes foul; . . . barren in one place, better soil in another: by woods, groves, hills, dales, plains, etc."

One of the ways that Burton achieves his intended effect is by using a mixture of literary styles. Thus, *The Anatomy* is a medical text because it contains discussions of the causes and cures of melancholy. Further, it is a psychological study, the first in the English language, because it discusses the mental difficulties to which melancholy gives rise. Additionally, the work is a theological meditation or a sermon because it posits The Fall as the primary cause of melancholy. Finally, *The Anatomy* is a satire because it mocks the ways of the world: "If Democritus were alive now," Burton writes in his preface, "and should see the superstition of our age, our religious madness . . . what would he say?"

The book is also autobiographical, for Burton is interested in his own melancholy as much as he is interested in melancholy in general. "When I first took this task in hand," he tells the reader, "this I aimed at . . . to ease my mind, for . . . I was not a little offended with this malady, shall I say my mistress Melancholy."

The overall affect of Burton's use of multiple genres is that his *Anatomy* risks seeming like "an amorphous literary digression, an infinite digression upon an infinity of subjects," to cite the scholar Rosemary Colie. Colie goes on, however, to defend Burton's method, noting that "a subject such as melancholy, in which cause, symptom, and cure are so confused and so confusing, . . . demands the mixture of mode and genre." Burton's seemingly chaotic approach to his subject, in other words, has been followed in order to imitate the seemingly chaotic nature of melancholy itself. Decorous or not, *The Anatomy*, according to Colie, "reflects the confusion and chaos that [Burton] sees in the world." Many modern readers have found Burton's work difficult and confusing, because of its use of numerous Latin quotes and the outdated nature of its subject. However, *The Anatomy of Melancholy* remains an important milestone in the history of psychology and a favorite of ambitious readers.

Works about Robert Burton

Breitenberg, Mark. *Anxious Masculinity in Early Modern England.* New York: Cambridge University Press, 1996.

Schmelzer, Mary Murphy. *'Tis All One: "The Anatomy of Melancholy" As Belated Copious Discourse.* New York: Peter Lang, 1999.

Vicari, Eleanor. *The View from Minerva's Tower: Learning and Imagination in* The Anatomy of Melancholy. Toronto: University of Toronto Press, 1989.

Butler, Samuel (1612–1680) *poet*

Samuel Butler was born at Strensham in Worcestershire, England, to a farming family. He was educated at King's School, Worcester, and possibly at either Oxford or Cambridge—the record is inconclusive.

Butler held several secretarial posts before becoming steward, or manager, of Ludlow Castle in 1661. Among those he served was Sir Samuel Luke, a rigid Presbyterian who was a colonel in the Parliamentary army that fought against the forces of King Charles I during the English Civil War (1642–51). Many scholars believe that Luke was the model for the title character in Butler's satirical poem *Hudibras* (1661–78).

After the publication in 1661 of the first volume of *Hudibras,* the recently restored king, Charles II—pleased by the poem's merciless satire of the Puritans, who were his enemies—promised Butler a pension of 100 pounds a year, but it seems that it was never paid. Butler published the second volume of *Hudibras* in 1663 and the third in 1678. In the meantime he wrote a number of shorter poems and a series of prose "characters," or character sketches; these were not published until long after

his death in *The Genuine Remains in Verse and Prose of Mr. Samuel Butler* (1759). Butler died in poverty.

Critical Analysis

Butler's *Hudibras* is a poem of 10,000 lines that is both a satire and a burlesque. Satire is a literary form that uses irony and sarcasm to criticize human behavior that the author considers foolish. A burlesque is a literary work that criticizes through grotesque exaggeration or comic imitation.

Hudibras is loosely based on *Don Quixote* by Miguel de CERVANTES SAAVEDRA. Instead of the elderly cavalier and his earthy squire, Sancho Panza, it features a Presbyterian colonel named Hudibras and his squire, Ralpho; instead of arguing about chivalry, these two discuss theology and church government, often disagreeing bitterly. Hudibras is described as:

> . . . in Logic a great critic,
> Profoundly skill'd in Analytic. . . .
> He'd undertake to prove by force
> Of argument a man's no horse.

Butler goes on to identify Hudibras with religious militants:

> Such as do build their faith upon
> The holy text of pike and gun;
> Decide all controversies by
> Infallible artillery;
> And prove their doctrine orthodox
> By apostolic blows and knocks.

Furthermore, the poem reveals Hudibras to be stupid, greedy, and dishonest.

Butler pretends to write an epic poem, that is, a long, serious poem about the exploits of a hero, in praise of Hudibras, but the poem is a mock epic, or parody—a work that ridicules through imitation. Although the main target is Puritan hypocrisy, Butler finds plenty of other types of human folly and vice to lampoon along the way.

The poem is written in iambic tetrameter (a line with four beats of alternating stressed and unstressed syllables) in rhyming couplets, a verse form now known as "Hudibrastic." Butler also used this form for his poem *The Elephant in the Moon* (1676), in which the object of the satire is the Royal Society. Founded in 1660, the society was a group of prominent scientists and philosophers who advocated investigating nature through reason and experimentation. Its members (who included John AUBREY, John DRYDEN, and Isaac NEWTON), were mostly Puritan sympathizers, which made it a ready target for Butler. In the poem the savants (wise men) mistake the flies and gnats that are trapped in their telescope for inhabitants of the moon, called the Privolvans and the Subvolvans. As they take turns pressing their eyes to the telescope to observe the warring factions on the moon, including a spectacular elephant, they agree

> *That 'twas more noble to create*
> *Things like Truth, out of strong conceit,*
> *Than with vexatious pains and doubt,*
> *To find, or think t' have found, her out.*

Butler was not impressed by the Royal Society's early attempts to develop the modern scientific method. In his universally skeptical view, all opinion was self-deception or could be bought.

The posthumously published prose "Characters," modeled on *Ethical Characters* by the ancient Greek writer Theophrastus (ca. 300 B.C.), may have provided material for *Hudibras.* They include "A Modern Politician," "An Hypocritical Non-conformist," "A Modern Statesman," "A Small Poet," "A Lawyer," "A Virtuoso," "A Justice of Peace," and "A Fanatic." This quip from "A Degenerate Nobleman" gives a taste of Butler's method: "A degenerate nobleman, or one that is proud of his birth, is like a turnip. There is nothing good of him but that which is underground."

Hudibras was immensely popular during its author's life and for about 100 years after his death. In the 19th century people began to take a different view of the Civil War, seeing the Puritan rebels as champions of liberty against tyranny, and Butler's jaundiced view of them fell out of favor. He is due for new recognition. As the critic Hugh Walker writes, "On his own ground, that of satire in the grotesque vein written in doggerel verse, Butler is supreme in English."

Other Work by Samuel Butler

Prose Observations. Edited by Hugh De Quehen. New York: Oxford University Press, 1979.

Works about Samuel Butler

Wasserman, George Russell. *Samuel Butler and the Earl of Rochester: A Reference Guide.* Boston: G. K. Hall, 1986.

Wasserman, George Russell. *Samuel "Hudibras" Butler.* Boston: Twayne, 1989.

Byrd, William (1543–1623) *composer, poet*

William Byrd was one of the most important composers of English madrigals during the Elizabethan era. Little is known about the details of Byrd's early life, although he may have been born to a musician in Lincoln, Lincolnshire, England. He studied under the famous composer Thomas Tallis and was appointed organist of Lincoln Cathedral. In 1572 he moved to London and was sworn a gentleman of the Chapel Royal, a private religious establishment. Though he lived in Protestant England and wrote music for Anglican services, Byrd was probably a dedicated Roman Catholic throughout his lifetime.

In 1575 Queen ELIZABETH I granted Byrd and Tallis sole publishing rights to print music. Later that year the two published the first volume of *Cantiones Sacrae* (*Sacred Songs*). In 1588 Byrd published *Psalmes, Sonets, & Songs,* a collection of English madrigals, songs that followed a strict poetic form and were generally sung by two to four people. The madrigals enjoyed much popularity in England after Byrd published his collection. In 1589 he published another collection, *Songs of sundrie natures,* and in 1589 and 1591 he published two further books of church music, *Cantiones Sacrae*

Byrd is well known for his beautiful lyrics as well as for his music. The sorrow seems genuine in this simple lament for Sir Philip SIDNEY:

> Come to me, grief, for ever,
> Come to me, tears, day and night,
> Come to me, plaint, ah helpless,
> Just grief, heart's tears, plaint worthy.

"Though Amaryllis Dance in Green" is a love song by a shepherd because the beautiful Amaryllis does not return his love:

> Ah, wanton eyes, my friendly foes,
> And cause of woes,
> Your sweet desire
> Breeds flames of ice and freeze in fire.
> Ye scorn to see me weep so sore,
> Hey ho, 'chill [I'll] love no more.

A man of many talents whose music is still played today, Byrd wrote masses, secular works including sonnets and madrigals, and more than 120 works for the keyboard. With John DOWLAND, he remains the supreme musician of his era.

Caldwell, Elizabeth (d. 1603) *nonfiction writer*

Elizabeth Caldwell, née Duncalffe, was born in Chester County, England. She is known to literature as the subject and author of a work published by Gilbert Dugdale in 1604: *A True Discourse of the Practises of Elizabeth Caldwell.* The first half of this work contains an account of her life by Dugdale, a minister who came to know Caldwell when she was in prison; the second half is a letter by Caldwell, addressed to the husband for whose attempted murder she was executed.

In simple prose, Dugdale describes how Caldwell, married to Thomas Caldwell at a young age, was semi-abandoned by her husband, who, very young himself, spent long periods traveling in foreign countries. In her husband's absence, Caldwell succumbed to the temptation of an affair, and she was persuaded by her lover, Jeffrey Bownd, to murder Thomas on one of his brief stays at home. She baked rat poison into oatmeal cakes; Thomas vomited the poison and survived, but one of the cakes fell into the hands of a neighbor's small child, who died, and it was for this death that Caldwell and Bownd paid with their lives.

Caldwell's letter, by contrast with Dugdale's direct style, is impassioned and somewhat confused.

She begins by adopting a posture of repentance and subservience:

> Although the greatness of my offence deserves neither pity not regard, yet give leave unto your poor sorrowful wife to speake unto you, what out of her own woeful experience, with abundance of grief and tears, she hath learned in the School of affliction. . . .

However, she goes on to show in detail how badly Thomas treated her and to call upon him to repent:

> I speak it not to lay any thing to your charge, for I do love you more dearly, then I do my self, but remember in what a case you have lived, how poor you have many times left me, how long you have been absent from me, all which advantage the devil took to subvert me.

Caldwell's position captured the public imagination. Sometimes 300 people a day came to see her in prison. After hearing her story, Dugdale was willing to give her the benefit of the doubt. He included in the book a description of the speech Elizabeth gave from the scaffold on the day of her death. Her voice is one of the few surviving from before the 19th century that address the problem of economic abuse of wives.

A Work about Elizabeth Caldwell

Tebeaux, Elizabeth, and Mary M. Lay. "The Emergence of the Feminine Voice, 1526–1640: The Earliest Published Books by English Renaissance Women." *JAC: A Journal of Composition Theory* 15, no. 1 (1995).

Calvin, John (Jean Calvin) (1509–1564)
nonfiction writer

John Calvin was born in Noyon, France, on July 10, 1509. He was one of four sons born to Gerard Calvin, a notary and administrator in the town's Roman Catholic cathedral. His mother, Jeanne LeFranc Calvin, was a pious woman who often took her sons to visit holy shrines. As a youth, Calvin so distinguished himself in scholarship that he was given stipends, or clerical benefices, by the church to help finance his studies. At the age of 14, he enrolled at the University of Paris, where he met many of the leading humanist thinkers of the period and where he may have begun to question the Roman Catholic religion.

By the age of 18, Calvin had received his master's degree. Instead of pursuing a career in the church, as he had originally intended, he embarked on the study of law in Orléans, France. He completed his doctoral degree in 1532 and, in the same year, published his first book, a commentary on *De Clementia* (*On Clemency*), a work by the Roman philosopher Seneca.

Sometime in 1533, Calvin experienced a sudden conversion that led him to reject Roman Catholicism completely. Not one to reveal details about his personal life, he never specified precisely where or when he experienced this conversion. In the same year, he was forced to leave Paris to escape the possibility of persecution for his beliefs. For the next three years, he lived in various places in Italy, France, and Switzerland.

The year 1536 saw the publication of the first edition of Calvin's most famous work, *Institutes of the Christian Religion.* The prologue to this edition was a letter, dated 23 August 1535, to King Francis I of France. In this letter, Calvin attempted to persuade Francis that Protestants did not threaten the monarchy and urged him to "make an utter end of popery," or Roman Catholicism. Over the years, Calvin rewrote and expanded *The Institutes* several times, from an original six sections to 79. This work outlines the basis for the Calvinist system of belief.

In July 1536 Calvin was on his way to Strasbourg, Germany, when he was forced to detour from his original route because of the outbreak of war between Francis I of France and the Holy Roman Emperor, Charles V, over the succession to the throne of Milan. He entered Geneva, Switzerland, intending to spend only one night there, but Guillaume Farel, a French-born religious reformer, begged Calvin to stay and help him in the process of converting the newly independent populace to Protestantism; somewhat reluctantly, Calvin agreed. Over the next two years, the pair attempted to institute a number of reforms. However, Farel and Calvin's proposed changes, which included mandatory communion four times a year and excommunication as a punishment for those who did not conform to the moral code, proved to be too radical for the city council. Calvin and Farel were expelled from the city in May 1538.

For the next three years, Calvin lived and worked in Strasbourg, where he was pastor to a church of French refugees and married Idelette de Bure. Little is known about his wife, except that she bore Calvin a son in 1542. The boy died shortly after birth, and Idelette died in 1549. Calvin was very happy in Strasbourg, but when he was invited to return to Geneva, in 1541 he felt it was his duty to go and continue the work he had begun.

In a much stronger position than he had been during his earlier stay in Geneva, Calvin was now able to convince the council to enact his Ecclesiastical Ordinances, with which he established a theocracy in Geneva. The word *theocracy* comes from the Greek and means "rule by the deity"; it refers to governments that claim to represent God's will on earth. The ordinances provided for religious education for all citizens, and especially for children. They also established a group of ministers to rule the church and a group of ministers and lay people to rule the city. Between 1542 and 1555, Calvin instituted various reforms designed to remove traces of Catholicism, such as candles, incense, and images of saints. He also installed a strict moral code of behavior. Eventually the city council was able to punish sins as crimes. For example, failing to "keep the Sabbath" could be grounds for civil prosecution; punishment could include excommunication and banishment from the city.

Calvin supported improvements in the day-to-day lives of the citizens of Geneva, including hospitals, an improved sewer system, and the introduction of new industries to the area. In addition, he founded a college, which became the University of Geneva. According to English theologian Richard Hooker, Calvin's "most important work involved the organization of church governance and the social organization of the church and the city . . . so that clergy would be involved in municipal decisions." Calvin's social organization became the model of the original Puritan settlers in North America and through them influenced social and moral life in America in its early history.

Calvin lived in Geneva for the rest of his life, continuing to write and preach. In his later years he suffered from many illnesses; he died in 1564. He asked to be buried in an unmarked grave so as to discourage idolatry on the part of religious pilgrims. Calvin's literary legacy includes commentaries on most of the books of the Bible and more than 2,300 sermons. His influence extended throughout Europe as preachers trained in Geneva brought his ideas to their homelands. The Puritans of England, the Presbyterians of Scotland, and the Huguenots of France, among others, were influenced by Calvinist theology.

Critical Analysis

Calvin's *Institutes* were widely read in his own day and were a powerful force in the development of Protestant theology. His thinking was based entirely on his reading of scripture, and his reading of the Bible was literal. The fact of the omniscience of God led Calvin to assert that the fate of humankind must be predestined:

> God has once and for all determined, both whom He would admit to salvation, and whom He would condemn to destruction. We affirm that this counsel, as far as concerns the elect, is founded on His gratuitous mercy, totally irrespective of human merit; but that to those whom He devotes to condemnation, the gate of life is closed by a just and irreprehensible, but incomprehensible, judgment.

Thus, according to Calvin, only God's grace can guarantee salvation; neither good deeds nor faith can change an individual's destiny. Someone who is predestined for salvation is a member of "the elect" and can never fall from grace. Although no one can ever really know for sure whether he or she is a member of the elect, living a virtuous life can bring an individual a measure of hope. Predestination is one of what has come to be called "the five points of Calvinism."

The second point is that the grace of God is "irrestible." Hard as members of the elect may try to avoid living a life of virtue, God's grace will penetrate to their core, causing a complete and sincere conversion. The elect cannot escape their destiny.

Third is the concept of "total depravity," which is the result of Adam and Eve's fall from grace in the Garden of Eden. This original sin, according to Calvin, has corrupted every aspect of humanity—intellect, senses, and emotions. Through this concept Calvin wanted to emphasize the need for people to depend entirely on Christ for their salvation. The famous sermon by the American preacher, Jonathan Edwards, "Sinners in the Hands of an Angry God," exemplifies this aspect of Calvinism. In his sermon Edwards explains that each person is held in God's hands over the flames of hell. It is only by God's grace that we are not thrown immediately into those fires. Moreover, we deserve this punishment because of our total depravity.

The fourth point of Calvinism outlined in the *Institutes* is the concept of limited atonement, which is related to the concept of predestination. According to Calvin, Christ was sent by God to atone for the sins of mankind, but he died not for all but only for the elect.

The fifth point is the perseverance of the saints. By this Calvin means that members of the elect will persevere by the grace of God and will in fact be rewarded in heaven and become saints. Thus, Calvin enjoins the elect never to doubt their salvation.

Calvinism has had an immense effect on the modern world. Because Calvin emphasized that virtues such as hard work and thrift were signs of election, he is often seen as having influenced the rise of the middle class—which, in turn, began to move governments from monarchy to democracy. As European nations broke with the Roman Catholic Church, the concept of nationalism redrew geographic boundaries and changed the relationship of the individual to the state.

Works about John Calvin

Battles, Ford Lewis, and John Walchenbach. *Analysis of the Institutes of the Christian Religion of John Calvin.* Nashua, N.H.: P & R Press, 2001.
Cottret, Barnard. *Calvin: A Biography.* Translated by M. Wallace McDonald. New York: Eerdmans, 2000.

Cambridge Platonists (fl. mid-1600s)

The Cambridge Platonists were a group of Cambridge University teachers who attempted to synthesize Renaissance HUMANISM and Christian ethics. They drew their ideas from NEOPLATONISM but went beyond it in assuming that God reaches downward to lift humans to him through love and reason. They formed in part as a reaction to Thomas HOBBES and his materialistic views, which tended to reject the supernatural.

The Cambridge Platonists were out of step with two dominant forces of their era, Puritanism and empiricism. Although all were educated in the Puritan tradition, the Cambridge Platonists tended to shy away from dogmatism and encourage toleration of differing viewpoints, while Puritans tended to be more dogmatic. The Cambridge Platonists also rejected the idea of predestination, a central tenet of Puritan belief. Their objection to empiricism at first seems odd, because they supported experimental science. However, empiricists find truth by investigating the material world, while the Platonist believes that knowledge is inborn. The Cambridge Platonists believed that contemplation lifted the soul to God. The end of learning was the Godly life, not practical application.

The writings of these men illuminate the unpopular positions they defended. Benjamin Whichcote (1609–83) preached Christian tolerance at a time when denominations hotly contested interpretations of scripture. Whichcote argued that God in his goodness would not allow anyone to be condemned based on interpretation of scripture. Only three essentials existed: love of God, faith in God's goodness, and imitation of God. Anyone practicing these essentials was Christian. By contrast, Puritanism stressed the importance of living by complicated doctrines and following the letter of the interpreted scripture.

John Smith (1616–52) argued that reason and faith are not adversaries: Reason is "a light flowing from the fountain and father of lights . . . it was to enable man to work out of himself all those notions of God which are the true Groundwork of Love and Obedience to God and conformity to Him."

The writings of Ralph Cudworth (1617–88) explain the Cambridge Platonists' complaint against predestination: It changes God's nature from all-good to arbitrary, and it negates the possibility of sin. If God will save whom he chooses regardless of that person's actions, why live in moral obedience?

Henry More (1614–87) stressed the need for purity of heart. Only by "the purgation of the mind from all sorts of vices whatsoever" could this purity be achieved, and only then could the soul perceive the truth of God. Without reason, Christians must "foot it in the dark and tumble into the next ditch"—often led there by disputed church doctrines.

Calls for reason as a path to faith and mutual tolerance were opposed to the prevailing religious beliefs of the day, and the Cambridge Platonists were largely ignored. However, the historian Frederick Powicke argues that their ideas resonate in the 18th-century movements of rationalism, deism, and tolerance; these "went the way and took the form they did, because directed, more or less, by the principles or spirit of the Cambridge men."

Camden, William (1551–1623) *historian*

William Camden was born in London, the son of Sampson Camden. Although his family was without means, he received his early schooling at Christ's Hospital and at St Paul's School in London before attending Oxford University. Returning to London in 1571, he began doing historical research and began teaching at the Westminster School, a prestigious boys' school in London, becoming its headmaster in 1593.

Camden was one of the founders of the Elizabethan Society of Antiquaries in 1586. This was a group of scholars who were interested in the material artifacts of the past and other types of historical investigations, the first of its kind in England. In 1622, just a year before his death, Camden founded the Camden Chair of ancient history at Oxford.

In 1577 Camden commenced a project that was to occupy him for the rest of his life: writing and researching a comprehensive history and geography of Britain. Unlike earlier historians who often crafted their accounts from mythological or legendary sources, Camden took pains to base his work on primary sources, documents, and systematic investigation, thus making him a precursor of the modern "scientific" historian. In the following year he traveled through Norfolk and Suffolk, gathering evidence and making detailed observations, doing the same in Yorkshire and Lancashire in 1582 and in Wales in 1590. Camden recorded such diverse matters as the origins both of personal names and local place names, the inscriptions on coins and other artifacts from Britain's Roman and Celtic pasts, and genealogical information. His scholarship on place names remained an authoritative sourcebook for centuries afterwards.

Camden wrote his first historical accounts in Latin, in a treatise entitled *Britannia* (1586). Although the publication of *Britannia* helped establish the foundations for more systematic and objective historical research, Camden did not shrink from expressing his personal enthusiasm for his native land. In his preface he refers to "this Isle of Britaine" as being "the most flourishing and excellent, most renowned and famous Isle of the whole world. So rich in commodities, so beautiful in situation, so resplendent in all glorie, that if the most Omnipotent had fashioned the world round like a ring, as hee did like a globe, it might have beene most worthily the onely gemme therein." The preface is replete with admiration for England's rich mines and farms ("aboundant in pasture, replenished with cattell both tame and wild") and its rural and urban amenities ("plentifully wooded . . . beautified with many populous Citties, faire Borroughs, good Townes, and well-built Villages . . ."). His enthusiasm reflects the unbridled self-confidence of an era of expansion and discovery that was rapidly outstripping the narrow horizons of the medieval period. Implicit in Camden's preface was a consciousness of the earth as a globe, a notion that had gained popular acceptance only in the 16th century.

Camden's research also helped formulate notions of national identity and linguistic uniformity that were beginning to come together in important new ways during the Elizabethan era. Although he wrote some of his earlier works in Latin, he used a plain style and contemporary vocabulary in his English *Remains* (1605) and other works. Twentieth-century scholar R. D. Dunn wrote of *Remains* that "There is, scattered throughout the book, a wealth of contemporary phrases, nonce [nonsense] words, and idiomatic expressions some of which cannot readily be found elsewhere. The *Oxford English Dictionary* drew heavily upon the *Remains* for examples and often Camden's is the earliest cited for a particular usage."

In 1596 Camden was asked to write a history of the reign of Queen ELIZABETH I, then in its fourth decade. The fruit of this labor, *Annales Rerum Anglicarum et Hibernicarium Regnante Elizabetha* (1615), was published in English as *Annales. The True and Royall History of the Famous Empresse Elizabeth, Queene of England, France and Ireland, &c. . . .*

In recent years scholars have paid tribute to Camden's groundbreaking work, as when Sir Maurice Powicke wrote in 1948: "A great book might be written about Camden, his life and his works, his wide circle of friends and correspondents and his humanity. . . . Here I would emphasize Camden's humanity as revealed in the width of his interests, his part in the generous intercourse of scholars and his capacity to lean back and think about the best way to write what he wished to say."

Campion, Thomas (1567–1620) *poet, composer*

Thomas Campion was born in London to affluent parents. His father, John Campion, was an attorney and a diplomatic courier. Both his parents died when Campion was a child, but they left enough money for him to be educated at Cambridge University (1581–84) and to study law at Gray's Inn in London beginning in 1586. Gray's Inn was a lively center of artistic activity, and Campion contributed songs to at least two musical events while he was a student there. There is no record of his having qualified as an attorney or practiced law.

The first poems Campion wrote, probably while he was at Cambridge, were in Latin. Five of his English poems were published in 1591, in an unauthorized edition of Sir Philip SIDNEY's *Astrophel and Stella,* but the first publication devoted to Campion's own work was a collection of his Latin epigrams, *Poemata,* published in 1595. His English lyrics were published in five volumes with music; the first, *A Book of Ayres to Be Sung to the Lute, Orpherean, and Bass Viol,* was issued in 1601, the remaining four in 1613–17. Campion composed the music, setting his poems in four or five parts, but always keeping a clear top line so that the music never obscured the words. Though the music is sophisticated, the lyrics often have a directness that reminds one of folk songs. Most are secular, but there are a few devotional pieces.

In 1602 Campion published a prose work, *Observations in the Art of English Poesie.* In it he attacked the "vulgar" custom of rhyming. Latin poetry relies primarily on meter for its auditory effects, and Campion suggested that English poetry should do the same. (It is noticeable that in his own English verse Campion does not follow his own advice.) Samuel DANIEL attacked Campion's views in his *Defense of Rhyme* (1603), and Ben JONSON may have weighed in with his own opinion, but if he did the text has been lost.

In 1602 Campion began a three-year stay on the European continent; he studied medicine at the University of Caen in France, receiving his M.D. degree in 1605. On his return to London, he practiced as a doctor but continued to write. He wrote several masques (dramatic pageants with music) that were performed at the court of JAMES I. *The Lords' Masque,* written and performed in honor of a royal wedding in 1613, is considered the best. In it, Orpheus, the great musician of Greek mythology, pleads with Mania (an allegorical personification of madness) to set the hero, Entheus, free—that is, to free him from his mental illness; Orpheus will complete the cure with music. The slight plot is interspersed liberally with songs, and the published version includes detailed descriptions of the lavish sets designed by the scenographer and architect Inigo Jones.

Campion had not forgotten music: In 1613 he published a work of music theory, *A New Way of Making Fowre Parts in Counterpoint.*

In 1615 Campion was arrested for questioning about the murder of Sir Thomas OVERBURY, but he was soon cleared of suspicion and released. He died in London, probably of the plague, minor epidemics of which occurred throughout the 17th century until the Great Plague of 1665.

Campion did not consider himself a professional; poetry and music were, for him, delightful pastimes. His light and graceful attitude to life and death is summed up in these lines from "My Sweetest Lesbia":

> When timely death my life and fortune
>   ends,
> Let not my hearse be vexed with mourning
>   friends,
> But let all lovers rich in triumph come,
> And with sweet pastimes grace my happy
>   tomb.

Other Work by Thomas Campion

The Essential Campion. Edited by Charles Simic. New York: Ecco Press, 1988.

Works about Thomas Campion

Davis, Walter R. *Thomas Campion.* Boston: Twayne, 1987.

Eldridge, Muriel T. *Thomas Campion: His Poetry and Music.* New York: Vantage Press, 1971.

Lindley, David. *Thomas Campion.* Leiden: Brill Academic Publishers, 1986.

Carew, Thomas (ca. 1594–1640) *poet, critic*

Thomas Carew (pronounced Carey) was probably born in Kent, England, but his father, Matthew Carew, a lawyer, moved the family to London about 1598. Matthew Carew did well in London, and he was knighted in 1603. Thomas Carew was well educated, receiving bachelor's degrees from both Oxford and Cambridge Universities; he enrolled at the Middle Temple in London, but he "studied the law very little," as his father complained.

When an opportunity arose to enter the service of the diplomat Sir Dudley Carleton, his father's friend, Carew took it. He traveled with his employer on embassies to Italy and the Netherlands between 1613 and 1616, learning several languages during this time. In 1616 he lost his job with Sir Dudley, apparently because of having insulted Lady Carleton, and returned to England to seek other employment. Sir Matthew, angry at his son and in financial straits himself, offered no help; he died in 1618.

In spite of his unstable position, Carew soon became noted at the court of JAMES I for his elegance and wit. In 1619 he found work with Sir Edward HERBERT, and went with him on a diplomatic mission to Paris. During the 1620s Carew seems to have been in London, associating with the court and also with the group of poets surrounding Ben JONSON. His first published poem appeared in 1622.

In 1630 Carew was appointed to an official court position: Sewer in Ordinary (responsible for the royal eating arrangements) to King Charles I, who had ascended to the throne in 1625. He continued to write poetry, not for publication (only 10 of his 130 poems were printed during his lifetime) but for circulation around the court in manuscript and for musical settings.

Most of Carew's poems may be grouped in two categories: the love poems, many of them addressed to the mysterious "Celia"; and the "occasional" poems (written to mark particular occasions, such as deaths or births). Many of the love poems are sexually explicit or cynical, reinforcing Carew's reputation as a libertine. Others advance the standard poetic arguments for why the mistress should yield to the poet's desires, with conventional imagery, rhetorical devices, and classical allusions handled gracefully to make a charming but slight whole. For example, these lines from "The Complement" make a delightful use of the device of listing the loved one's attributes:

> I love not for those eyes, nor haire,
> Nor cheekes, nor lips, nor teeth so rare;
> Nor for thy speech, thy necke, nor breast,
> Nor for thy belly, nor the rest:
> Nor for thy hand, nor foote so small,
> But wouldst thou know (deere sweet) for
>   all.

The occasional poems, on the other hand, are more serious, and Carew's "An Elegy upon the Death of Dr. Donne, Dean of Paul's," regarded by Lynn Sadler as "his most important poem," is both a moving tribute to John DONNE's poetry and an exemplar of Donne's influence:

> Here lies a King, that rul'd as hee thought fit
> The universall Monarchy of wit.

In many of his poems in addition to "An Elegy upon the Death of Dr. Donne, Dean of Paul's," Carew discusses the works of other poets. The critical views expressed are an interesting window on the literary values of his time. In a religious vein, he wrote verse translations of nine of the Psalms.

In addition to his CAVALIER POETRY, Carew was interested in the theater and contributed song lyrics to dramatic works by several of his friends. He also wrote a masque, *Coelum Britannicum* (The British Heaven), produced at court in 1634 in a lavish production in which the king himself took part. The masque is set in the heaven of classical mythology. In it, King Charles and Queen Henrietta Maria are appointed to rule in a reformed heaven by Jove himself, who has recognized the moral failings of the Olympian gods and has chosen the British monarchs because of their exemplary virtues. The masque is written in blank verse and includes topical allusions and humorous passages in addition to its royalist propaganda.

The monarchy was in fact precarious. In 1639 the king led a military expedition against Scotland, the first episode of the English Civil War, which culminated in Charles's execution and the temporary abolition of the monarchy in Britain. Carew was probably part of the king's army in 1639. He seems to have fallen ill during the expedition; he died in March the following year.

Other Works by Thomas Carew

Crofts, Thomas, ed. *The Cavalier Poets: An Anthology.* New York: Doer, 1995.
Poems of Thomas Carew. Edited by Rhodes Dunlap. New York: Oxford University Press, 1985.

Works about Thomas Carew

Martz, Louis L. *The Wit of Love.* Notre Dame, Ind.: University of Notre Dame Press, 1969.
Miner, Earl. *The Cavalier Mode from Jonson to Cotton.* Princeton, N.J.: Princeton University Press, 1971.
Sadler, Lynn. *Thomas Carew.* Boston: Twayne, 1979.
Selig, Edward I. *The Flourishing Wreath: A Study of Thomas Carew's Poetry.* Hamden, Conn.: Archon Books, 1970.

Carey, Elizabeth, Lady, Viscountess Falkland (Elizabeth Cary) (1585–1639)
dramatist, poet, biographer

Elizabeth Carey, or Cary, was born in Oxford, England, to Sir Laurence and Lady Elizabeth Tanfield. Carey had an isolated childhood, but she immersed herself in studies, learning French, Spanish, Latin, and Hebrew. She married Henry Carey in 1602.

Carey's play *The Tragedy of Mariam* was written in 1602–03, and in 1613 it became the first English play by a woman to be published. She wrote *The History of the Life, Reign, and Death of Edward II* in 1627 or 1628 but never completely finished the play.

The Tragedy of Mariam tells the story of King Herod's second wife, Mariam. Written to be read aloud to a small group rather than to be performed, the play explores the power struggles within Herod's kingdom and the position of women, particularly the wives of prominent men. Despite the fact that Herod's right to rule is obtained largely through his marriage to Mariam, she is required by law to obey him. He has further secured his throne by murdering Mariam's brother, Aristobolus. When Herod is called to Rome to explain the death of Aristobolus, he orders his servant to kill Mariam in the event he is killed while he is away.

The play opens with a soliloquy by Mariam in which she contemplates her duties as wife and her well-founded reasons for resenting Herod. At this point she believes Herod has indeed been put to death, and she knows of his intention to have her executed:

> Oft have I wished that I from him were free;
> Oft have I wished that he might lose his
>   breath . . .

But now his death to memory doth call
The tender love that he to Mariam bare,
And mine to him.

Eventually, however, Herod returns and executes Mariam for adultery, based on false accusations by Herod's sister, Salome. From the very beginning of the play, the audience is allowed inside Mariam's thoughts, so that Herod's actions against her seem even more unjustified.

Mariam is not only significant for its place in literary history as the first original drama by a woman, but as critic Betty Travitsky points out, it is a "significant intellectual effort—a most interesting and individual handling of materials by a woman . . . It is a subtle and penetrating criticism . . . of the consequences to even the most seemingly exalted of women of their dependent position." Critics have also noticed the obvious parallels between the story of Herod and Mariam and the execution of Anne BOLEYN by Henry VIII.

The History of Edward II exists in two versions, both being a combination of prose and verse. The second version is more dramatic than the first, though it, too, contains a great deal of narration, as opposed to dialogue and action. Like *Mariam, Edward II* features a woman, Queen Isabelle, at the center of the action.

Carey also wrote verse biographies about female saints, including Mary Magdalene, Agnes the Martyr, and Elizabeth of Portugal. These works reflected her interest in the lives of outstanding women and her conversion to Catholicism in 1626. She was also a poet and translator of several works from Latin and French.

Other Work by Elizabeth Carey

Elizabeth Cary, Lady Falkland: Life and Letters. Edited by Heather Wolfe. Cambridge, U.K.: RTM Publications, 2001.

Works about Elizabeth Carey

Raber, Karen. *Dramatic Difference: Gender, Class, and Genre in the Early Modern Closet Drama.* Newark, Del.: University of Delaware Press, 2001.

Walker, Kim. *Women Writers of the English Renaissance.* New York: Twayne, 1996.

Carey, Mary (1609–1680) *poet, nonfiction writer*

The daughter of Sir John Jackson Berwick, Mary Carey lived in a fashionable manner during her youth, but she became seriously ill while only a teenager, which awakened her religious sensibilities. She was first married to Sir Pelham Carey, who had been an Oxford scholar, but was widowed by 1643. That year she wedded George Payler, a Parliamentarian officer whose official duties forced them to travel to garrison towns throughout the country during the years of the English Revolution and Civil War (1642–48).

In 1653 Carey began collecting her compositions to be bound in one manuscript volume, which she dedicated to her second husband. The work included primarily religious meditations and poems, the dominant subject matter of which was her grief at losing five children. In a poem she penned in May 1652 upon the death of her son Peregrine Payler, Carey laments, "I thought my All was given before / But Mercy order'd me one more." Despite her obvious distress, the tone she takes at the end of the piece is representative of her belief in God and her acceptance of his actions: "My dearest Lord, has thou fulfill'd thy will, / Thy Hand-Maid's pleas'd, compleately happy still." Carey's volume of writings has never been published in full, but the manuscript remains a testament to her religious humility, as well as her capabilities as an introspective author.

Carleton, Mary (1642–ca. 1673) *nonfiction writer*

Labeling Mary Carleton a "nonfiction writer" is a convention of literary identification, because her fame comes from her ability to create and sustain fictions of various kinds in her life. She was born Mary Moders, or Meders, to a chorister, or singer in a choir, in Canterbury. She was evidently an avid reader and was especially fond of romances, in which she often saw herself as the heroine. Her life of deception began when she married a shoemaker, Thomas Stedman, and then, without divorcing him, married Thomas Day, a surgeon. Tried for bigamy, she got off by claiming to have believed that Stedman had died. Next, she pretended to be a "German princess" born in Cologne to Henry von Wolway, Lord of Holmstein. In this guise she married John Carleton. As a result of this marriage she was tried for polygamy but was not convicted because Carleton's family could not find witnesses to prove that she was already married. In addition to her marriages, Carleton also engaged in a variety of other fraudulent activities. She was arrested and tried for a third time for stealing a silver tankard. She was convicted and sentenced to be transported out of England and to live the rest of her life in Jamaica. After two years she returned to England illegally and for this was eventually arrested, tried, and hanged.

The writing for which Carleton is known consists of accounts explaining her identity and experiences. They claim to be nonfiction but demonstrate the same audacity of invention as did her life. In 1663 Carleton defended herself in *The Case of Madam Mary Carleton lately styled "The German Princess."* In this explanation she introduces herself as "a foreign and desolate woman" suffering from "injured innocence." Although she sticks to her story about her origins, she also brags about her successful career as an imposter: "What harm have I done in pretending to great titles? . . . If the best things are to be imitated, I had a good precept and warrant for my assumption of such a personage as they were willing to believe me to be." The writer of Mary's story in *The Newgate Calendar,* a series of sensational stories about prisoners held in that infamous prison, says she was a "prodigious woman, who, had she been virtuously inclined, was capable of being the phoenix of her age; for it was impossible for her not to be admired in everything she said and did."

Works about Mary Carleton
Kietzman, Mary Jo. *The Self-Fashioning of an Early Modern Englishwoman: Mary Carleton's Lives.* Burlington, Vt.: Ashgate Publishing Company, 2004.
Todd, Janet M., and Elizabeth Spearing, eds. *Counterfeit Ladies: The Life and Death of Mal Cutpurse: The Case of Mary Carleton.* New York: New York University Press, 1994.

Cartwright, William (1611–1643) *poet, playwright*

William Cartwright was born in Gloucestershire, England, to William and Dorothy Coles Cartwright; his family's wealth and social position declined during his childhood. At the time of Cartwright's birth, his father was living as a landed gentleman, but by the time the young William was of school age, his father had become an innkeeper. He nonetheless received the education of a gentleman's son, and in 1625 he entered Oxford, where he remained for the rest of his life. After receiving a B.A. in 1632 and an M.A. in 1635, he took holy orders and began lecturing on religious subjects. During his stay at Oxford, Cartwright wrote a number of poems and four plays.

In the early 1640s the English Civil War broke out. This conflict was sparked by disagreement between the king and Parliament over religious issues and questions about the rights of the monarchy. Cartwright was a royalist—supporter of the king—and actively defended the traditional order that he celebrated in his writing.

As with so many poets of the mid-17th century, especially those with royalist sympathies, Cartwright owes much to the example of Ben JONSON. Like Jonson's work, Cartwright's poems are highly polished, something made evident in these lines from "A Bill of Fare" (1651): "Troth, I am like small Birds, which now in Spring / When they have nought to eat, do sit and sing." The poet places himself above worldly care here, singing in the face of hardship, the very position many of the old gentry found themselves forced to take as the middle class gained power and prestige in England.

Cartwright is at his best when he writes compliments to royalty. Indeed, his "use of the courtly compliment," the scholar G. Blakemore Evans writes, "is unsurpassed even by avowed court poets." The following lines from "On the Lady Newburgh" (1651) demonstrate Cartwright's success in the mode:

> Pardon, thou Soul of Goodness, if I wrong
> Thine Ample Virtues with a sparing
>   Tongue,
> Alas, I am compell'd, speaking of thee,
> To use one of thy Virtues, Modesty.

This poem is written in a modest style in imitation of a modest subject, which allows Cartwright to downplay the importance of his role as writer and to credit his subject, Lady Newburgh, with endowing his poem with the virtue that its reader finds in it. The poem's virtue and that of Lady Newburgh are thus one and the same.

What is also interesting about the poem is how Cartwright gives life to one of the clichés of the compliment. Like so many poets before him, Cartwright suggests that he does not have the words to praise his subject adequately: He is obliged to use a "sparing tongue." His inability to find the words to express himself, however, is a compliment for an unexpected reason. Cartwright is not saying that there are no words to describe Lady Newburgh because she is so perfect. Rather, he is saying that to offer abundant praise, though deserved, would be inappropriate because the lady is so modest.

Cartwright's plays are similar to his poems in that most of them are positive illustrations of fashionable court literature. All but one of them—a middle-class comedy called The Ordinary (ca. 1635), set at a boarding house (which, in the 17th century, was called an ordinary)—are Platonic dramas, characterized by exotic settings and characters.

Cartwright's most important play of this type, which is perhaps the most successful of the kind, is The Royal Slave, first performed in 1636 before Charles I. Set in Persia, The Royal Slave deals with a fictional Persian law that requires the king to make one of his prisoners of war a pretend king. According to the law, the prisoner is to enjoy the benefits of kingship for three days and is then to be sacrificed to the sun god. Cartwright's other plays, never performed but published posthumously in Comedies, Tragi-Comedies, With Other Poems (1651), are the romantic comedies The Lady Errant and The Siege, or Love's Covert.

Cartwright's work has commanded little attention over the last 300 years, perhaps because his writing style is too dated for modern tastes. Still, his writing contains, as the scholar R. Cullis Goffin writes, "all the elements which at that time commanded particular admiration . . . Hence it repays study . . . as being so altogether typical of the age."

Cary, Patrick (ca. 1623–1657) poet

Patrick Cary was the son of Sir Henry Cary, first Viscount Falkland, and his wife, Elizabeth Tanfield, Lady Cary. The Cary family were well known as Royalists, or supporters of the monarchy during the English Civil War.

In 1651 a notebook was found containing 30 poems composed by Cary. They were not published at that time, but eventually the notebook came into Sir Walter Scott's possession. Scott published Cary's collection Trivial Poems and Triolets [an eight-line poetic form] in 1819. As the title implies, Cary focuses on commonplace subjects, as in the poem "For God's Sake Marcke [take note of] That Fly." The verse cautions the reader not to underestimate the power of small things, for "This little, poore, weake Fly/Has killed a Pope; can make an Emp'rour dye." Much of Cary's poetry is overtly religious: "Great God! I had been Nothing but for Thee; / Thy all-creating Power first made mee Bee." Other of his poems include ballads that express conventional romantic sentiments.

> Some prayse the Browne, and some the
>   Fayre;
> Some best like Blacke, some Flaxen Hayre:
> Some love the Tall, and some the Low;
> Some choose who's quicke; and some, who's
>   slow.

Cary's poetry is more interesting for its publishing history and the high rank of its author than for the literary merit of the poems. However, his poems are of interest to those interested in religious verse in the 17th century.

Other Work by Patrick Cary
The Poems of Patrick Cary. Edited by Veronica Delany. New York: Clarendon Press, 1978.

Castiglione, Baldassare (Baldasar Castiglione) (1478–1529) *nonfiction writer*
Baldassare Castiglione was born in Casatico, near Mantua, Italy, to Count Cristoforo Castiglione and Luigia Gonzaga. He was educated in Milan and later worked in the court of the marquis of Mantua. He also served as a military commander, diplomat, adviser, and papal nuncio (emissary) for the pope. His experience in these positions and his connections with members of the Italian court and papacy provided the raw material for his masterpiece *The Courtier* (1528). He spent much of his life revising the work, which he originally began in 1516. When it was finally published, it was a huge success both in Italy and abroad.

The Courtier is a "courtesy book" that seeks in dialogue to describe proper aristocratic behavior. It takes the form of a conversation between several of Castiglione's closest friends. To pass the time, they discuss the characteristics of the ideal courtier, or person who attends a member of the royalty at court. Because the personalities of the speakers differ, they disagree over many issues. However, what emerges is a general image of what is now known as the Renaissance man: a well-educated, well-dressed, and well-spoken soldier and gentleman.

The key phrase that describes the perfect courtier is *sprezzatura*, which translates loosely as "nonchalance"—that is, as having a casual manner. The courtier, Count Lodovico explains, should "practice in all things a certain sprezzatura, so as to conceal all art and make whatever is done or said

appear to be without effort and almost without any thought about it." Although everyone in the book acknowledges that the courtier should have an education and have undergone training in such matters as dance, riding, and war, each claims that these skills should appear to come naturally. In addition to describing the skills and education required to become a successful courtier, Castiglione's book also describes how a lady of the court should behave:

> For many vertues of the minde I recken be as necessary for a woman, as for a man. Likewise noblenesse of birth, avoidinge Affectation or curiositie, to have a good grace of nature in all her doinges, to be of good condcyons, wyttye, foreseeyng, not haughtie, not envious, not yll tunged, not light, not contentious, not untowardlye, to have the knowledge to wynn and kepe the good wyll of her Ladye and of all others, to do well and with a good grace the exercises comely for women.

Castiglione also discusses the ideals of platonic love, a love based on spiritual, rather than physical, union.

The Courtier was translated into English in 1561 by Thomas HOBY. It not only set the tone of the English court, but it was used by such writers as William SHAKESPEARE and Edmund SPENSER to describe aspects of court life. *The Courtier* was extremely influential in determining proper courtly behavior, as it provided an essential bridge between the chivalric code of the Middle Ages and the courtly behavior of the RENAISSANCE. As critics Robert Hanning and David Rosand explain, Castiglione's *The Courtier* influenced "so many aspects of Renaissance culture—from language and literature to art and music, courtiership and politics to humor and feminism, Neoplatonic idealism to the most cynical realism." Castiglione, they say, "stands as the truest, because most complex, reflection of the complicated cultural phenomenon and historical moment we call the High Renaissance."

Works about Baldassare Castiglione

Falvo, Joseph D. *The Economy of Human Relations: Castiglione's Libro del Cortegiano.* New York: P. Lang, 1992.

Hanning, Robert W. *Castiglione: The Ideal and the Real in Renaissance Culture.* New Haven, Conn.: Yale University Press, 1983.

Cavalier poetry

The aristocratic supporters of King Charles I in the English Civil War were known as the Cavaliers, these being gentlemen trained in arms and horsemanship. The poets among this group included Thomas CAREW, William CARTWRIGHT, Charles COTTON, Abraham COWLEY, John DENHAM, Sidney GODOLPHIN, James GRAHAM, William HABINGTON, Robert HERRICK, James HOWELL, Richard LOVELACE, Thomas RANDOLPH, Thomas STANLEY, John SUCKLING, Henry VAUGHAN, and Edmund WALLER. They were not a formal literary school, but all were influenced by the high valuation of friendship and integrity found in the works and life of the playwright and poet Ben JONSON, and their poetry is distinguished by elegance, wit, and occasional cynicism.

In his influential study *The Cavalier Mode from Jonson to Cotton,* the scholar Earl Miner distinguishes the Cavalier poets by their use of the social mode (focused on friendship and social events) as opposed to the private mode (focused on the poet's private relations with a lover or with God) of the METAPHYSICAL POETS and the public mode (focused on the larger society beyond the poet's own acquaintance) of such later 17th-century poets as John MILTON and John DRYDEN. There is some overlap with the metaphysical poets; for example, Andrew MARVELL and Robert Herrick have been mentioned in both groups. In formal terms, the Cavaliers, like the metaphysical poets, favored short lines and complex rhyme schemes, as in this example from Herrick's "The Bracelet to Julia":

> WHY I tie about thy wrist,
> Julia, this my silken twist;

> For what other reason is 't,
> But to show thee how, in part,
> Thou my pretty captive art?
> But thy bondslave is my heart . . .

Many of the poems were written as songs, and their rhythmic suppleness reflects this. Several types of subject matter were especially favored by the Cavaliers. Love poems, typically addressed to a nymph with a name that recalls the classical Greek pastoral (a poem about the simple lives and loves of imaginary shepherds and shepherdesses), addressed sensual pleasure, such as Lovelace's "Song: To Amarantha, That She Would Dishevel Her Hair":

> Amarantha, sweet and fair,
> Ah braid no more that shining hair!
> . . . Like the sun in's early ray
> Shake your head and scatter day.

Poems addressed to real, named people celebrated the pleasures of friendship. Poems about places, often the country seats of the nobility, celebrated the culture of the English aristocrats who patronized music and literature, a culture that seemed precarious at many times during the turbulent 17th century. As the scholar Earl Miner remarks,

> Cavalier seduction poems and drinking songs have held appeal for three centuries, not merely because sex and drink still give pleasure, but because such poems raise their formal topics into visions of happiness. The world we look upon through Cavalier poetry is that of an England at peace . . ., dedicated to ancient rights of king and subject, liberal to friends and dependents, given to love, drink, song, angling and hunting, certain of the value of learning.

It is a world that is still seductive and pleasurable to explore.

Works by the Cavalier Poets

Crofts, Thomas, ed. *The Cavalier Poets: An Anthology.* New York: Dover, 1996.

MacLean, Hugh, ed. *Ben Jonson and the Cavalier Poets: Authoritative Texts, Criticism.* New York: Norton, 1975.

Works about the Cavalier Poets

Corns, Thomas N., ed. *The Cambridge Companion to English Poetry: Donne to Marvell.* New York: Cambridge University Press, 1993.

Miner, Earl. *The Cavalier Mode from Jonson to Cotton.* Princeton, N.J.: Princeton University Press, 1971.

Cavendish, Jane (1621–1669) *playwright, poet*

Jane Cavendish was one of five children born to Elizabeth Basset and William Cavendish, Duke of Newcastle. Her paternal grandmother was Bess of Hardwick, one of the wealthiest women of the Elizabethan period, best known for her attempts to place her family in line to inherit the throne of England. In her youth, Cavendish spent much of her time at Welbeck Abbey, in Nottinghamshire, England, one of the family's expensive homes. Although she was certainly aware that women of her era were not expected to be "literary," her father, who wrote verse and plays, encouraged Cavendish to express herself through writing. In fact the Cavendish family contained at least five other women who produced written works. As scholar Marion Wynne-Davies points out in *Women Poets of the Renaissance,* the huge output of the Cavendish family means they "must rank . . . as one of the key groups of women writers in the early modern period."

Cavendish is primarily remembered for the play *The Concealed Fancies,* which she coauthored with her sister Elizabeth BRACKLEY around 1645. At the time the sisters were confined at Welbeck by enemy forces during the English Civil War, which was sparked by conflict between the king and Parliament over religious issues and questions about the rights of the monarchy. *The Concealed Fancies* centers on two sisters who disguise their true feelings toward their suitors in hopes of retaining control over their relationships in spite of being married; hence the work's title. War-related themes, such as

feelings of doubt about the outcome of the war and sorrow over the absence of loved ones, also appear. For instance, in a subplot, three cousins besieged in a castle seek something to help them forget their condition, one of them lamenting, "I wish I could not think, that I might not remember, I had been once happy."

Scholars believe that Cavendish continued writing throughout her life, though this speculation comes from references made in an elegy upon her death by Thomas Lawrence. Besides *Concealed Fancies,* the only other known Cavendish works are a handful of poems; a masque, or short allegorical play performed by masked actors; *A Pastorall,* which she composed with her sister Elizabeth; and a verse written on the occasion of Elizabeth's death in 1663.

Nevertheless, Cavendish is particularly important for the unusual nature of her artistic efforts. Her writings were not, as acknowledged by the scholars S. P. Cerasano and Marion Wynne-Davies, part of an "isolated excursion into the world of literary activity," but "a contribution to a familial discourse in which women were capable of asserting an independent subjectivity."

Cavendish, Margaret

See NEWCASTLE, MARGARET CAVENDISH, DUCHESS OF.

Caxton, William (ca. 1422–1491) *printer, translator*

Little is known of William Caxton's early life other than that in 1438 he was apprenticed to a wool merchant. For about 30 years, beginning in 1441, Caxton found success working in Europe's wool trade. During this time he also developed interests in literature, and around 1470 he learned to print books in Cologne. His translation, *The Recuyell of the Histories of Troye* (1475), was the first book printed in English. By 1476 Caxton had returned to England to set up his press at Westminster. He spent the rest of his years establishing the English printing trade.

Caxton's books are not known for innovations in type or particular beauty; rather, he cared more for readability and durability. Still, his press's output is of remarkable importance for several reasons. First, Caxton's press published 108 books (87 titles) over about 20 years. These books represent a variety of fields of knowledge, such as science, history, religion, and literature. Caxton's stated goal in publishing was "the betterment of the human lot not only in time but also in eternity." He shaped English thought and reading tastes by publishing what he thought people *should* read.

Second, although Caxton published books at the request of powerful patrons, for the most part he decided for himself what to print. The spoken word, he wrote, is "perishing, vain, and forgettable"; but printed "writings dwell and abide permanently" and can have great impact. Caxton published practical texts such as the *Governal of Health* (1491). He published moral texts such as *Aesop's Fables.* He put the record of England's history before the public and published important poets such as Geoffrey Chaucer, John Gower, and Thomas Malory. Biographer Frieda Penninger notes, "Caxton was, first, a moralist and a critic who considered books to be instruments of instruction. For Caxton . . . history was a series of lessons which would enable the human race to find the clue to civilization and to right action."

Finally, Caxton broadcast his philosophy of education in two ways: in the 26 works he chose to translate into English and in the prologues and epilogues of many of the books he printed. He provided English readers, at a time of growing literacy, with a reason to read and a method of reading. Through his fine translations, Caxton also established a simplified prose style that influenced other English writers. Penninger argues that without Caxton's publications, our understanding of 15th-century England would be seriously diminished. "Caxton's books enable us to capture the quality of life in his century with far more wholeness than do the stories of kings and killings."

A Work about William Caxton

Penninger, Frieda. *William Caxton.* Boston: Twayne, 1979.

Cecil, Mildred, Lady Burghley (Mildred Cooke) (1526–1589) *translator*

Mildred Cooke Cecil was the oldest of the nine children who survived to maturity born to Sir Anthony Cooke and his wife, Anne Fitzwilliam Cooke, at Gidea Hall near Romford, Essex, England. Five of these children were daughters, each of whom would become notable in her own right. Around 1545 Mildred married William Cecil, who was a member of Parliament and a privy councillor, and who would later become Lord Burghley and principal secretary to Queen Elizabeth I.

According to the scholar Pearl Hogrefe, Mildred Cecil was her husband's "equal in scholarship," although, as explained by the scholar Sheridan Harvey, "while the Cookes' upbringing and classical education gave them certain capabilities, the outlets for their knowledge often depended on their husbands." Cecil and her sisters were educated with a firm foundation in the classics, and she was often praised for her fluent command of the Greek and Latin languages. (Roger Ascham once commented that Cecil spoke Greek as if it were English, and poet Christopher Ockland referred to her as "most famous, most learned, most skilled in Greek and Latin literature, and in other literature.") But as Hogrefe says, "She made no display of her learning," and the one remnant that demonstrates Lady Burghley's command of the classics is an unpublished manuscript translation of a homily by Saint Chrysostom from Greek into English. Unfortunately, despite these acknowledgements of her mastery over Greek and Latin, Cecil refused to publish her translation when she learned that the work had already been translated by John Cristopherson.

While Mildred Cecil, Lady Burghley, was know for her active role in her husband's political life and for her philanthropic pursuits, her intellect was what earned her the highest praise. She and her sisters were, according to biographer George Ballard, "the wonders of the age."

A Work about Mildred Cecil

Hogrefe, Pearl. "Mildred Cooke Cecil, Lady Burghley." *Women of Action in Tudor England: Nine*

Biographical Sketches. Ames: Iowa State University Press, 1977.

Cellier, Elizabeth (ca. 1650–1693)

nonfiction writer

Elizabeth Cellier, later known as "the Popish Midwife," was born into a Protestant Buckinghamshire family who had supported King Charles I in the English Civil Wars. In fact, her father and brother both died while fighting for the king. Partly because of the persecution her family suffered as royalists, Cellier converted to Catholicism. She worked as a midwife to members of the aristocracy and became the center of controversy upon her involvement in the storm surrounding the Popish Plot of 1678.

The Popish Plot was a hoax designed to stir up anti-Catholic feeling in England. Titus Oates, a former Anglican clergyman, claimed to have uncovered a conspiracy to murder Charles II and replace him with his Catholic brother James. The panic that resulted from Oates's claim led to the arrest and execution of several Catholics. Cellier became involved in the crisis by helping imprisoned Catholics and soon became embroiled in the controversy herself when a man in her employ, Thomas Dangerfield, joined in a conspiracy to entrap her. The "Meal-Tub" Plot, in which Cellier was implicated, received its name from the meal-tub in which Dangerfield placed forged documents that claimed that the Whig politician Shaftesbury planned to murder the king.

In 1680 Cellier was imprisoned for her supposed role in this plot, an event that provided the basis for her most famous work, *Malice Defeated: or a Brief Relation of the Accusation and Deliverance of Elizabeth Cellier,* which she wrote within three weeks of her release. *Malice Defeated* is, in the words of scholar Anne Barbeau Gardiner, a "spirited vindication of her conduct during the Popish Plot." Cellier begins by explaining her conversion to Catholicism and goes on to describe her interrogations and imprisonment. She tells, for example, of one interrogator who tries to persuade her

to confess by asking her pointedly if she would prefer to be home. She answers him:

> I am prisoner for truth sake, and that cause, and the joy I have to suffer for it, makes this dirty, smoky hole to me a palace, adorned with all the ornaments imagination can think upon; and I assure you, this is the most pleasant time of my whole life, for I have thrown off all care of earthly things, and have nothing to do but to serve God.

She also alleges that the Catholic prisoners were tortured. Despite a great deal of evidence that she was accurate in these allegations, she was imprisoned for libel as a result of this publication. In that same year she published the pamphlet *The Matchless Rogue,* a biting satire about Thomas Dangerfield, whom she mockingly refers to as "the Virtuoso who accus'd Me."

After her release from prison, Cellier devoted herself to humanitarian and medical pursuits. She may have been, according to Gardiner, "the most outspoken and indomitable woman of the Restoration."

Cervantes Saavedra, Miguel de

(1547–1617) *fiction writer, playwright, poet*

Miguel Cervantes was born in Alcalá de Henares, Spain, the fourth of seven children born to Rodrigo de Cervantes, a surgeon, and his wife, Leonor. Cervantes's education was unsettled because his father moved frequently in search of employment, but he spent some time studying with the humanist scholar Juan López de Hoya, a student of ERASMUS.

In 1569 Cervantes went to Italy to serve an Italian nobleman, and a year later he joined the Spanish military to assist his country in its conflict with the Islamic Ottoman Empire. He lost the use of his left hand at the battle of Lepanto (1571). After some time recovering from his wounds and further military service, he was kidnapped by pirates on his way home to Spain in 1575. Ransomed in 1580 after five years as a slave in Algiers, he returned to

Spain, where he married and obtained a government post as a tax collector. He also began to write. Several of his plays were produced on the stages of Madrid in the 1580s, but without great success. They include the tragedy *Numancia* (*The Siege of Numantia*), which depicts the mass suicide of the people of ancient Numantia, who chose death over being ruled by imperial Rome.

Cervantes's first novel, *La Galatea* (1585), is a pastoral romance (a work whose main characters are country folk who are supposed to be more innocent and pure than city dwellers). The book features a beautiful maiden, Galatea, who is pursued by several suitors whom she alternately taunts and encourages. *La Galatea* was not a popular success, and Cervantes never wrote the promised second part.

Cervantes lost his government job in 1597 and was briefly imprisoned on charges of dishonesty. It is thought that he conceived the idea for *Don Quixote* while he was in prison. When *Don Quixote* was published in 1605, it was an immediate and huge success, bringing him international fame. His *Novelas ejemplares* (*Exemplary Tales*), a collection of short stories, was published in 1613, and his satirical poem *Viaje del Parnaso* (*The Journey to Parnassus*) in 1614. His work on the second part of *Don Quixote* was hurried by the appearance of a spurious sequel (by another writer) in 1614; Cervantes' own Part 2 was published in 1615. He also collected his plays for publication in the volume *Ocho comedias y ocho entremeses* (*Eight plays and eight interludes,* 1615). He died the next year, shortly after completing the prose romance *Los trabajos de Persiles y Sigismunda* (*The labors of Persiles and Sigismunda,* 1617), which he considered his best work.

Critical Analysis

Don Quixote, Part 1 (1605) is a picaresque novel— that is, it follows a less-than-ideal central character through a series of adventures. It tells the story of an elderly knight from La Mancha, Alonso Quesada, or Don Quixote, "who is mad past recovery, but yet . . . has lucid intervals." Quixote's madness

comes from his having steeped himself in chivalric fiction—the romances about Arthurian knights that were popular throughout Europe in the RENAISSANCE. In the company of his neighbor, Sancho Panza—an illiterate peasant who thinks only of eating and drinking but is persuaded to act as Don Quixote's squire by promises of booty—Don Quixote sets off in quest of glory. He hopes to right the wrongs of the world with his lance and sword; however, his perceptions are so compromised by his madness that he often takes the wrong side, and his actions are frequently harmful to the people they are meant to help. He perceives a group of windmills as giants and attacks them with his lance, only to be thrown to the ground by their great sails, whereupon he declares that a magician must have changed the giants into windmills, "in order to deprive me of the glory of overcoming them." Along their way, he and Sancho stay in inns, which Don Quixote always sees as castles.

The work creates two contrasting worlds: the one in Quixote's imagination and the drab and distinctly unheroic world that the other characters live in. Although Don Quixote is constantly defeated by the real world, with consequences that are often hilariously funny, his persistence in seeing things through the lens of his idealism comes to seem noble as well as ridiculous, and it is the world of the cynical operators Don Quixote meets that seems poor by comparison. There is a great deal of social criticism in the novel in addition to its humor.

An English translation of *Don Quixote,* Part 1, was published in 1612, and this was followed by many others, including one by Peter Motteux (1703) and one by Tobias Smollett (1755). The work's influence was profound, so much so that the word *quixotic* entered the language to describe anyone who is dreamy and idealistic. Many 17th-century dramatists drew plots from *Don Quixote;* as the English novel developed in the 18th century, *Don Quixote* was the most useful model. Henry Fielding said that his *Joseph Andrews* was inspired by Cervantes, and Laurence Sterne's *Tristram Shandy* clearly responds to the questions raised in

Don Quixote, Part 2, about the relation between fiction and reality. The contemporary novelist Milan Kundera (b. 1929) has called Cervantes "the founder of the modern era" and has observed that "Don Quixote is practically unthinkable as a living being. And yet, in our memory, what character is more alive?"

Cervantes's *Novelas ejemplares* is a collection of stories imitating the Italian tradition of "novellas" and includes, most famously, "The Colloquy of the Dogs" and "The Deceitful Marriage." "The Colloquy of the Dogs" is often cited as an example of Cervantes' skill in creating complex realities. It is a story about two dogs who gain the power of speech and are just as mystified by it as the human who overhears them. For instance, one dog says, "I truly think, that what we are experiencing is a dream, and that we are dogs. But don't let us for that reason fail to enjoy this blessing of speech."

Overall it is Cervantes' ability to create complex balances in his work that sets him apart as one of the greatest storytellers ever. Whether it is a blend of tragedy and humor, as in *Don Quixote,* or the profound and the absurd, Cervantes is consistently able to strike a chord within that has resonated for four centuries with ordinary readers and scholars alike.

Works about Miguel de Cervantes Saavedra

Riley, E. C. *Cervantes's Theory of the Novel.* Newark, Del.: Juan de la Cuesta, 1992.

Saffar, Ruth El., ed. *Critical Essays on Cervantes.* Boston: G. K. Hall & Company, 1986.

Weiger, John G. *The Substance of Cervantes.* Cambridge, U.K.: Cambridge University Press, 1985.

Chamberlain's Men *theater troupe*

The Chamberlain's Men was the company of actors that included William SHAKESPEARE as both actor and playwright. Under the protection of the Earl of Leicester, the Chamberlain's Men was originally known as the Earl of Leicester's Men. Having a patron ensured actors a living, so when the earl was awarded the title Lord Chamberlain in 1585, the acting troupe changed its name accordingly.

Few acting troupes, however, were under the protection of aristocratic patrons. In fact, until the middle of the 16th century, acting companies roamed the countryside, putting on plays at fair grounds, in inn yards, or in meadows. The actors, all male, passed the hat for payment, depending on the generosity of the audience for their livelihood. Occasionally they were called upon to stage a private performance at the home of a wealthy person, who guaranteed payment and who provided an indoor space in which to perform.

In 1574 a law that had previously forbidden theater performances on weekdays was repealed. Playhouses now became profitable enterprises, and the first private amphitheater in England, The Theater at Shoreditch, was built by James Burbage as the home of the Chamberlain's Men. Before having their own theater, the troupe had had an ever-changing membership. Now the Chamberlain's Men included the popular clown Will Kempe and Burbage's son Richard.

The Chamberlain's Men performed plays in repertory, including works by Shakespeare, Ben JONSON, Thomas DEKKER, and Thomas KYD. For Will Kempe, Shakespeare wrote the roles of Bottom in *A Midsummer Night's Dream,* first performed in 1595, and Dogberry in *Much Ado about Nothing* in 1598. Burbage was one of the great dramatic actors of the period, and for him Shakespeare wrote the *Henry* plays, which were first staged from 1590 to 1592; *Richard III* in 1592; *Romeo and Juliet* in 1594; and *Richard II* in 1595.

Extremely popular, the Chamberlain's Men performed more often for ELIZABETH I than any other acting troupe. The scholar Peter Hyland states that "the Lord Chamberlain's Men did have good material as well as good actors, and from the season of 1595–6 they dominated court performance."

The Chamberlain's Men were shareholders in their repertory company. When the GLOBE THEATER was built in 1598, the members owned shares in it as well. Since the Globe housed 3,000 people, it ensured a handsome living for the troupe. In 1603

JAMES I OF ENGLAND took over the PATRONAGE of the company and renamed it the KING'S MEN.

Works about the Chamberlain's Men

Gurr, Andrew. *Playgoing in Shakespeare's London.* New York: Cambridge University Press, 1987.

Hyland, Peter. *An Introduction to Shakespeare: The Dramatist in his Context.* New York: St. Martin's Press, 1996.

Chamberlayne, William (1619–1689) *poet*

William Chamberlayne was born in Shaftesbury, Dorsetshire, England, to Peter Chamberlayne, a doctor, and his wife. Little else is known of his early years except that he became a physician at Shaftesbury. Throughout his life he remained poor, and because of his poverty he was unable to associate with the literary elite of his time.

In 1659 Chamberlayne published *Pharonnida,* an epic, or long poem of heroic deeds, much in the style of Sir Edmund Spenser's verse romances. *Pharonnida* tells the adventures of the hero Argalia and his love for the princess Pharonnida. Chamberlayne describes Argalia as a "worthy lover" but notes that his love for Pharonnida is

> like that amorous vine,
> When crawling o'er the weeds, it strives to
> twine
> Embraces with the elm, he stands; whilst she
> Desires to bend, but, like that love-sick tree,
> By greatness is denied.

The 19th-century critic Thomas Campbell called the poem "one of the most interesting stories that was ever told in verse." The Greek writer Heliodorus's romance *Aethiopica* was a significant influence on Chamberlayne's other major work, *Love's Victory* (1658), a tragicomedy.

Chapman, George (ca. 1559–1634)
playwright, poet, translator

George Chapman was born in Hitchin, Hertfordshire, England, to Thomas and Joan Nodes Chapman. In 1574 he entered Oxford University, which he left without a degree. For the next 20 years, little is known of him, except that he worked as a tutor in an aristocratic household for a short time and probably served in the military.

Chapman's first published work, *The Shadow of the Night* (1594), consists of two poems: "Hymn to Night" and "Hymn to Cynthia," goddess of the moon. The poems celebrate the quiet serenity of night. *Ovid's Banquet of Sense* (1595) is one of many RENAISSANCE erotic poems claiming inspiration from the Roman poet Ovid. The banquet described has five sections, one to tempt each sense.

Chapman achieved wide success with his additions to Christopher MARLOWE's *Hero and Leander* (1598). Marlowe had left unfinished an adaptation of the Greek myth, telling the story of a secret love between Hero, a nun of the goddess Venus, and Leander, her lover, who swam a strait every night to see her. Chapman did not attempt to match his deceased friend's style, but his contemporaries greatly appreciated his completion of the story. *Hero and Leander* has remained popular for four centuries.

Chapman began what was to be his most famous work in 1598. *Seven Books of the Iliad* was his first translation of the Greek poet Homer. He then stopped translating for 11 years, perhaps because such painstaking work required PATRONAGE, the financial support of a wealthy person, which Chapman lacked.

Chapman turned to writing drama. *Sir Giles Goosecap* (1603) featured a comedy of humors (in which characters have distinct personality traits determined by their balance of bodily fluids) in the subplot. The main plot was a reworking of Geoffrey Chaucer's *Troilus and Criseyde,* a story of illicit love arranged with the help of the woman's uncle.

The Gentleman Usher (ca. 1602) is notable as one of the earliest examples of tragicomedy on the English stage. Featuring a serious plot, including brushes with death, yet a happy ending, the genre of tragicomedy was to be developed and perfected by Francis BEAUMONT and, especially, John FLETCHER. In *The Gentleman Usher,* Duke Alphonso and his son Vincetio are both in love with the same woman, Margaret. She barely escapes marrying the duke by disfiguring her face, but she is miraculously healed in the end.

Experiencing some financial problems, Chapman left the Admiral's Men, a theatrical company, to write for a successful children's company, the Children of St. Paul's. It was here that his most famous plays were written and first performed, including *Bussy D'Ambois* (1604). The title character has an affair with the Countess of Montsurry. When her husband finds out, he pulls her onstage by the hair and stabs her several times before she finally writes D'Ambois a letter—in her own blood–that will lure him into the way of hired murderers. The play was a big success.

Chapman collaborated with Ben Jonson and John Marston on 1605's *Eastward Ho.* The satirical city comedy's jokes at the expense of Scots, many of whom had come to London with James I of England, landed Chapman and Jonson in jail briefly. The play—carefully censored—remained popular, however, and was even performed for the king several years later.

The Widow's Tears (ca. 1605), along with *Bussy D'Ambois,* is one of Chapman's greatest works. It features a character of low station who rises in rank. Tharsalio, a former servant, manages by his wits to woo and wed his beautiful employer, Duchess Eudora. Meanwhile, Tharsalio's brother, Lysander, mistrusts his virtuous wife Cynthia and disguises himself as a soldier in an attempt to seduce her.

The Conspiracy and Tragedy of Charles Duke of Byron (1608) was a play of court intrigue. Once again, Chapman found himself in trouble with the authorities, who objected to the disrespectful portrayal of royalty in the play. *The Revenge of Bussy D'Ambois* (ca. 1610) capitalized on the success of *Bussy D'Ambois.* Bussy's brother Clermont is an idealized hero who avenges his brother's death only for the sake of duty, not out of passion.

In 1611 Chapman finished translating *The Iliad,* the work he had left 13 years earlier. Its companion epic, *The Odyssey,* was published in 1615.

After translating several other Greek poems, Chapman finally produced *The Crown of All Homer's Works* in 1624. It consists of *Batrochomyomachia* (an account of a fanciful battle between the frogs and the mice) and several shorter poems. Having translated all the works attributed to Homer, Chapman wrote in a prefatory poem, "The Worke that I was borne to doe, is done." He died 10 years later.

Critical Analysis

It is no surprise that an author who spent a good deal of his life translating Greek literature wrote excellent dramas. *The Widow's Tears,* based on a Greek romance, serves as Chapman's farewell to comedy, and a sad farewell it is. As biographer Charlotte Spivack writes, "A mood of tragedy underlies this bitter but powerful 'comedy.'" For example, the scene in which Tharsalio wins Eudora is similar to Richard's wooing of Lady Anne in William Shakespeare's *Richard III* (1593). Indeed, Tharsalio's speech in which he reflects on "how short-lived widows' tears are, [and] that their weeping is in truth but laughing under a mask" is reminiscent of Hamlet's disgust at his mother's brief period of mourning. Later, Tharsalio's planting doubt in Lysander's mind about his wife's chastity clearly recalls the similar relationship between Iago and Othello in Shakespeare's *Othello* (1603). Despite these dark elements, however, Cynthia's turning the tables on her husband, his subsequent pardon, and, especially, the imminent marriage of Lysander's son and Eudora's daughter mark this play as a comedy.

The tragedy *Bussy D'Ambois* is Chapman's best-regarded play. Featuring ghosts, monstrous spirits, and elevated verse speeches, the play recalls Marlowe and likely influenced John Webster. Although no exact source for the play has been found, it is based on real events in the life of a French courtier whose greatness and flaws are his own doing and undoing. Like Marlowe's Tamburlaine, Bussy rejects society's standards: "Who to himself is law, no law doth need, / Offends no king, and is a king indeed." His supreme confidence is engaging. He possesses, in the words of A. R.

Braunmuller, "a secular grandeur to match his claim of transcendental stature."

Chapman began and ended his career attending to Greek poetry. His translation of the complete works of Homer is a very remarkable feat, showing impressive knowledge of Greek, mastery of the preferred English mode of verse translation (the rhymed couplet), and great stamina. Chapman's translation was the first complete one, but even after the great poet Alexander Pope completed his translation in 1726, Chapman's was preferred by many. Chapman's *Iliad* is mostly rendered in 14-syllable lines, as when Trojan hero Hector predicts his wife's sufferings at the hands of the Greeks:

> Thus will thy nourish thy extremes: "This
>   dame was Hector's wife,
> A man that, at the warres of Troy, did
>   breathe the worthiest life
> Of all their armie." This again will rub thy
>   fruitfull wounds
> To misse the man that to thy bands could
>   give such narrow bounds.

The Odyssey's 10-syllable couplets make for more forced syntax. Chapman's style has been frequently criticized as "dense," packing too much into one line: "hony-sweetness-giving-minds-wine-filled." The translations are rather free in places, as Chapman felt it was important to convey the feeling of the original, not just provide a literal translation.

One of the most famous tributes to Chapman is John Keats's 1816 sonnet "On first looking into Chapman's Homer," in which the poet compares hearing about Homer's works to actually reading them in Chapman's translation:

> Oft of one wide expanse had I been told
> That deep-brow'd Homer ruled as his
>   demesne:
> Yet did I never breathe its pure serene
> Till I heard Chapman speak out loud and
>   bold:
> Then felt I like some watcher of the skies
> When a new planet swims into his ken.

Critic Douglas Bush, writing in the 20th century, goes so far as to claim that "if Homer could return from Elysium to read all the English renderings, he would surely find in Chapman his truest son."

Chapman's works as a dramatist and a translator are often neglected today. Those who read Chapman, however, will find, as Charlotte Spivack says, "an infallible theatrical instinct, and a wavering poetic sensibility capable of . . . towering pinnacles of glorious language."

A Work about George Chapman

Huntington, John. *Ambition, Rank, and Poetry in 1590s England.* Urbana: University of Illinois Press, 2001.

Chettle, Henry (ca. 1560–ca. 1607)
playwright, editor pamphleteer

Henry Chettle was born in London, the son of Robert Chettle, a dyer. Apprenticed to a stationer, he worked as a printer, editing works by prominent authors of the period. Chettle himself came to prominence in 1592 with his posthumous edition of Robert GREENE's *Greene's Groatsworth of Wit: Bought with a Million of Repentance,* in which his contemporary, Shakespeare, was famously described as an "upstart Crow." Chettle apologized for this comment in his 1593 pamphlet *Kind-Hart's Dreame,* a prose work that features ghosts criticizing the living.

Chettle is credited with having been the sole author of 13 plays, though only one of them, *The Tragedy of Hoffman: or a Revenge for a Father* (written 1602, published 1631) has survived. This play is a revenge tragedy set in Prussia. In it, a son seeks to avenge his father's murder:

> Revenge I kisse thee, vengeance y'are at
>   liberty,
> Wouldst thou having lost a father as I have,
> Whose very name dissolves my eyes to
>   teares.

Chettle is believed to have contributed to as many as 50 other plays, collaborating with John

DAY, Thomas DEKKER, William Haughton, Anthony MUNDAY, and others. *The Tragedy of Hoffman* bears some similarities to *The Danish Tragedy*, another play in which Chettle had an interest, leading to speculation that *Hoffman* might have been written as a competitor to Shakespeare's *Hamlet*.

Chettle's 1603 prose and verse elegy *Englande's Mourning Garment* was occasioned by the death of Queen ELIZABETH I. Soon after Chettle's death, he was mentioned in Thomas Dekker's *Knight's Conjurer* as having recently arrived in limbo.

Works about Henry Chettle

Carroll, D. Allen, ed. *Greene's Groatsworth of Wit: Bought with a Million of Repentance (1592)/Attributed to Henry Chettle and Robert Greene.* Binghamton, N.Y.: State University Press, 1994.

Jenkins, Harold. *The Life and Work of Henry Chettle.* London: Sidgwick & Jackson, 1934.

Chevers, Sarah

See EVANS, KATHERINE, AND CHEVERS, SARAH.

Chidley, Katherine (fl. 1640) *nonfiction writer*

Little is known of Katherine Chidley's early life. In Shrewsbury in 1626 she married Daniel Chidley, with whom she had seven children. Through her writing, Chidley became a controversialist. Her first rebellion coincided with the birth of her first child. The common practice at the time was for women to be "churched" after childbirth, a humiliating process in which the woman was not allowed to touch anything sacred in the church, as she was "unclean," and had to wait—and make an offering to the church—to be purified. This practice offended some women, including Chidley, and in 1626 she caused a stir by refusing to be "churched."

In 1640 the family moved to London, where Daniel attempted to open an Independent church and Katherine began her political and religious writing. She aligned herself with the radical Lev-

eller party, which advocated democratic reforms so advanced that they were not realized in England until 1884, and wrote of the injustices of the CHURCH OF ENGLAND. In 1641 she published a pamphlet, "The Justification of the Independent Churches of Christ." She addressed "churching": ". . . for befor the mother dare goe abroad, shee must have their blessing, that the Sun shall not smite her by day, nor the Moone by night for which the *blessing* of theirs, they must have an *offering,* and the like they require for all the children that be borne into this world." Thus Chidley was as much offended by having to pay for the privilege of being blessed as she was by the idea that there was something unclean about her and her child.

Chidley's writing specifically accused Presbyterian preacher Thomas Edwards of misunderstanding the Bible; she, along with many dissenters, believed the Bible should be accessible to anyone, even the poor and women. Many dissenters, including Chidley, believed that women should be allowed to prophesy and preach. Edwards was infuriated and in 1645 charged that Chidley wrote with "violence and bitterness against all Ministers." He added that she was a "brazen-faced, audacious old women."

Undaunted by her critics, Katherine Chidley continued to write and dared to define herself as a minister. She often cited biblical passages in which women overcame men, such as the story of Jael, whose wife, Heber, nailed his head to the ground while he slept. Chidley wrote with an entertaining, aggressive style that was an effective method of addressing the flaws of the Anglican clergy.

A Work about Katherine Chidley

Gillespie, Katherine. *Domesticity and Dissent in the Seventeenth Century.* Cambridge, U.K.: Cambridge University Press, 2003.

Chillingworth, William (1602–1644) *nonfiction writer*

William Chillingworth was an Anglican religious thinker. He was born in Oxford, England, and was educated at Trinity College, Oxford University where he became a fellow in 1628. Chillingworth was known for his theological debates with the Jesuit John Fischer, who in 1630 convinced him to convert to Roman Catholicism. In 1634, however, Chillingworth rejoined the Anglican Church as a fervent spokesman for the Protestant faith. He served as a chaplain to the Royalist army in the English Civil War, was captured, and died in prison.

Chillingworth is best known for writing *The Religion of Protestants a safe way to Salvation . . .,* in which he asserts the Protestant view that the Bible is the sole authority in religious matters and that any person has the right and ability to interpret the Bible on his or her own and without the help of the church. In his book he says that "God does not, and therefore that men ought not to, require any more of any man than this, to believe the Scripture to be God's word, and to endeavor to find the true sense of it, and to live according to it."

Chillingworth was a member of a small group of religious thinkers known as the Tew Circle that sought to determine the essential elements required of a Christian in order to reach salvation. Chillingworth asserted that a Christian has that right to use reason and logic in thinking about spiritual matters, a position that earned him the admiration of philosopher John LOCKE.

Church of England (Anglican Church)
religious establishment

The Church of England was created in 1533 when King Henry VIII broke with the Roman Catholic Church and declared himself supreme head of the church in England. Henry's actions stemmed from the refusal of the pope to grant the English king an annulment of his marriage to Catherine of Aragon, who had failed to produce a son and heir to the throne. After severing his ties with the Vatican, Henry divorced his wife and married Anne BOLEYN. In 1534 the Church of England became a legal entity when Parliament issued the first Act of Supremacy, legitimizing the king's position as

leader of the Church. The English people had long been dissatisfied with Roman Catholicism, and many members of Parliament were anticlerical, so it did not take much urging on Henry's part to convince Parliament to take these steps.

The Church of England, in its earliest manifestations under Henry, was still very like Catholicism, the only real difference being that Henry, not the Pope, was the official head of the church. In fact, Henry sought to underscore his ties with Catholicism by creating the Six Articles, which affirmed many important doctrines of Catholicism, such as transubstantiation (the idea that Christ's body is actually present in the communion wafer), celibacy for priests, and the sacrament of confession. Under Henry's son, Edward VI, who reigned from 1547 to 1553, the church became more Protestant, in that some aspects of doctrine and ritual were changed. For example, priests were allowed to marry and the BOOK OF COMMON PRAYER, written by Thomas CRANMER, was used for all church services.

When Edward died in 1553, his sister Mary, a staunch Catholic, took the throne and attempted to return England to Catholicism. Her forceful methods included the execution of Protestant leaders, angering many. Thus when ELIZABETH I came to power in 1558, the nation was sharply divided on religious grounds. Elizabeth attempted to effect a compromise, creating a church that stood somewhere between Protestantism and Catholicism. She instituted the Act of Uniformity (1559), which repealed many of the changes Mary had instituted and restored the Book of Common Prayer as the standard text for worship. In the same year, Parliament passed another Act of Supremacy, declaring Elizabeth the head of the church in England. In 1571, the Thirty-Nine Articles of faith were published, establishing accepted Anglican doctrine, most of which was very similar to Catholic doctrine.

By the time of Charles I (1625–48), Puritans, who dissented from the Church of England, became concerned that Charles and William Laud, then the archbishop of Canterbury, were leading the nation back to forms of worship that were distinctly Catholic. They also suffered persecution under Charles, and therefore religious differences were among the causes of the English Revolution and Civil Wars (1642–49). Many of those who supported the king (Royalists) were Catholic; while many of his enemies, the Parliamentarians, were Puritan, such as Oliver Cromwell, who served as lord protector of England from 1651 to his death in 1658. During this period, called the Interregnum (or time between kings), the Anglican Church was effectively dismantled. But with the Restoration and accession to the throne of Charles II, the Anglican Church was reinstated, and Puritans were again persecuted for their beliefs. Anglicanism remained the official state religion until the passage in 1690 of the Toleration Act, which allowed those who dissented to hold meetings.

Churchyard, Thomas (ca. 1520–1604)
poet, prose writer

Born in Shrewsbury, England, the son of a farmer, Thomas Churchyard devoted much of his life to a military career as a soldier of fortune, serving various causes in Ireland and Scotland as well as on the European continent. As a young man, Churchyard was tutored in poetry and prose by his patron, the Earl of Surrey, in whose household he resided. Beginning about 1540 and continuing for the rest of his life, he wrote a great deal of both poetry and prose. His style was elaborate, with many figurative embellishments, and his playfulness was evident in the title he gave to collections of his poetry, *Churchyard's Chippes* (1575), a pun on the chips of gravestones to be found in a churchyard. During the reign of ELIZABETH I, he wrote pageants in 1574 and 1578 to celebrate her visits to Bristol, but whatever royal approval he gained as a result of the pageants was erased in 1579 when the queen became offended by a passage in his collection of poems, *Churchyard's Choice*. As a result of the royal displeasure, Churchyard was forced to seek exile in Scotland for the next three years.

Churchyard's first published works were *The Myrrour of Man* (ca. 1552) and *Davy Dicar's Dream* (ca. 1552), both poems with religious elements. His most critically acclaimed work, *The Legend of Shore's Wife*, a long poem narrated by Jane Shore, the mistress of Edward IV, was published in 1563 in *A Mirror for Magistrates*. This work influenced Nicholas Rowe's play based on Shore's life. Churchyard drew upon his military experiences for a number of his works, including *The Wofull Warres of Flanders* (1578) and *Generall Rehearsall of Warres* (1579), which describes the exploits of English warriors from the reign of Henry VIII. In "The Siege of Leith," (1560), Churchyard describes a Scottish battle. He vividly portrays the soldiers' lack of preparation:

> *And most of those, not trained for the field,*
> *More rawe than rype, unready out of use:*
> *And some men say, ech leader was not skild.*

Later works include *The Worthines of Wales* (1587), a description of that country; and *The Praise of Poetrie* (1595), a literary treatise.

Other Work by Thomas Churchyard
A Description of the Warres in Flaunders. Norwood, N.J.: W. J. Johnson, 1976.

Cleveland, John (1613–1658) *poet*

John Cleveland was born in Loughborough, England, to Elizabeth Hebbe and Thomas Cleveland, a clergyman. Cleveland attended Cambridge University, where he studied law and religion and was eventually appointed rhetoric reader, a prominent teaching post.

Cleveland became a major Royalist poet during the English Civil War, which was sparked by conflict between the king and Parliament over religious issues and questions about the rights of the monarchy. The Royalists were those who supported the king. Cleveland wrote verse on political topics, such as "To P. Rupert," (published 1647) which glorified Prince Rupert, the dashing nephew of Charles I who led the Royalist troops; and "Epitaph on the Earl of Strafford" (1647), a poem mourning the execution by Parliament of the king's chief military adviser.

Much of Cleveland's poetry, however, is satire (attacks on people or institutions in which humor is used like a weapon). According to biographer Lee A. Jacobus, "Cleveland set a style, through his own enormous popularity, of satirical attack which became the vogue of the Restoration and early eighteenth century satirists."

Cleveland frequently satirized the Puritans' religious and political beliefs. Puritans rejected the rites of the CHURCH OF ENGLAND and opposed the monarchy during the war. In "Square-Cap" (1647), for instance, referring to the traditional square cap by which many Puritans identified themselves, Cleveland describes a Puritan's conduct toward a Sister, a fellow believer:

> Next Comes the Puritan in a wrought-Cap
> With a long-wasted conscience towards a
>   Sister,
> And making a Chappell of Ease of her lap,
> First he said grace, and then he kist her.

Cleveland uses religious language, "making a Chappell of Ease," to make fun of the Puritan's unreligious conduct, reclining in his lady's lap.

Cleveland employs his characteristic poetic device of the conceit, an extended metaphor or comparison that joins together unlike things. The Puritan compares his mistresse to his "Text," a reference to the Puritans' devotion to the Bible, to justify his "Use" of her (that is, his romantic conduct):

> Beloved, quoth he, thou art my Text,
> Then falls he to Use and Application next:
> But then she replied, your Text (Sir) I'le be,
> For then I'm sure you'l ne'r handle me.

Her reply mocks the Puritan's false piety and obvious lack of biblically proper conduct. She tells him that if she were a Bible, she would never need worry about his touching her since he never reads it.

Critics classify Cleveland with the METAPHYSICAL POETS, a group of 17th-century poets who typically employ extended conceits and wordplay. Immensely popular in the 1640s, Cleveland stands out among the metaphysicals for his entertaining political wit.

Other Work by John Cleveland
J. Cleveland Revived. Edited by W. H. Kelliher. Brookfield, Vt: Scolar Press, 1990.

A Work about John Cleveland
Jacobus, Lee A. *John Cleveland*. Boston: Twayne, 1975.

Clifford, Anne (1590–1676) *nonfiction writer*

Anne Clifford was born in Westminster, England, to George Clifford, third Earl of Cumberland, and Margaret Russell Clifford, daughter of the second Earl of Bedford. Her father died in 1605, leaving the family estates to his brother. This loss sparked Anne's lengthy legal battles to regain her estates, remarkable for a woman of her time. She wrote about this struggle in her diary, which spanned both of her marriages, first to Richard Sackville, Earl of Dorset, in 1609; and, after his death, to Philip Herbert, Earl of Pembroke and of Montgomery, in 1630.

Clifford's personal diary from 1616 to 1619 is one of the few surviving personal records by an early 17th-century woman. It reveals that she was remarkably well-read as it includes references to such authors as Edmund SPENSER and Geoffrey Chaucer, as well as classical and biblical writings.

Clifford's diary displays the private, domestic existence that defined women's lives in the period. As the critic Mary O'Connor comments, "This early diary is engaged with . . . the expression of confidences—the disappointments, pain and secrets she might share with a friend." For example, following an argument with and separation from her first husband over a proposed agreement to settle her legal claims, Clifford confides her resulting isolation and sorrow: "my Lord was at London where he had infinite & great resorte [variety of visitors] coming to him. He went much abroad to Cocking, to bowling Alleys, to Plays and Horse-races . . . I stay'd in the Country having many times a sorrowfull & heavy heart, and being condemn'd by most folks because I would not consent to the agreements, so as I may truly say I am like an owl in the Desert."

Clifford's prose is personal and describes domestic and social events. She writes about the society life of the aristocrats of her era, as well as her needlework and her care of her daughter. Her reflections upon her private and public existence are a valuable illustration of a remarkable RENAISSANCE woman's life.

A Work about Anne Clifford

Lewalsky, Barbara. *Writing Women in Jacobean England.* Cambridge, Mass.: Harvard University Press, 1994.

Clinton, Elizabeth (fl. 1620) *nonfiction writer*

Elizabeth Clinton, the Countess of Lincoln, was the author of *The Countesse of Lincoln's Nurserie* (1628), a book originally addressed to her daughter-in-law, but one that reached a much wider audience. The book is an extensive justification of breast-feeding one's children, a task Clinton neglected in her own life but hoped her daughter-in-law would not. For women of Clinton's class, breast-feeding was not common; most babies were sent out to wet nurses (women who breast-fed children not their own). In her book Clinton criticizes this practice, saying, "The mothers then that refuse to nurse their owne children, doe they not despise Gods providence?" She stresses that it is God's will and woman's nature to raise and nurture children, and she claims nursing is a key factor in children's care.

Unlike other writers of mothers' handbooks or manuals, Clinton is not on her deathbed as she writes, nor does she make multiple apologies or excuses. She is modest and calls primarily on the

higher authority of God, but she is not hesitant to be direct. For instance, she alludes to the reason she did not breast-feed her own children: "[P]artly I was overruled by another's authority." Presumably "another's authority" is her husband. This allusion daringly questions the husband's and perhaps all men's authority over their wives.

A Work about Elizabeth Clinton

Burke, Mary E., et al., eds. *Women, Writing and the Reproduction of Culture in Tudor and Stuart Britain.* Syracuse, N.Y.: Syracuse University Press, 2000.

Coke, Sir Edward (Edward Cooke) (1552–1634) *nonfiction writer*

Edward Coke was born in Mileham, Norfolk, England, to Robert and Winifred Knightley, Coke the only son in a family of eight. He entered Cambridge University in 1567 and then went on to study law in the Inner Temple. In 1578 he qualified as a lawyer.

Coke was involved in some of the most famous political trials of the period. He conducted the prosecution's cause against ELIZABETH I's disgraced favorite Robert Devereux, Earl of Essex; against Sir Walter RALEIGH; and against those involved in the Gunpowder Plot, a 1605 attempt to restore England to Roman Catholic rule by blowing up the House of Parliament when they were in session. However, he did not merely practice law, he also wrote about it.

Coke's *Reports,* a vast, 13-volume work, was published serially between 1600 and 1615; he had begun to collect the material in it, for his own use, while still a student. Coke was the first to attempt a written record of court cases as they unfolded. Within the volumes he presents specific cases, repeats their arguments, and then writes a short commentary on the various points of law that each case raises. The cases are written up in the archaic Norman French that was still use in the English court system at the time, but the prefaces Coke attached to 11 of the volumes are in English. In one of them he explains the need for not leaving cases "to slippery memory, which seldom yieldeth a certain reckoning. In troth, reading, hearing, conference, meditation, and recordation are necessary." His purpose in collecting and organizing these materials was educational, and the texts proved popular with lawyers of the period. They were reprinted again and again over the next 200 years.

Coke's other major work is *Institutes,* its four volumes being published between 1628 and 1644. This text did not focus on the workings of the contemporary courts in the same way that the *Reports* had. Instead, *Institutes* attempts to uncover the importance of legal history and its origins, and to define English law as it stood in Coke's own time. Unlike the *Reports* it was written in English, with a view to making the law accessible to any literate inhabitant of the country.

Coke's procedure in the first and most famous *Institute,* fully titled *I. The First Part of the Institutes of the Laws of England; or a Commentary upon Littleton* and generally known as *Coke-Littleton,* is illustrative. Sir Thomas Littleton wrote his short book *Tenures,* about land rights, in the 15th century. Coke elaborates on the implications of every statement, every phrase in Littleton's book. When Littleton mentions a contract that lasts for a day, Coke discourses for a page about the different ways of reckoning days that have prevailed in different societies throughout history. Mastering the intricacies of *Coke-Littleton* was a rite of passage for law students in England and the United States until well into the 19th century.

Thomas HOBBES objected to Coke's elevation of legal precedent and statute above the authority of the monarch. It is not hard to see why King Charles I prevented the publication of the second *Institute;* it was not published until 1642, when the Civil War had begun and the Parliamentarians had control of London. There have been many other criticisms of Coke's work, but his influence in the legal systems of both Britain and the United States is indisputable. As the legal historian William Holdsworth put it: "What Shakespeare has been to literature, what Bacon has been to philosophy, what the translators of the authorized [King James] version of the Bible have been to religion, Coke has been to the public and private law of England."

A Work about Sir Edward Coke

Boyer, Allan D. *Sir Edward Coke and the Elizabethan Age.* Stanford, Calif.: Stanford University Press, 2003.

Colet, John (1467–1519) *nonfiction writer*

John Colet was a theologian and humanist of RENAISSANCE England. He studied at Oxford University before traveling to France and Italy to further his studies. While he was abroad, Colet became interested in the classics and in new ideas about education. In 1505 he was named dean of St. Paul's Cathedral in London, and in 1509, using his own fortune, he founded the St. Paul's School, where his good friend William LILLY served as the first headmaster. The St. Paul's School was the first in England to be solely devoted to the "New Learning," a form of teaching based on the study of Latin and Greek.

As a humanist, Colet was interested in the pursuit of knowledge that was based on rational thinking. Renaissance HUMANISM is a broad term that is associated with a renewed interest in classical Greek and Roman thought and a belief that people can discover the truth about intellectual questions by applying reason, rather than by merely accepting the word of authorities.

Colet, along with Lilly and the famous Dutch humanist Desiderius ERASMUS, wrote a textbook on Latin grammar that was used well into the 19th century and eventually became known as the Eton Grammar, after Eton College. In *A Literary History of England,* Albert C. Baugh says the textbook would "prove the most influential of all English textbooks." Colet also wrote a treatise on the sacraments of the church as well as a commentary on the biblical books of Romans and Corinthians. He gave lectures at Oxford on the New Testament and was known to have been a harsh critic of corruption within the Catholic Church and an advocate of reform.

Collier, Jeremy (1650–1726) *nonfiction writer*

Jeremy Collier was a nonjuror, that is, a member of the clergy who would not take an oath of allegiance to William III and Mary II after the revolution of 1688, in which James II was removed from the throne of England. He is remembered for writing tracts against English theater, of which one was particularly popular: *Short View of the Immorality and Profaneness of the English Stage* (1698).

Collier was influenced by *Short View of Tragedy*, in which Thomas RYMER lambasted Shakespeare as profane and immodest. Collier's *Short View* takes Rymer's argument further to attack all theatrical displays. In his attack Collier critiques those who write base and immoral material, by which he seems to mean nearly any depiction of vice, even if the vice is condemned. As he says of the playwright Juvenal, "He teaches those vices he would correct, and writes more like a pimp than a poet . . . Such nauseous stuff is almost enough to debauch the alphabet, and make the language scandalous." He praises Greek playwright Euripides for not portraying his heroine Phedra as "lewd," then adds "Had Shakespeare secur'd this point for his young virgin Ophelia, the play had been better contriv'd. Since he was resolved to drown the lady like a kitten, he should have set her swimming a little sooner." As a result of the furor stirred up by Collier's pamphlet, dramatists William CONGREVE and Thomas D'URFEY were prosecuted by magistrates in Middlesex, and other playwrights were fined.

Collier's *Short View* is remembered today primarily because of the poets who responded to it, namely, John DRYDEN, John VANBRUGH, and George Farquhar. As Vanbrugh says of Collier and his kind in the preface to *The Relapse*, "I despair of them; for they are friends to nobody: They love nothing but their altars and themselves." Farquhar may have had the most pointed response, saying "that the best way of answering Mr. Collier was not to have replied at all; for there was so much fire in his book, had not his adversaries thrown in fuel, it would have fed upon itself, and so gone out in a blaze."

A Work about Jeremy Collier

Self, David. *The Single Source of All Filth: A Consideration of the Opinions of Revd Jeremy Collier, Ma, on the English Stage, Together With the Views of His Defendants, Critics and the Dramatists.* London: J Garnet Miller, 2001.

Congreve, William (1670–1729) *playwright, poet, essayist*

William Congreve was born to a landed family in Bardsey, Yorkshire, England, the son of William Congreve, an officer in the British army, and his wife, Mary Browning. He grew up in Ireland, where his father was posted, and attended the prestigious school at Kilkenny, excelling in a curriculum that included Greek, Latin, Hebrew, rhetoric, and oratory. One of his fellow pupils was Jonathan Swift.

Congreve wrote his first poems while a student at Kilkenny, one of them being an elegy occasioned by the death of the headmaster's magpie. By the time he entered Trinity College, Dublin, in 1686, Congreve was "already a student of the stage," according to one of his professors.

The Congreve family returned to England in 1688. English drama at the time was recovering its energy and authority after the long period of Puritan suppression in mid-century. Comedies of manners—works that satirize the customs, attitudes, and behaviors of a particular society—and witty farces were especially popular at this time. It was in the midst of this cultural flowering that Congreve wrote his first offerings for the stage.

In 1691 Congreve entered London's Middle Temple with the idea of becoming an attorney. During this period Congreve frequented Will's Coffee House and met John DRYDEN, who admired Congreve's literary gifts and commissioned him to contribute some translations of works by the Roman poet Juvenal (ca. A.D. 60–ca. 136) for Dryden's new edition of classical works. The budding author also contributed some odes and songs to Charles Gildon's *Miscellany of Original Poems* as well as translations from Homer's *Iliad* for a collection called *Examen Poeticum*.

Congreve's first play, *The Old Batchelor* (1693), as revised by Dryden and others, made an instant celebrity out of its 23-year-old author. It had an unprecedented 14-day run at a London theater, and the script went through three printings in one month. It is a farce that celebrates and exemplifies the joys of frivolity and of wit (verbal humor):

> Come come, leave Business to Idlers, and
>   Wisdom
> to Fools; they have need of 'em: Wit, be my
>   Faculty; and
> Pleasure, my Occupation.

Congreve's next play, *The Double-Dealer,* opened later in the same year. It mocked the pretensions of London society by presenting a character who deceives her skeptical peers by telling them the complete truth, something that her cynical associates cannot fathom. Congreve also wrote songs for other playwrights, including one for Dryden's *Love Triumphant* that was set to music by Henry Purcell, and contributed a prologue to George Powell's *A Very Good Wife.*

Queen Mary II died during 1694. Congreve wrote an elegy for her, *The Mourning Muse of Alexis: A Pastoral Lamenting the Death of Queen Mary.* The queen's grieving spouse, William III, was so pleased with this poem that he made Congreve a gift of £100, a considerable sum at the time. For 200 lines of heroic couplets—five-beat iambic lines rhymed in pairs—Congreve develops the idea that all of nature is in mourning for "Pastora," the poem's name for the queen; in the last section Pastora is seen to ascend into the sky as a shining star:

> Fairest it shines of all that light the Skies,
> As once on Earth were seen Pastora's Eyes.

Although with its blatant flattery of the powerful it is not likely to appeal to modern taste, it is skillfully crafted, and it is regarded as Congreve's best poem.

Congreve's comedy *Love for Love* (1695) was written for performance by a new company at Lincoln's Inn Fields that was set up and managed by Congreve. The play is one of Congreve's most durable offerings, an echo of the RESTORATION comedies that attracted audiences for their wit, wordplay, satire, and risqué allusions. In February 1697 his only tragedy, *The Mourning Bride,* opened at Lincoln's Inn Fields. Although to modern readers this play seems immensely stilted and artificial, it was an immense critical success at the time and was also the most commercially successful of all Congreve's plays. In 1697, too, Congreve began work on a nondramatic poem, *The Birth of the Muse.* In addition to his own plays Congreve continued to contribute prologues and other materials to plays by his colleagues.

Soon after the success of *The Mourning Bride,* Congreve came under attack by Jeremy COLLIER, a clergyman who was leading a campaign against what he saw as frivolity and vice on the London stage in general and in Congreve's plays in particular. Congreve replied to these objections in a rejoinder titled *Amendments of Mr. Collier's False and Imperfect Citations* (1698). The controversy did not deter Congreve from moving forward with what was to become his most celebrated work, *The Way of the World,* which opened in March 1700, several weeks before the death of his friend and mentor John Dryden.

After *The Way of the World* Congreve's days as a playwright were essentially over, although he remained involved in the world of the London theater. Congreve's libretto for *The Judgment of Paris* was performed at the Dorset Garden theater in 1701. Another libretto, *Semele,* based on a story from the Roman poet Ovid (43 B.C.–18 A.D.), was written in 1705–06; it was not produced but was published in 1710. In 1704 Congreve and Sir John VANBRUGH collaborated on a translation of MOLIÈRE's *Monsieur de Porceaugnac,* produced under the title *Squire Trelooby.* In the same year Congreve and Vanbrugh went into partnership to build and manage a new theater in the Haymarket.

In the last 20 years of his life, Congreve was less active in theater. Supported by a variety of court appointments, he devoted his time to writing essays, odes, and translations. He published a collection of his *Poems Upon Several Occasions* (1710) and a translation of Ovid's *Art of Love, Book III* that same year. He also penned an issue of the *Tatler* (no. 292, February 17, 1711). He maintained a lively association with leading literary figures, including Richard Steele, Joseph Addison, Alexander Pope, and the French intellectual Voltaire, who visited him in 1726. Among his later works are an introduction to Dryden's *Dramatick Works* (1717) and a translation of Ovid's *Metamorphoses, Book X* (1717). Other prominent writers, such as Steele and Pope, admiringly dedicated their own works to Congreve. In his last years Congreve spent a great deal of time with the widowed Duchess of Marlborough, and it is almost certain that he was the father of the daughter she bore in 1723.

Critical Analysis

In *Love for Love* most of the characters demonstrate the shallowness and untrustworthiness of city society with gleeful cynicism. For example, in an early scene Tattle, a sophisticated man about town, undertakes to educate Miss Prue, recently arrived from the country, about how to carry on a flirtation:

> *Tattle.* De'e you think you can Love me?
> *Miss Prue.* Yes.
> *Tattle.* Pooh, Pox, you must not say yes already;
>   I shan't care a Farthing for you then in a
>   twinckling.
> *Miss Prue.* What must I say then?
> *Tattle.* Why you must say no, or you believe not,
>   or you can't tell—
> *Miss Prue.* Why, must I tell a Lie then?
> *Tattle.* Yes, if you would be well-bred. All well-
>   bred Persons Lie—

Yet at the same time the two main characters, Angelica and Valentine, are learning to overcome their worldly cynicism and to take the risk of loving one another. The scholar Harold Love comments, "Despite its preoccupation with the least sublime of human passions . . . the overall sense given by *Love for Love* is of an immense and heartening liveliness."

The Way of the World, considered one of the most enduring and best-written English comedies of manners, describes the romantic intrigues surrounding the courtship of a young woman named Millamant by a beau named Mirabell, who has earned the displeasure of Lady Wishfort, Millamant's wealthy aunt and guardian. By manipulating the situation with the assistance of his former mistresses, Mirabell succeeds in thwarting Lady Wishfort's control and winning the hand of his beloved. Meanwhile, Millamant uses stratagems of her own to reform Mirabell into the kind of husband she would like to have. Like other plays of its era, *The Way of the World* uses sparkling dialogue, fashionable theatrics, and a complicated plot line to entertain its audience while slyly poking fun at stodgy conventions and pompous behavior. Some critics see greater depth in it; the 19th-century critic Lytton Strachey, for example, called it "among the most wonderful and glorious creations of the human mind." Except for the 19th century, when such plays fell out of fashion, *The Way of the World* has remained a familiar staple of the English-speaking theater the world over.

In his day Congreve's poetry was highly regarded, but it has not survived critics of the 18th century and beyond who find it deficient in comparison with works by Pope, Dryden, and other neoclassical writers. It is on his work as a dramatist that Congreve's reputation solidly reposes.

Other Work by William Congreve
The Comedies of William Congreve. Edited by Eric S. Rump. New York: Penguin, 1986.

Works about William Congreve
Novak, Maximilian E. *William Congreve.* New York: Twayne, 1971.
Thomas, David. *William Congreve.* New York: St. Martin's, 1992.
Bartlett, Laurence. *William Congreve.* Totowa, N.J.: Rowman & Littlefield, 1996.
Lindsay, Alexander and Howard Erskine-Hill, eds. *William Congreve: The Critical Heritage.* New York: Routledge, 1989.

Constable, Henry (1562–1613) *poet*

Henry Constable was the son of Sir Robert and Christiana Dabridgecourt Constable. After graduating from St. John's College, Cambridge University, in 1580, he lived in Paris and converted to Roman Catholicism. It was during his sojourn in France that he began to write poetry. His first collection of 23 sonnets, *Diana* (1592), was reprinted four centuries later as *Resolved to Love* (1980). Like other sonnets of the period, these poems celebrate an idealized and inaccessible love, as in "To His Absent Diana," which addresses his beloved as a creature "Severed from sweet Content, my life's sole light; / Banished by overweening wit from my desire." He dedicated another of the sonnets "To the Princess of Orange," of whom he wrote: "Your sacred head which wisdom doth indue, / Is only fit a diadem to wear." He also published a sonnet entitled "On the Death of Sir Philip Sidney," whom he admired and to whom his work has been compared.

A devout Catholic, Constable also published a collection of *Spiritual Sonnets: To the Honour of God and His Saints* (1594), which included verses "To God the Father," "To God the Son," "To God the Holy Ghost," several "To Our Blessed Lady," and to saints as varied as Michael the Archangel, John Baptist, Mary Magdalen, and Margaret, whom he addressed as "Fair Amazon of heaven" for her steadfast faith. "To Our Blessed Lady" uses royal imagery to shower praise on her as queen of heaven, concluding: "What honour should unto that Queen be done / Who had your God for father, spouse, & son."

Constable had strong political and religious convictions. As early as the 1580s, he served as a secret service agent for the English government, and in 1598 he went to Scotland on a mission from the pope to present the Catholic viewpoint on the possible accession of King James VI (later JAMES I) to the English throne (which happened in 1603, after the death of ELIZABETH I). Returning to England during James's reign, he was arrested and returned to France as an exile.

A Work about Henry Constable

Fleissner, Robert F. *Resolved to Love: The 1592 edition of Henry Constable's Diana, critically considered by Robert F. Fleissner.* Salzburg, Austria: Institut für Anglistik und Amerikanistik, Universität Salzburg, 1980.

Conway, Ann (1631–1678) *nonfiction writer, philosopher*

Ann Conway, née Finch, was born in London in 1631. Her father, Sir Heneage Finch, sergeant-at-law, Recorder of the City of London, and Speaker of the House of Commons, died a week before she was born, and his second wife, her mother, Elizabeth Craddock, raised her. Her eldest stepbrother, Heneage Finch II, was also a politician and eventually became Earl of Nottingham. Conway received no formal education but was tutored at home, where she learned Latin, Greek, and Hebrew. In 1651 Conway married Edward Conway, who later became Viscount Conway (1655) and Earl of Conway (1679). Conway was afflicted with severe headaches and spent most of her adulthood in the Warwickshire countryside at her estate, Ragley Hall.

One of Conway's brothers, John, introduced her to his tutor at Cambridge, Henry More, with whom Conway became close friends and who taught her the philosophy of Descartes. More said that Conway was gifted with "a singular quickness and apprehensiveness of understanding" and in 1652 dedicated his *Antidote against Atheism* to her. Conway developed another intellectual friendship with Francis Mercury van Helmont, the son of scientist Jean Baptiste van Helmont. Van Helmont moved to Conway's estate to try to cure her headaches, and he stayed at Ragley Hall with her for nine years until she died. During this time Conway and van Helmont studied Quakerism and the writings of the mystic Christian Knorr von Rosenroth. It was during this time that Conway converted to Quakerism and wrote the work for which she is remembered, a treatise entitled *The Principles of the Most Ancient and Modern Philosophy.* Van Helmont found this work in a journal after Conway's death, and it was published in 1690. In her treatise Conway is particularly interested in mutability, or change. She says "that all creatures in their own nature are changeable" and that this quality must exist in order to create "distinction between God and creatures." Conway's philosophy is both religious and scientific, and philosophers continue to study it today.

Other Work by Ann Conway

Coudert, Allison P. A., and Taylor Corse, eds. *Anne Conway: The Principles of the Most Ancient and Modern Philosophy.* New York: Cambridge University Press, 1996.

Copernicus, Nicolaus (1473–1543)
nonfiction writer

Nicolaus Copernicus (the Latinized spelling of Nikolaj Kopernik) was born at Thorn in what is now Poland, to Niclas Kopernik, a wholesale trader, and Barbara Watzelrode Kopernik. Copernicus entered the University of Cracow in 1491 and began studying mathematics. Five years later he traveled to Bologna, Italy, where he studied church law and attended astronomical lectures. In 1501 he entered the medical school of Padua, Italy, graduating in 1505, at which time he returned to his native country. Over the next 38 years he practiced medicine, wrote on currency reform, and studied astronomy.

In 1513 Copernicus began his great work, *The Revolution of the Heavenly Spheres,* which was finished around 1530 and was circulated in manuscript for some years before it was finally printed in 1543, as Copernicus lay on his deathbed. In this work he proposed that the earth spun around on its own axis and revolved around the sun.

Copernicus's theories were not exactly new. As the scholar Thomas Docherty notes, "the idea of the Earth's movement, spinning on its own axis was also not entirely new. Copernicus indeed claimed some degree of authority for his propositions in the writings of ancient philosophers." However, the ancient Greek philosopher Aristotle, who lacked an understanding of gravity, had argued that, if the Earth moved, objects would fly off its surface. The Alexandrian astronomer Ptolemy, among others,

believed that the Sun and the other planets revolved around the Earth. Indeed, all the heavenly bodies revolved around the Earth, which sat still and motionless at the center of the universe.

Ptolemy had needed a very complex mathematical system to explain the way objects in the sky moved. Many astronomers, including Copernicus, found such complexity dissatisfying. After much thought, Copernicus decided that a simpler model would have the Sun at the center of the universe. He discovered that he could more accurately predict when and where the planets would appear in the heavens. Copernicus concluded that the universe was laid out thus:

> The first and the highest of all is the sphere of the fixed stars, which contains itself and everything, and is therefore immovable . . . It is unquestionably the place of the universe, to which the motion and position of all the other heavenly bodies are compared.

Copernicus's ideas had uses beyond astronomy. As Docherty points out, RENAISSANCE social and religious thought "stressed . . . the centrality and primacy of the human on Earth in the divine order of things." To question the position of the Earth in the heavens was to question not only astronomical thought but also the structure of society and the church. Thus the Catholic Church, Lisa Jardine tells us, declared Copernicus's theory to be heresy, or opposed to Church teaching and therefore forbidden. The English poet John DONNE later lamented that the "new philosophy calls all in doubt." Copernicus, in short, "displaced man and his planet," in the words of the critic Jonathan Dollimore, "from their privileged place at the center of the universe." Copernicus's theory is perhaps the most important scientific discovery of the Renaissance. It laid the foundation for the Scientific Revolution that followed and radically redefined the common understanding of the universe.

Other Works by Nicolaus Copernicus
Complete Works. 3 vols. London: Macmillan, 1972.

Minor Works. Translated by Edward Rosen. Baltimore, Md.: Johns Hopkins University Press, 1992.

Works about Nicolaus Copernicus

Gingerich, Owen. *The Eye of Heaven: Ptolemy, Copernicus, Kepler.* New York: American Institute of Physics, 1993.

Moss, Jean Dietz. *Novelties in the Heavens: Rhetoric and Science in the Copernican Controversy.* Chicago: University of Chicago Press, 1993.

Rosen, Edward. *Copernicus and the Scientific Revolution.* Malabar, Fla.: Krieger, 1984.

Corbet, Richard (Richard Corbett)
(1582–1635) *poet*

Richard Corbet was born in Ewell, Surrey, England, the son of Vincent Corbet, a gardener. He was educated at Westminster School; Broadgates Hall; and Pembroke College, Oxford University, completing his M.A. in 1605. As proctor of the university and senior student, he gave funeral orations for Prince Henry and Sir Thomas BODLEY (1612).

Corbet, who became bishop of Oxford in 1628 and bishop of Norwich in 1632, was known for his wit and preaching as well as for his strong opposition to the Puritan faith. He married Alice Hutton, daughter of the vicar of Flower, Northampton.

Corbet's major work was a collection of satiric and amusing poems published in two parts: *Certain Elegant Poems written by Dr. Corbett, Bishop of Norwich* (1647) and *Poetica Stromata* (1648). Although Corbet's poetry was very popular in his own time, today he is more well known as a wit than as a poet.

Coryate, Thomas (Thomas Coryat)
(1577–1617) *nonfiction writer*

Thomas Coryate was born in Somersetshire, England, son of the Reverend George Coryate, prebendary (a member of the clergy who receives a stipend) of York Cathedral. After attending Oxford University, Coryate eventually became part of the household of Henry, the eldest son of JAMES I OF ENGLAND. There he was the unofficial court jester, perhaps because of his physical appearance, which has been described as odd.

In 1608 Coryate set off on a solo walking tour round France and northern Italy. His adventures resulted in the publication of *Coryate's Crudities* in 1611. This work is a unique combination of poetic verse and satirical travel observations. The published version is different from Coryate's original manuscript. Under orders from Prince Henry, who had insisted on approving the book before publication, a committee of poets and wits, including Ben JONSON and John DONNE, was established to make edits and add humorous verses to the manuscript in order to enhance the tales of Coryate's encounters abroad.

This "travel adventure" book was the first of its kind and was quite popular. The work is credited with introducing the fork to Britain after Coryate wrote about its widespread use in Italy:

> The Italian and also most strangers that are commorant in Italy, do always at their meales use forke when they cut their meat for while with their knife which they hold in one hand they cut the meate out of the dish, they fasten their forke, which they hold in their other hand, upon the same dish; so that whosoever he be that sitting in the company of any others at meale, should unadvisedly touch the dish of meate with his fingers which all at the table doe cut, he will give occasion of offence unto his company, as having transgressed the lawes of good manners, insomuch that for his error he shall least be brow beaten if not reprehended in wordes.

He is also credited with coining the word *umbrella.*

In 1612 Coryate set out on a walking tour of India, Persia, Egypt, Greece, Jerusalem, and Agra. A number of his travel letters from this journey were published under the title of *Letters from Asmere* (1616) as well as *Purchas his Pilgrimes* in 1625. Coryate's contribution to English literature was the creation of a new literary genre: comic travel and adventure writing.

Works about Thomas Coryate

Moore, Tim. *The Grand Tour: The European Adventures of a Continental.* New York: St. Martin's Press, 2001.

Moraes, Dom, and Sarayu Srivatsa. *The Long Strider.* New Delhi, India: Penguin-Viking, 2003.

Cotton, Charles (1630–1687) *poet, translator*

Charles Cotton was an English poet and translator who is best known for his poetical burlesques, or mock poems. Born at Beresford Hall in Staffordshire, England, he may have studied at Cambridge University, knew French and Italian, and studied ancient Greek and Roman texts. Cotton married his cousin Isabella Hutchinson in 1656, with whom he had three sons and five daughters. His father died in 1658, leaving the estates of Beresford and Bentley, which are near Staffordshire, to Charles. It was there, on the River Dove, that he developed a love of fly-fishing that would serve as an inspiration for much of his poetry.

Cotton's best-known work was *Scarronides, or Virgil Travestie* (1664–65), a poetical burlesque (parody) of books one and four of Virgil's ancient Roman epic, the *Aeneid,* translated from a French original by Paul Scarron. The often bawdy work became widely popular and ran to 14 editions. Cotton is often credited with sparking the trend in burlesque writing among poets of his age.

Cotton also wrote a treatise on fly-fishing, which was appended to his friend and fellow poet Izaak WALTON's *Compleat Angler* (1676). The two men were known to have spent time fly-fishing on the River Dove together. Their friendship is highlighted in these lovely lines by Cotton on the perfect day for a fisherman:

> *A day without too bright a Beam,*
> *A warm, but not a scorching Sun,*
> *A Southern gale to curl the Stream,*
> *And (master) half our work is done.*

Cotton also translated several works from French into English, including his finest work in translation, *Essays of Michael Seigneur de Montaigne* (1685) and *Corneille's Horace* (1671). A collection entitled *Poems on Several Occasions* was published posthumously in 1689. These poems reflect his appreciation for simplicity and beauty in life.

As Albert C. Baugh says in his *Literary History of England,* Cotton's "love poems [are] . . . natural and genuine, and his other verses are influenced frequently by French lyrists of the century, and while he produces charming effects in these imitations and translations, the country details of his descriptive poems are what one values most." For example, in his poem *The Retirement and The Ode to Winter,* Cotton paints a vivid picture of a flock of sheep at sunset, the land covered with odd shadows, food for the imagination:

> *A very little, little flock*
> *Shades thrice the ground that it would*
> *stock;*
> *Whilst the small stripling following them,*
> *Appears a mighty Polypheme.*

Cotton, Sir Robert Bruce (1571–1631) *antiquarian, pamphleteer*

Robert Bruce Cotton, the son of Thomas and Elizabeth Cotton, claimed descent from the Scottish royal house. He was educated at Westminster School and Jesus College, Cambridge University, where he received his bachelor's degree in 1585.

Cotton was most famous as an antiquarian (someone who collects ancient manuscripts and artifacts). He joined the Antiquarian Society with historian William CAMDEN and others, and they held meetings at Cotton's home until 1604.

Cotton collected coins, Roman stones, and ancient books and manuscripts from many sources, including the Catholic monasteries that were destroyed during the reigns of Henry VIII and ELIZABETH I. Eventually he amassed a larger collection of government records than the government itself had. He knew the leading men of his day, including Francis BACON, Ben JONSON, and King JAMES I. His library and his generosity in lending books to scholars were famous, and his advice was widely sought on matters of ancient custom, such as boundary disputes and heraldry. He was knighted by James I on his accession to the throne of England in 1603.

Cotton stood for Parliament in 1604 and was re-elected three times. As a member of Parliament, he was opposed to the arbitrary nature of the rule of Charles I, and he was imprisoned for political intrigue in 1615 and released the next year. A pamphlet entitled "The Danger in which the Kingdom now standeth and the Remedy" (1628), in which Cotton asks the king to put his faith in Parliament, led him to be perceived as an enemy of the monarchy. He was arrested, and his library was sealed. Some scholars suggest that the charges against Cotton were trumped up because the king wanted Cotton's magnificent collection of records and artifacts for the Crown. C. J. Wright of the British Library explained why the king was so interested in Cotton's library: It was "arguably the most important collection of manuscripts ever assembled in Britain by a private individual. Amongst its many treasures are the Lindisfarne Gospels [a beautifully illustrated manuscript, created around 715] two of the contemporary exemplifications of Magna Carta and the only surviving manuscript of *Beowulf*." While the government was inventorying the contents of his library, Cotton died, some say of a broken heart.

Coverdale, Miles (1488–1568) *translator*

Miles Coverdale was born near Middleham in Yorkshire, England. He studied at Cambridge University, received his doctorate at Tübingen, Germany, and was ordained a Catholic priest in 1514. He then became a monk at the Augustinian Convent in Cambridge, where he began studying the works of Augustine, an early father of the church and the saint for whom the convent was named. This led to intensive Bible study with others of what was called "the New Religion," or what we know today as Protestantism.

Soon after his prior, Robert Barnes, was arrested on a charge of heresy, Coverdale left the convent and began preaching against many Catholic practices such as confession and the worshipping of images. As a result, he had to leave England, probably around 1529. In Europe he met William TYNDALE and became part of a group of zealous Bible translators. Using Tyndale's translations, as well German and Latin works, Coverdale produced the first complete English translation of the Bible in 1535. While his scholarship is not equal to Tyndale's, his superior style created a beautiful and flowing work. Coverdale extended Tyndale's idea that the English Bible should be rendered in everyday language that anyone could read, not full of pedantic, obscure words.

Examples of Coverdale's musical and smooth translations are the word *lovingkindness* (*see* Psalm 63:3) and the phrase *the valley of the shadow of death* (Psalm 23:4). He revised awkward phrasings of Tyndale's, such as changing "shadowed them" in the gospel account of the transfiguration to "a bright cloud overshadowed them" (Matthew 17:5).

Coverdale also subsequently worked on several other English Bible translations, including Thomas CRANMER's Great Bible of 1539, and translated theological works and hymns from German. His version of the psalms, gospels, and New Testament epistles from the Great Bible were included in the CHURCH OF ENGLAND's *BOOK OF COMMON PRAYER* (1549). Ultimately, though, Coverdale's major contribution to English literature was his profound influence on the King James Bible (*see* BIBLE, KING JAMES VERSION) of 1611, the most influential Bible in English. Scholar J. H. Gardiner notes in *The Bible as English Literature* that

> Coverdale's work . . . was a counterbalancing influence in favor of expressiveness in English rather than a slavish rendering of the literal words and order of the Hebrew and Greek. Since the deep and thorough permeation of the English Bible and its language into our literature and our everyday speech is largely due to this exquisite happiness and expressiveness of phrase, Coverdale too must have his niche in the temple of English literature.

A Work about Miles Coverdale

Mozley, James F. *Coverdale and His Bibles.* London: Lutterworth, 1953.

Cowley, Abraham (1618–1667) *poet*

Abraham Cowley was born in London to Thomas and Thomasine Cowley; his father died before he was born. When he was young, Cowley read Edmund SPENSER and decided that he wanted to be a poet. Spenser's *Fairie Queene* (1590, 1596), he later wrote, filled his head "with such chimes of verse, as have never since left ringing there." When he was 15, he published his first poems, some of which were written before he was 12, in a book entitled *Poetical Blossoms* (1633). In 1637 he entered Cambridge University, where he earned a B.A. in 1639 and an M.A. in 1642.

After receiving his degrees, Cowley remained as a lecturer at Cambridge, but in 1643 he was forced to leave. His sympathy for Charles I in the English Civil War was unwelcome at that university. This conflict was sparked by disagreement between the king and Parliament over religious issues and questions about the rights of the monarchy.

Cowley is one of the METAPHYSICAL POETS, who were followers of the school of John DONNE. His poetry, like Donne's, is intellectually charged and exploits all forms of knowledge: philosophical, religious, and practical. He is also notorious for his use of the metaphysical conceit, a poetic device in which two apparently dissimilar images are, to use T. S. Eliot's formula, "compelled into unity by the operation of the poet's mind." In his poem "The Muse," for example, Cowley compares time to a body of water, a snake, a piece of ice, and a mirror:

> If past and future times do thee [the muse]
>   obey.
> Thou stop'st this current, and dost make
> This running river settle like a lake;
> Thy certain hand holds fast this slippery
>   snake.
>   . . .
> This shining piece of ice,

> Which melts so soon away
> With the sun's ray,
> Thy verse does solidate and crystallize
> Till it a lasting mirror be.

Cowley's most widely read poem is "Ode: Of Wit." Using "wit" to mean both the creative imagination and the products of such an imagination, Cowley contrasts false wit, which yokes very different ideas together, to true wit, which fashions all things into a unified whole. True wit, Cowley contends, does not "work upon all things to obtrude, / And force some odd Similitude"—that is, it does not forcibly create odd resemblances between completely dissimilar things:

> In a true piece of Wit all things must be,
> Yet all things there agree.
> As in the Ark, joyn'd without force or strife,
> All Creatures dwelt; all Creatures that had
>   Life.

Cowley does not insist here that dissimilar things should be excluded from a piece of wit. Rather, he claims that one with true wit will be able to unite dissimilar things, just as God was able to unite all the animals on Noah's Ark. "Of Wit" itself demonstrates the ability of true wit to fashion "all things" into a unity, "for Cowley," the critic James G. Taffe observes, "successfully blends false wit" into the whole that is his poem.

Although Cowley was known as "that incomparable poet" during his life, his reputation, like Donne's, waned during the Restoration and the 18th century. Metaphysical conceits came to be regarded as confusing or cold, and the poems in which they appeared went unread by all but the most avid readers. Donne and other metaphysics, including Cowley, were rediscovered in the 20th century as the more complex styles of modernism came into fashion.

Cowley's influence, however, never completely disappeared because he introduced what has come to be called the irregular ode. The regular, or Pindaric, ode is a lyric with a serious subject, a serious style, and a recurring three-stanza pattern. The scholar M. H. Abrams has observed that "Cowley, who imitated the Pindaric style and matter, disregarded the recurrent . . . triad, allowing each stanza to establish its own pattern of variable line lengths, number of lines, and rhyme scheme. This type of irregular stanzaic structure, which is free to alter in accordance with shifts in subject and mood, has been the most common for the English ode ever since."

Other Works by Abraham Cowley

The Collected Works of Abraham Cowley. Newark: University of Delaware Press, 1995.
Selected Poems of Abraham Cowley, Edmund Waller, and John Oldham. Edited by Julia Griffin. New York: Penguin, 1998.

A Work about Abraham Cowley

Taaffe, James G. *Abraham Cowley.* New York: Twayne Publishers, 1972.

Cranmer, Thomas (1489–1556) *religious writer*

Thomas Cranmer was born in Nottinghamshire, England, to Thomas Cranmer, a minor landowner, and Agnes Hatfield Cranmer. Educated at Cambridge University from the age of 14, Cranmer took holy orders in the Catholic Church and was lecturing at Cambridge in ecclesiastical law when he came to the attention of King Henry VIII, who was seeking to divorce his wife, Catherine of Aragon. Cranmer developed an ingenious legal argument by which the church could grant the king a divorce without breaking its own statutes, and Henry sent him to the pope to present the case. The pope was not receptive, and the king established a separate CHURCH OF ENGLAND, with himself as its head. In 1533 Henry appointed Cranmer archbishop of Canterbury—the leader of the Anglican Church.

Cranmer is often regarded as a mere puppet of Henry, but he had his own ideas and beliefs. One of these was that people should be able to read the word of God in their own language, a radical idea

for the times. Previously the Bible had been available only in Latin, and people were expected to let the priests tell them about the contents. Cranmer not only created one of the first translations of the Bible into English but used his influence to secure a royal proclamation providing a copy for every parish church. The creators of the King James Bible (*see* BIBLE, KING JAMES VERSION) built on his work.

During the reign of Henry's son Edward VI (1547–53), Cranmer had more opportunity to carry out reforms in the Church of England. In his *Book of Homilies* he promoted the idea that priests should, through their sermons, lead their congregations to engage personally with the Bible. His new order of service, the BOOK OF COMMON PRAYER, written in a dignified and melodic English, introduced English-language worship to English churches.

Edward VI died at 16 and was succeeded by his Catholic sister Mary, the daughter of the cast-off Catherine of Aragon. Obedient to the pope, Mary set out to undo the establishment of the Church of England. As a leading Protestant, Cranmer was arrested, tortured, and forced to write a recantation of his work for the English church. Despite his submission, he was sentenced to be burned at the stake. His last act, related dramatically in John FOXE's *Book of Martyrs,* was to repudiate his recantation and to thrust into the fire the hand with which he had written it.

In his compendious biography, Diarmaid Mac-Cullough concludes that Cranmer's most lasting legacy was the *Book of Common Prayer,* which contributed so much to the English language:

> Through his connoisseurship, his appreciative pilfering of other people's words and his own adaptations, he created a prose which was self-consciously formal and highly crafted. . . . He stands prominently amid a select band of Tudor writers, from Tyndale to Shakespeare, who set English on its future course.

A Work about Thomas Cranmer

MacCulloch, Diarmaid. *Thomas Cranmer: A Life.* New Haven, Conn.: Yale University Press, 1996.

Crashaw, Richard (ca. 1613–1649) *poet*

Richard Crashaw was born in London to William Crashaw, a well-known Puritan minister, and his wife. Crashaw received a strong education at Charterhouse, a private school for boys, then entered Cambridge University in 1631. At Cambridge he was noteworthy for his fervent religious devotion, which he exhibited later in his poetry. While still at the university, Crashaw anonymously published, in Latin, his first volume of verse, *Epigrammatum Sacrorum Liber* (*A Book of Sacred Epigrams,* 1634), a collection of short religious poems.

In 1635 Crashaw was appointed a fellow at Peterhouse, a college at Cambridge noted for its reverence of ceremony and church ritual. Eight years later the English Civil War, a conflict between the monarchy and Parliament over religion and the rights of the king, broke out. Crashaw, being a Royalist, lost his position and fled to France, where he converted to Catholicism and eventually gained the favor of Queen Henrietta Maria, the wife of England's Charles I. Through her influence, Crashaw obtained a position at the cathedral at Loreto, Italy, but he died shortly thereafter.

Before his death, Crashaw prepared for publication *Steps to the Temple, with Other Delights of the Muses* (1646), which contains both religious and nonreligious verse. The collection's title is a nod to *The Temple,* by his contemporary George HERBERT, who was famous for his sacred poetry.

In his preface to *Steps to the Temple* Crashaw describes his intentions for his poetry: "maist thou take a Poem hence, and tune thy soule by it, into a heavenly pitch; and thus refined and borne up upon the wings of meditation, in these Poems thou maist talk freely of God, and of that other state." Crashaw conceives of his poetry as a way to be transported to an "other state," which is the elevated awareness of God, or grace. He exalted this experience of expanded religious consciousness, achieved through meditation upon a poem, image, or even music, in much of his verse.

The "Divine Epigrams," found in *Steps to the Temple,* are short poems focused on one brief, religious image for meditation. They contain some of Crashaw's most graphic images. "On the Wounds of Our Crucified Lord," for example, begins with typically extravagant Crashaw metaphors, which are comparisons between unlike things: "O these wakefull wounds of thine! Are they mouths? Or are they eyes?" Comparing the wounds of the crucified Christ to mouths or eyes, Crashaw humanizes Christ's wounds as signs through which the worshipper can identify with Christ. The poem continues the comparison: "To pay thy tears, an Eye that weeps" describes how Christ's wounds weep for humanity as the religious weep for his suffering. The image of a crucified Christ, in all of his pain, blood, and human suffering, is for Crashaw an important symbol throughout his poetry that demonstrates God's immense love for mankind.

Crashaw is considered one of the METAPHYSICAL POETS, a group of 17th-century poets whose work employed elaborate conceits, or extended metaphors. Crashaw is often compared to an earlier metaphysical poet, John DONNE. Both poets adopted the language of love poetry to their religious verse. In RENAISSANCE love poetry, intense pain, sickness, or being pierced by Cupid's arrow is often symbolic of the state of being in love. For example, in "The Flaming Heart" Crashaw uses the violent image of Christ's arrow, described as "Heavn's great artillery," piercing the heart of the mystic and martyr St. Teresa. The arrow (like Cupid's arrow) brings to her an intense love of God. The poem closes with Crashaw requesting, "Leave nothing of myself in me. / Let me so read thy life, that I / Unto all life of mine may dy [die]." He seeks to be emptied of selfhood and transformed by a loving God, as was St. Teresa, by contemplating her life and death.

In addition to St. Teresa, other women such as Mary and Mary Magdalene occupy a privileged place in Crashaw's poetry. They become intermediaries between the poet and God. By contemplating women's sorrow and devotion in "The Weeper," about Mary Magdalene mourning for Christ at his crucifixion, and "Sancta Maria Dolorum, or The Mother of Sorrows," about Mary as a mother mourning her son Christ, the poet seeks religious enlightenment through examples of feminine religious love. In "Sancta Maria Dolorum," for example,:

> O Mother turtle-dove!
> Soft sourse [source] of love
> That these dry lidds might borrow
> Something from thy full Seas of sorrow!

Crashaw praises Mary as an example of love and sorrow whom he hopes to emulate.

Of Crashaw's nonreligious poetry, the best-known is "Musicks Duell," which narrates a competition between a nightingale and lute player. The poet portrays the bird's song in lush, elaborate verse that earned him a label as a baroque poet. The baroque was a movement in art, architecture, and music that began in Italy and spread throughout Europe, and which was noted for its ornate and dramatic style. Crashaw was particularly influenced in this style by the Italian poet Giambattista Marino. He describes the nightingale's song thus:

> . . . thundering volleyes float,
> and roule [roll] themselves over her
>   lubricke [liquid] throat
> In panting murmurs, still'd out of her
>   Breast
> That ever-bubling Spring; the sug[a]red
>   Nest
> Of her delicious soule.

Crashaw's elaborate portrayal, using multiple sensuous images to describe the bird's song, is characteristic of his poetry influenced by baroque trends. His poetry represents, in the words of Paul Parrish, "a unique fusion of various theological, aesthetic, and personal forces that result in a truly eclectic art."

Other Work by Richard Crashaw

The Complete Poetry of Richard Crashaw. Edited by George Walton Williams. New York: New York University Press, 1972.

Works about Richard Crashaw

Parrish, Paul A. Richard Crashaw. Boston: Twayne Publishers, 1980.

Roberts, John R., ed. New Perspectives on the Life and Art of Richard Crashaw. Columbia: University of Missouri Press, 1990.

Crowne, John (1640–1712) dramatist

John Crowne was born in Shropshire in 1640 to William Mackworthe Crowne, a member of Parliament and relative of the Earl of Arundel, and his wife, Agnes. In 1657 Crowne moved with his family to America and began studying at Harvard College. Because of his time at Harvard Crowne is now known as "Harvard's first playwright."

In 1660 Crowne returned to England to pursue a literary career. After writing several plays in various forms, including a romance and a romantic comedy, he gained favor with King Charles through his masque Calisto (1675), which began a long-term relationship between Crowne and the king; he became, in fact, the King's favorite playwright. This particular masque, or short play, mostly in verse and performed by masked players, is memorable because John DRYDEN, who was poet laureate at the time, should have been asked to write the play. The Earl of Rochester, who was once Dryden's patron, was angry at Dryden for having chosen a different patron and recommended Crowne for spite.

Of his 17 plays Crowne is today best remembered for Sir Courtly Nice (1685), which Charles II specifically asked Crowne to write based on a comedy of the Spanish dramatist Moreto. Crowne hoped the play would so please the king that he would be granted a small pension so he could retire from professional playwriting. Unfortunately, Charles died before the play was finished. Nevertheless, Sir Courtly Nice was among the most popular Restoration comedies, and Sir Courtly is among the best-known fops, or extraordinarily vain men, in English comedy, taking his place among several others including Colley Cibber's Sir Novelty Fashion and John VANBRUGH's Lord Foppington.

Other Work by John Crowne

The Comedies of John Crowne: A Critical Edition.
    Edited by B. J. McMullin. New York: Garland Pub-
    lishing, 1984.

Cudworth, Ralph (1617–1688) *nonfiction writer, poet*

Ralph Cudworth was the son of Dr. Ralph and
Machell Cudworth. He was educated at Emmanuel
College, Cambridge University, where he received
his master's degree in 1639 and where he served as
Regius Professor of Hebrew from 1645 until his
death.

Cudworth used his knowledge of Hebrew to
advise the preparers of the Polyglot Bible
(1653–57), which contained Latin translations of
some oriental texts of the Bible. During the years
of Oliver Cromwell's regime (1649–58), Cudworth
advised the government on various matters, including religion. After the restoration of the
monarchy, he was allowed to keep his university
position, despite his service to Cromwell's antimonarchist government.

Cudworth was also a leader of the CAMBRIDGE
PLATONISTS, a group of idealists who opposed extreme religious views and the materialism of
Thomas HOBBES. The arguments of the group were
compatible with Cudworth's main work, *On the
Intellectual System* (1678), which set out to refute
the concept of determinism. Cudworth's plan for
the work included proving three main points: that
God exists, that people are capable of and should
make moral distinctions, and that human freedom
is real. Cudworth deals only with the first of the
points in the unfinished work. He discusses the
second and third points in *Treatise on Eternal and
Immutable Morality* (1791) and *Treatise on Free
Will* (1838), both published after his death. The
American philosopher Ralph Waldo Emerson was
deeply influenced by Cudworth's belief in the
power of intuition to uncover truth.

Dampier, William (1652–1715) *nonfiction writer*

William Dampier was born in East Coker, Somersetshire, England. Little is known about his early life. His father, a farmer, died when he was 10, and his mother when he was 16. At her death Dampier joined the navy but later found he preferred to hitch a ride with pirates, giving many the impression he was a buccaneer himself.

On a voyage to Jamaica Dampier joined with his first buccaneer ship, captained by Richard Sawkins. He later joined up with the pirate John Cooke on the ship *Revenge.* On the west coast of Africa the crew captured and commandeered a Dutch ship and continued on to Chile. There they rescued a member of the Miskito tribe, whose story would inspire Daniel Defoe to create the character Friday in *Robinson Crusoe.* Alexander Selkirk, a crew member with Dampier, later became captain of his own ship. When his crew threatened to mutiny against him, he was marooned at his own request and later was the main subject of Defoe's novel.

In 1697 Dampier published his detailed journal, *A New Voyage Round the World.* It was an immediate best seller. The book contained such a wealth of valuable information that Dampier was hailed as a scientist. Not only did he include keen observa-tions about local flora, fauna, and inhabitants, he also created highly accurate maps.

Of the Miskitos Dampier wrote: "They are tall, well-made, raw-bon'd, lusty, strong, and nimble of Foot, long-visaged, lank black Hair, look stern, hard favour'd and of a dark Copper-colour Complexion." While Dampier wrote of his respect for the Miskitos, his second journal, *Voyage to New Holland* (1699), contained less kind appraisals of the native people. Dampier described Australian natives as the world's "miser-ablest People."

Because of the popularity of his books, his journeys were financed by the British admiralty. Admiral Burney wrote of Dampier: "it is not easy to name another sailor who has supplied such valuable information to the world." Along with her praise, Marjory Stoneman Douglas added: "He was also a pirate."

Other Work by William Dampier

Dampier, William. *Voyage to New Holland.* Amherst, N.Y.: Prometheus Books, 1982.

A Work about William Dampier

George, Alex S. *William Dampier in New Holland: Australia's First Natural Historian.* Hawthorn, Australia: Bloomings Books, 1999.

Daniel, Samuel (1562–1619) *poet, dramatist, historian*

Samuel Daniel was born in Somersetshire, England, the son of a music teacher. Though poor, he managed to be admitted to Oxford University, where he studied history and philosophy for three years. It is not known if he graduated.

In 1591 his first poems were published without his knowledge, included in a volume with Philip SIDNEY's *Astrophil and Stella*. Though Daniel was upset about what he considered the premature publication of his verse, his association with Sidney proved to be advantageous. His work was widely circulated, and he gained the favor of Philip's sister, Mary SIDNEY, Countess of Pembroke, who became his patron. As a result of the Countess's friendship, he was able to spend time at Wilton, the Pembroke estate, a place he called "my best school."

In 1592 Daniel published his sonnet sequence "Delia" and "The Complaint of Rosamond" in a single volume, dedicating it to Mary Sidney. The volume contained revisions of his earlier sonnets and 31 new ones. Many of the poems are noteworthy for their lyric brilliance. In fact, Daniel's sonnets may have been a model for those of William SHAKESPEARE. Like Shakespeare, Daniel tells his beloved that her beauty will be eternal because it has been enshrined in his verse. In Sonnet 33, for example, Daniel reminds Delia of how beautiful she is now and forever will be in his verse:

> Goe you, my verse, goe tell her what she was,
> For what shee was shee best shall finde in
>   you.
> Your fierie heate lets not her glorie passe,
> But (Phenix-like) shall make her live anew.

In addition to poetry, Daniel also wrote several plays, including two dramas, *Cleopatra* (1594) and *Philotas* (1605). *Cleopatra* tells the story of the Egyptian queen after her lover Anthony's death. A scene that may have caught Shakespeare's eye and influenced his own *Antony and Cleopatra* describes Cleopatra's death. Although the story is told to the audience, rather than shown, it is still vivid, as the queen discovers the snakes among the figs and prepares to die:

> Therefore come thou, of wonders wonder
>   chiefe,
> That open canst with such an easie key
> The doore of life; come gentle cunning
>   thiefe
> That from our selves so steal'st our selves
>   away.

Daniel's other tragedy, *Philotas*, tells the story of a military officer who was executed for plotting against Alexander the Great.

Daniel's later dramas were masques and pastorals rather than tragedies. Masques were elaborately staged dramas usually performed for royalty upon a specific occasion; they were more spectacle than drama, with little plot or dialogue. Daniel wrote two masques for King JAMES I, *The Vision of Twelve Goddesses* (1604) and *Tethys Festival* (1610). Daniel's pastoral plays, *The Queenes Arcadia* (1605) and *Hymen's Triumph* (1614) are, in keeping with the form, set in an idealized shepherd's world.

Daniel was also a historian who wrote a verse history, *The Civil Wars* (1609), and prose histories such as *The First Part of the Historie of England* (1612) and an expanded edition, *The Collection of the Historie of England* (1618). In addition, he wrote *A Defense of Rhyme* (1603), an argument for rhyme and accentual rhythm rather than quantitative verse, which is based on length of syllables.

Twentieth-century writer C. S. Lewis aptly observed that Daniel is "a poet of ideas" who "actually thinks in verse; thinks deeply, arduously; he can doubt and wrestle . . . he is the most interesting man of letters of his century."

Other Work by Samuel Daniel

Hiller, Geoffrey G., and Peter L. Groves, eds. *Samuel Daniel: Selected Poetry and A Defense of Rhyme*. Asheville: University of North Carolina Press, 1998.

A Work about Samuel Daniel

Evans, Maurice, ed. *Elizabethan Sonnets.* London: Everyman, 1994.

Davenant, Sir William (William D'Avenant) (1606–1668) *playwright, poet, opera writer*

Sir William Davenant was born in Oxford, England, to tavern keeper and future mayor of Oxford John Davenant and his wife, Jane. At age 12 Davenant wrote one of his first poems, "Ode in Remembrance of Master Shakespeare." William SHAKESPEARE stayed many times at John Davenant's inn while traveling between Stratford-upon-Avon and London. The playwright became close to the family, eventually becoming Davenant's godfather (rumor had it that Shakespeare was Davenant's actual father).

Between 1627 and 1630 Davenant produced four plays: *The Cruell Brother* (1627), a tragedy; *The Tragedy of Albovine, King of the Lombards* (1626); *The Siege* (1629); and the tragicomedy *The Just Italian* (1629). After a period of illness, in 1633 he registered a new play, *The Witts,* which is considered his masterpiece. It tells the story of a pair of lovers, separated by the young man's poverty, who trick their families into helping them out financially and allowing them to marry. After *The Witts* Davenant became prolific, producing, between 1634 and 1638, five plays and five masques (pageants produced at court or in great noble households, acted by aristocratic amateurs, and involving song, dance, and elaborate costumes and scene designs). Two of the masques were collaborations with the highly respected scene designer Inigo Jones (1573–1652).

In 1638 Davenant published a collection of poems, *Madagascar; with Other Poems.* The title poem celebrates an imagined victory of Elizabeth Stuart's son Prince Rupert over the exotic island; Davenant envisions his own spirit hovering over the island to view the glorious conquest. (An expedition had been suggested, but the plan had been quickly scuttled.) The other poems in the collection are mostly occasional poems (celebrating particular events) addressed to the queen or to Davenant's personal friends. That year King Charles I, pleased with the book and Davenant's work in general, granted Davenant a yearly pension of 100 pounds.

At the onset of the Civil War in 1642, Davenant began military service for the king. Although he would be involved in military action until the war's end—he was knighted for his courage—it did not prevent him from pushing forth with more literary works between assignments. It is assumed that Davenant began work on one of his more famous works, an epic romance (long poem that follows its lovers through a series of adventures) entitled *Gondibert,* when on brief military leave in Paris in 1646. The preface to this work, which thanks Thomas HOBBES for his assistance with the piece, highlights the fact that many men of letters had left England at the time and gathered in Paris to work and write. The preface includes a catalogue of the epic works that preceded *Gondibert* and is regarded as one of the most important critical works of the 17th century.

After the Civil War, during the Commonwealth years, Davenant was imprisoned by the parliamentary government, and he used this time to continue his work on *Gondibert.* He was transferred to the Tower of London to await trial for treason, but the trial never came and after a time he was released; John MILTON, who had a high position in the Commonwealth, is rumored to have brought this about. Davenant was still in the Tower in 1651 when he published *Gondibert,* with some 1,700 four-line stanzas telling the story of a noble hero who is the chosen mate of a great princess but who loves Birtha, the unassuming daughter of a poor philosopher. The work was published in an unfinished state, and Davenant never resolved the complications. He did hint at looming tragedy:

> *And thou (what ere thou art, who doth*
>   *perchance,*
> *With a hot Reader's haste, this Song*
>   *pursue)*

*Mayst find, too soon, thou dost too far
    advance,
And wish it all unread, or else untrue.*

Although many critics have made fun of *Gondibert*, citing its wooden characters, pedantic literary references, and repetitive rhythms, it has many beautiful passages—for example this evocation of "the weary World's great Med'cin, Sleep":

*It loves the Cottage, and from Court
    abstains,
It stills the Sea-man though the Storm be
    high,
Frees the griev'd Captive in his closest
    Chains,
Stops Want's loud Mouth, and blinds the
    treach'rous Spy!*

Theater was banned under the Commonwealth, but Davenant, with the encouragement of his friends, ingeniously invented a new form of private entertainment, which he called opera (the first use of this term in English) and which the authorities did allow. He wrote several examples of this genre between 1656 and 1660, including *The Siege of Rhodes* (1656), with music by Henry Lawes, which tells the story of the siege of the island by Suleiman the Magnificent and the devotion and bravery by which Ianthe, the governor's wife, saves her husband and the defending islanders. This work introduced three innovations to the English stage: sung drama, a female performer, and the painted set.

After the RESTORATION of the monarchy in 1660, Davenant thrived as a theatrical manager, one of the few links between the Jacobean theater and that of the Restoration. He staged performances of many Shakespearean plays, insisting that he was performing these plays as Shakespeare wished. However, unlike the Jacobean practice, Davenant employed women instead of boys to play female roles and used movable scenery. Many of his adaptations are now considered tasteless and even comic.

A large folio of Davenant's works appeared in 1673, five years after his death. The volume contains *Gondibert*, several nondramatic poems, and almost all of his plays and masques.

Other Work by Sir William Davenant

The Shorter Poems, and Songs from the Masques. Edited by A. M. Gibbs. New York: Oxford University Press, 1997.

A Work about Sir William Davenant

Edmond, Mary. *Rare Sir William Davenant: Poet Laureate, Playwright, Civil War General, Restoration Theatre Manager.* New York: St. Martin's Press, 1987.

Davies, Lady Eleanor (1590–1652)
nonfiction writer

Lady Eleanor Davies was born in 1590, the fifth daughter of George Touchet and his wife, Lucy. Her father was the 11th Baron of Audeley and, later, the Earl of Castlehaven. In 1609 Eleanor married poet John DAVIES. In July 1625, soon after Charles I became the king of Great Britain, she came to believe that the voice of the prophet Daniel had awakened her and informed her of the day of the Last Judgment. As a result of this experience, she published a tract called "Warning to the Dragon," detailing her vision, and ending by saying "There is nineteen yeares and a halfe to the day of Judgment . . . And I think that I have also the Spirit of God." It was seven years before she published her next tract, in 1633, but from that time on she published with increasing frequency, particularly during the 1640s, issuing about 70 tracts in her lifetime and 13 in 1649 alone.

Often signed with the name "The Lady Eleanor," Davies's tracts relied on graphic biblical imagery, often referring to Daniel and Revelations. She frequently criticized the conduct of King Charles I, as a result of which she was twice imprisoned. In many of her tracts, she reiterated her prediction of the Day of Judgment. For example, in "Star to the Wise," she told her readers that "a great voice from Heaven then . . . [spoke] to her, revealing in what yeer the day of Judgment; and so at what time of the yeer, or how long that time." Some of her later writings, such as "Hell's Destruction," "Restitution of Prophecy," and "Bethlehem Signifying the House of Bread," described her imprisonments and attempted to defend herself against charges of madness made by people such as Sir John Lambe, who rearranged the letters in her name, "Dame Eleanor Davies," to form the phrase "Never Soe Mad a Ladie." Although there were other female prophets at the time, Eleanor Davies was unique because she did not belong to a movement or attempt to develop followers. Her writings serve to illustrate her own experiences as a woman in her era and to speak what she believed to be the truth about the times in which she lived.

Other Work by Eleanor Davies

Prophetic Writing of Lady Eleanor Davies. Edited by Esther S. Cope. New York: Oxford University Press, 1995.

A Work about Eleanor Davies

Cope, Esther S. *Handmaid of the Holy Spirit: Dame Eleanor Davies, Never Soe Mad a Ladie.* Ann Arbor: University of Michigan Press, 1992.

Davies, John (1569–1626) *poet, historian*

John Davies was born in Wiltshire, England, to John Davies, a tanner or one who works with animal hides, and Mary Davies. In 1595 he began a legal career that almost ended three year later when he got into a brawl with his onetime friend, Richard MULCASTER. After JAMES I OF ENGLAND became king, Davies embarked on a successful political career, becoming attorney general for Ireland in 1606, a member of the Irish Parliament in 1612, and the speaker of the Irish Parliament's Lower House in 1613.

Davies's first collection of poetry, *Epigrams and Elegies* (1595), was well received, but he is primarily remembered for two philosophical poems. In the unfinished *Orchestra, or A Poem of Dancing* (1596) and *Nosce Tiepsum* (Know Thyself, 1599) he defended traditional Elizabethan beliefs.

Orchestra is a lengthy commissioned poem about dancing. Promising to tell a tale that Homer omitted from *The Odyssey,* Davies proceeds to relate how Antinous attempts to convince Penelope, the wife of Ulysses (or Odysseus), to dance. Penelope refuses because she associates dancing with "disorder and misrule." Antinous counters with a long demonstration of dancing's function in the order of the universe and within civilization:

> The fire, air, earth, and water did agree,
> By Love's persuasion, nature's mighty king,
> To learn their first disordered combating:
> And, in a dance such measure to observe,
> As all the world their motion should
>   preserve.

In these lines Antinous asserts that the four elements that were believed to make up the universe—earth, air, fire, and water—were taught by God, or Love, to dance in harmony. The harmonious dance of the elements is that which keeps the universe from lapsing back into chaos. "Kind nature," Antinous continues, "first doth cause all things to love; / Love makes them dance and in just order move." Thus, Antinous argues that he and Penelope should join this universal dance and participate more fully in the order of creation.

The poem ends with a vision of ELIZABETH I's court, which shows, Elizabethan scholar E. M. W. Tillyard argues, "the cosmic dance reproduced in the body politic." In so doing, Davies suggests a relationship between the order of the universe and the order of the English state. And indeed, for the Elizabethans the social order was a mirror of the natural order and thus should not be changed.

Nosce Tiepsum is mostly about the immortality of the soul. This poem is similar to *Orchestra* in that it assumes the existence of a God-centered, orderly universe. However, the poem also demonstrates some of the strain that this worldview was undergoing as Elizabeth's reign came to a close.

Other works by Davies include *Discovery of the True Causes Why Ireland Was Never Entirely Subdued* (1612), a historical analysis of English rule in

Ireland. Today, Davies is remembered as much for this work on Ireland as for his two major poems.

Other Work by John Davies

The Poems of Sir John Davies. Edited by Robert Krueger. Oxford, U.K.: Clarendon Press, 1975.

Works about John Davies

Pawlisch, Hans S. Sir John Davies and the Conquest of Ireland: A Study in Legal Imperialism. New York: Cambridge University Press, 2002.
Sanderson, James L. Sir John Davies. New York: Twayne, 1975.

Davies of Hereford, John (ca. 1565–1618)
poet, nonfiction writer

John Davies of Hereford was born between 1560 and 1565 in Hereford, Herefordshire, England, but little is known of his family. He was an eminent teacher of penmanship in England, and he eventually became master of penmanship to Prince Henry, son of King JAMES I OF ENGLAND. According to author Thomas FULLER, "John Davies of Hereford . . . was the greatest Master of the Pen that England in her age beheld." Davies's occupation influenced some of his poetical works. In the sonnet "Against Flauius His Unconstancy and Promise-Breaking," from Scourge of Folly (ca. 1611), for instance, he takes aim at an ungrateful pupil:

> So, you passe me in [giving] skill for skill,
> But to [give] ill for good is passing ill.
> Well go your way, I learne of you this lore,
> Still to [deceive] but bee [deceived] no
>   more.

Davies's first publications were Mirum in Modum: A Glimpse of God's Glory and the Soul's Shape (1602) and Microcosmos (1603), both of which are philosophical treatises written in verse. According to the scholar Alexander B. Grosart, these poems, along with other philosophical works by Davies, such as Summa Totalis (The Sum of All, 1607), exhibit the poet dealing with "the crucial problems of nature and human nature and destiny—with 'common sense' . . . as the final appeal."

In 1603 Davies published Humour's Heau'n on Earth. This three-part work, inspired by Dante, contains "The Triumph of Death," which consists of vivid descriptions of the destruction caused by the plague of 1603 in which more than 30,000 people died, as well as of Death personified:

> Cast out your Dead, the Carcasse-carrier
> cries, Which he, by heaps in groundlesse
>   [graves] interres!
> Now, in his Murdring, he [observes] no
>   meane, But
> tagged and ragge he strikes, and striketh
>   sure.

Davies displays a much different tone in Wittes Pilgrimage (1610), a collection of love sonnets including "Love Sovran," "Love-delays," "Wooing-Words," "Blushes," and "Marriage." In "Some Blaze the Precious Beauties of their Love," Davies rejects the elaborate comparisons of other poets and says that while others say their lovers are like jewels or flowers,

> by none of these will [I] blazon mine,
> But only say her self herself is like,
> For those similitudes I much mislike
> That are much used, though they be divine.
> In saying she is like herself, I say
> She hath no like, for she is past compare.

In Scourge of Folly Davies takes satirical aim at many contemporaries through his series of epigrams (concise poems dealing pointedly and often satirically with a single thought or event and usually ending with an ingenious turn of thought). Some of these epigrams, however, are complimentary, as is "To Our English Terence, Mr. Will." SHAKESPEARE:

> Some others raile; but raile as they thinke
>   fit;
> Thou hast no ralying, but, a raging Wit:

And honesty thou sow'st, which they do
      reape;
So, to increase their Stocke which they do
      keepe."

In addition to his poetic works, Davies wrote the penmanship manual *Writing Schoolmaster or The Anatomy of Fair Writing,* of which the original publication date is unknown, though it was published subsequently in later editions (1633, 1663, and 1669). Though not often regarded as one of the great English poets, Davies was, according to Grosart, "a Singer of genuine quality."

Davis, John (John Davys) (ca. 1550–1605)
nonfiction writer

John Davis was born in Sandridge, England, where his neighbors included Humphrey GILBERT and his half brother, Sir Walter RALEIGH, both of whom became famous explorers. After a classical education, Davis set out to become a seaman and explorer himself. He traveled extensively during his life, searching for new lands to colonize and new sea passages. He made three voyages to Greenland and also sailed to Asia as chief pilot for the first expedition of the East India Company. He was killed by Japanese pirates off the coast of Malaysia in 1605.

In 1594 Davis published *The Seaman's Secrets, divided into Two Parts.* This work is an account of his voyages and a detailed sailing manual that includes drawings, definitions, and mathematical calculations. For example, in the following passage, Davis explains how to calculate latitude when so far north that the sun never sets:

[Y]ou must by your Instrument seek the Suns height from the Horizon, subtract that height from his Declination, and the remaining number sheweth how far the Equinoctial is under the Horizon up-on the point North for so much is the opposite part of the Equator above the Horizon upon the point South, subtract that Meridian Latitude of the Equinoctial from 90, and the remaining number is the Poles height desired.

The wealth of practical information in *The Seaman's Secrets* served as an impetus for further exploration in North America. Davis is also remembered for inventing a quadrant, an instrument for measuring altitude, and his log books served as a model for other sailors for more than 300 years.

Day, Angel (Angell Daye) (b. ca. 1550)
nonfiction writer, translator, poet

Angel Day was born the son of a parish clerk, Thomas Day, in London. Though little is known about his life, it can be gathered that he received literary influences rather early in his life, as his interests were perhaps sparked by an apprenticeship to bookseller Thomas Duxwell in 1563. Although there are only a handful of publications to Day's name, his memory rests firmly upon the 1586 publication *The English Secretary,* which was reprinted three times before the popular 1599 edition (*The English Secretary; Or Methods of Writing Epistles and Letters with A Declaration of Such Tropes, Figures, and Schemes as either usually or for ornament sake are therein required*) and holds an important place in studying the history of correspondence and letter-writing rhetoric in the English language.

The English Secretary (sometimes spelled *Secretorie*) was a manual not only directed at those whose occupation was to write business transactions and correspondences for another (as is the modern definition ascribed to the word *secretary*), but also at those who wished to improve their skills in writing epistles (elegant letters) for various purposes. According to the scholar Elbert N. S. Thompson, "Until the beginning of the eighteenth century, at least, the letter as a form of literature held a position of importance that it possibly never can regain," and such formularies as *The English Secretary* were extremely influential in exhibiting the proper ways in which letter-writing, which had become an organized literary genre, should be done.

According to Day, "Seeing an Epistle hath chieflie his definition here of, in that it is tearmed the familiar and mutuall talke of one absent friende to another: it seemeth the character thereof, shoulde according thereunto bee simple, plaine, and of the lowest and meanest stile, vtterly deuoid of any shadow of hie and lofty speeches." He does, though, provide guidelines and models for writing several types of epistles, including those "descriptory," "laudatorie," and "hortatorie," as well as explaining and classifying rhetorical "Tropes, Figures, and Schemes."

In 1587 Day published the pastoral *Daphnis and Chloe*, translated from Jacques Amyot's French version of Longus's original Greek publication. Day also published two poems, "Upon the Life and Death of Sir Phillip SIDNEY" and "Wonderfull Strange Sightes seene in the Element over the Citie of London and other places," in addition to the sonnet added to William Jones's translation of Giovanni Battista Nenna's *Nennio, or a Treatise of Nobility* (1595) (to which verses were also added by Edmund SPENSER, Samuel DANIEL, and George CHAPMAN). However, Day is primarily remembered for *The English Secretary,* which was among the very important treatises that, according to the scholar Robert O. Evans, "surely found their places on many a writing table."

Day, John (ca. 1574–ca. 1640) *playwright*

John Day was born in Cawston, Norfolk, England, the son of Walter Day. Day entered Cambridge University in 1592 but was expelled a year later for stealing a book from the library. He began writing plays for theater owner Philip Henslowe around 1598 and collaborated on over 20 plays with Henry CHETTLE and Thomas DEKKER. With Chettle, Day wrote such plays as *The Conquest of Brute, The Orphan's Tragedy,* and *The Blind Beggar of Bednall Green.* With Dekker, Day is thought to have written *The Spanish Moor's Tragedy,* and *The Seven Wise Masters.* The plays, most of them comic, were slight amusements and have been lost.

Little is known about Day's life. His career churning out plays for Philip Henslowe prevented him from developing his own style, as he was but one of the low-paid group of playwrights Henslowe employed. He appears to have been frequently in debt. Henslowe, in his diaries, mentions lending small amounts of money to Day. Others thought him a ne'er-do-well, including Ben JONSON who called Day "a rogue" and a "base fellow".

Day and his fellow playwrights wrote what appeared to be popular at the moment and would amuse their audience. His best-known play, *Parliament of Bees,* was probably written and performed in 1608 although not published until 1641. In the prologue Day describes the play as "Being an Allegorical description of the actions of good and bad men in these our days." In the play itself the bees hold court, listening to complaints about the wasp, the drone, and the bumblebee. In the end justice is meted out by the fairy king. The critic Arthur Symons says that Day's plays have ". . . that special charm of fancy and wit and bright invention." Day states that *Parliament of Bees* is "golden moments from a golden hive . . ."

According to the critic Arthur Henry Bullen, Day's play *Law-Trickes* contained "witty writing and touches of quiet pathos." Bullen calls another play, *Humour out of Breath,* written mainly in rhyme, "a delightful comedy with vivacious dialogue."

The exact year of Day's death is not known, but an elegy written by John Tatham was published in 1640. Bullen wrote of Day: "His gift was for delicate fancy but his job was to collaborate on comedies . . ."

Other Works by John Day

The Blind Beggar of Bednall Green. New York: AMS Press, 1970.

The Isle of Gulls: A Critical Edition. Edited by Raymond S. Burns. New York: Garland, 1980.

Pericles and the Sherley Brothers. Edited by H. Neville Davies. Dover, N.H.: Revels Plays Companion Press, Manchester University Press, 1986.

Parr, Anthony, ed. *Three Renaissance Travel Plays.* Dover, N.H.: Revels Plays Companion Press, Manchester University Press, 1995.

Dee, John (1527–1608) *nonfiction writer*

John Dee was born in London, the son of a merchant named Rowland Dee. He was educated at St. John's College, Cambridge University, and at Louvain in the Netherlands, where he met many of the great minds of the day, including the geographer Gerardus Mercator. Dee made it his business to master every branch of knowledge from mathematics to astrology, and he maintained important connections among the powerful. His wife was an intimate friend of one of the queen's ladies-in-waiting. Queen ELIZABETH I consulted him both as an astrologer—to determine the luckiest date for her coronation—and as a medical man. Another service Dee performed for the queen was to develop a legal argument, bolstered by detailed, perhaps imaginative, genealogical work, to prove that she had a right to claim dominion over vast lands in the Western Hemisphere.

Dee was also involved with the Elizabethan theater. He not only created special effects that earned him the reputation of being a magician, but as the scholar Joy Hancox claims, Dee was the architect for the unprecedented wooden theaters in the round that were built at this time. His personality appealed to the imaginations of dramatists; it is said that he was the model for William SHAKESPEARE's characters Prospero and King Lear and also for Ben JONSON's scheming Alchemist.

At his house of Mortlake, outside London, Dee amassed the greatest library that England had ever seen, with over 4,000 books—more than either Oxford or Cambridge could boast at the time. The notes he made in the margins of his books, many of which survive, provide fascinating material for understanding the ways in which Elizabethan scholars approached reading.

Dee spent the years from 1583 to 1589 away from England, mostly at the Holy Roman Emperor Rudolph's court in Bohemia; he was accompanied by a man named Edward Kelley, who was apparently a medium. With Kelley's help, Dee produced the *Libri Mysteriorum* (*Books of Mysteries*), part of which was published in 1659 with the title *A True and Faithfull Relation of what passed for many years between Dr. John Dee and Some Spirits.* Today occultists still mine these texts for revelations; another interpretation of them is that they were coded messages addressed to Queen Elizabeth's intelligence service, for whom (it is suggested) Dee was spying at Rudolph's court. The critic William Sherman comments, "These texts make for fascinating—if difficult and often disturbing—reading, packing together with little direction or demarcation Dee's devout prayers, his transcripts of the angelic voices that spoke through Kelley, and his narrative of political progress at the Rudolfine court."

Other Work by John Dee

The Private Diary of Dr. John Dee. Edited by James O. Halliwell. Whitefish, Mont.: Kessinger Publishing Co., 1997.

Works about John Dee

Sherman, William H. *John Dee: The Politics of Reading and Writing in the English Renaissance.* Amherst: University of Massachusetts Press, 1995.

Woolley, Benjamin. *The Queen's Conjuror: The Science and Magic of John Dee, Advisor to Queen Elizabeth I.* New York: Henry Holt, 2001.

deism

Deism has taken many forms since it first arose in England in the 17th century. Its basic tenets, however, remain essentially the same. Deists, influenced in part by the rise of science, believe in a Creator but do not accept the idea that this being is actively involved in the daily lives of people or in the regular workings of nature and the universe. Influenced by Isaac NEWTON's theories of a machinelike universe running on its own principles, deists favor the concept of a "watchmaker" God, who established the laws of nature but does not interfere with them. Thus, deists typically do not believe in the usefulness of prayer or in the possibility of miracles. Since God works through the unchangeable laws of nature, deists believe, miracles are impossible. And since God does not interfere in human life, prayers will not change anything.

Epitomizing the rationalist tendencies of the 17th century, deists deny that there is any aspect of religion that is beyond reason. Deists, then, believe that one need not have faith to believe in God; such belief is completely rational and self-evident. According to Thomas Paine "When we see a watch, we have as positive evidence of the existence of a watchmaker, as if we saw him; in like manner the creation is evidence to our reason and our senses of the existence of a Creator." Sometimes called "natural religion," deism teaches that essential religious truths can be learned through the study of nature, God's creation. As Paine says, "The creation is the Bible of the true believer in God. Everything in this vast volume inspires him with sublime ideas of the Creator." Deists also tend to regard the Bible as merely a compilation of stories and do not accept many of the central tenets of Christianity. For example, they accept Jesus as a historical personage but do not believe that he is the "Son of God."

Among English deists Lord Herbert of Cherbury is counted among the first. He vigorously opposed the idea of revealed knowledge and believed that the Creator could best be worshipped by living a good and moral life. Thomas HOBBES's political philosophy was also deist in its foundations. He sees differences in religion as the result of fear and superstition and attempts to provide rational explanations of miracles. John LOCKE also questioned revealed religion and asserted that religious truth was valid only if it could be deduced rationally. Like Hobbes, Locke hoped to reduce the strife between various religious sects by eliminating what he saw as nonessential differences among them, these differences being based on superstition, not reason. Deism influenced various poets, including Alexander Pope, Percy Shelley, and William Wordsworth, and had a profound influence on the development of the democratic ideology in America.

A Work about Deism

Stephens, William. *An Account of the Growth of Deism in England.* New York: AMS Press, 1995.

Dekker, Thomas (ca. 1570–1632)
playwright, pamphleteer

Little is known about the life of Thomas Dekker. Most scholars assume that he was born in London around 1570, and some feel that he may have been born to Dutch immigrants since his name is likely Dutch. Dekker is first mentioned in the diary of theatrical manager Philip Henslowe in 1597. His name is cited in connection with a number of plays that he wrote, either by himself or in collaboration with contemporary playwrights, including Ben JONSON, Thomas HEYWOOD, John WEBSTER, and Thomas MIDDLETON. Dekker's name is also mentioned in connection with money that he borrowed from Henslowe, and there are other records that suggest he was often jailed for debt, including three years (1616–19) in the King's Bench prison.

Dekker was quite a prolific writer, penning more than 50 plays, only 20 of which survive. His most famous play, which is still performed, is *The Shoemaker's Holiday* (1599). The central plot of the play is based on Thomas Deloney's *The Gentle Craft* (1597), in which shoemaker Simon Eyre becomes Lord Mayor of London. In his preface Dekker describes the play as "a merry conceited comedy" in which "nothing is proposed but mirth." The play is notable not only for its comedy but also for its focus on hardworking middle-class characters and on the development of guilds, which were early trade unions. *The Shoemaker's Holiday* is set in London, which becomes an important presence in the play. Dekker, like Charles Dickens, has the ability to make the city come alive with all sorts of odd and wonderful characters, many of whom are introduced in the first act by Simon Eyre, the shoemaker of the title, as he tries to keep one of his journeyman from being sent to France for military service:

Gentlemen, captains, colonels, commanders! Brave men, brave leaders, may it please you to give me audience. I am Simon Eyre, the mad shoemaker of Tower Street; this wench with the mealy mouth that will never tire, is my wife, I can tell you; here's Hodge, my man and my foreman; here's Firk, my fine firking journeyman, and this is blubbered Jane. All we come to be suitors for this honest Ralph. Keep him at home, and as I am a true shoemaker and a gentleman of the gentle craft, buy spurs yourselves, and I'll find ye boots these seven years.

In addition to plays, Dekker is remembered today for a series of pamphlets he wrote that provide an excellent historical record for scholars interested in day-to-day life in RENAISSANCE England. *The Wonderful Year* (1603) sets out to document the death of ELIZABETH I and the accession of JAMES I to the English throne. But Dekker turns to the effects of the plague on the city, and there are passages that paint a picture of almost unbelievable horror, with worm-ridden corpses rotting in the street and stacked in charnel houses (chambers where dead bodies were housed before burial):

What an vnmatchable torment were it for a man to be bard [boarded] vp euery night in a vast silent Charnell-house? hung (to make it more hideous) with lamps dimly & slowly burning, in hollow and glimmering corners: where all the pauement should in stead of greene rushes, be strewed with blasted Rosemary: withered Hyacinthes, fatall Cipresse and Ewe, thickly mingled with heapes of dead mens bones: the bare ribbes of a father that begat him, lying there: here the . . . hollow scull of a mother that bore him: round about him a thousand Coarses [corpses], some standing bolt vpright in their knotted winding-sheets: others halfe mouldred in rotted coffins, that should suddenly yawne wide open, filling his nosthrils with noysome stench, and his eyes with the sight of nothing but crawling wormes.

The Gull's Hornbook (1609) is a satiric book of advice to London gentlemen on how to behave in playhouses, taverns, and other popular haunts of the day. Dekker advises young men entering an inn to salute not any but those of your acquaintance: walk up and down by the rest as scornfully and as carelessly as a gentleman-usher [a person who ushers visitors into the presence of royalty]: select some friend, having first thrown off your cloak, to walk up and down the room with you; let him be suited, if you can, worse by far than yourself; he will be a foil to you; and this will be a means to publish your clothes.

Another of Dekker's pamphlets is *The Seven Deadly Sins of London* (1606). In this work he describes daily life in London through a portrait of its most common sins. *The Bellman of London* (1608) focuses on the rogues and vagabonds of the city.

Dekker is also remembered for the fine lyric quality of songs that he included in his plays. Overall, Dekker's work is a charming combination of fairy tale and realism.

A Work about Thomas Dekker

Champion, Larry S. *Thomas Dekker and the Traditions of English Drama.* American University Studies, Series IV, English Language and Literature, Vol. 27. New York: Peter Lang, 1985.

Denham, Sir John (1615–1669) *poet, dramatist*

Sir John Denham was born in Dublin, Ireland, to Sir John Denham, a baron of the exchequer (a judge in one of the three ancient courts of England), and his second wife, Eleanor Moore Denham. Educated at Oxford University (1631), the younger Denham studied law at Lincoln's Inn in London and was admitted to the bar in 1639. The outbreak of the Civil War between Charles I and the Parliament prevented Denham's pursuit of his legal ambitions, and in 1642 he took up arms for the Royalists. After the Restoration in 1660, he was knighted (1661) and later served as a member of Parliament.

Denham's first major work, *The Sophy,* performed in 1641, was a historical tragedy of the Turkish court. The play was written in unrhymed iambic pentameter, known as blank verse. Its publication prompted poet Edmund WALLER to state that the author of this tragedy, "admired by all ingenious men, . . . broke out like the Irish Rebellion, threescore thousand strong, when no body was aware, or in the least suspected it."

In 1642 Denham published his best-known poem, *Cooper's Hill,* a work in rhymed couplets that established his literary fame and reputation. *Cooper's Hill* helped established a new English genre: the leisurely meditative poem that describes a particular landscape while combining moral reflections. The following excerpt demonstrates this balance:

> My eye, descending from the hill, surveys
> Where Thames amongst the wanton valleys
>   strays;
> Thames, the most lov'd of all the Ocean's
>   sons
> By his old sire, to his embraces runs,
> Hasting to pay his tribute to the sea,
> Like mortal life to meet eternity.

Denham helped develop the closed heroic couplet (a two-line verse rhyming *aa* and containing a complete idea, not dependent upon the preceding or following couplet). The poet John Dryden considered Denham an influential poetic voice who was instrumental in popularizing the closed couplet. Dryden particularly admired the following four verses from *Cooper's Hill* in which Denham compares his poetry to the Thames:

> O could I flow like thee, and make thy
>   stream
> My great example, as it is my theme!
> Though deep, yet clear; though gentle, yet
>   not dull;
> Strong without rage, without o'erflowing
>   full.

Samuel Johnson noted that because of Dryden's admiration of Denham's verses, many writers have imitated them and thus increased their popularity.

Descartes, René (1596–1650) *nonfiction writer*

René Descartes was born in La Haye, France, to Joachim Descartes, a counselor in the French parliament. In 1606 he entered the Jesuit school of La Flèche in Anjou, where he studied classics, logic, philosophy, and mathematics. He then enrolled at the French University of Poitiers, where he received a law degree and a B.A. in 1616. In 1620 he began a life of leisure, traveling throughout Europe. Eight years later he moved to Holland, where he remained for the next 20 years, writing and thinking.

After settling in Holland, Descartes began work on a scientific work, *The World or Treatise on Light,* which argued that the Earth revolves around the Sun. However, he decided not to publish it after he learned that the Italian scientist Galileo was being tried for defying church teaching for publishing similar scientific beliefs, which built upon Nicolaus COPERNICUS's theories about the Earth's movement around the Sun.

Descartes's first two published works, and the ones for which he is best known, are *Discourse on Method* (1637) and *Meditations on First Philosophy* (1641). At the beginning of *Meditations* he writes, "I should withhold from assent no less carefully from opinions that are not completely certain and indubitable than I would from those that are patently false."

With this statement Descartes sets out his underlying purpose, to establish a methodology that is based on skepticism, eventually labeled "Cartesian doubt." He denies, for the sake of argument, that anything can be taken for granted. Since one's senses can deceive one, Descartes supposes "that everything I see is false. . . . I have no senses whatever." From this piece of reasoning he concludes that the only thing of which he can be certain is that he thinks. *Cogito, ergo sum,* or "I think therefore I am," is thus the first principle of Descartes's philosophy. As he explains in *Discourse on Method:*

> I resolved to assume that everything that ever
> entered into my mind was no more true than

the illusions of my dreams. But immediately afterwards I noticed that whilst I thus wished to think all things false, it was absolutely essential that the "I" who thought this should be somewhat, and remarking that this truth *"I think, therefore I am"* was so certain and so assured that all the most extravagant suppositions brought forward by the skeptics were incapable of shaking it, I came to the conclusion that I could receive it without scruple as the first principle of the Philosophy for which I was seeking.

According to the scholars Marjorie Grene and Roger Ariew, "This pronouncement obliged those in the West" to reach "a new level of awareness, at which [one] could ask . . . reflective questions about [one's self]." Such questions lead to considering how thought determines the way one sees the world rather than assuming that the world really is exactly the way it is seen.

There is a split in Cartesian thought between the evidence of the senses, which must remain uncertain, and pure thought. Descartes announces his distrust of the bodily senses in *Meditations on First Philosophy:* "All that up to the present time I have accepted as most true and certain I have learned either from the senses or through the senses; but it is sometimes proved to me that these senses are deceptive, and it is wiser not to trust entirely to any thing by which we have once been deceived." The philosopher, according to Descartes, is required to progress from a simple idea, one which can be known without any prior knowledge, to ideas that can be known only because of one's knowledge of the chain of ideas that proceeds from the first one. Hence, as the scholar Emily R. Grosholz points out, "the argument of the *Meditations* [the basis of all Descartes's thought] critically limits the extent of human knowledge to ideas proportional to the 'I think' with which it begins." This limitation requires the Cartesian philosopher to ignore other possibilities, excluding, for example, considerations of the body.

This limitation may seem extreme, but whatever problems Descartes's thought might have, it has remained extremely important and influential. Cartesian philosophy took hold in France almost immediately. In England, however, Descartes's influence was less immediate. The Cartesian distrust of the evidence of the senses ran directly contrary to British empiricism, a philosophy built on direct sensory evidence and typified by the work of Francis BACON and John LOCKE. Later skeptical philosophers such as David Hume renewed interest in Descartes in the 18th century. Descartes's thought is one of the most important stages in the history of philosophy: "Over the centuries and with currently renewed intensity," as Grosholz observes, "his *Meditations* has never failed to inspire serious discussion among philosophers."

Other Work by René Descartes
The Philosophical Writings of Descartes: Volume 1. Edited by John Cottingham, et al. New York: Cambridge University Press, 1985.

Works about René Descartes
Cottingham, John, ed. *The Cambridge Companion to Descartes.* New York: Cambridge University Press, 1992.
Sorell, Tom. *Descartes: A Very Short Introduction.* New York: Oxford University Press, 2000.

de Vere, Edward
See OXFORD, EDWARD DE VERE, EARL OF.

Digby, Sir Kenelm (1603–1665) *nonfiction writer, natural philosopher*
Sir Kenelm Digby was the son of Sir Everard and Lady Mary Digby. Sir Everard was among those involved in the Gunpowder Plot, a conspiracy by Catholics against KING JAMES I and Parliament, for which he was executed. Although Kenelm Digby attended Oxford University in 1618, he did not complete his degree.

Digby's varied writings reflect his life and interests. In 1625 he secretly married Venetia Stanley, a famous beauty he had known since childhood.

His account of their romance, *Private Memoirs*, was not published until 1827.

Digby led a naval expedition to the Mediterranean and defeated the French and Venetian fleets in Scanderoon Harbour, Turkey, in 1628. His *Journal of a Voyage into the Mediterranean* (1868) tells this story. He was imprisoned for Royalist and Catholic activities during the English Civil War, and during this time wrote his *'Observations' from a Catholic point of view of Sir Thomas BROWNE's Religio Medici*, which was published without the author's approval in 1642. Digby disagreed with Browne on several points, such as the mortality of the soul. Digby believed in an immortal soul, and he argued his ideas in *A Treatise on the Nature of Bodies* (1644) and *Of the Immortality of Man's Soul* (ca. 1643). At this time he also published *'Observations' on the Twenty-Second Stanza of Spenser's Faerie Queen* (1644).

Digby knew René DESCARTES and admired and corresponded with Thomas HOBBES. It is believed that he discovered oxygen is necessary to plant life (1662–63); he wrote about this discovery in his paper *A Discourse concerning the Vegetation of Plants* (1661). His science also included alchemy and the use of a "powder of sympathy" for curing wounds. *Chemical Secrets and Rare Experiments in Physick and Philosophy* (1668) was published in his name after his death, but it may not have been his work.

Kenelm Digby's writings are of historical interest. They reflect the intellectual life of his day, as well as the insecurities of England's political turmoil during the Civil War period. However, his most significant contribution to literature lies in valuable medieval manuscripts from his former Oxford tutor, Thomas Allen, which he donated to the Bodleian Library in 1632.

Dillon, Wentworth (Earl of Roscommon)
(ca. 1633–1685) *translator*

Wentworth Dillon was the fourth Earl of Roscommon. He was born in Ireland and educated at Wentworth Woodhouse in Yorkshire, England, and the Protestant University at Caen, Normandy, France. His father died in October 1649, and after the Restoration of the monarchy and the accession of Charles II to the throne, Dillon returned to inherit his estates in Ireland; however, he had to sell many of them to pay his debts. He received an honorary law degree from Cambridge University in 1680 and an honorary doctorate in canon law from Oxford University in 1683. He was appointed master of the horse to the Duchess of York in the early 1680s.

Dillon's main work was a translation of Horace's (68–5 B.C.) *Ars Poetica in Blank Verse* (1680; 1684; 1709). He also wrote an *Essay on Translated Verse* (1684), which was included in the second and third editions of the Horace translation. Dillon's verse is workmanlike but not profound or moving. In *Translated Verse*, for example, he says:

> *Good Translation is no easie Art*
> *For tho Materials have long since been*
>   *found*
> *Yet both your fancie, and your Hands are*
>   *bound;*
> *And by Improving what was writ Before;*
> *Invention Labours' less, but Judgment,*
>   *more.*

Although Dillon's meter and rhyme are careful and correct, his work lacks emotion. Still, he recognizes greatness. In 1685 he became the first professional critic publicly to praise John MILTON's *Paradise Lost*. His opinion was added as a final passage to his second edition of the essay on translation.

Dillon produced several other poems and translations, which were collected into a first edition in 1701. He died in 1685, quoting two forthright lines from his own translation of the *Dies Irae*,

> *My God, My Father, and My Friend*
> *Do not forsake me at my end.*

Some time before his death, Wentworth Dillon founded a literary academy modeled on the famous one in France. The purpose of the French academy was to honor literary achievement and help to preserve the language. Scholar Greg Clingham says that the English version was similarly intended to improve and purify the native language through poetry and through translation from classical Greek and Latin. Unfortunately Dillon died before he could ensure the survival of the academy, and the plans were abandoned.

The poet John DRYDEN had been the "principal assistant" in the endeavor, and Clingham suggests that his appreciation of the importance of "fundamentally new poetic and cultural work in translation" led Dryden to praise Dillon as follows:

> The wit of Greece, the Gravity of Rome
> Appear exalted in the British Loome;
> The Muses empire is restor'd agen,
> In Charles his Reign, and by Roscommon's
> pen.

Donne, John (1572–1631) poet, nonfiction writer

John Donne was born in London, the son of John Donne, a prosperous Roman Catholic iron and hardware dealer. His mother, née Elizabeth Heywood, was related through her mother to Thomas MORE. Donne's uncle was executed in 1594 for performing masses, and his brother died while in prison for harboring a priest. Despite this Roman Catholic tradition in the family, Donne in his youth seems to have exhibited little interest in religious affairs.

Donne attended Oxford University without taking a degree and then studied law in the Inns of Court. He joined the Earl of Essex and other adventurers in the raid on Cadiz in 1596 and participated in a second military expedition to the Azores in 1597.

Since most of Donne's poetry was published only after he died, it is difficult to tell when he wrote specific poems. However, he is generally thought to have written most of his love lyrics and satires during this early period of his adult life. During the same time he probably wrote *Paradoxes,* a short col-

lection of outrageous arguments on such topics as "That Nature is our worst guide" or "That it is possible to find some virtue in some women."

Donne's early poetry was modeled on the verse of classical Roman authors. He wrote five satires and a number of verse letters in imitation of Horace and love lyrics in the style of Catullus and other Roman lyricists. Ovid's *Amores* probably inspired Donne's 20 elegies: long, rhymed, erotic poems that sometimes address a lover, sometimes describe an amorous situation, and sometimes develop a philosophy of love.

In 1601, when he was employed as secretary to Sir Thomas Edgerton, Donne eloped with Edgerton's niece, Anne More. Donne's father was furious, as was Edgerton, who actually had Donne imprisoned for a period. The scandal forced Donne to spend much of the next decade living away from London. During this period Donne read voluminously and wrote (but did not publish) a collection of *Problems,* a kind of tame version of *Paradoxes;* and *Biathanatos,* a treatise on the church and suicide. During this time he published two anti-Catholic tracts, *Pseudo-Martyr* (1610) and *Ignatius his Conclave* (1611). In 1611 and 1612 he commemorated the death at age 14 of Anne, the daughter of his then-patron, Sir Robert Drury, by publishing *Anniversaries,* two long poems about the decay of the world and the progress of the soul.

Around 1610 JAMES I OF ENGLAND, who admired *Pseudo-Martyr,* began urging Donne to enter the ministry. When Donne declined on the grounds that the office was, as Izaak WALTON put it in his *Life of Dr. John Donne* (1640), "too weighty for his abilities," the king pressured him by shutting off all other career routes. Donne finally took orders in 1615.

Donne's ecclesiastical career was very successful, and in the last decade of his life, as dean of St. Pauls in London, he became the most famous preacher of his age. Walton describes him as

> A Preacher in earnest; weeping sometimes for his Auditory [audience], sometimes with them:

always preaching to himself, like an Angel from a cloud, but in none; carrying some to Heaven in holy raptures, and inticing others by a sacred Art and Courtship to amend their lives.

Several of Donne's sermons saw print during his lifetime, and in 1624 he published *Devotions,* a series of 24 meditations and prayers on his own near-fatal illness. In his last years he made his impending death the subject of his meditations. He was said to have preached his own funeral sermon in "Death's Duel" (1630), and near the very end he posed for his sepulchre's monument in his funeral winding sheets.

Donne himself described his career as falling into two phases: that of the early *Jack* Donne, writer of witty erotic lyrics and paradoxes; and the later *John* Donne, the preacher concerned with decay, death, and salvation. It is, nevertheless, not certain that all the secular lyrics were early or all the divine poems late. Soon after Donne's death, the poems on which much of his later fame rests were published in book form as *Poems, by J. D.* (1633). The poems were accompanied by elegies, often verses that honor the dead, written by other important poets including Ben JONSON and Thomas CAREW.

Critical Analysis

Despite their difficulty, Donne's intellectual and often dramatic poems have been very influential. Many poets who followed him later in the 17th century imitated him in writing what a later age would call metaphysical poetry, lyrical verse characterized by wordplay and unusual images (*see* METAPHYSICAL POETS). Invented by John DRYDEN, the label represented a criticism of Donne, who Dryden felt wrote about love with too little emotion and too much intellect. However, during the early 20th century, under the endorsement of the American poet T. S. Eliot, metaphysical poetry became a model for what lyrical poetry should be, and Donne came to be regarded as its greatest practitioner.

In Elegy 19, "To His Mistress Going to Bed," the speaker urges his beloved to undress and describes the process in ingenious images. In famous lines he compares caressing the naked woman to the excitement of global exploration:

> *Licence my roving hands, and let them go*
> *Before, behind, between, above, below.*
> *O my America, my new found land,*
> *My kingdom, safeliest when with one man*
> *   manned,*
> *My mine of precious stones, my empery,*
> *How blessed am I in this discovering thee!*

Sexual and territorial exploration share an extraordinary moment here. Donne's mind, never content with the single comparison, pushes the metaphor, testing other ways it can be made to work: By asking the woman to "license" his "roving hands," he makes her the equivalent of the queen who gives charters—that is, licenses—to explore and prey on the outer world.

As the scholar Achsah Guibbory observes, however, the woman who begins as the queen ends up a colony: "The man becomes not only explorer but conquerer, and she becomes *his* land and kingdom." Thus, the thought of America as the equivalent of the hidden parts of a woman leads to thoughts of conquest and rule: "one man manned" is about monarchy, male possessiveness, and sexual dominance. "Manned" ingeniously links the single man with control and sexuality, to ideas of new world treasure ("precious stones"), and finally to expectations of honor. Like Columbus, the discoverer is "blessed" by being recognized by the queen, by other men, and by history; his fortune is made. It is a thoroughly male triumph.

This elegy reveals an important characteristic of Donne's poetry: It is intensely intellectual even as it describes and engages in highly emotional situations. It is distinguished in part by a love of ingenious metaphors, often drawn from extravagantly remote fields. Perhaps the most famous of these, which has been used frequently to characterize metaphysical poetry in general, is the simile of the drafting compass as an image of true lovers in "A Valediction forbidding Mourning":

> If they [i.e., our souls] be two, they are two
>   so
> As stiff twin compasses are two,
> Thy soul the fixed foot, makes no show
> To move, but doth, if th'other do.
>
> And though it in the centre sit,
> Yet when the other far doth roam,
> It leans, and hearkens after it,
> And grows erect, as that comes home.
>
> Such wilt thou be to me, who must
> Like th' other foot, obliquely run;
> Thy firmness makes my circle just,
> And makes me end, where I begun.

The compass image suggests a connection between the lovers even as they are apart. Yet Donne ingeniously finds further meanings. He considers the difference between a central, "fixed" foot at "home" and a roaming, "obliquely" moving foot. He suggests ideas of desire: "leans," "hearkens," and "grows erect." He concludes with an idea of love as the perfect ("just") circle that ends where it began.

The image with its many meanings remains open for further interpretation. For instance, while traditionally scholars have read the image as a tribute to the faithful woman who stays at home while the man wanders, more recently the scholar Thomas Docherty has pointed out that the text itself confuses the gender roles: "In some manuscript versions of this poem, its title suggests that it must be spoken by a male to a mistress; but there is nothing within the text itself to necessitate that." Thus, the meaning of the compass image remains open and suggestive.

Along with sensuality and conceit, Donne loves ingenious argument. Perhaps the most notorious poem in this respect is "The Flea." In the first stanza the speaker tries to convince his lady to make love by arguing that her concern for "honor" is beside the point since their bloods have already

been mixed in the flea that has bitten them both. In the second stanza, when she threatens to squash the flea, he stops her by asserting that it has become a sacred temple of their marriage. In the third and final stanza, after she has killed the flea, the speaker triumphs yet again by arguing that her "honor" is just as trivial as the flea. In this poem the ingenuity that is seen in the single conceit is developed into an argument with dramatic stages.

The surprise that characterizes such poetry is neatly displayed in "Song." The poem begins as if it were anticipating a romantic song, but as the lines accumulate, the purpose of the list becomes increasingly confusing:

> Go, and catch a falling star,
> Get with child a mandrake root,
> Tell me, where all past years are,
> Or who cleft the Devil's foot,
> Teach me to hear mermaids singing,
> Or to keep off envy's stinging,
>   And find
>   What wind
> Serves to advance an honest mind.

The last line here is typical in that it seems a distant allusion to the proverbial "it is an ill wind that blows no good," but it turns out to suggest something much more cynical and pessimistic: There is no wind that helps honesty. Only at the end of the second stanza does it become clear that this strange set of commands is a list of impossibilities, the last of which is to find "a woman true and fair," that is, both honest and beautiful.

In the third and last stanza of this poem, Donne plays a typical trick and heightens the insult. A moment after being told of a miraculously true and fair woman, the speaker begins to have second thoughts. Do not tell me of such a woman, the poet says,

> I would not go,
> Though at next door we might meet,
> Though she were true when you met her,
> And last till you write your letter,

Yet she
Will be
False ere I come to two, or three.

The slander begins quietly but becomes over-whelming. The speaker starts by imagining such a woman next door. He even concedes she may be faithful right up to the moment she is reported, but in the time it takes him to get the letter and to go next door she will betray her lover, and not just once nor twice, but thrice. At the end of the poem, how-ever, the reader may suspect that the poet's cynicism is a trick of the male mind, not a general truth about women but the expression of a disappointed man.

Donne is a poet writing about the central con-cerns of his age and of our own. As the scholar Janel Mueller argues, "By casting desire and love as physical operations actually endured, Donne in-vigorates stock tropes [figures of speech]." The very energy of his intellect and ego makes him both exciting and disturbing. Against those who might find Donne too dominating, Mueller makes the case that, while Donne's forceful male speaker inevitably "reinscribes the inequality of the sexes," "to his personal credit, Donne lends no credence to . . . views of sexual difference, for his poetry is unmarked by their major premise—that a woman's capacity to bear children defines her and her rela-tion to a man." Certainly, Donne's speakers tend to triumph over their women and even insult them on occasion, but they also take them more seri-ously than any other poetry of the period.

There is in Donne a sense of self-dramatization. In the Divine poems he can even criticize himself for playing at piety and for enjoying catastrophe. For the first eight lines of "At the round earth's imagin'd corners, blow" he enthusiastically antici-pates the Judgment Day, but in the final six lines he abruptly catches himself and in doing so brings to awareness the shortness of life and the need to re-pent now. He asks God to hold off Judgment Day and let the dead sleep on:

But let them sleep, Lord, and me mourn a
space,

For, if above all these my sins abound,
'Tis late to ask abundance of thy grace,
When we are there; here on this lowly
ground,
Teach me how to repent; for that's as good
As if thou hadst sealed my pardon, with thy
blood.

The drama of the break in the middle of the third-to-last line pits heaven, Judgment Day, and eternity ("there") against this ordinary moment, "this lowly ground"—that is, "here." The aware-ness of the mystery of grace plays against the poet's terrifying sense of his own worthlessness. He sees himself as the greatest sinner and possi-bly worries about when it might be too late to re-pent. The phrase "'Tis late" may be a compressed way of saying, "'Tis *too* late," or it may simply be an observation that one's chances of forgiveness are better if one does not wait literally to the last minute to repent.

Donne's sermons and meditations, written in the last two decades of his life, are extended reflec-tions on just these sorts of issues. Like the poems, these prose compositions are dramatic perform-ances, yet even when they seem to be terribly per-sonal, they also consciously instruct the audience. Like his poetry, Donne's prose exhibits a restless, probing, and daring imagination. In the famous "Meditation 17" of the *Devotions,* the sick speaker hears a funeral bell tolling and thinks about its re-lation to himself.

All mankind is of one author, and is one vol-ume; when one man dies, one chapter is not torn out of the book, but translated into a bet-ter language; and every chapter must be so translated.

Calling God the "author" leads to seeing God's cre-ation as a book.

A little later in this same meditation, the idea of the unity of humanity, first imagined as a book, gets developed by a different metaphor. Donne writes:

No man is an island, entire of itself; every man is a piece of the continent, a part of the main. If a clod be washed away by the sea, Europe is the less, as well as if a promontory were . . .: any man's death diminishes me, because I am involved in mankind, and therefore never send to know for whom the [funeral] bell tolls; it tolls for thee.

It is not surprising that these lines have become famous. The mysteries, not just of death but of life and our relations to each other, are explored through this constant probing and revising of metaphors. Such an intellectual exercise never lets the reader rest. Critic Stanley Fish terms this kind of writing a "self-consuming artifact" that forces us to confront issues by denying us the deceptive comfort of thinking too easily that we understand.

Donne remains a striking instance of an artist of fantastic self-dramatization who created work that is charged with intellectual energy, that knows what is happening, and that is always aware of the whole earthly and spiritual world in which he lived. It is this very complexity of Donne's energetic poetry and prose that makes him important. Arthur Marotti, a major Donne critic, asserts, "It is no accident that such a self-conscious, performative writer, whose works so often call attention to their own modes of operation and . . . dynamics, should appeal . . . to literarily sophisticated readers prepared for the challenges and pleasures of difficult texts."

Other Works by John Donne

The Complete Poetry and Selected Prose of John Donne. Edited by Charles M. Coffin. New York: Modern Library, 2001.
John Donne: Devotions Upon Emergent Occasions together with Death's Duel. New York: Vintage Books, 1999.

Works about John Donne

Corthell, Ronald. *Ideology and Desire in Renaissance Poetry: The Subject of Donne.* Detroit: Wayne State University Press, 1997.
Fish, Stanley. *Self-Consuming Artifacts: The Experience of Seventeenth Century Literature.* Berkeley: University of California Press, 1972.
Marotti, Arthur F., ed. *Critical Essays on John Donne.* New York: G. K. Hall, 1994.
Marotti, Arthur F. *John Donne, Coterie Poet.* Madison: University of Wisconsin Press, 1986.
Warnke, Frank J. *John Donne.* Boston: Twayne, 1987.

Dorrell, Hadrian
See ROYDON, MATTHEW.

Douglas, Gavin (Gawin Douglas)
(ca. 1475–1522) *poet, translator*

Gavin Douglas was a Scottish poet who translated Virgil's epic, the *Aeneid.* Where he was born is not known, but he was the third son of Archibald Douglas, the fifth Earl of Angus, and became connected with the Scottish royal family when his nephew, the young Archibald, sixth Earl of Angus, married Queen Margaret of Scotland. Douglas was educated at St. Andrews in Scotland and at the University of Paris. In 1513, after the Battle of Flodden, in which English forces defeated Scottish invaders led by the Scottish king James IV, he became involved in Scottish politics. He died of the plague in London.

Douglas established himself as a poet with his *Palice of Honour* (1501), in which he imitates the famous medieval poet Geoffrey Chaucer's *Hous of Fame.* His version of the Roman poet Virgil's *Aeneid* is an accurate albeit loose translation. This work, in heroic couplets, has the distinction of being the first translation into English of any classical work. Douglas opens each book of the *Aeneid* with an original prologue consisting of a variety of his own poems. For example, he opens the first book with this praise of the great poet:

> Laude, honor, prasingis, thankis infynite
> To the, and thi dulce ornate fresch endite,
> Mast reverend Virgill, of Latyne poetis
>   prince,

Gemme of ingine and fluide of
   eloquence . . .
(Honor, praise, and infinite thanks to thee
and thy sweet ornate fresh tale,
Most reverend Virgil, Prince of Latin poets,
gem of genius and flood of eloquence . . .)

Douglas's *King Hart* (date of publication unknown) is an allegory about the stages of life, touching on themes of life, death, and aging. A modern reader needs a glossary to understand Douglas's Middle Scots, the dialect in which he wrote.

Douglas's work is considered to be characteristic of the transition period between the Middle Ages and the RENAISSANCE. Literary historians Emile Legouis and Louis Cazamian note that Douglas "was not in the full stream of the Renascence. He stood on its brink marking the transition from one age to another."

Dowland, John (1563–1626) *composer, poet*

Little is known of John Dowland's early life, but in the preface to his *A Pilgrim's Solace* (1612) he notes that he had studied music from childhood. In 1588 he received a degree in music from Oxford University. Dowland seems to have been recognized as an important talent by then, and there is a record of his song "Thy Golden Locks Time Hath to Silver Turned" being sung to Queen ELIZABETH I in 1590. However, no court position opened up for him, and he went to the European continent, where he traveled widely and where he seems to have been more appreciated than in England.

Although Dowland's *First Book of Songs,* published in London in 1597, was a great success (and was followed by the *Second Book* in 1600 and the *Third Book* in 1603), there was still no job for him in England. In 1598 he entered the service of King Christian IV of Denmark, who paid him a high salary as royal lutenist and permitted him to spend periods of time in his native country. In 1603 Dowland went again to try his luck at the court of England's new king, JAMES I, to whose wife Dowland dedicated his new collection of consort pieces.

Dowland left the Danish court in 1606. He was one of the most famous musicians and keyboard experts in Europe by this time and was able to find enough PATRONAGE in England to support himself, but as he makes clear in the preface to *A Pilgrim's Solace,* a collection of part-songs that was the last of his work published in his lifetime, he felt unappreciated in his own country: He complains that in spite of his "Kingly entertainment in a forraine climate" he "could not attaine to any (though never so meane) place at home." His friend Henry PEACHAM wrote in a poem published in 1612,

How few regard thee, whom thou didst
   delight,
And farre and neere, came once to heere
   thee sing;
Ingratefull times.

Finally, in May 1612 Dowland received the English court appointment he had sought for so long. He apparently achieved recognition in his last years and remained an active and sought-after musician until his death, when his son Robert succeeded him in his court position.

Dowland is considered by many to be the greatest of all English songwriters. Many of his songs are set to texts by well-known poets of the day, but most are by unknown writers, possibly by Dowland himself. His most famous tune, "Lachrimae," (ca. 1595) which was originally written as a piece for solo lute, became a song, "Flow My Teares," with words that were probably written by Dowland. They capture the essence of the melancholy that had such a grip on the Elizabethan and Jacobean imagination:

Flow my tears fall from your springs,
Exiled for ever: Let me mourn
Where night's black bird her sad infamy
   sings,
There let me live forlorn.

A Work about John Dowland

Poulton, Diana. *John Dowland.* Berkeley: University of California Press, 1982.

Dowriche, Anne (ca. 1550–1613) *poet*

Few details regarding the life of Anne Dowriche, author of *The French History* (1589), are known, a problem compounded by the fact that she has been repeatedly confused with a niece who bore the same name. Nevertheless, it is clear that she was the daughter of Sir Richard and Elizabeth Tregian Edgecombe, prominent inhabitants of the English West Country, though her date of birth is indefinite. In 1580 she married Hugh Dowriche, a rector with whom she had four children. Her husband, a graduate of Oxford University, was also literary, composing *The Gaoler's Conversion* in 1596, which includes some introductory verses written by his wife.

Dowriche was a devout Protestant, and her writing reflects her religious beliefs in lines such as "No tempting tryall from the Lord, / No griefe or dire annoye, / Can sever once the faithfull hart, / From Christ, his onely joye." Religion also plays an integral role in Dowriche's primary work, *The French History*. This is a lengthy poem that relates events in France leading up to the murder of tens of thousands of Protestants on St. Bartholomew's Eve in 1572 (known as the SAINT BARTHOLOMEW'S DAY MASSACRE) *The French History* written during a period when the situation of English Protestants, who had been persecuted by Catholics for many years, was finally improving. The work is often credited as the inspiration of Christopher MARLOWE's *The Jew of Malta*.

Dowriche is exceptional in that, as Marion Wynne-Davies points out in *Women Poets of the Renaissance,* she is "one of the first English women writers to adopt a political topic and tone." Indeed, she does not disguise her political leanings, making comments like, "O poor unhappy place, O France how art thou led" and "The mother Queen as chief does promise to begin, / By treason joined with flattery to trap them in her gin." These last lines express Dowriche's dissatisfaction with the fate of France under the rule of Catherine de Medici, a resolute Catholic.

For *The French History,* Dowriche relied heavily on the account of historical events in Thomas Tymme's *The Three Partes of Commentaries, Containing the whole and perfect discourse of the Civill warres of Fraunce* (1574), which was a translation of an earlier work of Jean de Serres. Yet she manages to make the work distinctly her own by utilizing original verse, lengthening and adding numerous fictive speeches, and creating an innovative frame story that many see as a reflection of her source because it involves two narrators, one English and the other French.

Drake, Judith (fl. 1690) *nonfiction writer*

Little is known about Judith Drake's life. She was probably the daughter of Robert Drake, an attorney. Like Mary ASTELL, Drake was concerned with the place of women in intellectual and political life.

In "An Essay in Defense of the Female Sex," Drake declines to "enter into any dispute, whether Men, or Women be generally more ingenious, or learned; that Point must be given up to the advantages Men have over us by their Education, Freedom of Converse, and variety of Business and Company." Instead, she says, "The Question I shall at present handle is, whether the time an ingenious Gentleman spends in the Company of Women, may justly be said to be misemploy'd or not?" Drake concludes that keeping company with women could indeed benefit men and along the way makes a variety of astute observations about the balance of power and ability between men and women. For example, she remarks: "As the world grew more Populous, and Men's Necessities whetted their Inventions, so it increas'd their Jealousy, and sharpen'd their Tyranny over us, till by degrees, it came to that height of Severity, I may say Cruelty, it is now at . . . where the Women, like our Negroes in our Western Plantations, are born slaves, and live Prisoners all their Lives."

Drayton, Michael (1563–1631) *poet, playwright*

Michael Drayton was born in the village of Hartshill, England. At the age of 10 he decided he wanted to become a poet, and he spent the rest of his life writing, publishing, and revising his poems. In publishing his verse, Drayton was unusual because most Elizabethan poets were either aristocrats who wrote verse when they were not occupied with matters of state or courtiers who wrote to gain advancement through PATRONAGE or sponsorship from the monarch or another noble person. In addition, they generally circulated their poetry in manuscript and were published rarely.

Along with Edmund SPENSER and Ben JONSON, Drayton was among the few poets who regarded poetry as a profession. In the introduction to *Poly-Olbion* (1612, 1622), he went so far as to look down on those whose "verses are deduced to chambers . . . kept in cabinets, and must only pass by transcription."

Drayton experimented with all the principal poetic forms popular in his day. He wrote a collection of sonnets, *Idea* (1594–1619); pastoral poems, or poems of idealized country life; poems based on mythology; and verse letters. Between 1597 and 1602 he even dabbled in the drama. He is believed to have worked on 20 or 21 plays, only one of which, *Sir John Oldcastle* (1600), has survived.

Critical Analysis

Drayton's early work has been criticized for its overly complex and abstract language. The 20th-century poet T. S. Eliot, for instance, complains that Drayton succeeds only when he "drops his costume for a moment and talks in terms of actuality." Eliot's criticism concerns Drayton's dressing his verse in traditional images. Eliot regarded this method of composition as an unnatural, or inauthentic, method of expression. The woman addressed in *Idea,* for example, has an "arched, ivory, polished brow," a "cheek, now flush with roses," and "pearly teeth." There is little that distinguishes her from the women addressed in a number of other sonnet sequences.

But Drayton is following standard Elizabethan poetic practice. The scholar Rosemond Tuve notes that Drayton's images illustrate "the normal methods used to satisfy the primary requirement of for-mal design" that Elizabethans expected to find in poetry. Poetic imagery, Tuve goes on to argue, imitates "not the visible world but the intelligible" world—the world of thought. Elizabethan imagery was not meant to create naturalistic pictures of the world but to give expression to ideas. Thus, it is often traditional for this reason.

Drayton wrote not just for self-satisfaction. He also, as the Drayton scholar Joseph A. Berthelot observes, "sought to bring further glory to England through his poetic muse." To achieve this objective, he composed a number of nationalistic poems, including *England's Heroic Epistles* (1597, 1598, 1599), a series of fictional verse letters from famous English historical figures (such as Mary Tudor) to their lovers. In one such letter, the imprisoned Lady Jane Grey writes to her lover Lord Gilford Dudley:

> Mine owne deare Lord, sith [since] thou art
>   lock'd from me,
> In this disguise my love must steale to thee,
> Since to renue all Loves, all Kindnesse past,
> This Refuge scarcely left, yet this the last.

In *Poly-Olbion,* a topographical (or geographical) poem, Drayton mingles haunting descriptions of the English and Welsh countryside with British legendary and historical tales. In *The Battle of Agincourt* (1627) he tells the tale of Henry V's early 15th-century victory over the French.

In each of these works Drayton contributed to the sense of nationalism that had been growing in England since Henry VIII's break with the Catholic Church in the 1530s. Henry's establishment of the CHURCH OF ENGLAND as independent of the pope helped to promote the independence of the English people. Elizabethan writers, of which Drayton is among the longest-lasting, responded by writing about glorious English figures, both legendary and historical, and glorious moments in England's past. Such works helped to forge a sense of the individual character of the English nation.

Poly-Olbion is perhaps the most ambitious example of such a work. It is a long poem divided into 30 songs (the first 18 of which were published in 1612, the last 12 in 1622). Thus it does not merely celebrate England and its past; it also draws attention to the importance of such celebrations, as in the 10th song:

> But, in things past so long (for all the
>   world) we are
> Like to a man embarqu't and travelling the
>   deep:
> . . . So, of the ages past;
> Those things that in their age much to be
>   wondered were,
> Still as wing-footed time them farther off
>   doth bear,
> Do lessen every hour.

As the scholar Richard Hardin observes, "The sea, the present," as it is represented in these lines, "is an eternally shifting place for man; the rocks of the past should provide him with both a reference point for navigating, and a model for stability." The traveler, however, loses sight of the rocks, the monuments of history. Historical narratives must take the place of the monuments that will become covered by the mists of time and prevent the past from becoming swallowed in the chaos of the present.

Drayton would not be making statements about history's value if he felt his contemporaries were treating the historical monuments with the respect they deserved. The other major theme of *Poly-Olbion* is the relationship between modern English society and the past. He suggests that although some historical records may not be completely accurate, this is no reason to discount all history. "I cannot choose," Drayton writes in the poem, "but bitterly exclaim / Against those fools that all Antiquity defame." To combat such fools, the scholar George Parfitt argues, Drayton fashioned a "moving ideal" for his readers: "its truthfulness lies in its ability . . . to make that ideal feel both desirable and attainable."

Although Drayton's works are very infrequently studied and republished today, he was one of the major poets of his day. His versatility and ambition make him one of the most interesting and underappreciated Elizabethan writers.

A Work about Michael Drayton

Hardin, Richard. *Michael Drayton and the Passing of Elizabethan England.* Lawrence: University of Kansas Press, 1973.

Drummond of Hawthornden, William
(1585–1649) *poet*

William Drummond was born at Hawthornden, Scotland, to Sir John Drummond and Susannah Fowler Drummond, the sister of a Scottish poet. After earning an M.A. in 1605 at Edinburgh University, Drummond went to France to study law. He abandoned these studies upon his father's death in 1610, when he inherited Hawthornden. He remained on this estate for the rest of his life, reading widely and writing poetry.

Drummond's finest poetic achievements are *Teares on the Death of Meliades* (1613), written upon the death of Prince Henry, the oldest son of JAMES I OF ENGLAND; *Poems* (1616); and *Flowers of Sion* (1623), a collection of religious poems. Drummond is among the first Scottish poets to have written in English rather than Middle Scots, the common idiom of Scotland in his day. His poems won him the admiration of poets such as Michael DRAYTON and Ben JONSON. Jonson, Drummond reports, said of his verses, that they were "all good, especially [his] Epitaph of the Prince, save they smelled too much of the schools and were not after the fancy of the time."

Jonson's criticism, slight when compared with his criticism of other prominent poets, calls attention to Drummond's strengths. His poetry, influenced by Italian poets, carries on the tradition of 16th-century poets such as Philip SIDNEY. Indeed, Drummond's sonnet sequence, published in the 1616 *Poems,* closely resembles Sidney's *Astrophel and Stella* (1582), and "some of his sonnets," Drummond scholar William C. Ward observes, "would not seem at all out of place among those sonnets to Stella."

In Sonnet XVIII, for example, Drummond, like Sidney, writes about the eyes of his mistress, whose name, Auristella, contains "Stella." Some of the lines are also very similar to those Sidney wrote. Drummond's "Mars and Apollo first did her [Nature] advise / In color black to wrap those comets" is similar to Sidney's "In color black why wrapped she [Nature] beams so bright?"

However much Drummond imitated his predecessors, especially Sidney, his verse has struck readers as valuable. The critic French Roew Fogel notes "the melody and felicity [grace] of the lines themselves. It is this trait that has led critics to speak so fully of his 'sweetness'."

Other Work by William Drummond of Hawthornden
Poems. New York: AMS Press, 1988.

Dryden, John (1631–1700) *poet, dramatist, translator*

John Dryden was born at Aldwinkle, near Oundle, Northamptonshire, England, to Erasmus Dryden and Mary Pickering, both members of established rural gentry families. Dryden's family had strong Puritan and antiroyalist sympathies, and Dryden absorbed this influence early in life. He received his initial education at Westminster School, where he was a classmate of the philosopher John LOCKE and where he received a thorough grounding in classical literature under the famous headmaster Richard Busby. In 1650 he entered Cambridge, from which he earned a bachelor's degree in 1654.

While still at Westminster Dryden published his first poem, "Upon the Death of Lord Hastings" (1649), an elegy (poem of mourning) written in the metaphysical style of poetry then popular. Metaphysical poetry, as practiced by writers such as John DONNE and Abraham COWLEY, tended to use elaborate images and far-fetched comparisons, as Dryden does when describing the marks of smallpox on Hasting's body:

> Like rose-buds, stuck I' th' lily skin about.
> Each little pimple had a tear in it,
> To wail the fault its rising did commit.

Dryden soon abandoned this style and helped to create and popularize a new mode of poetry that would profoundly influence English verse for the next century. In works such as "Heroic Stanzas" (1659), written to commemorate the funeral of the Puritan leader Oliver Cromwell, and "Astraea Redux" (1660), which celebrated the RESTORATION of Charles II to the throne, Dryden drops the complexity of Donne and Cowley. Instead, he strives for a smoother, plainer, and more harmoniously regular style, which is often called neoclassic, or Augustan, because of its emphasis on rules, order, and decorum and because of its frequent references and borrowings from writers of ancient Greece and Rome. Dryden's new poetic mode also focuses on the public world of society, politics, and religion, as opposed to the inward, mystical, and often intensely personal world of the metaphysical poets.

Dryden used his new poetic mode in *Annus Mirabilis* (1667), a poem he wrote in praise of the reign of Charles II during the difficult times following the plague of 1665, the Great Fire of 1666, and the defeats suffered by the English during the Second Dutch War. In one stanza he predicts Britain's rise to imperial greatness:

> Now, like a maiden queen, she will behold,
> From her high turrets, hourly suitors come:
> The East with incense, and the West with
>   gold,
> Will stand, like suppliants, to receive her
>   doom [command].

Dryden, now a Royalist, continued to prove himself a valuable supporter of Charles II. As a reward for his services, in 1668 he became poet laureate, England's highest honor for a poet, and a year later the Historiographer Royal, or official historian of the court. Dryden now began writing plays, which became his primary means of financial support. He was a prolific playwright, writing and staging some 28 plays, both comedies and tragedies in verse.

In the 1670s Dryden began writing the type of poetry for which he is best known today: political and literary satires, works that ridicule human folly. In 1681 he published *Absalom and Achitophel,* one of his greatest satires.

Dryden wrote two other major satires: *The Medal* (1682) and *Mac Flecknoe* (1684), which attacks his rival and sometimes collaborator, the dramatist Thomas SHADWELL. Dryden also wrote two important religious poems, *Religio Laici* (1682) and *The Hind and the Panther* (1687). *Religio Laici* explores Dryden's religious faith, while *The Hind and the Panther* celebrates and defends his conversion to Catholicism. These poems demonstrate Dryden's great facility for reasoning and arguing in verse.

In 1685 Charles's brother James ascended the throne. Because of his Catholicism, he was overthrown three years later and succeeded by the Protestant William of Orange and his wife, Mary, James's daughter.

Dryden, as both a Catholic and a supporter of James, lost all his official positions and his privileged relationship with the government. During this difficult, even perilous, time he began doing translations. After rendering the ancient Roman chronicler Plutarch into prose, in 1693 he produced poetic translations of the classical Roman poets Juvenal and Persius, and in 1697 the classical author Virgil. In 1700 Dryden published *The Fables.* which offered translations of authors such as Homer, Ovid, BOCCACCIO, and Chaucer.

Dryden's late translations, which in terms of sheer length make up most of his entire poetic output, made accessible to an increasingly literate public the great works of antiquity. His translation of Virgil was hailed as an immense and invaluable contribution to English letters. Alexander Pope, himself the translator of Homer's work, called it "the most noble and spirited translation that I know of in any language."

However, as recent scholars have come to realize, Dryden's decision to shift from original com-

position to translation was not politically neutral. By writing in the voice of other authors, Dryden offered disguised critiques of contemporary events, such as the removal of James from the throne, that he otherwise could not publish. The critic Paul Hammond notes that translation allowed other opportunities: "It was translation, too, which gave Dryden further scope to explore psychology: to represent the human mind in disorder as it is taken over by forbidden desire in Ovid and Boccaccio, or by fear of death in Lucretius."

In addition to his career as poet, playwright, and translator, Dryden was a major literary critic. Samuel Johnson remarks: "Dryden may be properly considered as the father of English criticism, as the writer who first taught us to determine upon principles the merit of composition." Dryden's three greatest contributions to literary criticism are *An Essay of Dramatic Poesy* (1668), "Preface" to *The Fables* (1700), and "Dedication to the *Aeneis*" (1700). In the *Essay* four fictitious characters Lisideius, Crites, Eugenius, and Neander (who speaks for Dryden), discuss the principles of drama, comparing the ancients and moderns and the English and French theaters. Neander voices early praise for SHAKESPEARE, which would become a critical commonplace later in the 18th century: "He was the man who of all modern, and perhaps ancient poets, had the largest and most comprehensive soul." Dryden's prose in these works, like his poetry, is clear, lucid, and plain.

Critical Analysis

Dryden's plays are rarely staged today. Even in his own time he was ridiculed for the exaggerated language of his heroic dramas. However, a few of Dryden's plays are powerful dramas. One of his best plays is *All for Love,* a tightly constructed and unified rewriting of William Shakespeare's *Antony and Cleopatra,* a tragedy about the famed ancient lovers. Some critics even prefer the Dryden version to Shakespeare's.

Even Dryden's dramas that are not theatrically successful contain some excellent verses, such as the following address from *The Indian Queen* (1664), semiopera with music by Henry Purcell:

> Must I feell tortures in a humane brest,
> While Beasts and Monsters can enjoy their
>   Rest?
> What quiet they possess in sleeps calm bliss!
> The Lions cease to roar, the Snakes to hiss,
> While I am kept awake—
> Only to entertain my Miseries.

Sometimes considered Dryden's greatest poem, *Absalom and Achitophel* is a complex work, which the critic Morris Freedman calls a "miniature epic." It was prompted by the political event known as the Exclusion Crisis (1678–84). In 17th-century England Roman Catholics were considered political subversives who threatened the stability of state and church. When it became known that the heir to the throne, Charles's brother James, was a Catholic, tensions began to build and culminated in the so-called Popish Plot. In 1678 the Protestant fanatic Titus Oates claimed that Catholics planned to assassinate Charles II and massacre Protestants. While Oates's claims were dubious, they stirred widespread hysteria and prompted a movement to exclude James from the British throne, and indeed the Earl of Shaftesbury nearly succeeded in this aim.

Dryden's poem was written to support Charles and James. Dryden recasts the events of the crisis by retelling the biblical story of Achitophel's rebellion against King David, thus summoning the biblical authority of David's heroic kingship to buttress the Stuart regime. Additionally, Dryden paints harshly satirical portraits of the king's enemies, such as Shaftesbury and Oates, thus deflating their dignity and popularity.

Dryden also used the poem to attack the Duke of Buckingham for the duke's earlier attack upon him in *The Rehearsal*. Buckingham, portrayed as Zimri in the poem, is

> Stiff in opinions, always in the wrong;
> Was everything by starts, and nothing long;

> But, in the course of one revolving moon,
> Was chymist, fiddler, statesman, and
>   buffoon:
> Then all for women, painting, rhyming,
>   drinking,
> Besides ten thousand freaks that dies in
>   thinking.

Dryden's satirical poem *Mac Flecknoe* has proven to be one of his most entertaining and enduring works. Dryden's principal motivation in writing this satire was to humiliate Thomas Shadwell, a literary rival. Although Dryden had praised Shadwell in his *Essay of Dramatic Poesy*, the latter had ridiculed Dryden as the impotent Dry Bob in his play *The Humorists* (1671) and offered veiled abuse in the preface to the drama *The Virtuoso* (1676). Dryden did not wait long before retaliating in *Mac Flecknoe*.

Mac Flecknoe is the first example in English of a mock heroic poem. In it Dryden uses a high, serious style and models the work on the epics [long heroic poems] of Virgil and MILTON. However, the poet employs these elements for satiric rather than epic purposes.

Dryden pairs Shadwell with the notoriously poor Irish poet Richard Flecknoe and casts them as epic "heroes." Shadwell is the "Mac Flecknoe" of the title, or son of Flecknoe (Mac is an Irish prefix meaning "son of"). As the poem opens Flecknoe is dying and decides on Shadwell as his worthy successor in dullness and ignorance:

> Sh—— alone, of all my sons, is he
> Who stands confirm'd in full stupidity.
> The rest to some faint meaning make
>   pretense,
> But Sh—— never deviates into sense.

While analysis of the poem's rhythm suits "Sh——" to "Shadwell," Dryden also implies that excrement, or feces, symbolizes his rival.

After anointing Shadwell as his successor, Flecknoe offers a speech explaining why Shadwell is the best candidate to become the king of dunces. He belittles Shadwell's appearance ("nor let thy mountain-belly make pretence"), his intelligence ("thoughtless as monarch oaks that shade the plain"), and his talent ("thy inoffensive satires never bite"). At the end of the poem Flecknoe is awkwardly swept away—falling through his throne, a toilet—as Shadwell steps forward to take his place on the throne as king of the dunces.

Because of *Mac Flecknoe,* Shadwell's name has become synonymous with bad writing. However, while he is not a great writer, he is by no means as poor a one as Dryden pictures him.

More significantly for literary history, *Mac Flecknoe* provided a model and inspiration two generations later for one of Alexander Pope's greatest poems, *The Dunciad.* Like Dryden, Pope also selects a mediocre writer and makes him king of the dunces. Even without this literary legacy, *Mac Flecknoe* stands on its own as a major work that remains accessible to modern readers.

Dryden is third only to Shakespeare and Milton as the most influential poet during the 17th century, and his importance has led scholars to label the period in which he flourished the Age of Dryden. He established a new mode of writing, satirical, public oriented, and neoclassical, that would decisively shape and define the literature of the 18th century. The greatest poet of the 18th century, Alexander Pope, acknowledged Dryden as his master and sought to refine and polish the tradition that Dryden began. Scholar William Frost has attempted to summarize Dryden's many achievements: "Dryden's literary excellence . . . lies in his wit and his vigor; in the psychological penetration of his satire; in the rapidity of his narrative, and the clarity of his argumentative verses; in the fluency, melody, and variety of all his poems; and in the translucent ease of his essays."

Other Work by John Dryden

Selected Poems. Edited by Steven N. Zwicker and David Bywaters. New York: Penguin, 2002.

Works about John Dryden

Bywaters, David. *Dryden in Revolutionary England.* Berkeley: University of California Press, 1991.

Frost, William. *John Dryden: Dramatist, Satirist, Translator.* New York: AMS Press, 1988.

Hammond, Paul and David Hopkins, eds. *John Dryden: Tercentary Essays.* Oxford, U.K.: Clarendon Press, 2000.

Winn, James Anderson, ed. *Critical Essays on John Dryden.* New York: G. K. Hall, 1997.

Dugdale, Sir William (1605–1686)
nonfiction writer

William Dugdale was born at Shustoke, Warwickshire, England. He was educated in Coventry and at Oxford University, receiving his M.A. in 1642. He was associated with the Herald's College from 1638 and became Garter King-of-Arms, or chief of the official heralds, in 1677. These duties were interrupted during Oliver Cromwell's regime (1653–58) but resumed in 1660, after the RESTORATION.

Dugdale's main work, *Monasticum Anglicanum* (1655), was written with Roger Dodsworth, who died in 1654 before publication of the first volume was complete. The second volume was published in 1661, the third in 1673. The work describes the legal charters and grants of monasteries back to Anglo-Saxon times. It was popular with Roman Catholics, who were interested in their pre-Reformation property rights.

Dugdale wrote impressively on a variety of subjects. His second book, *Antiquities of Warwickshire* (1656), acknowledges the work of Sir Symon Archer, a fellow antiquary. *The History of St. Paul's Cathedral* (1658) describes the original building before it was destroyed in the Fire of London (1666). *The History of Imbanking and Drayning of divers Fenns and Marshes, both in foreign parts and in this Kingdom . . .* (1662) is still of historical agricultural interest.

Legal historians have also benefitted from Dugdale's work, especially *Origines Judicales: A History of English Legal Matters* (1666) and *The Baronage of England* (1675–76), as well as his *Catalogue of Lord Chancellors and Keepers of the Great Seal of England* (1666). Dugdale's extensive research has thus provided useful historical records in the areas of law, property, and genealogy.

Dunbar, William (ca. 1460–ca. 1520) *poet*

William Dunbar has sometimes been called the "Chaucer of Scotland." The exact date and location of his birth are unknown, although it is believed that he was educated at St. Andrews University in Scotland. He went on to become a Franciscan novice and traveled and preached throughout England and possibly in France. By the turn of the century, he was receiving a pension, or salary, as a member of the court of King James IV.

Along with Robert HENRYSON, Gavin DOUGLAS, and Sir David LYNDSAY Dunbar belonged to a group of poets often called "Scottish Chaucerians," who emulated and reacted to the style of Geoffrey Chaucer during a time that was considered the golden age of Scottish poetry. The Scottish Chaucerians, who were also called the Makaris, or makers, were influenced by and extended the themes of Chaucer's poems about love and dreams.

One of Dunbar's best-known works is the poem *The Thrissil and the Rois* (*The Thistle and the Rose*, 1503) celebrating the union of two parts of England through the marriage of the Scottish king James IV to Margaret Tudor of England, daughter of Henry VII. Because of his close ties with the Scottish court, Dunbar may even have helped to arrange this marriage. The poem, a 27-stanza allegory, is reminiscent of Chaucer in its descriptive language and its treatment of courtly matters. For example, it includes this stanza of praise for the queen in which her crown is imagined as a glorious light illuminating the landscape, and she is dubbed the queen of flowers:

> *A coistly croun with clarefeid stonis brycht*
> *This cumly quene did on hir head inclois,*
> *Quhill all the land illumynit of the licht:*
> *Quihairfor me thocht all flouris did rejos,*
> *Crying attonis, Haill be thow, richest Ros,*
> *Haill hairbis empryce, haill freschest quene*
>   *of flouris;*
> *To thee be glory and honour at all houris.*
>
> (*A costly crown with clarified stones bright*
> *This lovely queen did on her head enclose,*

> *From which all the land is illuminated by*
>   *the light:*
> *Wherefore I thought, all flowers did rejoice,*
> *Crying, Hail be you, richest Rose,*
> *Hail empress, hail freshest queen of flowers;*
> *To thee be glory and honor at all hours.*)

Dunbar uses vivid language to describe the landscape in another Chaucerian allegory, *The Goldyn Targe (Shield)*:

> *The crystal air, the sapphire firmament,*
> *The ruby skies of the orient*
> *Cast berial [beryl, or pale green] beams on*
>   *emerald boughes green . . .*
> *With purple, azure, gold and gules [red]*
>   *gent [graceful].*

The Goldyn Targe is nearly 300 lines long and deals with the triumph of love over the golden shield of reason. The poet describes a dream in which Reason unsuccessfully attempts to protect a sleeping poet from the arrows of King Cupid.

Dunbar also wrote gloomy and satirical poems. *The Lament for the Makaris* deals with the theme of death. Each stanza of the poems ends with the Latin line "Timor mortis conturbat me," or "the fear of death throws me into confusion." His satire, *Flyting [or dispute in verse] of Dunbar and Kennedie*, humorously criticizes his rival poet, Walter Kennedy. *Tretis of the Tua Mariit Wemen and the Wedo* (*Treatise of the Two Married Women and the Widow*) satirizes women with shocking descriptions and provides a response to Chaucer's "Wife of Bath."

English historians Emile Legouis and Louis Caziman have noted that Dunbar "has to a rare degree—one never reached before him and seldom since—virtuosity of style and versification. No one hitherto had put so much color in pictures; no one, above all, had given such a swing to lines and stanza. He dazzles the eyes and ravishes the ears."

Other Work by William Dunbar

The Poems of William Dunbar. Edited by Patricia Bawcutt. Glasgow: Association of Scottish Literary Studies, 1999.

Dunton, John (1659–1733) *nonfiction writer*

John Dunton was born to the rector of the parish of Graffham, Huntingdonshire, England, John Dunton, and his wife, Lydia Carter, who died soon after her son's birth. His father subsequently moved to Ireland, while Dunton was sent to school at Dunsgrove. On his father's return Dunton left school to be educated at home. His father had intended Dunton for the clergy, but because of his son's poor academic progress he was apprenticed to a London bookseller at 14. Dunton did well at his apprenticeship and eventually set up his own shop.

Dunton is best remembered for one of his early publishing ventures, the *Athenian Gazette,* later the *Athenian Mercury* (1689–96). This periodical answered questions of all kinds sent in by readers "to satisfie all *Ingenious and Curious Enquirers* into *Speculations,* Divine, Moral, and Natural." His publication was a precursor to modern advice columns, answering questions from readers on everything from matters of etiquette to factual queries about science and geography. According to the critic J. Paul Hunter, *The Athenian Mercury* is notable for "the extraordinary attention to novelty and innovation that Dunton and many others articulated around the turn of the century."

Dunton continued to publish a variety of work throughout his life. His autobiography, *Life and Errors of John Dunton, Late Citizen of London, Written in Solitude* (1705) is a remarkable source of information on the book trade during this time. Other works include *Dunton's Whipping-Post, or a Satire upon Everybody* (1706), and *Athenianism, or the New Projects of John Dunton* (1710), a collection of pamphlets that included satirical verses. In 1717 he produced a weekly paper, *The Hanover Spy,* with Daniel Defoe. Dunton is a minor literary figure of the period but one who is of particular interest to historians of publishing.

Other Work by John Dunton

The Dublin Scuffle. Edited by Andrew Carpenter. Dublin: Four Courts Press, 2000.

D'Urfey, Thomas (Thomas Durfey) (1653–1723) *dramatist, poet*

Thomas Durfey was born in Exeter, England, to John Durfey and his wife, Frances. In 1683 D'Urfey added the apostrophe to his name to suggest an association with the aristocracy. He planned to study law, but as D'Urfey said of himself, "My good or ill stars ordained me to a knight-errant in the fairy field of poetry."

D'Urfey was one of the most popular songwriters of his age. He entertained five monarchs and wrote more than 32 plays and 500 songs in his career. His songs were of three styles: political songs, court songs, and songs about country folk. D'Urfey developed a reputation for writing crude and vulgar lyrics and for being careless in his composition. As D'Urfey himself said, however: "irregularities disappear when . . . [my] songs are sung." Despite these criticisms, D'Urfey's songs were extremely popular. Alexander Pope in a letter wrote: "Dares any Man speak against him who has given so many Men to eat? So may it be said of Mr. Durfey to his Detractors: What? Dares any one despise him, who has made so many Men drink? Alas, Sir! This is a Glory which neither you nor I must ever pretend to."

As a playwright and poet D'Urfey's greatest contribution to English literature remains his comedic plays for the stage, which were early versions of the ballad operas that would soon become popular. D'Urfey's *Wit and Mirth; or, Pills to Purge Melancholy,* in fact, was a major source for John Gay's *Beggar's Opera. Wit and Mirth* comprises songs with suggestive lyrics set to popular tunes of the day. For example, "The Comical Dreamer" begins with this bawdy stanza, which is actually quite mild in comparison with most of D'Urfey's lusty lyrics:

> *Last Night a Dream came into my Head,*
> *Thou wert a fine white Loaf of Bread;*
> *Then if May Butter I cou'd be,*
> *How I wou'd spread,*
> *Oh! how I wou'd spread my self on thee.*

D'Urfey's songs were set to music by more than 40 composers, including Henry Purcell.

Dyer, Sir Edward (1543–1607) *poet*

Edward Dyer was born in Somersetshire, England, to Sir Thomas Dyer and was educated at Oxford University. In the 1570s he became a member of ELIZABETH I's court and soon acquired the PATRONAGE of the Earl of Leicester. Dyer was a friend to Sir Philip SIDNEY. Despite his life at court, he was more interested in cultivating the life of the mind than in pursuing a life of action. Nonetheless, he was obliged to serve as an ambassador to Denmark in 1589 and to become chancellor (an honorary title) of the Order of the Garter, an order of knights, in 1596, the year he was knighted.

Although few of his poems have survived, Dyer's poetry was admired by his contemporaries. The Elizabethan literary critic George PUTTENHAM cites a number of Dyer's poems in his *Art of English Poesy* (1589).

Dyer's most famous poem is "My Mind to Me a Kingdom Is," a song that appeared in an anthology called *Psalms, Sonnets, and Songs of Sadness and Piety* (1588) and was also issued as a broadside, an inexpensive pamphlet containing one poem. The poem, which some regard as a commentary on Dyer's life, praises the life of the mind above that of action:

> *I press to bear no haughty sway,*
> *I wish no more than may suffice,*
> *I do no more than well I may,*
> *Look, what I want my mind supplies.*
> *Lo! thus I triumph like a king,*
> *My mind content with anything.*

Dyer's reputation as a poet declined after the 16th century as his works became unavailable to readers. However, the biographer Ralph Sargent observes that, as "the earliest of the Elizabethan 'courtly makers,' [that is, poets] Dyer brought forth possibly the first fine lyrics of the RENAISSANCE in England."

A Work by Edward Dyer

May, Steven W., ed. *The Elizabethan Courtier Poets: The Poems and Their Contexts.* Columbia: University of Missouri Press, 1991.

Earle, John (ca. 1601–1665) *nonfiction writer, translator*

John Earle was born in York, England, and in 1616 began studying at Oxford University where he became a fellow. Earle rose to fame for tutoring Charles II as a prince; he was later appointed chaplain to the king. As a loyal supporter of Charles II, he was exiled from 1644 to 1660—during most of the English Civil Wars and during the entirety of Oliver Cromwell's rule. Earle was devoted to the Anglican Church, and in 1633 he returned to England to become the bishop of Salisbury.

Earle's most famous work, *Microcosmographie, or A Piece of the World Discovered in Essays and Characters,* was first published anonymously in 1628 and went on to gain such popularity that it went through several editions throughout his lifetime. In this book he humorously describes such characters as "the old college butler," "the child," "the good old man," "the young raw preacher," and many others. Like many of the 17th-century English character writers, including Thomas OVERBURY, Joseph HALL and John CLEVELAND, Earle was an admirer of the psychological works of the Greek philosopher Theophrastus (d. 287 B.C.). Many British thinkers of the Jacobean era revered the classics but also sought to improve on them by incorporating the moral values of the Anglican Church. Theophrastus's *Characters* was a se-

ries of sketches that examined the social conduct of man. It brought to light the consequences of excessive forms of certain social behavior. Drawing on this concept, the English character writers often examined the absurdity of human conduct for satirical purposes. Earle's *Microcosmographie,* however, not only pokes fun at human behavior but also observes the moral significance of the day-to-day activities of the common man.

With the description of his first character, "the child," one can see such religious and moral overtones. Earle describes the child as being "a man in a small letter, yet the best copy of Adam before he tasted of Eve, or the apple . . . The elder he grows, he is a stair lower from God; and like his first father much worse in his breeches."

Earle is also known for translating several works. Charles II commissioned him to translate Charles I's *Eikon Basilike,* or *Royal Image,* into Latin. The work was then published in 1649. Earle also translated Richard HOOKER's *Of the Laws of Ecclesiastical Polity,* but the translation was accidentally destroyed.

Eden, Richard (1521–1576) *translator*

Richard Eden was born in Herefordshire, England, and studied at Queens' College, Cambridge

University, which nurtured his lifelong expertise in European languages. He worked for several years in the English treasury and then traveled through Europe from 1562 to 1573, a time when he became familiar with the work of many continental writers and explorers. Fueled by patriotic fervor during the Age of Exploration in the 16th century, Eden wanted the English people to know about the accounts and journals written by Spanish, French, and Portuguese explorers, so he translated many of these works into English. Thanks to Eden's work, many of these authors became available for the first time to English-speaking readers.

Among his translations was a large part of Pietro d'Angluera's *De Nouo Orbe,* which Eden called *The Historie of the West Indies* (1612); and of Martín Cortés's *Arte of Navigation,* published in London in 1615. He also published an adaptation of Sebastian Munster's *Cartographie,* which Eden called *A Treatyse of the Newe India* (1553), and translated a collection of stories from New World explorers, published under the title *The Decades of the New World* (1555). In this work Eden urged the English to follow the Spanish in exploring the New World: "The kynges of Spayne of late dayes . . . may so much the more for theyr just desertes and good fortune be compared to those goddes made of men." Indeed, Eden's translations of Spanish travel writings helped to inspire the English to begin their own explorations.

Eden's last translation, posthumously published, was *The History of Trauayle [travel] in the East and West Indies* (1577).

A Work about Richard Eden

Hadfield, Andrew, ed. *Amazons, Savages, and Machiavels: Travel and Colonial Writing in English, 1550–1630: An Anthology.* New York: Oxford University Press, 2001.

Egerton, Sarah Fyge (1670–1723) *poet and satirist*

Sarah Fyge Egerton was one of six daughters born in London to Thomas Egerton, a physician, and Mary Beacham. Egerton's first publication, written at the age of 14, launched her controversial literary career. *The Female Advocate* (1686), a satirical poem, was a response to Robert Gould's poem *Love Given O'er: Or, a Satyr Against the Pride, Lust and Inconstancy of Women* (1682). Published anonymously, Egerton's work included a preface signed *S. F.* (for Sarah Fyge) in which she wrote, "I think when a Man is so extravagant as to Damn all Womankind for the Crimes of a few, he ought to be corrected." Thomas Egerton, embarrassed by his daughter's ideas and her success, banished her from London, sending her to relatives in the country. He also arranged for Egerton's marriage, against her desires, to Edward Field, a lawyer. These actions did not keep Egerton from publishing a second, expanded edition of *The Female Advocate* in 1687.

By 1700 Field had died, leaving Egerton childless and well-off. Egerton published *Poems on Several Occasions* in 1703. This collection of poems criticizes social institutions, such as marriage, that exploit women:

> *From the first dawn of life unto the grave,*
> *Poor womankind's in every state a slave . . .*
> *Then comes the last, the fatal slavery:*
> *The husband with insulting tyranny*
> *Can have ill manners justified by law,*
> *For men all join to keep the wife in awe.*

The poems also show Egerton's weakness for romantic love, which she tries to overcome but cannot.

Despite her love for another man, Egerton married Rev. Thomas Egerton, her second cousin, a man 20 years her senior. From the start the marriage was unhappy, and she eventually sued for divorce on the grounds of cruelty. He in turn accused her of desertion. The divorce was not granted, and Egerton returned to live with her husband until his death in 1720. She herself died in 1723. In the years between the publication of *Poems on Several Occasions* and her death, she published very little. Some scholars wonder why: Was she dejected over her marriage and imprisoned intellectually by her husband, or did she choose to stop writing?

Egerton wrote her own epitaph: "I could only in the grave find rest." But though Egerton saw herself as a victim of her times, the critic Constance Clark sees her as a "strong-willed and aggressive woman. . . . In a society where the education of women was suspect, and writing not approved of, Egerton flaunted her learning, and not only wrote, but dared to publish."

Other Works by Sarah Fyge Egerton

Poems on Several Occasions. (Orig. 1703) Introduction by Constance Clark. Delmar, N.Y.: Scholars' Facsimiles and Reprints, 1987.

Blain, Virginia, Patricia Clements, and Isobel Grundy, eds. *The Feminist Companion to Literature in English: Women Writers from the Middle Ages to the Present.* New Haven, Conn.: Yale University Press, 1990.

Uphaus, Robert W., and Gretchen M. Foster, eds. *The "Other" Eighteenth Century: English Women of Letters 1660–1800.* East Lansing, Mich.: Colleagues Press, 1991.

Eliot, John (1604–1690) *theologian, translator*

John Eliot was born in Widford, Hertfordshire, England, to Bennett Eliot, a landowner. He graduated from Jesus College, Cambridge University, in 1622, and first earned his living as a schoolteacher before subscribing to Puritan beliefs, influenced by his reading of the Puritan theologian Thomas Hooker. As a Puritan missionary, Eliot went to New England in 1631 and soon became involved in the lives of the indigenous Algonquian peoples around Roxbury, Massachusetts, where he had settled. He became known as the "Apostle to the Indians."

In order to better communicate with the people he was attempting to convert, Eliot learned the Algonquian language. His dictionary and grammar of the language were an important early contribution to the study of Native American languages and the science of linguistics. In 1654 Eliot published a catechism, or summary of religious doctrine, in Algonquian, and by 1658 he had completed a translation of the Old and New Testaments. Published from 1661 to 1663, this was the first Bible published in North America. Among his other published works is *The Christian Commonwealth* (1659).

Eliot believed that the white settlers in New England should assimilate the Native Americans into their own "praying towns," of which 14 were established. In his *Brief Narrative* (1670), a pamphlet about "the Propagation of the Gospel amongst the poor blind Indians in New-England," Eliot describes the progress of Christianity in the 14 towns, which included Natick, Ponkipog, and Hassunnimesut. *Indian Dialogues* (1671) is a dialogue meant to explain Christianity to the Indians. In this book Eliot's characters discuss Christianity and argue against the common objections of Native Americans: "The Book of God is no invention of Englishmen. It is the holy law of God himself, which was given unto man by God, before Englishmen had any knowledge of God."

Much of Eliot's work was curtailed by the outbreak of King Philip's War in 1675. He died in Roxbury 15 years later.

Works about John Eliot

Bowden, Henry W., and James P. Ronda, eds. *John Eliot's Indian Dialogues: A Study in Cultural Interaction.* Westport, Conn.: Greenwood Press, 1981.

Winslow, Ola Elizabeth. *John Eliot: Apostle to the Indians.* New York: Houghton Mifflin, 1968.

Elizabeth I (1533–1603) *orator, poet*

Although the birth of Elizabeth I, daughter of Henry VIII and his second wife, Anne BOLEYN, was a bitter disappointment to Henry, who had prayed for a son, she was treated kindly at court and given a fine education. Tutored by the brilliant scholar Roger ASCHAM, Elizabeth studied logic, rhetoric, and music, and became fluent in Greek, Latin, French, and Italian. Ascham commended her intellect: "Her mind has no womanly weakness, her perseverance is equal to that of a man, and her memory long keeps what it quickly picks up." Of her writing style he said that it "grows out of the subject, chaste in its appropriateness, beautiful in its clarity. She admires, above all, modest metaphors and comparisons of contraries well put together and contrasting felicitously with one another."

As queen of England from 1558 to 1603, Elizabeth not only mastered the art of governing and diplomacy but also the art of public speaking. In *Elizabeth Tudor* (1975) Lacey Smith writes, "Her public speeches, though posing as sudden, extemporaneous outbursts of pleasure or anger, were in fact carefully rehearsed, the results of endless deletion, insertion and stylistic amendment." George Rice in *The Public Speaking of Queen Elizabeth* (1951) observes: "She stressed love of country, loyalty, reverence for religion, obedience, the wisdom of the ancestors, respect for precedent, and freedom from foreign oppression."

Excerpts from several of Elizabeth's most famous speeches illustrate her command of situation and of rhetorical technique, such as the art of persuasion through direct appeals. In 1588, when she reviewed her soldiers who were preparing for a Spanish invasion of England, her aim was to inspire and encourage her troops by appealing to their loyalty and patriotism. What better way than to declare that she, the queen, was brave enough to die with them: "Wherefore I am come among you at this time but for my recreation and pleasure, being resolved in the midst and heat of the battle to live and die amongst you all, to lay down for my God and for my kingdom and for my people mine honor and my blood even in the dust." She then uses a metaphor that subtly compels the troops to recall two valiant English kings: Richard the Lionheart and Henry VIII. "I know I have the body but of a weak and feeble woman, but I have the heart and stomach of a king and of a king of England too. . . ." As further incentive, because she knew that officers sometimes pocketed soldiers' salaries, she promised "in the word of a prince" that her soldiers' salaries would be paid.

Elizabeth's ability to sway, surprise, and delight her audience by using appeals to emotion, reason,

and credibility reached its zenith in 1601 when she gave her last speech to members of Parliament. It was a speech so dazzling in its concession to audience expectations that it became known as her "Golden Speech" and was copied and cited for years as an example of royalty giving in to parliamentary demands—in this case, a demand that Elizabeth repeal grants of royal monopolies that had stifled business competition. She begins by earnestly declaring her love for her subjects and accepting their love: "I do assure you there is no prince that loves his subjects better, or whose love can countervail our love. . . . This I count the glory of my crown: That I have reigned with your loves." And to prove her love she promises to abolish royal monopolies and punish those grant holders who have profited unfairly. She then uses a strikingly sinister image to support her reason for not having addressed the problem sooner, namely that grant holders had lulled her with false assurances to mask reality, not unlike "physicians who, ministering a drug, make it more acceptable by giving it a good aromatical savor; or when they give pills, do gild them over."

She makes several persuasive ethical appeals (a rhetorical device to establish credibility and strength of character): "I was never so much enticed with the glorious name of a king or royal authority of a queen as delighted that God has made me His instrument to maintain His truth and glory, and to defend this kingdom from peril, dishonor, tyranny, and oppression." She closes her speech with a generous and dramatic gesture, saying, "before these gentlemen depart into their countries . . . bring them all to kiss my hand." Lord Harrington, a member of the audience that day, spoke for many when he was heard to say, "We loved her, for she said she did love us."

Although Elizabeth inspired many poets (Edmund SPENSER dedicated *The Faerie Queen* to her), only a dozen or so of her poems survive. They reveal her courage, self-confidence, sorrow over loss of love and the brevity of life, and even occasional humor.

Of Elizabeth's place in literature, editors of *Elizabeth I: Collected Works* (2000) say, "During her forty-five-year reign as queen of England, she continued to be a prolific letter writer and occasional poet; but her greatest literary achievement is a series of speeches that are often remarkable for their beauty and power."

Works about Elizabeth I

Smith, Lacey Baldwin. *Elizabeth Tudor: Biography of a Queen.* Boston: Little Brown, 1990.

Somerset, Anne. *Elizabeth I.* New York: Knopf, 1991.

Elyot, Sir Thomas (ca. 1490–1546)
nonfiction writer, translator

It is not clear where or when Thomas Elyot was born, but his mother was Alice Fynderne, the first wife of Richard Elyot, a landowner with connections at the royal court who owned extensive property in Wiltshire. Although Elyot was educated at home, he acquired fluency in Latin, Greek, and Italian and devoted much of his life to bringing the knowledge of the ancient Greeks and Romans to England.

In an age when many women, even in the upper classes, were illiterate, Elyot married an educated woman, Margaret Barrow, who had been a student of Sir Thomas MORE. Elyot held government positions from 1511 on, and in 1530 King Henry VIII honored him with a knighthood.

Elyot's first and most famous work, *The Boke Named the Gouvernour* (*The Book Named the Governor*), was published in 1531, with a dedication to Henry. The king was pleased, and honored Elyot further by appointing him ambassador to Holy Roman Emperor Charles V. Elyot's specific mission was to try to persuade the emperor of the merits of Henry's projected divorce from Queen Catherine of Aragon, so that the emperor, in turn, would persuade the pope to permit the divorce. The expenses Elyot incurred on this unsuccessful mission were never reimbursed, and after he returned, his plea to be excused from another appointment that was sure to involve further expense was ignored. It is likely that Elyot's friendship with More had made him unpopular with the king, even though

Henry recognized his ability. Elyot was on a second embassy to Charles V in 1536 when he heard of More's execution.

Elyot continued in public service and also wrote. His works include *The Castle of Health* (1534), a digest of the medical knowledge of the ancient world, which had largely been forgotten during the Middle Ages; and *The Dictionary of Sir T. Elyot, Knight* (1538), the first comprehensive Latin-English dictionary. He also published many translations from Latin, Greek, and Italian, among them *Rules of a Christian Life,* based on the work of the Italian philosopher Pico della Mirandola (1534); *The Doctrine of Princes,* based on the work of the Greek rhetorician Isocrates (1534); and *The Education or Bringing up of Children* based on the work of the Greek biographer Plutarch (1535). All these were popular throughout the 16th century, bringing the excitement of the rebirth of the wisdom of antiquity to people who had no opportunity to learn languages. In 1542 Elyot represented the borough of Cambridge in Parliament. He died at his manor near Cambridge.

Today Elyot is remembered most of all for his first work. *The Book Named the Governor* is considered the first educational treatise in English. It begins with a survey of the various ways a country can be governed and a discussion of the relative merits of monarchy, aristocracy, and democracy. Elyot concludes that monarchy is the best, but that its success depends on the monarch's having a class of wise and virtuous men at his disposal from whom to choose his deputies. From this point on the book is devoted to the educational system needed to produce that class, beginning at birth. The child is to be put under the care of a carefully chosen tutor at the age of seven. He is to be inspired with a love of reading by beginning with enjoyable material such as Aesop's fables and Homer's epics. Discipline is to be gentle: "I would not have them enforced by violence to learn, but . . . to be sweetly allured thereto with praises and such pretty gifts as children delight in."

The arts—music, painting, and carving—are an essential part of Elyot's curriculum, and the body is not neglected. Elyot recommends wrestling, swimming, hunting, archery, and tennis, but not football because of the risk of injury—"rancor and malice do remain with them that be wounded." Dancing merits several chapters, including one called "How Dancing may be the Introduction into the First Moral Virtue, Called Prudence."

In all his works Elyot took great care with his writing style and made a point of molding the English language to accommodate the concepts of the Renaissance, coining a word if he could not find the right word in English for what he wanted to say. For example, in *The Book Named the Governor,* to describe one of the ultimate aims of education, he introduced a word from Latin that quickly became part of the English language: *maturity.*

Other Work by Thomas Elyot

A Critical Edition of Sir Thomas Elyot's "The Boke Named the Governour." Edited by Donald W. Rude. New York: Garland, 1992.

Works about Thomas Elyot

Dees, Jerome S. *Sir Thomas Elyot and Roger Ascham: A Reference Guide.* Boston: G. K. Hall, 1981.
Kennedy, Teresa. *Elyot, Castiglione, and the Problem of Style.* New York: Peter Lang, 1997.

Ephelia (fl. 1679) *poet, playwright*

Ephelia is a pseudonym for a writer whose true identity is unknown. Her poetry suggests that she may have come from an upper-class London family, and she may have been orphaned as a child.

Ephelia's main work is *Female Poems on Several Occasions,* first published in 1679. The volume explores her misadventures in love and traces her journey from self-doubt to self-confidence.

The need for the pseudonym "Ephelia" is clear: The poetry is bold and occasionally racy, enough so that if the author's true identity were known, she might have been forbidden to continue writing by a shamed male relative. Ephelia writes openly about her feelings, reversing the convention of the shy virgin pursued by the amorous lover. In "The Change or Miracle," for example, Ephelia is the one longing for a kiss while the man is coy: "Though all I sue for, be the empty bliss / Of a kind Look, or at the most a Kiss, / Yet he's so cruel to deny me this."

Another of Ephelia's themes has to do with the loss of freedom that accompanies falling in love. In "Love's First Approach" she says, "Great love, I yield; send no more darts in vain, / I am already fond of my soft chain."

The manuscript of her play *The Pair-Royal of Coxcombs [fools],* is lost, but selections of it were printed in the 1682 edition of *Female Poems,* along with several songs now not believed to have been written by Ephelia.

Her style of writing is unpretentious, while playing with rhyme-schemes, forms, and line lengths. *Female Poems* also includes four acrostics made up from the names of her female friends. An editor of a recent edition of *Female Poems,* Maureen Mulvihill, has commented on Ephelia's versatility: "Her small body of verse flaunts an impressive diversity of styles and genres."

A Work about Ephelia

Hobby, Elaine. *Virtue of Necessity: English Women's Writing, 1649–88.* Ann Arbor: University of Michigan Press, 1989.

Erasmus, Desiderius (1466–1536)
nonfiction writer, translator

Desiderius Erasmus was born Gerrit Gerritsoon in Rotterdam, Holland, to an unmarried woman, Margarethe Rogers, and a priest. He chose for himself the name by which he is known, which means "loved" in both Latin and Greek. His mother died when he was a child, but she left him in the care of guardians who were careful about his education. As a youth Erasmus attended a monastery school in Gouda and then in Deventer. He later complained that he was very poorly instructed as a child, and, like many of his contemporaries, he would later sponsor educational reform. However, his education did give him fluency in Latin, the language of scholars. In 1492 he became a monk and was ordained a priest.

In 1495 Erasmus entered the University of Paris to study theology. He was unhappy there, complaining about the harsh approach of many of the instructors. He also objected to the excessive emphasis on authority and tradition in Roman Catholic universities of the day, feeling that students should think for themselves. He eventually left without receiving the degree he desired.

Erasmus's obsession with learning eventually led to his association with the humanists. HUMANISM was dedicated to rescuing and reviving classical Greek and Roman literature and art that had been neglected during the Middle Ages. Humanists also focused attention on the human individual, rather than retaining the medieval emphasis on the place of the individual in the universe as ordered by God.

Among the private students he taught in Paris was an Englishman who invited Erasmus to visit his country, which he did in 1499. England was a center of humanism, and this visit would change Erasmus's life. He lived in Oxford, where he studied Greek with Thomas LINACRE and became a friend and admirer of John COLET. As the tutor of two noble boys, Erasmus made the acquaintance of Sir Thomas MORE, who introduced him to the English court. Erasmus's admiration for the atmosphere of learning that was developing in and around the English court inspired him.

Although he was happy in England, Erasmus did not stay long on this visit. Throughout his life he was on the move. He loved to meet new people and always resisted taking on any responsibilities, however prestigious or financially tempting, that might interfere with his independence of action or thought. With his complete command of the Latin language, Erasmus could, and did, communicate with scholars anywhere in Europe. He corresponded with more than 500 people in the course of his life, including the greatest scholars and some of the most politically powerful people of his time. His letters were greatly admired; a col-

lection of them was published in 1518. He gained immense influence and prestige through his personal contacts and, later, through his published writings.

From 1500 to 1506 Erasmus lived mostly in Paris. His first important book was the *Adagia* (*Adages,* 1500), a collection of proverbs and extracts from classical writers; Margaret Mann Phillips describes it as an "enormous bedside book for the would-be classical scholar." *Adagia* proved popular and was reprinted in an enlarged edition in 1508. About the same time, Erasmus was working on *Enchiridion Militis Christiani* (*The Manual of the Christian Knight,* 1503), a short work designed to help the reader live a truly Christian life. Although it is a devotional work, it contains hints of the author's later sarcastic criticism of the Catholic Church.

From 1506 to 1509 Erasmus traveled in Italy. In Rome he was disgusted by the corruption he observed among officials of the church. Back in England in 1509 as a guest of Sir Thomas More, he produced *Encomium Moriae* (*The Praise of Folly*). In the book's dedicatory letter to More, Erasmus asserts that he wrote it in nine days. It is ironic that this has become his most famous work, since he seems to have regarded it himself as a playful product of his leisure hours.

Erasmus took far more seriously his work as an editor and translator of biblical and classical texts. He was a prolific translator. Although all churchmen of the time learned Latin, ancient Greek had been almost forgotten. Erasmus made Latin versions of works by such Greek authors as the dramatist Euripides (ca. 480–406 B.C.), the historian Plutarch (ca. A.D. 45–125), and many others. He also issued an edition of the New Testament in its original Greek, with his own commentary and translation (1516).

Erasmus was in England from 1509 until 1514, for some of the time teaching at Cambridge. In 1514 he accepted an invitation from the Archduke Charles of Brabant, who was to become the Holy Roman Emperor Charles V, to become one of his counselors. In his new job Erasmus wrote

Institutio principis christiani (*The Education of a Christian Prince,* 1515), a humanistic portrait of the ideal ruler, dedicated to Charles. Soon after that he published the *Colloquia* (*Colloquies,* or *Dialogues,* 1518).

In 1517 Erasmus moved to Louvain, Belgium. The conflict between Martin LUTHER and the Roman Catholic Church was beginning at this time. Because Erasmus had attacked corruption and stupidity in the church in print many times, Luther and his supporters expected Erasmus to align himself with them. But Erasmus hated conflict and never considered breaking with the church. He wrote to Luther in 1519, "I observe as strict a neutrality as possible, in order to advance scholarship, which is again beginning to flourish, by my modesty rather than by passion or violence." His attitude disappointed many, and he was attacked from both sides.

Luther's supporters made Erasmus's life in Louvain so uncomfortable that in 1521 he moved away, spending most of the rest of his life in Basel, Switzerland. Although he is often considered to have started the Protestant REFORMATION with his criticism of the abuses in the Roman Catholic Church, he saw Luther's split with the church and the religious conflict that followed, with the intolerance it brought on both sides, as a tragedy.

Critical Analysis

In Praise of Folly is spoken entirely from the character of Dame Folly, or Foolishness. The text begins on a lighthearted note. Folly explains that she has earned a bad reputation for being the master of foolishness when, in fact, she is more a master of pleasure. "But tell me, by Jupiter" she exclaims, "what part of man's life is that that is not sad, crabbed, unpleasant, insipid, troublesome, unless it be seasoned with Pleasure, that is to say, Folly?" Folly goes so far as to say that there would actually be no life if she were not around since people would be entirely too rational to endure the pains of childbirth.

This upbeat tone begins to change as Folly's speech proceeds. In the latter sections of the text,

Folly launches bitter attacks on church officials, particularly in their weakness for following Folly's path. Of monks, Folly remarks:

> . . . they believe it's the highest form of piety to be so uneducated that they can't even read. . . . Many of them too make a good living out of their squalor and beggary, bellowing for bread from door to door. . . . This is the way in which these smooth individuals, in all their filth and ignorance, their boorish and shameless behaviour, claim to bring back the apostles into our midst! . . . Most of them rely so much on their ceremonies and petty man-made traditions that they suppose heaven alone will hardly be enough to reward merit such as theirs. They never think of the time to come when Christ will scorn all this and enforce his own rule, that of charity.

However, even within these passages, Folly maintains the pose that she is only teasing, a rhetorical move that allows for humor and also affords Erasmus protection against anyone's taking serious offense.

Colloquies started as a text meant to assist young students of Latin to express themselves with ease. Other works of this sort provided dialogues largely consisting of demonstrations of verbal etiquette, ways for people to greet one another and ways to express thanks. Erasmus's volume starts out within this tradition but then brings in conversations about politics, literature, and women, and in later editions making fun of some of the practices of the church and the superstitions of its adherents. For example, in one of the dialogues, Adolph is telling Antony about a shipwreck he experienced. He describes the panicked appeals to the saints that went up as the storm raged:

Adolph One chanted *Salve Regina* [Hail Mary], another *Credo in Deum* [I believe in God]. Some had certain queer beads, like charms to ward off danger.

Antony How devout men are made by suffering! In prosperity the thought of God or saint never enters their heads. What were you doing all this time? Making vows to any of the saints?

Adolph   Not at all.

Antony   Why?

Adolph   Because I don't make deals with saints. For what else is that but a bargain according to the form "I'll give this if you do that"?

School officials censored portions of Erasmus's text that were seen as too controversial, and eventually the book itself was banned.

Erasmus was a central figure in the development of English humanism. His influence (especially through *The Education of a Christian Prince*) is direct and obvious in the educational works of Thomas ELYOT and Roger ASCHAM. Indirectly, he influenced generations through the way he affected the practice of education in England. Michel de MONTAIGNE loved Erasmus's rationalism, and this strain of Erasmus's thought had successors in René DESCARTES, Thomas HOBBES, and John LOCKE. His religious humanism was central to the vision of John MILTON, and he continues to capture the imaginations of writers and social thinkers. As Margaret Mann Phillips says, Erasmus "stands before us still as the apostle of common sense, and a great liberator of the mind."

Other Works by Desiderius Erasmus

An Erasmus Reader. Edited by Erika Rummel. Buffalo: University of Toronto Press, 1990.

Erasmus on Women. Edited by Erika Rummel. Buffalo: University of Toronto Press, 1996.

Works about Desiderius Erasmus

Huizinga, Johan. *Erasmus and the Age of Reformation.* New York: Dover, 2002.

Jardine, Lisa. *Erasmus, Man of Letters: The Construction of Charisma in Print.* Princeton, N.J.: Princeton University Press, 1993.

McConica, James. *Erasmus.* New York: Oxford University Press, 1991.

Phillips, Margaret Mann. *Erasmus and the Northern Renaissance.* Totowa, N.J.: Rowman & Littlefield, 1981.

Tracy, James D. *Erasmus of the Low Countries.* Berkeley: University of California Press, 1996.

Etherege, George (ca. 1636–1692)
dramatist

George Etherege was born in London to Capt. George Etherege, a member of the court of Charles I and Queen Henrietta Maria, and his wife, Mary. Etherege was apprenticed to an attorney from 1654 to 1658 and then studied law at Clement's Inn. In 1662 Etherege began writing plays to provide financial assistance to his widowed mother as well as to support his extravagant lifestyle.

Etherege's first play, the popular *The Comic Revenge* (1664), contains an upper and a lower plot. In the upper, or main plot, Graciana, engaged to Beaufort, is encouraged by her siblings, Aurelia and Lovis, to wed the heroic Bruce. After being disarmed by Beaufort in a duel, Bruce falls on his sword but recovers to marry Aurelia, leaving Beaufort and Graciana free to wed. In the lower, or subplot, Sir Frederick Frollick humorously tricks the Widow Rich into revealing her love for him. Believing "women, like fishes," must be skillfully fooled into hanging "themselves on the hook" of love, he feigns first his own death and, when that fails, his arrest. Frollick also saves the incompetent Sir Nicholas Cully from being conned out of his fortune by the swindler Wheadle.

The scholar J. Douglas Canfield notes that multiple plots are typical of the "divided plays" of Etherege's era: "In the heroic plot, beleaguered constancy is finally rewarded; in the gay-couple plot, the inconstant rake is finally converted to marriage; and in the farcical plot, some pretending fool or some nouveau knight raised by Cromwell" is made a fool of. This plot structure served a political purpose in the wake of Charles II's RESTORATION to the throne in 1660, as it underscored the monarchists' claim that born aristocrats like Beaufort and Sir Frederick were inherently superior to men like Cully who were knighted by Cromwell, the Puritan who dethroned and beheaded Charles I in 1649. A lifelong supporter of monarchy, Etherege revels in what Canfield calls "the wish fulfillment of class triumph."

Etherege's next play, *She Would If She Could,* was poorly received by audiences in 1668 but praised by many writers of the time. The play follows Ned Courtall and Frank Freeman as they pursue the witty country heiresses Ariana and Gatty. Prior to winning the women's love, the men endure much taunting, as when Ariana scolds them for "the unpardonable sin of talking." In the process they avoid Lady Cockwood's "foolishly fond and troublesome" attempts at seduction and her husband Oliver Cockwood's debauched lifestyle. The play's reliance on the humor of clever banter and hypocrisy, rather than on turns of plot, has led contemporary critics to see it as the first comedy of manners, a genre whose focus is primarily on conduct and social codes. Critic Michael Cordner, a contemporary scholar suggests that this might account for the play's initial unpopularity, since only "a relatively narrow community" would be familiar with the elaborate social conventions represented.

Etherege's well-received *The Man of Mode* (1676) opens with the libertine Dorimant planning to pursue Bellinda. At the same time Dorimant's friend young Bellair discovers that his father, old Bellair, loves Emilia, whom young Bellair is secretly courting. After seducing Bellinda Dorimant pursues Harriet, a country heiress fascinated by his reputation as "a wild extravagant fellow." Unaffected by Dorimant's attempts at seduction, Harriet convinces him to accompany her to her "great rambling lone house" in the countryside. Young Bellair and Emilia secretly marry, and old Bellair finally gives them his blessing. This comedy has some unusually dark elements, as exhibited in the seduction of Bellinda, who rather than displaying stereotypical traits of the fallen woman, resembles the heroines of other Restoration comedies in all aspects except her downfall. Bellinda's dismay and her request that the still-flirtatious Dorimant "take no notice of" her after he marries, cause a degree of discomfort with,

rather than amusement at, Dorimant's treatment of her. As the critic Robert Markley suggests, the play's comic conclusion "pits our expectations of a happy ending against our knowledge of the characters and the world they inhabit."

Etherege also wrote several popular poems, some of which were set to music but which fell into obscurity after the 18th century. In 1685 he moved to Ratisbon, Germany, to serve as a political correspondent for King James II. When James was deposed in 1688 by William of Orange, Etherege followed his king to Paris and died soon afterwards. Denounced as immoral by the mid-19th century, Etherege's comedies began to be performed again in the 1970s and 1980s. Like earlier audiences, contemporary readers are again savoring, in the critic Arthur Husboe's words, the "troublesome questions of the individual versus society that are raised by the comedy" of George Etherege.

Works about George Etherege

Huseboe, A. R. *Sir George Etherege.* Boston: Twayne Publishers, 1987.

Mann, D. D. *Sir George Etherege: A Reference Guide.* Boston: G. K. Hall, 1981.

Young, Douglas M. *The Feminist Voices in Restoration Comedy: The Virtuous Women in the Play-worlds of Etherege, Wycherley, and Congreve.* Lanham, Md.: University Press of America, 1997.

Evans, Katherine (d. 1692), and Chevers, Sarah (d. 1664) *nonfiction writers, poets*

Katherine Evans (from Bath, England) and Sarah Chevers (from Slaughterford, England) are remembered for their joint religious writings. Both were affluent Quaker women who traveled extensively preaching their religion. In 1658 they decided to leave their husbands and children in order to travel east, intending to follow in the footsteps of Saint Paul. Once they arrived in Malta, however, they found themselves accused of witchcraft and imprisoned by the Inquisition. Although they were in captivity for more than three years, both refused to convert to Roman Catholicism and withstood their captivity, taking solace in each other. Their story was published twice, first while they were imprisoned in 1662 as *This is a Short Relation of some of the Cruel Sufferings of Katherine Evans and Sarah Chever in the Inquisition of the Isle of Malta* and then later, when they were released in 1663.

Their writings are a moving collection of poems, letters, and prophesies that demonstrate the women's true devotion and belief in their religion. For instance, Katherine writes to her husband that, "In our deepest affliction, when I looked for every breath to be the last, I could not wish I had not come over sea, because I knew it was my eternal Father's will to prove me, with my dear and faithful friend." Evans and Chevers's story is particularly inspirational in its portrayal of how the two women took care of one another, earned a meager living knitting stockings and mending the clothes of other prisoners, and turned their prison into something resembling a home by sheer strength of will.

In the end, the two women's works remain as a testament to their faith and to their ability to maintain their faith in the face of danger and deprivation.

Evelyn, John (1620–1706) *diarist, nonfiction writer*

John Evelyn was born at his father's estate of Wotton in Surrey, England, the second son of Richard and Elianor Standsfield Evelyn. He was educated at home until he joined the Middle Temple in 1637 to study law. The following year he began studies at Balliol College, Oxford University. His father died in 1640, his mother having died several years earlier, and with some income from his parents' estate Evelyn decided to travel. Over the next few years he visited the Netherlands, France, Italy, and Switzerland. During this time the English Civil War raged, ending with the execution of King Charles I and the establishment of a republic, or commonwealth, under the leadership of Oliver Cromwell.

In France, Evelyn met Sir Richard Browne, who was serving as ambassador to France for the exiled King Charles II; he married Browne's daughter Mary in 1647. Evelyn decided that he would prefer to start his family in England in spite of the unfavorable political climate. He bought the manor house of Sayes Court, in Deptford, near London, from his father-in-law, and he and Mary, pregnant with their first child, settled there in 1652.

As a royalist, Evelyn kept a low profile. He began to write and set about making Sayes into a showpiece of landscaping. This was for him much more than a pastime or an opportunity for display; he believed that a garden could be not just a joy but a spiritual discipline. He wrote to his friend Sir Thomas BROWNE in 1657: "The air and genius of gardens operate upon human spirits towards virtue and sanctity."

In 1660 Evelyn joined with several other scientifically curious men, among them John AUBREY, to found the Royal Society. When Evelyn read a paper at a meeting of that society about the damage that had been done to Britain's forests during and after the Civil War, the society commissioned him to write a study of forests and how to restore them. This commission became the work for which Evelyn was most famous in his lifetime: *Sylva; or, a Discourse of Forest Trees* (1664). He crammed into this book his thoughts about the varieties of trees and how they grow, about how landowners should manage their estates, and about his own philosophy of life. Other Evelyn works include *The Character of England* (1659), a disapproving comparison of the manners of the English with those found on the European continent; *Fumifugium* (1661), an early treatise about the harmfulness of air pollution as Evelyn experienced it in London; and *Kalendarium Hortense* (1664), a gardening calendar.

After the RESTORATION, Evelyn was able to enter public life as he could not before. King Charles II commissioned writings and invited him to court, but though he respected the king, Evelyn was uncomfortable with the dissipated atmosphere at court and preferred public service. He took the job of commissioner for sick and wounded seamen and performed his duties conscientiously, even during the panicky time of the plague (1665–66).

In middle age, Evelyn, who by all accounts was an attentive husband, embarked on a platonic relationship with a young woman named Margaret Blagge. Their friendship seems to have revolved around devotional activities—prayer and Bible study—yet when Margaret became engaged to Sidney GODOLPHIN she kept that relationship secret from Evelyn for as long she could. Margaret died in childbirth only three years after her marriage. In his *Life of Mrs. Godolphin* (not published until 1847), Evelyn wrote, "Friendship is beyond all relationships of flesh and blood, because it is less material."

Evelyn is best known today for his diary, in which he wrote almost daily for most of his life. Unlike his friend Samuel PEPYS, who confided his most private thoughts to his diary, Evelyn avoids personal revelations and concentrates on matters of general interest, like the subjects of discussion at the Royal Society and the political events of his day. His diary, though less racy than Pepys's, is at least as valuable as a window on the 17th century, and it covers a much longer period.

Still, it is to Pepys's diary that one must turn for a glimpse of Evelyn's sense of humor, in his record of a gathering at which "Mr Evelyn's repeating of some verses made up of nothing but the various acceptations of may and can, and doing it so aptly upon occasion of something of that nature, and so fast, did make us all die almost with laughing." And it is Pepys who allows a feeling for the affection Evelyn could inspire, when he remarks of him: "A most excellent person he is, and must be allowed a little for conceitedness; but he may well be so, being a man so much above others." Pepys also said, "The more I know him, the more I love him."

Other Works by John Evelyn

De la Bédoyère, Guy, ed. *Particular Friends: The Correspondence of Samuel Pepys and John Evelyn.* Rochester, N.Y.: Boydell Press, 1997.

———. *The writings of John Evelyn.* Rochester, N.Y.: Boydell Press, 1995.

A Work about John Evelyn

Harris, Frances. *Transformations of Love: The Friendship of John Evelyn and Margaret Godolphin.* New York: Oxford University Press, 2003.

Evelyn, Mary (1665–1685) poet

Mary Evelyn was born in 1665, the daughter of the royal diarist John EVELYN and Mary Browne Evelyn. She died of smallpox when she was only 19, and her literary legacy can be attributed to the efforts of her father. After her death he found among her letters and diaries a manuscript for a long poem that he helped to publish five years after her death, in 1690.

The work, entitled *Mundus Muliebris: Or, The Ladies Dressing-Room Unlock'd and Her Tiolette Spread,* is a burlesque of the vanity of "the women's world" that also satirizes women's concerns with silly entertainments such as theater-going and novel-reading. The poem includes a preface and a "fop dictionary" of terms common and particular to the world of women's fashion in the last years of the 17th century. Some argue that John Evelyn wrote these sections of the work, which included an antifeminist warning:

> Whoever has a mind to abundance of
>   trouble.
> Let him furnish himself with a Ship and a
>   Woman.
> For no two thing will find you more
>   Employment.
> If once you begin to rig them out with all
>   their steamers.

Whether or not those words came from her father, the entire poem reflects Mary Evelyn's conservative outlook on her own sex.

In his diaries John Evelyn commented on what a great "abundance of witt" young Mary possessed. The poem reflects her flair for comedy and satire, cataloging in detail the ridiculous lengths women take to satisfy their vanities:

Gold is her Toothpick, Gold her Watch is,
And Gold is everything she touches
But tir'd with numbers I give o're,
Arithmetick can add no more,
Thus rigg'd the Vessel, and Eqippp'd,
She is for all Adventures Shipp'd,
And Portion e're the year goes round,
Does with her vanity Confound.

Mary Evelyn took great pains to educate herself. It helped that her parents encouraged her far beyond the usual limits for young women of that time. Besides her poems, Evelyn busied herself with devotional reading and writing. A manuscript found among her papers was entitled "Rules for Spending My Pretious Tyme Well," which was perhaps a result of the influence of the devotional writings of Margaret Godolphin, her father's spiritual protégée.

Evelyn was also, according to her father, popular at court, sought out for her sharp wit and charming conversation. She even spent a summer at Windsor with her cousin Lady Tuke.

Mundus Muliebris was published in 1690 and was reprinted three times before being reissued in 1700. It is one of the few female contributions to the burlesque genre of the time.

Fage, Mary (fl. 1637) poet

Recent evidence suggests that Mary Fage was the wife of Robert Fage of Doddinghurst parish, Essex, England, and the daughter of Edward Fage, also from Doddinghurst. Robert Fage, a translator, was the son of a lawyer and related by marriage to a powerful family of lawyers, the Barkers, one of whom served in Parliament, another of whom was a serjeant-at-law.

If Mary Fage's husband did in fact belong to this prominent family, it helps explain *Fame's Roule* (1637), her single surviving text, which contains more than 400 acrostic poems, each with an anagram and every one directed to a powerful person of the day. In an acrostic, the first letter of each line of the verse forms a name when read top to bottom, while an anagram consists of the letters of a word or name rearranged to form a different word or phrase. For example, in "To the High and Mighty Princess Anne, Third Daughter of Our Sovereign Lord King Charles. Anna Stuarte" Fage makes an anagram of Anna's name and the first letters of the first four lines spell "Anna."

> *Annagramma: A NU NEAT STAR*
> *A Star remain you in our firmament*
> *Newly sprung forth, having the luster lent*
> *Newly wherewith your excellence doth*
>   *shine*
> *(Ah still increase you) from that Sol of*
>   *thine.*

Fage shows proper deference to those in power by arranging her verses in order of the rank of their subjects. Although her anagrams, acrostics, and wordplay may seem clumsy to the modern ear, they reflect the taste of her day. Queen ELIZABETH I was fond of anagrams on her name. Even the title *Fames Roule* may be read as either *Fame's Roll* or *Fame's Rule*.

Fairfax, Edward (ca. 1568–1635) translator, poet

Edward Fairfax was born in Leeds, Yorkshire, England, probably as an illegitimate son to Sir Thomas Fairfax. In 1600 he produced the first complete translation of *Jerusalem Delivered as Godfrey of Bulloigne done into English Heroicall Verse.* This work, originally published by Torquato TASSO in 1581, is a story of the First Crusade, which Godfrey led, and is full of fable and knightly romance.

English heroic verse is written in iambic pentameter. Fairfax's poem is comprised of eight-line stanzas in iambic pentameter, rhyming *ab ab abcc.*

The subject matter and the verse are both noble and heroic. Here Fairfax introduces Godfrey and his task:

> [of] The sacred armies, and the godly
>   knight,
> That the great sepulchre of Christ did free,
> I sing; much wrought his valor and
>   foresight,
> And in that glorious war much suffered he;
> In vain 'gainst him did Hell oppose her
>   might,
> In vain the Turks and Morians armed be:
> His soldiers wild, to brawls and mutinies
>   prest,
> Reduced he to peace, so Heaven him blest.

Fairfax is chiefly known for *Jerusalem Delivered*, which had a profound effect on the development of heroic verse in English. Critics agree that Fairfax translated loosely, but the scholars Kathleen Lea and T. M. Gang, in their 1981 edition of the poem, conclude that his narrative in English has "order and power; regularity and variety." The poem influenced other poets, and the editors of Edmund WALLER's *Poems* (1711) admitted his debt to Fairfax. William Collins, in his *Ode on the Popular Superstitions of the Highlands of Scotland* (1750), admires Tasso and says of Fairfax ". . . at each sound imagination glows."

Fairfax also wrote *Daemonologia* (1621), in which he mistakenly described his daughters' seizures as owing to witchcraft. Elizabeth Cooper, editor of *The Muses Library* (1737), mentioned 12 pastoral poems by Fairfax but published only *Eglon and Alexis* and *Hermes and Lycaon*.

Falkland, Viscountess of
See CAREY, ELIZABETH, LADY, VISCOUNTESS FALKLAND.

Fanshawe, Ann (1625–1680) *nonfiction writer*
Ann Fanshawe (née Harrison) was born in London to Margaret and Sir John Harrison, one of the richest men in England. Her education befitted her so-cial position: instruction in dancing, singing, playing music, speaking French, and doing fine needlework, in addition to the horseback riding and other outdoor exercise that she preferred.

The English Civil War changed Fanshawe's life dramatically. This struggle was sparked by the conflict between the king and Parliament over religious issues and questions about the rights of the monarchy. Fanshawe's father's support for the king led to his wealth being seized by parliamentary forces.

In 1644 Ann married Sir Richard FANSHAWE, diplomat and secretary of war for the Prince of Wales. Fanshaw would later describe their relationship in her memoirs: "I more valued myself to be call'd by his name than borne a princess, for I knew him to be very wise and very good, and his soule doated on me." In her writing she shows the deep regard they had for each other, which lasted through their adventurous life during the Civil War followed by diplomatic journeys abroad to Spain.

Fanshawe documented her life in her memoirs, which she wrote for her only surviving son, Richard, to record the "most remarkable actions & accidents" of the family's history. Her memoirs were not published until 1829, nearly 150 years after her death, although they had circulated in manuscript much earlier. In an era that afforded little support for women's writing, female authors frequently turned to private, family-oriented forms of writing as creative outlets. Fanshawe, however, had a clear sense of herself as an agent in history during the turbulent political events of her life. As she writes, "we appeared upon the stage to act what part God destined us, as faith is the evidence of things not seen, so we upon so righteous a cause cheerfully resolved to suffer what that would drive us to, which afflictions were neither few nor small."

In her writing Fanshawe eloquently displays the fortitude and faith that saw her through numerous trials during the war. Her exploits include escaping from parliamentary forces just two days after giving birth, enduring naval battles while fleeing to

France, and dodging bullets with her husband as they landed on the beach at Calais.

Although her memoirs focus on her husband, Fanshawe demonstrates a strong-willed and adventurous sensibility of her own. While her prose is at times unpolished, as the scholar John Loftis comments, Fanshawe "permits glimpses of her innermost life," and her memoirs "are important for the record they provide of persons, events, and places."

A Work about Ann Fanshawe

Rose, Mary Beth, ed. *Women in the Middle Ages and the Renaissance: Literary and Historical Perspectives.* Syracuse, N.Y.: Syracuse University Press, 1986.

Fanshawe, Sir Richard (1608–1666) *poet, translator*

Sir Richard Fanshawe, the son of Sir Henry Fanshawe, was educated at Cripplegate School and Jesus College, Cambridge University. Fanshawe had a love of the classics and poetry and was devoted to King Charles I, which led to his imprisonment in 1651 after the battle of Worcester during the English Civil War. After the RESTORATION, when Charles II acceded to the throne, Fanshawe became ambassador to Portugal and Spain.

The year 1655 saw the publication of Fanshawe's translation of the Portuguese epic *Lusiadas,* its first appearance in English. This poem by Luis de Camões (1524–80), who is considered the greatest of all Portuguese poets, describes the travels of explorer Vasco da Gama. Fanshawe's translation includes this vivid personification of storm clouds coming out of the Cape of Good Hope: "His crispt Hayre filled with earth, and hard as Wyre / A mouth cole-black, and Teeth two yellow Tyre."

As a poet, Fanshawe is perhaps best known for "The Rose," a sonnet that mixes classic themes of beauty and death. The poet addresses the rose:

> BLOWN in the morning, thou shalt fade
>   ere noon.

> What boots a life which in such haste
>   forsakes thee?
> Thou'rt wondrous frolic, being to die so
>   soon,
> And passing proud a little colour makes
>   thee.

Parodoxically, Fanshawe tells us that the rose's beauty is precisely why it must die so soon, "For the same beauty doth, in bloody leaves, / The sentence of thy early death contain."

Fanshawe's official correspondence from his time as ambassador was published in 1701. Letters written to his wife Ann FANSHAWE were published in her *Memoirs of Lady Fanshawe* (1829).

A Work about Sir Richard Fanshawe

Fanshawe, Lady Ann. *Memoirs of Lady Fanshawe.* Cambridge, Mass.: IndyPublish.com, 2003.

Fell, Margaret (Margaret Fox) (1614–1702) *pamphleteer*

Margaret Fell was born in Dalton-in-Furness, Lancashire, England, to John Askew; her family was landed gentry. First married in 1632 to Thomas Fell, she later married George FOX, the founder of the Quaker faith. Quakers flourished along with other dissenters during the period following the English Civil War, a conflict between the king and Parliament.

Quaker theology emphasized the spiritual equality of women and men and the necessity of prophecy, important beliefs that led Fell to write pamphlets as a Quaker activist in 1655. Although 17th-century society sometimes viewed women's public outspokenness negatively, Fell, along with many other women, found increasing opportunities to enter public debate through their religion. Her family background included a history of speaking out on matters of religion: She was descended from Anne ASKEW, a 16th-century Protestant MARTYR.

Fell's pamphlet "Women's Speaking Justified" (1667) confronted contemporary doctrine against women as orators and preachers. Drawing on the Bible, Fell argues that Christ was "made of a woman," that "Women labour in the Gospel," and that both "Sons and Daughters do Prophesie."

Fell was also inspired by her faith to political action. In 1559 she presented to Parliament a petition asking for the religious toleration of 7,000 Quaker women. This was a remarkable instance of women's collective political action. The following year, when the restoration of Charles II to the crown brought renewed fears of persecution for religious dissenters, she published "A Declaration and an Information From us the People of God called Quakers, To the present Governors, the King and Both Houses of Parliament" (1660). This pamphlet criticized the government's persecution of the Quakers and called for religious freedom.

Fell continued writing religious pamphlets, even though at one point, from 1664 to 1668, she was imprisoned for her dissenting views. As the scholar Bonnelyn Young Kunze writes, "If Fell's literary output is compared, not only to other Quaker female writers, but to other literate Englishwomen of the period, she stands out as one of the exceptional women of the seventeenth century."

A Work about Margaret Fell

Kunze, Bonnelyn Young. *Margaret Fell and the Rise of Quakerism.* Stanford, Calif.: Stanford University Press, 1994.

Felltham, Owen (ca. 1604–1668) *poet, essayist*

Owen Felltham was probably born in the village of Mutford, Suffolk, England, in 1604, the son of Thomas Felltham, a wealthy gentleman, and his wife, Mary. Few details are known about Felltham's life. He was largely self-educated, with the occasional help of tutors, and spent a large part of his life as a steward to the Earl of Thomond, at whose Northamptonshire estate he died in 1668. He married Mary Clopton, who likely died before her husband, leaving him no children.

After a trip to Holland in the 1620s, Felltham wrote a pamphlet entitled "A Brief Character of the Low-Countries Under the States," which describes that country and proved quite popular. It was published in English and Dutch editions throughout the rest of the century.

Felltham is best known as the author of *Resolves: Divine, Morall, Politicall,* a collection of essays on religious topics such as Man's Imperfection, Faith, and Death. It was first published in 1623, and he continued to revise it in eight editions over his lifetime. The essays were written in a formal, moralistic style and demonstrated that Felltham was widely read in classical and religious literature. In "How He Must Live, that Lives Well," for example, Felltham writes, "He who neglects his duty to himself, his neighbour, or his God, fails in something, that should make life commendable. For ourselves, we need order; for our neighbour, charity; and for our God, our reverence, and humility." As the scholars Ted-Larry Pebworth and Claude J. Summers point out in their 1973 monograph: "His world view is a conservative one, dominated by a preference for the old order. . . . This concept of the universe teaches him that 'order and degree' are of paramount importance in questions divine, moral, and political." It is perhaps not surprising that Felltham was a royalist and partisan of the established church who welcomed the 1660 RESTORATION of the Stuart king Charles II, a monarch he called "Christ the Second."

In a section of the 1661 edition of the *Resolves* called "Lusoria: Or Occasional Pieces, With a Taste of Some Letters," Felltham included 42 poems (some of them in Latin) that he had written over his lifetime, prefacing them with a disclaimer that he looked upon the verse as "sports" that "rather improve a man by preserving him from worse."

Though he is regarded as a minor poet, Felltham's lyrics are representative of their period. As Pebworth and Summers point out, "His poems include a distinguished collection of love lyrics and a body of occasional poetry in which are represented almost all the subgenres popular in the earlier seventeenth century." The love lyrics are often embellished with imagery that draws on both spiritual and erotic images, as when Felltham writes: "For when two souls shall towre so high, / Without their flesh their rayes shall flye, / Like Emanations from a Deity."

One of the *Lusoria* poems, "To the Memory of immortall B E N," was originally written in 1637 and published in a collection of elegies that various poets had written upon the death of Ben JONSON. It is full of allusions to classical authors so common to poems of the 16th century, as when Felltham compares Jonson to "*Pindar*'s height, / *Plautus* his wit, and *Seneca*'s grave weight, / *Horace* his matchless Nerves, and that high phrase / Wherewith great *Lucan* doth his Readers maze." Commenting on Jonson's laborious ways, Felltham must "Admit his Muse was slow" while comparing the deceased poet to "Those Planets placed in the higher Sphœres / [that] End not their motion but in many yeares; / Whereas light Venus and the giddy Moone, / In one or some few days their courses run." Allusion to astronomy was also a favorite metaphor in 16th-century verse.

Critics consider Felltham's best poem to be his "On the Duke of Buckingham . . ." George Villiers, the Duke of Buckingham, rose to favor under JAMES I OF ENGLAND and served as Charles I's chief minister. In 1628 he was assassinated because of his mismanagement of a war against Spain and France. In the poem, Felltham contrasts Buckingham's high station with the low estate to which he had fallen ("so huge a pile / Of State") to portray the fate of a tragic figure whose humiliation can be eased only by Christian attitudes of forgiveness and reconciliation.

Although Felltham is regarded as a minor poet, his lyrics epitomize the spirit and purpose of the secular poetry of the period. As Pebworth and Summers conclude: "Felltham's measure as poet is not his originality, but his ability to make fresh and personal poems which derive from a fertile and various milieu. His may not be a distinctive voice, but it is a fine one nevertheless."

Fenton, Geoffrey (ca. 1539–1608) *translator*
Geoffrey Fenton was born around 1539 in the town of Fenton, Nottinghamshire, England, to Henry and Cecily Beaumont Fenton. No evidence exists to suggest he was educated at Oxford or Cambridge, but at some time he had learned French, Latin, and some Italian and Spanish.

Fenton was living in Paris in 1567 when he translated and published *Certain Tragical Discourses,* a collection of stories by the Italian writer Matteo Bandello. Fenton's work was a very free translation, and his versions of the stories bear little resemblance to Bandello's. Unlike the original work, Fenton's translation takes on a moralizing tone. He writes of the moral corruption of the Italians and the weaknesses of women in general. This moral tone appealed to contemporary English readers, and his sharp attention to detail and his addition of soliloquies improved upon the psychological realism of his sources.

Certain Tragical Discourses is Fenton's most famous work, largely because it marked the introduction of the continental novella (short novel) to English literature. Many of these continental novellas served as sources for English dramatists. Fenton's translation of "Albanoys Captain," which tells of "an insanely jealous foreign military man who murders his wife and then commits suicide," is a possible source for William SHAKESPEARE's *Othello.*

Fenton translated other works, including *A Discourse of the Civil Wars and Late Troubles in France* (1570); *Acts of Conference in Religion* (1571); and *Golden Epistles, Containing Variety of Discourse Both Moral, Philosophical, and Divine* (1575), the last originally written by Antonio de Guevara (1480–1545). His works have strong Protestant— and thus very anti-Catholic—stances. In *Acts of Conference in Religion,* Fenton writes of the "rude sophistry of the Papists and mild simplicity of the reformed side." The book starts out as a dialogue and transforms into an exchange of letters that debate the validity of the Catholic mass versus the Protestant sacrament of the Last Supper. Fenton's last work was *The History of Guicciardin* (1579), another free translation of an Italian work, Guicciardini's *Storia d'Italica*.

Field, Nathan (1587–1619) *playwright*

Nathan Field was born in London to John Field, an outspoken Puritan minister, and his wife, Joan. Field attended St. Paul's school before transferring to the Chapel Royal in 1600. There he became a member of the Children of the Queen's Revels, an acting troupe of young boys who performed during the reign of Queen ELIZABETH I and King JAMES I OF ENGLAND. Field became a protégé of Ben JONSON, playing lead parts in Jonson's plays *Cynthia's Revels* (1600) and *Poetaster* (1601). He remained with the Children of the Queen's Revels until 1616, when he joined the KING'S MEN. Field's name appears in William SHAKESPEARE's First Folio as one of the original actors to perform his plays.

During his time with the Children of the Queen's Revels, Field wrote two plays, *A Woman is a Weathercock* (1609) and *Amends for Ladies* (1611). At the time the troupe was in need of new plays, and, as Field said in the preface to the play, "I have been vexed with vile plays myself a great while, hearing many; now I thought to be even with some, and they should hear mine too." *A Woman is a Weathercock* was a success for the Children of the Queen's Revels. It is an intricately plotted comedy characterized by many of the popular conventions of the time, including disguises, duels, and plot twists in the grand recognition scene, combined with Field's own comic satire. It expresses the ironic sentiment of "how slight a thing woman is" who changes like a weathercock with every breeze, and it concludes with a masque, or a short form of dramatic entertainment performed by masked actors.

Amends for Ladies follows *A Woman is a Weathercock* in its intricate structure, use of stock characters and situations, and contemporary satire, while, as the title implies, intending to retract the playwright's earlier charges against women. Field satirizes women and men, fashion and decorum, and religious hypocrisy, through the presence of a hypocritical Puritan. The play has three heroines—Honor, Perfect, and Bright—who personify the maiden, the wife, and the widow, respectively. These characters attempt to vindicate their sex and lay claim to the virtue of constancy.

In addition to these two plays, Field collaborated with Philip MASSINGER and John FLETCHER on *The Jeweller of Amsterdam* (1616), and with Massinger once again on *The Fatal Dowry* (1632).

Flecknoe, Richard (ca. 1600–ca. 1678) *poet*

Few facts are known about Richard Flecknoe's life. He was of Irish extraction, but no one is sure if his parents were living in Ireland or England when he was born. He seems, however, to have been brought up in England. He is said to have been a Catholic priest, though he apparently ceased to present himself as one after 1660.

Although Flecknoe was one of the most prolific writers of the century, he published infrequently. Many of his works of poetry and drama were printed only for private circulation. His first published work was a religious piece, *Hierothalamium, or the Heavenly Nuptials of our Blessed Savior with a Pious Soul* (1626). Other works include the collection *Miscellania, or Poems of all Sorts* (1653); *The Idea of his Highness Oliver, Late Lord Protector* (1659); a poem in praise of English leader Oliver Cromwell; and *Love's Kingdom* (1664), the only one of his dramas to be performed.

Flecknoe has the dubious distinction of being satirized by two of the greatest poets of the 17th century, Andrew MARVELL and John DRYDEN (1631–1700). In "Flecknoe, An English Priest at Rome" (ca. 1645), Marvell recalls listening to him read his "hideous verse . . . in a dismal tone"; and Dryden, in his "Mac Flecknoe" (1682) notes that

> *this Flecknoe . . .*
> *had governed long;*
> *In prose and verse was owned, without*
>   *dispute,*
> *Throughout the realms of nonsense,*
>   *absolute.*

Thereafter, Flecknoe's name became linked with bad poetry, and even today critics continue to take Dryden at his word. The scholar George Parfitt, discussing the power of 17th-century satire, asserts that Dryden's "obliteration of Richard Flecknoe . . . is perhaps unnecessary, given the self-obliteration of the untalented."

Fletcher, Giles, Jr. (ca. 1585–1623) *poet*

Giles Fletcher, Jr., was probably born in London, the son of the poet and diplomat Giles FLETCHER, Sr., and the brother of Phineas FLETCHER, who was also a poet. Young Giles began his studies at Trinity College, Cambridge University, in 1605 and stayed there as a fellow, teaching Greek for more than a decade. Around 1618 he became the rector of Alderton, Suffolk, where he remained until his death. He excelled in sermon writing and preaching, though his parishioners discouraged him from pursuing literary matters.

As befitting his position as a clergyman, religious imagery is a prominent feature in Fletcher's poems. His most prominent work, the epic *Christs Victorie, and Triumph in Heaven, and Earth, Over and After Death* (1610), is divided into four cantos. In this poem Fletcher employs allegorical devices to describe the temptation of Christ in the desert; his passion, death, and resurrection; and his final triumph over sin and evil. Fletcher wrote this work in eight-line stanzas reminiscent of the style of Edmund SPENSER, to whom his work is often compared. As Spenser did in *The Faerie Queene*, Fletcher crafted elaborate conceits to describe semi-allegorical characters like the Lady of Vain Delight or the embodiments of Mercy and Justice.

It has been suggested that John MILTON was indebted to *Christs Victorie* for some of the imagery and rhythms of his *Paradise Regained*. Here is a stanza from the fourth canto, in which Fletcher's use of imagery is at its finest and in which his majestic tone seems to foreshadow Milton's:

> So long . . . [Christ] wander'd in our lower
> sphere,
> That heav'n began his cloudy stars despise,
> Half envious, to see on earth appear
> A greater light, than flam'd in his own skies:
> At length it burst for spite, and out there
> flies
> A globe of winged angels, swift as thought,
> That on their spotted feathers lively caught
> The sparkling earth, and to their azure
> fields it brought.

Fletcher contributed an elegy on the death of Queen ELIZABETH I to the commemorative collection *Sorrows Joy* (1603). Shortly before his death, he wrote a devotional tract in prose, *The Reward of the Faithfull* (1623).

Fletcher, Giles, Sr. (1546–1611) *historian, poet*

The second son of Richard Fletcher, vicar of Cranbrook, and his wife, Joan, Giles Fletcher was educated at Eton. His first published work was a collection of verses honoring Queen ELIZABETH I's visit to the school in 1563. Fletcher was a fellow at King's College, Cambridge University, from which he received his bachelor's degree in 1569. Later he lectured in Greek at King's and also served as public orator, bursar, and, in 1580, dean of arts. In 1581 he married Joan Sheafer; among their seven children were the writers Giles FLETCHER, Jr., and Phineas FLETCHER. After his marriage, Fletcher and his family settled in Cranbrook. In 1584 he was elected to Parliament from Winchelsea, and he was later appointed by the Queen as Remembrancer of the City of London, an office that required him to write letters and other official correspondence.

Fletcher's most renowned work is *Of the Russe Common Wealth: The History of Russia, or, The Government of the Emperour of Muscovia: With the Manners and Fashions of the People of that Countrey.* The work represents the first comprehensive overview of Russia published in English and continues to be of interest to scholars; in fact, it was included in a 2001 anthology of Elizabethan-era travel writing. Fletcher's account was a firsthand one, derived from his diplomatic service as the English ambassador to Russia in 1588. Fletcher was not treated well by the Russians, and the book's publication was initially suppressed in England by commercial interests who feared that Fletcher's candid comments might have a negative impact on trade relations. It was not published in its entirety until 1856.

Fletcher wrote other historical works, including *Israel Redux, or The Restauration of Israel, Exhibited in Two Short Treatises* (1609–11), in which he maintained that the Tartars were the 10 lost tribes of Israel. He also wrote a history of King Richard III, using Sir Thomas MORE and Raphael HOLINSHED as source material. A collection of Fletcher's verse, *Licia, or Poems of Love,* based on Latin verse forms, appeared anonymously in 1593. It includes an oft-quoted sonnet on the frailty of life and the constancy of love, which begins, "In time the strong and stately turrets fall, / In time the rose and silver lilies die . . .'"

After his service in Moscow, Fletcher unsuccessfully tried to secure access to public records so that he could write a Latin history of Queen Elizabeth's reign. Later in the 1590s, he helped negotiate a commercial treaty with the Netherlands. After the Essex rebellion in 1601, in which Robert Devereux, the Earl of Essex, tried to seize the throne from Elizabeth I, Fletcher fell out of favor with the court and was arrested. Though he did not participate in the rebellion, he wrote a letter that suggested that Sir Walter RALEIGH caused Devereux's downfall. He died on March 11, 1611.

A Work about Giles Fletcher

Hadfield, Andrew, ed. *Amazons, Savages, and Machiavels: Travel and Colonial Writing in English, 1550–1630: An Anthology.* Oxford, U.K.: Oxford University Press, 2001.

Fletcher, John (1579–1625) *playwright*

John Fletcher was born in Rye, Sussex, England, to Elizabeth Holland and Richard Fletcher; his father was a prominent clergyman until he fell out of favor with Queen ELIZABETH I. Fletcher apparently entered Cambridge University in 1591, earning a master's degree in 1598. Afterward, he moved to London, but nothing else is known of his life until he published the romantic comedy *The Woman Hater* with Francis BEAUMONT in 1607. The following year saw the performance of Fletcher's *The Faithful Shepherdess.* As the title suggests, the play is a pastoral—that is, a play that features country folk, including shepherds and shepherdesses. The plot of *The Faithful Shepherdess* is very complex, involving four couples whose disagreements center mostly on mismatches of chastity and wantonness.

Fletcher's name will forever be linked with that of Beaumont, his friend and collaborator. Indeed, their shared labor produced some of the most popular plays of the time. Seventeenth-century biographer John AUBREY wrote of their close association: "They lived together on the Bankside, not far from the Play-house [presumably the Globe], both batchelors; lay together; had one Wench in the house between them, which they did so admire; the same cloathes and cloake, etc.; between them."

Philaster (1609), Beaumont and Fletcher's first success, is partly a revival of certain elements from the unsuccessful *Faithful Shepherdess.* Questions of jealousy and chastity are featured, and, as in the earlier play, confusion and danger lurk in the woods. The tragicomic plot involves a disinherited prince, Philaster, who listens to lies about his beloved Arathusa's involvement with his page Bellario. In a jealous rage he stabs both of them but, true to Fletcher's rules, no one dies. Forgiveness, marriage, and the restoration of Philaster's status as heir to the throne provide a harmonious ending.

In *The Maid's Tragedy* (1610) a vicious King takes one of the ladies of the court, Evadne, as his mistress. The King arranges to cover up any possible children from the relationship by marrying Evadne to the loyal soldier Amintor, despite his previous engagement to Aspatia, a courtier's daughter. When Evadne reveals the truth to Amintor, his duty to the King prevents him from seeking vengeance. Evadne's brother Melantius is more concerned with family honor than political loyalty, and he forces his sister to take matters into her own hands. Evadne ties the King to the bed; he is convinced that her actions are a "pretty new device" of lovemaking until she stabs him.

A King and No King (1611) explores the theme of sibling incest. Arbaces, king of Iberia, falls in love with his sister Panthea and spends most of the play resisting or guiltily cherishing his feelings. As in many plays by Fletcher and his collaborators, a last-minute plot twist resolves the tension.

These three plays made Beaumont and Fletcher the toasts of the London theater. All three were taken up by the KING'S MEN (William SHAKESPEARE's company), and, as Shakespeare eased into semiretirement, the company hired Beaumont and Fletcher to replace him. Beaumont, however, soon married a rich heiress and retired himself, leaving Fletcher as the principal dramatist of the company.

Fletcher wrote *The Woman's Prize* (1611) (also called *The Tamer Tamed*) as a sequel to Shakespeare's *The Taming of the Shrew* (ca. 1593), the play in which Petruchio had married and tamed the unmanageable ("shrewish") Katherine. In Fletcher's sequel, Katherine has died, and Petruchio has married a woman named Maria, who promises she will do what Katherine "dare[d] not do"—tame Petruchio. It seems Maria accomplishes her goal, but her epilogue, in which she encourages husbands and wives "to love mutually," places "both Sexes" in a state of "due equality."

Fletcher actually collaborated with Shakespeare on two plays, *Two Noble Kinsmen* and *Henry VIII* (both ca. 1613). The plot of *Two Noble Kinsmen*, taken from Geoffrey Chaucer's *The Canterbury Tales*, tells of two imprisoned cousins who fall in love with the same woman; while *Henry VIII* paints a rather flattering portrait of Elizabeth I's father.

Fletcher worked with other dramatists as well, most notably Philip MASSINGER, in such plays as *Sir John van Olden Barnavelt* (1619), *The Custom of the Country* (1620) and *The Wild Goose Chase* (ca. 1621). *Sir John van Olden Barnavelt* was based on recent political events in the Netherlands. *The Custom of the Country*, a bawdy tragicomedy, and *The Wild Goose Chase*, an unconventional romantic comedy in which the young lady Oriana must chase the wandering "wild-goose" Mirabel, were popular but less serious plays.

Fletcher continued writing prolifically until his death. Aubrey reports that Fletcher delayed leaving town to have a new suit made, "and while it was making, fell sick of the plague [that was ravaging London at the time] and died."

Critical Analysis

Although *The Faithful Shepherdess* was a failure on stage and is not widely read today, the printed edition (ca. 1609) contains Fletcher's important explanation of the new genre of tragicomedy: "it wants [lacks] deaths, which is ingough to make it no tragedie, yet brings some neere it, which is ingough to make it no comedie." Additionally, Fletcher indicates that it should include characters of low and high degree. Tragicomedy, as Fletcher and his collaborators developed and popularized it, emphasizes issues of loyalty, morality, and forgiveness, often spotlighting female characters in crucial situations. The comic ending is often touched with irony.

While some of Fletcher's characters may seem unrealistic to modern readers, they serve the playwright's ends, representing certain virtues or vices and advancing the plot. Certain of Fletcher's characters, however, are well developed and complex. The jailer's daughter in *Two Noble Kinsmen* (believed to be entirely Fletcher's creation) is likable as she fulfills her simple tasks, believable as she falls in love, and pitiful as she loses her sanity. Arbaces, the title character in *A King and No King*, is one of the most interesting characters in the plays of Fletcher and his collaborators. Through his asides (speeches supposedly unheard by other characters onstage) and soliloquies (speeches given by a character alone onstage), Beaumont and Fletcher allow the audience to see into Arbaces's troubled mind. After allowing himself to exchange kisses with Panthea, Arbaces admits to himself, "I wade in sin, / And foolishly entice myself along." Two scenes later, he resolves, "I will not do this sin. / I'll press it here till it do break my breast." However, he eventually is controlled by his passions "as the wild ocean that obeys the winds." Especially remarkable is that such a flawed character still gains sympathy from the audience.

Another way of looking at *A King and No King* is to see it as a play that focuses on a monarch who lets his personal vice interfere with ruling the country. Likewise, the character known only as "King" in *The Maid's Tragedy* has followed his passions to the detriment of the state. Amintor and Melantius, both worthy soldiers, are distracted and eventually ruined by the relationship of Evadne and the King. Calianax, a trusted elderly courtier, the holder of a strategic fort, and the father of the wronged Aspatia, spends most of the play stirring up dissension. Writing a scene in which a king is murdered, no matter how justified, was touchy business. Beaumont and Fletcher point out, in the last lines of the play, that "suddene deaths from God are sent" to "lustful Kings"; however, "curst is he that is [the] instrument" used to kill even a bad king.

Another politically sensitive play was *Sir John van Olden Barnavelt.* In one scene of the play, the Prince of Orange is locked out of a meeting of Parliament, which is plotting to revolt against the prince. Such a scene made the Master of the Revels, the government official charged with censoring plays, nervous. He wrote in the margin, "I like not this." The revolt does occur against the haughty prince, but all the rebels, including the attractive ringleader Barnavelt, are put to death. Thus, as scholar Gordon McMullen observes, Fletcher's plays "demonstrate the potential energy of popular unrest in the face of failed responsibility," as well as "the dangers inherent in political instability."

Fletcher's work remained popular until the 18th century and then fell into obscurity. However, both critics and performance companies have recently shown fresh interest in the works of one of the most prolific and popular playwrights of the English RENAISSANCE. According to the biographer Charles L. Squire, "Fletcher was a thorough professional, a master craftsman" who "pleased the audiences of his day and for half a century beyond," and who "can still be read with pleasure and profit."

A Work by John Fletcher

Bowers, Fredson, gen. ed. *The Dramatic Works in the Beaumont and Fletcher Canon.* New York: Cambridge University Press, 1966.

Works about John Fletcher

McMullan, Gordon. *The Politics of Unease in the Plays of John Fletcher.* Amherst: University of Massachusetts Press, 1994.
Squire, Charles L. *John Fletcher.* Boston: Twayne, 1986.

Fletcher, Phineas (1582–1650) *poet*

Phineas Fletcher was born in Cranbrook, Kent, England, to Giles FLETCHER, Sr., author and politician, and Joan Fletcher. He attended Eton and then Cambridge University, from which he received a B.A. in 1604 and an M.A. in 1608.

Fletcher composed most of his poetry in English during his graduate career. As a poet he is chiefly remembered for *The Purple Island, or the Isle of Man,* which is an allegorical (or symbolically representative) poem on the human body and mind, including descriptions of the mind, the veins, and the bones. In 1627 Fletcher published *Locustae Vel Pietas Iesuitica* in Latin, along with an English version, *The Apollyonists;* this was an attack on the Jesuits. In 1628 he revised his erotic poem *Venus and Anchises* and published it under Edmund SPENSER's name as *Brittain's Ida.* This was followed by *Sicelided* (1631), a fanciful and imaginative play about fish; *Joy in Tribulation* (1632); *The Way to Blessedness* (1632); and the *Sylvia Poetica* (1633). Fletcher's final work, *A Father's Testament,* a devotional manual interspersed with several metaphysical (or abstract and speculative) poems, was published posthumously in 1670.

Like other poets of the day, Fletcher wanted to use the pastoral as a means of self-expression, as a source of amusement for his friends, and as a way of advancing his career by showcasing his classical learning as well as traditional religion and politics. His literary antecedents are not difficult to recognize. Apart from the Latin classics, in which he was thoroughly immersed, Fletcher was swept up in the 1590s vogue for epigrams that imitated the Roman satirist Martial. He was so deeply influenced by Edmund Spenser that he rearranged the letters in his own name to spell "Spenser hath life." His eclogues (pastoral poems) show, even in their choice of names, a strong admiration for Spenser's *The Shepheardes Calender*. In his eclogues Fletcher was inspired by the pastorals of Virgil, Sannazaro, and Theocritus. Izaak WALTON described Phineas Fletcher as "an excellent divine, and an excellent angler; and the author of excellent Piscatory Eclogues, in which you shall see the picture of this good man's mind: and I wish mine to be like it."

Florio, John (ca. 1553–1625) *translator*

John Florio was probably born in London to an exiled Italian Protestant family. At the accession of the Catholic queen Mary I (1553), the Florio family had to leave England, and they settled in Switzerland. Florio was probably educated at Tübingen University, Germany, but by 1576 he was again in England (now ruled by the Protestant ELIZABETH I).

In 1578 Florio published an instruction manual for learning Italian, called *First Fruits*. In this book a grammar is supplemented by 44 dialogues, graded in difficulty, and printed in parallel columns in Italian and English. The characters wander around London, buy things, flirt with ladies, invite each other to visit, and discuss life in England. Both *First Fruits* and its sequel, *Second Fruits* (1591), are entertaining and reveal much about Elizabethan life.

For a while Florio taught French and Italian at Oxford University, where he met Samuel DANIEL, who was to become his brother-in-law and lifelong friend. He also met Richard HAKLUYT, for whom he translated Jacques Cartier's account of his first two voyages to North America. But the poorly paid life of an Oxford lecturer did not satisfy Florio's am-

bitions. In 1583 he went to work at the French embassy in London as tutor to the ambassador's young daughter and secretary to the ambassador. In this position he was well placed to build up his network of powerful acquaintances. He also met Giordano BRUNO, who was the ambassador's guest at the time and who figures as a character in some of the dialogues in *Second Fruits*.

Queen Elizabeth made a point of conversing with foreign visitors in their own languages, so interest in learning French and Italian was high among the upper classes. By the 1590s Florio's pupils included Sir Fulke GREVILLE and the Earl of Southampton, patron to many poets, including William SHAKESPEARE. Florio became most noted in his time for his great Italian-English dictionary, *The World of Words* (1598). For this work he drew vocabulary from Italy's great writers but also from specialized works in such fields botany, military strategy, and other fields. The book contains 46,000 definitions, often with six English synonyms for one Italian word, and sometimes a whole paragraph explaining the use of the word by different writers. There is much to be learned about RENAISSANCE English, as well as Italian, from this book. A much expanded version was published in 1611—when Florio was employed as personal secretary to King JAMES I's queen, Anne of Denmark—as *Queen Anna's New World of Words*.

In 1603 Florio published his most influential work: his translation of the *Essays* of Michel de MONTAIGNE. Since English intellectuals were very curious about Montaigne, Florio's book was read everywhere. Ben JONSON owned a copy; Walter RALEIGH had a copy with him in his imprisonment in the Tower of London. Shakespeare, who had earlier made fun of Florio by including him as the comic character Holofernes in *Love's Labors Lost* (1595), made a thorough study of Florio's Montaigne and drew ideas and images from it for his plays.

A Work about John Florio

Yates, Frances. *John Florio: The Life of an Italian in Shakespeare's England.* New York: Octagon Books, 1968.

Ford, John (1586–ca. 1639) *dramatist, poet, pamphleteer*

John Ford was born in Islington, Devonshire, England, to Thomas Ford, a gentleman landowner. There is evidence that he entered Oxford University in 1601 and was associated with the Middle Temple, a legal training institution, from 1602 onwards.

Before embarking on his dramatic career, Ford wrote several occasional poems (dealing with specific events or observances), including *Fame's Memorial* (1606), an elegy on the death of the Earl of Devonshire. Several Ford pamphlets, such as *Honour Triumphant* (1606) and *The Golden Mean* (1613), discuss moral virtues. His major works, however, were his plays, written later in his life.

The Witch of Edmonton (1621) was a collaboration with William ROWLEY and Thomas DEKKER. Based on historical events, this play tells the story of Elizabeth Salter, who had been executed only months earlier as a witch. A subplot, believed to have been written by Ford, features a man who commits bigamy in order to save the family land.

Ford's most popular works, sometimes termed "tragedies of forbidden love," are *The Broken Heart* (ca. 1629), *'Tis Pity She's a Whore* (ca. 1630), and *Love's Sacrifice* (ca. 1631). The main plot of *The Broken Heart* involves a woman who is pressured by her family into a loveless marriage. To this extent, it is believed to reflect the real-life events elsewhere described in Sir Philip SIDNEY's sonnet sequence *Astrophil and Stella*. The play's heroine, Penthea (whose name suggests Penelope Devereux, Sidney's real-life "Stella") has been ordered by her brother Ithocles to marry a repulsive older man, Bassanes. Bassanes's irrational jealousy motivates him to accuse the siblings of incest, causing the touching and violent ending.

In *'Tis Pity She's a Whore* the incest is real. By the second scene, brother and sister Giovanni and Annabella have entered into an incestuous relationship. As they emerge from their chamber together, Giovanni speaks to Annabella:

> *Come, Annabella: no more sister now,*
> *But love, a name more gracious; do not blush,*

> *Beauty's sweet wonder, but be proud to know*
> *That yielding thou hast conquered, and inflamed*
> *A heart whose tribute is thy brother's life.*

This speech shows the intensity of the emotions in the relationship and also foreshadows the violent ending, one of the most shocking in RENAISSANCE theater.

Love's Sacrifice seems largely to be a reworking of William SHAKESPEARE's *Othello*. Shakespeare tells the story of a husband, Othello, who unjustly suspects his wife Desdemona of committing adultery with a trusted friend due to the evil influence of the villain Iago. In Ford's play, however, the main character, Caraffa, has reason to suspect his wife Bianca of having an affair with his best friend Fernando because the two are actually in love. However, they are determined not to act on their feelings. The character of D'Avolos plays the Iago figure; his language quite closely parallels that of Shakespeare's villain.

The "forbidden love" (incest or adultery) themes in these three plays and the intense suffering and violence the characters endure have created a variety of reactions in modern readers. Ford's plays have often been said to exemplify the "decadence" of late Renaissance theater. The scholar Roland Wymer points out Ford's odd position in history, following playwrights such as Christopher MARLOWE, Shakespeare, and John WEBSTER: "All writers of tragedy must engage with and surpass their predecessors in order to achieve the desired emotional effects." The controversial and shocking elements in Ford's plays are thus his way of reaching the audience of his day.

Quite different from Ford's other plays is the history *Perkin Warbeck* (1632). This work stages a true story from English history, featuring, as Ford's prologue notes, "the threats of majesty, the strength of passion, hopes of an empire, [and] change of fortunes." The title character Ford creates is much more appealing than the historical

Warbeck, who pretended he was heir to the throne in order to depose his enemy, Henry VII. Ford's character, however, as the scholar Norman Rabkin states, is "an attractive rebel" whose "belief in the truth of his cause radically changes the way in which one must respond to him." By presenting such a likable character who nevertheless had no real claim to the throne, the play subtly raises questions about hereditary monarchy.

Perkin Warbeck was Ford's last important play and has retained the interest of scholars through the years. *The Broken Heart* and, especially, *'Tis Pity She's a Whore* have been performed with some regularity. The biographer Donald K. Anderson finds a common ground between *Perkin Warbeck* and the tragedies of forbidden love. In Anderson's words, Ford "puts us in the ambivalent position of admiring an attractive champion of an unacceptable cause," producing a drama that is both "provocative and esthetically satisfying."

Other Work by John Ford

'Tis Pity She's a Whore and Other Plays. Edited by
    Marion Lomax. New York: Oxford University
    Press 1995.

A Work about John Ford

Hopkins, Lisa. *John Ford's Political Theatre.* New York:
    St. Martin's Press, 1994.

Fortescue, John (ca. 1531–1607) *nonfiction writer*

John Fortescue, second cousin to ELIZABETH I, was the eldest son of Sir Adrian Fortescue (executed in 1539 for his commitment to the Catholic Church) and his second wife, Anne Reade. During the reign of Mary I, Fortescue was a tutor to his cousin, Princess Elizabeth. When Elizabeth became queen in 1558, she appointed Fortescue keeper of the great wardrobe, an appointment that proved the beginning of a long and fruitful political career. He went on to serve in Parliament beginning in 1572. In 1589 he was appointed chancellor of the exchequer—that is, the English treasury—and be-

came a member of the queen's advisory committee, the Privy Council.

After Elizabeth's death, Fortescue suggested that JAMES I OF ENGLAND's powers be restricted, possibly in an attempt to limit the king's ability to appoint Scots to positions in the English government. His suggestion was ignored, and he was removed from his position as chancellor of the exchequer. He seems, however, to have retained the king's favor, for he entertained James a number of times at his home.

Having devoted his life to public service, Fortescue wrote simply to fulfill his duties, and his existing writings reveal the often boring nature of those duties. In July 1591, for instance, he wrote to the officers of the Custom House, London and informed them that the government was aware "that Great quantities of cloths, kersies &c., are weekly conveyed overland to divers ports, and thence exported, and small customs paid." He went on to direct the officers "to see that, before any person carries cloth or other wares from London to be exported, he delivers to them a true entry of the same, in the owner's name, with the place to which they are carried."

There is little scholarship on Fortescue, and no edition of his speeches. There is a manuscript of his letters in the British Library. No other manuscripts appear to exist. However, as Fortescue was a major political figure, his speeches, lost or not, were important political documents during his lifetime.

Fowler, Constance Aston (ca. 1621–1664) *nonfiction writer, poet*

Constance Aston Fowler was probably born in Tixall, Staffordshire, England, the youngest daughter of the 10 children of Walter, Lord Aston, Baron of Forfor, and Gertrude Sadlier Aston, his second wife. Both the Astons and the Sadliers were prominent and influential families with connections to the royal family. Aston married Walter Fowler when she was 14 years old.

Constance Fowler began writing at an early age, keeping, from the time of her youthful marriage, a commonplace book, or scrapbook, in which she included poetry and letters. She soon found herself at the center of a literary group that included her mother; her brother, Herbert Aston; and her sister, Gertrude ASTON Thimelby; as well as Katherine THIMELBY; several other women; and the CAVALIER poet Richard FANSHAWE. Fowler, serving as an unofficial editor and publisher for the group, collected and circulated their works, which included original works and copies of the works of other writers that the group members liked. Many of the poems Fowler included in her commonplace book were religious in nature, relating to her Catholic faith. Others were about family members, friends, and miscellaneous subjects. Four of the religious poems were by the imprisoned Jesuit Robert SOUTHWELL, and others were similar to those penned by the metaphysical poet John DONNE. The works she chose show her fondness for wordplay, alliteration, and metaphysical conceits, or extended comparisons.

In her introduction to *The Verse Miscellany of Constance Aston Fowler* (2000), Deborah Aldrich-Watson writes that "Aston's volume . . . provides the present-day reader with a document important to the study of creative thought in early modern women, as well as to the study of manuscript transmission among women and seventeenth-century literary society in general." Another literary historian, H. R. Woudhuysen, has termed her manuscript "one of the important collections of verses put together by families."

Though none of the poems in her commonplace book have been definitively attributed to Fowler, it seems probable that she may have authored a few of them, including one entitled "On the Passion of our Lord and saviour Iesus," which expresses personal remorse for the sufferings inflicted upon Christ. It concludes, "Once euery day to fix a sorrowed Looke / vpon the place, and say o there I strooke: / His sacred flesh thus all to peices torne."

Other Work by Constance Aston Fowler

The Verse Miscellany of Constance Aston Fowler. Edited by Deborah Aldrich Watson. Tempe: Arizona Center for Medieval and Renaissance Studies in conjunction with Renaissance English Text Society, 2000.

Fox, George (1624–1691) *nonfiction writer*

The son of a weaver, George Fox was born in Leicester, England. He was apprenticed to a shoemaker but left home when he was 19 "at the command of God," as he explains in his *Journal* (1694). Opposed to state control of the CHURCH OF ENGLAND, he traveled around the country, eventually discovering that his purpose in life was to proclaim the gospel. He gave sermons and formed a group called The Friends of Truth, which was soon nicknamed the Quakers but later came to be known as the Society of Friends. He married the widow Margaret FELL in 1669. The central tenet of the religion he promoted was that each individual possessed an inner light that was conveyed directly to his soul by Christ. The convictions of Fox and his adherents led them to refuse to honor officials or to pay tithes, actions that resulted in their frequent persecution and imprisonment. By the time of Fox's death, however, the Quakers had received some relief from maltreatment through the Toleration Act of 1689.

Fox's *Journal,* compiled and published by William Penn three years after Fox's death, is his most compelling literary work. The piece portrays his personal experiences, recounting a number of important events in the rise of Quakerism while at the same time providing a unique account of 17th-century England. In one interesting incident, Fox attends a service in Leicester in which the preacher tells the congregation that they may ask questions. When a woman of the parish speaks, however, the minister chastises her, saying, "I permit not a woman to speak in the church." Fox is outraged by this and disputes with the minister, who is so upset that he actually comes down from his pulpit. (As Quakerism developed in later years, it became unique in the freedom it granted to its female adherents.) Although Fox's *Journal* also contains numerous lengthy and dry passages, it has been well received and published in numerous editions over the past 300 years.

Fox was also a prolific letter writer, and much of his correspondence has been published as well, most recently *The Power of the Lord Is Over All: The Pastoral Letters of George Fox* (1989). The letters primarily address theological questions and explicate the path that Fox's followers should take. Sometimes the proclamations he makes are of a broadly religious nature: "Friends, everyone of you having a Light from the Son of God, wait in it, that you may . . . receive Power from him to be the sons of God [by] faith in him." At other times Fox marks out distinct, concrete actions that his "Friends" should or should not undertake. For instance, in a letter condemning sloth, he proclaims that beggars should not be "suffered to wander," but should "be kept in diligence"—that is, provided with work to do. Fox even wrote letters on such subjects as whether or not Quakers should wear hats at prayer. Fox spent his final years in London continuing to preach until just days before he died, on January 13, 1691.

A Work about George Fox

Bailey, Richard. *New Light on George Fox and Early Quakerism: The Making and Unmaking of a God.* San Francisco: Mellen Research University Press, 1992.

Fox, Margaret

See FELL, MARGARET.

Foxe, John (1516–1587) *nonfiction writer*

John Foxe was born in Boston, Lincolnshire, England, to a prosperous middle-class family. He was educated at Magdalen College, Oxford University, and subsequently became a clergyman and fellow (lecturer) there. According to some accounts, he was forced to leave Oxford because of doctrinal differences with his superiors. The CHURCH OF ENGLAND had broken away from the Roman Catholic Church in the 1530s, but Foxe's Protestantism was more radical than that of some of his superiors.

Foxe found employment as tutor to the children of the recently beheaded Henry Howard, Earl of SURREY, and stayed with the family for five years. During this time he published several religious tracts, and after the accession of the Catholic queen Mary I (1553), he felt it necessary to flee to the Continent. He made a living as a printer's proofreader, but he continued writing. In Strasbourg, France, he published *Commentarii Rerum in Ecclesia Gestarum* (1554), a 212-page work in Latin about the persecution of reformers from the time of John Wycliffe in the late 14th century to 1500. Foxe was in touch with refugees from England and was brought news of the more than 300 people who were burned alive for heresy during Mary's brief reign. All he heard went into his great work on Protestant MARTYRS, which was published in Latin in Basel, Switzerland, in 1559.

After ELIZABETH I's accession to the throne (1559), Foxe returned to England. He spent some years living in the home of the Duke of Norfolk, one of his former pupils, who settled an annuity of 20 pounds a year on him. Although this amount continued to be paid after the duke had been executed for conspiring with Mary, Queen of Scots, and although he had a minor appointment at the cathedral of Salisbury, Foxe remained poor all his life.

The first English edition of *Acts and Monuments* was published in London in 1563, in four volumes totaling about 1,800 pages. It became known at once as the *Book of Martyrs*. There were many subsequent editions, which grew in scope. For example, the 1570 edition had more than 2,300 pages. Although it covers a period that includes the early Christian Church, the accounts of the sufferings of Protestants in the 16th century, including the painful deaths of Anne BOLEYN and Thomas CRANMER, were what drew the attention of Foxe's contemporaries. Written in a direct, homely style, and illustrated copiously with gruesome woodcuts of the tortures described, the book had mass appeal. Queen Elizabeth even ordered that a copy be placed in all the colleges and chapels throughout her kingdom. Foxe's work did much to foment English anti-Catholicism.

The scholar Charles Whibley comments in *The Cambridge History of English Literature* that "it is idle . . . to expect accuracy or a quiet statement from Foxe." He goes on:

> The dramatic turn which Foxe gives to his dialogues, the vitality of the innumerable men and women, tortured and torturers, who throng his pages—these are qualities which do not fade with years. Even the spirit of bitter raillery which breathes through his pages amazes, while it exasperates, the reader.

Foxe is still an icon for evangelical Protestantism. Many editions of *The Book of Martyrs* are in print today.

Works about John Foxe

Highley, Christopher, and John N. King, eds. *John Fox and His World.* Burlington, Vt.: Ashgate, 2002.

Loades, David, ed. *John Foxe: An Historical Perspective.* Burlington, Vt.: Ashgate, 2002.

Wooden, Warren W. *John Foxe.* Boston: Twayne, 1983.

Fraunce, Abraham (ca. 1558–1633) *poet*

Born in Shrewsbury, Shropshire, England, Abraham Fraunce was educated at Shrewsbury school. Sir Philip SIDNEY, who had entered the same school eight years before, took an interest in Fraunce and sent him to St. John's College, Cambridge University, where he earned his M.A. degree in 1583. Fraunce became a protégé of Sidney, and this relationship would last until Sidney's death in 1568. Sidney's sister, the Countess of Pembroke, to whom most of Fraunce's works are dedicated, then took up his PATRONAGE. After 1588 Fraunce practiced law, although his first love was always poetry.

Fraunce became intimate with the literary circle which included Edmund SPENSER, Sir Edward DYER, and Gabriel HARVEY. All of his verse was written in classical hexameters (verse lines of six feet, or accented syllables). This made his poetry rather awkward for reading, because the natural rhythm of English tends to be better expressed in iambic pentameter; nonetheless Fraunce's skill as a poet was highly commended by many of his contemporaries at the time. However, changes in literary taste resulted in a loss of popularity for Fraunce and others who wrote in hexameters. Ben JONSON had stronger feelings about it than most, saying, "Abram Francis in his English hexameters was a fool."

In 1587 Fraunce published his first work, *The Lamentations of a myntas for the death of Phyllis.* Fraunce's reputation exists today mainly because of his *Arcadian Rhetorike* (1588), a critical textbook designed to illustrate the beauties of Sir Philip Sidney's *Arcadia.* Fraunce also wrote *The Lawiers Logike* (1588), illustrating logic in law; and *The Countesse of Pembrokes Emanuel* (1591), a book of verse. The Latin comedy *Victoria* is also attributed to Fraunce, most likely written while he was still a student at St. John's College.

Fuller, Francis (1637–1701) *nonfiction writer*

Francis Fuller was born in London. His father was John Fuller, a minister. Fuller received his master's degree from Cambridge University in 1660, became a preacher, and settled in Cheapside, England. It was there that he began his writing career.

Fuller's works are mainly of a religious nature. A *Treatise of Faith and Repentance* (1684) is a deep meditation on faith that reminds readers that "Faith and repentance are necessary conditions required on our part." Similarly, in *A Treatise of Grace and Duty* (1688) Fuller deals with the idea of religious conditions and obligations, stating that "there are two things that keep up friendship betwixt God and us, the receipt of grace from him, and the return of duty to him."

Fuller also published several sermons in a shorter pamphlet format, including *Peace in War by Christ the Prince of Peace* (1696). Fuller's son, also named Francis (1670–1706), went on to write important works about exercise.

Fuller, Thomas (1608–1661) *nonfiction writer*

Thomas Fuller was an Anglican clergyman known as a staunch supporter of the Crown during the English Civil Wars of 1642–51. He was born at Aldwincle in Northamptonshire, England, and educated at Queens College, Cambridge University. In 1641 he was appointed as preacher at the Chapel Royal in London. In 1643, with the first of the English civil wars underway, he left for the Royalist headquarters at Oxford, where he served as a chaplain to the army of Charles I. In 1646 he wrote *Andronicus, or the Unfortunate Politician,* a satire that humorously criticizes Oliver Cromwell, the leader of the parliamentary forces during the war.

Considered by many literary historians to be his most popular work, Fuller's *The Holy and Profane State* (1642) is a collection of humorous character sketches that describe ideal types of people, including the good merchant, the good husband, and the true gentleman, as well as profane (or irreverent) types, including the atheist and the witch. He describes the good yeoman as "a gentleman in ore, whom the next age may see refined; and is the wax capable of a gentle impression, when the prince shall stamp it." Fuller's work is biographical in that many of these characters are based on historical figures. For instance, his "good sea captain" draws on the life of Sir Francis Drake.

Fuller's writing, while entertaining, attempts to serve as moral instruction. In fact, in his *History of Englich Humour,* Alfred Guy L'Estrange notes that for early British humorists, including Fuller, "Pleasantry was with them little more than a vehicle of instruction; the object was not to entertain, but to enforce and illustrate their moral sentiments."

Fuller's other most popular work, *The Worthies of England* (published in 1662, after his death), is a collection of biographical descriptions of important English people as well as a compilation of antiquarian information on various countries of the world. In this book he describes the "Lark" as "a harmless bird while living, not trespassing on grain, and wholesome when dead, then filling the stomach with meat, as formerly the ear with music." Fuller also includes a chronicle of English proverbs, a task for which he is well known. Such proverbs include "Enquire not what boils in another's pot," "Learning makes a man fit company for himself"; "Some have been thought brave because they were afraid to run away"; and "No man can be happy without a friend, nor be sure of his friend until he is unhappy."

Some of Fuller's other works include *Church History of Britain* (1655) and *The Holy War* (1639). Many of his contemporaries admired Thomas Fuller's wit and historical knowledge. English poet and critic Samuel Taylor Coleridge praised him for "surpassing that of the wittiest in a witty age" and for his "sound, shrewd good sense and freedom of intellect."

Garth, Samuel (1661–1719) *poet*

Samuel Garth was born in Yorkshire, England, to William Garth, a landowner, and his wife. Garth received both a bachelor's and master's at Cambridge before he began studying medicine at the University of Leiden. In 1691, after some traveling, Garth returned to Cambridge and received a doctorate of medicine. He was subsequently elected a fellow at the Royal College of Physicians in 1693, where he became a censor (an officer who grants licenses) of the college. It was his role at the college that inspired his greatest and most remembered poem, *The Dispensary* (1699).

The *Dispensary* is a response to and critique of the controversy that raged in the late 17th and early 18th centuries between the Royal College of Physicians and the Society of Apothecaries, or pharmacists. For many years the Royal College had controlled apothecaries to prevent them from practicing medicine without licenses, therefore limiting their income to what they earned as pharmacists. The issue came to a head in 1698, when the Royal College opened a dispensary, a place where medicine and medical help were distributed at a low cost to the poor. The apothecaries were outraged that medication was being distributed so inexpensively, and it is this out-

rage that Garth deals with in his poem. The poem is a mock-epic, a poem that treats an ordinary debate in a grand heroic style, and, as such, it influenced another, much more famous mock epic, Alexander Pope's *The Rape of the Lock*. More important, *The Dispensary* was a model for the sort of rhyming couplet and poetic diction that became so popular with Pope and other poets in the 18th century. In *The Dispensary* the god Sloth attempts to disrupt the harmony between the apothecaries and the Royal College by sending Envy to create tension. Here Mirmillo, a surgeon, boasts like an epic hero of his prowess at killing patients.

> *Oxford and all her passing Bells can tell,*
> *By this Right Arm, what mighty Numbers*
>   *fell.*
> *Whilst others meanly ask'd whole Months*
>   *to slay,*
> *I oft dispatch'd the Patient in a Day.*

The Dispensary was extremely successful at the time it was published and went through 10 editions. Although Garth never gained the acclaim of Pope, *The Dispensary* ensured that he will continue to be remembered as an influential satirist and writer.

Works about Samuel Garth

Sena, Joseph F. *The Best-Natured Man: Sir Samuel Garth, Physician and Poet.* New York: AMS Press, 1986.

Cook, Richard I. *Sir Samuel Garth.* Boston: Twayne, 1980.

Gascoigne, George (ca. 1525–1577) *poet, playwright, prose writer*

George Gascoigne was born in Cardington, Bedfordshire, England, the eldest child of Sir John Gascoigne, a well-connected landowner. He was educated at Cambridge University and later enrolled at Gray's Inn in London to study law. He was present at ELIZABETH I's coronation in 1558 and spent much of his life thereafter attempting to win a position at court. In 1561 he met and married a wealthy widow, Elizabeth Bretton. Unfortunately a prior engagement of Elizabeth's involved Gascoigne in a costly lawsuit brought by her rejected fiancé.

There was a lively interest in literature, especially drama, at Gray's Inn. Gascoigne and another law student, Francis Kinwelmarshe, collaborated on a play: a translation of Lodovico Dolce's Italian version of *The Phoinissae* by Euripides, which they entitled *Jocasta*. It tells the story of the tragic queen who was the mother and wife of Oedipus and was the first representation of any Greek drama to appear in English. The play was produced at Gray's Inn and was followed soon after by a play Gascoigne completed alone, a comedy he entitled *Supposes*. This too is a translation from an Italian work, *I Suppositi* by Ludovico ARIOSTO, but the translation is far from slavish. Ariosto wrote two versions of the play, one in prose and one in verse; Gascoigne evidently studied carefully and drew from both, alternating prose and verse in his version. William SHAKESPEARE drew the subplot for *The Taming of the Shrew* from this play.

Gascoigne made little progress at Gray's Inn in the study of law. An autobiographical poem composed later in life, "The Green Knight's Farewell to Fansie," devotes a stanza to each of his early efforts

to find a career: the pursuit of courtly success, farming, writing, soldiering. The first stanza gives a feeling for his tone:

> The gloss of gorgeous courts, by thee did
>   please mine eye,
> A stately sight me thought it was, to see the
>   brave go by:
> To see their feathers flaunt, to marke their
>   straunge device,
> To lie along in ladies lap, to lisp and make
>   it nice:
> To fawn and flatter both, I liked sometimes
>   well,
> But since I see how vain it is, Fancy (quoth
>   he) farewell.

By 1570 Gascoigne had been imprisoned for debt. It may have been to escape his creditors that in 1571 he volunteered for the army and was sent to serve in the Netherlands. Holland had been annexed by Spain, and England was backing a Dutch rebellion against the hated Spanish overlords, the so-called War of the Spanish Succession. Gascoigne probably hoped to make his name as a military officer and his fortune as well. He made neither; this first excursion to the Netherlands resulted in the antiwar poem *Dulce Bellum Inexpertis* ("War is sweet to those who have not experienced it"), which points out how little heroism and how much cowardice, greed, and bribery are involved in war as it is fought in the real world.

Gascoigne's best-known work is a collection he put together and published in 1571, *A Hundreth Sundrie Flowres,* probably in the hope of attracting the attention of a patron (*see* PATRONAGE). The collection contains the texts of *Jocasta* and *Supposes;* a large collection of poems in various styles and on various topics—hunting, love, gardens, friendship, among others; and an unusual, in fact unprecedented, work, *The Adventures of Master F. J.*—the first secular prose narrative to be published in English. It tells of a young man who spends a summer visiting relatives in the north of England, falls in love with a married woman, seduces her, and as the summer draws to a close is rejected by her in favor of another lover. It is told in passages of prose narrative and of witty dialogue alternating with poems that advance the story.

A Hundreth Sundrie Flowres failed to find a patron and got Gascoigne into trouble. In fact, it was banned by the Queen's Commissioners because of "wanton speeches and lascivious phrases." For Gascoigne's revised and enlarged edition, *The Posies of George Gascoigne Esquire* (1575), he took out some poems, added new ones, took out sexually explicit sections of *The Adventures of Master F. J.,* and changed the story's setting from England to Italy so that he could claim it was a translation and not his own work. But even this version displeased the censors.

After this experience Gascoigne's works took on a more sober cast. He wrote a play, *The Glass of Government* (1575), set in the Netherlands, which tells of two pairs of brothers who succumb to the temptations that beset youth and come to a bad end. The two fathers are left to grieve for their lost boys and to find comfort in the virtuous survivors. The moralizing strain is tempered by lively dialogue and a sympathetic understanding of how exuberance, innocence, and a longing for experience can lead the young into trouble.

The Steel Glass (1576), a satire about corruption in English society, looks back nostalgically to an earlier time when the social hierarchy was clearer and people paid more attention to their obligations. It evidently reflects Gascoigne's bitterness at being unable to find his own place in the social upheaval of Tudor society, but its wealth of realistic detail makes it lively. In technical terms, after Lord Surrey's translation of Virgil, it is the first nondramatic English poem to be written in blank verse (unrhymed iambic pentameter) and as such foreshadows the work of John Milton.

In 1576 Gascoigne's long search for a government position bore fruit. He was employed by Elizabeth's chancellor, Lord Burghley, to go to the Netherlands on a fact-finding mission. There he was a witness to the total breakdown of law and order due to a mutiny in the wealthy Dutch city of Antwerp. Gascoigne wrote a prose pamphlet about it, *The Spoyle of Antwerp* (1577), which his biographer, C. T. Prouty, describes as "an early example of news reporting." It includes vivid descriptions of the cruelties of war and some self-deprecating humor. In a passage describing the movements of a panicking crowd, Gascoigne writes:

> I might see a great troupe coming in greater haste . . . as . . . a flock of sheep: who met me on the farther of the Bourse . . . and . . . bare me over backwards, and ran over my belly and my face, long time before I could recover on foot. At last when I was up, I . . . began thus to bethink me. What in God's name do I here which have no interest in this action? . . . And whilst I stood thus musing, another flock of flyers came so fast that they bare me on my nose, and ran as many over my back, as erst had marched over my guts.

In fact, Gascoigne's actions in Antwerp helped save the English Merchant Aventurers' House in Antwerp, where he was staying, from being sacked by looters. Thus, his government position was secure on his return. But he was not to enjoy this success for long before he died of an unknown illness.

Other Work by George Gascoigne
A Hundreth Sundrie Flowres. Edited by George Pigman III. Oxford, U.K.: Oxford University Press, 2000.

A Work about George Gascoigne
Johnson, Ronald C. *George Gascoigne.* New York: Twayne, 1972.

Gerard, John (1545–1612) *nonfiction writer*
John Gerard was born in Nantwich, Cheshire, England, and educated at nearby Willaston. He studied medicine and was connected with the Barber-Surgeons' Company (a guild) from 1562 on. He was an herbalist (one who uses herbs for

healing) as well as superintendent of gardens for Lord Burghley, the Elizabethan statesman.

Gerard's first publication, a *Catalogue of the Plants Cultivated in the Garden of John Gerard* (1596), is the first known catalogue of any garden. He followed this with his very popular *Herball or Generall Historie of Plantes* (1597), which is partly a translation of Rembert Dodoens's *Pemptades,* but which Gerard adapted to describe the location of rare plants. He describes his work in his Proem, or preface: "In three books therefore, as in three gardens, all our plants are bestowed: sorted as near as might be, in kindred and neighborhood." The first book is for grasses, the second for herbs, and the third "hath trees, shrubs, bushes, fruit-bearing plants, Rosins, Gums, Roses, Heath, Mosses, Mushrooms, Coral, and their several kinds."

Gerard's work was in a tradition of herbals that began in ancient Greece and was not the first of its kind. However, it was among the first in early modern English and was highly regarded for several generations. The book remains significant to us for the beauty of its 1,800 woodcuts, including what is believed to be the first-ever picture of a potato, as well as for the historical information it provides about plants and their uses. The Swedish botanist Carl Linnaeus paid Gerard the compliment of naming after him the herb *Gerardia,* which is found in North America.

Gibbons, Orlando (1583–1625) *composer, poet*

Orlando Gibbons was born in Oxford, England, the youngest of four sons of the musician William Gibbons. Gibbons's brother Edward was master of choristers at King's College, Cambridge University, and Gibbons was a chorister there for several years in the 1590s. He became a student at the university in 1598 but did not receive his bachelor of music degree until eight years later. In 1603 he entered the service of the new king, JAMES I OF ENGLAND, as a musician at the Chapel Royal, advancing to senior organist by 1625. In 1606 he married Elizabeth Patten, whose father was an official of the

Chapel Royal and with whom he had seven children. He died suddenly at Canterbury, where he had gone with the royal entourage of King Charles I to meet Charles's new queen, Henrietta Maria, who was arriving from France.

Gibbons was most famous in his time as a virtuoso keyboard player, but as a composer he attracted the respect of the great William BYRD, who collaborated with him on a collection of keyboard pieces, *Parthenia* (1613). His first published collection of music was *Madrigals and Motets* (1612). He also wrote sacred choral music. However, it is as a composer of madrigals—secular songs for four to six solo voices—that Gibbons is remembered today. The words he set to music are mostly by unknown poets, though one of the pieces in *Madrigals and Motets* is Sir Walter RALEIGH's "What Is Our Life?" which had not been previously published. This song compares life playfully to a turn on the stage, concluding with a sudden change of mood. "Only we die in earnest, that's no jest." The text of his most famous madrigal, "The Silver Swan," is thought to have been written by Gibbons himself:

> The silver swan, who living had no note.
> When death approach'd, unlock'd her silent
>   throat;
> Leaning her breast against the ready shore,
> Thus sung her first and last, and sung no
>   more.
> Farewell, all joys; O Death, come close mine
>   eyes;
> More geese than swans now live, more fools
>   than wise.

A Work about Orlando Gibbons

Harley, John. *Orlando Gibbons and the Gibbons Family of Musicians.* Brookfield, Vt.: Ashgate, 1999.

Gilbert, Humphrey (ca. 1539–1583) *nonfiction writer*

Sir Humphrey Gilbert, the second of Otho and Katherine Gilbert's four children, was born in southern England at Greenway on the River Dart. Katherine later remarried following Otho's death and give birth to three more children, including Gilbert's half brother and fellow explorer Sir Walter RALEIGH. Gilbert was educated at Eton College and Oxford University before entering into the service of Princess Elizabeth, later to be Queen ELIZABETH I, in 1555. He joined the military in 1562, fighting at New Haven and in Ireland, where he put down rebellions and obtained the rank of colonel.

Gilbert had long been interested in maritime discovery, and in 1566 he wrote *The Discourse of a North-West Passage,* which was published by the poet George GASCOIGNE 10 years later as a pamphlet entitled *A Discourse of a Discoverie for a New Passage to Cataia [China].* In this treatise, Gilbert attempts to prove the existence of a Northwest Passage to China; encourages a search for this passage, stressing the various advantages to be obtained from trade with China; and suggests that "we might inhabit some part of [Asia and America] and settle there such needy people of our country which now trouble in the Commonwealth, and . . . are inforsed to commit outragious offences whereby they are dayly consumed of the gallows." Following its publication in 1576, *Discourse* inspired the voyages of Martin Frobisher and John DAVIS, and subsequently helped set into motion various other attempts at finding the Northwest Passage.

In the intervening years between the writing of *The Discourse* and Gilbert's first expedition in 1578, he was knighted for military service in Munster, Ireland, was elected to Parliament, and fought in the Netherlands. In 1573 he presented to Queen Elizabeth a plan for a military academy, in an unpublished treatise entitled *Queen Elizabeth's Academy,* although such a plan would not come to fruition until centuries later. Gilbert also wrote the unpublished manuscript *Discourse How Hir Majesty may annoy the King of Spain* in 1577, in which he suggested plans by which the English might undermine Spanish power over trade routes.

Upon securing a patent from Queen Elizabeth in 1578, Gilbert set out to found an English colony in America. His first attempt failed, and in 1583 he and his crew set sail once again, this time arriving in and taking possession of Newfoundland. While returning to England, his vessel disappeared at sea. The influential *Discource of a Discoverie for a New Passage to Cataia* remains Gilbert's only published work out of the "commendable exercises perfected by his own penne," referred to by Gascoigne.

Gilbert, William (1544–1603) *nonfiction writer*

William Gilbert was born in Colchester, Essex, England, to Elizabeth and Jerome (or Hierome) Gilbert, a prosperous magistrate. He attended Cambridge University, earning a bachelor's degree in 1561, a master's in 1564, and eventually a doctor of medicine degree in 1569. Sometime during the 1570s, Gilbert opened a medical practice in London, where he became much sought after by the aristocracy. Elected president of the Royal College of Physicians, he was appointed personal physician to Queen ELIZABETH I and later King JAMES I.

In addition to his work as a physician, Gilbert also studied magnetism. In fact, he spent 17 years developing his six-volume treatise *De Magnete, Magneticisque Corporibus, et de Magno Magnete Tellure (On the Magnet, Magnetic Bodies, and the Great Magnet of the Earth,* 1600), which quickly became the standard comprehensive work on electricity and magnetism throughout Europe. The work begins with a declaration by Gilbert about his use of the scientific method of hypothesis and experimentation.

> In follies and fables do philosophers of the vulgar sort take delight; and with such like do they cram readers a-hungered for things obtruse, and every ignorant gaper for nonsense. But when the nature of the lodestone [magnetic iron ore] shall have been by our labours and experiments tested, then will the hidden and recondite but real causes of this great effect be brought forward, proven, demonstrated . . . and the foundations of a grand magnetic science

being laid will appear anew, so that high intellect may no more be deluded by vain opinions.

In this work, Gilbert was the first to distinguish between magnetism and the so-called amber effect (static electricity). He goes on to outline a theory of magnetism based on a comparison of the earth's polarity, or magnetic field, with that of a magnet. Among Gilbert's contributions to the study of magnetism is the first scientific explanation of the ability of a compass needle to point north. Gilbert came to his conclusions by conducting many experiments over the years, including one that debunked the myth that garlic could affect the function of a compass. Gilbert's experiments led to the conclusion that, when aligned with the earth's poles, a perfectly spherical lodestone would spin on its axis, just as the earth does. This idea challenged the belief current at the time that the earth was in a fixed position and lent support to COPERNICUS's controversial theory that the earth revolves around the sun.

Gilbert died of the plague in 1603, and his younger half brother posthumously published two of his manuscripts under the title *De Mundo Nostro Sublunari Philosophia Nova* (*New Philosophy About Our Sublunary* [terrestrial] *World,* 1651). This work, however, had little impact on the 17th-century scientific community.

Known as the father of magnetism, Gilbert introduced the word *electricity* to scientific discourse, and the "gilbert," a unit of magnetomotive force, is named for him. Stephen Pumfrey and David Tilley, in an article entitled "William Gilbert: Forgotten Genius," say that *On the Magnet* still "stands as the first great work of experimental physics."

Glanvill, Joseph (Joseph Glanvil)

(1636–1680) *nonfiction writer, philosopher*
Joseph Glanvill was born in Plymouth, England, to a Puritan family. He was educated at Exeter and Lincoln Colleges, Oxford University, and became chaplain to Francis Rous, provost of Eton College. In 1666 he transferred to the Abbey Church, Bath,

and was made prebendary (a member of the clergy who received a stipend for his work) of Worcester Cathedral.

He also became a member of the Royal Society of Science, an organization that helped to nourish Glanvill's ideas about witchcraft and ghosts, which would later become an important aspect of his work. Glanvill became chaplain to King Charles II in 1672.

Opposed to the university teaching methods current at the time, Glanvill became an advocate of more experimental scientific inquiry. In 1661 he published *The Vanity of Dogmatizing,* also known as *Confidence in Opinions* and later recast as *Scepsis scientifica* (*Scientific skepticism,* 1665). This work encouraged an entirely new way of learning. It defended Glanvill's ideas, especially with respect to experimental philosophy, against detractors and argued for the effectiveness of the scientific method in gaining knowledge of the natural world. This work was extremely controversial in that it completely contradicted then-current theories of education. Glanvill later published *Progress and Advancement of Knowledge Since the Days of Aristotle* (1668), a work that attempted to demonstrate that experimental research methods were not inconsistent with religious faith.

In 1667 Glanvill published the first version of his book titled *Some Philosophical Considerations Touching Witchcraft,* which was reprinted again in 1681 as *Sadducismus Triumphatus.* (The title refers to a Jewish sect, called Saducceas, which did not believe in the resurrection of the dead. Thus, Glanvill's title suggests the triumph over those who do not believe in spirits.) This work defined Glanvill's belief in the supernatural power of witchcraft: "The Question, whether there are Witches or not, is not a matter of vain Speculation, or of indifferent Moment; but an Inquiry of very great and weighty Importance." He argued that there was no inherent contradiction between modern science and a belief, and he is often seen as an early proponent of modern research into psychic phenomena. *Sadducismus Triumphatus* is an important work that not only presents Glanvill's philosophical views but also contains a significant collection of 17th-century folklore about witchcraft. As the scholar James Sutherland states, the book "remains a curious reminder of the uncertainty all through this period of what are now called 'climates of opinion.'"

Works about Joseph Glanvill

Burns, Robert M. *The Great Debate on Miracles: From Joseph Glanvill to David Hume.* Lewisburg, Pa.: Bucknell University Press, 1981.

Redgrove, I. M. L. and H. Stanley Redgrove. *Joseph Glanvill and Psychical Research in the 17th Century, 1921.* Whitefish, Mont.: Kessinger Publishing, 2003.

Globe Theatre

The Globe Theatre was erected on the south side of the Thames River in Bankside, a suburb of London, in 1599. It was constructed from the building materials of the first amphitheater built for staged plays, the Theater at Shoreditch.

Through 1574 the London theater district had been in a residential neighborhood in London proper, but people who lived near the theaters were annoyed by the noise and crowds of the theater-going public. This increasing hostility from the neighborhood and a dispute with his landlord is what led Richard Burbage, the owner of the Shoreditch Theater, to dismantle and float the building's timbers and ironwork across the Thames River to a new location, where he erected the Globe.

The true dimensions of the Globe are not known since no architectural plans exist. Construction notes for The Fortune, another 17th-century theater modeled on the Globe, however, have survived. Additionally, illustrations of theaters of the time and a recent excavation of the Rose, another 16th-century theater, provide clues as to the Globe's physical appearance.

The Globe was 20-sided and nearly cylindrical, with a diameter of around 105 feet. A large rectangular stage in the center of its amphitheater measured 43 by 23 feet. Three overhanging tiered galleries seated the audience. The top gallery had a thatched roof, but the rest of the theater was open to the elements. The least expensive area in the theater surrounded the stage on three sides and was for standing room only. Here was where the "groundlings," as they were called, watched the plays.

Above the stage at the back was another gallery, used for such scenes as the balcony sequence from *Romeo and Juliet* and for sitting musicians. Under this gallery was the "tiring-house," which served as dressing room, prop and costume storage, the waiting area for actors about to enter the stage, and a place for the prompter to cue the performers' lines. Underneath the stage was the trap door through which actors disappeared from the stage and descended into "hell." Above the stage were the mechanisms for producing special effects like thunder and lightning and the suspension apparatus used to "fly" the actors.

The Globe held 3,000 people, and its audiences were composed of members from all social classes. Lords and ladies, whores and thieves, and barristers, professors, and students, and just about everyone in between attended plays at the Globe.

Unlike today, Elizabethan theater was a rowdy event, and the Globe's audiences were more like spectators at a sporting event than respectful and passive observers. Equally vocal and enthusiastic in their support and their criticism, audience members cheered their favorite actors and threw garbage at those they did not like. The playwright Ben JONSON mentions this practice in the prologue to his play *Volpone,* first performed at the Globe in 1605:

> Yet thus much I can give you, as a token
> Of his playes worth, no eggs are broken
> Nor quaking custards with fierce teeth
>   affrighted,
> Wherewith your rout are so delighted.

The CHAMBERLAIN'S MEN, later called the KING'S MEN, was the resident company of the Globe. The theater was also the home of William SHAKESPEARE, who in addition to being the major playwright at the Globe was a member of its acting troupe and one of the shareholders in the playhouse.

The Chamberlain's Men put on about 30 plays a year at the Globe; generally, two of these productions were new Shakespearean plays. Thus in the 1599–1600 season at the Globe *Hamlet* had its premiere performance as did *The Merry Wives of Windsor.* That same season, Ben Jonson's *Every Man Out of His Humour* had its debut.

In 1613, during a performance of Shakespeare's *Henry VIII,* a cannon shot during a staged battle ignited the thatched roof, and the Globe burned to the ground without serious casualties. Within a year the theater was rebuilt, this time with a tile roof, and it continued to host performances until 1642 when the Puritan government, strongly opposed to all forms of entertainment, shuttered every theater in London. The Globe was torn down two years later.

A Work about the Globe Theatre
Gurr, Andrew. *Playgoing in Shakespeare's London.* New York: Cambridge University Press, 1987.

Godolphin, Sidney (1610–1643) *poet*
Sidney Godolphin was born in Cornwall, England, the son of William and Thomasine Godolphin. He was educated at Exeter College, Oxford University (1624) and at one of the Inns of Court, and was first elected to the House of Commons in 1628. A devoted Royalist, Godolphin was a supporter of the Earl of Strafford and was one of the last to leave the Commons when Charles I ordered his supporters to withdraw in 1642. During the first Civil War, he joined the Royalist forces of Sir Ralph Hopton and, at age 33, was killed in action while advancing into Devon.

As Thomas HOBBES noted in the dedication of *Leviathan* (1651), Godolphin was a man of "remarkable promise." Sidney Godolphin left several poems that were never collected in any volume, his chief work being *The Passion of Dido for Aeneas* (1658), a translation from Virgil's fourth book of the *Aeneid,* apparently unfinished at his death and completed and published by the poet Edmund WALLER. Other poems survived in manuscript collections. The following is a passage from "When the Wise Men Came from Far," in which the soldier Godolphin reveals his gentle and religious side:

> Lord, when the wise men came from far,
> Led to thy cradle by a star,
> Then did the shepherds too rejoice,
> Instructed by thy angel's voice.
> Blest were the wise men in their skill,
> And shepherds in their harmless will.

The first complete collection of Godolphin's poetry was edited by George Saintsbury, in *Minor Poets of the Caroline Period,* Vol. 2 (1906).

Golding, Arthur (ca. 1536–ca. 1606)
translator, nonfiction writer
Arthur Golding came from a family of considerable wealth and connections. He associated with nobility and royalty, including Queen ELIZABETH I, and even helped raise Edward de Vere, the 17th Earl of OXFORD. Even though his family and friends were quite wealthy and Golding's writing was moderately successful, his finances were never stable. He often owed money and was even thrown into Fleet Prison for debt in 1593.

Golding is famous for his translations of classical literature and religious tracts. By far his most successful translation was Ovid's *Metamorphoses,* which he published in four books beginning in 1565. While the translation has been both lauded and attacked by critics for changing Ovid's graceful, ironic poetry into awkward verse, it was read widely both during Golding's lifetime and after his death. And while some critics disliked Golding's verse, others praised him for his use of heptameter, or a verse line of seven feet. In the story of Venus and her love for Adonis, Golding's style has vigor and movement. When Adonis is killed, for example, Venus

> turned her Cygnets backe, and when shee
>   from the skye
> Beehilld him dead, and in his blood
>   beweltred for to lye,

She leaped downe, and tare at once hir
garments from her brist,
And rent her heare, and beate uppon her
stomack with her fist.
And blaming sore the destnyes, sayd: Yit
shall they not obteine
Their will in all things. Of my greefe
remembrance shall remayne
(Adonis) whyle the world doth last. From
yeere too yeere shall growe
A thing that of my heavinesse and of thy
death shall showe
The lively likenesse. In a flowre thy blood I
will bestowe.

As a strong believer in Puritan and Calvinist values, Golding's goals in translating works like Ovid's and others were to teach his fellow citizens true godliness and virtue. To this end he begins *The Preface to the Reader* for Ovid's *Metamorphoses* with a word of caution to his reader, "I would not wish the simple sort offended for too bee, / When in this booke the heathen names of feyned Godds they see."

In addition to his translations, Golding also wrote several original works, such as *A Discourse upon the Earthquake that happened through this realme of Englande and other places of Christendom the sext of Aprill, 1580.* However, these writings were not as popular as his translations.

Among authors influenced by Golding's work were William SHAKESPEARE and Sir Philip SIDNEY, with whom Golding shared a long friendship. In fact, in 1587 Golding completed Sidney's translation of Philippe de Mornay's *De la verite de la Religion Chrestienne,* which was interrupted by Sidney's death in 1586. The work was published as *Trueness of the Christian Religion.*

Googe, Barnabe (1540–1594) *poet, translator*

Barnabe Googe was born in Lincolnshire, England, to Robert and Margaret Mantell Googe. He entered Christ's College at Cambridge in 1555. There is no record of his graduation.

Googe's friend John BALE encouraged him to translate into English an Italian poem by Marcellus Palingenius, *Zodiake,* which used the 12 signs of the zodiac to explain the mysteries of life. The task took Googe several years to complete and was published in installments, the first three books in 1560, the final books in 1565. The translation is said to have influenced the works of William SHAKESPEARE, Edmund SPENSER, and John MILTON. In gratitude to Bale, Googe wrote the short poem "To Doctor Bale," which chides his friend for working too hard. The poem begins with the verse, "Good aged Bale, that with thy hoary hairs Dost yet persist to turn the painful book."

In the mid-17th century it was not gentlemanly to have one's own work in print, but in 1563 Googe's friends gathered his poems and had them published. This poetry collection, titled *Ecologues, Epitaphs and Sonnets* was the first book of poetry by a single author published in England. Googe's collection, as the scholar William E. Sheidley states, ". . . did much to prepare the way for the later successes of the English literary RENAISSANCE." Two lines from one of the poems in the collection, *Of Money,* state: "Fair face show friends when riches do abound; / Come time of proof, farewell, they must away." According to Sheidley, the poem is written "as a praise of money rather than a dispraise of fair weather friends (and so) he enlivens the poem with irony."

A poetic satire about the voyage of life, *Shippe of Safeguard,* was published in 1569. About this work, Sheidley states, ". . . sixteen years before the publication of SPENSER's 'Shepheardes Calendar,' Googe was already handling moral, political and religious questions under the cover of shepherd's songs."

Gorges, Arthur (1557–1625) *poet, nonfiction writer, translator*

Sir Arthur Gorges was born in southwest England to Sir William Gorges and Winifred Budockshed. From very early on in his education, Gorges learned to read and speak French, a knowledge that would manifest itself in much of his later poetic and translational work. He was admitted into Oxford University in 1574, and although his date of graduation is unrecorded, by 1612 he was counting himself among the distinguished Oxford alumni. By 1576 he had served in the court of Queen ELIZABETH I, and by 1580 he was a Gentleman Pensioner, or one of 40 gentlemen who attended the sovereign on state occasions, keeping company with such noted figures as Sir Walter RALEIGH (his mother's first cousin), Sir Robert Carey, and Sir Philip SIDNEY, and eventually serving in Parliament.

In Edmund SPENSER's poetry Gorges is known as "Alcyon" (described in the poem *Colin Clouts Come Home Againe* as mourning the loss of his "Daphne," or his wife), and, as scholar Helen Estabrook Sandison explains, this "high place . . . was won by his genuine poetic touch." Gorges's translation of Lucan's *Pharsalia* into English appeared in 1614, and his translations into French of Sir Francis BACON's *The Wisdom of the Ancients* and *Essays* both followed in 1619. While his translations, as well as some practical nonfiction tracts, including the *Relation of the . . . Iland Voyage* (1625) and *The Publique Register for generall Commerce* (1611), were printed during his lifetime, his poems, for the most part, remained unpublished until years later.

In the collection *Sir Arthur Gorges his Vannetyes and toyes of youth* (1953), many of the poems, or "sweet lays of love," focus on the figure of Gorges's first wife in one form or another ("No meaner hope shall haunte my breste / than dearest Daphnes grace"), with the sonnet being the dominant poetic form throughout the collection.

Scholar Sandison describes Gorges's place in literary history as follows: "Talented as writer of verse and of prose, and as translator into French as well as into his own tongue, courtier, and gentleman-mariner, he holds his place . . . in the rank lead by the great figures . . . Spenser, Ralegh, Bacon."

A Work about Arthur Gorges

Sandison, Helen Estabrook, ed. *The Poems of Sir Arthur Gorges.* Oxford, U.K.: Clarendon Press, 1953.

Gosson, Stephen (1554–1624) *nonfiction writer, playwright, poet*

Stephen Gosson was born in Canterbury, England, to Cornelius Gosson. He graduated from Oxford University in 1576 and then moved to London, where he began writing poetry and plays. None of his plays survive, although he refers to at least three of his own works in his later tracts critiquing the theater: *Captain Mari,* an Italian comedy; *Praise at Parting,* a moralizing play; and *Catilines Conspiracies,* a play about Roman politics, which Gosson later disparaged as "a pig of mine own sow." He also acted for a short time.

In 1579 Gosson began writing the antitheater tracts for which he is now known. His first pamphlet, *The School of Abuse* (1579), was an attack on actors, playwrights, and poets that criticized the social and moral disorder of the theater. The poet and playwright Thomas LODGE responded with a *Defense of Plays* (1580), and acting companies revived Gosson's plays to expose his inconstancy in changing his position on the theater.

Gosson's second tract was *Plays Confuted in Five Actions* (1582), his most sustained critique of the theater. Here he continued the debate about the morality of the theater and its social effects, claiming that it drew the public away from religion and taught vice. As the critic Stephen Hilliard observes, "Gosson's argument changed from a witty attack in *The School of Abuse* (1579) to outright condemnation in *Plays Confuted in Five Actions* (1582), but he was consistent in his view that drama was helping to cause undesirable social changes (such as spreading immorality and distracting the public from religion), by miseducating the common people."

Gosson included the theater in the same category with other behaviors he disapproved of: dancing, drinking, loose morals, and distraction from work. He also considered commoners to be easily swayed and misled:

The meaner sort tottre [waver], they are carried away with every rumor, and so easily corrupted, that in the Theatres they generally take up a wonderfull laughter, and shout altogether in one voyce, when they see some notable cosenedge practiced, or some slie [sly] conveighance [trick] of baudry brought out of Italy. Wherby they showe themselves rather to like it then [than] to rebuke it.

Referring to the popular theater's tendency to represent dishonest trickery (cosenedge) or sexual themes (baudry), Gosson voices a common RENAISSANCE concern about the function of literature. Literary critics of the period argued over the capacity of literature and drama to entertain versus their responsibility to teach virtue and elevate readers morally and intellectually.

By 1584 Gosson had abandoned his literary career and become a priest. His work demonstrates the Renaissance concern for the power and appeal of the theater as a cultural and literary institution that many feared could undermine traditional values.

Graham, James (James Graham, Marquis of Montrose) (1612–1650) poet

James Graham was born in Scotland, the only son of John Graham, a Scottish nobleman, and his wife, Margaret Graham. He was brought up at Kincardine Castle, the family seat, and inherited the title of fifth Earl of Montrose in 1626. He later attended St. Andrews University and married Magdalene Carnegie in 1629.

In the early 1630s Graham spent some time in France and Italy studying military arts. Later, as a general, he participated in several military campaigns in support of the king during the period of the English Civil War; Charles I appointed him lieutenant general, and later lieutenant governor, of Scotland. The king also awarded him the title of first Marquis of Montrose in 1644. In 1650 he was hanged in Edinburgh by the Scots, who opposed the king, for being disloyal to the cause of Scottish nationalism.

Though essentially a warrior, Graham wrote a number of poems that express his courageous attitude toward life. He is known to have composed 12

or 13 poems, which were not published until after his death. Among them are "My Dear and Only Love," with the famous lines "He either fears his fate too much, / Or his deserts are small / That dares not put it to the touch / To gain or lose it all." When he was in prison awaiting execution, he wrote a stirring appeal to divine mercy, with the lines, "Let them bestow on ev'ry airt a limb; / Open all my veins that I may swim / To Thee my Saviour, in that crimson lake; / Then place my purboil'd head upon a stake." His other poems include brief verses inscribed in copies of books by classical authors such as Caesar and Lucan and poems addressing issues of love, war, and grief. Graham was memorialized by an inscription on his tomb, written by William Faithorne, that calls him "Scotland's glory, Britain's pride."

Other Work by James Graham
The Collected Poems of James Graham, First Marquis of Montrose. Edited by Robin Graham Bell. New York: David Lewis, 1970.

Works about James Graham
Brown, Chris. *The Battle for Aberdeen, 1644.* Stroud, Gloucestershire, U.K.: Tempus, 2002.
Wedgwood, C. V. *Montrose.* New York: St. Martin's Press, 1995.

great chain of being

The great chain of being is a RENAISSANCE concept that categorized all of life, observable and unobservable, according to an elaborate and remarkably consistent ordered system. God was, of course, at the top of the system, with angels, humans, animals, plants, and inanimate matter completing the chain in that order.

Within each part of the chain (except the top) there are many subgroups, such as the divisions of angels which are seen, for example, in John MILTON's *Paradise Lost.* Among animals (which did not include humans), mammals were superior to birds, fish, reptiles, amphibians, and insects (in that order). Similarly, among mammals the lion was seen to be the "primate," i.e., highest ranking, member of the group, with others following. The eagle was primate among birds, and the Sun ranked highest among heavenly bodies.

Human beings, located in the center of the great chain, had the unique potential to participate in the spiritual realm of angels but also might lower themselves to the level of beasts by yielding to animal desires. Within human society, of course, there were the usual subdivisions. The monarch was at the top, nobility and gentry next, followed by common folk and servants.

A correspondence was understood to exist between the members of the various levels of the chain. Thus the Sun, lions, and eagles (as the primates of their respective levels) also often served as symbols of monarchy. Likewise, disturbances in the natural order often indicated disturbances in the human order. Comets, seen as disorderly intruders among the orderly movements of the night sky, were signs of trouble. Ulysses, in Shakespeare's *Troilus and Cressida*, refers to the great chain of being when he discusses Achilles' defiance of Agamemnon; comparing Agamemnon's leadership to the Sun's domination over the sky:

> When that the general is not like the hive,
> To whom the foragers shall all repair,
> What honey is expected? Degree being
>   vizarded, [hidden]
> Th' unworthiest shows as fairly in the mask.
> The heavens themselves, the planets, and
>   this centre,
> Observe degree, priority, and place,
> Insisture [permanence], course, proportion,
>   season, form,
> Office, and custom, in all line of order;

Further correspondence was seen between the family and the state. The husband/father was the monarch of the family and the wife and children the subjects. Thus, the term "petty [i.e., little] treason" was used to describe the crime of a wife attempting to murder her husband.

NEOPLATONISM, the revival and adaptation of the ideas of the ancient Greek philosopher Plato,

encouraged viewing the world in ranked categories and thus helped form the concept of the great chain of being. Although the belief in the great chain of being seems quaint to 21st-century minds, it was partly based on scientific observation of the natural world—classification of living beings is still a scientific pursuit—and the cosmos, as the science of astronomy was developing. Thus, as the scholar Arthur O. Lovejoy has noted, "the idea of the Chain of Being . . . has had many curiously happy consequences in the history of Western thought."

Greene, Robert (1558–1592) *dramatist, fiction writer, nonfiction writer*

Robert Greene was born in Norwich, England. Who his parents were is not known, although they do seem to have been well off as Greene entered Cambridge University in 1575 as a sizar, a scholarship student. He received his B.A. three years later and an M.A. in 1583. After receiving his M.A., Greene moved to London, where he published a prose romance, *Mamillia* (1583), a fictional love story about a wayward husband. (The romance is a form of fiction that preceded the novel; it is set in an idealized world and often involves magic.)

Greene is often grouped among the UNIVERSITY WITS, writers who earned degrees at Cambridge or Oxford and turned to writing for the stage to earn a living. Between 1583 and 1592, he wrote plays, pamphlets, and prose fiction. He is even said to have written during the last weeks of his life, when he apparently composed *Greene's Groats-worth of Wit, Bought with a Million of Repentance* (1592), the famous pamphlet in which he targeted William SHAKESPEARE as an "upstart crow" and plagiarist. *Groats-worth of Wit* is the story of "Roberto" Greene's hedonistic life. This work enhanced Greene's reputation for wild living, a reputation he had already fostered in *Never Too Late to Mend* (1590), in which he confesses "forasmuch as [my wife] would persuade me from my willful wickedness, after I had a child by her, I cast her off, having spent up the marriage-money which I obtained by her." Greene's cony-catching pamphlets—tracts that reveal the tricks of criminals, which he published in the last three years of his life—also provide suggestive evidence of his knowledge of the seedier side of London life.

Greene is best remembered for his prose fiction and plays. The majority of his fiction, which includes *The Mirror of Modesty* (1584), a retelling of the biblical story of Susanna and the elders, and *Planetomachia* (1585), a collection of tales based on astrology, was written early in his career. Greene was very much a follower of John LYLY in that he used the balanced syntax and complex and flowery language of Lyly's Euphuistic style, named for Euphues, the main character in Lyly's books. Indeed, Greene announced his debt to Lyly in titles such as *Euphues his Censure to Philautus* (1587), a series of moral tales. His most famous work of prose is *Pandosto, The Triumph of Time* (1588), a tale about a jealous king, Pandosto, which provided Shakespeare with much of the plot for *A Winter's Tale* (1610–11).

Greene's plays were all based on historical sources: *Selimus, The Emperor of the Turks* (ca. 1588), a historical tragedy; *Alphonsus of Aragon* (ca. 1588), based on Spanish history; *Friar Bacon and Friar Bungay* (1589–90), based on the lives of two 13th-century Oxford scholars; and *James IV* (ca. 1592), which tells the story of the king of Scotland.

Friar Bacon and Friar Bungay is based on Christopher MARLOWE's play *The Tragedy of Doctor Faustus*. However, where Marlowe created the tragic figure of a man seeking to overreach human boundaries, Greene wrote a comedy, blending the story of Friar (Roger) Bacon, a medieval English philosopher, with a courtly love story.

James IV is probably Greene's most successful play. It tells the story of the unlawful passion of King James IV of Scotland for the virgin Ida. To possess Ida, James attempts to kill his wife, Dorothea, who escapes to her father, Henry VII of England. Henry declares war upon James. As the play concludes, Dorothea reconciles the two kings:

> *Give me that hand, that oft hath blest this*
> *   head,*
> *And clasp thine arms, that have embraced*
> *   this [neck],*
> *About the shoulders of my wedded spouse.*
> *Ah, mighty prince, this king and I are one!*
> *Spoil thou his subjects, thou despoilest me.*

Thus, Dorothea demonstrates her essential goodness and lives up to a traditional ideal of womanhood.

Greene's plays display his moral purpose. As the scholar Tetsumaro Hayashi observes, Greene's work may offer "a glimpse of wickedness that triumphs temporarily . . ., [but] the virtuous and innocent, who function temporarily as misunderstood victims of circumstance, are ultimately rewarded." This combination of his moral purpose and immoral lifestyle make Greene one of the most fascinating English playwrights before Shakespeare.

Other Work by Robert Greene
Greene's Groats-worth of Wit, Bought with a Million of Repentance. Edited by D. Allen Carroll. Binghamton, N.Y.: Medieval and Renaissance Texts and Studies, 1994.
Menaphon: Camilla's Alarm to Slumbering Euphues in His Melancholy Cell. Toronto, Canada: Dovenhouse Editions, 1996.

A Work about Robert Greene
Grupi, Charles W. *Robert Greene*. Boston: Twayne, 1986.

Greville, Sir Fulke, Baron Brooke
(1554–1628) *poet, dramatist, nonfiction writer*
Fulke Greville was born in Warwickshire, England, to a wealthy family. He entered Shrewsbury School at age 10, on the same day in 1564 as Philip SIDNEY, who became a close friend. From Shrewsbury he went on to Cambridge University (as did Sidney) and then to the court of Queen ELIZABETH I. He was highly regarded by Elizabeth and her successor, King JAMES I, and served their governments in various administrative positions. Elizabeth

knighted him for his services in 1597, and James made him Baron Brooke in 1621.

Greville's writing was a hobby, and very little of his work was published during his lifetime, though it probably circulated in manuscript form among his friends. At Elizabeth's court he was a member of a literary society called the Areopagus Club, whose other members included Sidney and Edmund SPENSER. Sir Edward DYER and Samuel DANIEL were also friends of his. Daniel was among the many writers whom Greville helped with his influence and financial support.

Apart from a few poems published in anthologies and an elegy on the death of Sidney, the only work of Greville's to be published before his death was the tragedy *Mustapha* (1609). Five years after he died, *Certain Learned and Elegant Works* (1633) was published, containing several works of Greville's: three long philosophical poems, *An Inquisition upon Fame and Honour, A Treatie of Wars,* and *A Treatie of Humane Learning;* two tragedies, *Mustapha* and *Alaham;* and a set of 109 short poems under the collective title *Caelica.* His most famous work, *The Life of the Renowned Sir Philip Sidney,* was published in 1652, and a volume of poems on mainly religious themes appeared in 1670.

Mustapha was based on actual events that occurred in 1553 when the Ottoman emperor Suleyman II murdered his son and heir, Mustapha, to forestall a plot. *Mustapha* and Greville's other tragedy, *Alaham* (1633), which also has a Middle Eastern setting, were *closet dramas*—meant to be read, perhaps aloud among friends, rather than performed on stage. In both tragedies, Greville followed Greek and Roman models, including using a chorus to comment on the action, but drew upon his own observations of Tudor and Stuart political life for his point of view. Greville explained his intentions in a disgression in his biography of Sidney, distinguishing his own plays from those of both the ancient and contemporary writers in their focus on people rather than Providence or God: "My purpose in them was . . . to trace out the high ways of ambitious governors, and to show in the

practice, that the more audacity, advantage, and good success such sovereignties have, the more they hasten to their own desolation and ruin." In its intensity, solemnity, and spareness, Greville's dramatic verse is unlike any other of his era. In fact, the scholar Ronald Bayne, writing in the *Cambridge Encyclopedia of English and American Literature* (1907–21), compares Greville's dramatic verse with John MILTON's *Samson Agonistes.*

The Life of the Renowned Sir Philip Sidney is not quite what its title (given by its anonymous editor) suggests. It does contain invaluable information about Sidney's life (though it leaves out material a modern biographer would find essential, such as any mention of Sidney's wife and child), but it also includes discussions of Elizabethan and Jacobean politics, literature, and Greville's own writing. In his political passages, Greville uses Sidney as a model to attack the corruption he saw in the post-Elizabethan world around him. He contrasts Sidney with men who pursue honors only for their own selfish purposes. He writes, "Sir Philip Sidney is none of this number; for the greatness which he affected was built upon true Worth; esteeming Fame more than Riches, and Noble actions far above Nobility itself."

The poems of *Caelica,* most of which are sonnets, appear to have been written over many years, and they reflect a variety of moods. Some are courtly love poems that may have been addressed to Queen Elizabeth herself. There are ribald lyrics that joke against women as well as a number of protests, charming or cynical, against the loved one's inconstancy; overall, the attitude toward love is one of deep distrust. Some of them—for example, *Caelica 22*—draw for their effects on Greville's knowledge of country courtship customs:

> *I, with whose colors Myra drest her head,*
> *I, that ware posies of her own hand*
>   *making . . .*
> *Must I look on, in hope time coming may*
> *With change bring back my turn again to*
>   *play?*

Greville's later poems turn toward religion and the pull between the religious and the political life. They express a deep sense of personal guilt and also a personal assurance of God's mercy, as in *Caelica 99*:

> Down in the depth of mine iniquity,
> That ugly center of infernal spirits;
> Where each sin feels her own deformity,
> In these peculiar torments she inherits,
> Deprived of human graces, and divine,
> Even there appears this saving God of mine.

Greville died tragically, stabbed by a deranged servant who believed that he had been cut out of his master's will and who killed himself immediately after the stabbing. Greville died four weeks later and was buried in St. Mary's Church, Warwick, under a tombstone carved with his own summary of his life: "Fulke Grevil—Servant to Queene Elizabeth—Councellor to King James—and Frend to Sir Philip Sydney."

Other Work by Sir Fulke Greville
The Prose of Sir Fulke Greville. Edited by Mark Caldwell. New York: Garland, 1987.

Works about Fulke Greville
Kemp, Paul. *Fulke Greville and Sir John Davies.* Boston: G. K. Hall, 1985.

Larson, Charles Howard. *Fulke Greville.* Boston: Twayne, 1980.

Raber, Karen. *Dramatic Difference: Gender, Class, and Genre in the Early Modern Closet Drama.* Newark: University of Delaware Press, 2001.

Grimald, Nicholas (1519–1562) *poet, dramatist, translator*

Nicholas Grimald was born in Leighton Bromswold, England, to John Baptista and Anne Grimaldi. (The lack of spelling standards in his day may be why the final "i" was dropped from his name, although Grimald may have dropped it himself to make his name sound more English.)

His literary career began around 1539 when he went to Oxford University and wrote the Latin play *Christus Redivivus The Resurrection of Christ* (1543), the earliest known experiment in the use of mixed genres (the use of comedic and tragic elements in one play) in England. He was granted M.A.s from both Oxford and Cambridge in 1544.

Grimald's best-known works are the 38 poems he contributed to *Songs and Sonnets* (1557), an anthology of poems more commonly known as *Tottel's Miscellany.* These poems consist of a number of love poems, a few narrative poems based on classical subjects, and some moral poems on topics such as "Of Laws" and "Of Friendship." Tottel had published Grimald's translation of Cicero's *De Officiis* (*Of Duty*) in 1556.

The *Miscellany* established Grimald's reputation as a poet; the 16th-century literary historian John BALE wrote that Grimald was "not the least illustrious [i.e., one of the finest] of his time." Grimald's poems demonstrate his interest in advancing the art of English poetry. Two of them, "The Death of Zoroas," a war poem based on classical sources, and "Marcus Tullius Ciceroes Death," a narration of the death of the famous Roman orator, employ blank verse, that is, unrhymed iambic pentameter (lines of 10 syllables alternating unstressed and stressed), a poetic form that had, until then, only been used by Henry Howard, Earl of SURREY.

Grimald, however, is at his best when he employs the poulters measure, which is composed of two lines, one with 12 syllables and the second with 14. The following lines from "A True Love," a short love poem, reveal his skill with this meter: "As mellow pears above the crabs esteemed be: / So doth my love surmount them all, whom yet I hap to see."

Because Grimald's poetic achievement was surpassed by later poets, he has been all but forgotten. Still, the scholar L. R. Merrill observes, "as a contributor of two specimens of blank verse to a volume of which there were eight editions within thirty years . . . his influence on the poetry in that form" must have been far-reaching.

Grymeston, Elizabeth (d. 1603) *nonfiction writer*

Elizabeth Grymeston was a Catholic living in Protestant England during the reign of ELIZABETH I. While on her deathbed, she wrote *Miscelanea, Meditations, and Memoratives* (1604) to her son Bernye. Grymeston's work is written out of love for her son and in the knowledge that she will not always be present to give maternal advice. Thus she tells him:

> My dearest sonne, there is nothing so strong as the force of love; there is no love so forcible as the love of an affectionate mother to hir naturall childe: there is no mother can either more affectionately shew hir nature, or more naturally manifest hir affection, than in advising hir children out of hir owne experience.

Although Grymeston writes specifically for her son, her advice can also apply to others:

> Arme your selfe with that modestie that may silence that untemperate tongue, and controll that unchaste eye, that shall aime at passion. Be mindfull of things past; carefull of things present; provident of things to come. Goe as you would be met. Sit as you would be found. Speak as you would be heard: and when you go to bed, read over the carriage of your selfe that day. Reforme that is amisse; and give God thanks for that which is orderly: and so commit thy selfe to him that keepes thee.

Grymeston's book was published in four editions, indicating its popularity. Modern critics have praised her work for depicting the inner workings of the mind of a 16th-century woman, including what she read, her religious beliefs, and her love for her son.

Works about Elizabeth Grymeston

Otten, Charlotte F. *English Women's Voices 1540–1700.* Miami: Florida International University Press, 1992.

Travitsky, Betty, ed. *The Paradise of Women: Writings by Englishwomen of the Renaissance.* New York: Columbia University Press, 1989.

Guilpin, Everard (Edward Guilpin) (ca. 1574–ca. 1601) *nonfiction writer, poet*

Not much is known of Everard (or Edward) Guilpin's life. He is known to have been a cousin as well as friend of John MARSTON. Scholars think that Guilpin attended Highgate Grammar School before entering Cambridge University in 1588. He later turned to the law and began legal training at Gray's Inn in 1591. However, there is no record of his having become a lawyer.

Guilpin's literary reputation is founded mainly on the satirical compilation *Skialetheia, or a Shadow of Truth*, published anonymously in 1598. A satire is a work that criticizes human folly and vice by making fun of them; the satires of the Roman poet Juvenal (A.D. 60–136) provided a model that was much admired in the 16th century, and Guilpin imitates Juvenal in the cynical tone of *Skialetheia*. Likewise, in *Skialetheia* Guilpin warns the reader of his "harsh stile" and notes that he will "onely spit my venome, and away."

Skialetheia is composed of 70 numbered epigrams (witty short poems, some of only two lines), each addressed to a person with a Latin-sounding name, followed by a "Satyre Praeludium" ("Preface to the Satires") and six much longer satires (about 100 lines of verse apiece), numbered in Latin. The Latin names were all understood by Guilpin's contemporary readers to apply to actual people, and it is a sport for today's literary historians to identify the people Guilpin makes fun of: "Chrysogyne" in number 30 is Ben JONSON, teased for making his naturally ugly features still uglier by forcing them into frightening expressions:

> *Chrysogonus each morning by his glass,*
> *Teacheth a wrinkled action to his face,*
> *And with the same he runs into the street,*
> *Each one to put in fear that he doth meet. . . .*

Guilpin was especially interested in the theatrical world, and mentioned specifically in the work are several of London's playhouses. Scholars have identified among Guilpin's characters such writers as Philip SIDNEY, Edmund SPENSER, Christopher MARLOWE, and Thomas NASHE. But it is not always necessary to know the reference to enjoy the humor, which is at times very broad, as in number 4, "To Livia":

> Livia, I can thee thank, when thou dost kiss
> Thou turn'st thy cheek: see what good
>   nature is!
> For well thou knowest thy breath's
>   infection,
> Able to turn my stomach upside down.

In "Satira Quinta" ("Satire Five") he makes fun of an Elizabethan dandy:

> Here comes Don Fashion, spruce formality,
> Neat as a Merchants ruff. . . .
> Oh brave! what, with a feather in his hat?
> He is a dancer you may see by that;
> Light heels, light head, light feather well
>   agree.

The pointed personal references in *Skialetheia* and other satires resulted in a satiric battle in the last years of the 16th century. An anonymous satire called *The Whipping of the Satyre* appeared in 1601, making fun of Guilpin, Marston, and Jonson under the names of "the Epigrammatist," "the Satirist," and "the Humorist." Guilpin responded to this in another satirical piece, *The Whipper of the Satyre, His Penance* (1601), his last publication.

H

Habington, William (1605–1654) *poet, playwright, historian*

William Habington was the son of Thomas Habington of Hindlip, Worcestershire, England. The family was Catholic, and he was educated at St. Omer and Paris. He married Lucy Herbert in 1634.

Habington's principal work was *Castara* (1634), a book of poems to his wife, in which he celebrates courtship followed by married love. He added elegies, or poems written to commemorate the death of an individual, to the second edition (1635). Among the elegies added were those written on the occasions of the deaths of George Talbot, the sixth Earl of Shrewsbury, and Venetia Digby, wife of natural philosopher Kenelm DIGBY. In his third edition (1640) Habington included sacred poems. This excerpt from "To Roses in the Bosom of Castara" cleverly describes the wonderful effect of their location on the roses:

> *Transplanted thus how bright yee grow;*
> *How rich a perfume doe yee yeeld?*
> *In some close garden, Cowslips so*
> *Are sweeter then i' th' open field.*

Of this sonnet sequence Victorian poet Arthur Henry Hallam said that it makes the English "proud of living in the same land, and inheriting the same association, with its true-hearted . . . author."

The third edition of *Castara* also contains "Prologues, Epilogues and Songs from *The Queen of Arragon*" (1640), a romantic tragedy in blank verse which was first produced at court for Charles I and Henrietta Maria. Kenneth Allott, a modern editor of Habington's work, sees the play as a forerunner of "the heroic tragedy and light comedy" of the Restoration. He suggests that it presents a "satirical contrast between the ideal pretensions [of the courtly world] and reality."

Habington also studied history and wrote, at the request of King Charles I, *The Historie of Edward the Fourth* (1640). He published six other essays in *Observations Upon Historie* (1641), introducing his subject, Charles I, as "that faithfull preserver of things past, that great instructor of the present, and certain Prophet of the future."

While some contemporaries accused Habington of disloyalty to the king during the Civil War, this seems unlikely, since all his writing suggests that he particularly valued loyalty. Furthermore, editor and compiler of *England's Parnassus* Robert Allot (fl. 1600s) provides historical evidence that Habington fought alongside other Royalists in one of the early battles of the war. His home was plundered after their defeat, and little else is known of his life. He was buried in his family vault at Hindlip Church.

Critics generally seem to agree that Habington was a minor poet but, both technically and morally speaking, a good one. Having lived through the execution of Charles I and seen the beginning of Cromwell's regime, Habington said of his experience, "I have seen Comets, threatning all/Vanish themselves: I have seene Princes so."

Hakluyt, Richard (ca. 1552–1616)
nonfiction writer

Richard Hakluyt was probably born in London, where he was educated at Westminster School. While he was at Westminster, a visit to an elder cousin, also named Richard Hakluyt, inspired his lifelong passion for learning and writing about voyages of discovery. In the preface to his major work, *The Principal Navigations,* (1589), Hakluyt describes how intrigued he was by a table piled with books about cosmography and a huge "universal map." The elder Hakluyt answered the boy's questions in detail and also pulled down a Bible to share with him a text from Psalm 107: "They which go down to the sea in ships and occupy the great waters, they see the works of the Lord, and his wonders in the deep."

Hakluyt never let go of the passion sparked by these experiences. While at Oxford University, he read everything about sea travel he could get his hands on, in any language. Soon after taking his bachelor's degree in 1574, he lectured on geography at Oxford. Ordained as a priest in 1578, he seems to have regarded his clerical career as secondary to his real interest in exploration. The various church positions he was appointed to over the years supplied income but do not appear to have occupied much of his time.

In 1582 Hakluyt published his first book, *Divers Voyages Touching the Discovery of America and the Islands Adjacent Unto the Same,* which he dedicated to Sir Philip SIDNEY. For this book Hakluyt collected whatever information he had been able to gather on the subject, making the point that

there was room between the South and Central American colonies of the Spanish and the Canadian colonies of the French for the English to make their own influence felt. The book brought Hakluyt to the attention of Sir Francis Walsingham, Queen ELIZABETH I's secretary of state, and the following year Walsingham appointed Hakluyt chaplain to the English embassy in Paris. Hakluyt seems to have had a covert mission, which he embraced, to find out what he could about French activities in America, such as the Canadian fur trade.

While in Paris, Hakluyt discovered a manuscript about Florida, which he published in English, with a dedication to Sir Walter RALEIGH, in 1587, under the title *A Notable History Containing Four Voyages Made by Certain French Captains unto Florida.* Hakluyt translated and published several other works that had not previously been available in English. One of his aims was to disseminate the knowledge of the science of navigation, not just to curious scholars but to sailors as well, and so make sea voyages safer.

Hakluyt returned to England in 1588. In 1589 the first edition of his great work, titled *The Principal Navigations, Voyages, and Discoveries of the English Nation . . .,* appeared, dedicated to Walsingham; the second edition, updated to cover "These 1600 Years," appeared in three volumes in 1598, 1599, and 1600. There was much to add, because the accomplishments of English mariners in the 16th century far surpassed their whole previous history.

Hakluyt's labor on this work was huge; he combed the account books of merchant companies, traveled great distances to interview voyagers and copy out their original journals and log-books, and maintained a lengthy correspondence. In the dedication of the first volume of the second edition, he describes how he

brought to light many rare and worthy monuments which long have lien miserably scattered in musty corners, and retchlessly hidden in misty darkness, and were very like . . . to have been buried in perpetual oblivion. . . . For the bringing of which into this homely and rough-hewn shape which here thou seest; what restless nights, what painful days, what heat, what cold I have endured; how many long, and chargeable journeys I have traveled . . . what expenses I have not spared . . . thyself can hardly imagine, yet I by daily experience do find and feel.

The Principal Navigations is a compilation rather than an original work, but Hakluyt edited the components and supplied connecting and introductory material that amply conveyed his enthusiasm for his subject. He thus had a great influence on the development of the British Empire, especially the colonization of America, and also on the imagination of English writers, among them William SHAKESPEARE, most notably in *The Tempest.*

Hakluyt died at Eaton, in Herefordshire, and was buried in Westminster Abbey. His unpublished manuscripts came into the hands of Samuel PURCHAS, who edited and published some of them in *Pilgrims* (1625). To this day, the Hakluyt Society, founded in 1846, honors Hakluyt's memory by publishing books about exploration.

Other Works by Richard Hakluyt
The Original Writings and Correspondence of the Two Richard Hakluyts. Edited by G. Taylor. Reprint, Millwood, N.Y.: Kraus International Publications, 1988.
Voyages and Discoveries. Edited by Jack Beeching. New York: Viking Penguin, 1982.

A Work about Richard Hakluyt
Quinn, David B. *The Hakluyt Handbook.* Two volumes. London: The Hakluyt Society, 1974.

Hale, Matthew (1609–1676) *nonfiction writer*
Matthew Hale was a scholar of English common law who served as lord chief justice of England. He was born at Alderley in Gloucestershire, England,

and orphaned at age five. He went on to study at Magdalen College, Oxford University, before he was admitted to Lincoln's Inn, where he studied law.

Hale quickly established a successful legal career and became an important member of the reform movement of 1651–52, which sought to improve the English legal system. In 1653, during Oliver Cromwell's rule as lord protector, Hale became a judge in the English court of common pleas, and in 1655 he took a position in Parliament and subsequently played an important role in restoring the monarchy. In 1660 Charles II appointed him chief baron of the Exchequer, and in 1671 he became chief justice of the King's Bench.

Hale's *History of the Pleas of the Crown* (1715) and *History of the Common Law of England* (1736) were both published after his death. These are rather dry works that attempt to set down all that was known of English law. In *History of the Pleas of the Crown,* Hale writes, among other things, about how judges should handle certain situations. For example, he considers what to do if a criminal should become insane:

If a man in his sound memory commits a capital offense, and before his arraignment he becomes absolutely mad, he ought not by law to be arraigned during such his phrenzy, but be remitted to prison until that incapacity be removed; the reason is, because he cannot advisedly plead to the indictment.

In *The History of Common Law,* Hale attempts to find the origins of many of Britain's laws and to discuss the different methods by which concepts become law. He also reveals his pride in the English judicial system as he discusses trial by jury:

I shall now with more Brevity consider that other Title of our Law which I before propounded . . . viz. The Trial by a Jury of Twelve Men; which upon all Accounts, as it is settled here in this Kingdom, seems to be the best Trial in the World: I shall therefore give a short Account of the Method and Manner of that Trial.

In summarizing Hale's view of the law, historian J. G. A. Pocock notes,

> [W]e aim at no more than establishing rules of conduct to which all can agree and which will give satisfaction in the greatest possible number of the cases which come before the courts.

A Work about Matthew Hale

Cromartie, Alan. *Sir Matthew Hale: 1609–1676.* Cambridge, U.K.: Cambridge University Press, 1995.

Hales, John (1584–1656) *nonfiction writer*

John Hales was born in Bath, England; his father was a servant for a wealthy family. Hales was educated at Oxford University, where he earned a B.A. in 1603 and an M.A. in 1609, the same year he took orders as a clergyman. At Oxford he lectured on Greek and belonged to an intellectual discussion group known as the Great Tew Circle.

Hales attended and recorded the proceedings at the Synod of Dort in Holland, a series of theological debates that took place from 1618 to 1619. Unimpressed by the Calvinist concept of grace argued at the meeting, Hales "bade John CALVIN a good night." His letters from the Synod of Dort were later published in *Golden Remains of the Ever Memorable Mr. John Hales* (1659), in which he condemns the "great and irremediable inconvenience this free and uncontroulable venturing upon Theological Disputes hath brought upon us."

As a theologian, Hales connected to the latitudinarians, a group which believed that charity, mutual tolerance, and the imitation of Christ's life were the essence of Christianity. In *A Tract concerning the Power of the Keys, and Auricular Confession* (1677). Hale writes dismissively of dissension, "All these questions concerning the notes, the visibility, the government of the church, if we look upon the substance and nature of the church, they are merely idle and impertinent; if upon the end why learned men do handle them, it is nothing else but faction." Andrew MARVELL called him "one of the clearest heads and best-prepared breasts in Christendom."

Hales refused to write for publication, and all works issued prior to his death were published without his authorization, including *A Tract Concerning Schisms and Schismatics,* (1642) which advocates tolerance in religion, and his collected *Works* (1765).

Scholar M. Kaufmann, in *Latitudinarianism and Pietism,* says of Hales that he was

> a typical Latitudinarian, gifted with acuteness of intellect, a most delicate perception of the proportion of things, and a profound spiritual insight, viewing the current of religious partisanships from the elevated standpoint of a candid observer rather than from that of a chief actor in the turmoil of political and religious warfare.

Halifax, Marquis of

See GEORGE SAVILE.

Halkett, Anne (1622–1699) *nonfiction writer*

Anne Halkett, née Murray, was born in London, the daughter of Jane Drummond Murray, a governess to the royal family, and Thomas Murray, secretary to Prince Charles (later Charles II). In 1656 she married Sir James Halkett, and the couple settled at his estate in Pitferrane, Scotland.

Most of what is known about Halkett comes from *The Autobiography of Anne Lady Halkett* (1875), which portrays her as a strong-minded and adventurous woman. Among other things, the memoir describes her love affair with Col. Joseph Bamfield before her marriage. Halkett met Bamfield when he was a secret agent for King Charles I during the English Civil Wars, in which Parliamentary forces succeeded in executing the king and taking over the government. The young Duke of York, Charles's third son, who would eventually be crowned James II, was being held in St. James Palace in London by Parliamentary forces. In order to try to preserve the succession, he had to be rescued. Halkett claims that she and Bamfield were part of the successful plot to get James out of the country.

Halkett's memoirs are particularly interesting to students of the Civil War, as Halkett was a Royalist, or supporter of the monarchy. In her journal Halkett writes about "the earnest desire I had to serve the King" and says her loyalty "made me omit no opportunity wherein I could be useful."

Halkett also included a number of devotional meditations in her journal that reveal the spiritual underpinnings of her political beliefs. In the meditation titled *Upon the disbanding of the Army, and the disorder that followed,* she writes "There is a time for all things, says the wise man . . . there was a time for the King to suffer exile, and all his subjects to be enslaved, and a time for him to be restored; but till this time came that God had appointed for it all industry was fruitless." Scholar John Loftis believes Halkett wrote "in an effort to sort out the pattern of her life, above all in its spiritual dimension."

Hall, Edward (ca. 1498–1547) *nonfiction writer*

Edward Hall was born in London—where he lived for most of his life—to John Hall, a grocer and merchant, and his wife, Katherine. Educated at Cambridge University, where he received a B.A. in 1518, he went on to become a lawyer and served as undersheriff of London and as a member of Parliament.

Hall's great work, *The Union of the Noble and Illustrious Families of Lancaster and York,* commonly called *Hall's Chronicle,* narrates the history of England from the beginning of Henry IV's reign in 1399 to the end of Henry VIII's in 1547. An unfinished version may have been published in 1542. However, the first edition is more likely to be the one issued by the printer Richard Grafton in 1548, the year after Hall's death. Indeed, Hall left his *Chronicle* "late made" to Grafton with instructions that he should "set it forward." Grafton was obliged to complete it, for what he received was a narrative that broke off in 1532, along with notes covering the next 15 years.

The *Chronicle* was once regarded as an eyewitness account of several events in Henry VIII's reign, but more recent scholars have shown this notion to be unlikely. Janet Dillon, for instance, notes that Hall, like all historians of his time, repeated published sources, often word for word, even "for that period of the reign for which he was a potential eyewitness." Hall, in fact, did not aspire to be an original historian. Rather, he described himself as one who "compiled and gathered (and not made) out of divers writers . . . this simple treatise."

Hall's Chronicle nonetheless remains a valuable document. It was, for example, a major source for William SHAKESPEARE's history plays, especially the three *Henry VI* plays. Shakespeare's representation of Queen Margaret, Henry VI's wife, is taken from Hall, who describes her as "a manly woman, used to rule not to be ruled."

Hall's work also illustrates the importance of 15th-century histories to those living in the 16th, for his was one of the texts responsible for justifying the reign of the Tudors (Henry VIII and ELIZABETH I, among others). The Tudors, Hall argues, brought unity to England, releasing it from an imagined political disorder of the previous century. This act alone, in Hall's mind and the minds of other defenders of the Tudors, was proof that they were placed on the throne by God. In other words, Hall structures his discussion of the civil wars of the 15th century, in which the Tudor family emerged victorious and assumed the throne of England, as inevitable and ordained by God.

Although such a politically motivated use of history may seem biased by modern standards of balanced history writing, this was the way histories were written in the 16th century. What makes Hall a notable historian is the clarity and force of his account of a turbulent century.

A Work about Edward Hall

Dillon, Janet. *Performance and Spectacle in Hall's Chronicle.* London: Society for Theatre Research, 2002.

Hall, Joseph (1574–1656) *poet, nonfiction writer*

Joseph Hall was born the second of 12 children at Ashby-de-la-Zouch in Leicestershire, England, and was educated at Emmanuel College, Cambridge University. In 1601 he was offered the rectory of Halsted, in Suffolk, and after serving several other high posts in the church, he became bishop of Exeter in 1627.

In 1597 Hall published the first three of the six books that constituted his *Virgidemiarum* (*A Harvest of Blows*). These were a series of satirical verses modeled after the poems of the Roman satirists Horace and Persius. Hall called the first three books "toothless satires" because they chastised institutions and customs with a gentle humor. In the following passage, for example, he mocks playwrights, suggesting that they receive their inspiration from alcohol:

> So doth the base, and the fore-barren
>   [previously empty] brain,
> Soon as the raging wine begins to reign.
> One higher pitch'd doth set his soaring
>   thought
> On crowned kings, that fortune hath low
>   brought;
> Or some upreared, high-aspiring swain,
> As it might be the Turkish Tamberlain [an
>   allusion to MARLOWE's play Tamburlaine]

The second three books were published in 1598 and were modeled on the works of the Roman satirist Juvenal. Hall called these books "biting satires" because they sharply criticized specific individuals. In Book V of his collection, Hall describes the qualities he believes a satire should possess and goes on to praise the ancient writers of the form:

> The Satire should be like the Porcupine,
> That shoots sharp quills out in each angry
>   line,
> And wounds the blushing cheek and fiery
>   eye,
> Of him that hears and readeth guiltily.

Hall prided himself on being one of the early English writers to emulate the ancient Greek and Roman character writers. In 1608 he published his *Characters of Vices and Vertues,* one of the earliest imitations of the Greek Aristotelian philosopher Theophrastus. In this book Hall portrays a series of vices and virtues through his characters. As with much of his writing, he uses satire as a way of instructing readers on moral behavior. One of the characters he satirizes is the "busybody" whose "estate is too narrow for his mind, and therefore he is fain to make himself room in others' affairs; yet ever, in pretence of love. No news can stir but by his door; neither can he know that which he must not tell." Hall's other works include *Heaven upon Earth* (1606), a book of moral philosophy, and *Mundus Alter et Idem* (*The World Different and the Same,* ca. 1605).

Hammond, Henry (1605–1660) *nonfiction writer*

Henry Hammond was an English theologian known for his critical analysis of the Bible and his sermons about the duties of Christians. He was born in Chertsey, Surrey, England, and educated at Magdalen College, Oxford University. He spent his career serving the church and became a distinguished orator who won the praise of King Charles I.

Hammond wrote several books of religious instruction, sometimes called catechisms, including *Paraphrase and Annotations on the New Testament* (1653) and *Practical Catechism* (1644). Writing during a time when Protestants and Catholics bitterly disputed the right of an individual to interpret the Bible, Hammond urged all Christians to avoid attacking each other and remain mindful of their responsibilities as Christians. In his *Practical Catechism,* he warns against Christian rivalry and says that the issue "may piously be believed on either side." He went on to say that Christians ought to treat the dispute with meekness and charity. Of Hammond, the scholar Timothy James says he was "The Theologian who rallied Anglicans less willing to compromise with the Puritan rulers of England . . . It was a real tragedy that he died . . . before the RESTORATION movement began."

A Work about Henry Hammond

Green, Ian M. *The Christian's ABC: Catechisms and Catechizing in England ca. 1530–1740.* Oxford, U.K.: Oxford University Press, 1996.

Harington, Sir John (1561–1612) *poet, translator*

John Harington was born in Kelston, Somerset, England, the son of John Harington and his second wife. The senior Harington had a connection to the royal family in that his first wife was the illegitimate daughter of King Henry VIII. Harington was educated at Eton College; Cambridge University; and Lincoln's Inn, London. He spent most of his career in the court of his godmother, Queen ELIZABETH I, developing a reputation for high-spirited humor, fine poetry, and wit.

In his early 20s, Harington translated the story of Gioconda, a rather "racy" part of Ludovico ARIOSTO's *Orlando Furioso,* and circulated the translation among the ladies of Elizabeth's court for amusement. As punishment for this act, the queen banned Harrington from court until he had finished translating the entire work of almost 40,000 lines. In 1591 he completed the job and it stands to this day as one of the finest translations of the poem ever made. Around this time Harington also invented the flush lavatory, or modern-day toilet, and installed one for Queen Elizabeth.

In 1596 Harington published *A New Discourse of a Stale Subject, The Metamorphosis of Ajax,* a rather obscene yet comical discourse on his invention of the toilet, "jakes" (which sounds like Ajax) being another word for toilet. The poem is written in an ornate style and filled with literary allusions, or references to other literary works. At the same time Harington describes the technical design and workings of the toilet, he also examines the larger question of obscenity. At the end of the work, he tells his readers that he hopes they find a method

as good as the toilet "to cleanse, and keep sweete, the noblest part of themselves, . . ."

Harington's biographer, D. H. Craig, points out that this comic poem has a serious moral, that "the truly dangerous sinners are those who deny the animal side of humanity and disguise it with finery." As punishment for this publication, Harington was again banished from court, but in 1599 he went on a military expedition to Ireland that earned him a knighthood. His spirited personality and bold (though often offensive) writing style failed to gain him advancement beyond his status—characterized by King JAMES I—as Elizabeth's "saucy godson."

A Work about John Harington

Scott-Warren, Jason. *Sir John Harington and the Book as Gift.* New York: Oxford University Press, 2001.

Hariot, Thomas (Thomas Harriot) (1560–1621) *nonfiction writer*

Thomas Hariot was born in Oxford, England, and later studied at St. Mary's Hall, Oxford University. After graduating, he became a mathematics and science tutor in Sir Walter RALEIGH's household.

Hariot is known to modern readers today as the author of *A Briefe and True Report of the New Found Land of Virginia* (1588), which was written during his expedition to America with Richard Grenville in 1585–86. Hariot was sent along to help with navigation, make astronomical observations, study the native people and lands, and supervise the mapping of the territory. His report appeared along with other chronicles of explorations in Richard HAKLUYT's *Principal Navigations* (1589).

In his report, Hariot pays careful attention to the economic possibilities of the land. The first part consists of a list of commodities with brief descriptions, how they were then used, and how they might be exploited further or exported for use by the English. For example, Hariot discusses the healthful properties of tobacco, which became a profitable export for the eventual British colonies. He explains that tobacco users take the fume or smoke thereof by sucking it through pipes made of claie into their stomacke and heade; from when it purgeth superfluous fleame [phlegm] and other grosse humors [or bodily fluids], openeth all the pores and passages of the body ... wherby their bodies are notably preserved in health, and know not many greevious diseases wherewithall wee in England are oftentimes afflicted.

Much of the report is factual and scientific, but it also borders, as this passage does, on promotion. Primarily, Raleigh and his associates, including Hariot, were interested in assuring their ventures in America would succeed. Hariot's report, however, gives a unique and intelligent glimpse into America's past.

Beginning in about 1609, Hariot began a correspondence with the astronomer Johannes Kepler, and together the two formulated an explanation for how light is dispersed in rainbows. Hariot also developed several powerful new telescopes through which he was able to observe the phases of Venus and complete drawings of the Moon. In addition, he figured out how to calculate the distance from the Sun to the Moon.

Harley, Brilliana (1598–1643) *letter writer*

Brilliana Harley, née Conway, was born to Sir Edward and Dorothy Conway in Brill, England. Raised in an aristocratic, politically connected family, Harley was well educated in English, French, and Latin, as well as in history, literature, and the Protestant religion. In 1623 she married Sir Robert Harley, an influential Puritan parliamentarian.

Harley left a legacy of unpublished letters spanning the years 1625 to 1643. Most were addressed to her eldest son, Edward, while he attended Oxford and later lived in London. In part her correspondence recounts her domestic management of the family estates at Bromton Castle, but she also advises her son on matters of health, religion, and politics: "My deare Ned, be carefull of your health; vse exersis and a good diet; . . . but above all, my deare Ned, looke to that precious part of you, your

soul." (1639) Harley's concern with both physical and spiritual well-being pervades her letters, many of which document her own frequent ill health, including pregnancy and miscarriage. But it is her concern with religion, for she was a staunch Puritan, that led her away from typically gendered topics and motherly advice to discussing the religious matters and politics of her day.

The critic Jacqueline Eales observes, "Lady Brilliana conformed to the conventional contemporary image of the dutiful wife and godly mother, but her letters also demonstrate her active involvement in the religious and political disputes of the [English] civil war." The civil war occurred because of differences between the king and Parliament over religious matters and the rights of the monarchy. The Harley family's Puritan politics lead to conflict with the king's forces, culminating in the siege of their estate. Harley's letters document the events leading up to the civil war; some were about sensitive local politics and were even written in code. They culminate in her extraordinary endeavors to defend her estates while her husband and son were away. Throughout her ordeals she emphasized her faith: "[D]eare Ned, if God weare not mercyfull to me, I should be in a very miserabell condistion. I am threatened every day to be beseet with soulders [soldiers]. My hope is, the Lord will not deliver me nor mine into theair hands; for surely they would use all cruellty towards me." (1642)

Although Harley successfully defended her home, shortly thereafter her letters ended abruptly when she died of pneumonia.

A Work about Brilliana Harley
Daybell, James, ed. *Early Modern Women's Letter-Writing, 1450–1700.* New York: Palgrave, 2001.

Harrington, James (James Harington) (1611–1677) *nonfiction writer*

James Harrington was born in Northampton, England, to Sir Sapcotes and Jane Harrington. He attended Trinity College, Oxford University, but never completed his education, opting to travel instead.

In 1656 Harrington's life changed when he published *The Commonwealth of Oceana,* a work that earned him both instant fame and instant notoriety. *The Commonwealth of Oceana* is a thinly veiled allegory that suggests to the English government the need for political reform. The work focuses on the nation of Oceana (or England), where Olphaus Megaletor (Oliver Cromwell), struggles to decide what is right for his country.

In Harrington's ideal commonwealth as portrayed in *Oceana,* a natural aristocracy based on merit will emerge to rule, but upward mobility must also be possible, for "Where a man from the lowest may not rise unto the due pitch of his unquestionable merit . . . the commonwealth is not equal." Harrington proposes a legislature made up of two houses, much like the Congress of the United States, and emphasizes the importance of term limits, based on his idea that power should not remain in the same hands for too long a period of time. He also recommends land reform so that there is a more equal distribution of property, a condition he believes is necessary for the commonwealth to thrive.

Oceana sparked an immediate controversy and left Harrington defending his work in various pamphlets for the rest of his life. He was even imprisoned in the Tower of London for a time, an experience that left him mentally unstable for the rest of his life. A hundred years after Harrington's death, however, many of his ideas found their way into the Constitution of the United States.

Harvey, Gabriel (ca. 1550–1630) *nonfiction writer, poet*

Gabriel Harvey was born in Saffron Walden, Essex, England, to John Harvey, an Essex rope maker. He entered Cambridge University on a scholarship in 1566, eventually earning his M.A. in 1573. Harvey remained an academic his entire life. Among his students may have been Edmund SPENSER, with whom he formed a close friendship.

In 1576 Harvey became a lecturer in rhetoric, or the art of argumentation. The first of his lectures, *Ciceronianus* (*The Ciceronian,* referring to the ancient Roman orator Cicero), was published in 1577. In this work Harvey condemns the common practice of imitating Cicero's sentence structures and vocabulary, insisting that Cicero's wisdom also needed to be imitated. Those who contented themselves with merely imitating Cicero's style, Harvey pointed out, could succeed at the task even if they were "dumber than the very fish." However, it took real intelligence to master the content of Cicero's writing.

Harvey's involvement in the intellectual life of 16th-century England went beyond scholarship. Along with other poets such as Sir Philip SIDNEY, he sought to reform English poetry and claimed to have brought it new poetic techniques. In 1579 and 1580 Harvey and Spenser exchanged letters, published in 1580, in which they discussed the reformation of poetry. In one of his letters Harvey refers to "those two excellent gentleman Mr. Sidney and Mr. [Edward] DYER . . . [who have helped] forward our new famous enterprise for the exchanging of barbarous . . . rhymes with artificial verses." Harvey praises the metrical smoothness of Dyer's and Sidney's verses, something he is perhaps overly concerned with in the letter. At one point he criticizes Spenser for having one syllable too many in a line of some unnamed poem.

Harvey's nitpicking over things such as syllable counts has helped to give him a reputation as a hairsplitter. This reputation was cemented in a feud he had with the dramatist Robert GREENE and the fiction writer Thomas NASHE in the 1590s. The feud began when Harvey's brother Richard satirized Greene, Nashe, and other UNIVERSITY WITS, a group of writers centered around Oxford University. Greene responded by attacking the Harveys in *A Quip for an Upstart Courtier* (1591), a pamphlet that was suppressed and later reprinted without the references to the Harveys in it.

Harvey then attacked Greene after his death in *Four Letters and Certain Sonnets* (1592), which discusses in spiteful detail the misery of Greene's last years. Harvey concludes the book with a vindictive sonnet sequence. In "John Harveys Welcome to Robert Greene," for example, he writes:

Come, fellow Greene, come to thy gaping
*   grave:*
Bidd Vanity, and Foolery farewell:
Thou over-long hast plaid the madbrain'd
*   knave:*
And over-loud hast rung the bawdy bell.
Vermine to Vermine must repair [return] at
*   last:*
No fitter house for busy folk to dwell.

Nashe, whose talent for satire was much greater than Harvey's, took up his pen to defend Greene's memory. "Harvey," Nashe writes in *Strange News* (1592), "goes twitching and hopping in our language like a man running upon quagmires, up the hill in one syllable, and down the dale in another." Nashe goes on to parody his target in a verse that mocks Harvey's claim to have brought a new poetic meter into English: "But eh! What news do you hear of that good Gabriel Huffe-Snuffe, / Known to the world for a foot [that is, a metrical foot with a pun on a human foot], and clapt in the fleet for a runner?" The controversy turned so bitter that the state censor was compelled to issue a decree that "all Nash's books and Dr. Harvey's books be taken wheresoever they may be found, and that none of the same books be ever printed hereafter."

Nashe's portrait of Harvey has obscured his importance. The scholar Kendrick W. Prewitt defends Harvey's memory by noting that he "was a noteworthy figure in his own right as one of the most learned humanists . . . and his treatises, letters, and marginalia [that is, the marginal notes that he left in his books] constitute a rich testimony to academic life in his day."

A Work about Gabriel Harvey

Stern, Virginia. *Gabriel Harvey: His Life, Marginalia, and Library*. Oxford, U.K.: Clarendon Press, 1979.

Harvey, William (1578–1657) *nonfiction writer*

William Harvey was born at Folkestone, Kent, England, the eldest child of well-to-do merchant Thomas Harvey and his wife, Joan. After earning a B.A. at Cambridge University in 1596, he received a medical degree from the University of Padua in Italy (the center for anatomical research at the time) six years later. He then returned to London, where in 1613 he became a member of the College of Physicians, responsible for regulating medical practice. He also served as physician to JAMES I OF ENGLAND.

In 1615 Harvey became lecturer in anatomy at the College of Physicians. It was as a lecturer that he began to consider ideas that would lead him to discover how the blood circulates through the body. As early as 1616 he had concluded that the heart acted as a pump that actively pushed out blood as it contracted. The idea was not new, but most doctors believed the heart sucked blood in but did not actively expel it. In 1628 Harvey published his findings in *Exercitatio Anatomica de Motu Cordis et Sanguinis in Animalibus* (*Anatomical Exercises on the Motion of the Heart and Blood in Animals*).

Harvey's discovery would dramatically transform medical theory, yet he was in many ways a conservative thinker. He deferred, like many doctors in his day, to the authority of the ancient Greek philosopher Aristotle. Aristotle's theories, however, would be debunked by the new learning to which Harvey's discovery contributed. As Harvey scholar Andrew Wear puts it, "when the leading figures of the scientific revolution constructed their new science, they explicitly rejected the philosophy of Aristotle, replacing his . . . view of the world and life . . . with one that was mechanical and quantitative."

Harvey thus seems to be a contradiction in that he is simultaneously a conservative and a major innovator who committed, in the words of the critic John Rogers, "an act of rebellion against contemporary medical orthodoxy that easily qualified [him] as the century's premier 'disturber of the quiet of Physicians'." The contradiction is not difficult to explain. Harvey's discovery grew out of his studies in comparative anatomy, which he took up in imitation of Aristotle. These studies required him to observe the objects that he was investigating, an act that placed him at odds with traditional Aristotelian practices. During the Middle Ages, when authors wrote about a subject, they included everything that previously had been said about it into their writings, whether or not the authors they cited contradicted each other. Medieval scholars were not expected to say anything original. Indeed, observation was often ignored in favor of book knowledge.

In the RENAISSANCE, however, things changed, especially in medical circles. Medical theorists began to question age-old authorities. Still, many theorists seemed more interested in proving ancient notions wrong than in arguing for new ideas.

More so than many of his contemporaries, Harvey was interested in exploring new ideas about the human body. In *Anatomical Exercises* he explains how he came to realize the truth about the workings of the heart and the movement of the blood by describing the experiments that have led him to his conclusions. For instance, in his experiments with ligatures, or tightened bandages, he first makes a distinction between a tight ligature, which completely stops blood from flowing into the arm, and a medium tight one, which allows some blood to flow into the arm. Harvey writes:

> [I]f a tight ligature is made by compressing the arm as is bearable, it can first be noted that beyond the ligature, that is toward the hand, there will be no arterial pulsation [blood flowing from the arteries] in the wrist or anywhere else; secondly that directly above the ligature the artery . . . exhibits a kind of tidal swell as if it were trying to burst through an impediment to its passage and to reopen a channel. Harvey goes on to explain that if one makes the ligature medium tight, one will see the blood flow into the arm through the arteries. Such a ligature, however, continues to block the veins, preventing blood from leaving the arm. Harvey thus concludes, "So from these facts any reasonably careful observer can readily learn that the blood enters through the arteries" and exits through the veins.

Harvey's final experiments were studies of the female reproductive system, the uterus and the ovaries. His last published work, *Exercitationes de Generatione Animalium* (*Experiments Concerning the Generation of Animals,* 1651), is a study of the fertilization of eggs.

Harvey's work is important not only because it showed that the blood circulates but also because it demonstrated the value of describing repeatable experiments. By describing his experiments in detail, Harvey allowed those whom he was teaching to perform and therefore confirm his findings themselves. Medical professor Eric Neil writes that Harvey also "turned anatomical facts into physiological [scientific] language," and therefore helped to develop the language of modern medicine.

A Work about William Harvey
Yount, Lisa. *William Harvey: Discoverer of How Blood Circulates.* Hillside, N.J.: Enslow Publishers, 1994.

Hawes, Stephen (ca. 1475–1511) *poet*
The published works of Stephen Hawes describe him as a "groom of the chamber" to King Henry VII, and official records of payments made to him support this claim. He is otherwise known only through his work. Like John SKELTON, a late medieval writer, Hawes admired the morality of John Gower, Geoffrey Chaucer, and John Lydgate, and he continued their tradition of allegorical poetry. He adapted this to the HUMANISM of his day by, showing that a person's morality can be improved by education.

Hawes's principal poetic works are *The Example of Vertu* (1504) and *The Pastime of Pleasure* (1509), dream visions in which a young hero sets off to find and win his lady through debates, adventures, and trials. In *The Example of Vertu* Youth, guided by Discretion, becomes Virtue and rescues his lady, Cleanness, from a dragon. The dreamer in the second poem is Grand Amour (Great Love), who begins his education at the Tower of Doctrine. He falls in love with La Belle Pucelle (The Beautiful Virgin), and then studies at the Tower of Chivalry, which prepares him for his quest to win her. Both poems include the death of the dreamer after marriage, and *The Pastime of Pleasure* takes this as an opportunity to warn readers about the inevitability of death:

> O mortall folke! you may beholde and se
> Howe I lye here, sometyme a myghty
>   knyght;
> The end of joye and all prosperyte
> Is dethe at last, through his course and
>   smyght;
> After the day there cometh the derke night;
> For though the day be never so longe,
> At last the belles ryngeth to evensonge.

Hawes wrote two shorter poems: "The Conversion of Swearers," in which Christ protests against swearing by His wounds, blood, and so on; and "A Joyful Meditation of the Coronation of Henry the Eighth," celebrating the beginning of the new reign. *The Comfort of Lovers* was Hawes's last work. Here the young lover, Amour, dreams of his lady, who is promised to another. She warns him not to continue loving her, and he agrees but asks: "But right dear lady, whom I long have sought / Forget me not, remember love dear bought."

Hayman, Robert (1575–1629) *poet*

Robert Hayman was born in Devon, England, in 1575, the son of Nicholas Hayman, a prosperous landowner. His mother, Alice Gaverocke Hayman, died when he was just five, and his father remarried a few months later. His father became a member of Parliament in 1586. Hayman received his B.A. from Exeter College, Oxford University, in 1590, and then studied law at Lincoln's Inn in London, though it is unknown if he finished his studies there. A letter from his father, dated July 1600, mentions the fact that Hayman was studying at the University of Poitiers in France.

In the early years of the 17th century, records indicate that Hayman was living in Bristol with his wife, Grace Spicer Hayman. Hayman's brother-in-law, John Barker, was one of those responsible for settling the land in Newfoundland called Bristol Hope, in and around 1617. Hayman traveled there, and this visit became the source for his one published work, *Quodlibets* (1628).

The book of epigrams (brief, witty poems), whose full title was *Quodlibets, lately come over from New Britaniola, All of them Composed and done at Harbor-Grace in Britaniola, anciently called Newfoundland,* is dedicated to King Charles I. Many of the epigrams are addressed to other influential women and men of the time, many of whom were concerned with the settling of Newfoundland. The work can be seen as a plea to the king and other powers to help support and save the colony. Hayman stressed the riches of the new land—its fish, minerals, furs, abundant forests—but at the same time expressed disgust for those who came to the new land solely for profit. He wrote, "*Send forth your Sonnes unto our New* Plantation; / *Yet send such as are Holy, wise,* and *able.*" In the end, his work did little to secure royal support, mainly because graver matters were distracting the king.

Hayman recognized the fact that his epigrams paled in quality next to those of Ben JONSON: "My Epigrams come after yours in time; / So doe they in conceipt, in forme, in Ryme . . . / There never had beene better Verses writ, / As good as *yours,* could I have ruled it." Still, he believed in the future of Canada and saw *Quodlibets* as a small contribution to a future, great nation. He died during an expedition up the River Wyapoko in Guiana in 1629.

Hayward, John (ca. 1560–1627) *nonfiction writer, historian*

John Hayward was born in Suffolk, England, and educated at Cambridge University, where he earned a B.A. in 1581, an M.A. in 1584, and a doctorate some time later. In 1599 he published *The First Part of the Life and Reign of King Henry IV,* a history which tells how Henry Bolingbroke overthrew King Richard II in 1399 and became Henry IV. The book was dedicated to Robert Devereux, second Earl of Essex, who attempted to overthrow ELIZABETH I in 1601. Because it was determined to be treasonous, the book was burned, and Hayward was imprisoned for three years.

The Elizabethan authorities felt Hayward had constructed a comparison between the past and the present in *Henry IV*. Thus, in the words of the scholar Phyllis Rackin, the "description of Richard II's inadequacies as a ruler could be taken to apply to Elizabeth," while the positive description of Henry as "courteous and familiar respectively towards all men, whereby he produced great reputation and regard, especially with the meaner sort" seemed to apply to Essex. At Essex's trial, a passage from Hayward's book was used as evidence against the earl. Hayward accused Richard II of using benevolences, or forced loans, to raise money. This practice, however, was not begun until the second half of the 15th century. Therefore, according to Rackin, "the times of Elizabeth rather than those of Richard II were in question" in Hayward's history. Apparently for Hayward, history could be used to comment on the present.

After his release from prison, Hayward sought the favor of JAMES I OF ENGLAND by publishing two pamphlets. Both *An Answer to the First Part of a Certain Conference Concerning Succession* and *A Treatise of Union of England and Scotland*, flattered the king by repeating his belief in the divine right of kings, the theory that the monarchs of England had been placed on the throne by God. In 1610 Hayward was appointed historian at a college that James founded; he was knighted in 1619.

Hayward wrote a number of histories, including *Lives of the Three Norman Kings of England* (1613), which told the lives of William I, William II, and Henry I; and *The Life and Reign of King Edward VI* (1630). In the latter work, Hayward constructs a compelling narrative out of the materials of King Edward's life: "This noble prince, whose Storie is here delivered, seems to have had the same adversity of fortune in his life and death, which he had at his birth."

Hayward was a competent RENAISSANCE historian who (like many historians) used the events of the past as a way of discussing present politics. Although he does not rank with the great historians of the age such as John STOW and Raphael HOLINSHED, he is of interest as a historical figure in his own right.

Head, Richard (1637–1686) *fiction writer*

Richard Head was born in Ireland and witnessed the murder of his father, a chaplain to a nobleman, by Irish rebels in 1641. Head and his mother fled to England, where he studied briefly at Oxford University before opening a bookstore in London. Due to drinking and gambling, Head lost his business and moved to Dublin to escape his debts. He later returned to London, where he again opened and lost a bookstore and made a very modest living from writing before drowning while crossing to the Isle of Wright.

Head wrote fictional biographies of rogues and criminals that were popular amongst the lower classes he served as a bookseller. His first and most popular work, *The English Rogue* (1665), was highly autobiographical. *The English Rogue* details the antics of a young man in a series of crude stories. Head describes an unwelcome intruder while the character Meriton Latroon is in bed with a prostitute: "The bulk of his body began to heave like an earth-quake, whilst his mouth, Aetna-like [volcanic, after Mount Etna], belched out all manner of sulphurous oaths, which roared so loud as if his belly had contained a barrel of gunpowder, and the linstock of his nose had fired it." Head depicts Meriton as immoral and selfish. He steals his mistress's money because "it was better for one to want than two." Critic James Seigel calls *The English Rogue* "base, crude and over-obvious." The bookseller Francis Kirkman wrote several sequels to the book, and a total of four parts were published under the same title by 1671. Head's first part is considered the least offensive of the set.

Head produced a number of vulgar works on the rogue theme (which includes characters who are mischievous, scoundrelly, or rascally), including *Floating Island* (1673), *The Life and Death of*

Mother Shipton (1677), and *Nugae Venales* (1686), all of which Seigel suggests were popular among the Puritans. Shinagel writes that Head's life and work "typify the wretched existence of scores of hack writers during the . . . period."

Henryson, Robert (ca. 1424–ca. 1506)
poet

Nothing beyond his poetry is known of Robert Henryson, who wrote in Middle Scots, a dialect used for writing rather than for speech. One of Henryson's major works is *The Morall Fabillis of Esope the Phrygian* (1568), a collection of animal fables. The 13 fables that comprise the collection are Henryson's versions of stories that had been popular in Britain since the Norman Conquest and that can be read as moral allegory. One of the finest of these tales is the story from Aesop of the country mouse and the city mouse. This tale, like all the others, ends with a moral:

> *Grit aboundance and blind prosperitie*
> *Oftymes makis ane evill conclusion.*
> *The sweitest lyfe, thairfoir, in this cuntrie,*
> *Is sickernes, with small possessioun.*

> (*"Great abundance and blind prosperity*
> *Often make an evil conclusion.*
> *The sweetest life, therefore, in this country*
> *Is security with few possessions."*)

Henryson is best known for his *Testament of Cresseid*, a sequel to Geoffrey Chaucer's *Troilus and Criseyde*. Chaucer took his version of the story from the Greek legend about the Trojan prince Troilus, who falls in love with Cressida. Though Cressida swears to be true, she betrays Troilus. Henryson follows Chaucer but invents an explanation of what happens to Chaucer's Criseyde after Troilus dies, and makes leprosy the punishment for her sins. In his new ending Henryson is sympathetic as well as stern when he describes Cressida's father's reaction to her disease: He luikit on hir uglye lipper face, / The quhylk befor was quhite as lillie flour; / and knowing that there was no cure for her sickness, / Thus was thair cair aneuch betuix thame twane ("He looked on her ugly leprous face, / Which before was as white as a lily; / And knowing there was no cure for her sickness, / Thus was their care enough between the two of them"). Henryson's poem is not merely a sequel to Chaucer; it is a great work in its own right, as the poet parallels the physical degeneration of Cressida with her spiritual redemption.

Henryson wrote a third long poem, *Orpheus and Euridice*, based on the classical myth about two lovers: Orpheus, a musician, and his wife, Euridice. When Euridice dies, Orpheus plays the lyre so beautifully that the gods are moved to allow him to bring her back from the dead, but they stipulate that he must not look on her until they reach the upper world. Orpheus forgets the condition and turns to check on Euridice, thereby losing her again to death. Henryson's work can also be read as comment about society, since it makes Orpheus a king and begins by suggesting that men in high positions should not be overproud of their ancestry but should be more inclined to turn their hearts "The moir to vertew and to worthiness." The poem also often refers to rulers who have fallen, such as Nero and Julius Caesar.

Henry the Minstrel
See BLIND HARRY.

Herbert, Edward (1583–1648) *poet,*
nonfiction writer

Edward Herbert was born at Eyton in Shropshire, England, the older brother of the famous religious poet George HERBERT and the oldest son of Richard Herbert, the sheriff of Mongomeryshire, and his wife, Magdalen, who was later a patron of the poet John DONNE. Educated at University College, Oxford, Herbert mastered writing in Latin and later went on to serve in a variety of diplomatic positions, including ambassador to France (1619–24), before being created Baron Herbert of Cherbury in 1629.

Herbert discusses his religious ideas in his three philosophical works, *De veritate* (1624), *De religione laici* (1645), and *De religione gentilium* (1663). The first of these works is considered his greatest; however, in all three he examines what he considers the truths of religion. Herbert argues there are several ideas that all religions have in common. These are: (1) that there is a supreme Deity; (2) that this Deity ought to be worshipped; (3) that virtue combined with piety is the chief part of divine worship; (4) that men should repent of their sins and turn from them; and (5) that reward and punishment follow from the goodness and justice of God, both in this life and after it. For these ideas Herbert has come to be considered "the father of English deism. He believed that it was possible to find a logical formula that one could follow in order to guarantee a place in heaven. Herbert's analysis of religion from a rational or logical point of view, rather than one based on the pure faith in God, unquestioning belief in the Bible, or mere acceptance of religious authority, earned him criticism from both Protestant and Catholic theologians of his day.

Herbert also wrote from a philosophical perspective in much of his metaphysical poetry (*see* METAPHYSICAL POETS). Although his younger brother George is more famous than he, Edward wrote several metaphysical poems that examine the world through rational analysis. This is apparent even in the title of his love poem "An Ode upon a Question moved, Whether Love should continue for ever?" One of the lovers in the poem, Celinda, asks the question, and her beloved Melander responds with a reassurance that love does last:

> These eyes again, then, eyes shall see,
> And hands again these hands enfold,
> And all chast pleasures can be told
> Shall with us everlasting be.
>
> For if no use of sense remain
> When bodies once this life forsake,
> Or they could no delight partake,
> Why should they ever rise again?

A man of many talents, Herbert was admired by many of his contemporaries, including the philosopher René DESCARTES who said that Herbert's "mind had few equal."

Works about Edward Herbert

Bedford, R. D. *The Defence of Truth: Lord Herbert of Cherbury and the Seventeenth Century.* Princeton, N.J.: Princeton University Press, 1987.

Butler, John A. *Lord Herbert of Chirbury: An Intellectual Biography.* Lewiston, N.Y.: Edwin Mellen Press, 1990.

Herbert, George (1593–1633) *poet, nonfiction writer*

George Herbert was born in Montgomery, Wales, the fifth son of Richard and Magdalen Newport Herbert. His father died in 1596, and Herbert was educated by his mother, a woman known for her piety as well as her PATRONAGE of John DONNE, among other writers. Herbert attended Westminster School in London and went on to receive both bachelor's and master's degrees from Cambridge University. He subsequently taught at Cambridge and was appointed to the prestigious post of public orator for the university. This could easily have led to a political career, but he gave up secular ambition to study for the priesthood; he was ordained in 1630. (His older brother, Edward HERBERT, took the secular route as a diplomat and was rewarded with a peerage in 1629.)

Herbert took over the church at Bemerton, near Salisbury, England, in 1630. He began to rebuild the decaying church with his own hands and, mostly, his own funds. But his priestly career was short-lived, as he contracted and died of tuberculosis.

Herbert had been writing poetry, in English and Latin, since his university days. During his life, however, he published only a few poems. The majority of Herbert's writings were published after his death. A 1652 volume entitled *Herbert's Remains* contained his prose work *A Priest to the Temple, or the Country Parson, his Character or Rule of Holy Life,* a practical manual for parish priests. Herbert's verse translations of eight psalms were published in a 1671 volume entitled *Psalms and Hymns.*

Herbert's most important poetic work was *The Temple: Sacred Poems and Private Ejaculations* (1633). This collection, which appeared not long after Herbert's death, contains religious poems that he wrote during the last few years of his life. *The Temple* proved popular, with many editions appearing over the next century.

Critical Analysis

Herbert is considered, with Donne, the most important of the METAPHYSICAL POETS. The metaphysicals broke with the conventions of Elizabethan poetry to produce poems that were forceful, surprising, and intellectual, rather than delicate, charming, and melodious. Unlike Donne, who wrote some of the language's great love poems, Herbert confined himself to devotional verse, but his emotional range is great, from the agonies of religious doubt to the insecurity of a priest wondering if he has the strength to lead his parishioners, to the bitterness of repentance, to the occasional intense joy of feeling at one with God.

Herbert shares much with the religious poetry of Donne and Fulke GREVILLE, particularly a tendency toward complex thought. As is characteristic of the metaphysical poets, he often used images whose connection to the subject at hand is far from obvious; readers must exercise their intellects to follow the argument.

The uniqueness of *The Temple* lies in its structure, which is modeled on that of a church. The titles of various poems are parts of the church: "The Church-Porch," "Sepulchre," "Church-Monuments," "Churchlock and Key," "The Church-Floor," and "The Windows" all speak to specific parts of the church's structure, while other titles refer to events that happen in the church or objects used by church officials.

In "The Windows," Herbert addresses the preacher's sense of inadequacy before his task:

> LORD, how can man preach thy eternal
> word?
> He is a brittle crazie glasse. . . .

The comparison with glass seems to be introduced for the connotations of fragility, but it quickly becomes apparent that the transparency of glass is the nub of the image: the preacher is to be the window through which God's light can flow:

> Yet in thy temple thou dost him afford
> This glorious and transcendent place,
> To be a window, through thy grace.

But it is not enough to be transparent; it is much better if the church windows have colors and can tell a story as they let the light through. The preacher's colors are his living relationship with God, without which any truth he speaks will not reach the listener's heart:

> Doctrine and life, colours and light, in one
> When they combine and mingle, bring
> A strong regard and awe: but speech alone
> Doth vanish like a flaring thing,
> And in the ear, not conscience ring.

In "The Pulley," Herbert uses the idea of a homely mechanical thing that a church warden might set up to raise the blinds in the church to convey God's care for humankind. The conceit (elaborate metaphor) is that God has set up a pulley to bring people home. In making man, God has given him every gift except one; he has carefully withheld the gift of rest, which is the pulley:

> If goodness leade him not, yet weariness
> May toss him to my breast.

Herbert was interested in how a poem looks on the page—that is, how, when it is set in type, its final shape ties into its meaning. For example, the very lines of "The Altar" take the shape of this church structure. The poem's shape is a symbol. The altar may seem to be made of stone, but it is actually "made of a heart, and cemented with tears," not merely a "workman's tool." Since the poem is printed in the traditional shape of an altar, each word can be seen as a brick in the overall structure. Herbert suggests that it is not only the poet who builds this altar but the reader who constructs it by reflecting upon each word read.

"Easter Wings" also develops a relationship between the poem's physical shape on the page and its meaning. Originally printed so that a reader of *The Temple* would have to turn the volume sideways to read the lines, the two stanzas, or verses, of "Easter Wings" actually look like two sets of wings upon the page. The poem's content depends on this image since it speaks to the subject of man's fall and its relationship to Christ's resurrection from the dead.

In each stanza the lines grow steadily smaller until the middle, and then they once more grow longer. Thus the first stanza reads:

> *Lord, who createdst man in wealth and stone,*
> *Though foolishly he lost the same,*
> *Decaying more and more*
> *Till he became*
> *Most poor'*
> *With thee*
> *O Let Me Rise*
> *As larks, hamoniously*
> *And sing this day thy victories:*
> *Then shall the fall further the flight in me.*

In this stanza words such as "lost" and "decaying" give the impression of a dwindling away, a process of whittling down to nothing. At the same time Herbert whittles his stanza down, bit by bit, to further emphasize this point.

However, in the second set of five lines the poet regains hope as he sees the possibility for rejuvenation and resurrection. In response to this renewed hope, the lines increase in length until the last line is as long as the first. The last line expresses the thought, familiar in religious poetry for centuries before, that the tragedy of the fall actually led to greater happiness, as without it Christ would never

have made his sacrifice and conquered Satan and death.

The last two lines of the poem's second stanza, "For, if I imp my wing on thine, / Affliction shall advance the flight in me" speaks directly of the importance of the wing imagery to the poem. (To "imp" is a term from falconry, meaning to repair a damaged wing by grafting in a new feather.) The flight symbolism counters the decay of the poem's first part.

When turned on its side, the poem also has the shape of an hourglass. This shape is equally appropriate since the poem is also concerned with the passage of time, from the fall to the resurrection and the ultimate release into eternity.

Herbert's poems need to be read with a careful eye since it is easy to miss some of his subtle craftsmanship. In his style Herbert is nothing if not understated. His poems are simple in their tone but should not be quickly passed over because of their simplicity. Because Herbert was dedicated to the project of fashioning poetry into something new and spiritual, one of the main themes a reader encounters when reading his work is the relationship between complexity and simplicity. He suggests, time and time again, that things are not always as simple as they seem: There is meaning in the smallest gesture, the smallest object, the smallest prayer. In *The Temple* this theme is always at work, primarily when Herbert questions the formalism of public religious practices and whether they are an adequate partner to private reflective meditation.

Other Work by George Herbert
The Complete English Poems. Edited by John Tobin. New York: Penguin, 1992.

Works about George Herbert
Charles, Amy M. *Life of George Herbert.* Ithaca, N.Y.: Cornell University Press, 1977.
Malcolmson, Cristina. *Heart-work: George Herbert and the Protestant Ethic.* Stanford, Calif.: Stanford University Press, 1999.

Patrides, C. A., ed. *George Herbert: The Critical Heritage.* London: Routledge, 1983.

Ray, Robert H. *A George Herbert Companion.* New York: Garland, 1995.

Stewart, Stanley. *George Herbert.* Boston: Twayne, 1986.

Wall, John W., Jr. *Transformations of the Word: Spenser, Herbert, Vaughan.* Athens: University of Georgia Press, 1988.

Herbert, Mary

See SIDNEY, MARY.

Herrick, Robert (1591–1674) poet

Robert Herrick was born in London to Nicholas Herrick, a wealthy goldsmith, and his wife, Julian Stone Herrick, the daughter of a prosperous textile merchant. Little is known of Herrick's childhood and early education, although he may have received instruction in Latin poetry and prose. In 1607, when he was 16, he was apprenticed to his uncle, Sir William Herrick, a successful goldsmith and jeweler.

Herrick's earliest datable poems are from the years of his apprenticeship. "A Country Life: To his Brother M. Tho. Herrick," which celebrates the pleasures of "the Countries sweet simplicity," was written around 1610, when Herrick's brother left London to farm in Leicestershire. "To my dearest Sister M. Mercie Herrick" must also have been written around this time. In this poem Herrick conveys a blessing to his sister:

> Prosper thy basket and therein thy dough.
> Feed on the paste of filberts, or else knead
> And bake the flour of amber for thy bread.
> Balm may thy trees drop, and thy springs
>   run oil,
> And everlasting harvest crown thy soil!

In 1613 Herrick went to Cambridge University, where he studied the classics as well as rhetoric and logic. He earned a B.A. degree in 1617 and an M.A.

three years later. In 1623 he became an Anglican priest.

Herrick made a name for himself as a poet during the 1620s, when his poems were circulated in manuscript, as was the custom of the time. According to his own poems, he frequented London taverns, where he made many literary friends, among them the dramatist and poet Ben JONSON and the poets William BROWNE and Richard CORBET. Jonson was a particularly important influence on Herrick, who was one of the Sons of Ben, a group of young poets who clustered around the older man. "Ah, Ben!" Herrick wrote in "An Ode for Him" (1648), "each verse of thine / Out-did the meat, out-did the frolic wine."

Among the people Herrick met at these gatherings was the Duke of Buckingham, for whom in 1627 Herrick served as chaplain during a failed military expedition to aid French Protestants on the Isle of Rhé. In 1639, as a reward for his services, Herrick was made vicar at the village of Dean Prior in southwest England.

Herrick's poems reveal his mixed reaction to living in the country. He deplores the isolation of "this dull Devonshire," in "Discontents in Devon" but elsewhere celebrates its folk customs of "Maypoles, Hock-carts, Wassails, Wakes."

Herrick, who was loyal to the British monarchy, was ejected from his post as vicar by Parliament in 1647, during the English Civil Wars, which were fought between those who supported the monarchy and those who wanted rule by Parliament. He returned to London, where in 1648 he published *Hesperides: or the Works both Humane & Divine of Robert Herrick Esq.,* a collection of 1,400 poems. Its title, *Hesperides,* refers to Greek mythology's Daughters of Evening, nymphs who guarded a tree with golden apples in the far western regions of the earth. Paralleling this mythical region, Devonshire is in the west of England and is famed for its apples. *Hesperides* includes poems in imitation of Roman verse; epigrams, which are short poems often ending with a witty twist; love poetry; and folk songs. Within this collection, as a separate book, are Herrick's religious poems, entitled "Noble Numbers."

In 1660, when the monarchy was restored under Charles II, Herrick returned to the vicarage at Dean Prior, where he lived until his death. In the last decade of his life, however, he apparently wrote no further poetry. He was buried in an unmarked grave in the cemetery of the church he had served.

Critical Analysis

Robert Herrick is the author of one of the most famous lines in English poetry, "Gather ye Rosebuds while ye may," which comes from his brief lyric poem "To the Virgins, to Make Much of Time." The line's message that both beauty and time are fleeting and that enjoyment must be seized immediately before it is lost is a common one in Herrick's nonreligious poetry. Its origins go back to the Roman poets Horace, Catullus, and others whose works Herrick studied and admired. This kind of poetry is often referred to as "carpe diem," from the Latin for "seize the day."

Another of Herrick's "carpe diem" poems is among his most famous, "Corinna's Going a-Maying." It begins with these lovely images and charming alliteration:

> Get up, get up for shame, the blooming
>   Morn
> Upon her wings presents the god unshorn.
> See how Aurora throws her fair
> Fresh-quilted colours through the air;
> Get up, sweet slug-a-bed, and see
> The dew bespangling herb and tree.

Among Herrick's "flower poems," "To Daffodills" may be the most read, perhaps because of its melancholy yet apt comparison of the brevity of the daffodil's life to human life. It ends:

> We have short time to stay, as you,
> We have as short a spring;
> As quick a growth to meet decay,
> As you, or anything.
> We die,
> As your hours do, and dry

> Away,
> Like to the summer's rain;
> Or as the pearls of morning's dew,
> Ne'er to be found again.

The range of Herrick's poetry is wide, from exquisite love lyrics to salty epigrams, from pastoral poems (celebrations of country life) to racy drinking songs. Some of his finest pieces are his love poems, although the Julias, Antheas, and Corinnas to whom they are addressed were probably imaginary. Love poems such as "Upon Julia's Haire Fill'd with Dew" vividly conjure up the effect the sight of the beloved has on the poet: "Dew sat on Julia's hair / And spangled too, / Like leaves that laden are / With trembling dew." In "Upon Julia's Clothes," Herrick conveys a delicate sensuality through both his words and their languid sounds: "When as in silks my Julia goes, / Then, then (me thinks) how sweetly flowes / That liquefaction of her clothes."

Herrick's religious poems are, essentially, love poems addressed to the deity. They have much the same sweetness and lyric quality as do his secular verses. In "To His Sweet Savior," for example, Herrick writes about a long night of worry and sickness of the soul. He begs:

> O Saviour! do Thou please
> To make my bed soft in my sicknesses:
> Lighten my candle, so that I beneath
> Sleep not for ever in the vaults of death;
> Let me Thy voice betimes i' th' morning
>   hear:
> Call, and I'll come; say Thou the when, and
>   where.

"I make no haste to have my Numbers read. / Seldome comes Glorie till a man be dead," wrote Herrick, who was confident of the immortality of his work. In fact he was recognized in his own lifetime: In 1625, when Herrick was 34, the poet Richard James in his *The Muses Dirge* ranked Herrick with Ben Jonson and Michael DRAYTON as the leading poets of the day.

Nevertheless, for 150 years after his death, Herrick's poetry was often neglected or underrated. The very range of tone and subject matter of Herrick's poetry was a problem for some readers. Those drawn to the rosebuds, tulips, and daffodils of his polished love lyrics were repelled by such coarse verses as the description of a drunkard's pimpled nose. Those who appreciated his earthy gusto found his depictions of fairy revels in poems like "Oberon's Feast" insipid. Thus, some like the 19th-century English poet Robert Southey criticized Herrick as "a coarse-minded and beastly writer," while the 20th-century English critic F. R. Leavis pronounced Herrick "trivially charming."

Still, Herrick did have his admirers. The English critic George Saintsbury, in his introduction to the *Poetical Works of Robert Herrick* (1893), wrote, "It is not easy to find a poet who is in his own way so *complete* as Herrick." The poet Algernon Swinburne, in *Studies in Prose and Poetry* (1894), hailed Herrick as "the greatest song-writer ever born of English race." Composers ranging from Herrick's contemporaries William and Henry Lawes to the modern masters Paul Hindemith and Benjamin Britten have been inspired to set his poems to music.

In the past century there has been a deepening appreciation of Herrick's poetry. The scholar J. Max Patrick writes that "Herrick's place as one of the greatest English lyric poets is now secure."

Other Work by Robert Herrick

Robert Herrick. Edited by Douglas Brooks-Davies. New York: Everyman's Library, 1997.

Works about Robert Herrick

Rollin, Roger B. *Robert Herrick.* (Twayne English Author Series) New York: Twayne, 1992.

Scott, George Walton. *Robert Herrick: The Life of a Poet, 1591–1674.* New York: St. Martin's Press, 1974.

Heylyn, Peter (Peter Heylin) (1600–1662)
historian, nonfiction writer

Peter Heylyn was an English theologian and historian best known for writing a history of the English reformation. He was born in Burford, Oxfordshire, England, and studied at Hart Hall and Magdalan College, Oxford University. Heylyn's lectures on geography and cosmography at Oxford were published in 1621. He went on to serve as the king's chaplain for Charles I before the English Revolution and Civil Wars broke out in 1642. After the Restoration, Heylyn retired to Westminster, where he continued to write.

Heylyn's *Cosmographie* (1652) incorporated his previous work *Geography* (1621) and was intended to be a comprehensive history of the world. Reportedly Heylyn wrote this work after a stranger told him, "Geography is better than divinity." He organizes *Cosmographie* by country, giving as much information as is known about the land, the people, customs, and so on. As is often the case among early geographers, Heylyn does not carefully distinguish between fact and fable. Here is part of his description of the Swedish people:

[They] are naturally strong and active, provident, patient, and industrious; *hospitable* towards strangers, whom they entertain with great humanity: so healthy, that if they doe not shorten their dayes by excess and riot, they live commonly to 140 years of age; and so laborious that a Begger is not seen amongst them.

In 1659 Heylyn published his *Examen Criticum,* the first part of which criticizes Fuller's *Church History* for being inaccurate. His most notable work, *Ecclesia Restaurata, or The History of the Reformation* (1661), covers the history of the CHURCH OF ENGLAND from the accession of Edward VI in 1553 to the Elizabethan settlement (1559), when Queen ELIZABETH I declared herself the Supreme Governor of the Church of England.

Two of Heylyn's works were published posthumously: *Cyprianus Anglicus, or The History of the Life and Death of Archbishop Laud* (1668); and *Aerius Redivivus, or The History of Presbyterianism* (1670), in which he blames England's internal troubles and civil war on a group of radical Puritans who lived in London.

Heywood, John (ca. 1497–ca. 1580)
playwright, poet

John Heywood, the son-in-law of Sir Thomas More and the maternal grandfather of John Donne, grew up in Hertfordshire, England, although he may have been born in London. He was educated at Oxford University. In the early 1520s he became a musician, a singer, and an actor at the court of Henry VIII.

Heywood rejected England's turn away from Roman Catholicism in the 1530s. He must, however, have publicly professed acceptance, for he avoided becoming a MARTYR like his friend and in-law Thomas More.

When the Roman Catholic Mary I came to the throne, Heywood published a long poem called *The Spider and the Fly* (1556), which endorsed Mary's restoration of Catholicism to England. The flies in the poem are said to stand for Roman Catholics and the spiders for Protestants. Mary is represented by a maid obeying the commands of Christ. Heywood's life seems to have continued as usual after Mary died in 1558, but his staunch Catholicism finally caught up with him in 1564 during the reign of Elizabeth I, and he fled to France to escape persecution.

Heywood was a prolific poet, writing 600 epigrams, or very short poems that are terse and to the point. His epigrams are comedic in nature, as the representative "Jack and His Father":

> Jack (quoth his father) how shall I ease
>   take?
> If I stand, my legs ache; and if I kneel
> My knees ache; if I go, then my feet ache;
> If I lie, my back ach'th; if I sit, I feel
> My hips ache; and lean I never so weel,
> My elbows ache. Sir (quoth Jack) pain to
>   exile,
> Since all these ease not, best ye hang awhile.

Heywood's importance as a writer, however, stems from his contribution to the theater. His interludes are considered the earliest comedies written in English. The interlude was an early 16th-century dramatic form in which characters debate among themselves. Heywood's dramas lack any real plot, and the characters are simplistic. The scholar Russell A. Fraser declares that Heywood writes "primitive comedy," yet he also notes that Heywood's interludes are "where it [English comedic drama] begins."

Heywood's comedies are actually quite advanced for their day, as they have something that other dramatic works of the period lack: conflict. Heywood develops conflict "through the process of dialogue and mutual judgment . . ., [and] argument and view point," according to the scholars Richard Axton and Peter Happé. The plays end with the resolution of the central argument rather than plot.

The Four P's is typical of Heywood's plays. It presents a contest among three typical medieval figures: a Palmer, or pilgrim; a Pardoner, or one who sells pardons for sins from the pope; and a Pothecary, or pharmacist. The fourth P, a Pedlar, serves as a judge who involves the other three in a lying contest. The lying contest, however, is a diversion from the more serious debate over which figure offers the best way to salvation. The Palmer argues that salvation is achieved by going on pilgrimages

> for Christ's sake
> And namely such as pain do take
> On foot to punish their frail body
> Shall thereby merit more highly.

The Pardoner, by contrast, has a quicker means to salvation: "At home is remedy, / For at your door myself doth dwell" dispensing pardons. Finally, the Pothecary claims superiority over both:

> No soul ye know, entereth heaven-gate
> Till from the body he be separate;
> And whom have ye known die honestly
> Without help of the pothecary. Heywood's
>   play concludes with an affirmation of
>   conservative values. The function that
>   the Palmer and the Pardoner is meant to
>   serve is declared valuable.

In this and his many other works, Heywood displays a keen moral sense and a gift for language. Although his plays seem primitive and overly simplistic by more modern standards, his pioneering comedies helped lay the foundations for later writers such as Ben JONSON and William SHAKESPEARE.

Other Work by John Heywood

The Plays of John Heywood. Edited by Richard Axton and Peter Happé. Cambridge, U.K.: D.S. Brewer, 1991.

Heywood, Thomas (ca. 1573–1641)
playwright

Thomas Heywood was born into the family of a Lincolnshire clergyman, Robert Heywood, and his wife, Elizabeth. It is unclear whether the family was related to the earlier dramatist John HEYWOOD. Educated at Cambridge University, Heywood had one of the longest writing careers of his age: His first payment for a play was recorded in 1596 (although he probably started writing earlier), and his final work was *Love's Masterpiece,* staged in 1640. During this half-century of writing, he produced at least 24 plays that are known to be his. Heywood's own account of his output is staggering: in the preface to *The English Traveller* (1633), he reports having had "an entire hand, or at least the main finger" in writing 220 plays. Though widely viewed as an exaggeration, the statement has encouraged various scholars to suggest Heywood as the author of most of the anonymous plays of the period.

Heywood established himself on the London stage with *Edward IV* (1599), a history in two parts. The first part opens with Edward and the citizens of London staving off a rebellion, and the second part ends with the events William SHAKESPEARE chronicled in *Richard III* (1593). Heywood, in the spirit of the times, did not hesitate to borrow liberally from other playwrights, particularly Shakespeare. In what would become a commonplace among histories of the period, the royal plot of *Edward IV* is balanced by a working-class subplot. In this case, the subplot features apprentices,

a group with which Heywood seemed to have a special affinity.

The Four Prentices of London, with the Conquest of Jerusalem (1599) was a remarkably influential play. It tells of four noble English youths who are forced to take apprenticeships in the time of William the Conqueror and then wander the world to seek adventure. In the sentimental ending, all "four prentices" happen to meet again. This sort of sentiment, as well as the chivalric elements in the play, are parodied by Francis BEAUMONT in *The Knight of the Burning Pestle* more than 10 years later.

Heywood's most enduring play has proven to be his domestic tragedy *A Woman Killed With Kindness* (1603). The play begins with indications of a happy marriage between John Frankford and his wife Anne, people of the middle class. When Frankford invites his friend Wendoll into their home, however, Wendoll seduces Anne, and the play turns tragic.

Heywood generally took a positive view toward his country and its government. Queen ELIZABETH I's life furnished the material for two successful plays staged in the two years following her death in 1603. *If You Know Not Me You Know Nobody* (in two parts) honors the queen's struggle to establish Protestantism as the religion of England, the building of the Royal Exchange (a commercial center), and the defeat of the Spanish Armada. Part One shows the queen giving her famous address to the troops at Tilbury before they went out to defeat the Spanish. *The Fair Maid of the West, Part One* (before 1609) features a title character, Bess Bridges, a barmaid whose name is compared to that of "Good Queen Bess" (Elizabeth I). In her basic goodness as well as her savvy dealings with Londoners and foreigners alike, the barmaid mirrors her namesake. The second part of *The Fair Maid of the West,* which appeared years later in 1631, was not as successful as the first part.

In *The Wise Woman of Hogsdon* (1604), the title character provides homes for illegitimate children and advice to young immoral men who want to obtain beautiful women while avoiding legal marriage.

The plot is very complicated, involving a "wild-hearted" young man named Chartley, who is outsmarted by the Wise Woman with the help of two young women named Luce and several disguises.

Many RENAISSANCE playwrights were able to capitalize on the success of a popular play by writing a related play. Heywood exploited a successful idea—dramas based on Greek and Roman myths—in five plays with the word *Age* in the title (*Golden, Silver, Brazen,* and *Iron, Part One* and *Part Two*) written between 1611 and 1632. These plays told familiar stories such as the exploits of Jupiter and the labors of Hercules, depending to a large extent on elaborate stage spectacle. In the preface to the first part of *The Iron Age* Heywood cannot resist pointing out his success with the *Age* plays, which were, he says, "often (and not with the least applause,) Publickely Acted by two Companies, upon . . . Stage at once, and have at sundrey times thronged three severall Theaters." Therein lay one of Heywood's secrets to his impressive productivity: Although he sometimes worked for one theater or another, he mostly remained a free agent, selling to all the major theater companies.

In the middle of his career, Heywood took an 11-year break from writing that has never been explained. Among plays written in the second part of his career, one of the most notable is *The English Traveller* (ca. 1627). Heywood called this play a tragicomedy (a play whose characters celebrate a happy ending after enduring danger and hardship), but it is, in fact, a return to the domestic tragedy he had mastered in *A Woman Killed with Kindness.* The main female character, Mrs. Wincott, once again dies after committing adultery, this time with a character named Dalavill. The name, sounding like "Devil," evokes the old morality plays, in which symbolic characters were tempted by devils to do wrong. (The play even acknowledges in the prologue that it hearkens back to an earlier age where dumb shows [silent enactments of key scenes], drums, and trumpets set the tone.)

In *Love's Mistress* (1634), Heywood revives many of the successful features of the *Age* plays: a story based on mythology (in this case, Cupid and Psyche), along with elaborate staging and spectacle. *Love's Mistress* is actually a masque, a staged work with music and dance performed privately, often for royalty, in which order is affirmed after a disorderly beginning. The success of *Love's Mistress,* written for the birthday of Charles I, is proved by the fact that it was performed three times during the extended celebration. As was the case with many other royal masques, sets and costumes were designed by the brilliant Inigo Jones.

Critical Analysis

Heywood is respected today for presenting what scholar Otelia Clark has called "the Elizabethan drama of everyday life." Heywood often features everyday people in his plays: barmaids, apprentices, middle-class merchants, and servants. Taverns also figure prominently in many Heywood plays.

A Woman Killed with Kindness is by far Heywood's most-read and most-performed play. It is widely seen as the best example of the popular Elizabethan genre of domestic tragedy. It is different from other plays in the genre, however. First, it appears that, unlike most such dramas, the main plot is not based on a historical source. Second, the play begins with the scene of Frankford and Anne's wedding, but later in the play the couple's children appear on stage (a common device). Thus, several years have passed during the course of the play as opposed to the several weeks typical in such plays. Third, although violence is threatened, vengeance is never carried out; the title refers to the fact that Anne starves herself in response to her husband's forgiveness. The biographer Barbara J. Baines notes that this is an "appropriate symbolic punishment for [Anne's] sin of sexual appetite." There is a sort of reconciliation at the end of the play when Frankford tells his wife,

> *Though thy rash offence*
> *Divorced our bodies, thy repentant tears*
> *Unite our souls.*

Anne dies, in most productions, in her husband's arms.

The Wise Woman of Hogsdon has been described by the scholar Norman Rabkin as "one of the best tragicomedies of the entire period." Editor Sonia Massai, meanwhile, points out that the "radical quality" of the play "never undermines its light-hearted tone."

Heywood's vast experience in writing and acting, as well as his honesty and the generally moral tone of his plays, made him the natural choice for the theater industry to refute Puritan arguments against the theater in 1612's *Apology for Actors.* In this play Heywood defends the theater on several grounds, especially emphasizing that theater can instruct as well as entertain.

No collected works of Heywood were published in his day or for many years after his death, and thus many of his plays have been lost. His remaining plays have been studied less than those of many less-important authors. The 19th-century critic Charles Lamb called Heywood a "prose Shakespeare." The poetry of Heywood's ideas, however, is evident to scholars such as Baines, who sees in his dramas the progress of "the wayward, deluded, disobedient soul" toward the "acknowledgment of the redeeming power of love."

Other Work by Thomas Heywood

Thomas Heywood: Three Marriage Plays. Edited by Paul Merchant. New York: Manchester University Press, 1996.

A Work about Thomas Heywood

Baines, Barbara J. *Thomas Heywood.* Boston: Twayne, 1984.

Hilliard, Nicholas (ca. 1547–1619) *artist, nonfiction writer*

Nicholas Hilliard was born in Exeter, England, to John Hilliard, a goldsmith, and Laurence Hall Hilliard. In 1562 he became an apprentice to Robert Brandon, the jeweler and goldsmith of ELIZABETH I. Hilliard's apprenticeship ended in 1569, and his career as a miniature portrait painter, or limner, began shortly thereafter. By 1572, the year his earliest known portrait of Elizabeth was painted, he had gained the queen's PATRONAGE.

For the rest of his life Hilliard painted court figures, yet he never ceased calling himself a goldsmith and a jeweler. Elizabethans regarded miniature portraits as jewelry and often wore them on necklaces or had them painted on brooches. Thus, for Hilliard the difference between jewelry and his paintings was slight. In *A Treatise Concerning the Art of Limning* (ca. 1597) he writes at length about the relationship between precious stones and the colors miniaturists use: "I saye for certayne truth, that ther are besides whit, and black, but five pefect cullors in the world which I prove by the five principall precious stones . . . [such as[*Rubie* for red, *Saphire* for blewe, *Emrod* [emerald] for greene." The colors, the scholars R. K. R. Thornton and T. G. S. Cain note, "can be seen as surrogates for the stones themselves." Hilliard was, in fact, able to imitate precious stones with uncanny exactness. In a miniature of Queen Elizabeth, art historian Mary Edmond notes, a real diamond set in the work cannot be distinguished from Hilliard's representations of diamonds.

The most important thing about a miniature is the portrait, and Hilliard was a master at painting realistic faces in small spaces. The trick as Hilliard understood it—based, to some extent, on the style of the German painter Holbein the Younger—is to use lines rather than shadows, which painters of large portraits use to create a sense of depth.

Hilliard is important not because of the influence that he had on those who came after him but because of the artifacts he has left. They give us a sense of how Elizabethan aristocrats wanted to be viewed. Similarly, Hilliard's writing is remembered more for what it says about the art of limning than as a piece of writing. At times, however, his style, the art historian Erna Auerbach observes, "warms and the perfect teacher speaks, eager to pass on his own skill to his charges."

A Work about Nicholas Hilliard

Edmond, Mary. *Hilliard and Oliver: The Lives and Works of Two Great Miniaturists.* London: Robert Hale, 1983.

Hobbes, Thomas (1588–1679) *nonfiction writer, translator*

Thomas Hobbes was born to a clergyman also named Thomas Hobbes near Malmesbury, Wiltshire, England. He graduated from Oxford University in 1608. An esteemed mathematician who was also well versed in ancient and modern languages, Hobbes was employed for much of his life as a tutor and secretary to the family of William Cavendish (who would eventually marry Margaret Cavendish, Duchess of NEWCASTLE). Thus Hobbes's social circle included prominent English writers such as Francis BACON and Ben JONSON. On trips to Europe, he made the acquaintance of some of the great minds of the day, including the scientist Marin Mersenne, the philosopher René DESCARTES, and the astronomer Galileo.

Hobbes's first published works were translations of and commentaries on classical works. An unsigned essay (1620) about the careers of several Roman emperors has recently been identified as Hobbes's work. In 1629 he published a translation of the Greek historian Thucydides's *History of the Peloponnesian Wars.* His choice of text is significant because the *History* is a major work in the history of political thought. In 1637 an adaptation of Aristotle's *Rhetoric* showed some of the bluntness that would become Hobbes's trademark: "The end of *Rhetorick* is victory," he declared, and the speaker should appeal more to the audience's preconceptions than to the truth.

When civil war threatened England in 1640, Hobbes and the Cavendishes, staunch Royalists, fled to France. There, he began *The Elements of Philosophy,* the work that he himself (though not history) would consider his major contribution to philosophy. This study, which was finally published in Latin in 1668, contains three sections entitled *Matter, Man,* and *The Citizen.* This systematic progression shows how Hobbes sees human beings both as part of the scientifically defined physical world and the socially defined political world.

Hobbes returned to England in 1651, the same year his masterwork, *Leviathan,* was published. The title of the work is taken from the Bible, which refers in several places to a great sea monster called the "leviathan." In Hobbes's work, the word becomes a tongue-in-cheek metaphor for the civil state, and the work primarily concentrates on the theory and practice of government.

Hobbes lived a long life for his time, and he continued writing until his death at 91. His *Behemoth: the History of the Causes of the Civil Wars in England,* a sort of postscript to *Leviathan,* remained unpublished until 1679, the year of his death. In his last years, Hobbes composed his autobiography in rhymed Latin and translated Homer's *Iliad* and *Odyssey.*

Critical Analysis

Although Hobbes is primarily viewed today as a political philosopher, the great scope of his work, from rhetoric to moral philosophy to history, should be kept in mind. Indeed, as the editor G. A. J. Rogers has noted, "Hobbes is one of the few English philosophers, and perhaps the only one of note, who has constructed what can be seen as a grand philosophical system."

Thus it is no surprise that the first section of *Leviathan* is entitled "Of Man." Hobbes presents human beings in a secular, scientific light. He states in the first chapter that all the ideas of humankind are the products of sense, that is, rational observation of the world around us. Our ideas do not arise from some naturally occurring internal knowledge or from divine revelation. Thus Hobbes sets himself up against the common views of his day, especially religious views.

Likewise, in discussing the passions, Hobbes expounds a relativistic moral and aesthetic philosophy. Words like *Good* and *Evil,* according to Hobbes, "are ever used in relation to the person that useth them: There being nothing simply and absolutely so; nor any common Rule of Good and

Evill." Desires for gain, safety, and reputation set humans, who are basically equal, in natural competition with each other, producing a "warre . . . of every man against every man."

In perhaps the most famous passage of *Leviathan,* Hobbes paints a dreary picture of human beings in the state of Nature: "no Arts; no Letters; no Society; and which is worst of all, continuall feare, and danger of violent death; And the life of man [is] solitary, poore, nasty, brutish, and short." It should be remembered, however, that Hobbes uses this description of the state of nature for the sake of argument in order to show how strongly humans are impelled to form governments, which provide safety and order. The passage hardly describes Hobbes's view of life within society.

In order to avoid the horrors of this state of nature, as Hobbes sees it, people enter into agreements or social contracts with each other, saying, in effect, "I Authorise and give up my Right of Governing my selfe, to this Man, or to this Assembly of men, on this condition, that thou give up thy right to him, and Authorize all his Actions in like manner." Thus Hobbes explains the origin of "that great Leviathan," also known as a commonwealth, government, or state. It arises out of a sort of grudging necessity.

At times, Hobbes seems to approve of and respect government and its authority. Since the primary responsibility of government is to provide peace and safety for its citizens, and since this duty is so important, rebellion or even dissension is not to be tolerated. Moreover, no ruler "can justly be put to death, or otherwise in any manner by his Subjects punished." Here, Hobbes may be expressing his disapproval for the execution of Charles I during the English Civil War.

Indeed, for Hobbes absolute monarchy, rather than a monarchy in which power is shared with a parliament, is the preferred form of government because "in Monarchy, the private interest is the same with the publique." Furthermore, "a Monarch cannot disagree with himselfe," thus avoiding civil strife and possible civil war.

This reverent attitude toward state powers, especially in a nonelective monarchy, makes Hobbes seem quite traditional, but other aspects of his philosophy have appealed to progressive minds. Individuals may not enjoy freedom of expression, but basic physical freedom is strongly upheld. Slaves, he writes, "have no obligation at all; but may break their bonds, or the prison; and kill or carry away captive their Master, justly." The individual's right to self-preservation is also absolute: Even a guilty prisoner may try to escape or resist the executioner. Thus, later readers of widely different political persuasions have found something appealing in Hobbes's work. As the editor Richard Tuck has stated, "The states we inhabit were to a great extent formed by the conflicts of [Hobbes's] period, and *Leviathan* is thus still one of the foundational texts of our politics," whatever our political beliefs may be.

Leviathan was controversial in its day, especially since it was perceived to be secular, despite many biblical quotations and two entire sections that discuss the role of religion in the state. Even Hobbes's acquaintance Henry Hammond, a Church of England clergyman, described the work as "a farrago [hodgepodge] of Christian Atheism." Whatever Christian elements were present in the work did not impress the authors of an anti-blasphemy bill of 1667: *Leviathan* was one of only two books explicitly mentioned in it. Hobbes could thank his acquaintances among the nobility for the fact that the bill never passed the House of Lords. He even wrote several defenses of his work on religious grounds, but they were never published in his lifetime, whether by Hobbes's own choice or the publisher's.

Today, as the scholar Thomas A. Spragens, Jr., notes, Hobbes is regarded as "perhaps the greatest political philosopher to write in the English Language," adding that modern readers "stand to learn much from him—about politics and about ourselves—even if we find his prescriptions ultimately unpalatable."

Works about Thomas Hobbes
Condren, Conal. *Thomas Hobbes.* New York: Twayne, 2000.

Rogow, Arnold A. *Thomas Hobbes: Radical in the Service of Reaction.* New York: Norton, 1986.

Hoby, Margaret (1571–1633) *nonfiction writer*

Margaret Hoby (née Dakins) was the only child of Arthur Dakins, a wealthy landowner, and his wife, Thomasin. Married and widowed twice before the age of 25, she married the Puritan Sir Thomas Hoby in 1596.

Although Hoby may have written diaries throughout her life, only one survives; it covers the period from 1599 to 1605. Scholars believe that this journal is the earliest English diary to have survived. It is primarily a record of Hoby's daily religious practice, but it allows glimpses of her secular daily life on the Hoby estate in north Yorkshire as well. For example, we learn that she shared with other women the responsibilities of midwifery:

> Wednesday 15 August 1599—In the morning at 6 o'clock I prayed privately: that done, I went to a wife in travail of child, about whom I was busy till 1 o'clock, about which time she being delivered and I having praised God, returned home and betook myself to private prayer two several times upon the occasion.

There are also entries about local politics and legal conflicts, including a Star Chamber case that took the Hobys to London. Margaret Hoby's work is considered an important window on the life of the English Reformation.

A Work about Margaret Hoby

Lamb, Mary Ellen. "Margaret Hoby's Diary: Women's Reading Practices and the Gendered Reformation Subject." In *Pilgrimages of Love,* edited by Sigrid King. Tempe, Ariz.: Center for Medieval and Renaissance Studies, 1999.

Hoby, Thomas (1530–1566) *translator*

Thomas Hoby was born in Leominster, Herefordshire, England, to William Hoby and his second wife, Katherine Forden Hoby. He went to Cambridge University in 1545 but appears not to have earned a degree. In 1566 Queen ELIZABETH I knighted him, and he became the ambassador to France, the country in which he died.

Hoby is chiefly remembered for his translation of Baldesare CASTIGLIONE's *The Book of the Courtier* (1561), a philosophical dialogue that served as a manual of ideal courtly behavior throughout Europe in the 16th century. The purpose of translating this book, Hoby explained in 1556, was to extend its influence into England:

> Englishmen are much inferior to well most all other nations: for where they set their delight and bend themselves with an honest strife of matching others, to turn into their mother tongue, not only the witty writings of other languages . . . our men weene [think] it sufficient to have a perfect knowledge, to no other end, but to profit themselves.

In other words, Hoby laments the fact that English men translate foreign books without publishing them. They thereby force those who follow them to retranslate the same books. Thus Hoby published his translation of *The Courtier* in order to relieve future readers of the need to translate it again, and by doing so he hoped to make its influence more lasting.

Hoby seems to have achieved his purpose. "In describing the soldier, courtier, scholar, the versatile and graceful RENAISSANCE man," the scholar Burton A. Milligan writes, "Castiglione created a pattern for Elizabethan courtiers like Sir Philip SIDNEY and Sir Walter RALEIGH, influenced English courtesy books like ASCHAM's *The Schoolmaster,* [and] helped shape the courtly ideals of SPENSER's *Faerie Queene.*"

Holinshed, Raphael (ca. 1520–1580) *nonfiction writer*

Raphael Holinshed was probably born in Cheshire, England. It is believed he entered Cambridge

University in 1544 and was eventually ordained a clergyman.

About 1560 Holinshed went to London and entered the employ of the printer Reginald Wolfe, who had been compiling, since 1548, an ambitious history of the world. Holinshed was put to work assisting Wolfe as a translator. When the printer died in 1573, Holinshed and his colleagues Richard HOOKER, Richard STANIHURST, and William Harrison continued the work, but they limited the scope of the project to England, Ireland, and Scotland.

In 1578, with the financial assistance of three other publishers, *Chronicles of England, Scotland and Ireland* was finally published. The massive work included illustrations, maps, and battle plans, and it ran over 4,000 pages. The book contained inaccuracies and sometimes made no distinction between real events and myths. According to the scholar Michael Best, one of "Holinshed's primary source[s] was the work of the 12th-century canon-priest Geoffrey of Monmouth (the *Historia Regum Britanniae*, or *History of the Kings of Britain*). Monmouth's own sources were oral tradition and earlier manuscripts with a similar basis. Thus, although truth peeps through, these stories are mainly legends that have been embellished by their various chroniclers to glorify English history."

Chronicles was an instant success. According to the critic Peter Hyland, the Elizabethans thought that "[h]istory provided a vast array of examples and models through which contemporary events could be understood."

Holinshed retired from publishing to become steward for Thomas Burdet in Warwickshire. In 1587, seven years after his death, *Chronicles* was revised and published, without illustrations, as *Holinshed's Chronicles of England, Scotland and Ireland.* Queen ELIZABETH I and her ministers found passages relating to the rebellion of Ireland offensive and demanded that they be excised. In 1808 *Chronicles* was published in a revised edition with the censored parts restored.

According to Hyland, "The second edition of Holinshed's work (1587) is the source of most of SHAKESPEARE's historical material." Critic Richard Holsley adds that Holingshed provided Shakespeare with " . . . the basic material for no fewer than thirteen plays: the ten plays dealing with English history and three others, *King Lear, Cymbeline,* and *Macbeth.*" As Holsley says, "Holinshed tells a good story."

Indeed, Shakespeare often borrowed wholesale from Holinshed, as with *Macbeth.* Here Holinshed describes the meeting of Macbeth with the three witches:

> *It fortuned as Makbeth and Banquho*
> *iournied . . . [that they met] three women*
> *   in*
> *strange and wild apparell, . . . whome . . .*
> *   the*
> *first of them spake and said: "All*
> *haile, Makbeth, thane of Glammis!" . . .*
> *   The*
> *second of them said: "Haile, Makbeth,*
> *thane of Cawder!" But the third said:*
> *"All haile, Makbeth, that heerafter*
> *shalt be king of Scotland!"*

Shakespeare followed Holinshed's version very closely:

> *MACBETH: Speak, if you can. What are*
> *   you?*
> *1. WITCH: All hail, Macbeth! Hail to thee,*
> *   Thane of Glamis!*
> *2. WITCH: All hail, Macbeth! Hail to thee,*
> *   Thane of Cawdor!*
> *3. WITCH: All hail, Macbeth! That shalt be*
> *   King hereafter!*

Many other Elizabethan dramatists, including Edmund SPENSER and Christopher MARLOWE used Holinshed for plot sources and inspiration. The scholar Alison Taufer writes that *Holinshed's Chronicles* is "An anthropological treasure hoard, it contains detailed descriptions of the history, daily lives, customs, beliefs, and traditions of Scotland and Ireland as well as England."

A Work about Raphael Holinshed

Patterson, Annabel. *Reading Holinshed's Chronicles.* Chicago: University of Chicago Press, 1994.

Holland, Philemon (1552–1637) *translator*

Philemon Holland, the son of a clergyman, was a man of many talents. He studied medicine at Cambridge University and, while practicing as a doctor, took on the position of director at the free school of Coventry. In addition, and most famously, Holland translated many classical Latin works into English for the first time.

Holland's translations of Latin historians and poets such as Livy, Suetonius, Plutarch, and Pliny, remain some of the best English translations of these authors. Holland did not rely on French or German translations to assist his work as some translators of the day were known to do. Many of these same translators attempted to rewrite classical authors in their own voice in the hope of achieving literary fame, but Holland preferred to recreate the meaning of the original and did not worry about the literary tone.

It is from Holland's translations that many Elizabethan citizens learned of Rome and its Empire. In fact, Holland's reasons for translating these works was to give readers access to the ideas and culture of the Romans. As he explains in "The Preface to the Reader" in his 1601 translation of Pliny's *The History of the World,* "Well may the newest songs and last devised plaies delight our ears at the first, and for the present ravish our senses; like as horarie and early Summer fruits content our tast and please the appetit: but surely it is antiquitie that hath given grace, vigor, & strength to writings; even as age commendeth the most generous and best wines."

Holland, Richard (Richard De Holande) (fl. 1450) *poet*

Hardly anything is known of the life of Richard Holland, a Scottish clergyman and poet who wrote during the middle of the 15th century. During a period of civil strife in Scotland when the nobles clashed with the monarchy, Holland was a supporter of the earls of Douglas, perhaps serving as a chaplain to them, and went into exile with them when their power was ultimately defeated by King James II.

Holland's only surviving poem, *The Buke of the Howlat* (*The Book of the Owl,* ca. 1450) was dedicated to Elizabeth Dunbar, the wife of Archibald, the seventh Earl of Douglas. An edited version was published by David Laing in 1823. Written in Northern Scots and employing an alliterative format (a type of verse that uses alliteration, or the repetition of the initial letters of words), *The Buke* is an allegory consisting of 1,001 lines, in which the birds of the poem represent various human foibles. Its central character is an owl dressed in borrowed plumage, and some scholars believe the poem contains allusions to the political intrigues of the period. Holland's support of the Douglas cause is seen in the lines: "O Dowglass, O Dowglass / Tender and trewe!" The poem is also embellished with much information about heraldry, musical instruments, and some of the Scottish bards who were prominent in the period. There are references to Holland's work in the writings of later poets such as William DUNBAR, Sir David LYNDSAY, Robert Burns, and Sir Walter Scott.

Hooker, Richard (1554–1600) *nonfiction writer*

Richard Hooker was born the son of Robert Hooker in Heavitree, near Exeter, England. He began his education under the guidance of his uncle John Hooker, who, finding him a diligent student, presented him to the bishop of Salisbury. Salisbury was so impressed by the young man that he helped get him into Oxford University on a scholarship. In 1581 Hooker entered the church and occupied a number of church posts over the years.

Hooker's great work was *Laws of Ecclesiastical Polity* (1593–97, 1647), a detailed account of Elizabethan religious and social thought. Among other things, Hooker attempts in this book to defend

Christian religion against the charge that its sole function is to get people to obey social rules with threats of punishment. Hooker explains that the reason "heathens, Turks [that is, Muslims], and infidels, impute to religion a great part of the same effects which ourselves ascribe thereunto" is because Christian truths are "entwined" in their false religions.

Hooker's view of the cosmos assumes that divine law generates natural law and that natural law generates social law. He thus assumes that we will inevitably discover Christian truths in so-called false religions and in non-Christian societies because all thought, religious and social, is generated by the divine word. Christianity and Christian societies, in Hooker's mind, are superior to other religions and societies because they provide direct access to God's word. Christians therefore have the means to transcend the corruption generated at The Fall if they follow their reason and accept the laws of God, nature, and society.

The need for people to follow their reason is, in fact, a key theological concept for Hooker, for it is reason that binds humankind to God and people to each other. "The law of reason," Hooker writes, is "that which bindeth creatures reasonable in this world, and with which by reason they may perceive themselves to be bound." He goes on to note that human law is derived from both reason and God. In fact it is their use of reason that has made it possible for non-Christians to establish laws that harmonize with God's law. Thus, argues the Hooker scholar Nigel Atkinson, "the natural law of reason is able to discern a great deal [of God's truth] . . . without the need of special revelation but purely from the light of natural discourse."

Hooker's great work has lasted primarily because it lays the ground for the doctrine of the CHURCH OF ENGLAND. But he also continues to be read because of the power of his style. A passage from his sermon on righteousness illustrates this: "Concerning the righteous, there neither is nor ever was any purely natural person who was absolutely righteous, devoid of all unrighteousness, of all sin. We dare not exempt from this truth even the Blessed Virgin herself." Hooker avoids the complex sentences that many prose writers of his age favored. His sentences are, it is true, very long, yet they are so clear that JAMES I OF ENGLAND associated Hooker's style with reason itself. James remarked, "I observe there is in Mr. Hooker no affected language; but a grave, comprehensive, clear manifestation of reason, and that backed with the authority of the Scriptures, the fathers and schoolmen, and with all law both sacred and civil."

Other Work by Richard Hooker
The Sermons of Richard Hooker: The Power of Faith, the Mystery of Grace. Edited by Philip B. Secor. London: Society for Promoting Christian Knowledge, 2001.

Works about Richard Hooker
Booty, John E. *Reflections on the Theology of Richard Hooker: An Elizabethan Addresses Modern Anglicanism.* Sewanee, Tenn.: University of the South Press, 1998.
Secor, Philip B. *Richard Hooker: Prophet of Anglicanism.* Toronto: Anglican Book Centre, 1999.
Voak, Nigel. *Richard Hooker and Reformed Theology: A Study of Reason, Will, and Grace.* New York: Oxford University Press, 2003.

Hoskins, John (John Hoskyns)
(1566–1638) *nonfiction writer, poet*

John Hoskins was born to John and Margery Hoskins in the village of Mouncton in Hereford, England. After briefly attending the Latin grammar school at Westminster, Hoskins entered Winchester College in 1579 and received his bachelor's and master's degrees in 1589 and 1592, respectively, from New College, Oxford University. He went on to study law, eventually becoming a member of the first parliament under King JAMES I OF ENGLAND in 1604.

Hoskins's place in literary history rests primarily on a manuscript treatise, written between 1598 and 1600, from which Ben JONSON (who once said in praise of Hoskins, "'twas he that polished me") incorporated several extracts into his own posthumously published *Discoveries* (1640–41). Hoskins's treatise, eventually published in 1935 as *Directions for Speech and Style,* is a guide to prose theory presented primarily through analysis of Philip SIDNEY's *Arcadia.* In this work, Hoskins defines several literary terms and provides guidelines for the use of such devices in speech and writing, opening his discourse by stating the importance of the appropriate usage of prose:

> The shame of speaking vnskillfully were small if the tongue were only disgraced by it, But as the image of the kinge in a Seale of waxe ill represented, is not soe much a blemish to the waxe or the signet . . . as to the king whome it resembleth, Soe disordered speech is not sow much iniury to the lipps w[hich] giue it forth, or the thoughts w[hich] put it forth, as to the right [portion] and Coherence of things in themselues soe wrongfully expressed.

Also among Hoskins's extant works are several poems in both English and Latin. According to the scholar H. J. C. Grierson, there is "a not uninteresting link" in Hoskins's poetry between the metaphysical tradition, often associated with John DONNE (to whom many of Hoskins's poems were long attributed) and the style of Sidney's poetry. In one of his poems, "Absence, Hear Thou my Protestation," he says that in the face of true love absence cannot triumph. The poem ends with a witty paradox:

> *By absence this good means I gain,*
> *That I can catch her*
> *Where none can watch her,*
> *In some close corner of my brain.*
> *There I embrace and kiss her,*
> *And so I both enjoy and miss her.*

While Hoskins's poetic abilities were highly regarded in his own time, he is best remembered today for the influence of his *Directions,* which the scholar Louise Brown Osborn says provides "doc-umentary evidence of the literary opinions, standards, and fashions prevalent at the close of the sixteenth century." According to scholar Gary R. Grund, this puts Hoskins "among the forces in the development of English prose."

A Work about John Hoskins
Grund, Gary R. *John Hoskyns, Elizabethan Rhetoric, and the Development of English Prose.* New York: Garland Publishing, 1987.

Howard, Henry
See SURREY, HENRY HOWARD, EARL OF.

Howard, Sir Robert (1626–1698)
dramatist, poet

Sir Robert Howard was born in 1626. His father, Thomas Howard, was Baron Howard of Charlton, Viscount of Andover and Earl of Berkshire. His mother, Elizabeth, was daughter of William, Lord Burleigh. In the British Civil War between those who supported Parliament and those who supported the monarchy, Howard's father was captured, and his estates were confiscated. There is little record of Howard's early life or education, but many believe he may have studied at Oxford. He also had a significant military career. In 1644 he was knighted. In 1645 Howard married Anne Kingsmyll, and they had several children, all but one of whom died before Howard. Howard was also a successful politician and served as a member of Parliament from 1661 until his death in 1698.

Howard published his first work, a poetry collection, *Poems,* in 1660, the same year that his soon-to-be brother-in-law John DRYDEN published his *Astraea Redux.* Next Howard turned to writing plays. Howard's most famous play is a satirical comedy, *The Committee* (1665). The play is set during the Civil Wars and concerns a committee that was established to seize the lands of the Royalists, or those who supported the monarchy. The heroes of the play are those who refuse "to take the covenant," that is, "pledge . . . to support and further the reformed Protestant religion" (Puritanism). Comic relief is provided by the Irish servant Teague, who claims that stealing a copy of the pledge means that he and his master have in fact "taken" the covenant.

Howard's other notable work is *The Indian Queen,* written with Dryden. This is an operalike work that was set to music by the composer Henry Purcell. Howard had written the original drama, but Dryden revised what he thought was a silly plot, although he liked the exotic Mexican setting. The story involves Queen Zempoalla, who must defend her kingdom against invaders. The play was a great success, partly because the story was accompanied by an expensive and elaborate set. In 1665 Howard published *Foure New Plays* and in the preface to this work began a famous quarrel with Dryden, Howard maintaining that blank verse was preferable to rhymed couplets in drama.

Howell, James (ca. 1593–1666) *nonfiction writer*

It is believed that James Howell, best known for his letter writing, was born in Abernant, Carmarthenshire, Wales. He was educated at Oxford University and went on to become a member of the English parliament in 1627. In 1642 he was imprisoned for eight or nine years during the period of the English Civil Wars, but whether he was imprisoned for debt or for his loyalty to the Crown is uncertain. Howell spent much of his time in prison writing letters as well as several books, dictionaries, and political pamphlets. He was well traveled and spent the latter part of his life writing about his travels.

Howell's most famous work, *Epistolae Ho-Elianae (Familiar Letters),* was published in four volumes over the years 1645 to 1655 and remained popular for the following century. In his 1926 book *On Writing and Writers,* Walter Raleigh says of James Howell that "all things considered, he is the best of our 17th century letter-writers. His letters are full of laboured conceits after the polite manner of the age, and his conscious preoccupation with literary expression is unremitting."

Most of Howell's letters were not actually posted to anyone but were, rather, written for his own enjoyment. Many were essays on various social and literary subjects and many included verse. One letter, which was certainly never sent, was written to console King Charles I after a defeat, advising him that other kings had suffered worse. Howell also wrote extensively and in great detail about himself. For example, in one of his letters he writes,

I prostrate myself in the humblest and decentest way of genuflection I can imagine; nor do I believe there can be any excess of exterior humility in [church] . . ., therefore I do not like those squatting, unseemly bold postures upon one's tail, or muffling the face in the hat, or thrusting it in some hole, or covering it with one's hand; but with bended knee, and an open confident face, I fix my eyes on the east part of the Church, and Heaven. . . . Every day following I knock thrice at Heaven's gate, in the morning, in the evening, and at night. . . . By these steps I strive to climb up to Heaven, and my Soul prompts me I shall go thither; for there is no object in the world delights me more than to cast up my eyes that way, specially in a Star-light night.

Howell wrote about the gossip of the day and is recognized as a keen observer of people and their behaviors. Some of the historical accuracy of his work is questionable, as he is believed to have fabricated dates and copied some of his writing from other authors. His work, however, serves as a valuable window into 17th-century daily life.

Howell, Thomas (fl. 1560) *poet*

Little is known about the life of Thomas Howell, other than he was most likely born in Dunster, Somerset, England, and may have been educated at Oxford University. His best-known work is *Howell his Devices, for his Own Exercise and his Friends' Pleasure,* sometimes simply called *Devices* (1581), but he also published *The Arbor of Amitie* (1568) and *Newe Sonets, and pretie Pamphlets* (1568). All three are collections of his verse. One original copy of each of these volumes survives today. Howell admired the lyrical styles of the 14th-century Italian poet Francis PETRARCH and the medieval English poet Geoffrey Chaucer. His poetry is conventional in both theme and versification, as can be seen in this poem about a rose, entitled "All in a garden green":

> *Whenas the mildest month*
> *Of jolly June doth spring,*
> *And gardens green with happy hue*
> *Their famous fruits do bring;*
> *When eke the lustiest time*
> *Reviveth youthly blood,*
> *Then springs the finest featured flower*
> *In border fair that stood.*

One of the poems in *Devices* contains the earliest known reference to Philip SIDNEY's *Arcadia* (1581), indicating that Howell probably saw the work in manuscript form.

It is believed that Howell was a gentleman who had close relations with the Pembroke family, as his *Devices* is dedicated to Lady Pembroke (Mary SIDNEY), the wife of Henry Herbert, the second Earl of Pembroke and sister to the poet Sir Philip Sidney.

humanism

Humanism refers to a series of cultural changes that occurred throughout Europe in the 14th and 15th centuries. It was influenced by the discovery of Greek and Roman writings that had been "lost" for centuries. As scholars began to study these works, they discovered, among other things, that many classical Greek and Roman philosophers were interested in how to live good, moral, and happy lives and had little interest in the afterlife. This attitude contrasted sharply with medieval thinking, which was largely focused on ensuring salvation. Thus influenced by classical writers, humanist philoso-

phers began to shift their thinking, focusing their attention more on the here and now than on the end of life. This led such thinkers to emphasize worldly pleasures, the importance of learning—including scientific inquiry—and the power and dignity of the individual. Humanist thinking, in fact, was among the causes of the Protestant REFORMATION in that many of the founders of Protestant sects emphasized the importance of the conscience of the individual in religious matters, encouraging people to question church authority and to study the Bible for themselves.

Desiderius ERASMUS, a Dutch scholar, had a major influence on humanism in England with his *In Praise of Folly* (1509), in which he satirized the corruption of the clergy and demonstrated that their behavior was sanctioned neither by the Bible nor by classical moral philosophers. English scholar Thomas MORE's *Utopia* (1516) also satirized corruption and the abuse of power, including attempts to impose religious beliefs on people. Here he writes that the king of Utopia

> made a law that every man might be of what religion he pleased, and might endeavor to draw others to it by force of argument, and by amicable and modest ways, but without bitterness against those of other opinions; but that he ought to use no other force but that of persuasion, and was neither to mix with it reproaches nor violence.

More writes in the best humanist tradition when he advocates the freedom of the individual to choose and the use of individual reason ("argument") as a method of acquiring faith.

Many scholars emphasize that humanism was, above all, an educational system, which included the study of Latin and Greek. John COLET, the dean of St. Paul's Cathedral, founded St. Paul's School, the first in England where children could study these ancient languages. Along with William LILLY, Colet wrote a Latin grammar that was in use in England for more than 300 years; it was the text William SHAKESPEARE used to learn the language.

Because many of the classical authors emphasized rhetoric and the persuasive power of language, English scholars and poets began to emphasize the idea of eloquence in speaking and writing, leading to the amazing development of English in the RENAISSANCE, as seen in the works of such writers as Shakespeare and Christopher MARLOWE. The classical focus on the individual can be seen in the complex, realistic characters of Renaissance drama, who are so unlike earlier allegorical figures of drama—characters who merely stood for a simple concept, such as Lust or Greed. Humanism also influenced the studies of such scientists as Nicolaus COPERNICUS, Galileo, and, in England, Francis BACON and William GILBERT by encouraging a move away from unquestioning acceptance of information toward empirical study and experimentation.

A Work about Humanism

Nauert, Charles G. *Humanism and the Culture of Renaissance Europe.* Cambridge, U.K.: Cambridge University Press, 1995.

Hume, Anna (fl. 1644) *poet, translator*

The daughter of David and Barbara Johnstone Hume of Godscroft, Anna Hume came from a titled Scottish family. Her father wrote poetry, which she translated from Latin, and she also supervised the publication of her father's *History of Douglas and Angus* (1644).

Hume gained prominence through her 1644 translations of three poems by Francis PETRARCH, "Triumph of Love," "Triumph of Death," and "Triumph of Chastity." Hume writes in rhyming couplets, but each rhymed pair does not represent an individual thought. Rather, her sentences bridge several couplets, and a given line of poetry usually begins mid-clause. The following lines from "The Triumph of Death" demonstrate Hume's characteristic style:

> *The glorious Maid, whose soul to Heaven is*
> *gone*
> *And left the rest cold earth, she who was*
> *grown*
> *A pillar of true valor, and had gain'd*
> *Much honor by her victory, and chain'd*
> *That God which doth the world with terror*
> *bind,*
> *Using no armor but her own chaste mind.*

In adapting Italian poetry, and Petrarch in particular, Hume joins other British women writers spanning the 17th century, from Mary WROTH (*Pamphilia to Amphilanthus,* 1621) to Aphra BEHN ("Song" from *Abdelazer,* 1677), as well as a much larger group of writers who borrowed Italian images and poetic styles.

Hutchinson, Anne (1591–1643) *preacher*

Anne Hutchinson (née Marbury) was born in Alford, Lincolnshire, England, to Francis Marbury, an Anglican minister, and his wife, Bridget Dryden Marbury. Her father belonged to the Puritan wing of the CHURCH OF ENGLAND; he and other Puritans believed that the church, which had broken from the Roman Catholic Church in 1533, should move even further away from Catholicism. Queen ELIZABETH I, who by virtue of being queen was leader of the church, feared the disruptive influence of the Puritans, and Francis Marbury was among many who got in trouble for their views. He was arrested in 1578 and spent some time in prison; when Anne was born, he was free but forbidden to preach. Because of this, he was home more than he would otherwise have been and was closely involved in Anne's education. She learned to read using the Bible and a transcript of her father's trial.

Bridget Marbury gave birth to 12 children after Anne, and her oldest daughter helped care for them. Anne also assisted her mother in her work as a midwife and eventually became a midwife herself. At 21 she married William Hutchinson, a textile merchant in Alford. They soon started a family; 13 of their children lived to adulthood. Living in Alford, they heard about a preacher working in

Boston, Lincolnshire, 24 miles away, named John Cotton. They began to make trips to Boston to hear Cotton preach. His main theme was the central importance of faith and of the individual's direct relationship with God, as opposed to the Anglican emphasis on living a moral life and following the rules of the church. Cotton's doctrine became known as the "Covenant of Grace," as opposed to the "Covenant of Works."

Cotton was disciplined by the church for his views, and in 1633 he emigrated to the Massachusetts Bay Colony in New England in search of greater religious freedom. Anne and William Hutchinson followed him in 1634. They settled in Boston (which the settlers had named for the Boston in Lincolnshire). In England Anne Hutchinson had been in the habit of inviting the women of the congregation to her home after Sunday service to discuss the sermon, and she continued this custom in Boston. At first these gatherings were small, but word spread of Hutchinson's eloquence and soon they grew to include 30–60 people, both women and men.

Before long the men who ran the Massachusetts Bay Colony became anxious about Hutchinson's influence, especially when she began to criticize the ministers of the church for putting too much emphasis on the Covenant of Works. Like John Cotton, she upheld the Covenant of Grace and the worshiper's personal relationship with God. In November 1637 she was brought to trial before the General Court of Massachusetts on a charge of heresy. Hutchinson, pregnant with her 15th child, defended herself vociferously and angrily, which only strengthened the feelings against her. She was sentenced to be banished from the colony, although she was allowed to stay—under house arrest—until the birth of her child. In March she underwent a second trial by the Church of Boston, which resulted in her excommunication from the church.

Hutchinson and her husband moved to Rhode Island, where Roger Williams, another devout person who had been banished from the Massachusetts Bay Colony for heresy, had established a colony. The family prospered there, but after Williams's death in 1642, Hutchinson became anxious about the growing influence of the Massachusetts Bay Colony and moved with her six youngest children to present-day Westchester County, which belonged at the time to the Dutch colony of New Amsterdam, later New York. The Dutch had poor relations with the Native Americans in the area. Hutchinson and five of her children were killed in a Native American uprising against the Dutch.

No writings of Hutchinson's survive, but her voice can be heard in the record of her two trials. Reading the transcript, one is amazed at the tenacity with which she kept challenging her opponents and her total confidence in her direct communication with God:

> You have power over my body but the Lord Jesus hath power over my body and soul; and assure yourselves thus much, you do as much as in you lies to put the Lord Jesus Christ from you, and if you go on in this course you begin, you will bring a curse upon you and your posterity, and the mouth of the Lord hath spoken it.

Works about Anne Hutchinson
Bremer, Francis J., ed. *Anne Hutchinson: Troubler of the Puritan Zion.* Huntington, N.Y.: R. E. Krieger, 1981.
Lang, Amy Schrager. *Prophetic Woman: Anne Hutchinson and the Problem of Dissent in the Literature of New England.* Berkeley: University of California Press, 1987.
Williams, Selma R. *Divine Rebel: The Life of Anne Marbury Hutchinson.* New York: Holt, Rinehart and Winston, 1981.

Hutchinson, Lucy (1615–1664) *biographer, poet*

Born to Sir Allen Apsley and Lucy St. John Apsley, Lucy Hutchinson had an extraordinary education for a 17th-century woman. In *The Life of Mrs. Lucy Hutchinson, Written by Herself* (1664–70, published 1806), a fragment of her autobiography, she describes a precocious childhood in which she read by age four, loved books, and "was so apt [able] that I outstripped my brothers who were at school." In 1638 she married Sir John Hutchinson, a young Puritan about whom she wrote her major work, *Memoirs of the Life of Colonel Hutchinson* (1664–70, published 1806).

Written to preserve Sir John's memory for her children and to justify his political career, the *Memoirs* create a heroic narrative for Colonel Hutchinson, a leader of the parliamentary forces who sided against Charles I during the English Civil War, a conflict between the king and Parliament over religious issues and the rights of the monarchy.

Hutchinson draws on the colonel's wartime life to write passionately about politics and religion, using a sharp tongue: "If any gentleman in his country maintain'ed the good lawes of the land, or stood up for any publick interest of his country for good order or government, he was a Puritane; and in short, all that crost [crossed] the interest of the needie Courtiers, the proud encroaching priests, the thievish projectors, [businessmen] the lewd nobility and gentrie, whoever was zealous for God's glory or worship, . . . all these were Puritanes; and if Puritanes, then enemies to the king and his government." Here she uses irony, implying the opposite of what she states, to mock the opinions of those courtiers, priests, and nobility opposed to her Puritan faith. Critic James Sutherland comments, "A deeply religious woman, she appears to have had very little of Christian charity in her make-up, and her comments on the moral-backslider, the hypocrite, the self-seeker, the opportunist, the fainthearted, . . . can be trenchant and highly sarcastic."

In addition to prose history, Hutchinson wrote *Order and Disorder,* an epic poem, which is an extended narrative poem recounting heroic deeds, written in an elevated style. Like *Paradise Lost* by John MILTON, Hutchinson's poem retells the biblical legends of creation and the fall of man. Only five of 20 cantos were published during her life because the work was considered politically sensitive. For example, the mingling of political and religious imagery in her description of war between heaven and Satan, as in "Hell's gloomy princes the World's rulers made" (5.101) can be interpreted as

a critique of the monarchy. As a Puritan embroiled in the struggles of her times, Hutchinson's writings, as critic David Norbrook comments, "are in a fundamental sense passionately personal, but the passion was informed by a complex and coherent set of political and religious ideas."

Hyde, Edward (Earl of Clarendon)
(1609–1674) *nonfiction writer*

Edward Hyde was born in Dinton, Wiltshire, England, and was educated at Magdalen Hall, Oxford University, before receiving his legal training at London's Middle Temple. Hyde served a distinguished career as an English statesman, becoming the first Earl of Clarendon in 1661. He also had a relationship with the royal family through the marriage of his daughter Anne to James, Duke of York.

Hyde supported the monarchy during the revolution and the English Civil Wars (1642–49) between the Royalists and Parliamentarians. He began his political career in 1640 as a member of both the Short and Long Parliaments, which opposed Charles I in the years leading up to the first phase of the Civil Wars. During the war, however, Hyde acted as an adviser to the Crown. After Charles I was tried and executed on charges of treason, Hyde served as an adviser to Charles II, who fled to France at the end of the second phase of the wars. In 1660 Hyde was appointed lord chancellor after Oliver Cromwell, who had been ruling England during Charles II's exile, died. He played an influential role during the Restoration but was ultimately exiled to France after Parliament blamed him for the unsuccessful 1665 wars against the Dutch, despite his having opposed this conflict.

Hyde's *History of the Rebellion and Civil Wars in England* (1702–04) is an important account of the English Civil Wars, even though it is considered a biased narrative favoring the Royalist position. Hyde did not originally write his *History* to be a survey of the wars, but intended it to advise future kings about their relations with Parliament. The work is recognized for its character sketches; Hyde relied on elaborate descriptions of many of the important people involved in the wars.

James I of England (James Stewart, James Stuart, James VI of Scotland)

(1556–1625) *poet, nonfiction writer*

James Stewart was born in Edinburgh to MARY STUART, queen of Scotland, and her second husband, Henry, Lord Darnley. When James was six months old, Lord Darnley met his death in a murder that is unsolved to this day. Shortly thereafter the Roman Catholic queen, distrusted by Scotland's nobles because most Scots by this time were Presbyterian Protestants, abdicated the throne and fled Scotland. In England she sought the protection of ELIZABETH I, but Elizabeth, who feared that Mary might have designs on the English throne, placed the Scottish queen under house arrest and, 19 years later, had her executed. Meanwhile the infant James was crowned as James VI of Scotland; John KNOX preached at his coronation. A succession of regents ruled for him until he came of age.

James's formal education ended when he was 14, but he was tutored by some of Scotland's greatest scholars, among them George BUCHANAN. Although the curriculum was in effect limited to the study of languages—Greek, Latin, French, and English, in addition to his native Scots—James's education was much more thorough than that of most Scottish nobles of the time, and he grew up with a great reputation for learning, He had little companionship of his own age; his entertainment as a boy was composing verse in Latin.

As James grew into young manhood, he took poetry very seriously, translating the work of several contemporary French poets and publishing two collections of his own poetry. A poem printed in 1590, "Lepanto," describes a 1571 battle:

> *Which fought was in Lepantoes Gulfe*
> *Betwixt the baptiz'd race*
> *And circumcised Turban'd Turkes*
> *Rencountring in that place.*

These lines, with their heavy meter and alliteration, give an idea of what the scholar David Mathew calls James's "slender talent" as a poet.

In 1589 James went to Denmark to meet and marry the princess Anne of Denmark, the only time in his life he left Britain. The marriage was arranged by his courtiers for dynastic reasons, but James used poetry to court his bride. Anne bore James seven children, among them the future King Charles I.

After his marriage James stopped writing poetry, but he continued to write. He published a book about Satan and witchcraft, *Daemonologie,* in 1597. This was followed in 1598 by *Basilikon Doron* (Greek for "The kingly gift"), a book of advice for his eldest son, Prince Henry, which shows James's growing conviction of God's support for the monarchy:

> First of all things, learne to know and love God, whom-to ye have a double obligation; first, for that he made you a man; and next, for that he made you a little God to sit on his Throne, and rule over other men. Remember that this glistering worldlie glorie of Kings, is given them by God, to teach them . . . so to glister and shine before their people . . . that their persons as bright lampes of godlinesse and vertue, may, going in and out before their people, give light to all their steps.

Sections of practical advice throw interesting light on the daily life of the Scottish court:

> It becommeth a Prince best of any many to be a faire and good horse-man. . . . I debarre all rough and violent exercises, as the footeball. . . . Ye may lawfully play at the cardes or tables. . . . And as for the chesse, I thinke it over fond, because it is over-wise and Philosophicke a folly.

In 1603 Queen Elizabeth, the Virgin Queen, died without any closer heir than her distant cousin the Scottish king, who became James I of England. He moved to London with his family and thereafter only went back to Scotland on visits. He was not an entirely successful monarch of England, as he never quite grasped the complicated politics of his new kingdom. It was in England that someone dubbed him "the wisest fool in Christendom," after his learning and his impractical approach to life.

James was often accused of extravagance. He gave generously to his favorite courtiers, but he was also an important patron of the arts, especially of William SHAKESPEARE's dramatic ensemble, the KING'S MEN, and of Ben JONSON. Both the king and the queen enjoyed masques by Jonson and others as entertainment at court.

The king's interests in literature and religion combined when he encouraged the careers of John DONNE and Lancelot ANDREWS, both of whom preached before him. The most important and enduring achievement of his reign was the 1611 publication of the King James Version of the BIBLE.

James continued to write, producing *A Counter Blaste to Tobacco* (1604), in which he inveighed against the evils of smoking, recently introduced from North America by Sir Walter RALEIGH. Smoking, he says, is

> a custom loathsome to the eye, hateful to the nose, harmful to the brain, dangerous to the lungs, and in the black, stinking fume thereof, nearest resembling the horrible Stygian smoke of the pit that is bottomless.

James also published two works about the rights of kings and, in his last years, two devotional works. He died at his country house at Theobalds in Hertfordshire, 22 years after assuming the English throne.

A Work by James I
Sommerville, Johann P., ed. *Political Writings.* Cambridge, U.K.: Cambridge University Press, 1994.

Works about James I
Goldberg, Jonathan. *James I and the Politics of Literature: Jonson, Shakespeare, Donne and Their Contemporaries.* Baltimore, Md.: Johns Hopkins University Press, 1983.

Lee, Maurice. *England's Solomon: James VI and I in his Three Kingdoms.* Urbana: University of Illinois Press, 1990.

Mathew, David. *King James I.* London: Jonathan Cape, 1982.

Peck, Linda L., ed. *The Mental World of the Jacobean Court.* Cambridge, U.K.: Cambridge University Press, 1991.

Jessey, Henry
See WIGHT, SARAH.

Jocelyn, Elizabeth (Elizabeth Joceline, Elizabeth Jocelin, Elizabeth Joselin, Elizabeth Joscelin) (1596–1622)
nonfiction writer

Elizabeth Brooke Jocelyn was born in Norton, England, to Sir Richard and Joan Chaderton Brooke. Her maternal grandfather, Bishop Caderton of Lincoln, raised her. She had no formal schooling but learned languages, history, and religion under the tutelage of her grandfather.

When she was pregnant with her first child, Jocelyn wrote *A Mother's Legacie to her Unborne Childe* (1624). The mother's legacy was a popular type of writing at the time; other writers in this tradition include Dorothy LEIGH. Because she feared that she would die in childbirth, Jocelyn included in the tract detailed instructions about how her child should be raised. In fact, she died nine days after delivering her baby, and two years after her death, the letter was republished; it was reprinted later in the century.

Jocelyn's work goes into detail about the way her child should be raised and how that child should live his or her life. She advocates religious observance, hard work, and avoidance of the sin of pride. She tells her child, "When you have finished your private prayr be sure that you absent not your selfe from Publick prayr if it bee used in the house whear you live, which ended go and use any lawfull recreation eyther for thy profit or pleasure." Jocelyn notes the differences between the rearing of boys and girls, particularly in terms of education. In the letter to her husband that precedes the tract, she indicates that if the child is a boy, he should receive a religious education, and if a girl she should be educated in the Bible, housekeeping, and writing, things appropriate for a wife maintaining a household. Of other education, she says, "Though I admire it [education] in those whom God hath blest with discretion, yet I desire not much in mine owne, having seene that sometimes women have greater portions of learning, than wisdome." Her thoughts are in keeping with the period's views on education for women: Many believed that education might lead to vain displays.

Jocelyn's letter is an important historical document for discovering attitudes about education, religion, and child rearing in the early 17th century. The critic Sylvia Brown also notes its literary achievement: "The particular eloquence of Joscelin's testament derives from its reproduction of the intimate speech act of maternal praise or reproof."

Works about Elizabeth Jocelyn

Brown, Sylvia, ed. *Women's Writing in Stuart England: The Mother's Legacies of Dorothy Leigh, Elizabeth Joscelin, and Elizabeth Richardson.* Thrupp, Stroud, Gloucester, U.K.: Sutton, 1999.
Martin, Randall, ed. *Women Writers in Renaissance England.* New York: Longman, 1997.

Johnson, Edward (1598–1672) *nonfiction writer*

Edward Johnson was born near Canterbury, England, the son of a parish clerk. He was of the generation of Englishmen who immigrated to the American colonies in the middle of life. Very much a self-made man of the middle class, Johnson was a shipbuilder by trade. In the military he achieved the rank of captain.

In 1630 Johnson took an initial journey to America with John Winthrop; six years later he set sail for a second, permanent time with his wife and seven children. Arriving in Boston, Massachusetts, he moved his family to Charlestown and bought property. In 1640 he helped found the new town of Woburn, of which he became a prominent resident.

Johnson recorded his experiences in the New World in his spiritual history *The Wonder-Working Providence of Sions Saviour in New-England.* The work was published anonymously in London around 1648. At that time it was given the title *A History of New-England. From the English Planting in the Yeere 1628. Until the Yeere 1658.* Johnson's authorship was established by scholar William Frederick Poole in 1867.

Although he was neither a clergyman nor a university-educated man, Johnson was a forceful writer, and his book is considered an important source on the history of New England. Johnson introduces his work as "a short Epitome of the manner how they [Puritan settlers] placed downe their dwellings in this Desert Wildernesse, the Lord being pleased to hide from the Eyes of his people the difficulties they are to encounter withal in a new Plantation, that they might not thereby be hindered from taking the worke in hand."

Johnson's work can be distinguished from other contemporary accounts by William BRADFORD and Winthrop. Their accounts focused on the formation of the early governments. Johnson's *Wonder-Working* is an account of the daily lives of ordinary Puritans. His work also has a strong spiritual component, as he viewed the colonists as "servants of Christ" whose destiny was to establish the new land in Christ's name.

One other book, *Good news from New England* (1648), has often been attributed to Johnson, but scholars have never proved his authorship of this work.

Jonson, Ben (Benjamin Jonson)
(1572–1637) *playwright, poet, critic*

Born in London a month after the death of his father, Ben Jonson was raised by his mother and a stepfather, a master bricklayer who married his mother in 1575. Jonson was educated at the famous Westminster grammar school. Here he studied under William CAMDEN, to whom he owed, as he later wrote, "all that I am in arts, all that I know" and with whom he remained a close friend.

After leaving school in 1589 or 1590, Jonson was apprenticed to a bricklayer, perhaps his stepfather, but he abandoned his position in 1591 when he became a soldier and went to fight in Flanders, the region known today as the Netherlands. What Jonson did in the five years after he left the army in 1592 is uncertain. He later told William DRUMMOND OF HAWTHORDEN that he "betook himself to his . . . studies." This cryptic comment may not explain how he supported himself financially, but it does explain how he became one of the most learned men of his age.

Jonson took up acting and writing plays in 1597, and in the following year he had his first success with *Every Man in His Humor,* a comedy in which William SHAKESPEARE acted and in which Jonson introduced his theory of humors—a biological explanation for people's personalities. Jonson's intent in this play and the ones that followed was to mock the folly of his audiences so that they would be shamed into improving their behavior—a mode of dramatic writing known as satire. Through this technique Jonson began his lifelong interest in the educational possibilities of ridicule.

The plot of *Every Man in His Humor* revolves around a merchant named Kitely and his irrational jealousy of certain guests staying in his house, Edward Knowell and Bobadill. Kitely suspects them of attempting to seduce (and thus steal from him) his wife and his sister Bridget. Much of the action comes from the confusion produced by the characters' meddling in each other's affairs, as the troublemaking servants Brainworm, Matthew, and Stephen try to break up the couple and their household. All ends well however, with the restoration of Kitely's faith in his wife's innocence, thanks to the wise and kind Justice Clement. This manner of creating tension out of insecurities and mischief is typical of Jonson's satire in that the problems are at first imagined and then become real only as a result of human weakness. In this way the playwright can comment on mankind's foolish nature while inviting the audience to laugh at itself and also learn from its self-recognition.

Shortly after *Every Man* hit the stage, Jonson was imprisoned for killing the actor Gabriel Spenser in a duel. He admitted his guilt but was released after forfeiting his goods and being branded on the thumb. The following year he was once again writing plays, and *Every Man out of His Humor* (1599), which illustrates the shortcomings of jealous, overambitious people, appeared. The two humor plays, while not the only ones written by Jonson in the late 1590s, are perhaps the most important, for they spawned what has come to be known as the "comedy of humors," a dramatic mode later taken up by the playwrights Richard BROME, William CARTWRIGHT, and others.

In this follow-up to *Every Man in His Humor*, Jonson explores what happens when fools who are dominated by their own obsessions are forced to change. Some of the memorable characters of the play include the miser Macilente, the sarcastic clown Carlo Buffone, and Puntarvolo, a comically arrogant knight, all of whom come from the Italian tradition of the commedia dell'arte (a type of comedic drama popular in the Italian Renaissance). The onlookers Mitis and Cordatus comment on the ridiculousness of these characters so that the audience understands how to judge their faults. They are Jonson's moral compass, the holders of a perspective with whom we would like to identify, even if we see ourselves in the fools.

In 1605 Jonson, along with fellow playwrights George CHAPMAN and John MARSTON, again found himself in jail, this time for writing *Eastward Ho!* (1605), a play that in part attacks JAMES I OF ENGLAND and his Scottish favorites. Jonson was not immediately arrested. Initially, only Chapman and Marston were imprisoned, but Jonson voluntarily joined them in jail, acknowledging that he too had had a part in composing the play. The three were finally released. This episode illustrates Jonson's moral character and also his desire to be given credit for all that he wrote at a time when many contributed to plays anonymously.

Although Jonson began to make a name for himself as a playwright in the last years of ELIZABETH I's reign, it was during the kingship of James I that Jonson became a major figure on England's literary scene. By 1616 he had written his greatest plays, including *Volpone, or the Fox* (1605), a satire about greed and the respect accorded to the wealthy rather than the morally superior. Next came *Epicoene, or the Silent Woman* (1609), a critique of the contradictory view of women in the period, which represented the ideal woman as silent even as women were said to be incapable of keeping quiet.

The Alchemist (1610), a satire about RENAISSANCE superstition, specifically the belief in alchemy and the way tricksters manipulate such superstitions to con people out of money, is arguably Jonson's greatest achievement. In this play Jonson continues to investigate man's essential foolishness. He depicts the vice of greed in the fake alchemist—someone who is supposedly able to turn ordinary metals into gold—ironically named Subtle. The swindler cheats his victims, such as Sir Epicure Mammon (another blustery knight in the mold of Puntarvarlo)—until he is caught and punished through a marriage to the obnoxious Dame Pliant. Jonson's genius is evident here in his ability to punish his villain-heroes as a result of their own schemes. Justice is served in his plays because order—the way in which everyone gets what they deserve—is always restored in the end.

Jonson also composed masques—dramatic entertainments with dances, disguises and musical elements that overshadow plot and character—in conjunction with the renowned architect Inigo Jones. Jonson's best masques include *The Masque of Blackness* (1606), *The Masque of Beauty* (1608), and *The Masque of Queen* (1609). In addition to the masque proper, these works contain what Jonson called an anti-masque, an element of the performance that he invented and that was used to develop allegories of royal power. The anti-masques present comic versions of the forces of misrule, while the masque presents versions of the order that is produced by royal authority.

Not to be forgotten is Jonson's role as a prominent poet of the time. In fact, he was held in such high regard that in 1616 King James began giving him a yearly salary for producing poetry—the honor or position that was to become known as being England's poet laureate. Perhaps the most famous of Jonson's poems is his "Song: to Celia," a combination of five prose passages by the Greek writer Philostratus. The poem's opening lines, a passionate address to a female lover, are among the most famous in English literature:

> *Drink to me only with thine eyes,*
> *And I will pledge with mine;*
> *Or leave a kiss but in the cup,*
> *And I'll not look for wine.*

Unfortunately, Jonson's life ended unhappily. After suffering a stroke in 1628, he spent the remainder of his life as a bedridden invalid. Upon his death in 1637, he was accorded the honor of a burial in London's Westminster Abbey, where he remains to this day underneath a tombstone reading "O rare Ben Jonson." The epitaph serves as an appropriate reminder of the writer's unique stature and talent as a man of English letters.

Critical Analysis

Ben Jonson is credited with the invention and perfection of a specific type of drama known as "comedy of humors." His major plays portray characters who are dominated by a humor, or trait, such as greed or jealousy, and those who suffer from such character flaws are ridiculous or, worse, corrupt. The vanity of Stephen (a "country gull," or a simpleton) in *Every Man in His Humor,* for example, compels him to throw away money on a hawk, a bird used by hunters but which Stephen has no use for; and a Toledo, a sword that only an aristocrat would own but which turns out to be a rapier, a more common type of sword.

Jonson's major plays are not merely satires of social corruption. They are also demonstrations of Jonson's poetic ideals. In *The Alchemist,* for example, Jonson, observes the scholar John Mebane, "links highly imaginative, symbolic forms of poetry with the mystical characters and obscure language used by occult philosophers." According to Jonson, a writer who uses complex, symbolic language may believe that he has a special knowledge that sets him apart from other writers. Jonson, however, frequently dismisses such a notion as arrogant and deceptive, in that flowery language cannot replace true insight. Indeed, he explicitly equates such symbolic language with fraud when Subtle, the Alchemist, creates a magical symbol for the shop owned by Drugger, one of his dupes:

> I will have his name
> Form'd in some mystic character, whose
>   radii,
> Striking the senses of the passers by,

> Shall, by a virtual influence, breed
>   affections.,
> That may result upon the party owns it . . .

In the play's preface, Jonson forges a connection between the kind of gibberish illustrated here and fashionable poetic language. "For thou wert" he writes, "never more fair in the way to be cos'ned [tricked] (than in this age) in Poetry, especially in Plays."

Jonson demands that poetic language be clear. "The chief virtue of a style," he writes in his *Discoveries,* a collection of quotations from famous writers to which he adds commentary, "is perspicuity [clarity] and nothing so vicious in it, as to need an interpreter." Thus when he writes poetry, as the scholar L. A. Beaurline observes, "Jonson aims for normal word order in speech . . . and careful control of the connotations of words."

Jonson's famous elegy "On My First Son" (1603) is an exercise in straightforwardness. The poem is notable for its understated, even proselike, language. "Farewell, thou child of my right hand, and joy; / My sin was too much hope of thee lov'd boy" the poem begins. It takes advantage of the literal meaning of his son's name, "Benjamin" (that is, "child of the right hand"), to register not just Jonson's pride in his son but also his desire to fashion an image of himself.

Beyond Jonson's personal beliefs about poetic style, another quality for which he was famous was his obsession with being recognized as a critic, or literary expert. Jonson's desire to set himself up as an authority reveals itself in his assuming the stance of literary judge and his critiquing of almost every well-known literary figure of his day. "Samuel DANIEL," he observed, "was a good honest man, had no children, but no poet." He even asserted that "Shakespeare wanted [lacked] art." Jonson's opinions, however, were not consistent, for in another mood, he wrote, for example, that Shakespeare was "the star of poets." William Drummond of Hawthornden regarded Jonson's remarks as a reflection of the playwright's personality rather than a fair judgment of the quality of the poets he discussed. At the end of *Conversations with Jonson* (written 1619, published 1711), Drummond calls Jonson "a great lover and praiser of himself, a condemner and scorner of others." Jonson's criticism, however, was not arbitrary.

Jonson was a neoclassicist—that is, one who attempted to apply the artistic values of the ancient Greeks and Romans to RENAISSANCE literature. His criticism is often a reaction to the indifference of Renaissance playwrights to classical ideals, such as the dramatic unities, which require that a play contain one action that takes place in a single day and in a single location. If a playwright did not pay attention to these unities, the action of his work would seem improbable. Thus, when Jonson observes that Shakespeare "lacks art," he does not mean that Shakespeare is a bad writer; he means that Shakespeare's plays do not maintain the dramatic unities.

At the end of his life, Jonson was regarded by many as the greatest living writer in England, and a number of young poets, regarding themselves as "The Sons of Ben" or as members of "The Tribe of Ben," gathered around him to enjoy his wit and learn their craft. One such poet was Robert HERRICK, who acknowledged Jonson's importance to his art in these terms:

> When I a verse shall make,
> Know I have prayed thee,
> For old religion's sake
> Saint Ben, to aid me.

Today Jonson is remembered as the second greatest English dramatist of the late 16th and early 17th centuries, and perhaps the foremost writer of satiric drama in English history. If Shakespeare had not been a contemporary of Jonson, Jonson might be considered the most important literary figure of his time, considering his ability to merge poetic innovation and adherence to classical values. Although not all of his work and critical opinions are without fault, the variety and depth of his thinking is never lacking in evidence.

Other Works by Ben Jonson

The Alchemist and Other Plays. Edited by Gorden Campbell. New York: Oxford University Press, 1998. *The Complete Poems.* Edited by George Parfitt. New York: Penguin, 1988.

Works about Ben Jonson

Loewenstein, Joseph. *Ben Jonson and Possessive Authorship.* New York: Cambridge University Press, 2002.

Mickel, Leslie. *Ben Jonson's Antimasques: A History of Growth and Decline.* Brookfield, Vt.: Ashgate Publishing Company, 1999.

Summers, Claude J., and Ted-Larry Pebworth. *Ben Jonson Revised.* New York: Twayne, 2000.

Ken, Thomas (1637–1711) *poet*

Thomas Ken was born in Hertfordshire, England, to Thomas Ken, an attorney, and his wife. Both of his parents died by the time Ken was in his teenage years, and it is likely that his sister, Anne, and her husband, Issac Walton, raised him. Issac was deeply religious, and his spirituality and friendship were an important influence in Ken's life. Ken went to New College, Oxford, where he was awarded both bachelor's and master's degrees. In 1663 he began his religious career when he was appointed to a Protestant rectory in Essex. He was eventually appointed bishop of Bath and Wells in 1684. Later in life, however, he was relieved of his duties after refusing to take an oath of loyalty to King William III.

Ken's spirituality and his writing are deeply linked since his work consists mainly of hymns written for the church. These hymns were first published in *Manuel for Winchester Scholars* (1674). The work was not intended to make money but rather to meet the spiritual needs of his community. It contains prayers and instruction for a model scholar, Timotheus, about when he should pray and what type of prayers he should employ. Among the hymns found in the book are Ken's most famous, the morning, noon, and night hymns. The hymns are intended to be sung at the different parts of the day. For instance, these lyrics are from "The Morning Hymn," "Awake my Soul, and with the Sun / Thy daily stage of duty run; / Shake off dull Sloth, and early rise, / To pay thy Morning Sacrifice." These lyrics are from "The Evening Hymn," "Sleep that may more vig'rous make, / To serve my God when I awake!" The hymns are remembered for their beautiful language. Although Ken wrote some other poetry and a few notable letters, none are as well known as these hymns, some of which are still sung in Protestant churches today.

Killigrew, Anne (1660–1685) *poet*

Anne Killigrew was born in London to Dr. Henry and Judith Killigrew, both from families closely associated with the royal court. Her father was master of the Savoy, a hospital; he also wrote plays. A painter, Anne Killigrew produced a portrait of James II, which is still owned by the royal family. Her small volume of poetry, *Poems* (1686), was published after her death from smallpox.

Killigrew's poems, which reveal her own strength and ambition, often celebrate powerful women. The fragment "Alexandreis" depicts a meeting between an Amazonian "Martial Queen" and Alexander the Great. Here she tells of Alexander's grief at finding no more worlds to conquer:

This is the Prince (if Fame you will believe,
To ancient Story any credit give.)
Who when the Globe of Earth he had
*   subdu'd,*
With Tears the easie Victory pursu'd;
Because that no more Worlds there were to
*   win,*
No further Scene to act his Glorys in.

In "To the Queen" Killigrew writes to Mary of Modena, wife of James II, saying that compared with her virtue, Alexander's military greatness is nothing:

Behold an Eye wholly Divine
Vouchsaf'd upon my Verse to Shine!
And from that time I 'gan to treat
With Pitty him the World call'd Great;
To smile at his exalted Fate,
Unequal (though Gigantick) State.

Killigrew's own lack of authority appears in her best-known poem, "Upon the Saying that My Verses Were Made by Another." Killigrew writes that she dedicated herself to poetry and hoped for "Sweet Fame," but she was deceived in her hope:

But, ah, the sad effects that from it came!
What ought t'have brought me Honour,
*   brought me shame!*

Although others took credit for her verses, she says, she will not be discouraged:

But let 'em Rage, and 'gainst a Maide
*   Conspire,*
So Deathless Numbers from my Tuneful
*   Lyre*
Do ever flow; so Phebus I by thee
Divinely Inspired and possest may be;
I willingly accept Cassandras Fate,
To speak the Truth, although believ'd too
*   late.*

After Killigrew's death John DRYDEN praised the "noble vigor" of her poetry in his ode "To the Pious Memory of the Accomplished Mrs. Anne Killigrew" (1686). Killigrew is remembered today primarily as the subject of Dryden's poem, who said of her that

nothing to her Genius was deny'd,
But like a Ball of fire the further thrown,
Still with a greater Blaze she shone,
And her bright Soul broke out on ev'ry side.

Works about Anne Killigrew

Barash, Carol. *English Women's Poetry 1649–1714: Politics, Community, and Linguistic Authority.* New York: Clarendon Press, 1996.

Messenger, Ann. *His & Hers: Essays in Restoration and Eighteenth Century Literature.* Lexington, Ky.: University Press of Kentucky, 1986.

Killigrew, Thomas (1612–1683) *playwright*

Thomas Killigrew was born in London to Sir Robert and Anne Killigrew. His interest in theater was evident from an early age, when he volunteered to play a devil at the Red Bull Theatre in order to see plays. Killigrew's schooling was cut short when he left home as a young man to become a page to King Charles I, and he lightheartedly acknowledged (and exaggerated) his lack of education in the epilogue to *The Parson's Wedding* (1641), referring to himself as "the illiterate Courtier that made this Play."

Killigrew penned his first play, *The Prisoners*, between 1633 and 1635. This extravagant and romantic tragicomedy was one of many plays written by courtiers for Queen Henrietta Maria. It was followed by two more tragicomedies, *Claricilla* (1635–36) and *The Princess* (1635–36).

In 1641 Killigrew wrote *The Parson's Wedding*. The coarse tone of this comedy lies in stark contrast to the grand tone of his first three plays, as does its purpose, which was for production in front of the general public rather than to entertain and please the queen. The play's clever and often sardonic dialogue takes aim at various English institutions as well as at country life ("So you will spare us miserable men, condemn'd to London . . . and never travel'd those Countries that set Mountains on fire a purpose to light us to our lodging.") and the restrictions of "the spiritual Non-sence the age calls Platonick Love." *The Parson's Wedding* is Killigrew's most reprinted work, and it best demonstrates his satirical wit.

With the escalation of the English Civil War, Killigrew followed Prince Charles into exile in 1647. During this period he wrote *The Pilgrim* (1646–47), *Cicilia and Clorinda* (1649–50), *Bellamira her Dream* (1652), and *Thomaso or the Wanderer* (1654). The last is a semiautobiographical play that includes satirical commentary on conditions in England: "The Dogs are so muzled and ty'd up at home, with constables and [C]romwel, they fight for sport abroad."

In 1660, when Charles II was restored to the throne of England, Killigrew became groom of the royal bedchamber and received a patent, or paid position, to organize and house his own company of actors. Along with William DAVENANT, Killigrew was principally responsible for the reestablishment of the theater in England. (During the Commonwealth, 1649–60, London's theaters had all been closed.) Killigrew and Davenant each built theaters that were the only licensed venues for theatrical performance in London until the 19th century. Killigrew was appointed Master of the King's Revels in 1673. In 1677, however, financial problems forced Killigrew to turn his theatrical company and official position over to his son.

Throughout his career, Killigrew was primarily known for his wit rather than for his skill as a playwright. Anthony à WOOD remarked, "It was usually said of this noted person that when he took a pen in hand, it did not answer to the never-failing smartness he showed in conversation."

King, Henry (1592–1669) *poet, sermon writer*

Henry King was born in Worminghall, Oxfordshire, England, the son of Dr. John King, bishop of London. He was educated at Thame and Westminster schools and Christ Church, Oxford University, completing the doctor of divinity degree in 1625. He became archdeacon of Colchester in 1617 and married Anne Berkely in the same year. John DONNE was one of his greatest friends.

King was a royal chaplain to JAMES I and Charles I. When the Civil War against the monarchy began, the town King lived in, Chichester, was attacked by the Puritans in 1642, and he lost all his possessions. He stayed with various relations until the monarchy was restored in 1660, and during this time he translated some of the biblical Psalms into verse (1652; 1655). King preached at Whitehall in London in 1661, and his sermon was printed soon after, but he seems to have retired after that, except for giving occasional sermons before the king.

King's earliest known poem is "A Groane at the Funerall of . . . Charles the First" (1649), occasioned by the execution of Charles I by the Puritans. He laments the execution: "Alas! our Ruines are cast up, and sped / In that black Totall–Charles is Murthered." A revised and improved version, entitled "Elegy," was published with his first collection of poems (1656–57). Other collections were issued in 1664 and 1700.

King's best-known poem was "Exequy," in which he mourns the death of his wife in 1624 and looks forward to Judgment Day when "we shall rise / And view our selves with clearer eyes / In that calm Region, where no Night / Can hide us from each other's sight."

King wrote a variety of other poems, such as "On Being waked out of my Sleep by a Snuff of Candle," and "Sonnet," in which he says of an unnamed woman, "Were thy heart soft, as Thou art fair, / Thou wert a wonder, past compare. / But frozen Love and fierce Disdain / By their Extremes thy Graces stain." The poems, which were written between 1612 and 1657, show the steady development of King's life and poetry through a difficult period in English history.

Although less well known, King's sermons were recently published by Mary Hobbs as "fine examples of seventeenth-century prose," important for presenting "the true middle" position of the CHURCH OF ENGLAND at that time.

King's Men *theater troupe*

The King's Men was an acting company that was originally named the CHAMBERLAIN'S MEN and owned the GLOBE THEATRE. The death of ELIZABETH I in 1603 brought JAMES I OF ENGLAND to the throne. A theater lover, James took over the PATRONAGE of the Chamberlain's Men, which was the premier acting company of the time, and the company was renamed accordingly.

William SHAKESPEARE was the major playwright and an actor for the King's Men. The company also included Richard Burbage, one of the great dramatic actors of the period; and Robert Armin, a character actor who played parts such as the Fool, a role with tragic undertone, in Shakespeare's *King Lear*. According to the scholar Peter Hyland, "a play-goer went to the Globe to see *King Lear* . . . not . . . because it was a play by Shakespeare, but because it was performed by the King's Men and featured Burbage and Armin."

The King's Men staged plays at the Globe when not performing at the royal court for James. The Globe was a huge open-air amphitheater with seating for 3,000 people. Shakespeare and the other company members owned shares in both the company and the theater.

The King's Men performed approximately 30 different plays per season, with each play running for two weeks. Shakespeare wrote two new plays per year for the company, which continued to perform his older plays as well. Plays by other popular dramatists such as Christopher MARLOWE, Ben JONSON, and Thomas DEKKER were also performed.

In 1608 the King's Men took over a second theater, the BLACKFRIARS. Smaller, more intimate, and enclosed (the Globe was open to the air), the Blackfriars seated a more refined audience than the Globe because tickets to the indoor playhouse were more expensive. However, the same plays were performed at both theaters. In 1642 the Puritans, who were opposed to public entertainment, gained control of the London government. They succeeded in closing all theaters, and the King's Men disbanded.

A Work about the King's Men

Gurr, Andrew. *Playgoing in Shakespeare's London.* New York: Cambridge University Press, 1987.

Knolles, Richard (ca. 1550–1610) *historian*

Richard Knolles was born in Cold Ashby, Northamptonshire, the son of Francis Knolles. He graduated from Lincoln College, Oxford University, in 1565 and received his master's degree there the following year. After leaving Oxford, he embarked upon a teaching career and became headmaster of a grammar school at Sandwich, Kent.

Knolles's most significant publication was a historical work of nearly 1,200-pages: *The Generall Historie of the Turkes: From the First Beginning of that Nation to the Rising of the Othoman Familie* (1603), which took him 12 years to compile. In his subtitle, Knolles acknowledges his dependence on secondary sources by claiming that his manuscript was "Faithfullie collected out of the best Histories and digested into one continual Historie . . ." For his research he drew primarily on Jacques Boissard's *Vitae et Icones Sultanorum Turcicorum*, a history of the Turks that had been published in Frankfurt in 1596. While *The Generall Historie* lacked the rigorous scholarship demanded by modern historians, it is of interest for its ornate language and richly embellished prose style.

For nearly two centuries, Knolles's work was considered the definitive English-language source of information about the Ottoman Empire and related matters. Thomas Goffe used it as the source for *The Courageous Turk, or Amurath the First* (1619), a drama about the 1389 Battle of Kosovo. In the 18th century, Samuel Johnson praised *The Generall Historie* for a style that was "pure, nervous, elevated, and clear." Later, Lord Byron wrote admiringly of "Old Knolles," whose history he had so enjoyed reading as a child. Byron added, "I believe it had much influence on my future wishes to visit the Levant [the Middle East], and gave perhaps the oriental coloring which is observed in my poetry."

Knox, John (ca. 1513–1572) *nonfiction writer*

John Knox was born in Haddington, Scotland. Little is known about his childhood, and most of what is known about his life comes from his own work, *History of the Reformation in Scotland* (1563). We do know, however, that he was ordained as a Catholic priest around 1530.

A major turning point in Knox's life was the execution of his friend and mentor, Protestant preacher George Wishart, who was burned at the stake as a heretic in 1546. Less than three months later a group of young men revenged Wishart's death by murdering Cardinal Beaton, a Catholic. In *The History of the Reformation* Knox shocked many by introducing the story of Beaton's death with the words, "These things we write merrily [happily]." After Beaton's death in June 1546, French and Scottish Catholics seized Knox, who was imprisoned for almost two years, at first in Scotland, then aboard a French galley, and finally at Rouen, France.

By 1549 Knox was free to return to Scotland, but he chose instead to live in England, where he presented his religious beliefs in a number of sermons. Among other things, he objected to the use of incense, the mass spoken in Latin, church bells, kneeling to receive communion, and music during the service. He also did not accept the Roman Catholic belief in transubstantiation, that is, the belief that the body of Christ is physically present in the host.

Knox wrote a great many religious treatises, including *A Brief Exhortation to England for the Speedy Embracing of the Gospel* (1559), in which he advised the populace to rid themselves of all "dregs of popery." Perhaps the most controversial work of the period was *The First Blast of the Trumpet Against the Monstrous Regiment of Women,* published anonymously in 1559. By regiment Knox meant regime, and his target in this essay was several Catholic women rulers of the day, among them Queen Mary of England and MARY STUART, then heir to the Scottish throne. Knox's argument was, basically, that it was against scripture for women to rule over men and nations. ELIZABETH I had become England's ruler by the time this treatise was published, and she did not care for Knox's attitude toward women—of whatever religion.

Knox intended to put forth two additional "trumpet blasts" but never got to them. He was exiled from England and went to Geneva, where he met John CALVIN, who influenced him greatly. In 1559 he returned to Scotland, where he immediately became the leader of the Protestant faction. In 1560 Knox and his party of reformers presented *The Confession of Faith Professed and Believed by the Protestants within the Realm of Scotland* to the Scottish parliament. Its acceptance established Protestantism as the national religion. *The Confession* called for abolishing the authority of the pope, prohibiting mass under penalty of death, using church revenues to support the Protestant ministry, and monetary help for the poor. By December that same year Knox and three other ministers had published *The First Book of Discipline,* the Protestant plan of church government, which advocated a national system of education among other so-called reforms.

In 1561 the Catholic Mary Stuart sailed from France and arrived in Scotland to claim her crown. She and Knox were enemies from the first. Knox's rhetoric against Mary was legendary, and he criticized her both in person and from the pulpit, calling her "a slave of Satan" and a "Jezebel," and comparing her to the insane Roman emperor Nero. When he continued to criticize Mary in his sermons, he was commanded to stop preaching but ignored the order.

Knox's last sermon, preached in Edinburgh in August 1572, was an impassioned reaction to the SAINT BARTHOLOMEW'S DAY MASSACRE of Protestants in France. Although Knox was known by his contemporaries as an amiable and kind man, his writing had such a distinctly Old Testament quality that many were incited to violence by his sermons. The

Earl of Morton, then regent of Scotland, said at Knox's funeral, "Here lieth a man who in his life never feared the face of man."

Works about John Knox

Scott, Walter. *From Gileskirk to Grayfriars: Mary Queen of Scots, John Knox, and the Heroes of Scotland's Reformation.* Nashville, Tenn.: Cumberland House, 2001.

Wilson, Douglas, and George Grant. *For Kirk and Covenant: The Stalwart Courage of John Knox.* Nashville, Tenn.: Cumberland House, 2000.

Kyd, Thomas (1558–1594) *playwright, translator*

Thomas Kyd was the son of a London scrivener (copyist), Francis Kyd, and his wife, Anna. He was educated at the Merchant Taylors' school in London, where he learned to read and write both Latin and English, and where the headmaster, Richard Mulcaster, had his pupils act in plays to be performed at court. There is no evidence of his attendance at any university. A wisecrack by Thomas NASHE suggests Kyd worked as a scrivener for some time.

Little is known of Kyd's adult life, with the great exception of his involvement in the atheism scandal surrounding Christopher MARLOWE. In 1593, as London workers rioted against the perceived privileged status of foreign workers, Marlowe and Kyd shared living quarters. The government searched their room for antiforeigner propaganda, which they did not find, but they did find some "atheistical" documents. Under intense interrogation and torture, Kyd assured authorities that the writings belonged to Marlowe alone.

In 1592 one of the most successful plays of the RENAISSANCE theater opened at The Rose: Kyd's *The Spanish Tragedy* (probably written around 1588). The play opens with a conversation between the ghost of Don Andrea, a Spanish nobleman, and the allegorical figure Revenge. These two characters observe the entire action of the play. Don Andrea, who has been killed in the war between Spain and Portugal, laments his separation from his beloved Bel-imperia, who is now betrothed to Don Andrea's killer, Balthazar, as part of the peace settlement. Don Andrea is nevertheless assured that Revenge will prevail.

Before that revenge is accomplished, however, the plot becomes quite complex. Bel-imperia falls in love with Don Andrea's friend Horatio, who is then killed by Balthazar and Bel-imperia's evil brother Lorenzo. Hieronimo, Horatio's father, arranges for Bel-imperia, Lorenzo, and Balthazar to perform in a bloody tragic play in which, unknown to the watching kings of Spain and Portugal, the violence on stage is real, and all are killed.

The year 1592 also saw the performance of the comedy *Don Horatio* (perhaps written several years earlier), which functions as a sort of prequel to *The Spanish Tragedy*. The play was published anonymously, but the close relationship between the two plays points to Kyd as the author of both. (Thomas HEYWOOD identified Kyd as the author of *The Spanish Tragedy* in 1612.) *Soliman and Perseda* (performed 1592, but probably written several years earlier) is a full-length version of the play that Hieronimo performs at the end of *The Spanish Tragedy*. At the beginning of *Soliman and Perseda*, Turkish emperor Soliman competes with the young knight Erastus for the love of Perseda. Soliman has Erastus killed, but revenge belongs to Perseda. The close links between this play and *The Spanish Tragedy* have influenced scholars to attribute *Soliman and Perseda* to Kyd.

Although there is little evidence for it, Kyd is often mentioned as a possible author or coauthor of the anonymous *Arden of Faversham,* a domestic tragedy (a play involving an unfaithful wife who pays for her wrongdoing with her life) published in 1592, the same year as *The Spanish Tragedy. Arden* shares many themes with Kyd's plays, all of which, as Kyd scholar Lukas Erne points out, involve "loss, grief, and revenge"; his main characters are all "victim[s] of adverse fortune trying to cope with . . . loss."

Only one play of Kyd's was published under his name during his lifetime. (In addition, a translation from the Italian author Torquato TASSO, *The*

Householder's Philosophy (1588), appeared with the initials T. K.). The tragedy *Cornelia* (1594) was a translation of a play by the French dramatist Robert Garnier. In the dedication to this work, Kyd refers to "those so bitter times" he lived through while working on the piece. Besides the stress of the government's investigation of himself and Marlowe, Kyd was apparently abandoned by his patron, a wealthy nobleman who had provided financial support for Kyd while he wrote. Additionally, his health may have been irrevocably damaged by interrogation under torture. He died the same year *Cornelia* was published.

Critical Analysis

Thomas McAlindon, a scholar of English drama, called *The Spanish Tragedy* "the most important single play in the history of English drama" because of its pervasive influence. Its theme of revenge is in the tradition of Seneca, the most famous of Roman writers of tragedy. There are three principal figures who seek revenge in the play: Don Andrea, Bel-imperia, and Heironimo. The first two are seeking revenge for the killing of Don Andrea, which occurred before the play begins. The allegorical character Revenge assures Don Andrea in the very first scene, however, that his killer will be "deprived of life by Bel-imperia" herself. Thus Kyd takes away any doubt about the outcome of the play, allowing the audience to focus on further complications in the plot, and especially on the elaborate means by which the revenge is accomplished.

In contrast to Don Andrea and Bel-imperia, however, Heironimo seeks revenge for an event that takes place during the course of the play. He becomes the main character of the play after his son Horatio is killed. Heironimo's soliloquy (a speech spoken while alone on the stage) upon finding Horatio's body hanged in his arbor is touching in his heartbroken questioning:

What savage monster, not of human kind
Hath here been glutted with thy harmless
blood,

And left thy bloody corpse dishonored here,
For me, amidst . . . [these] dark and
deathful shades,
To drown thee with an ocean of my tears?

When his wife, Isabella, enters, however, Heironimo hints at the course of the rest of the play, stating, "[I]n revenge my heart would find relief." In the meantime he feigns madness while he meditates upon how to find justice. Heironimo's solution is as brilliant as it is ironic. The play he arranges is supposed to pass the time between Bel-imperia and Balthazar's wedding ceremony and the wedding night. Instead Heironimo and Bel-imperia take their vengeance publicly and gloriously, then kill themselves. Many of these elements would be followed by authors of other revenge tragedies: the play within the play, the feigned madness of the delaying main character, and the death of the avenger all became standard in other revenge tragedies.

The most famous work attributed to Kyd has never been found, but it is generally believed to have existed. The so-called *Ur-Hamlet* is understood by scholars to have been used by William SHAKESPEARE in writing his *Hamlet* (1600–01). A remark by Nashe, writing 12 years before Shakespeare's play was performed, pokes fun at a writer who peruses Seneca, finding "whole Hamlets, I should say handfuls of Tragicall speeches." Nashe says that the author in question has left "the trade of Noverint [scrivener]," has gotten involved with "Italian Translations," and, if another hint is needed, compares the author to a "Kid" in a fable. If it is true that Kyd actually wrote an *Ur-Hamlet*, his influence on the history of drama can hardly be overstated. Other contemporary references to the *Ur-Hamlet* mention the ghost of Hamlet's father, one of the essential features of Shakespeare's play that may have been borrowed from Kyd.

Whatever his other contributions, Kyd assured his place in the history of English drama with his masterpiece *The Spanish Tragedy*. As the editor Norman Rabkin states, that work "made audiences and playwrights aware of the possibilities of their medium"; the play "seizes . . . on precisely the most vital and rewarding elements of a developing theater to speak both to and for its age."

A Work about Thomas Kyd

Erne, Lukas. *Beyond The Spanish Tragedy: A Study of the Works of Thomas Kyd*. New York: Palgrave, 2001.

Kynaston, Sir Francis (Sir Francis Kenaston) (1587–1642) *poet, translator*

Sir Francis Kynaston was a member of the court of King Charles I. He translated Chaucer's *Troilus and Criseyde* from middle English into Latin, prompting fellow poet William CARTWRIGHT to note "we read Chaucer now without a dictionary."

Kynaston's most popular original poem was probably "To Cynthia, on concealment of her Beauty." The poem is an elaborate love poem, each stanza of which begins with the words, "Do not conceal," as the poet begs Cynthia to reveal her beauty and wryly predicts terrible consequences if she should fail to do so:

> *Do not conceal those tresses fair,*
> *The silken snares of thy curled hair,*
> *Lest finding neither gold no ore,*
> *The curious silk-worm work no more.*

Then, in the final stanza, the poet gives the ultimate compliment:

> *Do not conceal no beauty, grace,*
> *That's either in thy mind or face,*
> *Lest virtue overcome by vice*
> *Make men believe no Paradise.*

In 1635 Kynaston opened the Museum Minerve, a school for the children of nobles where they learned diverse talents such as painting, sculpture and knowledge of antiquities, besides the usual subjects such as science and languages. But the school was intended for Royalists only and consequently failed as this faction was defeated by Cromwell's forces during the English Civil War.

A mysterious document titled *A true presentation of forepast Parliaments, to the view of present times and posteritie* has been linked to Kynaston, although his name does not appear on the work. Several scholars, such as Esther Cope, believe Kynaston authored the piece, which gives an inside view of the important people close to Charles I.

Shortly after his death, Kynaston's poem *Leoline and Sydanis: An Heroick Romance* was published in 1642. This work tells the tale of lovers who are separated by black magic but later reunited by white magic.

Lanyer, Aemelia (1569–1645) *poet*

Aemelia Lanyer, born in London, was the daughter of Baptist Bassano, an Italian court musician to ELIZABETH I, and Margaret Johnson Bassano. Throughout her life, including her marriage to another court musician, Alphonso Lanyer, she remained on the fringes of the English court rather than holding an important position.

Lanyer's sole poetic work was *Salve Deus Rex Judaeorum*, (*Praise God King of the Jews*), published in 1611. This work opens with nine separate poems and two prose pieces dedicated to aristocratic women, such as Queen Anne, wife of JAMES I OF ENGLAND. Lanyer requests their PATRONAGE, or social and financial support for her poetry. In "To the Ladie Katherine Countesse of Suffolke" she writes,

> *Vouchsafe sweet Lady, to accept these lines,*
> *Writ by a hand that doth desire to doe*
> *All services to you.*

Lanyer deferentially submits her verse to her patrons, requesting their favor and attempting to establish her voice in an era when women's writing was discouraged. As the scholar Susanne Woods remarks, "these dedications provide Lanyer's principal authority for publishing her verse."

In a final appeal to these women, Lanyer closes her volume with the verse "The Description of Cookham." The poet praises the countess of Cumberland's estate as a haven for women's learning. Lanyer gained exposure to the literary circles of the period through such connections to influential aristocratic women.

The actual *Salve Deus Rex Judaeorum* is a long narrative poem about Christ. Wood observes that Lanyer's "central topic, Christ's Passion [crucifixion], provides another authority," namely religion, for her writing poetry. For RENAISSANCE women, writing about religion, unlike, say, about politics, was an acceptable literary activity.

Lanyer proclaims that she is "God's steward," or caretaker, and urges her readers to encounter Christ through her poetry. She adopts the language of romance to portray religious love for Christ, drawing on traditional depictions of the worshipper as the bride of Christ:

> *Put on your wedding garments every one,*
> *The Bridegroome stayes to entertaine you*
> *   all.*

Lanyer further argues that women have a special relationship to Christ because he was begotten of a woman, borne of a woman, nourished of a woman, obedient to a woman; and that he healed woman, pardoned women, comforted women: . . . after his resurrection, appeared first to a woman, sent a woman to declare his most glorious resurrection.

Continuing her focus on women and religion, Lanyer reevaluates women's roles in the Bible. She takes on controversial issues, as when she retells biblical stories as a way to participate in contemporary debates about the sexes. For instance, in the story of Adam and Eve, traditionally Eve leads Adam to sin by urging him to eat the forbidden fruit of knowledge. Lanyer argues that Eve, in "Giving to Adam what shee held most deare," was guiltless, for it was by Satan that she "(poor soule) by cunning was deceav'd, / No hurt therein her harmless Heart intended."

While Lanyer's Eve is presented as good-hearted and innocent, by contrast "Adam can not be excused" because "being Lord of all, the greater was his shame." She claims that, since Adam had been granted dominion over Eden, his was the greater responsibility and guilt. Placing the blame on Adam is part of Lanyer's goal of restoring women's reputations at the expense of men, and she ends her argument by writing that man's greatest crime was putting Christ to death.

In *Salve Deus* the tone of the verse changes as the poem shifts from arguments about gender roles to the contemplation of Christ. When depicting Christ's suffering on the cross, Lanyer asks her readers,

> Upon the Crosse depriv'd of life or breath,
> To judge if ever Lover were so true,
> To yeeld himselfe unto such shamefull
>   death.

Lanyer draws upon the language of love poetry repeatedly to describe Christ as a lover:

> This is that Bridegroome that appeares so
>   faire,

> so sweet, so lovely in his Spouses sight,
> That unto Snowe we may his face compare,
> His cheekes like skarlet, and his eyes so
>   bright

Lanyer represents Christ's body by using the blazon, a Renaissance poetic technique in which a woman's eyes, cheeks, lips, and so on are compared to beautiful things. Thus, a male poet might write that his lover has lips like roses. By feminizing Christ and by describing his relationship to women as a husband or lover, Lanyer appeals to her audience of aristocratic women.

By including women so prominently in this religious narrative poem, Lanyer left an important legacy in an era when few women wrote or had a voice in matters of religion. As the critic Marshall Grossman writes, "Lanyer claims our attention on her own poetic merits. Her poetry is varied, subtle, witty, and provocative."

Works about Aemelia Lanyer

Grossman, Marshall, ed. *Aemilia Lanyer: Gender, Genre and the Canon.* Lexington: University Press of Kentucky, 1998.
Woods, Susanne *Lanyer: A Renaissance Woman Poet.* New York: Oxford University Press, 1999.

Latimer, Hugh (ca. 1492–1555) *nonfiction writer*

Hugh Latimer was born in Thurcaston, Leicester, England, to a tenant farmer. He entered Cambridge University in 1506, receiving a B.A. in 1510 and an M.A. in 1514. In 1522 he was appointed one of 12 university preachers.

Cambridge was a breeding ground for reformist radicals, but for a long while Latimer was unaffected by their views. Indeed, in 1524 his dissertation for his bachelor's of divinity degree challenged the doctrines of Phillip Melanchthon, an associate of Martin LUTHER. Latimer's dissertation argument was later disputed by one of the Cambridge radicals, Thomas Bilney, who persuaded him to accept reformist ideas. Thereafter,

Latimer was grateful to Bilney for "opening his eyes."

In 1535 Latimer was appointed bishop of Worcester, in which position his common-sense sermons persuaded many of the need for religious reform. His contention was that true piety was in prayer and living a good life rather than in the idolatry of relics. Historian Harold Darby writes that Latimer's "forthright speech still rings from the page."

Eventually Latimer was forced to resign the Worcester bishopric when he argued against Henry VIII's Six Articles that upheld such Catholic rites as clerical celibacy, the private mass, and confessions to a priest. Released from the administrative duties of the diocese, he was free to preach in the streets of London and the surrounding countryside. Crowds flocked to hear him, his common dress and everyday speech making him accessible to all.

In 1547 Latimer was again installed in an official post, this time as Court Prophet to Edward VI. He preached some of his most eloquent sermons to the young king and his advisers. In one sermon he likens the devil to a Catholic priest:

> And now I would ask a strange question: who is the most diligent bishop and prelate in all England, that passeth all the rest in doing his office? . . . And will ye know who it is? I will tell you: it is the devil. . . . his office is to hinder religion, to maintain superstition, to set up idolatry, to teach all kind of popery.

When Edward died, his sister Mary, a Catholic, was installed as queen, and Latimer was condemned to death for heresy. As the fires were lit, Latimer offered these now-famous words of reassurance for a fellow MARTYR: "Be of good comfort, Master Ridley, and play the man. We shall this day light such a candle by God's grace in England as I trust shall never be put out!" The scholar Patricia Cricco states that "Latimer's basic message was the same time-honored message of all preachers . . . the proper correlation between inner commitments and their external expressions."

A Work about Hugh Latimer

Smith, Lacey Baldwin. *Fools, Martyrs, Traitors: The Story of Martyrdom in the Western World.* New York: Knopf, 1997.

Lead, Jane (1623–1704) *nonfiction writer*

Jane Lead was born in Norfolk, England, the daughter of Schildknap Ward. She had her first spiritual experience as a teenager: She was dancing at a Christmas party when she heard a voice that said "Cease from this, I have another dance to lead thee in, for this is vanity." Initially she was frightened by this event, but it eventually led her to seek greater spiritual wisdom. In 1644 she married a distant cousin, William Lead.

Throughout her life Lead experienced visions that she subsequently recorded in her spiritual biography, *A Fountain of Gardens* (1696–1701). In her first vision, which occurred in 1670, a female figure says,

> Behold I am God's Eternal Virgin-Wisdom, whom thou hast been enquiring after . . . out of my Womb thou shalt be brought forth after the manner of a Spirit, Conceived and Born again: this thou shalt know by a New Motion of Life, stirring and giving a restlessness, till Wisdom be born within the inward parts of thy Soul.

From this point forward Lead began to write about her visions and spiritual ideas. She was an extraordinarily prolific writer, publishing literally dozens of religious tracts. In 1694 Lead met Francis Lee of Oxford, and together they established the Philadelphian Society, a group that stressed spiritual life and the inner light. Lead said in 1696 "Christ rejected Episcopaleans, Presbyterians, Independents, Baptists, Fifth-Monarchists, and Rome, choosing only the Philadelphian Society as free from all forms." In 1699 Lead lost her eyesight and Lee, whom she had adopted, recorded her subsequent visions.

Lee, Nathaniel (1653?–1692) *dramatist*

Nathaniel Lee was born in Hatfield, Hertfordshire, England, the son of Dr. Richard Lee, who was the Presbyterian rector at Hatfield. Young Nathaniel received his early education at Westminster School and then Trinity College, Cambridge. In 1671 he moved to London in the futile hope of securing patronage from the Duke of Buckingham and tried to support himself as an actor on various London stages, another futile effort because he suffered from intense stage fright.

Despite his failure as an actor, Lee remained passionate about the theater, which was gaining new life after the RESTORATION of Charles II to the throne in 1660. With a good general knowledge of classical history, Lee chose as the subjects for his plays the lives and times of significant rulers from times past. His plays include *Nero, Emperour of Rome* (1675); *Sophonisba, or Hannibal's Overthrow* (1676); *Gloriana, or the Court of Augustus Caesar* (1676), the latter two being extravagant dramas written in rhymed heroic couplets; and *Mithridates, King of Pontus* (1678).

Lee's blank-verse tragedy, *The Rival Queens, or the Death of Alexander the Great* (1677), which examined the jealousy of the ruler's first wife for his second, established Lee's reputation as a popular dramatist and remained a staple of the English stage for generations. It earned him the praise and friendship of John DRYDEN, to whom the play was dedicated, along with the Prince and Princess of Orange. Lee and Dryden later coauthored *Oedipus: A Tragedy*, first performed in 1678, and *The Duke of Guise* (1682). Dryden also wrote the prologue to Lee's tragedy *Caesar Borgia: Son of Pope Alexander the Sixth* (1679) and the prologue to a revival of *Sophonisba*. Colley Cibber, a contemporary reviewer, criticized the "furious fustian and turgid rant" of Lee's writing, but the 20th-century scholar Allardyce Nicoll, author of *The History of the English Drama*, declared that Lee's plays "are of inestimable importance in any attempt to divine the quality of the tragedy of his age."

Other Work by Nathaniel Lee

Works, Edited with Introduction and Notes by Thomas B. Stroup and Arthur L. Cooke. New Brunswick, N.J.: Scarecrow Press, 1954.

A Work about Nathaniel Lee

Armistead, J. M. *Nathaniel Lee.* Boston: Twayne, 1979.

Leigh, Dorothy (fl. 1616) *nonfiction writer*

Like Elizabeth JOCELYN, Dorothy Leigh wrote primarily to leave behind a legacy to her children in case she died before she could counsel them. She explains in her *A Mother's Blessing* (1616) that she sees herself "going out of the world and you [her children] but coming in."

Leigh's work is in four parts: a dedication to Elizabeth, the daughter of JAMES I OF ENGLAND; a letter to her sons justifying her writing; a poem written for her sons; and, finally, 45 chapters on personal behavior. Leigh was a practicing Christian, and thus much of her writing focuses on the religious aspects of life such as prayer and sacred education. For example, when she advises her sons on how to choose wives, she tells them, "You must seek a godly wife, that she may be a help to you in godliness."

Leigh's work, however, went beyond simple advice to her sons. She counsels other women, addressing companionable marriage and child-rearing practices that encourage patience over strict discipline. Critic Naomi Miller points out that Leigh "supports the existence of bonds of friendship between men and women in marriage as well as bonds of fellowship among women." Despite its religious focus, Leigh's book provides practical advice for women whose primary roles were as wives and mothers. The popularity of the book, which was reissued 19 times from 1616 to 1640, indicates that many women looked to it for advice and comfort.

Works about Dorothy Leigh

Brown, Sylvia, ed. *Women's Writing in Stuart England: The Mother's Legacies of Dorothy Leigh, Elizabeth Joscelin, and Elizabeth Richardson.* Thrupp, Stroud, Gloucester, U.K.: Sutton, 1999.

Martin, Randall, ed. *Women Writers in Renaissance England.* New York: Longman, 1997.

Leland, John (John Leyland, John Leylande) (1506–1552) *historian*

John Leland is considered England's first antiquarian (a person who collects, studies, or deals in old books or other antiquities). He studied under the humanist scholar William LILLY at St. Paul's school in London before beginning a university career at Cambridge and Oxford. Later he went on to become chaplain and librarian to King Henry VIII.

In 1533 the Crown commissioned Leland to be the "King's Antiquary," a position that required him to record important historical manuscripts. In order to accomplish this task, Leland toured the country for more than six years, collecting artifacts and documents and helping to prevent, in part, the wholesale destruction of manuscripts following the closing of the Catholic monasteries. His work was edited in a volume entitled *The Laboryouse Journey and Serche of J. Leylande for Englandes Antiquities, Given of Hym as a Newe Yeares Gyfte to Kinge Henry the VIII* (1549). Leland continued to write about the antiquities of the British Isles until he died in 1552.

Leland's interest in reviving ancient historical texts rose out of his humanist education, which valued people's ability to use reason to answer scientific questions and favored the culture and literature of the ancient Greeks and Romans. His studies sparked an interest in the ancient Germanic authors, many of whom were monks, of the British Isles. Leyland said that he studied the ancient relics "to the intent that the monuments of ancient writers . . . might be brought out of deadly darkness to lively light."

Leonardo da Vinci (1452–1519) *scientist, painter, nonfiction writer*

Leonardo da Vinci was an Italian artist and scientist whose work was fundamental to the artistic and intellectual revolution of the RENAISSANCE. His parents, Ser Piero, a Florentine notary, and Caterina, a young peasant woman, were unmarried at the time of his birth in Vinci, Italy. Leonardo was raised by his father and, as a teenager, went to Florence to work as an apprentice to the Italian painter and sculptor Andrea del Verrochio. In 1482 he traveled to Milan to work for that city's duke. His architectural skills led him to become an engineer on a variety of military projects. In 1507 he was named court painter to King Louis XII of France, who then resided in Milan.

Over the course of his life, Leonardo produced numerous paintings, sculptures, and drawings, as well as a collection of scientific notebooks that are more than 4,000 pages long. His most famous paintings include *The Adoration of the Magi* (1481–82), *The Last Supper* (1495–98), and the *Mona Lisa* (1503–5). As a painter he was known not only for capturing subtle expressions in his subjects, but also for painting with a keen sensitivity to anatomical accuracy. This can be attributed to his scientific study of the human body. In his treatise entitled *On Painting* he wrote, "A good painter has two chief objects to paint, man and the intention of his soul. The former is easy, the latter hard because he has to represent it by the attitudes and movements of the limbs."

In addition to his artistic achievements, Leonardo made several important scientific contributions. He was a careful observer of the world around him, and his scientific drawings reflect his interest in human and animal anatomy as well as in plant life. He also created numerous mechanical drawings in which he sketched out his innovative ideas. The theories in his scientific treatises, which he never completed, would have been revolutionary to the scientific inquiry of the 16th century. It seems that Leonardo planned to publish them as a great encyclopedia of knowledge, but, like many of his projects, this one was never finished.

Because his notebooks were difficult to decipher, Leonardo's findings were not published completely until well after his death. The manuscripts are difficult to read; not only did Leonardo write in mirror-image script from right to left, he also used peculiar spellings and abbreviations, and his notes are not arranged in any logical order. After his death, his notes were scattered to libraries and collections all over Europe.

While portions of Leonardo's technical treatises on painting were published as early as 1651, the scope and caliber of much of his scientific work remained unknown until the 19th century. He described himself as "a man without letters," yet his notebooks reveal his sensitivity to language. He wrote frequently about his disdain for those who spent too much time studying from books and not enough time observing their surroundings.

Leonardo's extraordinary artistic and scientific talents were ahead of his time. In a study that is considered by many historians to be controversial, the famous psychologist Sigmund Freud eloquently described Leonardo as a man "who awoke too early in the darkness, while the others were still asleep."

Other Work by Leonardo da Vinci
The Notebooks of Leonardo Da Vinci. McLean, Va.: IndyPublish, 2003.

A Work about Leonardo da Vinci
Clark, Kenneth. *Leonardo Da Vinci: An Account of His Development as an Artist.* New York: Penguin, 1993.

L'Estrange, Roger (1616–1704) *nonfiction writer, translator*
Born to Sir Hamon L'Estrange and his wife, Alice Stubbe, Roger L'Estrange was an ardent Tory, a supporter of the Stuart dynasty, and like so many literary men of his day, L'Estrange's fortunes and situation depended on who was in power. Primarily a political journalist and pamphleteer, L'Estrange had to abandon his political writings and flee to Europe in 1648, after having been imprisoned at Newgate for four years for his efforts on behalf of the monarchy in the English Civil Wars. When James II was restored to the throne in 1660, L'Estrange became surveyor and licenser of printing presses for the government. After James II was deposed and William and Mary acceded to the throne in 1688, L'Estrange was once again out of political favor and

lost his government post. He then turned to translation to support himself. He is known for a translation of *Aesop's Fables* that is straightforward and readable today. Here, for example, is his version of the Ass and the Grasshopper:

> An Ass having heard some Grasshoppers chirping, was highly enchanted; and, desiring to possess the same charms of melody, demanded what sort of food they lived on to give them such beautiful voices. They replied, "The dew." The Ass resolved that he would live only upon dew, and in a short time died of hunger.

L'Estrange is also remembered for a nasty and personal attack on the poet John Milton, who was blind, entitled *No Blinde Guides,* a response to Milton's "Brief Notes upon a late Sermon titled 'The Fear of God and the King,' by Dr. Matthew Griffith." Even as Charles II was about to be restored to the English throne Milton continued to maintain his belief in a republican form of government.

Lilburne, John (1615–1657) *pamphleteer*
John Lilburne was born in Sunderland, England, to Richard and Margaret Lilburne. At the age of 15 he became apprentice to Thomas Hewson, a Puritan through whom he met Dr. John Bastwick in 1636. Bastwick had been imprisoned for printing pamphlets that opposed episcopacy, or rule of the church by bishops. In 1637 Lilburne himself was whipped and imprisoned for distributing illegal Puritan pamphlets. His punishment drew the attention of many revolutionaries, including Oliver Cromwell, who aided in Lilburne's release. During his imprisonment, Lilburne wrote his first pamphlets, *The Christian Mans Traill* (1638) and *A Worke of the Beast* (1638), both of which gave detailed accounts of his punishments.

Lilburne became active in the revolutionary fervor preceding the Revolution and Civil War, and at the outbreak of hostilities in 1642 he enlisted as a captain in the Roundhead army in opposition to the supporters of the king. During the battle at

Brentford, Lilburne was taken as a prisoner in Oxford, where he wrote the pamphlet *A Letter from Captain John Lilburne* (1643), in which he stated that Parliament was "still that strength of this Kingdome, and champion of true Religion . . ." In 1645 Lilburne wrote *Letter to Prynne* in response to his former ally William PRYNNE's *Truth Triumphing.* Lilburne saw Prynne's work as an attempt to enforce religious conformity, and in his response he pled for religious tolerance.

Lilburne resigned from the army in 1645 after refusing to sign the Presbyterian Solemn League Covenant. This document was presented to the English by the Scots as a condition of military aid and would have required that everyone in England and Wales adopt Presbyterian forms of worship. During an imprisonment in 1645 for sedition, Lilburne wrote *England's Miserie and Remedie* and *England's Birth-Right Justified,* the latter of which would be the basis for the formation of the radical Leveller Party in 1645 and their *Agreement of the People* in 1647, which firmly laid out the party's belief in free elections, freedom of speech and religion, and other social reforms.

In 1649, after the execution of King Charles I, the Levellers came into conflict with Cromwell's new government, as laid out in Lilburne's pamphlet *England's New Chains Discovered* (1649). In this work Lilburne, disappointed in the new republican government, asked, "Where is that liberty so much pretended, so deerly purchased?" The pamphlet led to his arrest along with three other leading Levellers. He was banished from England but later returned and was arrested again. After his release, he retreated from public life and became a Quaker. Nicknamed "Free-born John," Lilburne wrote 83 pamphlets, many of which demanded rights, such as trial by jury, that later became the basis for the American Bill of Rights.

Lilly, William (William Lyly) (1468–1523)
nonfiction writer

William Lilly was a Renaissance humanist who is known for his work in creating a Latin grammar textbook that was widely used into the 19th century. He was born in Odiham, England, educated at Magdalen College, Oxford University, and spent a considerable amount of time studying Latin in Italy. He was the grandfather of John LYLY, considered the father of euphuism.

Lilly was part of a movement known as HUMANISM, which sought to base learning on the study of classical Greek and Roman culture and literature. Along with his fellow English humanist John COLET and the Dutch humanist Desiderius ERASMUS, Lilly helped to establish the St. Paul's School in London, which sought to educate its students in Latin and Greek, a pedagogy that was known as the "new learning." Lilly served as the school's first headmaster. He, Colet, and Erasmus also wrote a Latin grammar book that came to be the standard for the next 30 years. The book, which some called *Lilly's Grammar,* used mnemonic devices to help students remember Latin passages. Thus, it combined the art of memory with notable quotations.

Linacre, Thomas (ca. 1460–1524)
nonfiction writer, translator

Thomas Linacre was born in Canterbury, Kent, England, and educated at Oxford University. Following his studies at Oxford, he traveled throughout Italy, studying Latin, Greek, and medicine. Beginning in 1509 he served as physician to Henry VIII.

Along with his fellow scholar John COLET, Linacre introduced to Oxford University the "New Learning," a form of teaching based entirely on the study of the Greek and Roman classics. Students of this method not only mastered Greek and Latin but also closely studied the ancient texts, with a particular interest in philosophy, logic, and scientific inquiry.

In 1518 Linacre and others founded the Royal College of Physicians of London, a group of physicians who practiced medicine in that city. This group also had the authority to examine and license physicians throughout England to impose fines and imprisonment on those who practiced medicine fraudulently.

Linacre wrote and published medical textbooks as well as several Latin grammars, works designed to help people to learn the Latin language, such as *Linacri Progymnasmata* (1525) and *Rudimenta Grammatices* (1523); the latter book was specifically written for the king's daughter, Princess Mary. He also translated works from Greek into Latin, particularly the works of the Greek physician Galen. His translation of Galen's *De Tempermentis et de Inaequali Intemperie* (1521) was one of the first books printed at Cambridge.

Lindsay, Christian (Lady Christian Lindsay) (1603–1629) *poet*

Lady Christian Lindsay was born in Bonniel, Scotland, the daughter of Robert and Christian Hamilton Lindsay. She married Adam Colquhoun in 1621 and died in Dumberton, Scotland. There is some question over whether she is the author of *To Robert Hudson,* her only surviving work, since there is another person of the same name who might have been living at the time the poem was written. The author of *To Robert Hudson* was part of the Castalian Band, a group of poets brought together by King James VI (later JAMES I OF ENGLAND) in the hope that they could help revive Scottish vernacular poetry. The group included Lindsay, the poet and musician Robert Hudson, Alexander MONTGOMERIE, John Stewart, and William Fowler.

To Robert Hudson is addressed to fellow poet Hudson and concerns the king's expulsion of Montgomerie from the group, perhaps because of a brush with the law while traveling abroad. Lindsay writes, "Oft haive I hard, bot ofter fund it treu, / That courteours kyndnes lasts bot for a vhyle; / Fra once our turnes be sped, vhy then adeu, / our promeist freindschip passis in exyle." ("Often I have heard but oftener found it true / That courtly kindness lasts but for a while / For once our turns be sped, why then adieu / Our promisd friendship passes in exile.") The scholar Sarah Dunnigan describes the poem as "an act of pity and homage" to Montgomerie.

As a member of this brotherhood of poets, Lindsay engaged in communal, or group, writing.

The group produced a body of poetry known for its smoothness of style and suitability to be put to music.

Lisle, Honor (fl. 1540) *letter writer*

Honor Grenville Bassett, the widow of Sir John Bassett, married Arthur Plantagenet, Viscount Lisle, in 1532. Her new husband was the illegitimate son of King Edward IV and a member of Henry VIII's court. Lady Lisle and her husband accompanied Henry to Calais, France, in 1532, to a meeting with King Francis I; she was one of five masked ladies, including Anne BOLEYN, who danced with the French king.

In 1533 the Lisles returned to Calais, which was at that time under English control, because Lord Lisle had been given a post there. We know of their lives from the letters written to friends and family back home during their time in Calais, from 1533 to 1540. The letters give a picture of the business of courtiers and diplomats as well as domestic and family life. The Lisles did not have their own children, but Lady Lisle had seven from her first marriage, and her husband had three daughters from a previous marriage. Much of the correspondence describes the arrangements for the fostering and care of the children while their parents were abroad. The letters also revealed that the family had to sell property to maintain themselves, and that they could not control their business arrangements efficiently from Calais.

The Lisles were in some financial difficulty in 1540 when Lord Lisle was recalled and imprisoned in the Tower of London, suspected of complicity in a Catholic plot to give Calais over to the pope. The Lisle letters were among the papers impounded by the Crown at that time, and they were consequently preserved. Many of them are official and business documents.

Lord Lisle was eventually found not guilty but died in the Tower the night he heard the news. When her husband was arrested, Lady Lisle is said to have been so mentally distressed that she did not recover for many years.

Honor Lisle's is a tragic story. However, her letters allow modern readers to see the happier times quite closely and to see her, as critic Wallace MacCaffrey did, as "a woman of dignity and honesty" who also had an acute understanding of court politics. She left a lasting legacy, full of details of daily life during times that were uncertain and tragic for many.

Lock, Anne Vaughan (Anne Vaughn Locke, Anne Vaughn Lok, Dering Anne Prowse) (ca. 1534–1590) *translator*

Anne Vaughan Lock (who also wrote under several other names, including Dering Anne Prowse) was born in London, the daughter of Stephen Vaughan, a dealer in fabrics, and Margaret Vaughan, a seamstress for the Tudor royal court, who died when Anne was about 10.

Anne's father was a supporter of the Protestant Reformation, and her stepmother, Margery Brinkelow, was the widow of Henry BRINKELOW, who had written Protestant pamphlets. Thus the young woman grew up in a household that was highly sympathetic to the Protestant cause, and she became acquainted with many of the leading figures of the Reformation. These included William TYNDALE, first translator of the New Testament into English; John CALVIN, the theologian who established a Protestant sect in Geneva; and John KNOX, the founder of Scottish Presbyterianism who was much influenced by Calvin.

In 1551 Anne married Henry Lock, who was from a wealthy Protestant family of cloth merchants. When Queen Mary I tried to restore Catholicism, the Locks were among a group of English Protestants who sought asylum in Geneva, where Anne Lock began to translate Calvin's sermons from French to English. She returned to London in 1559, after ELIZABETH I became queen. During this period, when Lock and John Knox were engaged in a lively correspondence about theological issues, she published her first book, a translation entitled *Sermons of John Calvin* (1560), which was dedicated to the Duchess of Suffolk. Calvin's text urges Christian believers to endure deprivation and suffering as a mark of their election, the belief that a certain number of people were predestined to go to heaven. Susan Felch, who edited Lock's *Collected Works* (1999), writes that Lock "gathers her materials and deploys them artfully."

Lock's second translation, written under the name of Dering Anne Prowse, was of Jean Taffin's *Of the Markes of the Children of God* (1590). Taffin was a Protestant reformer who led French-speaking churches in Holland. In his work he describes the doctrine of election: "There are two principall meanes by which [God] giveth us to understand who are his children: the one is outward . . . the other is inward. . . . The outward marke lieth in this, that we be members of the church of Christ." In other words, those chosen by God know they are chosen in part by belonging to a church that subscribes to the belief in election. Lock died soon after this book's publication, highly regarded within her community as a staunch defender of the Reformed faith.

Other Work by Anne Vaughan Lock

The Collected Works of Anne Vaughan Lock. Edited by Susan M. Felch. Tempe: Arizona Center for Medieval and Renaissance Studies in Conjunction with Renaissance English Text Society, 1999.

Locke, John (1632–1704) *nonfiction writer*

John Locke was born the son of a country lawyer at Wrington, Somerset, England. In 1647 he went to Westminster School in London, where he received an excellent education that led to his acceptance at Oxford, where he studied medicine and experimental philosophy.

Locke earned his degree from Oxford in 1665 and through an acquaintance met Lord Ashley, later the Earl of Shaftesbury. Locke served as Ashley's personal physician and also came to be the statesman's adviser on domestic and political affairs. The two were like-minded. They believed in constitutional monarchy, civil liberty, religious toleration, rule of Parliament, and economic expansion of Britain.

Locke's scientific abilities were recognized in 1668, when he was elected to the Royal Society, whose goal was the promotion of scientific investigation. The society's members were interested in conducting careful experiments and systematically collecting facts in order to make scientific generalizations, a method of learning that was new at the time.

Locke himself tells the story of the beginning of his interest in modern philosophy. He says he and some friends were discussing "principles of morality and revealed religion," when it occurred to him that "we took a wrong course, and that before we set ourselves upon inquiries of that nature, it was necessary to examine our own abilities, and see what objects our understandings were, or were not, fitted to deal with." In his search to understand how the mind worked, Locke read French philosopher René DESCARTES and spent the latter part of the 1670s living in France, where he refined his philosophy of human understanding. Locke did not, however, publish his ideas until rather late in life. His works include *An Essay Concerning Human Understanding* (1690), in which Locke pursues the question of knowledge, what it is, and precisely how humans acquire it; *Two Treatises of Government* (1690), in which he questions the divine right of kings; *Some Thoughts Concerning Education* (1693), in which he recommends a complete program of child rearing; and *Reasonableness of Christianity* (1695), in which he emphasizes that the existence of the deity can be discovered through reason, although he does not deny revelation. He also wrote numerous pamphlets on various religious, philosophical, political, and economic matters.

Critical Analysis

Locke's most important contribution to modern philosophy is *An Essay Concerning Human Understanding.* In this work Locke attempts to understand "the origin, certainty, and extent of human knowledge, together with the grounds and degrees of belief, opinion, and assent." He concerns himself with determining the limits of human understanding in respect to God, the self, the natural world, objects, and concepts. Locke analyzes what one can legitimately claim to know and what one cannot. In the *Essay* he introduced a new method of philosophical enquiry, which has come to be known as theory of knowledge, or epistemology.

Book I of the *Essay* argues that we have no innate knowledge. At birth the human mind is a "tabula rasa," or blank slate, on which experience writes.

Book II contends that ideas are the building blocks of knowledge and that all ideas come from experience. The term *idea,* Locke writes, "stands for whatsoever is the Object of the Understanding, when a man thinks." There are two types of experiences, according to Locke, sensation and reflection. Sensation tells us about things and processes in the external world, and reflection tells us about the operations of our own minds. Reflection is a sort of internal sense that makes us conscious of the mental processes in which we are engaged. We get some ideas from sensation, some from reflection, and some from both.

Book III deals with the nature of language—its connections with ideas and its role in knowledge. Book IV is the culmination of the previous books and explains the nature and limits of knowledge, probability, and the relation of reason to faith. On this latter topic Locke argues that reason tells us that whatever exists must have been created by a being that is superior to what it created.

Locke's *Two Treatises of Government* (1690) had a powerful impact on the political thinking of the Enlightenment and influenced the American and French Revolutions. His *First Treatise* refutes the concept of the divine right of kings, which allowed for absolute rule. In his *Second Treatise,* the more important of the two, Locke describes his positive theory of government, saying it is his obligation to do so, "lest men fall into the dangerous belief that all government in the world is merely the product of force and violence." In his *Second Treatise* Locke essentially reconciles the idea of civil liberty with political order by asserting natural rights theory and the idea of the social contract. Natural rights are those rights we are supposed to have as human beings before government ever comes into being. Such rights include the right to free thought, speech, and worship, as well as the right to survive. The social contract says that citizens agree to transfer some of their natural rights to a central government so that there may be political order. In exchange, the government is obligated to protect the natural rights of citizens. These ideas went on to become the underpinnings of European and American political thinking for the next several centuries.

Locke also had new ideas about learning and education. *Some Thoughts Concerning Education* (1693) was based on a series of letters to Edward Clarke from Holland, in which Locke advised Clarke on the best upbringing for his son. Building on his idea that the mind at birth is a tabula rasa, devoid of innate ideas, Locke emphasizes the importance of building good character in children and argues that children should be allowed to vent their feelings. In contrast to previous theories of education, Locke believed that children should rarely be restrained. As the scholar W. M. Spellman observes, "prior to Locke's work the theory and practice of child-rearing had generally emphasized control over the youngster's inherently evil nature, stressing the importance of obedience, restraint, authority, and even fear." After Locke, Spellman notes, people began to change their minds about how best to raise children. The parent became "gentle preceptor, affectionate counsellor, and sympathetic guide."

In summing up Locke's influence on 17th and 18th-century thought, Spellman argues that "Without Locke the supremacy of reason and the malleability of the human mind, so much a part of enlightened thought during the eighteenth century, would have been practically inconceivable." His influence on the evolution of democracy, on enlightened theories of education, and on philosophy is immeasurable.

Other Works by John Locke
An Essay Concerning Human Understanding. Amherst, N.Y.: Prometheus Books, 1994.

The Second Treatise on Civil Government. Amherst, N.Y.: Prometheus Books, 1986.

Works about John Locke
Lowe, E. J. *Locke on Human Understanding.* London-Routledge, 1995.
Simmons, A. John. *The Lockean Theory of Rights.* Princeton, N.J.: Princeton University Press, 1992.
Wood, Neal. *The Politics of Locke's Philosophy.* Berkeley, Calif.: University of California Press, 1983.

Lodge, Thomas (1556–1625) *poet, playwright, fiction writer, nonfiction writer*
Thomas Lodge was born in London to Sir Thomas Lodge, who served as mayor of London. He received a B.A. from Oxford University in 1577 returned to London the following year to study law, but his interest in becoming a writer lured him away from his studies. Eventually he took up the study of medicine, and in 1602 he began working as a doctor in London.

Lodge's earliest known work is *A Defense of Plays* (1580), an answer to Stephen GOSSON's antitheater tract *The School of Abuse* (1579). Lodge tried his hand at every type of writing available to an Elizabethan author. He wrote plays, the most famous of which is *A Looking Glass For London and England* (ca. 1588), a comedy that was coauthored by Robert GREENE. He also wrote *Phillis* (1593), a series of love sonnets or 14-line poems; *A Fig for Momus* (1595), a collection of poems with a satirical tone; and a number of works of prose fiction.

Lodge's greatest success was with his fiction. His most famous effort is his pastoral romance (a work set in an idealized rural world) *Rosalynd* (1590). It was reprinted 11 times between 1590 and 1642 and provided William SHAKESPEARE with the plot to *As You Like It* (1599).

Rosalynd is written in the euphuistic style, an elegant but flowery literary style developed by John LYLY. The book opens with a knight, John of Bordeaux, dividing his estate among his three sons, Saladyn, Ferandyn, and Rosader. Contrary to custom, the youngest son, Rosader, inherits most of the estate. However, Saladyn, the oldest, cheats Rosader out of his inheritance, and Rosader is eventually forced to flee to the forest to escape his brother's schemes.

As these events are unfolding, the false king Torismond banishes the true king's daughter, Rosalynd, who disguises herself as a boy named Ganymede. Then Rosalynd and her friend Alinda, Torismond's daughter, head for the forest. There the principal characters all concern themselves with love matters in a highly wrought style: "At gaze upon this gorgeous Nymph sat the Shepheard, feeding his eyes with her favors, wooing with such piteous lookes, and courting with such deep straind sighs, as would have made DIANA her selfe to have been compassionate."

Lodge's prose was successful and is typical of the fiction popular in the period. He was far more adventurous when it came to writing poetry. His poems were not only admired by his contemporaries, they also spawned some of the literary trends of the 1590s. *A Fig for Momus* (1595), for instance, "helped usher in a notable period of verse-satire," the Scholars J. William Hebel and Hoyt H. Hudson note. The poem satirizes some of Lodge's contemporaries, such as Edmund SPENSER and Michael DRAYTON, and it was an influence on later satirists such as Ben JONSON and John DONNE.

More important, Lodge is responsible for the creation of a poetic form with his *Scilla's Metamorphosis* (1589), the first English mythological narrative poem. Over the next few years other writers would write mythological narratives: Shakespeare in *Venus and Adonis* (1593), Christopher MARLOWE in *Hero and Leander* (1593), and Michael Drayton in *Endimion and Phoebe* (1595). Lodge's poem, the scholar Elizabeth Story Donno writes, "introduces many of the elements typical of the erotic-mythological verse narrative," such as a love-stricken main character and references to classical mythology. The opening of the poem illustrates these features:

> Walking alone (all onely full of grief)
> Within a thicket nere to Isis floud,

> Weeping my wants, and wailing scant
>   reliefe,
> Wringing mine armes (as one with sorrowe
>   wood).

The poem's atmosphere is charged with hothouse sexuality, much in the tradition of the ancient Roman Ovid's *Metamorphoses*. With *Scilla's Metamorphosis,* Donno observes, Lodge set "a new standard of poetic achievement" in England.

Lord Howard's Men
See ADMIRAL'S MEN.

Lovelace, Richard (1618–ca. 1657) *poet, playwright*

Richard Lovelace was the eldest of the eight children of Sir William and Anne Barne Lovelace of Woolwich, Kent. Born either in Woolwich or in the Netherlands, where his father was serving in the military, he was educated at Charterhouse School and subsequently at Oxford University. Anthony à WOOD, in *Athenae Oxoniensis*, reports that at Oxford, Lovelace "was accounted the most amiable and beautiful person that ever eye beheld." As a student he wrote a comedy, *The Scholars*, which was acted at his college and later in London, but only the prologue and epilogue have survived.

Lovelace received his degree at the age of 18 and went straight to the royal court, where he was universally admired and soon became one of the CAVALIER POETS who celebrated the rarefied elegance of King Charles I and his circle. But the king's fortunes were declining. Like his friend Sir John SUCKLING, Lovelace served as an officer in Charles's two unsuccessful campaigns to put down the Scottish rebellion in the Bishops' Wars, 1639–40. Somehow he found time in 1642 to write a tragedy, *The Soldier;* but 1642 was also the year the Puritans succeeded in closing all the theaters in England. They did not open again until 1660, and *The Soldier,* never performed or published, has been lost.

Lovelace returned to his family estate in Kent, which he had inherited, and became active in local political life. In 1642 he was chosen to present a royalist petition to the House of Commons. Parliamentary leaders found the petition so offensive that they arrested Lovelace. He was in prison for seven weeks, during which he wrote the lyric "To Althea, From Prison," with the famous lines

> Stone walls do not a prison make,
> Nor iron bars a cage. . . .

The English Civil War began in earnest later that summer. The conditions of Lovelace's release from prison prevented him from taking an active part in the fighting, but he sold much of his land to outfit two of his brothers with men and money to fight for the king. After Charles's surrender at Oxford, 1646, Lovelace went to the Netherlands to fight on behalf of the French king, Louis XIV, against the Spanish, and was wounded at Dunkirk.

Back in England in 1648, Lovelace was again arrested. In prison he once more turned to poetry, preparing the volume *Lucasta: Epodes, Odes, Sonnets, Songs, etc.* (1649) for publication. Seventeen of the poems in this collection are addressed to a "Lucasta" who was probably a real person. Anthony à Wood states that Lucasta was Lucy Sacheverell, who had married after hearing that Lovelace had died of his wounds at Dunkirk, thus leaving Lovelace bereft; but Wood may not be completely reliable. The best known of the *Lucasta* poems is "To Lucasta, on Going to the Wars," which explains the lover's departure in terms of honor, concluding,

> I could not love thee, dear, so much,
> Loved I not honor more.

In addition to the courtly love poems addressed to Lucasta, the collection includes several cynically erotic poems. There are also some delightful and unusual poems addressed to insects, in which the poet, ostensibly seeing large moral truths in the circumstances of the tiny creatures, actually draws the reader in to an appreciation of their reality.

Lovelace was freed after Charles I's execution in 1649, but he had sold his estates on behalf of the Royalist cause. His last 10 years were lived in poverty. The circumstances of his death are unknown, but in 1659 his brother Dudley Lovelace published *Lucasta: Posthume Poems* ("posthume" or "posthumous" meaning "after the author's death").

The scholar Manfred Weidman, while admitting that Lovelace is a minor poet, captures Lovelace's distinctive gift when he remarks that in his best poems "the man's serenity enables him to endure whatever fate presents to him. . . . the mind, the proper attitude, overcomes the distresses of isolation caused by confinement or separation."

Other Work by Richard Lovelace

Selected Poems. Edited by Gerald Hammond. Manchester, U.K.: Carcanet Press, 1987.

Ludlow, Edmund (ca. 1617–1692)
nonfiction writer

Edmund Ludlow was born in Maiden Bradley, Wiltshire, England, the son of Sir Henry Ludlow, who was opposed to the English monarchy and who supported republican rule in England. Edmund graduated from Oxford University and, following his father's political views, joined the rebellion against royal rule that culminated in the deposition and execution of King Charles I (1642). When the monarchy was restored in 1660 and the Stuart king Charles II ascended the throne, Ludlow went into exile in Vevey, Switzerland, where he remained for the rest of his life.

Ludlow's *Memoirs* (1698–99), published seven years after his death, provide a detailed chronicle of the English Civil War and of his conflicts with Oliver Cromwell, who ruled England after the deposition of Charles I and was succeeded by his son Richard. Although Ludlow had supported the struggle against the king, he took offense when the Puritan general Cromwell set himself up as lord protector of England, seeing this as another form of monarchy. He does not mince words in exposing the misdeeds of his own party, as when he describes how "the Major-Generals carried things with unheard of insolence in their several precincts, decimating to extremity whom they pleased," or when he termed Sir Anthony Ashley Cooper, who fought for the Parliamentary party, "a great instrument in this horrid treachery."

Ludlow could also rise to sentiments of noble patriotism, as when he wrote "of the necessity incumbent on us all to lay aside our private animosities, and to unite our whole strength to preserve the vessel of the Commonwealth from sinking." Written in a direct, first-person format, Ludlow's *Memoirs* remain an important primary source of information about the English Civil War and its aftermath.

A Work about Edmund Ludlow

Hunt, Tristam. *The English Civil War: At First Hand.* London. Weidenfeld & Nicolson, 2002.

Lumley, Jane (ca. 1537–1577) *translator*

Jane Fitzalan Lumley was the daughter of Henry Fitzalan, the Earl of Arundel, a prominent and powerful noble in Tudor England. Her mother, Catherine Grey Fitzalan, was the aunt of Lady Jane Grey, who was queen of England for nine days in 1553 during a period of turmoil after the death of King Edward VI. Jane became the first wife of Lord John Lumley.

Following a common practice of noble families at that time, young Jane was given a classical education by her father. As Diane Purkiss points out in her study *Three Tragedies by Renaissance Women* (1998): "Lady Lumley's facility in Greek and Latin seemed to both her father and husband not an unfeminine eccentricity, but the very vanguard of fashion."

Jane Lumley was schooled in the humanist tradition that drew liberally on classic models (*see* HUMANISM). Her only published work is a translation of Euripides' tragedy *Iphigeneia in Aulis,* probably completed in 1553, during the political and religious turmoil surrounding the royal succession that occurred when the Catholic Mary Tudor as-

cended the throne after the death of her brother, Edward VI, who was loyal to the Church of England. When Mary deposed the Protestant archbishop Thomas CRANMER, Lumley's father came into possession of Cranmer's library, and it is likely that Jane used it to research her translation.

Lumley's translation of this ancient Greek tragedy about conflict and bloodshed within the warring House of Atreus can be read as a commentary on similar occurrences in the 16th-century House of Tudor. It was the first translation into English of a Greek drama and the first classical translation by a woman. However, Lumley's work was not staged until 1997.

A Work about Jane Lumley

Purkiss, Diane. *Three Tragedies by Renaissance Women.* London, New York: Penguin, 1998.

Luther, Martin (1483–1546) *nonfiction writer, translator*

Martin Luther was born in Eisleben, Saxony (present-day Germany), to a poor but ambitious family, and educated at the University of Erfurt. In 1505 he began to study law, in accordance with his father's wishes, but a few months later, after an experience of religious conversion, he entered the Augustinian monastery at Erfurt. He studied devoutly and was ordained a priest in 1507. In 1508 his order sent him to the University of Wittenberg in Saxony to study and lecture; he became famous as a charismatic and powerful teacher as well as a leader of the REFORMATION.

In 1510 Luther went to Rome on business for his order and was shocked by the lack of religious conviction he observed among the church's highest functionaries; this triggered a period of intense and painful spiritual searching. Through intense study of the Bible, Luther became convinced that because people are inherently sinful, salvation can only be granted as a free gift from God through Christ, rather than being earned through good deeds or penance. Although he continued to see himself as a Catholic, he increasingly saw a divergence between the practices of the church and what the Bible was telling him about the reality of religious life.

Luther was especially upset by the sale of indulgences, a practice by which priests offered to intervene with God for remission of time in Purgatory—in return for financial contributions to the church. He assumed that this abuse would be condemned by the pope if the pope only knew about it. In 1517 he posted on the door of the church in Wittenberg a list of 95 theses condemning the sale of indulgences. He wrote the list in Latin, expecting to debate it with other priests and religious scholars, but it was quickly translated into German and passed around among lay people dissatisfied with the church. Consequently, Luther found himself in opposition to the church he revered. In 1521 the pope excommunicated him, and Charles V, the Holy Roman Emperor, summoned him to a special diet, or meeting, of the German princes, which convened at Worms. Charles V demanded that Luther renounce his teachings, but after a day of prayer Luther famously told the diet, "My conscience is bound by the word of God. Unless I am convinced from the sacred Scriptures that I am in error, I cannot and I will not recant. Here I stand. I cannot do otherwise. God help me."

The emperor declared Luther an outlaw. For his protection, the elector (hereditary ruler) of Saxony lodged him for a year in his fortress at Wattburg. Luther spent his time in hiding translating the Bible into vernacular German to make it available for ordinary people. In 1522 he emerged from hiding because there was civil unrest in Wittenberg. Luther's principled and moderate stand enabled a resolution of the conflict. He spent most of the rest of his life in Wittenberg, teaching, preaching, and writing.

Luther became famous, or notorious, throughout Europe. King Henry VIII of England wrote an eloquent attack on Luther's disobedience, earning a special commendation from the pope as "Fidei Defensor"—Defender of the Faith—an ironic achievement, given that within 10 years Henry would initiate his own move away from Catholicism. Luther became an important guide for such Anglican leaders as CRANMER, and by 1525 he had broken with ERASMUS, his former ally in decrying the abuses of the Catholic Church. That same year Luther turned his back on the vow of celibacy he had taken when he became a monk by marrying Katherine von Bora, a former nun. They had six children together.

Luther's voluminous treatises on religion and commentaries on the Bible spoke eloquently for the direct experience of God's word and had a profound influence throughout northern Europe. Although the Protestantism that took root in Britain was on the whole less radical than Luther's, the leaders of the Anglican Church were well aware of Luther's teachings, and John KNOX molded the Scottish kirk (church) after Luther's and John CALVIN's models. The many hymns that Luther wrote to help the faithful in their worship were translated into English and inspired the holy music of such 18th-century religious leaders as Isaac Watts and John Wesley.

Works about Martin Luther

Bainton, Roland Herbert. *Here I Stand: A Life of Martin Luther.* New York: Penguin, 1995.

McKim, Donald J. *The Cambridge Companion to Martin Luther.* New York: Cambridge University Press, 2003.

Luttrell, Narcissus (1657–1732) *nonfiction writer*

Narcissus Luttrell was born in London, the third son of Francis and Catherine Luttrell. His was a fairly comfortable childhood, and he was educated at St. John's College, Cambridge. He studied law at Gray's Inn and was admitted to the bar in 1680. He served in a number of public offices, including justice of the peace and land-tax commissioner, and was a member of Parliament in 1679–80 and 1690–95.

A bibliophile, or lover of books, from his earliest years, Luttrell amassed during his lifetime a substantial library of significant books, especially on English history and antiquities. Luttrell published nothing during his lifetime, but his diaries, published years after his death, offer an important eyewitness account to British history in the late 17th and early 18th centuries.

The Parliamentary Diary of Narcissus Luttrell (1691–93), edited by Henry Horwitz, was published by the Clarendon Press, Oxford, in 1972. The observations in this diary are so detailed that its editor has speculated they must have been originally taken down in some form of shorthand, but no evidence of this first draft has been found. Horwitz concludes that Luttrell's diaries offer "a much more detailed account of the House's activities than most other diaries of the later seventeenth and early eighteenth centuries" and offer valuable insights into the evolution of Parliament and the British political parties during a time of transition.

Lyly, John (ca. 1554–1606) *prose writer, dramatist*

John Lyly was probably born in Canterbury, England. His father, Peter Lyly, was a minor official who worked at Canterbury Cathedral, and his grandfather, William LILLY, wrote the Latin grammar text used by William SHAKESPEARE, who quoted him in *The Merry Wives of Windsor*. Lyly received his bachelor's degree (1573) and his master's (1575) from Oxford University.

After failing to gain a fellowship to continue his studies, Lyly left Oxford for London, where he became an instant success with the publication of his prose romances, colorful narratives that involve extraordinary characters in situations far removed from those of ordinary life. Early romances were in verse and based on legends, such as those told about King Arthur, and on stories about classical heroes. From the 15th century on, romances tended to be in prose, as were Lyly's.

Lyly's most famous works were *Euphues, or the Anatomy of Wit* (1579) and *Euphues and his England* (1580). The name *Euphues* comes from the Greek and means "witty"; the hero of these stories is a quick wit who must learn to accept the wisdom of his elders. Both works are considered forerunners of the novel and are written in an elaborate style called "euphuism." This consists of carefully balanced sentence structure, pervasive alliteration (beginning successive words with the same consonant sound), and the use of proverbs and elaborate similes drawn from the ancient natural historian Pliny the Elder and other sources. Here Lyly is describing his central character:

> This young gallant, of more wit than wealth, and yet of more wealth than wisdom, seeing himself inferior to none in pleasant conceits, thought himself [so] superior to all in honest conditions . . . that he gave himself almost to nothing [except] fine phrases, smooth quipping, merry taunting, using jesting without mean and abusing mirth without measure. As therefore the sweetest rose hath his prickle, the finest velvet his brack, the fairest flower his bran, so the sharpest wit hath his wanton will and the holiest head his wicked way.

Often Lyly goes so far in his attempts to alliterate and create parallelism that he ends up straining both the reader's credibility and truth, as in "The freshest colors soonest fade . . . finest cloth is soonest eaten with moths, and the cambric sooner stained than the coarse canvas."

Shakespeare, among others, imitated Lyly's style on occasion, but the playwright also parodied it, especially in the proverb-spouting talk of Polonius in *Hamlet* and in Falstaff's speech in *Henry IV, Part I*, which begins, "Peace, good pint pot; peache good tickle-brain." Lyly even parodied the style himself in the language of Sir Thopas in his play *Endymion* (1586–87). Despite the artificiality of this elaborate style, however, it became a fad in the court of Elizabeth I, and everyone competed to be able to "parley euphuisme."

The plots of both Euphues books are extremely thin and involve failed love affairs. Both books are also didactic, attempting to help young people avoid the mistakes Euphues makes, such as placing love between a man and a woman before platonic friendship between men.

About 1580 Lyly turned to drama. Although, like his prose, his dramatic style was artificial, it was less exaggerated and more elegant. Lyly primarily wrote dramatic love stories, taken from mythology or ancient history and which were performed both at the BLACKFRIARS theater and at the court of ELIZABETH I. His dramatic works include *Campaspe* (1584), the story of how the painter Apelles falls in love with Campaspe, who is beloved of Alexander the Great; *Endymion: The Man in the Moon* (1586–87), the story of Endymion, who falls in love with Cynthia, the moon; and *Love's Metamorphosis* (1589), a play about the relative merits of chastity and love.

Lyly's characters—though supposedly classical figures—are typical RENAISSANCE courtiers: witty, focused on trifles, idealizing the young women who are the objects of their love, and loving the idea of being in love. Along with Christopher MARLOWE and several other young dramatists, Lyly was one of the UNIVERSITY WITS, who changed English drama by structuring their plays more carefully than playwrights had in the past and by using the poetic power inherent in the English language. In so doing, the University Wits paved the way for Shakespeare.

The songs from Lyly's plays are especially lovely. "Apelles's Song" from *Campaspe,* for example, begins, "Cupid and my Campaspe played / At cards for kisses,—Cupid paid." This passage illustrates Lyly's witty use of alliteration and balanced sentence structure.

In 1583 Lyly married Beatrice Brown, and between 1589 and 1601 he was elected to Parliament four times. He always wished to be chosen as the queen's master of revels but was disappointed in that hope. Today he is chiefly remembered for *Euphues* and for the impact his elaborate style had on his contemporaries. As the scholar Leah Guenther notes, "The sustained popularity that Lyly enjoyed incited a Euphuistic frenzy; other well-known authors of the period decided that they, too, should try their hands at Lyly's trendy prose."

Other Work by John Lyly

The Complete Works of John Lyly. 3 vols. Edited by R. Warwick Bond. 1902. Reprint, New York: Oxford University Press, 1993.

A Work about John Lyly

Houppert, Joseph W. *John Lyly.* Boston: Twayne, 1975.

Lyndsay, David (David Lindsay)
(ca. 1486–1555) *poet, playwright*

David Lyndsay was born in Monmail, Scotland, to David Lindsay, a nobleman. At a fairly young age, he entered the service of the Scottish royal court. He is best known as a poet and playwright who wrote works critical of the Roman Catholic Church and the Scottish court. He supported the idea of the Scottish REFORMATION, or break from Catholicism through his writing.

Around 1512, Lindsay was appointed as an attendant to the infant king of Scotland, James V. Lyndsay addressed several poems to the boy, including "Answer to the King's Flyting" (ca. 1531), a work about flyting, a Scottish tradition of trading insults; and "The Complaint and Public Confession of the King's Old Hound called Bagshe" (ca. 1531), which complains of the life of a courtier.

Lyndsay's allegorical poem "The Dreme" (1528) criticizes the laziness, pride, and greed of the Scottish rulers, both religious and political. In the poem the narrator sinks into hell, where he finds multitudes of churchmen who are there as a result of their vices. Their corruption has found its way into the church through the acquisition of wealth. In the poem, Lindsay notes that Scotland, which he regards as so well endowed by nature and so superior in its population, is actually very poor, and he blames its princes and governors:

> the negligence
> Of our infatuate headis
> insolent
> Is cause of all this realm's indigence.

Lyndsay's long morality play *Ane Pleasant Satyre of the Thrie Estaitis* (1540) (*Satire of the Three Estates*) attacks political abuses and satirizes the practices of the church; it was so long it took an entire day to perform. The play comments on the same issues he addressed in *The Dreme,* attacking politicians, courtiers, and the clergy. Lyndsay condemns the corruption of the church. According to the scholar Hugh Walker, "Chastity is driven from the doors of monk and nun alike, and finds refuge with the common people." Walker considers *Ane Pleasant Satyre* to be Lyndsay's best work and calls it "one of the best moralities in the language."

In Lyndsay's long poem *The Monarchie* (1553), the poet tells "of the Miserabyll Estait of the World" from the fall of man to doomsday. His other notable works include *Testament and Complaynt of Our Soverane Lordis Papyngo* (1538) (that is, the world according to the king's parrot), which claims to be the dying speeches of a talking parrot; and *The Historie and Testament of Squyer Meldrum* (1549), a poetic biography of a squire.

Other Work by David Lyndsay

Selected Poems. Edited by Janet Hadley Williams. Glasgow, U.K.: Association for Scottish Literary Studies, 2000.

A Work about David Lyndsay

Edington, Carol. *Court and Culture in Renaissance Scotland: Sir David Lindsay of the Mount.* Amherst: University of Massachusetts Press, 1994.

M

Mabbe, James (1572–1642) *translator, poet*
James Mabbe was born near Winchester, Surrey,
England, the son of James Mabbe, whose own father, a jeweler, had served as the chamberlain of
London. Mabbe's mother's name is unknown.
Young James graduated from Magdalen College,
Oxford University, later studied civil law, and
probably also became a clergyman. In 1611 he
traveled to Spain on a diplomatic mission. While in
that country he learned Spanish and began his lifelong enthusiasm for Spanish literature, translating
novels and other writings by Mateo Alemán,
Miguel CERVANTES, and Fernando de Rojas. Mabbe
published no original works aside from some song
texts and Latin and English verses. His eight-line
poem "To the Memorie of M. W. *Shakes-speare*,"
which appeared in a 1623 edition of the Folio,
lamented "Wee wondred (Shakespeare) that thou
went'st so soone / From the Worlds-Stage, to the
Graves-Tyring-roome."

Mabbe's first significant translation was of
Alemán's *The Rogue; or, The Life of Guzman de Al-
faroche* (1623). *The Rogue* is a picaresque novel in
which the author moralizes about human nature.
Of this work, the scholar P. E. Russell has written,
"Mabbe's extensive critical comments on the purpose of Mateo Alemán's novel show an understanding of the book which has only recently been
recovered by more modern critics." Mabbe's most
successful translation was considered to be that of
Fernando de Rojas's *Celestina; or, The Tragick-
comedie of Calisto and Melibea* (1631), another picaresque novel. His last translation was of
Cervantes's *Novelas ejemplares,* published in English as *Exemplarie Novells in Six Books* (1640). Although Mabbe's translations of these authors were
not necessarily the first in English, his stature in
London's literary community helped make the
new Spanish literature popular there during and
after the Elizabethan era.

Critics have noted Mabbe's tendency to amplify
his translations with explanatory details that were
not found in the originals. Ben JONSON's poem,
"On the Author, Worke, and Translator" praised
Mabbe's contributions to English literature by suggesting that a good translation is also an important
work of art, as in such lines as "Who tracks this Authors, or Translators Pen, / Shall finde, that either
hath read Bookes, and Men: / To say but one, were
single."

A Work by James Mabbe

Rojas, Fernando de. *Celestine; or, The Tragick-comedie
of Calisto and Melibea.* Translated by James
Mabbe; edited by Guadelupe Martinez Lacalle.
London: Tamesis, 1972.

A Work about James Mabbe

Fuchs, Barbara. "Pirating Spain: Jonson's Commendatory Poetry and the Translation of Empire." *Modern Philology* (Feb. 2002). Available online. URL: www.geocities.com/magdamun/johnson-fuchs.html. Downloaded on January 15, 2004.

Machiavelli, Niccolò (1469–1527)
historian, philosopher

Niccolò Machiavelli was born in Florence, Italy, on May 3, 1469, to Bernardo Machiavelli, a lawyer, and Bartolomea de'Nelli Machiavelli. Although descended from one of Florence's most important families, Bernardo was not wealthy, but he was fortunate in having a good library that included the works of ancient philosophers and historians.

To understand Machiavelli's life and work, it is important to know that, in the late 15th and early 16th centuries, Italy was divided into four city-states that often became pawns in ongoing battles between France and Spain, captured first by one, then by the other power. All his life Machiavelli hoped that Italy would one day be united under a single strong ruler. As a young man he witnessed the fall of the Medici family and the rise of the first Florentine republic, whose government was based on the conservative religious ideas of the Dominican monk Savonarola. After Savonarola's execution in 1497, a second republic was established under Pietro Soderini. Machiavelli served this new government as a secretary to the Second Chancery and as a diplomat. But in 1512 the second Florentine republic was overthrown by Spain, and the Medicis again ruled the city, with Lorenzo de' Medici at the helm. Lorenzo fired Machiavelli and had him imprisoned as a suspected traitor. Eventually Machiavelli was banished to his country home at San Casciano.

It was during this period of exile that Machiavelli wrote his most famous—or infamous—work: *The Prince,* a handbook on how to gain and keep political power. Machiavelli wrote *The Prince* in an effort to impress Lorenzo de Medici, but the work outraged nearly all its readers and continued to offend for many years. Machiavelli's advice to princes was thoroughly practical and pragmatic, based on his study of history and of human nature. Until *The Prince,* most philosophers had regarded politics as having an ethical dimension; thus, rulers were advised to make decisions based on notions of right and wrong. Machiavelli, however, made his recommendations based on expediency—that is, on what worked—without reference to morality. For example, he advises princes to kill their enemies if they must but urges them to do a thorough job of it so they will not have to keep on killing over the long term:

> Hence it is to be remarked that, in seizing a state, the usurper ought to examine closely into all those injuries which it is necessary for him to inflict, and to do them all at one stroke so as not to have to repeat them daily. . . . He who does otherwise, either from timidity or evil advice, is always compelled to keep the knife in his hand; neither can he rely on his subjects, nor can they attach themselves to him, owing to their continued and repeated wrongs. For injuries ought to be done all at one time, so that, being tasted less, they offend less; benefits ought to be given little by little, so that the flavor of them may last longer.

Machiavelli is as pragmatic about virtue as he is about vice, and he says that it is more important for a prince to *seem* to have certain virtues than to actually possess them. He also advises princes to be stingy rather than generous with his people, noting that history features few successful monarchs who were not "mean." He adds that if a prince must choose between being feared and being loved, he is much better off to be feared.

In his own time and for many years after, Machiavelli was despised because readers felt he was advocating immoral behavior. More recently, however, readers have realized that Machiavelli's advice is amoral, based entirely on what will work rather than what is ethical, and his masterwork has become a standard text of political philosophy. His direct influence on British literature can be seen in John MARSTON's political tragicomedy *The Malcontent* (1603) as well as in John WILSON's tragicomedy *Belphegor* (1691).

Machiavelli was never able to work effectively in the political arena again. The Medici never trusted him completely, and when they were deposed in 1527, their successors were suspicious of his attempts to befriend them. Ill and unable to influence the direction of political life in his beloved Florence, Machiavelli died on June 21, 1527.

A Work about Niccolò Machiavelli

Viroli, Maruizio. *Niccolo's Smile: A Biography of Machiavelli.* Translated by Antony Shugaar. New York: Farrar, Straus & Giroux, 2002.

Maitland, Sir Richard (1496–1586) *poet, nonfiction writer*

Sir Richard Maitland was born in Haddingtonshire, Scotland, to William and Martha Maitland and into an ancient lineage whose name appears throughout Scottish history. Maitland studied law at St. Andrews University. He later entered the service of King James V of Scotland and, subsequently, James VI (later JAMES I OF ENGLAND). He remained in this service until 1584, and during these years he became a commissioner appointed to settle the differences between Scotland and England. He lost his sight around his 60th year, but according to scholar George Eyre-Todd, he was still able to carry out his duties at court: "The affliction which added his name to the honourable roll of blind Homers did not prevent his continuing to fulfill the duties of his position."

The bulk of Maitland's poetry comes from the period following the loss of his sight, in which he turned his focus to writing and collecting poetry. During these years he compiled *A Chronicle and Historie of the House and Surname of Seatone* published (1829) and the works for which he is primarily remembered today: the *Maitland Folio Manuscript* and the *Maitland Quarto Manuscript*, compiled with the help of his daughter Mary.

These latter manuscripts, which contain collections of Maitland's poetry as well as that of other Scottish poets, engaged much of Maitland's time from 1555 onward. Selections of the manuscripts were published in 1786 under the title *Ancient Scottish Poems,* and Maitland's complete poems were published in 1830.

Predominant among Maitland's poems included in these collections are moral pieces—many of which deal with political strife between Scotland and England—and social satires, often considered among Maitland's best work. His satires include "Satire on the Age"; "Against the Thievis of Lissidall"; and "Satire on the Toun Ladies," in which Maitland takes an amusing and lighthearted tone and, with a trace of cynicism, mocks contemporary female fashion: "Thair bodyes bravelie they atyir / Of carnal lust to [add to] the fyir." Although much of Maitland's poetry deals with problems particular to his age, Eyre-Todd points out that "his best pieces [are those] containing touches closely applicable to the human nature of all time."

Makin, Bathsua (1600–1675) *nonfiction writer, poet*

Little is known of the origins of Bathsua Makin other than that she was the daughter of a schoolmaster and that she was a precocious child. When she was 16, Makin published two books, one about a shorthand system called Radiography that she had developed with her father; and another, *Musa Virginea Graeco, Latino, Gallica* (*The Virgin Muse in Greek, Latin, and French,* 1616), with original poems lauding the Stuart royal family in these languages and in Hebrew. It is reputed that when King JAMES I OF ENGLAND was presented a copy of the latter book, he scoffed at this work with the comment, "But can she spin?" It was this sort of condescending attitude that Makin strove to overcome in her writings, advocating the education of women at a time when few others were doing so. Makin embraced both scholarship and motherhood as a career, having given birth to nine children while writing and tutoring King Charles I's daughter, Princess Elizabeth, and the children of other notables.

Declaring that she would be unconcerned with the "Scoffes and Taunts from inconsiderate and illiterate Men," Makin outlined a course of study for women that, oddly, emphasized language, music, and household skills over science, in which Makin herself was quite interested. In fact, she discussed astronomy in correspondence with her brother-in-law, the mathematician John Pell. Makin established her own school and for much of her life tutored children from aristocratic families. She also established a reputation as a healer, having been given Sir Walter RALEIGH's herbal recipes by his widow.

Makin's *An Essay to Revive the Antient Education of Gentlewomen in Religion, Manners, Arts & Tongues* (1673) is arguably the first tract written in English by a woman advocating gender equality in education. In its dedicatory preface to "All Ingenious and Vertuous Ladies" and to Mary, the daughter of the Duke of York, Makin wrote sarcastically about the contemporary fear of educated women: "A Learned Woman is thought to be a Comet, that bodes Mischief, when ever it appears. To offer to the World the liberal Education of Women is to deface the Image of God in Man, it will make Women so high, and men so low, like Fire in the House-top, it will set the whole world in a Flame."

Makin's ideas were generally welcomed by those who wanted to see women achieve a better education, though some later pedagogues narrowly focused only on her endorsement of domestic arts like needlework to justify curricula designed for the "women's sphere." Frances Teague, who has edited some of Makin's works, describes her as one of the women of the period who "cared passionately about learning and who obtained an education despite incredible obstacles."

Works about Bathsua Makin

Holdsworth, Ian. "Teaching Making: A Brief History of Secondary School Craft Education Textbooks." Available online. URL: <w4.ed.uiuc.edu/faculty/westbury/Paradigm/HOLDSWOR.PDF>. Downloaded on January 15, 2004.

Teague, Frances, ed. *Bathsua Makin, Woman of Learning* Lewisburg, Pa.: Bucknell, University Press, 1998.

———. *The Early Modern Englishwoman: A Facsimile Library of Essential Works.* Ashgate, U.K.: Aldershot, 2001.

Marguerite of Navarre (Marguerite d'Angoulême) (1492–1549) *poet, playwright, lyrics writer, fiction writer*

Marguerite of Navarre was raised in Angoulême, in western France, with her younger brother François by their widowed mother, Louise de Savoie, who ensured that her children were thoroughly educated. At 17, Marguerite was married to the duc d'Alençon and went to live with him at Alençon, in Normandy. In 1515 François succeeded his cousin Louis XII as king of France. He continued the military campaigns in Italy that Louis XII had begun; in his absences, his mother acted as regent, and Marguerite began to spend much of her time at court. She was interested in all the arts, supported writers, and transformed the court into a brilliant literary center. She was also deeply engaged by religious thought; she had contacts with many of the leaders of the movement for religious reform that was developing at the time, among them John CALVIN. In the early 1520s she began to write religious poetry.

The duc d'Alençon died in battle in 1525, and two years later Marguerite married Henri d'Albret, king of Navarre (a state in the Pyrenees mountains). After her marriage, she divided her time between François's court and her husband's. She and Henri had two children: a daughter, Jeanne d'Albret, who inherited the throne of Navarre, and a son who died a few months after birth.

The death of her son in 1530 and of her mother the following year seems to have made her writing more important to Marguerite. In 1530 she published her first poem, *Miroir de l'Ame Pêcheresse* (*Mirror of the Sinful Soul*). During the 1530s she wrote both religious and secular lyrics as well as plays that were staged at both courts. She also began this decade with a great deal of influence over François and his policies, but gradually they became estranged as François began to feel threatened by the religious reformers who were Marguerite's friends. By 1540 Marguerite was no longer welcome at François's court.

It was probably in the early 1540s that Marguerite wrote her two long philosophical poems, *La Coche, ou le Debat sur l'Amour* (*The Coach, or the Debate on Love*) and *Le Triomphe de l'Aigneau* (*The Triumph of the Lamb*). In 1547 she published two collections of her works: *Les Marguerites de la Marguerite des Princesses tres Illustre Royne de Navarre* (*The Pearls of the Pearl of Princesses, the Illustrious Queen of Navarre*) and *Suyte des Marguerites . . .* (*More Pearls . . .*) Each book contained examples of all the genres she had attempted: plays, lyrics, and longer poems.

At the time of her death, Marguerite was working on a collection of stories modeled on BOCCACCIO's *Decameron*. The plots are drawn from French folklore, and the focus is generally on the trials endured by women and their need to maintain their chastity and love of God, but they include much humor and a wealth of fascinating detail about everyday life. Only 72 of the planned 100 stories were finished, but the collection was published in 1558 under the title *Heptaméron des Nouvelles* (*Heptameron of Stories; Decameron* derives from the Greek for 10 days, and *Heptameron* means seven days). This is the work for which she is best known today.

Marguerite was highly regarded in England in her own day and in the decades following her death. Princess Elizabeth, who was to become ELIZABETH I, made a translation of *Miroir de l'Ame Pêcheresse* when she was only 11 years old; her letter to her stepmother, Katherine PARR, asking her to critique the work, is still extant. Marguerite's stories had a profound effect on the English stage and, indeed, on narrative romanticism in general.

Other Work by Marguerite of Navarre
The Heptameron. Translated by P. A. Chilton. New York: Viking Penguin, 1984.

Works about Marguerite of Navarre
Collett, Barry. *A long and troubled pilgrimage: the correspondence of Marguerite d'Angoulême and Vittoria Colonna, 1540–1545.* Princeton, N.J.: Princeton Theological Seminary, 2000.

Cottrell, Robert D. *The Grammar of Silence: A Reading of Marguerite de Navarre's Poetry.* Washington, D.C.: Catholic University of America Press, 1986.

Lyons, John D., and Mary B. McKinley, eds. *Critical Tales: New Studies of the Heptameron and Early Modern Culture.* Philadelphia: University of Pennsylvania Press, 1993.

Thysell, Carol. *The Pleasure of Discernment: Marguerite de Navarre as Theologian.* New York: Oxford University Press, 2000.

Wertheimer, Molly Meijer, ed. *Listening to their Voices: The Rhetorical Activities of Historical Women.* Columbia: University of South Carolina Press, 1997.

Markham, Gervase (ca. 1568–1637)
nonfiction writer, playwright, poet

Gervase Markham was born in Nottinghamshire, England, to Robert Markham, a nobleman, and Mary Leake Markham. In his early life he served as a soldier with the Earl of Essex in Ireland. He was a prolific, though unremarkable, writer. Most of his works fall into the category of courtesy (instructional) literature. He wrote four books on horses and horsemanship, six on husbandry (land and household management), four on military discipline, four on sports and recreation, and one on housewifery. He also wrote poetry and one play, *The Dumbe Knight* (1608), which was cowritten with Lewis Machin and based on an Italian novella.

Remarkable for their detail, Markham's handbooks give a glimpse into the life of a country gentleman. They present the daily activities to which gentleman and ladies attended. In describing these activities, Markham uses an extensive vocabulary and technical terms, which he is always careful to define.

The most popular work by Markham is *The English Housewife* (1611). Containing everything from recipes for medicine and food to instructions on how to make clothing, this book, like his other manuals, draws on previously published works. This particular work also relies upon extensive time spent on country estates.

Markham is sometimes thought by some critics to be the rival poet mentioned in William SHAKESPEARE's sonnets. However, the critic Michael Best says this belief is unlikely, given Markham's minor reputation as a poet in his lifetime. His greatest contribution, Best says, is his "pervasive curiosity and the genuine fascination which his subjects obviously held for him."

Marlowe, Christopher (1564–1593)
playwright, poet

Few British writers ever lived so infamous a life as Christopher Marlowe, though his early years were uneventful. He was born in Canterbury, England, to John and Catherine Marlowe; his father was a cobbler, or shoemaker. The couple was able to send the boy to The King's School, Canterbury, where he earned a scholarship to attend Cambridge University. At Cambridge, Marlowe's studies would have centered on logic, rhetoric, ethics, and theology, and he would have had plenty of opportunities to sharpen his already impressive language skills. He graduated with a B.A. in 1584 and was entitled, according to the terms of his scholarship, to pursue a three-year M.A. as long as he intended to become a priest upon graduation.

Apparently Marlowe missed so many classes during this period that the university initially refused to award him a degree. In his defense, a letter from ELIZABETH I's government explained that "Whereas it was reported that Christopher Morley [Marlowe] was determined to have gone . . . to Reames [a French city] and there to remaine, Their Lordships thought good to certefie that . . . in all his accions he had behaved him selfe orderlie

and . . . had done her Majestie good service." In 1586 Sir Francis Walsingham, Elizabeth's secretary of state, had stifled a Roman Catholic plot against the English monarchy by strategically placing spies in the large Catholic community at Rheims. The allusion to the French city suggests that Marlowe had served as a spy for the government.

Shortly after obtaining his degree, Marlowe set out for London to make his name writing for an acting troupe called the ADMIRAL'S MEN, which performed its plays at the Rose Theatre. He was wildly successful and quickly emerged as the most popular playwright in the city. Unlike the expensive and exclusive theaters of today's world, Elizabethan theaters existed alongside alehouses and brothels, and they often attracted the same customers. Marlowe seems to have fit right into this seedy underworld. Although many works have been credited to him, Marlowe is known today primarily for seven plays, which were very popular with Elizabethan theatergoers. In 1589 he was arrested with his friend, Thomas WATSON, who had stabbed to death a man named William Bradley. Both men were committed to Newgate prison, where they pleaded that Watson had acted in self-defense. While Watson served five months for his crime, Marlowe was released after two weeks, though this would not be the last time he would find himself in trouble with the authorities.

In 1593 Marlowe's friend and fellow playwright, Thomas KYD was arrested by authorities who suspected him of atheism. A search of his home turned up papers "Denyinge the deity of Jhesus," which Kyd said belonged to Marlowe. While it must be remembered that Kyd was tortured for information, he described in detail what he perceived to be "Marlowes monstruous opinions":

he [Marlowe] contynewd [continued] it in table talk or otherwise to jest at the devine scriptures [,] gybe [mock] at praiers, & stryve in argument to frustrate & confute what hath byn spoke or wrytt by prophets & such holie men.

Marlowe was apprehended and forced to report daily to the authorities. During the investigation the lord chancellor, Sir John Puckering, received from Richard Baines, another former acquaintance of Marlowe's, a letter testifying to the playwright's atheism: "He affirmeth . . . That the first beginning of Religion was only to keep men in awe . . . [and] That Christ was a bastard." Whatever the truth of Kyd's and Baines's accusations, the sensational nature of the reports, compounded with the controversial subject matter of some of Marlowe's writings, has led some scholars to view Marlowe as an atheist. Because many of his plays—most notably, *Doctor Faustus*—recognize the existence of a God, "atheism" is probably a misnomer; if anything, he was critical of formal religion.

On May 30, 1593, Marlowe spent a day with several gentlemen at a house in Deptford, eating, drinking, and talking. According to witnesses, there was a quarrel over who should pay the reckoning, or bill. Marlowe is said to have pulled his dagger and wounded Ingram Frizer before the injured man grabbed the dagger and, according to Frizer himself, "gave the said Christopher then & there a mortal wound over his right eye of the depth of two inches & of the width of one inch." Marlowe died instantly. Since Frizer was pardoned shortly after by Walsingham, and since the other two gentleman who were present seem to have served as government spies, it is often assumed that Marlowe's murder was planned by government officials, perhaps in response to his "monstruous opinions." Somewhat ironically, the life of England's first great tragedian ended tragically before the age of 30.

Critical Analysis

Christopher Marlowe was born two months prior to his great dramatic rival, William SHAKESPEARE. The timing has proven unfortunate for Marlowe, whose writings, despite their brilliance, have been judged in comparison with Shakespeare's. There also is a certain amount of irony in Marlowe's neglect since the Shakespeare we know today might not have written so many masterpieces had Marlowe not preceded him.

Not only is Marlowe the author of one of England's greatest epyllia (brief epics, or grand narrative poems about the deeds of heroes)—*Hero and Leander* (ca. 1592)—but he also penned what is perhaps the most famous lyric (short, nonnarrative poem) of the 16th century: "The Passionate Shepherd to His Love" (ca. 1587). In this poem the speaker invites his mistress to join him in an idealized rural setting that renders physical love an innocent part of the natural world:

> Come live with me, and be my love,
> And we will all the pleasures prove,
> That valleys, groves, hills and fields,
> Woods, or steepy mountain yields.

The simple, melodic rhyme scheme and vivid imagery combine to produce a seductive invitation that inspired many imitations and parodies throughout the RENAISSANCE and contributed to the 17th-century craze for *carpe diem* poetry (poems that argue "Seize the day" or "Enjoy yourself while you can").

Marlowe's greatest contribution to English poetry, however, would be his radical transformation of dramatic, not lyric, verse. When Marlowe decided not to write his plays in the poetic style of previous English dramatists (that is, in rhyme), he changed English literature forever. Instead, he appropriated the form invented by Henry Howard, Earl of SURREY, who earlier in the century had written in "blank verse," or poetry in unrhymed iambic pentameter (poetic lines consisting of five "iambs," or two-syllable units with a stress on the second syllable). Marlowe chose blank verse because it offered a naturalistic rhythm characteristic of English speech. Indeed, Marlowe's polysyllabic (words with more than one syllable) vocabulary, use of repetitive, consonantal sounds (i.e., alliteration), and flexible manipulation of word order resulted in a poetic form that paralleled the natural rapidity, power, and flow of the language.

Marlowe celebrates his stylistic breakthrough in the prologue of his first successful play, *Tamburlaine* (1587), by announcing that he will avoid the "jigging veins of rhyming mother-wits" in favor of the "high astounding terms" spoken by the title character. Indeed, Tamburlaine, like all of Marlowe's great characters, is distinguished by his persuasive power, a characteristic that led Ben JONSON to praise "Marlowe's mighty line." Regardless of whatever else Marlowe would accomplish in his career, the importance of his contribution to English poetic form and style is almost unparalleled in the history of English literature; it is likely that without Marlowe's mighty line Shakespeare's *Hamlet* (1601) and John MILTON's *Paradise Lost* (1667) would have constituted little more than imitations of the (rhymed) poetry of earlier generations.

Marlowe would, in fact, accomplish a great deal more before his brief career was over. *Tamburlaine* is merely the first in a series of successful Marlovian tragedies performed at the Rose Theatre between 1587 and 1593. A distinguishing feature of these plays is their focus on socially subversive protagonists. Marlowe understood the seductive appeal of troublesome and, in some cases, villainous behavior. If Greek tragedy focuses on powerful men who fall from great heights, Marlovian tragedy tends to focus on outsiders who never find their place in society. As the scholar Emily C. Bartels has argued, alienation is the tragic state of reality for most of Marlowe's protagonists, a fact that may explain the power of his writings for modern audiences.

Unlike Shakespeare's King Lear, say, who will fall from the most powerful position in his world, a position he is born into, Tamburlaine is a "Scythian shepherd" who rises to power by means of his own warrior skill and rhetorical brilliance. From the beginning of the play, he is perceived by the "natural" rulers as little more than a social upstart, a "base usurping vagabond." Over the course of the play and its equally successful sequel, *The Second Part of Tamburlaine*, the audience witnesses his rise from the lowly ranks of shepherd to the most powerful position in the world as he conquers Persians, Tartars, and Turks, among other peoples. His success as a warrior stems from his limitless ambition and ability to persuade would-be followers, which validates the critic Harry Levin's claim that Marlowe's great heroes are "overreachers." Tamburlaine speaks of such ambition as perfectly natural: "Nature . . . / Doth teach us all to have aspiring minds." But it is Tamburlaine's *exceptional* ambition, not the natural ambition felt by ordinary beings, that defines him as a great figure.

Although Part I ends with Tamburlaine's military triumph and marriage to the Egyptian princess, Zenocrate, Part II traces his demise and destruction. Particularly telling are the failures of his sons to carry on his legacy. In essence, Tamburlaine is so superior to those around him that he succeeds in creating a world no one else can sustain.

Tamburlaine is an outsider among characters within the play because of his lowly background. He is also an outsider to his English audience because he is a Scythian in a largely Islamic world. In one of the most controversial passages in Part II, Tamburlaine is blinded by the pride that stems from his triumph over various Islamic nations: "In vain, I see, men worship Mahomet: / My sword hath sent millions of Turks to hell, / Slew all his priests, his kinsmen, and his friends, / And yet I live untouched by Mahomet." He burns numerous copies of the Koran, which his men have seized from the temples they have destroyed. A few moments later, Tamburlaine announces, "I feel myself distempered [ill]," signaling the beginning of his downfall, which is directly tied to this blasphemous action.

The play forces its English audience to identify with the central protagonist, oftentimes against their will. Was Marlowe trying to say that the audience should cheer on the atheist Tamburlaine as he destroys the enemies of the Christian world? If so, why does the burning of the Koran lead to his destruction? Or perhaps Marlowe was writing from a more orthodox position, arguing that blasphemy against God (the Koran figures as the Bible in this case) will be punished in the end.

In *The Jew of Malta* (ca. 1590), Marlowe forces the same sort of identification by presenting a Jewish villain who is far more charming than his Christian counterparts. On the one hand, Barabas is a brutal Jewish stereotype, a miserly merchant who spends his time counting gold and stockpiling "[i]nfinite riches in a little room." He systematically plots and executes hideous crimes, including the massacre of an entire convent of nuns. On the other hand, Barabas's crimes constitute revenge against Christian aggressors since he commits them in reaction to a law that openly discriminates against Malta's Jews. Because the Roman Catholic Knights of Malta owe a tribute to the Turks that they cannot pay, they determine that all Jews will be taxed one half of their estate or else must convert to Christianity.

Furthermore, the play suggests that Barabas's villainy is not so much the result of an intrinsically evil nature as the result of his socialization within a corrupt Christian culture. In other words, he learns how to commit crimes from the Christians around him. As Barabas remarks, "Rather had I, a Jew, be hated thus / Than pitied in a Christian poverty; / For I can see no fruits in all their faith, / But malice, falsehood, and excessive pride."

Marlowe asks his audience to see through the eyes of a character who is oppressed by a society that closely resembles London, though the subversiveness of the move is lessened somewhat because the Christians in this case are Catholics, as opposed to English Protestants. Viewers are forced back and forth between a Jewish protagonist and his Catholic persecutors. In both cases, the audience must identify with individuals they have been conditioned to fear and despise. The ending of the play does little to resolve this tension. As Barabas is burned alive in a boiling cauldron, the Christian governor of Malta asks that "due praise be given . . . / . . . to heaven." One can only agree with the 20th-century poet T. S. Eliot who called *The Jew of Malta* a "savage farce," in that Marlowe seems to be laughing at the hypocrisy of his own society.

Marlowe's most famous play, *Doctor Faustus* (1593), would also appear to question the morality of Christianity, though far more subtly. Faustus is an overreaching genius, a scholar so bored by worldly knowledge that he determines to know of heavenly things by turning to black magic in order to "get a deity" (i.e., conjure up the devil). Faustus sells his immortal soul to the devil, Mephistopheles, for 24 years of power and knowledge. The play focuses on Faustus's vain pursuit of satisfaction as he experiences the pleasures and confronts the mysteries that the world has to offer. Time is a central character in the play, for the audience is always aware that eternal hellfire awaits Faustus at the end.

The hero's final moments are characterized by an impressive counting down of time until Faustus is yanked by demons through the floorboards of his study into hell. The Chorus that concludes the play would appear to offer a fairly simple moral: "Faustus is gone. Regard his hellish fall, / Whose fiendful fortune may exhort the wise / Only to wonder at unlawful things."

Marlowe, however, is never so simple. Throughout the play, two angels visit Faustus. Whereas the Good Angel implores him to repent because it is never too late for God's mercy—"Faustus, repent. Yet God will pity thee"—the Evil Angel insists that it is too late. In the final moments of the play, as hell opens beneath him, Faustus cries out to God: "Oh, I'll leap up to my God: who pulls me down? / . . . / One drop [of Christ's] blood would save my soul, half a drop. Ah, my Christ!" Christ does not answer, though, and Faustus's final four lines confuse the terrifying wrath of God with the horrors that await Faustus in hell:

> My God, my God, look not so fierce on me.
> Adders and serpents, let me breathe a
>   while!
> Ugly hell, gape not, come not, Lucifer!
> I'll burn my books. Ah, Mephistopheles!

If Faustus's call to Christ is sincere, then the Good Angel must be a liar, and there is little difference between God and Lucifer. If Faustus calls out to Christ merely to save himself, which is what the Elizabethan censors must have believed, then

Faustus dies because he fails to repent. As usual, Marlowe writes an ambiguous conclusion, causing his audience to question its most cherished beliefs.

Marlowe's other plays raise moral questions in similarly subversive ways: *Dido, Queen of Carthage* (ca. 1586) ponders the devastating effects of a hypermasculine, imperialist culture upon women; *The Massacre at Paris* (ca. 1590) hints that Protestant rulers are as corrupt as the Catholics they oppose; and *Edward II* (ca. 1592) is the tragedy of a homosexual king who is deposed and brutally murdered by thugs who sodomize him with a "red hot poker" as he prays to God, a twisted representation and condemnation of the homosexual act.

As plays such as *Edward II* and *Dido* would suggest, Marlowe's social criticism extended beyond religious matters. While it is easy to understand why contemporary moralists found in Marlowe's plays evidence of his atheism and immorality, modern commentators benefit from the clarity of hindsight. To call Marlowe immoral is to distort the writings of a man determined to expose the hypocrisy of his own time. In the end, it is difficult to disagree with Harry Levin, who claims that "no other poet has been, so fully as Marlowe, a fellow-traveler with the subversive currents of his age." In judging the character of the man, we should remember that he was called subversive in an age largely defined by its oppressive sexual, religious, and political mores. Marlowe is admired today for the same reasons he was then—because he challenges audiences to confront their inner demons as well as the demons that surround them on all sides.

Other Works by Christopher Marlowe

Christopher Marlowe: The Complete Plays. Edited by Mark Thornton Burnett. Rutland, Vt.: Tuttle, 1999.
Christopher Marlowe: The Complete Poems. Edited by Mark Thornton Burnett. Rutland, Vt.: Tuttle, 2001.

Works about Christopher Marlowe

Bartels, Emily C. *Spectacles of Strangeness: Imperialism, Alienation, and Marlowe.* Philadelphia: University of Pennsylvania Press, 1993.

Eliot, T. S. *Elizabethan Dramatists.* New York: Harcourt Brace, 1960.
Hopkins, Lisa. *Christopher Marlowe: A Literary Life.* New York: Palgrave, 2000.
Kuriyama, Constance Brown. *Christopher Marlowe: A Renaissance Life.* Ithaca, N.Y.: Cornell University Press, 2002.
Nicholl, Charles. *The Reckoning: The Murder of Christopher Marlowe.* New York: Harcourt Brace, 1992.
White, Paul Whitfield, ed. *Marlowe, History, and Sexuality: New Essays on the Life and Writings of Christopher Marlowe.* New York: AMS Press, 1998.

Marprelate, Martin *nonfiction writer*

Martin Marprelate is a pseudonym of unknown ownership used as the author of many religious tracts that appeared throughout England following a decree in 1586 from the Star Chamber, the high court of England. The decree required that John Whitgift, the bishop of London, approve all publications. Whitgift used this power to censor the Puritans—Protestants who believed in stricter religious discipline and simpler ceremonies than those of the CHURCH OF ENGLAND.

Marprelate responded to this decree by publishing tracts that were not approved by Whitgift. There are seven surviving Marprelate tracts: *The Epistle* (1588); *The Epitome* (1588); *Certain Mineral and Metaphysical Schoolpoints* (1589); *Hay [i.e., have you] Any Work for Cooper* [someone who makes barrels, as well as a pun on the name of Thomas Cooper, bishop of Winchester] (1589); *Martin Junior* (1589); *Martin Senior* (1589); and *The Protestation of Martin Marprelate* (1589).

Marprelate's tracts are best described as intelligent arguments against the church that use such literary techniques as sarcasm and irony. In *The Epistle,* for example, he uses sarcasm when he boldly compares the priests to antichrists, "pettie popes and pettie Antichrists whosoeuer vsurpe the authority of pastors ouer them." And he is ironic in the same work when he explains to the priests that his writing will be good for them to read: "[T]his worke I recommend vnto them [the priests] with all my heart with a desire to see them all so prouided for one day as I would wish which I promise them shall not be at all to their hurt."

As Eric Leonidas explains in his book *Making Much of Martin: The Marprelate Controversy, Verse Satire, and the Style of the Stage,* what made Marprelate's writing so popular is that "Martin's discourse . . . is made of the language he has experienced in the streets, taverns, tradeshops and, above all, the popular playhouses of London."

Critics consider Marprelate's writing as some of the best satire—or writing that uses wit and irony to attack a person or idea—from Elizabethan England. Often his wit is turned toward the church's laws and its leaders. For example, Marprelate tells his readers in *The Epistle* (1588) that they "are as mannerly as bishops in medling with that you haue nothing to doe as they do in taking vpon them ciuill [civil] offices."

The tracts were so powerful that they began what become known as the Marprelate Controversy, and the church hired professional writers to respond to the writings. These responses were never as powerful or well-crafted as those from Marprelate. However, Parliament succumbed to pressure from the Church of England in 1593 and passed an anti-Puritan law in which anyone who disobeyed a decree from the church could be severely punished and even be put to death. This action quickly silenced the Puritan opposition.

The actual author of the Marprelate tracts was never discovered, although a number of candidates exist such as a clergyman named Udell as well as John Penry and Job Throckmorton, two known Puritan writers from the Marprelate period whose writing and views resembled Marprelate's. Indeed, Penry was eventually put to death for his beliefs.

Works about Martin Marprelate

Appleton, Elizabeth. *An Anatomy of the Marprelate Controversy 1588–1596: Retracing Shakespeare's Identity and That of Martin Marprelate.* New York: Edwin Mellen Press, 2001.

Carlson, Leland Henry. *Martin Marprelate, Gentleman: Master Job Throkmorton Laid Open in His Colors.* San Marino, Calif.: H. E. Huntington Library & Art, 1981.

Marston, John (ca. 1575–1634) *playwright, poet*

John Marston was born in Wardington, Oxfordshire, England, the son of John Marston, a lawyer, and Mary Guarisi Marston, whose father was an Italian doctor. Marston received a bachelor's degree from Oxford University in 1594 and later lived with his father at the Middle Temple, a legal training institute. The elder Marston lamented, however, that his son would probably never study the law, devoting himself instead to "playes[,] vayne studdyes[,] and fooleryes."

The "vayne studdyes and fooleryes" refer to Marston's satirical writings, such as *The Metamorphosis of Pygmalion's Image* and *The Scourge of Villainy* (both 1598). The former is an erotic poem, perhaps a parody of traditional love poetry; the latter harshly criticizes human frailties of vanity and lust. The two works, along with many similar ones by other satirists, were burned when satire was banned by the archbishop of Canterbury and the bishop of London in 1599.

Marston then turned to playwriting. In the comedy *Antonio and Mellida* (1599) the two title characters have to overcome the opposition of Mellida's father to their love, with the hero putting on a disguise in order to gain access to his beloved. There are several unusual aspects of the play, however. Mellida's father Piero seems too serious a villain for a comedy, as he gloats that he "is heaved up / On wings of fair success to overlook / The low cast ruins of his enemies." Another unusual element of the play is that Antonio's disguise is that of a female Amazon warrior. Most unusual of all, however, is the fact that the sequel to this comedy, *Antonio's Revenge,* (1602) is a full-fledged revenge tragedy in the tradition of Thomas KYD's *The Spanish Tragedy.* The wedding expected at the end of the previous play is not yet performed when

Piero appears on stage covered with blood, fresh from a murder. Many other murders follow, but, unlike most such tragedies, the revenger himself (Antonio) does not die at the end. As in other revenge tragedies, including Hamlet (which appeared about the same time), a ghost demands revenge and the hero pretends to be insane before that revenge is taken.

Marston's next play, *The Malcontent* (1603), is a political tragicomedy (a play that brings its main characters through dangers to a happy ending) set in Italy. Altofronto has been deposed as the duke of Genoa by Pietro and his scheming accomplice Mendoza. The latter soon aspires to the throne himself, but unluckily he employs Altofronto, disguised as Malevole, to help him. The play included the then-trendy themes of melancholy and Machiavellianism. Indeed, malcontentedness (the play's title refers to Altofronto in his disguise as Malevole) and melancholy were hard to distinguish. A great mind like Altofronto's was considered especially subject to the listless sadness of melancholy. Machiavellianism refers to applications of the ideas expounded in Niccolò MACHIAVELLI's *The Prince.* In popular understanding, Machiavellianism was a world view in which the ends justified evil means, as exemplified by Mendoza. His line "Fortune still dotes on those who cannot blush" could serve as his motto.

Parasitaster, or The Fawn (1604–05), like *The Malcontent,* features a duke in disguise. Here, Duke Hercules disguises himself to check up on his son, who is supposed to be arranging a marriage between Hercules and Dulcimel, the daughter of a neighboring duke. However, the witty Dulcimel prefers the son to the father, and Hercules is wise enough to give his blessing to the love of the young people. The play is the first of several of Marston's works to make extensive use of John FLORIO's translation of Michel de MONTAIGNE's *Essays,* passages from which form the basis for several speeches in the play.

Eastward Ho! (1604–05), a comedy written in collaboration with George CAPMAN and Ben JONSON, stirred up serious trouble with JAMES I OF ENGLAND for poking fun at things Scottish.

Marston managed to avoid spending time in jail, though his colleagues did not.

The Dutch Courtesan (1605) examines female sexuality. A one-sentence summary at the beginning of the published play states that "the difference betwixt the love of a courtesan [prostitute] and a wife is the full scope of the play." Young Freevill has enjoyed a long relationship with Franischina, the title character, but is now intent on marrying Beatrice. He offers Franischina to his Puritan friend Malheureux, who is at first horrified and then quickly falls in love with her. The plot turns serious when Franischina tries to enlist her new lover to kill his friend and drive Beatrice insane. Sexuality being, as the scholar T. F. Wharton notes, "the most insistent preoccupation of [Marston's] work, the three main female characters in the play show three versions of female sexuality: Franceschina is the courtesan, Beatrice the meek virgin, and Beatrice's sister Crispinella a witty young woman determined to choose for herself among her suitors."

Phillip J. Finkelpearl, Marston's biographer, notes that Marston's "subjects, his language, his tones and attitudes, his aesthetic preferences all show that he was bound and preoccupied by the problems of his immediate environment"; yet, his "visions of the dark but comic battle between a corrupt world and the integrity of the individual still convey an urgent power."

Works about John Marston

Finkelpearl, Phillip J. *John Marston of the Middle Temple: An Elizabethan Dramatist in his Social Setting.* Cambridge, Mass.: Harvard University Press, 1969.

Wharton, T. F., ed. *The Drama of John Marston.* New York: Cambridge University Press, 2000.

martyr

A martyr is someone who voluntarily suffers death as punishment for refusing to renounce a religion. From the beginning of the English REFORMATION until the succession of ELIZABETH I to the English throne in 1558, 350 Protestant believers were put to death for heresy. Other Protestants therefore considered them martyrs. The scholar Brad Gregory states, "Martyrs demonstrated their willingness to die for their beliefs, proclaiming that commitment to the truth outweighed the prolongation of their lives." In the 1530s, after King Henry VIII divorced his wife, Catherine of Aragon, several Catholic clerics, including Thomas MORE and John Houghton, refused to acknowledge Henry as head of the church in England and were hanged and disemboweled. John Fisher was beheaded for refusing to swear an oath of succession acknowledging that the children of Anne Boleyn and Henry were legitimate successors to the throne of England.

In 1563 John FOXE published *Acts and Monuments,* an account of Protestant martyrs such as Anne ASKEW, Thomas CRANMER, and Hugh LATIMER. Using woodcuts of heroic martyrs and fervent descriptions of their deaths, Foxe's book was a sensational best seller of its time. As author Robert Kolb states, "[T]ales of ultimate sacrifice and bold heroism for the sake of faith stunned and inspired pious hearts."

In *Acts and Monuments* Foxe offers this eyewitness account of the martyrdom of William TYNDALE: He was "brought forth to the place of execution, he was tied to the stake, strangled by the hangman and afterwards consumed with fire, crying at the stake with a fervent zeal, and a loud voice, 'Lord! Open the king of England's eyes.'"

Martyrdom was an effective tool that actually sparked Protestant conversions. The public places of execution provided excellent venues in which to seek converts. Since most of the martyrs were calm, some even joyful, in the face of death, they inspired many onlookers to embrace Protestantism.

A Work about Martyrs

Gregory, Brad S. *Salvation at Stake: Christian Martyrdom in Early Modern Europe.* Cambridge, Mass.: Harvard University Press, 1999.

Marvell, Andrew (1621–1678) *poet*

Educated at Trinity College, Cambridge University, Andrew Marvell received a B.A. degree in 1639. Despite his promising scholarly abilities, the death of his father in 1641 ended the possibility of an academic career. From 1642 to 1646 he traveled around Europe, primarily working as a tutor. Upon his return to England, although he was originally opposed to Oliver Cromwell's Commonwealth government, he became a supporter, eventually writing "An Horatian Ode upon Cromwell's Return from Ireland," a poem of both praise and warning to Cromwell that he must be ever vigilant: "The same arts that did gain / A pow'r, must it maintain" (1650). Marvell went on to serve as tutor to Cromwell's nephew and ward, William Dutton. By 1653 he had become friends with John MILTON, who wrote an extremely complimentary recommendation for him for the position of assistant Latin secretary to the Council of State. Marvell's long political career began with his appointment to that post in 1657. He was elected to Parliament in 1659 and remained in office for the remainder of his life, serving with distinction.

Throughout his political career, Marvell was an avid writer, composing lyric poems, odes, political satires, and pastoral poems. During his lifetime, however, his reputation as a poet was overshadowed by his high-profile political career. Although it is thought that the majority of his lyric poetry was written by 1650, few were actually published while he was alive. Had more of his work been published, his cutting political satires would have offended Royalists and republicans alike. It wasn't until 1681 that his nephew finished compiling and published Marvell's *Miscellaneous Poems*. During the 19th century, critic Charles Lamb rediscovered and reintroduced Marvell to the literary world. Since then, his fame as a poet has grown, and he is considered one of the greatest poets of his generation.

Critical Analysis

Marvell's poetry is a unique blend of metaphysical and classical poetry, using various aspects of both but committing to neither one nor the other. As David Daiches says in *A Critical History of English Literature,*

His best poetry combines true metaphysical wit with perfect classical grace and poise to a greater degree than any other poet of the century. . . . [He] stood alone, like Milton, creating his own synthesis out of the clashing elements swirling around him.

His range and style of poetry was wide and eclectic. While he is often considered one of the META-PHYSICAL POETS, his work is also marked by Puritan values and ethics, especially evident in his nature poems. Famously, in "The Garden," Marvell mocks the vanity of those who would win laurels by their worldly accomplishments when the garden with its natural beauty and repose invites one into a garlanded world of innocence and reflection in which the "soul into the boughs does glide / There like a bird it sits and sings."

"To His Coy Mistress" (1646) is a good examples of Marvell's metaphysical poetry; and his Cromwellian odes—"An Horatian Ode upon Cromwell's Return from Ireland" (1650), "The First Anniversary" (1655), and "On the Death of O.C." (1659)—are in the style of Pindar, a Greek poet known for his poems in celebration of victories in athletic contests. The first, "Horatian Ode," is an ambiguous work that is careful to balance both praise and criticism of Cromwell and the violence that he represents:

> So restless Cromwell could not cease
> In the inglorious arts of peace,
> But through adventurous war
> Urgèd his active star.

Marvell highlights with a warning what Cromwell represents: "The same arts that did gain / A power must it maintain." Through a skilled and careful balance and order of images, Marvell is able to both praise Charles I's conduct in defeat while treating Cromwell fairly as his executioner. In the end, Marvell's balance and fair-mindedness gives poetic dignity to both men, with neither loser nor victor. The work is a model example of the ambiguity that was often present in Marvell's work.

The carpe diem poem "To His Coy Mistress" remains the most famous of Marvell's poems, and one of the best known in the English language. The term *carpe diem* means "seize the day," and many poets have written on this theme in which an impatient poet encourages his love to give in to physical passion because time moves quickly and life is short. The poem begins with what may be Marvell's most famous lines: "Had we but world enough, and time / This coyness, lady, were no crime," after which the poet goes on to explain in great detail how much time he would like to spend courting the lady, including a hundred years to praise her eyes and forehead. In this extended conceit or comparison, Marvell, as do most of his fellow metaphysical poets, introduces into his poem many seemingly unrelated metaphors that enrich the work and cause it to extend its meaning far beyond just one pair of lovers into universal significance. He tells his lady that he'll wait for her love "Till the Conversion of the Jews." And in his most quoted and striking metaphor, he says his "vegetable love should grow / Vaster than empires and more slow." But unfortunately, says the poet wryly, "at my back I always hear / Time's winged chariot hurrying near." And he ends his plea to the lady with a characteristic, wry wit: "The grave's a fine and private place, / But none, I think, do there embrace."

After the Restoration of Charles II in 1660, Marvell began to write more political satires, his most notable being "Last Instructions to a Painter" and "The Rehearsal Transpos'd." As the scholar George Lord says about Marvell's change from lyric-based poetry to satire,

> The life and work of Andrew Marvell are both marked by extraordinary variety and range. Gifted with a most subtle and introspective imagination, he turned his talents in mid-career from incomparable lyric explorations of the inner life to panegyric and satiric poems on the men and issues involved in one of England's most crucial political epochs.

In fact, Marvell's scathing political satire, especially that which attacked religious intolerance and political corruption, was one of the main reasons he was published very little during his lifetime. An example of this is seen in his "The Character of Holland," a work written while England was preparing for war with Holland. It displays Marvell's satirical voice at its finest, exaggerating British views and mocking their attempt to justify war with Holland:

> HOLLAND, that scarce deserves the name
> of land,
> As but the off-scouring of the British sand;
> And so much earth as was contributed
> By English pilots when they heaved the lead;
> Or what by th' ocean's slow alluvion fell
> Of shipwrecked cockle and the mussel shell;
> This indigested vomit of the sea
> Fell to the Dutch by just propriety.

Marvell is today one of the best-known and most-read poets of the 17th century. "To His Coy Mistress" has become the model for metaphysical poetry, and his satire is considered some of the best ever written.

Other Works by Andrew Marvell
Complete Poetry of Andrew Marvell. Edited by George Lord. London: J. M. Dent & Sons, Ltd., 1984.
The Works of Andrew Marvell. Edited by Andrew Crozier. New York: Wordsworth Editions Ltd., 1998.

Works about Andrew Marvell
Chernaik, Warren, and Dzelzainis, Martin. *Marvell and Liberty.* New York: St. Martin's Press, 1999.
Patterson, Annabel. *Andrew Marvell: Writers and Their Work.* Oxford: University Press of Mississippi, 1996.
Wheeler, Thomas. *Andrew Marvell Revisited.* New York: Twayne, 1996.

Mary Stuart (Mary, Queen of Scots)
(1542–1587) *poet*
Mary Stuart was queen of Scotland (1542–67) and queen consort of France (1559–60). Although she is best known for her tumultuous po-

litical and marital life, Mary also wrote religious and romantic poetry. She was the daughter of Mary of Guise and James V, king of Scotland; her great-grandfather was King Henry VII of England. Six days after her birth, her father died, and she acceded to the throne. In 1548 Mary was sent to France, where she lived 13 years and became well educated, learning French, Italian, Greek, and Spanish. In 1558 she married the dauphin and later king, Francis II, who died of an ear infection in 1560, leaving his young queen to enter a period of mourning. The accession of ELIZABETH I to the throne of England in 1558 and Elizabeth's subsequent refusal to marry meant that Mary was, by virtue of her Tudor blood, heir to the English throne.

In 1561 Mary returned to a reformed Scotland under Protestant control. As a Roman Catholic, she was regarded by many, including the leading Scottish Calvinist preacher, John KNOX, as a foreign queen practicing an alien religion. In 1565 she married Henry Stuart, Lord Darnley, rousing controversy in the court of Elizabeth I.

In March 1566 Darnley and a group of Protestant rebels murdered David Rizzio, an Italian musician who was Mary's secretary. The murder greatly distressed Mary, who had witnessed the attack and who was pregnant with the future king, James VI (later JAMES I OF ENGLAND). In 1567 Darnley was assassinated, sparking accusations that Mary herself was involved in the murder. According to Mary's enemies, she planned the assassination with her adulterous liaison, James Hepburn, Lord Bothwell, whom she married later that year. In 1567 a silver casket was discovered, containing letters and poems allegedly written by Mary in which she suggested her part in the murder as well as Bothwell's. The letters were first made public in 1571, appended to George BUCHANAN's *Detectio Mariae Reginae.*

Public and private hostility deepened against Mary, and in 1567 she was imprisoned at Lochleven Castle. When she abdicated in favor of her son James, she was released from prison and fled to England, where she sought protection from

Elizabeth. For the remainder of her life, she was imprisoned by Elizabeth, who was fearful that Mary might serve as a rallying point for English Catholics hoping to replace her with the Scottish queen. It was the discovery in 1586 of a plot to assassinate Elizabeth and bring about a Roman Catholic uprising that convinced Elizabeth that her cousin would always be a threat to her position. Mary was tried in an English court at Westminster and found guilty of attempting to overthrow Elizabeth. She was executed in 1587 at Fotheringhay Castle in Northamptonshire.

Mary's turbulent life served as the inspiration for much of her poetry. She wrote poetry to each of her various lovers, to each of her three husbands, and to her rival, Queen Elizabeth I of England. The following is an excerpt of a sonnet written by Mary during her incarceration in Fotheringhay:

> Alas what am I? What use has my life?
> I am but a body whose heart's torn away,
> A vain shadow, an object of misery
> Who has nothing left but death-in-life.

In an ode upon the death of her first husband, the French king Francis II, aged only 16, Mary writes,

> In my sad, quiet song,
> A melancholy air,
> I shall look deep and long
> At loss beyond compare
> And with bitter tears,
> I'll pass my best years.

All of Mary's poetry was written in French and consists of an elegy, 16 sonnets, and a series of quatrains. She also wrote one essay.

Massinger, Philip (1583–1640) playwright, poet

Philip Massinger was the second of five children of Anne and Arthur Massinger, and their only son.

His father had received degrees from both Oxford and Cambridge, and was a trusted employee of the earls of Pembroke; Sir William Herbert, the fourth earl, paid for Philip Massinger's education at Oxford University, where he studied from 1602 to 1606.

The first documentation of Massinger's life after 1606 is a 1613 note in the diary of the theatrical manager Philip Henslowe that Massinger was asking for an advance payment for a play he was writing, which suggests that Massinger was already deeply involved in theatrical life. From 1621 on, his plays were frequently produced and published. Nothing is known of his personal life, except for a posthumous document mentioning a stipend from Sir Philip Herbert, to be paid to his widow in appreciation of a play he wrote in 1623. The identity of his wife, when he married, or whether there were any children are unknown.

Massinger frequently collaborated with other playwrights, especially at the beginning of his career. He worked with John FLETCHER after Francis BEAUMONT's retirement, and also with Nathan FIELD, Thomas MIDDLETON, and Thomas DEKKER. Fifteen plays that Massinger wrote independently have survived, including both tragedies and comedies, and historians know of 12 plays that have been lost. Massinger worked primarily for the KING'S MEN, where he was the company's principal dramatist after Fletcher's death in 1625.

The tragicomedy *The Maid of Honor* (acted 1621 or 1622, published 1632), based on a story from BOCCACCIO's *Decameron,* is considered one of Massinger's best plays. In it the heroine, Camiola, becomes a nun and gives away her property: one third to the convent, one third to the poor, and one third to the devoted and honest suitor who has failed to persuade her to marry him. It is partly on the basis of this play that Massinger has been thought to have had leanings toward the Roman Catholic Church.

The Renegado (1624, published 1630) may also support this notion. Its hero, a Jesuit priest, is portrayed as noble, generous, persuasive, and ultimately successful in leading other characters out of danger and wrongdoing: A European princess is rescued from Turkish captivity, a Turkish princess is converted to Christianity and brought to live in Venice, and the renegade of the title, an Italian officer who has deserted, is brought back to his duty. Although anti-Catholic, especially anti-Jesuit, feeling was high in London at the time, the play was popular.

The comedy *A New Way to Pay Old Debts* (1625 or 1626, published 1633) draws its plot from Middleton's *A Trick to Catch the Old One,* but the main character, Sir Giles Overreach, is Massinger's own brilliant creation. Overreach, the eloquent embodiment of avarice, cunning, and ambition, is the main reason why this play has been revived over the centuries, more than any others of Massinger's. The role provides a welcome vehicle for the talents of fine actors.

Massinger wrote in the dedication to *The Roman Actor* (1626) that this was his favorite play. A tragedy, *The Roman Actor* is a study of the Roman emperor Domitian and the social corruption brought about by his despotic rule. The actor of the title, Paris, is brought to trial before the Senate for libel. His speech in defense of his profession points out that while philosophers can discuss the nature of virtue, not many people will make the effort to read what they write, and among those, few are likely to be stirred by it. It is the actor who can have a real effect on people's consciences by working on their emotions so that they "go home changed men."

This speech by the Roman actor can be read as a description of what Massinger himself aimed at in his plays. The scholar Philip Edwards, in a 1962 essay, characterized Massinger as "a moralist, a sage and serious man determined to indicate what behavior was acceptable and what was not."

Massinger also wrote a number of poems. He died as the English Civil War was beginning; soon after his death the Puritans succeeded in closing the theaters, which did not open again until after the Restoration. According to tradition, Massinger was buried in Southwark Cathedral, in the same grave as his friend and mentor John Fletcher.

Other Work by Philip Massinger

The Plays and Poems of Philip Massinger. Edited by Colin Gibson and Philip Edwards. Oxford, U.K.: Clarendon Press, 1994.

Works about Philip Massinger

Adler, Doris. *Philip Massinger.* Boston: Twayne, 1987.
Clark, Ira. *The Moral Art of Philip Massinger.* Chester Springs, Pa.: Bucknell University Press, 1993.
Howard, Douglas, ed. *Philip Massinger: A Critical Reassessment.* Cambridge, U.K.: Cambridge University Press, 1985.

Medwall, Henry (fl. 1486) *dramatist*

Little is known about the life of Henry Medwall. He served as chaplain to Cardinal John Morton, archbishop of Canterbury, and was the rector of Balynghem during the English possession of Calais, France. In 1501 he seems to have been granted letters of protection allowing him to travel overseas, and a few months later he apparently resigned his post. Nothing else is known about his life.

Medwall's literary fame rests on the fact that he is one of the first known English vernacular dramatists in a period in which most drama was written in Latin. He composed his dramatic works for the entertainment of Cardinal Morton and guests. His *Nature* (1490) is an excellent model of an early morality play. This play tells the history of humankind in its struggle with the seven deadly sins. It is clear that this is a humanist rather than a medieval play, however, when Nature says that people must make choices based on both reason and sensuality. Sensuality is important because "If there be in him [humankind] no manner of feeling, / Nor no lively quickness, what lord is he? / A Lord made of clouts [rags] or carved out of tree."

Medwall's most famous work is *Fulgens and Lucrece* (1497), the earliest known secular English play and one of the first plays in English for which the date and place of its performance are known. The play, written to be performed for Cardinal Morton's household, is based on an Italian work.

Medwall translated the story of the heroine who must choose between two suitors and extended the original plot by writing a comic subplot into the story.

In later versions, Medwall's comedic subplot was often made into the main plot of the play. In the play, the heroine must choose between two suitors, one of humble origin but virtuous and the other of noble origin but evil.

When Cornelius asks Lucrece's father, Fulgens, for her hand, the older man replies, as any real father might,

> Syr, I shall do you the comfort that I can
> As far as she wil be advised by me.
> How be it, certeynly I am not the man
> That wyll take from her the liberte
> Of her owne choice—that may not be.
> But when I speke with her, I shall her
>   advyse
> To love you before other in all godely wyse.

Medwall's work was not only instrumental in anticipating a form of drama soon to become popular, but his work is also an important surviving example of 15th-century household drama.

Melville, Elizabeth (ca. 1570–ca. 1640)
poet

Elizabeth Melville, also known as Lady Colville of Culos, was born into a devout Presbyterian household, probably in Halhill, Scotland, the daughter of Sir James and Christina Boswell Melville. Few details are known about her personal life, but evidence of her religious piety is found in her chief work *Ane Godlie Dreame, Compylit in Scottis Meter* (1603). In this dramatic narrative, composed in 60 stanzas of *ottava rima* (eight-line stanzas most often found in Italian poetry), Melville imagines herself being guided in a pilgrimage through hell:

> The fyre was great, the heat did pearse me
>   sore,

> My faith grew weak, my grip was wondrous
>   small:
> I trembled fast, my feare grew more and
>   more.

The subject matter of Melville's poem makes it a sort of Calvinist version of Dante's *Inferno*, a Catholic devotional poem of the Middle Ages. *Ane Godlie Dreame* was not originally published under Melville's full name, just under the initials "M. M." for "Mistress Melville," in an edition that also included the text of her poem "A Verie Comfortable Song."

Melville's work was acclaimed by other writers of the period, including Alexander Hume, who dedicated his own *Hymnes or Sacred Songs* (1598) to this "Godlie daughter of a faithful father, . . . a tender youth . . . oft sighing & weeping through the conscience of sinne." Her work has also been compared to that of contemporary writers Aemelia LANYER and Rachel SPEGHT, women who also wrote religious poetry.

Some of Melville's other poems have been published in collections of Scottish verse of the period, such as a sonnet to the imprisoned Presbyterian John Welsch.

Works about Elizabeth Melville

Travitsky, Betty, and Patrick Cullen, eds. *The Early Modern Englishwoman: A Facsimile Library of Essential Works; Series 1, Printed Writings 1500–1640: Part 2; Volume 10.* Ashgate, Hants, England, and Burlington, Vt.: Aldershot, 2001.

Travitsky, Betty, *Paradise of Women: Writings by Englishwomen of the Renaissance.* Westport, Conn.: Greenwood, 1989.

Melville, Sir James (1535–1617) *memoirist*

James Melville began writing his memoirs when he was just 14 years old, serving as a page for Mary, Queen of Scots, while she lived in France, and continued writing for most of his very long life; he died at the age of 82. Thus, his memoirs serve as an invaluable source of detailed information about the period and are still used by scholars in their research.

Melville led an interesting life, traveling extensively throughout Europe. Bishops and royalty used him as a messenger, negotiator, and adviser. He discussed Queen Mary's marriage with Princess Elizabeth (later ELIZABETH I), went on a mission for Henry II of France, and witnessed the baptism of James VI of Scotland (later JAMES I OF ENGLAND). In one revealing passage, Melville tells about flattering Elizabeth. He is standing in a passageway, listening to her play the virginals, then steps into the doorway. Elizabeth, he says,

> Left off so soon as she turned about and saw me, and came forward, seeming to strike me with her left hand, and to think shame; alleging that she used not to play before men, but when she was solitary her alane, to eschew melancholy; and asked how I came there. I said, as I was walking . . . I passed by the chamber door. I heard such melody that ravished and drew me within the chamber I wist not how; excusing my fault of homelyness, as being brought up in the court of France, and was willing to suffer what kind of punishment would please her lay upon me for my offense.

Thus, in one ingenious swoop, Melville manages to insult Elizabeth's rival, MARY STUART—in whose French court he learned his so-called bad manners—and compliment Elizabeth's musicianship.

Melville spent the end of his life preparing his memoirs and living "a quiet contemplative life all the rest of his days." His memoirs were first published in 1683.

Other Work by Sir James Melville
Memoirs of His Own Life by Sir James Melville of Halhill: M.D.Xlix.–M.D.Xciii. From the Original Manuscript. New York: AMS Press, 1973.

Melville, James (1556–1614) *diarist, poet*
James Melville, nephew of the famous scholar and theologian Andrew Melville, was a regent of Glasgow University. He had a background in Greek and Hebrew, and, like his uncle, was a staunch Presbyterian.

From 1566 to 1601, Melville kept a journal, which not only captures life at that time, but the language as it was spoken in Scotland. For example, he describes a preacher at St. Andrews University who seemed weak and frail until he reached the pulpit, "bot or [but before] he haid done with his sermon he was sa active and vigorus, that he was lyk to ding that pulpit in blads and flie out of it."

Melville also wrote poems, many of them reflecting the religious strife in Britain. His journal was published in 1829. The original text was stored in Edinburgh's Advocates' Library and became part of the core collection of the National Library of Scotland when it was established in 1925 and absorbed the Advocates' Collection. The Melville journal has proved very useful for scholars and others who wish to understand daily life in the late 16th century.

Meres, Francis (1565–1647) *nonfiction writer, translator*
Francis Meres was born in Lincolnshire, England, and educated at Cambridge University, where he receive a B.A. in 1587 and an M.A. in 1591. In 1602 he became a vicar and a schoolmaster in Wing, Rutland.

Meres's first published works were his contributions to *Politeuphuia: Wit's Commonwealth* (1597), a series of books in which moral and philosophical quotations from classical Greek and Latin authors were collected. Meres's contributions to the series include chapters on books, philosophy, music, painting, religion, and poetry. The following year he published *God's Arithmetic* (1598), one of his sermons. Meres also published translations of the Spanish religious writer Luis de Grenada: *Grenado's Devotion* (1598) and *Sinner's Guide* (1614).

Meres is primarily remembered for his contributions to *Palladis Tamia, Wit's Treasury* (1598), a continuation of *Politeuphuia*. The most celebrated section of *Palladis Tamia* is a chapter entitled "A

Comparative Discourse of our English poets with the Greek, Latin, and Italian poets." To write this chapter, Meres strayed from the formula of the series, and instead of quoting authors, he judged English poets from Geoffrey Chaucer's time to his own by making comparisons between them and classical authors. His most famous statements concern William SHAKESPEARE, if only because they correspond to later evaluations of this playwright's work. Meres writes that "as Plautus and Seneca are accounted the best for Comedy and Tragedy among the Latins [the ancient Romans]: so Shakespeare among the English is the most excellent in both kinds for the stage." The scholars Richard Garnett and Edmund Gosse note that *Palladis Tamia* has thus "laid posterity under everlasting obligation by its notice of Shakespeare."

metaphysical poets

The term *metaphysical poets* is used to describe a group of poets of the 17th century who wrote lyric poetry in which wit, irony, and wordplay are applied to serious and emotionally resonant subjects. The term was first used, rather derisively, by John DRYDEN when he wrote of John DONNE in 1693:

> He affects the Metaphysics . . . in his amorous verses, where nature only should reign; and perplexes the minds of the fair sex with nice speculations of philosophy, when he should engage their hearts.

In Dryden's view, Donne's approach to love poetry was too artificial and intellectual. Samuel Johnson took up the term in the *Lives of the Poets* when he grouped Abraham COWLEY with "a race of writers that may be termed the metaphysical poets." Johnson saw the most characteristic feature of these poets' work as the use of far-fetched comparisons, a practice he disliked. It was not until the early 20th century, when T. S. Eliot took up their cause in his 1921 essay "The Metaphysical Poets," that the "metaphysicals" came to be appreciated as fully as they were in their own day.

Besides Donne and Cowley, the metaphysical poets usually included in the group are Richard CRASHAW, George HERBERT, Andrew MARVELL, Thomas TRAHERNE, and Henry VAUGHAN. Several were Anglican ministers by profession. Most of them wrote predominantly religious poetry, though, as Dryden noted, Donne wrote love poetry that was as knotty and intellectually demanding as his devotional work. The scholar Earl Miner, in several studies of 17th-century poetry, distinguished between the "private mode" of the metaphysical poets and the "social mode" of CAVALIER POETRY. Whether writing about God or a woman, the metaphysical focus is on the poet's private relationship, not on its social context. These poets did not write for publication, although they showed their work to friends who would be able to appreciate their sometimes obscure references. They reacted against the pretty rhythms and conventional imagery popular in much Elizabeth verse. Their rhythms are irregular and often reflect those of everyday speech. Their imagery is drawn not from literary tradition but from the current knowledge of the day, as in Donne's references to exploration, or from daily life, as in Herbert's references to a broom. In all their work, the intellect and passion are in creative tension. As Helen Gardner, one of the most influential scholars to study this movement, said in the 1957 introduction to her anthology *The Metaphysical Poets,*

> Argument and persuasion, and the use of the conceit as their instrument, are the elements or body of a metaphysical poem. Its quintessence or soul is the vivid imagining of a moment of experience or a situation out of which the need to argue, or persuade, or define arises.

Works about the Metaphysical Poets

Reid, David. *The Metaphysical Poets.* New York: Longman, 2000.

Williamson, George. *Six Metaphysical Poets: A Reader's Guide.* Syracuse, N.Y.: Syracuse University Press, 2001.

Middleton, Thomas (1580–1627)

playwright, poet

Thomas Middleton is recorded as having been baptized in London in April 1580, as the son of William Middleton, a master bricklayer, and Anne Snow Middleton. Middleton was already writing poetry in his teens; by 1600 he had published three volumes of verse. He entered Queen's College, Oxford University, in 1598, but apparently did not receive a degree. By 1602, when his play *Blurt, Master Constable* was published, he was probably already an established playwright.

Middleton was hardworking and prolific. He provided a steady stream of materials for the boys' companies (theatrical units that often performed at court), especially Boys of St. Pauls, as well as for the ADMIRAL'S MEN. He collaborated with many other playwrights, including Thomas DEKKER, with whom he wrote the comedies *The Honest Whore* (1604) and *The Roaring Girl* (1610); and William ROWLEY, with whom he wrote the comedies *A Fair Quarrel* (published 1617), *The World Tossed at Tennis* (1620), and the great tragicomedy *The Changeling* (acted in 1624 but not published until 1653). He is sometimes thought to have collaborated with William SHAKESPEARE on the scenes involving the witches and Hecate in *Macbeth* (1605–06).

Of the plays that Middleton wrote alone, 16 survive. The majority of them are comedies, often set in London's slums and portraying the conning of country people by city slickers. A frequent target of Middleton's satire is the hypocrisy of the middle class. *A Chaste Maid in Cheapside* is among the best of this group. It relates the efforts of the licentious Sir Walter Whorehound to arrange a marriage between his mistress (presented as his niece and as a "chaste maid") and the foolish young rich man whose lovely sister, Moll, Whorehound wishes to marry himself, and how Moll, with the help of the young man she loves, thwarts his schemes.

The political satire in *A Game at Chess* had an unprecedented success when it was produced in 1624, running for nine consecutive nights. Such a feat was unheard of in the days when the potential audience was small, and to keep people coming theaters usually changed the program every night. *Chess* concerned the relations between England and Spain and the unpopular project to arrange a marriage between Charles, Prince of Wales (the future King Charles I), and a Spanish princess. The characters are named for chess pieces, but it was obvious to everyone that the White King represented JAMES I, the Black King Philip IV of Spain, and the Black Knight the unpopular Spanish ambassador to London. The over-the-top characterization of the Black Knight especially delighted audiences. The Black Knight is so deep into intrigue that when confronted with "Your plot's discovered, Sir!" his response is, "Which of the twenty thousand and nine hundred / Four score and five, canst tell?" The Spaniards were understandably outraged by this characterization of their ambassador, and out of diplomatic necessity the play was closed by the authorities, and the actors and playwright mildly fined.

The tragedy *Women Beware Women* (ca. 1622) concerns the seduction of a middle-class wife by the profligate duke of Florence and its radiating consequences; the subplot involves the incestuous love of Hippolito for his niece, and both plots hinge on the machinations of the corrupt Livia. The final scene, hilarious yet so gory it verges on black humor, has prompted some scholars to suggest that Middleton is the true author of the macabre *The Revenger's Tragedy* (1607), which is traditionally attributed to Cyril TOURNEUR.

Middleton was not entirely dependent on the theater for his livelihood; he wrote many masques to be acted by noble amateurs in their homes. Beginning in 1613, he was frequently employed by the lord mayor to write pageants for the city of London, and in 1620 he won the post of city chronologer, or historian, which he held until his death. His successor in this job was Ben JONSON, whose opinion of Middleton, that he was "a base fellow" and not a true poet, has been overturned in recent years. The scholar Matthew Martin remarks in his introduction to a special issue of *Early Modern Literary Studies* devoted to Middleton that

Today Middleton is recognized as one of the most complex and perhaps the most versatile of early modern English dramatists . . . [S]everal recent critics have claimed Middleton as the early modern dramatist whose concerns are particularly resonant with our own.

Other Works by Thomas Middleton

Selected Plays of Thomas Middleton. Edited by David Frost. New York: Cambridge University Press, 1978.

Five Plays. Edited by Bryan Loughrey and Neil Taylor. New York: Penguin, 1988.

Works about Thomas Middleton

Heinemann, Margot. *Puritanism and Theatre: Thomas Middleton and Opposition Drama Under the Early Stuarts.* New York: Cambridge University Press, 1980.

Heller, Herbert Jack. *Penitent Brothellers: Grace, Sexuality, and Genre in Thomas Middleton's City Comedies.* Newark: University of Delaware Press, 2000.

Howard-Hill, T. H. *Middleton's "Vulgar Pasquin": Essays on "A Game at Chess."* Newark: University of Delaware Press, 1995.

Kistner, A. L. *Middleton's Tragic Themes.* New York: P. Lang, 1984.

Steen, Susan Jayne. *Ambrosia in an Earthern Vessel: Three Centuries of Audience and Reader Response to the Works of Thomas Middleton.* New York: AMS Press, 1993.

White, Martin. *Middleton and Tourneur.* New York: St. Martin's Press, 1992.

Mildmay, Lady Grace Sherrington

(1552–1620) *diarist, nonfiction writer*

Lady Grace Sherrington Mildmay was born into a noble family; her father was Sir Henry Sherrington. Her aunt schooled her at home, giving her an educational advantage over attending an elementary school, which only taught girls to read.

Sherrington kept a journal that recorded her daily activities. In one typical passage, she notes that when her aunt saw her "idly disposed, she would set me to cypher with a pen and to cast up and prove great sums and accounts." Clearly, part of her training included the ability to keep the household accounts. Also included in her journal are details of other lessons a young woman being groomed for society would receive, including the study of music, literature, and needlework.

In 1597 Sherrington married Anthony Mildmay, the son of Sir Walter Mildmay and nephew to Sir Francis Walsingham, who was secretary of state of ELIZABETH I. Shortly after their marriage, Anthony was knighted. The couple had one child, a daughter named Mary. Excerpts from Mildmay's diary, with a commentary by R. Weigall, were published in 1911.

Milton, John (1608–1674) *poet, essayist, dramatist*

John Milton was born in Cheapside, London, on December 9, 1608. His father, also named John, was a scrivener, or copyist of legal documents, who composed music and dabbled in poetry. His mother, Sarah Jeffrey (or Jeffries) Milton, was the daughter of a sailor. Milton's father came from a well-to-do family, but he had been disinherited because he rejected Catholicism and conformed to the CHURCH OF ENGLAND. Nevertheless, he did well for himself and was able to afford an excellent education for his son, whom he considered to be an especially apt student.

Milton began his formal education at St. Paul's Cathedral School, and he also worked with a tutor, Thomas Young, for many years. Young was a Scottish Presbyterian who influenced his pupil's religious philosophy, which Milton later articulated in both his prose and his poetry. Even as a very young man, he was known to study into the wee hours of the morning, a habit that some felt contributed to the loss of his eyesight later in life. Milton continued his studies at Christ's College, Cambridge University, beginning in 1625, but he was "rusticated," or sent home for a period, because he could not get along with his tutor there. After he returned to his studies with a new tutor, he graduated with a master's degree in 1632. While in the university Milton was dubbed the "lady of Christ's," a nickname that may have been either a compliment to his good looks or a slur on his masculinity.

After Milton graduated, his father further indulged him by allowing him to live at home for the next five years to continue his studies of literature, history, and languages. By the time this period had ended, Milton had written several of his most enduring poetic works: "On the Morning of Christ's Nativity" (1629), *Comus* (1634), *Lycidas* (1637), and *L'Allegro* and *Il Penseroso* (ca. 1632).

On the Morning of Christ's Nativity was written when Milton was just 21. In the opening lines of the poem, Milton imagines nature on the morning of Christ's birth, "in aw to him" and hiding her "guilty front," with "innocent snow . . . the Saintly Vail of Maiden white." As befits a hymn, this early work is written in regular, rhymed, eight-line stanzas, and its vision of the peace and harmony brought by the birth of Christ is youthful and beautiful:

> But peacefull was the night
> Wherein the Prince of light
> His raign of peace upon the earth began:
> The Windes with wonder whist,
> Smoothly the waters kist,
> Whispering new joyes to the milde Ocean.

Comus is a masque, or play in verse, dedicated to the Earl of Bridgewater, the lord-lieutenant of Wales, and acted by members of his family. The story tells how Comus, a supernatural creature, attempts to seduce a young girl, its theme being the value of chastity. Many critics see Comus himself as an early version of Milton's Satan—an eloquent tempter who tries to lure the Lady from the path of duty.

Lycidas is considered by many to be the greatest elegy, or poem of lamentation, ever written; in fact, one Milton biographer, the Rev. Mark Pattison, has called it "the high-water mark of English poetry." *Lycidas* was written in honor of Edward King, a classmate of Milton's at Cambridge, who had drowned on a voyage to Ireland in 1637. The poem has been praised for the unequaled beauty of its language and Milton's unconventional use of stanzas and lines of unequal length. *Lycidas,* though full of classical references, is a thoroughly Christian elegy in that the poet celebrates the immortality of the dead man's soul by reference to Christ's redemption:

> Weep no more, woful Shepherds, weep no
>   more,
> For Lycidas your sorrow is not dead . . .
> [he is] mounted high,
> Through the dear might of him that walk'd
>   the waves . . .
> In the blest Kingdoms meet of joy and love.
> There entertain him all the Saints above,
> In solemn troops, and sweet Societies
> That sing, and singing in their glory move
> And wipe the tears for ever from his eyes.

Lycidas is the first of Milton's poems to articulate his anticlerical views, in that St. Peter denounces corrupt clergy who are "swoln with wind" and who "Rot inwardly, and foul contagion spread."

The twin poems *L'Allegro,* and *Il Penseroso* are written in the classical tradition of *synchrisis,* in which the writer debates the value of two opposing ideas. In these paired poems, Milton opposes mirth and melancholy. *L'Allegro,* in favor of mirth, is written in a light and bubbling style, full of "Jest, and youth jollity," while *Il Penseroso,* in praise of "sage and holy" melancholy, is written in tones "sober, stedfast, and demure."

In 1638 Milton continued his education by traveling in France and Italy. He planned to spend time in Greece as well, but the political situation in England led him to cut his travels short; he returned home in August 1639, during the First Bishop's War. Scottish Presbyterians, outraged at Charles's attempts to impose English forms of worship on them, abolished bishops and rebelled. Charles himself led an army against them, first in 1639 and again in 1640. Milton opposed Charles in both religion and politics. Milton despised priests and bishops and believed that each individual could and should have a relationship with God without the intermediary of clergy or formal religion. Charles, of course, was head of the Anglican Church, and Milton rejected the doctrine of the divine right of kings—which Charles repeatedly invoked to sanction his high-handed imposition of taxes, declarations of war, and dissolution of Parliament.

Upon his return to England, Milton began to take in students to tutor, but eventually he became embroiled in a number of controversies and devoted most of his time to writing polemical tracts. The subjects of his prose works can be grouped into three major categories: religion—specifically attacks on the institution of bishops; social and political topics such as divorce, freedom of the press, and education; and justifications for the execution of Charles I.

In 1643 Milton married Mary Powell; he was 35 and she 17. After barely a month of marriage, Mary returned to her parents' home and refused to return to her husband. In that same year Milton wrote one of his most famous essays, "The Doctrine and Discipline of Divorce," in which he argued that "the mis-interpreting of some Scripture directed mainly against the abusers of the Law for divorce giv'n by *Moses,* hath chang'd the blessing of matrimony not seldome into a familiar and co-inhabiting mischiefe; at least into a drooping and disconsolate houshold captivity, without refuge or redemption." Using close argumentation and reference to scripture, Milton argued that the grounds for divorce should include spiritual incompatibility. This essay, and the fact that Milton was so sure of his righteousness that he asked another woman to marry him while he was still bound to Mary Powell, led to a firestorm of controversy—so much so that for some years the term *miltonist* was used to refer to someone who did not believe in the sacredness of marriage.

In 1644 Milton published "Areopagitica." The title refers to an essay of the same name by Isocrates, in which the Greek philosopher demands political reform and includes in his criticism the judges of the Athenian court of Areopagus.

Milton's essay is today regarded as one of the first and most powerful pleas for freedom of the press, though its original purpose was to argue against censorship of works before they were printed, and he does not include Catholics in his demand for tolerance.

In 1645, when Charles I's Royalist forces were defeated by parliamentarians, the Powell family, which had supported the monarchy, came to Milton for protection. Milton took the family in and his wife back. Mary bore her husband three daughters before her death in 1652 at the age of 27. Milton married twice more—in 1656 to Catherine Woodcock, who died in childbirth in 1658; and in 1663 to Elizabeth Minshull. Milton's sorrow at Catherine's death led to the composition of one of his most famous sonnets, which begins, "Methought I saw my late espoused saint / Brought to me like Alcestis from the grave."

In 1649, after the execution of Charles I, Milton was invited to become secretary for the foreign tongues (writer of diplomatic correspondence in Latin) for the new government under Oliver Cromwell. In the same year he published another of his famous essays, "Tenure of Kings and Magistrates," in which he argues that it is not wrong to depose and execute a tyrannical ruler.

Though he wrote little poetry during the years between the ascendancy of Cromwell and the Restoration, one of his most famous sonnets, "On His Blindness," was composed during this period. By 1652 Milton's eyesight, which had been failing for many years, was gone. In the poem he laments the loss of his vision and the limits this places on his ability to serve God, but he comforts himself in the final lines of the poem that "They also serve who only stand and waite."

When Charles II was restored to the British throne in 1660, Milton was arrested and imprisoned, but he was eventually pardoned and released. He moved his family to a home near Bunhill Fields, a military marching ground near London, where he lived for the rest of his life. His greatest works were published during the late 1660s and early 1670s—*Paradise Lost* (1667), *Par-*

adise Regained (1671), and Samson Agonistes (1671)—although parts of Paradise Lost were probably written earlier. Paradise Lost tells the story of the fall of Adam and Eve, Paradise Regained deals with the redemption of humanity through Christ, and Samson Agonistes portrays the revenge on the Philistines of the blind Samson as he pulls the temple down on them and himself.

John Milton died on November 8, 1674, of the gout.

Critical Analysis

Many consider Paradise Lost among the greatest poetic works in English, sublime in both subject and style. Milton summarizes the entire poem in his opening invocation to the muse. "Sing Heav'nly Muse," he says,

> OF Mans First Disobedience, and the Fruit
> Of that Forbidden Tree, whose mortal tast
> Brought Death into the World, and all our
>   woe,
> With loss of Eden, till one greater man
> Restore us, and regain the blissful Seat. . . .

He later says that his purpose is to "justifie the wayes of God to men."

The epic, written in unrhymed iambic pentameter—the same verse form used by William SHAKESPEARE—opens in hell, as Satan and his followers recover from defeat after their rebellion against God. Satan vows to continue his revenge on earth and to tempt Adam and Eve to evil. Despite specific warnings by Raphael against Satan, Eve succumbs, flattered by Satan's praise of her beauty, his rhetoric, and the seeming reasonableness of his arguments:

> Into her heart too easie [Satan] entrance
>   won:
> Fixt on the Fruit she gaz'd, which to behold
> Might tempt alone, and in her ears the
>   sound
> Yet rung of his perswasive words, impregn'd

> With Reason, to her seeming, and with
>   Truth.

Eve then tries to convince Adam to do as she has done and taste the forbidden fruit. Adam is horrified at her tale and laments that she is "lost / Defac't, deflourd, and now to Death devote." Despite his superior understanding of the consequences of Eve's act, Adam eats the fruit because he cannot bear to have eternal life while Eve is condemned to die. He is seduced by her charm as well as by fear of loneliness.

This episode in the poem highlights the central dilemma of faith that is the heart of Milton's epic. Human reason is flawed, more so after the fall. God's truth cannot be arrived at by reason; reason, in fact, may lead in the other direction. Faith can only be arrived at by faith.

Many scholars and critics who have read Paradise Lost have also been seduced by Satan fully as much as Eve herself. The romantics, in particular, found Satan to be magnificent in his defiance and admirable in his rebellion. According to Percy Bysshe Shelley in A Defence of Poetry (1821), for example,

> Milton's poem contains within itself a philosophical refutation of that system, of which, by a strange and natural antithesis; it has been a chief popular support. Nothing can exceed the energy and magnificence of the character of Satan as expressed in Paradise Lost. It is a mistake to suppose that he could ever have been intended for the popular personification of evil.

William Blake went so far as to say that Milton was "of the Devil's party without knowing it," and a critical debate has arisen between those who see Milton as sincere in his religious beliefs and those who felt that he too was seduced by his own creation into a kind of blasphemy. Stanley Fish, in Surprised by Sin (1967), goes far to resolve the debate by suggesting that Milton deliberately created an alluring Satan to put the reader through the same sort of temptation that the characters go through, precisely because humankind has inherited Adam and Eve's tendency to be drawn to Satan.

In keeping with the theme of good versus evil, the primary images in the poem are those of light and darkness. God is the "Bright effluence of bright essence increate," and hell is "darkness visible." Perhaps Milton's own blindness contributed to the power and glory with which he infuses images of light—the very privilege denied him in life. Many scholars also attribute the beauty of the poem's language to Milton's blindness. Because he dictated the poem, he was able to pay particular attention to sound.

In the 19th and 20th centuries, Milton's Eve has created almost as much controversy as his Satan. British critic Herbert Grierson called Milton "a sore, angry, intolerant, and arrogant critic of women," based largely on his portrayal of Eve. She is clearly portrayed as an example of the inferior sex. Adam and Eve are

> *Not equal, as thir sex not equal seemd;*
> *For contemplation he and valour formd,*
> *For softness shee and sweet attractive Grace,*
> *Hee for God only, shee for God in him:*

He adds that Eve's hair falls in "wanton ringlets wav'd / As the Vine curles her tendrils, which impli'd / Subjection." Without Adam by her side, Eve strays, and it is her vanity and weakness, according to Milton, that lead to the fall. Although Eve is beautiful, it is Adam who is made in God's image.

Some feminist readers have recently revisited Milton and taken a different view of his attitude toward women. For example, Stevie Davies, author of *Milton* (1991), says, that her "feminist approach is based on a perception that Milton at once identified himself with and vehemently disowned something female which was experienced as part of the self."

However, although modern readers may be somewhat put off by Milton's morality and his supposed chauvinism, no one with a taste for po-etry can ignore the sheer beauty of the verse. Here, for example, Christ describes his resurrection:

> *I shall rise Victorious, and subdue*
> *My Vanquisher, spoild of his vanted spoile;*
> *Death his deaths wound shall then receive,*
> *   and stoop*
> *Inglorious, of his mortal sting disarm'd*
> *   (Paradise Lost).*

Master of the majestic as well as the lyric, Milton is surely one of the two or three greatest poets in the English language.

Other Work by John Milton
The Riverside Milton. Edited by Roy Flannagan. New York: Houghton Mifflin, 1998.

Works about John Milton
Davies, Stevie. *Milton.* Harvester New Reading Series. London: Harvester Wheatsheaf, 1991.
Fish, Stanley Eugene. *How Milton Works.* Cambridge, Mass.: Harvard University Press, 2001.
Lewalski, Barbara. *The Life of John Milton: A Critical Biography.* Oxford, U.K.: Blackwell, 2002.
Parker, William Riley. *Milton: A Biography: The Life.* Oxford, U.K.: Clarendon Press, 1996.

Molière (Jean-Baptiste Poquelin)
(1622–1673) *playwright, actor*
Molière was born the oldest of six children at the so-called Monkey House, an ancient dwelling in an elegant quarter of Paris near the Louvre, to Jean Poquelin the younger, King Louis XIV's *tapissier* (master merchant upholsterer/furnisher) and Marie Cressé. As an adolescent Molière attended the Collège de Clermont, located in the Latin Quarter near the Seine River. This large Jesuit school offered a rigorous curriculum including Latin and Greek, rhetoric, acting, debate, philosophy, science, and theology. Evidence suggests Molière later studied law, possibly at Orléans, and perhaps philosophy as well.

On December 14, 1637, Molière inherited his father's title and office of *tapissier du roi* and spent at least one summer with the royal military, which was camped on the shores of the Mediterranean, in charge of arranging one of two tents that served as royal field palaces. But the lure of the stage proved too intense for Molière. In 1643 he ceded his royal office to his brother Jean and formed the Illustre Théâtre troupe with his mistress, Madeleine Béjart, a beautiful and talented actress. The troupe's beginnings, however, were fraught with difficulty. Soon they could not make ends meet. Molière was arrested and jailed until a friend posted bail, and after only two years the Illustre Théâtre was doomed.

For the next 13 years Molière and Madeleine lived the lives of itinerant artists, mostly in the southern provinces, where they obtained the PATRONAGE of the prince de Conti, under whom Molière embarked on his career as a playwright. In 1658 the actors returned to Paris to perform at the court under the protection of King Louis XIV's brother. Molière's first successful play, *Les Précieuses ridicules* (*The Folly of Affection*), which ran for 34 consecutive performances, testified to the author's extraordinary talent for comedy. The play portrays two young men who are trying to win the affections of two women, Magdelon and Cathos, who have elevated ideas about courtship based on their readings of popular romances. King Louis XIV was enthralled by the play, and henceforth Molière was destined to become, as Judd Hubert remarks in his *Molière and the Comedy of Intellect,* "by far the greatest creator of dramatic forms in the entire history of French literature, comparable in this respect to Shakespeare."

Molière worked incessantly, writing 19 plays in quick succession, including some of his masterpieces: *The Misanthrope, Dom Juan, Tartuffe, The School for Wives, The Would-be Gentleman,* and *The Miser.* Molière was not only an author but also functioned as manager and accountant of his troupe, as well as the producer, director, and main actor of its plays. Molière's company performed theater in Paris but also provided elaborate entertainments featuring sophisticated set designs, music, dance, fireworks, reflecting pools, fountain shows, and dramatic amusements at the king's behest.

When he was 40 Molière married Armande Béjart, 20 years his junior and daughter of his former mistress, Madeleine. Although he was an extraordinarily popular playwright, his plays' increasingly satirical tone and pungent social criticism often questioned traditional morality as well as religious and social norms. He mocked the aristocracy, the nouveaux riches (newly wealthy people), physicians, pedants (people who like to show off their knowledge), cuckolds (men whose wives cheat on them), the *précieuses* (women espousing a style of excessive refinement), and, of course, religious hypocrites. *Tartuffe,* a play concerning one such hypocrite, a con artist who plays on people's religious beliefs, created a major controversy. For five years Molière had to fight with church authorities, until Louis XIV finally allowed a modified version of the play to be staged. Although Molière had many enemies as a result of his satiric pen, he also had influential courtly and literary allies at the French court, including the king himself.

On February 17, 1673, an ill and weak Molière was to act the role of the Hypochondriac. Aware of his feebleness, his wife begged him not to perform that day, but he refused to let down all the theater workers who depended on him for their livelihood. He managed to get through nearly all his lines until he was seized with a convulsion, which he attempted to cover up with laughter. He died an hour later while awaiting the arrival of a priest. The chair in which Molière acted during this last performance remains on display to this day at the Comédie-Française. Molière's troupe merged with the other two Parisian companies seven years after his death, giving birth to the illustrious Comédie-Française.

Critical Analysis

The Molière biographer Grimarest recounts this exchange between Louis XIV and Molière at a court dinner: "Look, isn't that your doctor? What does he do for you?" "Sire," answered Molière, "we reason together; he orders remedies for me; I don't take them, and I get well." Discouraged by his declining health and the inability of the medical profession to cure him, Molière satirizes its inefficient and dogmatic procedures in his last play, entitled *Le Malade imaginaire* (*The Hypochondriac*). The hypochondriac of the title is Argan, who lives among his potions and drugs and surrounds himself with a bevy of doctors and druggists. They rule his world, often confusing medicine with religion, as they require a strict adherence to a barrage of ritual bleedings, purges, and prescriptions. When Argan misses one of his treatments, an irate doctor Purgon chastises him and condemns him to a litany of ailments, such as "dysentery, dropsy, and deprivation of life." As is common in Molière's plays, a servant provides the voice of reason amid the madness. The chambermaid Toinette impersonates an illustrious physician:

> TOINETTE: What on earth are you doing with
> this arm?
> ARGAN: What?
> TOINETTE: There is an arm I would cut off
> straight away if I were you.
> ARGAN: But why?
> TOINETTE: Don't you see that it is taking all
> of the nutrients, and that it is keeping the
> other side from benefiting?

Toinette does not succeed in her goal of scaring Argan straight, proposing such ridiculous treatments that he is cured of his hypochondria. Instead, the play ends in a frenzied grand finale where the hypochondriac decides to become a doctor himself in order to provide himself treatment during a farcical music and dance ceremony conducted in hilariously bad Latin. Here comedy and entertainment reign supreme, and while it is perhaps the greatest comedic irony and paradox that Molière died just after playing this role, this fact underscores, in Hallam Walker's words, that "his final physical efforts, like his whole existence, had been dedicated to the service of his art."

Molière's influence on British theater can hardly be overestimated. Many of his plots were borrowed for the British stage and many British playwrights wrote adaptations of his works. For example, Henry Fielding wrote *Miser* (1733) based on Molière's *L'Avare,* the character of Manly in WYCHERLEY's *The Plain Dealer* is based on Molière's *Misanthrope,* and Colly Cibber's *Non-Juror* is an adaptation of *Tartuffe.* Perhaps more important, however, British playwrights borrowed the very idea of comedy about social aberrants, such as misers and misanthropes, from Molière.

Other Works by Molière

The Misanthrope, Tartuffe, and Other Plays. Translated by Maya Slater. Oxford: Oxford University Press, 2001.
Eight Plays by Molière. Translated by Morris Bishop. Mattituck, N.Y.: Aeonian Press, 1986.

Works about Molière

Walker, Hallam. *Molière.* Boston: Twayne, 1990.
Scott, Virginia. *Molière, A Theatrical Life.* Cambridge: Cambridge University Press, 2000.

Mollineux, Mary (1651–1691) *poet*

Quaker poet Mary Southworth Mollineux of Liverpool was a voice of religious opposition in 17th-century England. In the preface to Mollineux's only published volume of poems, *Fruits of Retirement; or Miscellaneous Poems, Moral and Divine* (1702), her cousin Frances Owen describes her childhood, in which Mollineux's "weak eyes" resulted in her father's bringing her up to "more Learning, than is commonly bestowed upon our Sex," as she was "unfit for the usual Employment of Girls." Although much of her education was based in the classical tradition, she was one "who loved to read the Holy Scriptures," and much of her poetry focuses on biblical subjects.

In 1684 Mollineux met her future husband, Henry Mollineux, while both were imprisoned in Lancaster Castle for attending Quaker meetings, and they were married the following year. The scholar Sharon Achinstein points out that, perhaps as a result of Mollineux's prison experiences, "her poems repeatedly imagine open spaces and enclosures, confinements, and the dizzying heights of rocks and towers."

Though Mollineux's collection of poems was published posthumously in 1702, the first poem of the volume, "The Fall of Men," based on the book of Genesis, dates to 1663. Her poetic volume contains many other retellings of biblical stories, including "On Elijah," "On Daniel," "On Israel's Rebellion," and "On David and Jonathan"; as well as poems focusing upon moral preservation, including "Of Chastity," "Of Charity," and "Of Modesty." Also included are several hymns, epistles, and meditations in which Mollineux often invokes biblical references. In such poems as "Meditations in Trouble," Mollineux laments her sense of isolation:

> O Whither is he gone? Or where
> Shall I go mourn, till he appear,
> Who is my life, my love?
> Alas, how shall I move
> Him to return, that's secretly retired
> Like unto one displeased,
> Who, till he be appeased,
> My heart cannot be eased?
> He is one lovely, and to be admired!

In "A Meditation," Mollineux describes her hope that her persecutors will be brought to justice, condemning her "Tyranizing Foes / Who did her Children dear expose / T'exile and Banishment." According to Achinstein, Mollineux's work exemplifies "how personal anguish and social protest converge in acts of poetic devotion."

Montaigne, Michel Eyquem de
(1533–1592) *nonfiction writer*

Michael de Montaigne was born not far from Bordeaux, France, to Pierre Eyquem, a herring merchant, and Antoinette Lopez Eyquem. In 1539 he was sent to the College de Guienne at Bordeaux, and eight years later he took up the study of law. In 1554 he was made a counselor in the Bordeaux parliament, and he later spent much time at the French court.

In 1571 Montaigne retired to his country estate, resolved to pursue a life of study and contemplation. His plans, however, were interrupted by travels throughout France and official business. Despite these interruptions to his contemplative life, he managed to write three volumes titled *Essais* (*Essays*), two of which were published in 1580 and the third in 1588.

At least at first, Montaigne's writings seem to have been written by gathering together some thoughts and quotations on a particular subject, without any effort to follow a plan. Montaigne labeled each of these efforts an "essai," which simply means "attempt" or "trial" in French, because he was attempting to explore a particular subject in each piece of writing. These apparently haphazard meditations were a completely new literary form.

Critical Analysis

Throughout Montaigne's essays, he questions the accepted truths of his age, and this skepticism proved very influential to later writers, as did his essay form. John FLORIO first translated Montaigne's essays into English in 1603. They were read by, among others, William SHAKESPEARE and Francis BACON, the latter of whom was among the first in English to adapt the essay form to his own purposes. As the scholar Jonathan Dollimore observes, Montaigne participated in "a process of demystification"—that is, he exposed the social origin of customs that were traditionally said to have been established by God.

Montaigne pointed out that there was a diversity of customs in the world, and that this diversity showed there were no universal natural laws, because there is no law that is not "impugned or disallowed, not by one nation, but by many." Montaigne was suggesting that laws could be changed to improve society. Yet Montaigne remained a conservative thinker, keeping, as the critic David Norbrook writes, "a respect for custom and tradition" and believing that change would likely lead to social chaos.

The *Essais* begin with a short address to the reader in which Montaigne describes the purpose of his writing. One sentence in this address reveals what is perhaps the source of both his conservatism and his skepticism: "[I]f my fortune had been to have lived among those nations, which yet are said to live under the sweet liberty of Nature's first and uncorrupted laws, I assure thee, I would most willingly have portrayed myself fully naked."

Montaigne's assertion is conservative because it draws upon RENAISSANCE philosophers, influenced by NEOPLATONISM, or the revival of the idealist philosophy of Plato. These philosophers argued, in the scholar Frances Yates's words, that "the old, the primary, [was] nearest to divine truth" because God's influence, it was believed, was more powerful the closer one was to The Fall. In other words, the oldest laws of society are the best, and as time progresses the new laws that are created grow further away from God's intentions.

Montaigne also suggests that we cannot simply revive the original laws. The idea of presenting a portrait of himself "in all his nakedness," after all, calls attention to the inappropriateness of following the laws humans were originally expected to follow in the present. The world's corruption has made it impractical for us to follow those laws.

The *Essais* themselves cover a diverse collection of subjects, and what is most striking about them is their doubt about finding certainty. In "Of Prognostications," or prophesies, for instance, Montaigne ridicules astrological almanacs and those "who study and comment on their almanacs and cite their authority in current events": "With all they say, they necessarily tell both truth and falsehood. *For who is there who, shooting all day, will not sometimes hit the mark?*" . . .

Montaigne explains why people continue to accept such beliefs: "This I have seen with my own eyes, that in public disorders men stunned by their own fate will throw themselves back, as on any superstition, on seeking in the heavens the ancient causes and threats of their misfortune." He adds that the language of prophecy is so vague that

those who are trained in this subtle trick of tying and untying knots would be capable of finding, in any writings, whatever they want. But what gives them an especially good chance to pay is the obscure, ambiguous and fantastic language of the prophetic jargon, to which their authors give no clear meaning, so that posterity can apply to it whatever meanings it pleases.

Montaigne, however, cannot rest in such certainty. Rather than simply accept the truth of his own assertions, he concludes by admitting that the divine inspiration needed to give correct prophecies exists: "I have had some as weak in reason as violent in persuasiveness . . . by which I let myself be carried away so usefully and fortunately that they might be judged to have in them something of divine inspiration."

Thus, the translator J. M. Cohen remarks, "One sees, as one reads [Montaigne], how broad his mind was, and how many of the ideas of the next two centuries he grasped by anticipation."

Other Works by Michael de Montaigne

Apology for Raymond Sebond. Translated by Roger Ariew and Marjorie Grene. Indianapolis: Hackett, 2003.

The Complete Works: Essays, Travel Journal, Letters. Translated by Donald M. Frame. New York: A. A. Knopf, 2003.

Works about Michel de Montaigne

Heitsch, Dorothea B. *Practicing Reform in Montaigne's Essais.* Boston: Brill, 2000.

Hugo, Friedrich, and Philippe Desan. *Montaigne.* Translated by Dawn Eng. Berkeley: University of California Press, 1991.

Leschemelle, Pierre. *Montaigne, or, the Anguished Soul.* Translated by William J. Beck. New York: P. Lang, 1994.

Levine, Alan. *Sensual Philosophy: Toleration, Skepticism, and Montaigne's Politics of the Self.* Lanham, Md.: Lexington Books, 2001.

Montgomerie, Alexander (ca. 1556–1610)
poet, pageant writer

Alexander Montgomerie was born on Easter Sunday at Hessilhead Castle, Argyle, Scotland. His father was Hugh Montgomerie, and his brother Robert later became the archbishop of Glasgow. Montgomerie was privately educated and later became the unofficial poet laureate of the court of King James VI of Scotland (later JAMES I OF ENGLAND), though he subsequently fell out of favor with the Scottish court.

Montgomerie's poetic style was influenced by the Scottish poet Alexander Scott and by English sonneteers such as Thomas WYATT and Henry Howard, Earl of SURREY. He also wrote several pageants that were enacted at court, including *The Navigation* (1579) and *A Cartell of Three Ventrous Knights* (1579), both speeches praising James.

Montgomerie's most famous work, *The Cherry and the Sloe* (1597), is a long allegorical poem written in complex 14-lined stanzas. Its central idea is a choice between convenience and ambition. Here, a young man must choose between a luscious crop of cherries on a distant crag and a less appealing sloe bush at his feet: "With earnest eye whil I espye / The fruit betwixt me and the skye." *The Cherry and the Sloe* was extremely well-received and remained a favorite of Scottish readers for the next two centuries. It appeared in several versions in different editions of his work, including a Latin translation.

Montgomerie's other works include *The Flyting Betwixt Montgomery and Polwort* (1621), a collection of 70 sonnets of insult humor; and *The Mindes Melodie,* a poetic version of King David's Psalms. He is noted for his adherence to Middle Scots poetic traditions—that is, to poetry in the Scots dialect rather than in English—and is considered the greatest Scottish poet of his time.

Other Work by Alexander Montgomerie
Poems. Edited by David J. Parkinson. Edinburgh: Scottish Text Society, 2000.

A Work about Alexander Montgomerie
Jack, Ronald D. S. *Alexander Montgomerie.* Edinburgh: Scottish Academic Press, 1985.

Montrose, Marquis of
See GRAHAM, JAMES.

More, Henry (1614–1687) *nonfiction writer, poet*
Henry More, the son of Alexander and Anne Lacy More, was born in Grantham, Lincolnshire, England. He was educated at Eton and Christ's College, Cambridge University, receiving an M.A. in 1639. He led a quiet life as a scholar and writer, and refused to advance his career in the larger world.

More's first major work was *Philosophicall Poems,* including "Song of the Soul" (1647), poetry based on the works of the Greek philosopher Plato. Plato's philosophy was also an influence on his first major work of philosophy, *An Antidote against Atheism* (1652), which attempted to use logic to prove the existence of God. Early in this book, however, More says that logic does not entirely work in this case: "Wherefore when I say that I will demonstrate that there is a God, I do not promise that I will produce such arguments, that the Reader shall acknowledge so strong, as he shall be forced to confess that it is utterly impossible that it should be otherwise."

In *The Immortality of the Soul* (1659), More attempts to use the same methods to prove that humans possess a soul that lives on after they die. The work concludes "that there is an incorporeal [bodiless] Substance, and that in Man, which we call his Soul. That this Soul of his subsists and acts after the deat of his Body."

Other of More's major works include the philosophical works *Enchiridion Ethicum* (*Handbook of Ethics,* 1667), *Divine Dialogues, . . .* (1668), and *Enchiridion Metaphysicum* (*Metaphysical Handbook,* 1671). He also wrote commentaries on the *Book of Revelation* (1680), and the *Prophecies of Daniel* (1681). After his death, *Letters on Several Subjects* were published in 1694.

In the General Preface to his *Philosophical Works,* More said that he could not accept the Calvinism of his parents, with its ideas of predestination, the belief that certain individuals were destined from birth to go to heaven. He became, instead, one of the CAMBRIDGE PLATONISTS, a group of philosophers who believed that the soul must purify itself through a search for truth and goodness. More agreed with John LOCKE that every person uses reason and free will to choose a path on this journey. However, he did not believe that an individual could succeed on a path that is materialist, immoral, or atheist. For this reason, More would eventually turn against René DESCARTES, although it had first seemed that they agreed about conscience and reason—that is, that the mind is naturally moral because it is spiritual and related to God.

More was interested in spiritual phenomena and in alchemy, the search for a means to turn lesser metals into gold using witchcraft. The critic John Hoyles says that More studied case histories looking for the reasons behind tales and hauntings. He was not skeptical about the stories but made it clear that he believed in spirits.

To do otherwise would be "a dangerous prelude to Atheism," he wrote, since "*No Spirit [means] no God.*"

More held the platonic and Christian belief that matter is inert but is brought to life by spirit. He thought this compatible with modern science and developed the idea that space links this world with God. This thinking influenced Isaac NEWTON in the development of his scientific ideas of space and time.

In his day, then, More provided a path from medieval to modern thought; a moderate way between the extremes of atheism and unquestioning belief. He was also important for his insistence that science and religion are joined and for realizing that new scientific ideas could be compatible with religion.

Other Work by Henry More

Major Philosophical Works. 9 vols. Edited by G. A. J. Rogers. Dulles, Va.: Thoemmes Press, 1997.

A Work about Henry More

Hall, A. Rupert. *Henry More: Magic, Religion, and Experiment.* Cambridge, Mass.: Blackwell, 1990.

More, Sir Thomas (1478–1535) *nonfiction writer, translator*

Thomas More was born in London to John More, a prominent lawyer and later a judge, and his wife,

Agnes Graunger More. At 13 More became a page (one who attends a knight) in the household of Cardinal John Morton, archbishop of Canterbury, who sent him to Oxford University the following year. He received a B.A. in 1494 and went on to read law at New Inn and Lincoln's Inn, completing his studies five years later. He married Jane Colt in 1605 and with her had three daughters and a son. Jane More died in 1511. Soon after his wife's death, More married Alice Middleton, a widow.

More was appointed under-sheriff of London in 1510, and in 1515 Henry VIII sent him on a diplomatic mission to the Netherlands. Three years later he became a member of Henry's Privy Council, or council of advisers. In 1529 More reached the height of his political career when Henry appointed him lord chancellor, the most powerful position in the nation with the exception of the king's. Three years later he resigned the position because of Henry's decision to split from the Catholic Church. By 1534 More, who remained a loyal Catholic, refused to take an oath acknowledging Henry as head of the CHURCH OF ENGLAND. He was convicted of treason the following year and beheaded. In 1935 the Catholic Church acknowledged his loyalty by making him Saint Thomas More.

In his lifetime More led a rich intellectual life and had an international reputation as a scholar. He was instrumental in introducing HUMANISM, a movement away from religious concerns and toward the humanities, to Britain. This was due to his friendships with European humanists such as Desiderius ERASMUS.

As early as 1505 More was translating into English from the Latin *The Life of Pico* (1509), the biography of the famous Italian humanist Giovanni Pico della Mirandola written by his nephew Giovanni Pico. His translation, the scholar Richard J. Schoeck notes, is an important early learned work in the English language. Latin was the language educated people all over Europe used at the time. More—who is believed to have learned Latin before English—defended English in the treatise *Dialogue Concerning Heresies* (1528): "For as for that our tongue is called barbarous, is but a fantasy. For so is, as every learned man knoweth, every strange language to other."

More was also a historian, writing *The History of Richard III* between 1514 and 1518. This book helped to establish the myth that Richard was an evil, physically deformed ruler who murdered his brothers and nephews in order to become king of England, something that is central to William SHAKESPEARE's play *Richard III* (1592–93) and continued to be taught as historical truth in British grammar schools well into the 20th century. "Richard the third son, of whom we now entreat," More writes, "was in wit and courage egall [equal] with either of them [his two older brothers], in body and prowess, far under them both, little of stature, ill featured of limbs, crook-backed, his left shoulder being much higher than the right."

More was not the first to report these details. His creation—the one that made the myth so attractive to the 16th century—was to forge a symbolic connection between Richard's physical and moral deformity: "[N]ature changed her course in his beginning, which in the course of his life many things unnaturally committed."

More is a fascinating and contradictory figure. He is both heretic and saint, who expressed views in his most famous work, *Utopia* (1516), that foreshadow both religious reform and communism. He is also a key figure in literary history for bringing the RENAISSANCE to England through his portrayal of an ideal society in *Utopia*.

Critical Analysis

More's most famous work is *Utopia* (1516), a dialogue in which he describes an ideal or nonexistent society. It is modeled partly after Plato's *Republic,* a dialogue in which the philosopher Socrates describes an ideal city. Written in Latin, this book spawned numerous imitations such as Francis BACON's *New Atlantis* and James HARRINGTON's *Oceana*. Utopia, which means both "good place" and "nowhere," is the name More gave to his fictional island.

Utopia is a dialogue between Raphael Hythlodaeus, who describes the imaginary society of Utopia, and a character named Thomas More, who questions Hythlodaeus closely about his ideas. The work reads like a call for social reform. "When I run over in my mind," says Hythlodaeus, "the various commonwealths flourishing today, so help me God, I can see nothing in them but a conspiracy of the rich, who are fattening up their own interests under the name and title of the commonwealth." The word *commonwealth* suggests both a political state and the common health of the 16th century. In this passage, according to the critic Jonathan Dollimore, More acknowledges not only that the laws are corrupt but "that law and morality have their origins in custom rather than with an eternal order of things." The argument is strengthened because of the book's comparison of Utopian with European society. More's acknowledgement of the differences among cultures thus obliges him to admit that the order of the world was created by man.

Hythlodaeus also advances religious views that are extremely and oddly liberal, especially since throughout early 16th-century Europe people were required to accept the pope's authority. The punishment for dissent, or heresy, was sometimes death. In Utopia, however, "there are different forms of religion throughout the island," Hythlodaeus explains, "and in each particular city as well. Some worship as a god the sun, others the moon, and still others the planets. There are some who worship a man of past ages who was conspicuous either for virtue or glory; they consider him not only a god but the supreme god."

Hythlodaeus's ideas make him seem like a supporter of the REFORMATION, the religious movement that undermined the hold that the Catholic Church had over Europe. Indeed, his ideas are more radical than those of many reformers, since in each place that a reformed church appeared the citizens of that place were required to conform to the tenets of the new church. The kind of religious toleration that More's character was proposing would not be achieved in England until the 18th century.

The liberal ideas expressed in *Utopia* contrast with More's later writings, for he not only rejected the views expressed in *Utopia* but also wrote a number of tracts denouncing Reformation theology. About a year after he had resigned from public office, he wrote, "As touching heretics, I hate that vice of theirs and not their persons, and very fain [happy] would I that the one were destroyed and the other saved."

The scholar Stephen Greenblatt notes that a "pattern is repeated again and again in Hythlodaeus's account: freedoms are heralded, only to shrink in the course of the description." Thus, while Utopians are allowed their own religious beliefs, most Utopians "believe in a single power, unknown, eternal, infinite, inexplicable, far beyond the grasp of the human mind, and diffused throughout the universe." Additionally, everyone is required to attend the same house of worship and to believe in life after death.

Indeed, Utopia is not a state of freedom but a state in which dissent is impossible. More's hatred of heresy would thus seem to be a logical product of the ideas that he proposed in *Utopia,* for the Reformation could be seen as further evidence of European corruption in that it demonstrated that European culture bred dissent and would breed even more if the Reformation were allowed to proceed.

Whatever More meant to suggest in *Utopia,* the work's readers have found different messages. The critic Russell A. Ames, for example, sees Utopia as a defense of Catholicism, pointing out that "the Utopians, though not in contact with Christianity, by reason and natural religion found their way to confession, and this proves that the confessional as ordained by the Church is both a godly and rational institution." Karl Kautsky, on the other hand, sees More as a radical secularist, one who is more interested in the human than the divine, and argues that as a thinker "he was in the front rank of his contemporaries, as a Socialist he was far ahead of them all."

Other Work by Thomas More

Last Letters of Thomas More. Edited by Alvaro de Silva. Grand Rapids, Mich.: W. B. Eerdmans, 2000.

Works about Thomas More

Ackroyd, Peter. *Life of Thomas More.* New York: Nan A. Talese, 1998.

Guy, J. A. *Thomas More.* New York: Oxford University Press, 2000.

Murphy, Anne. *Thomas More.* St. Louis, Mo.: Liguori Publications, 1997.

Morley, Thomas (ca. 1557–1602) *musician, lyric writer, nonfiction writer*

Thomas Morley, son of Francis Morley, a brewer, was born in Norwich, England. He received much of his early musical education from composer William BYRD, under whom he studied from about 1572 to 1574, before becoming master of the choristers at the Norwich Cathedral in 1574. After receiving a bachelor of music degree from Oxford University in 1588, Morley was appointed organist at St. Paul's.

Morley's earliest compositions were sacred works dating from 1576, and his first published work was *Canzonets or Little Short Songs to Three Voyces* (1593). According to the scholar W. A. Barrett, Morley "laboured to do for vocal music what was being done elsewhere for instrumental music," making a significant contribution to the English madrigal tradition through his use of an Italian musical style. Madrigals are complex, unaccompanied vocal pieces consisting of two or more parts. Morley's three-part canzonets, or songs which resemble madrigals but are less elaborate, contain some adaptations of Italian songs as well as verse written by contemporary poets. According to the scholar John Earle Uhler, however, the author of most of the poetic lyrics was likely Morley himself: "As SHAKESPEARE is credited with the authorship of the greatest part of his plays, so Morley, even though to a lesser degree of certainty, should be credited with the authorship of most of his songs." Thus, lyrics such as these from "April is in my Mistress' face" may be credited to Morley:

> April is in my mistress' face.
> And July in her eyes hath place.

Within her bosom is September,
But in her heart a cold December.

Morley's Italian influences were further reflected in subsequent publications such as *Madrigalls to Foure Voyces* (1594); *The First Book of Ballets to Five Voyces* (1595); two more books of canzonets from 1695 and 1597; and the *Triumph of Oriana* (1601), a collection of madrigals in honor of Queen ELIZA-BETH I, the Oriana of the title. Each madrigal ended with the words "Long life fair Oriana."

Morley's *First Book of Consort Lessons* appeared in 1599, followed by the *First Book of Ayres* (1660), which contains his musical setting of Shakespeare's "It was a lover and his lass" from *As You Like It* (1598). Critics have disagreed over whether or not a lyric from *Twelfth Night* (ca. 1600) was actually the basis for Morley's tune "Oh Mistress mine, I must" from his book of consort lessons. Since both Shakespeare and Morley were living in Bishopsgate in 1598, they may have known one another.

Morley's reputation is perhaps most dependent on his *Plaine and Easie Introduction to Practicall Musicke* (1597), a guide to music consisting of earnest discussion interspersed with musical examples and clever dialogue in which, according to Uhler, "there are discernable many sparks of poetry." Its purpose was clearly stated by Morley—that "any of but mean capacity, so that they can but truly sing their tunings . . . may, without any other help saving this book, perfectly learn to sing, make descant, and set parts well and formally together." The scholar Philip Brett described this work as "perhaps the most famous musical treatise in the English language."

Motteux, Peter Anthony (Pierre Antoine le Motteux) (1663–1718) *playwright*

Peter Motteux was born in Rouen, France, to Antoine le Motteux, a merchant, and his wife, Isabeau le Nud. Religious persecution against Huguenots (French Protestants) in his native France resulted in Motteux's emigration to London in 1685 and his subsequent name change. There he soon became involved in literary circles, and by 1692 he had begun publishing *The Gentleman's Journal*, a col-

lection of essays, poetry, and miscellaneous pieces of gossip and criticism. In the *Journal* Motteux published not only his own writing but that of such prestigious writers as Aphra BEHN and Matthew Prior. Despite its success, the journal abruptly ceased publication in 1694.

That same year Motteux's interlude, a play performed between the acts of another play, *The Rape of Europa by Jupiter,* was included in an adaptation of the tragedy *Valentian,* originally written by John FLETCHER. The performance required the use of elaborate mechanical contraptions so that characters portraying Roman gods might be carried down from the heavens. The play opens with the descent of Mercury, who relates that the god Zeus is coming to earth in search of love: "Drawn by Commanding Love, / Imperial Jove, / Designs to Visit some New tempting fair / There is no end of his Amours." In the scenes that follow the disguised god seduces Europa.

The majority of Motteux's subsequent dramatic works were of a similar nature, combining verse, music, and spectacle. He was particularly fond of Italian opera and attempted to merge that genre with the traditional English musical, creating innovative works that were extremely popular during the period. Some of his greatest successes include the romantic comedy *Love's a Jest* (1696) and *The Island Princess* (1699), an opera set in an island paradise: "We're now in those delicious Eastern Climes / Where ev'ry Wind diffuses balmy sweets." *Arsinoe, Queen of Cyprus* (1705) is particularly notable for being London's first opera to be influenced by Italian opera.

Besides his dramatic works, Motteux also authored a number of important translations. He was the first to translate books 3 through 5 (published 1694) of Rabelais's masterpiece, *Gargantua and Pantagruel.* His translation of CERVANTES's *Don Quixote* was considered the best translation of that classic novel up to that point.

Mulcaster, Richard (ca. 1530–1611)
nonfiction writer

Richard Mulcaster was an English schoolmaster best known for his progressive writing about the profession of teaching. It is believed that he was born near Cumberland, England, and it is known that he was educated at both Cambridge and Oxford universities. From 1561 to 1586 he was headmaster of Merchant Taylor's School in London, where he taught the poet Edmund SPENSER, among many others.

Mulcaster's most famous works include *Positions* (1581) and *The First Part of the Elementarie* (1582), both theoretical writings about the profession of teaching. His theories about education were ahead of his time in that he believed teachers should receive professional training similar to that received by doctors and lawyers. He also believed that women and men of all classes should receive an education and that parents should collaborate with their children's teachers in order to ensure the best possible education. Of his profession he said, "[T]he teacher's life . . . wrestles with unthankfullnesse above all measure. . . . One displeased parent will do more harme upon a head . . . than a thousand of the thankfullest will ever do goode."

Mulcaster emphasized the importance of reading, writing, drawing, singing, and playing a musical instrument for young students. He also thought that it was the responsibility of the teacher, particularly those teaching elementary education, to adapt their methods to the individual needs of each child. His ideas about the unique learning styles of children were not widely accepted until the beginning of the 20th century.

During the RENAISSANCE many scholars took a renewed interest in ancient Greek and Roman texts, believing that Latin and Greek were superior languages. Mulcaster, however, became a champion of the English language, arguing that one could argue as effectively in English as any other language: "But why not all in English, a tung of it self both depe in conceit, and frank in deliverie? I do not think that anie language, be it whatsoever, is better able to utter all arguments, either with more pith, or greater planesse, then our English tung is."

Mulcaster's ideas about the importance of using the English language played a pivotal role in helping spread the wealth of scientific and artistic knowledge that came out of the RENAISSANCE. In *History of the English Language* (1957), Albert C. Baugh says that "the Renaissance would have had but a limited effect if these ideas had remained the property solely of academic men. If the diplomat, the courtier, and the man of affairs were to profit by them, they had to be expressed in the language that everybody read."

Mulgrove, Lord
See SHEFFIELD, JOHN.

Munda, Constantia (fl. 1615) *nonfiction writer*
Constantia Munda is the pseudonym of the author (probably a woman) of *The Worming of a Mad Dog* (1617), written in response to Joseph SWETNAM's antifeminist treatise, *The Arraignment of Lewde, Idle, Froward, and Unconstant Women* (1615), which argued that women are inferior to men. Swetnam's treatise began what came to be known as the pamphlet wars over the nature of women.

Munda's pamphlet uses various strategies for arguing against Swetnam. She, like other female pamphleteers such as Rachel SPEGHT and Ester SOWERNAM, presents examples of virtuous and heroic women from the Bible or ancient history to prove the merits of women. Munda, moreover, attacks Swetnam's character, calling him "an untoward whelp" and saying that he foams at the mouth "like the triple dog of hell" (Cerberus, the protector of the classical world's Hades). Despite this type of name-calling, Munda shows herself to be quite learned, quoting Latin and Greek and exposing the fallacies of Swetnam's arguments. Her main criticism is of his style and diction, which she says show him to be unlearned and unable to argue thoughtfully.

Munda identifies herself as aristocratic, which may explain her extensive education. Her degree of education might also indicate that the author was a man posing as a woman and that booksellers commissioned "her" work in order to flame the controversy and thus sell more books. Whether male or female, however, Munda effectively puts Swetnam in his place.

A Work about Constantia Munda

Henderson, Katherine Usher, and Barbara F. Mc-
  Manus. *Half Humankind: Contexts and Texts of the
  Controversy about Women in England, 1540–1640.*
  Urbana: University of Illinois Press, 1985.

Munday, Anthony (1553–1633) *poet, playwright, prose writer, nonfiction writer, translator*

Anthony Munday was born in London to Christopher Munday, a cloth merchant. In 1576, after some early experiences on the stage, he was apprenticed to a stationer. At the time stationers were not only suppliers of writing materials but also printers, and this task led Munday to try his hand at writing. He first wrote a few small verses that he added to a volume he was printing.

In 1578 Munday made a trip to France and Italy. In Rome he stayed at the English College, which had been founded to train Jesuits. He writes about this experience in *The English Romayne Life* (1582), explaining that he desired to see foreign countries and learn their languages. It is thought that Munday may have provided secret intelligence about the English Catholic community in Rome to ELIZABETH I's government.

When Munday returned to England in 1579, he published *The Mirror of Mutability* and dedicated it, in an attempt to secure PATRONAGE, to Edward De Vere, Earl of OXFORD. It contains an acrostic—a 12-line poem in which the first letters of each line spell out the name EDWARD DE VERE.

At this same time Munday occasionally acted in plays. He also began writing news pamphlets, ballads, prose fiction, and plays. He wrote or collaborated on more than 15 plays between 1584 and 1602, among them the comedy *Mother Redcap*, with Michael DRAYTON. On his own he wrote the historical dramas *John a Kent and John a Cumber* (1595) and *The Downfall of Robert Earl of Huntingdon*, afterward called *Robin Hood of Merry Sherwood* (1599).

The 1600 poetry collection *England's Helicon* contains several of Munday's poems, printed under the name of "Shepherd Tony," among them the charming "Beauty Sat Bathing a Stream":

> Beauty sat bathing by a spring
> Where fairest shades did hide her;
> The winds blew calm, the birds did sing,
> The cool streams ran beside her.
> My wanton thoughts entic'd mine eye
> To see what was forbidden. . . .

In 1599 Munday collaborated on a two-part drama entitled *True and Honourable History of the Life of Sir John Oldcastle, the good Lord Cobham.* This play was so successful that the stage manager Phillip Henslowe gave each author an additional payment beyond what was originally agreed upon. Munday was subsequently commissioned to write the annual pageant for the City of London in 1605, 1609, 1611, 1614–16, 1618, and 1623.

In his later years Munday was best known as a translator of the Spanish Arthurian romances, which he probably knew in their French versions. The first of these translations, *Palladino of England*, appeared in 1588. In 1589 and 1595 he translated into English the first two volumes of *Amadis of Gaul*, by Garciá de Rodriguez de Montalvo and in 1609 he published a translation of *Palmerin of England.* by Francisco Vásquez de Ciudad Rodrigo. Like many of the other works produced by Munday, these translations were capable, but lacked stylistic flair.

Ben JONSON ridiculed Munday through the character Antonio Balladino in his very early undated play *The Case Is Altered*. Jonson famously commented on Munday's lack of innovation, noting that his work was often unoriginal and uninspired. Although Francis MERES's listing of Munday, in his account of writers of comic drama, as "our best plotter" suggests that Munday was highly regarded in his own time, Jonson's view is supported by most modern critics. Munday's productivity and versatility are extraordinary, but his work is of more historical than literary interest.

Murray, Ann

See HALKETT, ANNE.

Nashe, Thomas (1567–1601) *pamphleteer, playwright, prose writer*

Thomas Nashe was born in Lowestoft, a fishing village on England's east coast, the third son of William Nashe, a clergyman, and Margaret Witchingham Nashe. He was educated at Cambridge University. After taking his degree, in 1586, he moved to London, where he became a member of the group known as the UNIVERSITY WITS—the others being Thomas LODGE, John LYLY, Robert GREENE, and George PEELE. These young men struggled to make a living as writers in a time when the total absence of copyright laws made that extremely difficult, but they were proud of their education and used it in witty verbal sallies against their enemies.

Most of Nashe's work consists of short pamphlets commenting on and satirizing the customs of his time. For example, *Pierce Penniless, His Supplication to the Devil* (1592) is about a poor writer, unable to make a living by selling his work, who turns to the Devil for patronage. The pamphlet, which includes a variety of amusing portraits of contemporary types, sold well and made Nashe famous, though not rich. Nashe was often obliged to make ends meet by working for his publisher, John Danter, as a proofreader.

Other pamphlets include *Christ's Tears over Jerusalem* (1593), an exposé of the lamentable morals prevalent in London, including lively pictures of tavern life and the joys and miseries of gambling. *Terrors of the Night* (1594) pillories superstition in entertaining accounts of dreams, devils, and witchcraft.

Nashe's friend Robert Greene died of starvation, perhaps brought on by the plague, in September 1592. That month Gabriel HARVEY, whom Greene had attacked in a pamphlet earlier in the year, published *Four Letters,* defending himself from Greene's attack and mocking Greene's squalid death. Nashe responded in December with a pamphlet called *Strange News of the Intercepting of Certain Letters,* defending his friend's memory and ridiculing Harvey. The feud between Harvey and Nashe went on for four years of published invective, despite efforts of friends to make peace between the two.

Nashe also wrote plays. His masque *Summer's Last Will and Testament* (acted 1592, published 1600) about the court jester, Summers, includes the much-anthologized lyric "Spring, the Sweet Spring":

> *Spring, the sweet Spring, is the year's*
> *   pleasant king;*
> *Then blooms each thing, then maids dance*
> *   in a ring,*

Cold doth not sting, the pretty birds do sing,
Cuckoo, jug, jug, pu-we, to-witta-woo!

In 1594 *The Tragedy of Dido, Queen of Carthage* was published with the byline "written by Christopher MARLOWE and Thomas Nashe." It is not known how much Nashe contributed to it, and the work is most often considered an early work of Marlowe's. An elegy written by Nashe for Marlowe, who had died in 1593, was apparently included in some copies of the play, but none have survived.

Nashe's picaresque romance *The Unfortunate Traveler* (1594) is considered a precursor of the novel. It follows its rogue-hero, a page named Jack, through adventures at all levels of society in France, Spain, and Italy.

Nashe was constantly in trouble with the law. The authorities of London, stung by how he portrayed them (and, according to Nashe's complaints, prompted by Gabriel Harvey), jailed him after the publication of *Christ's Tears.* He was released after the intervention of Sir George Carey, a patron of the arts who was later instrumental in protecting William SHAKESPEARE's acting company from Puritan efforts to quell it. In 1597 Nashe collaborated with Ben JONSON, then an obscure actor, on a comedy about England entitled *The Isle of Dogs,* which gave such offense that all the theaters in London were closed for a time. Nashe escaped arrest on this occasion by leaving London, but Jonson spent some time in jail. The play was suppressed so thoroughly that no copies have survived.

It is not known where or how Nashe died, but two references in other writers' works indicate that he died sometime in 1601, when he would have been 34.

In his preface to his edition of *Thomas Nashe . . . Selected Writings* (1964), Stanley Wells says of Nashe:

> He offers a richness of fantasy and a fascinatingly original outlook that is always capable of surprising. . . . He had great intelligence, a vivid imagination, a brilliant wit, a keen eye for the absurdities of human behaviour, and a sensitive though somewhat inconsistent and imperfectly balanced response to spiritual experience . . . Of his contemporaries, only certain dramatists—Ben Jonson, Shakespeare, and perhaps John Webster—wrote prose as hard, as luminous, and as vital as his."

Indeed, the works of all the writers Wells mentions sometimes show Nashe's influence.

Other Work by Thomas Nashe
The Unfortunate Traveler and Other Works. Edited by J. B. Steane. New York: Viking, 1985.

Works about Thomas Nashe
Hilliard, Stephen S. *The Singularity of Thomas Nashe.* Lincoln: University of Nebraska Press, 1986.
Hutson, Lorna. *Thomas Nashe in Context.* New York: Oxford University Press, 1989.
McGinn, Donald J. *Thomas Nashe.* Boston: Twayne, 1981.

Neoplatonism
Neoplatonism—that is, "the new Platonism"—refers generally to uses and applications of the work of the ancient Greek philosopher Plato (ca. 428–348 B.C.) by people living centuries later. The RENAISSANCE witnessed a revival of Neoplatonism.

The basis of Plato's philosophy was his belief in a world of "Forms." The Forms are perfect realities of existence copied imperfectly in our earthly realm. Thus, there is a perfect Form of "circle" that exists in the world of Forms (also known as the world of "Being"). A circle in our imperfect world (the world of "Becoming") is only a flawed copy of the circle Form. Still, the fact that it is recognizable as a circle shows it does participate, however imperfectly, in the Form of a circle. More interestingly, human love is marred by problems because it is an imperfect copy of the Form of love. On the other hand, ideal love is at least partly accessible to humans through its imperfect copies.

The Christian thinker Augustine (ca. 400) recognized that Neoplatonism was an important influence on the Catholic Church. Christian mystics, who sought a direct relationship with the Divine apart from the material world, embraced a form of Neoplatonism.

In the Italian Renaissance, Neoplatonism became associated with ideas of the lofty potential of humanity. It taught thinkers and authors of the time to value mind over matter and to aspire to the ideal. It also produced a tendency to favor contemplation and to despise all fleshly and bodily impulses, which are linked to the world of Becoming. Thus, our term for nonsexual love, *platonic,* reflects the priority of mental intimacy over sexual intimacy.

In fact, Neoplatonism as it applied to male/female love relationships, outlined in Baldassare CASTIGLIONE's *The Courtier,* was very important to Renaissance literature. For example, in sonnet sequences like Sir Philip SIDNEY's *Astrophil and Stella,* the male speaker is first physically attracted to his beloved. Rejection teaches him to deny his physical impulses and to aim at contemplating the perfect idea of love, of which his beloved is, ultimately, only a symbol. William SHAKESPEARE's *Sonnets* portray a Neoplatonic contrast between the spiritual love for the Fair Youth and the sexual passion for the Dark Lady. Other writers influenced by Neoplatonism include Edmund SPENSER and John MILTON, the latter of whom was associated with the CAMBRIDGE PLATONISTS, a group of Neoplatonic thinkers at Cambridge University. The concept of the GREAT CHAIN OF BEING categorized the entire seen and unseen world in a Neoplatonic system. "In the history of ideas," writes the scholar Richard Hooker, "Renaissance Neoplatonism is . . . important for its diffusion into a variety of philosophies and cultural activities, such as literature, painting, and music."

Newcastle, Margaret Cavendish, Duchess of (1623–1673) *nonfiction writer, poet, playwright, prose writer*

Margaret Cavendish, Duchess of Newcastle, was the youngest child born to aristocratic parents Thomas and Elizabeth Leghton Lucas in Colchester, Essex, England. In 1644 the English Civil War drove her to Paris, where she married William Cavendish, Marquis of Newcastle, the following year.

Newcastle and her husband settled in Antwerp to wait out the war, and while living in the house of the deceased painter Peter Paul RUBENS, she met many of the day's greatest thinkers, such as René DESCARTES and Thomas HOBBES. She also probably began some of the works that would be published in 1653, two years after her return to England: *Philosophicall Fancies* and *Poems, and Fancies. Philosophicall Fancies* marked the beginning of Newcastle's thoughtful considerations on natural philosophy and contained her theories on the nature of matter.

Poems, and Fancies contains the bulk of Newcastle's poetry printed in her lifetime. She revised and augmented the volume twice, first in 1664 and then 1668. The poems are divided into six sections, loosely grouped around themes such as science, moral philosophy, poetry, fairies, conflict, and death. Between each section is a transitional poem that Newcastle terms a *Clasp,* which serves to hold the work together much like the fastener or hinge on a piece of jewelry. Most of the poetry is written in rhymed 10-syllable lines: "Give me a Free and Noble Style, that goes / in an Uncurbed Strain, though Wild it shows." Her poetic influences include Ben JONSON (who had been acquainted with her husband) and John DONNE. Several poems feature animals: Two long narrative poems describe "The Hunting of the Hare" and "The Hunting of the Stagg." In each of these, Newcastle breaks the hunting-poem tradition by giving the animals' perspectives, evoking pity or disgust in the reader. In the 1668 edition, she appended the prose work *The Animal Parliament,* a traditional work of debate.

In 1655 Newcastle published *The Worlds of Olio,* an assortment of meditations on natural philosophy, history, literature, and art, as well as on Newcastle as writer. Interestingly, the book contains a dedicatory poem by William Cavendish in which he gives a humorous account of his financial troubles and shows his full support for his wife's career as a professional author: "Censure your worst, so [i.e., so long as] you the book will buy."

Natures Pictures Drawn by Fancies Pencil to the Life (1656) represents, according to the critic Kate Lilley, Newcastle's "most ambitious and copious generic experiment." The work has been compared to Chaucer's *Canterbury Tales,* as much of Newcastle's work consists of verse stories by different narrators who analyze and question gender stereotypes. Among the prose works included is the autobiographical "A True Relation of my Birth, Breeding, and Life," which again asserts Newcastle's willingness to be known as an author in a time when such a profession was virtually closed to women.

Newcastle's *Plays* appeared in 1662. An additional volume of plays "never before printed" would appear six years later. Her plays exhibit traditional elements of romance, disguise, and a fair amount of music and gender issues.

Newcastle gathered her opinions on Hobbes, Descartes, Henry MORE, and others in *Philosophical Letters* (1664). Another philosophical work, *Observation upon Experimental Philosophy,* appeared in 1666. Her last work in the field was *Grounds of Natural Philosophy* (1668).

Something of a philosophical bent colors many of Newcastle's works, certainly *The Description of a New World, called The Blazing World* (1666), which in fact was originally published as an addendum to *Observations upon Experimental Philosophy.* This work, perhaps Newcastle's most popular among today's readers, describes a fantastic voyage by a noblewoman to the North Pole, where another planet is discovered, joined to the Earth by its South Pole and inhabited by intelligent beings. Some of the inhabitants have the appearance of bears and some of foxes as well as other animals. There is also an entire kingdom of humanlike creatures who come in many colors (green, violet, scarlet). Newcastle uses her new world to comment upon European society, much as Sir Thomas MORE had done in *Utopia* (1516). The scientific and philosophical ideas that she had spent decades refining are placed in the mouths of the book's speakers.

Newcastle's contributions to science and philosophy were recognized (after years of disdain) by an invitation in 1667 to attend a meeting of the Royal Society, one of Britain's early groups of learned scientists, mathematicians, philosophers, and other intellects interested in science and the natural world; she was the first woman to be so honored. In the same year her most widely read book, a biography of her husband entitled *The Life of the Thrice Noble, High and Puissant Prince William Cavendishe, Duke, Marquess, and Earl of Newcastle,* was published.

Twentieth-century novelist Virginia Woolf compared Newcastle to "some giant cucumber [spreading] itself over all the roses and carnations in the garden" of more traditional women's writing. In other words, Newcastle's work is important and beneficial in and of itself and should not be compared with other, perhaps more mainstream, literary works. Woolf mourned that Newcastle's "poems, her plays, her philosophies, her orations, her discourses . . . moulder in the gloom of public libraries." Unfortunately, Woolf did not live to see a revival of interest in Newcastle's work that is increasing today.

Other Work by Margaret Cavendish, Duchess of Newcastle

The Blazing World & Other Writings. Edited by Kate Lilley. New York: Penguin, 1994.

A Work about Margaret Cavendish, Duchess of Newcastle

Wilson, Katharina M., and Frank J. Warnke, eds. *Women Writers of the Seventeenth Century.* Athens: University of Georgia Press, 1989.

Newton, Sir Isaac (1642–1727)
nonfiction writer

Sir Isaac Newton was born in Grantham, Lincolnshire, England, to the elder Isaac Newton, who died before his son Isaac's birth, and his wife, Hannah. As a young boy Newton was educated at King's School, during which time he primarily lived with the Clarks, the family of a local apothecary from whom Newton would acquire some knowledge of primitive chemistry. Early in his education Newton showed little academic promise or interest in science but became interested in scientific inquiry at the age of 13 after reading John Bate's *The Mysteries of Nature and Art.*

In 1661 Newton entered Trinity College at Cambridge, where much of the curriculum was devoted to studying ancient Greek philosophers. Newton, however, became acquainted with and attracted to the concepts put forth in the works of more contemporary philosophers such as René DESCARTES, Thomas MORE, and Thomas HOBBES, as well as scientists such as COPERNICUS, Tycho Brahe, Galileo, and Robert BOYLE. In 1663 Newton began to record his thoughts and questions regarding accepted scientific and philosophical concepts in the notebook entitled *Quaestiones Quaedam Philosophicae* (Some problems in philosophy). Written in Latin below the title was the phrase, "I am a friend of Plato, I am a friend of Aristotle, but truth is my greater friend." The entries in *Quaestiones* would provide much of the basis for Newton's later research and included such topics as "Attraction Magnetical," "Of the Sun Stars & Planets & Comets," "Of Gravity and Levity," "Of Atoms," and "Of Light." Newton received his bachelor's degree in 1665, but an outbreak of plague delayed his return to Cambridge until 1667.

During this intervening period Newton returned to Woolsthorpe, the manor house of his childhood, and his studies in the quiet countryside would lead to revolutionary advances in science and mathematics. At Woolsthorpe, Newton made tremendous breakthroughs in his theories regarding gravity, optics, and mathematics, and, although legend has it that during his stay at Woolsthorpe an apple fell on his head and suddenly prompted him to develop his theory of gravity, Newton once stated that his great discoveries were made by "keeping the subject constantly before me, till the first dawnings open slowly, by little and little, into the full and clear light." Newton's studies at Woolsthorpe would lay the foundation for theories that were fully expanded upon in *Philosophiae*

Naturalis Principia Mathematica, better known as *Principia* (1687), and, later, in *Opticks* (1704).

Newton returned to Cambridge in 1667 and was elected to a major fellowship in 1668. That same year he wrote the treatise *De Analysi per Aequationes Infinitas* (On analysis by an infinite series), which outlined the concepts of integral and differential calculus. Newton continued his studies in optics, eventually constructing a reflecting telescope and in 1672 publishing his first scientific paper on the subject, "Theory of Light and Colours," in the scientific journal *Philosophical Transactions of the Royal Society.*

Encouraged by the astronomer Edmund Halley to fully expand upon his developments regarding motion in the universe, Newton published *Principia,* often regarded as the greatest work of science ever written, in 1687. In *Principia* Newton defined types of forces, proposed his three laws of motion, and, after establishing this framework, explained the gravitational forces governing orbiting bodies in the universe. He described the attraction that holds planets in their orbits and governs the orbits of comets, the variation of tides, and the motion of the moon in relation to the sun through a mathematical formula known as the inverse-square law: "all matter attracts all other matter with a force proportional to the product of their masses and inversely proportional to the square of the distance between them." According to the scholar Michael White, "The *Principia* laid the cornerstone for the understanding of dynamics and mechanics which would, within the space of a century, generate a real and lasting change to human civilization."

In the same year as the publication of *Principia* political and religious controversy surrounded Cambridge. King James II began appointing only Catholics to positions of importance, including positions at Cambridge and Oxford. Newton, a devoted Protestant, opposed the policy and was eventually sent by Cambridge University as a representative to Parliament.

A year before receiving his knighthood in 1705, the *Opticks* was finally published. In it Newton expanded on his theories of light and color, which he had first presented early in his career as a professor at Cambridge. *Opticks* consists of explanations of reflection and refraction, rainbows, mirrors, and prisms, the central idea being that white light is made up of many different colors. In a second edition of *Opticks,* published two years later, Newton explained how his theories regarding light were bound to the workings of the universe as a whole:

> Have not the small particles of bodies certain powers, virtues or forces, by which they act at a distance, not only upon the rays of light for reflecting, refracting and inflecting them, but also upon one another for producing a great part of the phenomena of Nature?

The scholar E. N. Da C. Andrade described Newton as a man "whose work, whose viewpoint [changed] the current of human thought" and as "one of the great intellectual figures of all time."

Works about Isaac Newton

Westfall, Richard S. *The Life of Isaac Newton.* New York: Cambridge University Press, 1993.

White, Michael. *Isaac Newton: The Last Sorcerer.* Reading, Mass.: Addison-Wesley, 1997.

Norris, John (1657–1712) *nonfiction writer*

John Norris was born at Collingbourne Kingston, Wiltshire, England, the son of John Norris, the local vicar, and a theologian who had leanings toward the Puritanism inspired by John CALVIN but wanted to remain in the Anglican Church. Norris was educated at Winchester College and at Exeter College, Oxford, where he was influenced by a wide variety of thinkers, including the ancient Greek philosopher Plato (427–347 B.C.), Thomas MORE, René DESCARTES, and the French rationalist Nicolas de Malebranche (1638–1715). In 1680 he became a fellow of All Souls College, Oxford, where he continued to study philosophy and theology. He was ordained an Anglican priest in 1684.

Norris's first original work was *An Idea of Happiness* (1683), which follows Plato in seeing the highest human happiness in the expression of the soul in the contemplation and love of God. Norris published many sermons, notably *Discourses upon the Beatitudes* (1690), a commentary on Christ's Sermon on the Mount. Other theological writings include *Reflections upon the Conduct of Human Life, with Reference to the Study of Learning and Knowledge* (1691) and *An Account of Reason & Faith: In Relation to the Mysteries of Christianity* (1697). Here he makes a distinction between things contrary to reason and things (such as religious truth) that are above reason. The human mind, Norris states, is not the measure of truth.

Norris was highly critical of the work of John LOCKE, which he attempted to refute in his *Cursory Reflections upon a Book Call'd, An Essay Concerning Human Understanding* (1691). He objected to Locke's materialist view that all human ideas originate in sensory experience and stressed the objective and eternal nature of some kinds of truth. Another prominent philosophical work, *An Essay Towards the Theory of the Ideal or Intelligible World* (1701–04), was a metaphysical treatise about the nature of knowledge and existence. Norris's concept of the intelligible world refers to the system of ideas eternally existent in the mind of God, according to which material creation was formed.

In his later years Norris planned to write a series of books on how Christian virtues could be applied in practical life but completed only one before his death, *A Treatise Concerning Christian Prudence* (1710). Norris was an important influence on John Wesley and through him on the development of Protestant thought throughout the 18th and 19th centuries.

Other Work by John Norris

Philosophical and Theological Writings. Edited by Richard Acworth. Chicago: University of Chicago Press, 2002.

A Work about John Norris

Acworth, Richard. *The Philosophy of John Norris of Bemerton.* New York: Olms, 1979.

North, Sir Thomas (ca. 1535–ca. 1601)
translator

Little is known about the early life of Thomas North, although he had an extensive military career as a captain and a trainer of fighters against the Spanish Armada. He was knighted in 1591, and became a justice of the peace in Cambridge.

During his military career, North began to hone his skills as a translator. In 1557 he translated Spanish author and moralist Antonio de Guevara's *El reloj de príncipes* (*The Dial of Princes*), a didactic novel that sets the life of Roman Emperor Marcus Aurelius as an example for rulers. He also translated an Italian collection of Eastern beast fables, *The Moral Philosophy of Doni*.

In 1579 North published his most famous work, *Lives of the Noble Grecians and Romans,* a translation of Plutarch's *Lives*. North did not translate from the original Latin but chose as his text a French translation by Jacques Amyot. While Amyot embellished Plutarch, North embellished Amyot. North's stories, style, and sense of drama influenced William SHAKESPEARE, who borrowed plots and even prose from North's work for *Anthony and Cleopatra; A Midsummer Night's Dream;* and *Julius Caesar,* which particularly shows North's influence.

North did not merely translate Plutarch; he added warmth and humanity to the characters. In the following passage North describes the banished Roman warrior Coriolanus when he calls upon his enemy Aufidius at his home:

> When he came . . . [to Aufidius's home], he got him up straight to the chimney harthe, and sat him down, and spake not a worde to any man, his face all muffled over. They of the house spying him, wondered what he should be, and yet they durst not byd him rise. For, ill-favoredly muffled up and disguised as he was, yet there appeared a certain majestie in his countenance, and in his silence; whereupon they went to Tullus who was at supper, to tell him of the strange disguising of this man.

North's style was vigorous and vivid, serving as a model for Shakespeare and others who followed him.

Norton, Thomas (1532–1584) *dramatist, translator, poet*

Thomas Norton was born in London to Thomas Norton, a wealthy merchant, and Elizabeth Merry Norton. He was educated at Cambridge University and studied law in 1556. That same year he married Margery Cranmer, the daughter of Archbishop Thomas CRANMER, who was an important figure in the early CHURCH OF ENGLAND. Later in his life, Norton became a fervent anti-Catholic. His extreme Puritanism eventually landed him in trouble with Elizabethan authorities, and he was imprisoned for a time in the Tower of London in 1584.

Norton began his writing career at age 18, when he translated *A Letter Which Peter Martyr Wrote to the Duke of Somerset* (1550) from the Latin. During the next decade, Norton published a handful of religious pamphlets and several poems in collections, but he is best remembered for the play *Gorboduc, or Ferrex and Porrex,* which he wrote with Thomas SACKVILLE in 1561. This work is the earliest known English tragedy and the first play to be written in blank verse, unrhymed lines of iambic pentameter (lines of 10 syllables alternating between unstressed and stressed), the dominant poetic form of Elizabethan and early 17th-century drama. *Gorboduc* tells the story of an ancient English king, Gorboduc, who, Elizabethan historians believed, divided England between his two sons, Ferrex and Porrex. Each brother then attempted to take control of the entire kingdom.

A part of Norton and Sackville's intent in the play was to urge ELIZABETH I to marry, have children, and insure a peaceful succession upon her death. This political element of the play becomes obvious when Hermon, Ferrex's evil adviser, observes:

> *Wise men do not so hang on passing state*
> *Of present princes, chiefly in their age.*

But they will further cast their reaching eye
To view and weigh the times and reigns to
  come.

Gorboduc failed to convince Elizabeth to marry and is remembered for its literary, not its political, importance. The scholar William Tydeman praises Norton and Sackville with providing "the stateliest literary form [that is, tragedy] . . . with a verse medium dignified enough to allow weighty and illustrious characters to speak without incongruity."

A Work about Thomas Norton

Walker, Greg. *The Politics of Performance in Early Renaissance Drama.* New York: Cambridge University Press, 1998.

Oldham, John (1653–1683) *poet*

John Oldham was born in Gloucestershire, England, to John Oldham, a vicar, and his wife. He was educated at Tetbury grammar school and entered St. Edmund Hall, Oxford, in 1670. He graduated in 1674, becoming a schoolmaster and a tutor to several prominent families.

Although John Oldham lived only a short time, he managed to produce an impressive amount of poetry, most of it satirical in nature. In 1677 he wrote *A Satire Against Virtue,* which purported to be a poem in praise of sin. Oldham also produced several imitative poems, including several pieces in the style of the Roman poet Horace (65–8 B.C.) and several in the pastoral tradition of the ancient Greeks. His most famous work, *A Satire upon the Jesuits* (1681), was inspired by the Popish Plot, an imaginary Catholic conspiracy to assassinate Charles II invented and publicized by a disreputable clergyman named Titus Oates in 1678 that led to a wave of anti-Catholic violence. Oldham fully participates in the anti-Catholicism of the day, seeing Catholic beliefs as hypocritical:

> *And here I might (if I durst) reveal*
> *What pranks are play'd in the confessional.*

Oldham made fun of the Catholic belief in transubstantiation, that is, the belief that the bread used in the mass is actually transformed into the body of Christ, which struck him as superstitious and absurd:

> *Hey jingo, Sirs! What's this? 'tis bread you*
>   *see?*
> *Presto, begone!, 'tis now a deity.*

Oldham's translations of works by the satirical Roman poet Juvenal (A.D. 55–127) and other poems were collected in *Poems and Translations,* which was published not long before his early death of smallpox. John DRYDEN memorialized Oldham in his poem "To the Memory of Mr. Oldham," with its well-known opening lines:

> *Farewell, too little and too lately known,*
> *Whom I began to think and call my own;*
> *For sure our souls were close ally'd; and*
>   *thine*
> *Cast in the same poetic mould as mine.*

Later in the poem Dryden, while conceding that Oldham's verse lacks polish and elegance, asserts that it succeeds without them:

But Satire needs not those, and Wit will
  shine
Through the harsh cadence of a rugged line.

Oldham is considered a pioneer of the imitation of the classical poets that became so important in the Augustan Age.

Other Work by John Oldham

The Poems of John Oldham. Edited by Harold Fletcher Brooks and Raman Selden. New York: Oxford University Press, 1987.

Works about John Oldham

Hammond, Paul. *John Oldham and the Renewal of Classical Culture.* New York: Cambridge University Press, 1983.

Zigerell, James. *John Oldham.* Boston: Twayne, 1983.

Osborne, Dorothy (1627–1695) *letter writer*

Dorothy Osborne, the daughter of Sir Peter and Dorothy Danvers Osborne, was probably born at the family's estate at Chicksands in southeastern England. Her father was a staunch Royalist (supporter of the monarchy) during the troubled Civil War era in England, and his family lived in difficult circumstances when the Puritan Party controlled England, 1649–60.

In 1648 Dorothy Osborne met Sir William Temple, and as he was traveling through Europe, the two engaged in a rich correspondence until their marriage on Christmas Day 1654, over the objections of their families. Osborne's letters offer insightful glimpses into the domestic life and personalities of the nobility in this period, sometimes with an ironic tone, or satire directed against the pomp and self-righteousness of others. In one letter, for example, she remarks on a woman who has just moved into the neighborhood: "She is one of my Lord of Valentia's daughters and has married an old fellow that is some threescore and ten [70 years old] whoe has a house that is fitter for the hoggs then for her." She also expresses her pleas-

ure at reading French romances, long works of fiction devoted to the love affairs of historical figures. In one letter Osborne explains her familiar letter-writing style: "Great Schollers are not the best writers (of Letters I mean, of books perhaps they are) . . . all letters mee thinks should be free and easy as one's discourse."

Osborne's surviving letters to Temple (77 of them, from 1652 to October 1654), were collected and published in several editions, the first by Edward Abbott Parry in 1888. More recent editions were edited by Kingsley Hart (1968) and Kenneth Parker (1987). Virginia Woolf admiringly devoted an essay in *The Common Reader* (1948) to Osborne's letters, writing: "Into these innumerable letters, lost now for the most part, went powers of observation and of wit that were later to take rather a different shape in *Evelina* and in *Pride and Prejudice*. They were only letters, yet some pride went into their making."

A Work by Dorothy Osborne

Letters to Sir William Temple. Edited by Kenneth Parker. New York: Penguin Books, 1987.

Otway, Thomas (1652–1685) *dramatist*

Thomas Otway was born in Sussex, England, to Elizabeth and Humphrey Otway, the rector of Woolbeding. An excellent student who attended Oxford, Thomas planned to join the clergy. However, distraught after his father's death, he left Oxford in 1672 and moved to London to become a playwright.

Otway's early plays were conventional. Produced in 1657, his first play, *Alcibiades,* features a hero who stabs himself after the queen of Sparta, who desires him, poisons his wife. In the more successful tragedy *Don Carlos* (1676) the irrationally jealous King Philip poisons his wife and drives his son, the title character, to suicide. *Friendship in Fashion* (1678) pairs a standard comic romance between the protagonists with a ribald subplot about the adulterous Mr. and Mrs. Goodvile. That year Otway joined the military and briefly became a lieutenant until the House of Commons dissolved the army.

At this time England was in an uproar because of the Exclusion Crisis. Fearing the possible ascendancy of his Catholic brother James to the throne, many members of the Whig party supported forcing King Charles II to name his illegitimate Protestant son, the Duke of Monmouth, his heir. Otway's next play, 1679's well-received *Caius Marius,* marks his turn toward the political, and its main romantic plot is intertwined with a subplot that criticizes Caius Marius's illicit acquisition of power. The critic Jessica Munns sees Otway's representation of Caius Marius as a "warning against deviation from monarchical rule." *The Soldier's Fortune,* a comedy produced the next year, celebrates the cuckolding of Whig merchant Sir Davy Dunce by a former Royalist soldier.

Even Otway's popular domestic tragedy *The Orphan* (1680) has political overtones. In this play twin brothers Castalio and Polidore vie for the love of their father's ward, Monimia. Castalio and Monimia secretly marry, but Polidore, believing their affair to be illicit, seduces Monimia in the guise of his twin. When all is revealed, the three remorseful characters commit suicide.

The twins' father, Acasto, had brought his family to the countryside to escape "Corruption, envy, discontent, and Faction," but as he dies, Castalio compares the family's inner turmoil to "States Rebellion" and "Churches Schism." This ending suggests a fear that rebellion and schism are inevitable. As the critic Laura Mandell suggests, the play can be read metaphorically as "a sort of cautionary tale, warning us of what will happen if merchants try to achieve status in their own way." The natural hierarchies, which place both kings and fathers in charge, must be kept in place, or chaos ensues.

Otway's best play, *Venice Preserv'd; or, a Plot Discovered* (1682), opens with Jaffeir and Belvidera's property having been taken by Belvidera's father, a Venetian senator who opposed their marriage. Jaffeir's friend Pierre invites him into a plot to overthrow the corrupt government, but Belvidera convinces Jaffeir to expose the plot to the senate in order to prevent bloodshed. Although the senate promises to spare the conspirators' lives, the plotters are condemned to execution by torture. Jaffeir saves Pierre from this dishonor by stabbing Pierre and then killing himself; Belvidera goes mad.

The precise political position of this complex play is difficult to determine. The critic Kerstin P. Warner notes that while British soldiers in New York "called for a revival of *Venice Preserv'd* as an expression of their Tory sympathies," nonetheless, "in the same year, in London, the play was banned for its 'dangerous republican tendencies.'" Modern critics have also been conflicted. The scholar Philip Harth, tracing the critical history of the play, notes that while some modern interpreters equate "the Venetian conspirators to the Whig exclusionists," others see Otway as "blackening the Senate as a means of attacking the Whig leaders in Parliament." Other modern critics see the senate as "the yet unrealized Whig ideal of government." Regardless of the specific political parallels, the attendance of both Charles II and his brother at the play suggests that *Venice Preserv'd* was meant to offer some critique of the Whigs.

Otway's final play, *The Atheist* (1683), was a failure. His final published work, the poem *Windsor Castle* (1685), eulogizes Charles II. Although some early biographers state that Otway died in a tavern or a debtor's prison, none of the accounts of his death are supported by persuasive evidence. It is certain, however, that he died impoverished.

Otway's reception has always been mixed. Although the 19th-century writer William Hazlitt found Otway "mawkish," John DRYDEN found him unsurpassed in his ability to "express the passions which are seated in the heart." Modern critics have found in Otway's tragedies a powerful representation of a changing world. This appraisal, as the critic Jessica Munns states, "charts, without sentimentality or approval, the replacement of an ethic of public virtue by a practice of personal interest."

Works about Thomas Otway

Taylor, Aline Mackenzie. *Next to Shakespeare; Otway's Venice Preserv'd, and The Orphan, and Their History on the London Stage.* Durham, N.C.: Duke University Press, 1950.

Warner, Kerstin P. *Thomas Otway.* Boston: Twayne, 1982.

Overbury, Thomas (1581–1613) *essayist, poet*

Thomas Overbury was born at Compton Scorpion Manor in Warwickshire, England, to Nicholas Overbury and Mary Palmer. He entered Oxford University in 1595 and received a B.A. three years later. He then turned to the study of law, something he abandoned to become a member of the court of JAMES I OF ENGLAND.

In 1606 Overbury became the secretary to Robert Carr, later the Earl of Somerset. In 1613 Carr proposed marriage to Frances Howard, the Countess of Essex. Overbury opposed the match because she was divorced, and Howard's family arranged to have him imprisoned in the Tower of London, where he grew ill and died. Rumors that Howard had conspired to have him poisoned spread quickly, and in 1616 she and Carr were convicted of Overbury's murder, though they were later pardoned.

Overbury's literary reputation rests on his *Characters* (1614), short essays modeled on prose pieces written by the ancient Greek philosopher Theophrastus in which a number of social types, such as "A Good Wife" and "A Soldier," are sketched. The essays are moralistic in tone. Some are meant to serve as guides to good behavior. In "A Virtuous Widow," for example, Overbury writes, "A virtuous widow . . . marries no more. She is like the purest gold, only employed for prince's medals: she never receives but one man's impression." Other essays are satiric, written with the intention of persuading their readers to avoid foolish behavior. "An Ignorant Glory Hunter" is thus mocked for being one who "entertains men with repetitions, and returns them their own words. . . . He gets the names of good wits,

and utters them for his companions. He confesseth vices that he is guiltless of, if they be in fashion."

Eventually 82 characters, many of them written by Overbury's friends, were published. "The station in English literature which Thomas Overbury occupies," the scholar James E. Savage thus observes, "is almost unique, for much of the writing associated with his name is not in reality his." It is impossible to tell how many of the character sketches Overbury wrote.

Overbury is also noted for his long poem *A Wife* (1616). This piece was written to dissuade Carr from marrying Frances Howard, and it was very popular at the time. Overbury describes the ideal wife, concluding that

> *All these good parts a perfect woman make:*
> *Adde love to me, they make a perfect wife:*
> *Without her love, her beauty should I take,*
> *As that of pictures; dead; that gives it life:*

Because of his opposition to the Carr-Howard marriage, Overbury's literary career was cut short. But that same opposition produced one of the most memorable poems of the 17th century.

Oxford, Edward de Vere, Earl of (1550–1604) *poet*

Edward de Vere, Earl of Oxford, was born in Essex, England, to John de Vere, the 16th Earl of Oxford, and Margaret Golding de Vere. He was tutored by his uncle, Arthur GOLDING, the translator of the Roman poet Ovid's *Metamorphoses*. As a young man, Oxford had the good fortune to secure the favor of Queen ELIZABETH I. However, his lavish lifestyle and constant clashes with his peers, the most famous of which was a quarrel with Sir Philip SIDNEY at a tennis court in 1579, prevented his being appointed to an important position at court.

Since the 1920s, a small group of scholars led by J. Thomas Looney have claimed that the earl wrote William SHAKESPEARE's plays. However, Shakespeare's later plays mention events that took place after Oxford died. Oxford was nonetheless a literary figure in his day. Not only did he provide PATRON-AGE, that is financial support, to both actors and writers, he was also a well-respected lyric poet. His poems circulated widely at court in manuscript, but only a handful of them remain. Of the surviving poems, most are love lyrics, as in the following stanzas from "Come Hither, Shepherd's Swain":

> Come hither, shepherd's swain;
> Sir, what do you require?
> I pray thee shew to me thy name.
> My name is Fond Desire.
>
> When wert thou born, Desire?
> In pride and pomp of May.

> By whom, sweet boy, wert thou begot?
> By Self-Conceit, men say.

Oxford received extravagant praise for writing such lines. For instance, the Elizabethan literary critic George PUTTENHAM noted that there were "sprung up another crew of Courtly makers [that is, poets] . . . of which number is first that noble gentleman, Edward Earl of Oxford." Puttenham may have been impressed because Oxford avoided the singsong rhythms that many of his fellow poets produced. Indeed, Oxford's poetry, the critic John Thomas Looney observes, "foreshadowed most distinctly, if it did not actually furnish, the generating impulse for the poetry of . . . [the] later years" of Elizabeth's reign.

P

Painter, William (ca. 1525–1595) *translator*
Nothing is known of the origins of William Painter, who entered St. John's College, Cambridge University, in 1543 and left without a degree in 1556. He became headmaster at Sevenoaks School in London, was ordained a deacon in 1560, and finally moved to London to become clerk of the ordnance in the Tower of London.

Painter is thought to have translated William Fulke's *Antiprognosticon* (1560), but his most important work was *The Palace of Pleasure* (1566), a collection of over 100 stories that he translated from Latin, Greek, French, and Italian. A second volume of 34 stories appeared in 1567, and both volumes were later published together in 1575. Painter's stories came from sources that included the classical authors Herodotus, Aelian, Plutarch, Aulus Gellius, and Livy as well as more recent Italian and French writers such as Bandello, Belleforest, and Marguerite of Navarre.

The Palace of Pleasure includes *Coriolanus,* from Livy and also *Romeo and Julietta* from Bandello, which Painter says is "The goodly history of the true and constant love between Romeo and Julietta, the one of whom died of poison, and the other of sorrow and heaviness."

Although modern scholars do not think Painter was Shakespeare's primary source for these two plays, they do know that Shakespeare was familiar with *The Palace of Pleasure* and probably used it for *All's Well that Ends Well.* Painter's translation of a French version by François de Belleforest of *The Duchess of Malfy* is accepted as the source for John WEBSTER's play *The Duchess of Malfi* (1614).

Parker, Matthew (1504–1575) *nonfiction writer, translator*
Matthew Parker, son of William and Alice Parker, was born in Norwich, England. Parker was educated at Corpus Christi College, Cambridge University, receiving a doctor of divinity degree in 1537. He married Margaret Harlestone in 1547.

Parker became a member of the Cambridge Reformers, a group of students who were interested in reforming the corrupt practices of the Catholic Church. Most of the group advocated a complete break with the church, inspired by the writings of German reformer Martin LUTHER, but Parker was more moderate in his views and remained so throughout his life.

In 1535 Parker was made chaplain to Anne BOLEYN, then queen of England and the wife of Henry VIII, and was also appointed dean of St. John the Baptist College at Stoke-by-Clare in Suffolk, a religious school. When ELIZABETH I succeeded to the

English throne, he was named archbishop of Canterbury.

Parker oversaw the compilation of the *Bishop's Bible* (1568). He may himself have translated the prefaces, Genesis, Exodus, Matthew, Mark, and the Gospels of St. Paul except for 1 Corinthians. This work was the version of the Bible used for reading in church during most of Elizabeth's reign, but it was later replaced by the King James Version (*see* BIBLE, KING JAMES VERSION).

Parker's most important work is *De Antiquitate* (1572), perhaps the first privately printed book in England, in which he traced the course of religion in the country from the time of Augustine. Among its six historic treatises, the book contains biographies of all the archbishops of Canterbury, including himself. Parker was attempting to demonstrate the evolution of an English church independent of Rome in order to legitimize the CHURCH OF ENGLAND. He collected many manuscripts from England's Anglo-Saxon past, and in so doing, he preserved many documents that might have been lost with the destruction of the monasteries under Henry VIII. He produced and preserved many other treatises and prayers and also published *The Whole Psalter translated into English Meter* (1567), a translation of the Book of Psalms.

After Parker's death, Corpus Christi College was endowed with his greatest legacy, a library of historic and ancient manuscripts, many rescued from the destroyed monasteries. In the Parker Library today are the earliest editions of works in Old English by Gildas, Asser, Aelfric, and Matthew Paris, as well as the *Anglo-Saxon Parker Chronicle*, a history of the early inhabitants of England. Matthew Parker could not complete a plan to revive the study of Old English language, but through his manuscript collection left the means for future scholars to do so.

Parkinson, John (1567–1650) *nonfiction writer*

John Parkinson's early life remains shrouded in obscurity, although it is likely that he was born in Nottinghamshire, England. He was an apothecary (druggist) and herbalist who cultivated many rare plant species in his garden at Long Acre in London and recorded his observations in several herbals (books about botany) that are considered among the finest early examples of this genre.

Parkinson's comprehensive *Theatrum Botanicum, The Theatre of Plantes* (1640) included detailed descriptions of 3,800 plants. More than a decade earlier he had published a similar work on garden flowers, *Paradisi in Sole Paradisus Terrestris: A Garden of All Sorts of Pleasant Flowers Which Our English Ayre will Permitt to be Noursed Up* (1629), which had descriptions of nearly 1,000 plants and some 700 illustrations. It was divided into three sections: on flower gardens, kitchen gardens, and orchard gardens. Parkinson was the first to identify and describe several new plants species, including the Welsh poppy, the strawberry tree, and the lady's slipper. He was also the earliest writer to "separately describe and illustrate" the orchard, vegetable, and flower garden. He was an early promoter of the art of gardening, which became a large part of English culture.

Parkinson served as the court apothecary to King JAMES I OF ENGLAND and was later given the title of Botanicus Regius Primarius (First Royal Botanist) by King Charles I. In this position he promoted the dissemination of botanical knowledge as an important tool for apothecaries to use in creating suitable medicines for their patients' maladies. He was also responsible for having introduced several new plant species into England. A genus of a tree found in Central America was named in his honor by the French botanist Charles Plumier.

Parr, Catherine (ca. 1513–1548) *nonfiction writer*

Catherine Parr was born in Kendal Castle, Westmoreland, in the north of England. Her father, Sir Thomas Parr, held a position at the court of King Henry VII; her mother, Lady Matilda Parr, was lady-in-waiting to Henry VIII's first queen, Catherine of Aragon. Parr was educated in the royal schoolroom, receiving a thorough training in Latin and theology. At 14 she married a wealthy landowner who was much older than she and died before she was 18. Another marriage left her a very wealthy widow at 30. At this point King Henry VIII proposed marriage. There was no denying the king's wishes, and they were wed in 1543.

As queen, Parr nursed the ailing king and promoted family harmony, taking on the role of mother to Henry's younger children, Edward and the future ELIZABETH I. She also took an interest in religious matters, which brought her into danger when a conservative court faction nearly succeeded in convincing the king that his wife was guilty of heresy. Parr's diplomacy diverted the king's suspicions from herself, but not from her friend Anne ASKEW.

In 1545 Parr's *Prayers or Medytacions* was published. Based on part of Thomas à Kempis's Latin work *The Imitation of Christ* (1471), it is a work aimed at helping lay Christians maintain an intimate and loving relationship with Jesus. This goal harmonized with the push of the new CHURCH OF ENGLAND toward making religious writing available in English as well as Latin and encouraging church members to approach God directly rather than through priests and saints. Parr uses à Kempis's ideas about conversion to and by Christ but employs her own metaphors to make them immediate, as in this passage where she evokes the sense of taste to convey the intimacy of God's presence: "O lorde, without thee, nothyng maie longe delite or please: for if any thyng should be lykyng and savorie, it muste be through helpe of thy grace, sesoned with the spice of thy wisedome."

Parr's second work, *The Lamentacion of a Sinner,* appeared in 1547. It is a much more original and personal work, recounting Parr's own process of conversion from Catholicism to Protestantism and foreshadowing the important genre of religious autobiography that was to develop hugely in the next 200 years.

Parr's works continued to be reprinted until well into the 17th century. Elizabeth I owned a miniature copy of *Prayers and Meditacyons* that she wore on her girdle.

Works about Catherine Parr

Martienssen, Anthony. *Queen Katherine Parr.* New York: McGraw Hill, 1974.
Starkey, David. *Six Wives: The Queens of Henry VIII.* New York: HarperCollins, 2003.

Pascal, Blaise (1623–1662) *philosopher, mathematician*

Blaise Pascal was born in Clermont (now Clermont-Ferrand), France, the only son of Étienne Pascal, a lawyer and member of the minor nobility, and Antoinette Bégon Pascal. His mother died when he was three, and Étienne decided to devote himself to the education of his three daughters and his son Blaise, who exhibited notably precocious intelligence. Étienne moved the family to Paris in 1631. He had original ideas about education, derived partly from his reading of MONTAIGNE. One of them was that mathematics was too much of a strain for young minds. Blaise Pascal therefore had no exposure to mathematics until he was 12, but he was then instantly fascinated. He went on to do important original work in the field. His first published work was an essay on the conic sections (1640).

In 1639 the family moved to Rouen, Étienne having been appointed tax collector for the province of Normandy. To help his father with his work, the young Pascal invented a calculating machine, one of the first ever. He also began to correspond with some of the great scientists and thinkers of the day, including René DESCARTES. In 1646 his father had an accident; his injuries were tended by two Jansenists—members of a strict and Puritanical Catholic religious order. Thereafter the whole family became adherents of Jansenism.

When Étienne died in 1651, Pascal wrote a letter to his sister Jacqueline elaborating on the religious meaning of death in general and their loss in particular. The ideas in this letter were developed much later in his work *Pensées* (*Thoughts*) (1660). Jacqueline entered the Jansenist convent at Port Royal in the year of her father's death, partly because of Pascal's persuasions, but Pascal himself fell away from religious observance for a while, spending time with gamblers and entrepreneurs. He did not, however, neglect his work in mathematics and physics. He corresponded with the great mathematician Pierre de Fermat (1601–65) about a mathematical problem involving dice, and together they worked out the basis of the theory of probability that is still viable today.

In late 1654 Pascal suffered a nearly fatal accident. He was riding in a carriage when the horses bolted, the traces broke, and the carriage was left teetering off a bridge over the Seine River. Soon after this incident, Pascal had an ecstatic conversion experience, a description of which he wrote on a piece of parchment that he wore next to his heart for the rest of his life. It was not long after this that he began to spend much of his time at Port Royal.

Jansenism came under attack from many in the Roman Catholic Church who felt that it resembled Protestant Puritanism too closely, and Pascal's Jansenist friend Antoine Arnauld was put on trial before the faculty of theology at the Sorbonne in Paris. Using a pseudonym, Pascal wrote and published 18 *Provincial Letters* in Arnauld's defense (1656–57), each addressing a different aspect of religious life. The *Provincial Letters* are described in the *Catholic Encyclopedia* (1913) as "the first prose masterpiece of the French language, in their satirical humour and passionate eloquence."

Pascal's health had never been good, and by 1659 he was in almost constant pain from an illness that might today be diagnosed as cancer. In the periods when the pain was lessened, he composed what has become his most famous work, his *Pensées*. As the title suggests, the work is less a unified whole than a collection of aphorisms and paragraphs, which he did not have the time to put into coherent form. Nonetheless, it gives a clear impression of Pascal's overall philosophical outlook.

One of the best-known sections, Pensée 233, contains the gambler's argument in favor of believing in God (known and argued about by philosophers as "Pascal's Wager"). In essence, Pascal says that one cannot know with rational certainty that God exists, but since, if God exists, believing in him will lead to eternal happiness, and not believing will lead to eternal suffering, it is reasonable to choose faith—if there is no God after all, nothing will have been lost.

Another important passage expresses the centrality of thought to human identity:

> Man is but a reed, the most feeble thing in nature, but he is a thinking reed. . . . All our dignity then, consists in thought. By it we must elevate ourselves, and not by space and time which we cannot fill. Let us endeavour then, to think well; this is the principle of morality.

But Pensée 277 shows that though Pascal valued rational thought highly, he knew that it was not everything: "The heart has its reasons, which reason knows nothing about."

Jacqueline died in 1661, and Pascal spent his last months at the home of one of his other sisters. Pascal's religious views influenced English letters, including Milton's *Paradise Lost*.

Other Works by Blaise Pascal

Christianity for Modern Pagans: Pascal's Pensées Edited, Outlined, and Explained. Edited by Peter Kreeft. San Francisco: Ignatius Press, 1993.
The Mind on Fire: An Anthology of the Writings of Blaise Pascal. Edited by James M. Houston. Portland, Oreg.: Multnomah Press, 1989.

Works about Blaise Pascal

Morris, Thomas V. *Making Sense of It All: Pascal and the Meaning of Life.* Grand Rapids, Mich.: W.B. Eerdmans, 1992.
O'Connell, Marvin R. *Blaise Pascal: Reasons of the Heart.* Grand Rapids, Mich.: W.B. Eerdmans, 1997.

Paston, Margaret (ca. 1423–1484) *letter writer*

Margaret Paston was born into a well-to-do family in Essex, England. Her father, John Mauteby, arranged her marriage to John Paston, a wealthy Norfolk landowner, in 1440. The Pastons owned several properties throughout Norfolk and also had business interests in London. John Paston was often away, and in his absence Margaret was often in charge of affairs at home, which involved not only the ordinary business of running a household but negotiating with tenants and merchants. She even represented the family's interests in local courts and commanded the family's private militia in defensive actions against raids by noble neighbors.

Seventy letters received or sent by Paston form part of a famous collection preserved by the family. It is likely that she could not actually write herself but used a scribe. Nonetheless, a very distinctive voice comes through. In a letter written to her husband in 1443 when he was sick and in London, she says,

> Right worshipful husband, I recommend me to you, desiring heartily to hear of your welfare. . . . And I thank you for the letter that ye sent me, for by my troth my mother [her mother-in-law] were nought in heart's ease from the time that we wist of your sickness, till we wist verily of your amending. . . . If I might have had my will, I should have seen you ere this time; I would ye were at home . . . lever than a gown, though it were of scarlet.

The formal and deferential opening gives way to a surprisingly direct expression of concern and care. Cloth dyed scarlet was prohibitively expensive and much sought after in the 15th century, and Margaret was, as other letters show, acutely aware of the prices of things. To value her husband's company above a scarlet gown was to value him highly indeed.

In a 1465 letter to John about her efforts to defend the family properties against aggression, Paston lets him know that though they parted at Caister, one of the family manors, she has moved the household to another property: "I had liefer, an it pleased you, be captainess here than at Caister." Though ever deferential, she has already decided what to do and knows that she is in charge as "captainess."

In 1469 Paston's daughter Margery displeased her mother by entering into an engagement with Richard Calle, one of the family servants. Paston, unable to prevent the marriage, wrote that "I charged my servants that she should not be received in mine house. I had given her warning."

Although Paston was thus unforgiving toward her daughter, she did remember Margery and Richard's child in her will. The will itself is a fascinating document, listing as it does an entire household's worth of items—beds, cups, spoons, a girdle—and matching them with a long list of relatives and dependents. Paston's letters provide matchless access to the reality of 15th-century life.

A Work by Margaret Paston
Private Life in the Fifteenth Century: Illustrated Letters of the Paston Family. Edited by Robert Virgoe. New York: Weidenfeld and Nicolson, 1989.

A Work about Margaret Paston
Cherewatuk, Karen, and Ulrike Wiethaus, eds. *Dear Sister: Medieval Women and the Epistolary Genre.* Philadelphia: University of Pennsylvania Press, 1983.

patronage
Patrons are powerful individuals who advance the causes of less-powerful individuals or groups. Patronage supported invention during the RENAISSANCE. Not only artists but also scientists had patrons, whose support of people of learning and talent not only helped those artists and scientists but reflected well on the character of the patrons themselves.

In England patronage was particularly important to actors. A 1572 law required acting companies to have patrons because, notes historian Margaret Chute, "nothing could have been more sinister to the Elizabethan mind than any group of men traveling about the country without proper credentials." People feared that vagabonds might be thieves. Although local companies might operate under a town's council, larger ones needed the protection of someone with the wealth and power of a baron.

Patrons provided financial support as well. Acting companies had to purchase plays and properties, pay actors, rent or build stages, and, above all, finance costumes. Out of patronage arose two great London acting companies in the 1590s. The first was managed by Edward Alleyn. Charles, Lord Howard, Lord High Admiral of England, was the patron to this group, called the ADMIRAL'S MEN. Chief rival to this company was the CHAMBERLAIN'S MEN, supported by Henry, Lord Hunsdon, lord chamberlain to Queen ELIZABETH I. Lord Hunsdon was a powerful advocate for the company, persuading London's mayor to allow plays to be performed in London inns. William SHAKESPEARE was a member of this company.

The Chamberlain's Men, which visited Edinburgh, became the KING'S MEN when James VI of Scotland ascended the English throne as JAMES I in 1603. James's family loved theater: a second company received the patronage of Queen Anne, and the Admiral's Men came under the patronage of James's eldest son Henry, becoming Prince Henry's Men. Thus three royal patrons helped to make possible England's great age of drama.

Writers often sought patrons by writing elaborate dedications flattering wealthy and powerful individuals. At this time the STATIONERS' COMPANY, the guild that regulated printing, was intensely watchful for any seditious writing. Having a royal patron ensured that a book would reach the public, and some books included dedications to more than one influential person.

Shakespeare had patrons who helped him in getting his poetry published. One of these was Henry Wriothesley, Earl of Southampton. Handsome and generous, the earl was the recipient of many dedications. Shakespeare's first dedication to him on the publication of *Venus and Adonis* shows remarkable restraint: "I know not how I shall offend in dedicating my unpolished lines to your Lordship, nor how the world will censure me for choosing so strong a prop to support so weak a burthen."

By the mid-18th century, the patronage system had changed radically. More publishers and more competition among publishers provided outlets for writers that had never existed before. The scholar Dustin Griffin, in fact, believes that publishers and booksellers essentially took over the role of the patron, choosing whose work would reach the public and whose would not, much as wealthy patrons had always done.

A Work about Patronage

Griffin, Dustin. *Literary Patronage in England, 1650–1800.* Cambridge, U.K.: Cambridge University Press, 1996.

Peacham, Henry (ca. 1576–ca. 1634)
nonfiction writer, poet

Henry Peacham was born in North Mimms, Hertfordshire, England, the son and namesake of a clergyman and rhetorician. After he acquired his bachelor's and master's degrees from Trinity College, Cambridge University, he served as a schoolmaster for a few years in Wymondham, Norfolk.

Peacham was a RENAISSANCE man, well read in various disciplines. He wrote treatises on rhetoric and grammar and various artistic and scientific subjects. He also produced verse in both English and Latin. His *Garden of Eloquence* (1577) was a dictionary of classical rhetorical terms and figures of speech—a "great might" of them, as he wrote in his introduction—mostly drawn from Greek and Roman models. Peacham defined dozens of such rhetorical devices in this encyclopedic book, so that "the orator may lead his hearers which way he lists; and draw then to what affection he will; and briefly to be moved with any affection that shall serve best for his purpose."

Others of Peacham's books dealt with the subjects of heraldry, art, and personal development; these included *Minerva Brittana: Or a Garden of Heroycal Devices* (1612) and *The Art of Drawing with the Pen and Limming in Water-colors* (1616). His *Compleat Gentleman* (1622) offered a practical primer for well-born young men eager to cultivate their social and intellectual lives. This work was specifically written for William Howard, a son of Lord Arundel, but its message proved relevant to others of his generation, and it went through several editions in just a few years. In *Compleat Gentleman,* Peacham referred to the Elizabethan era as "a golden age (for such a world of refined wits and excellent spirits it produced whose like are hardly to be hoped for in any succeeding age)." Although none of his individual works stands out as a masterpiece of the time, Henry Peacham is most notable for the wide range of topics he wrote on.

Works about Henry Peacham

Espy, Willard R. *The Garden of Eloquence: A Rhetorical Bestiary.* New York: Harper & Row, 1983.

Young, Alan R. *Henry Peacham.* Boston: Twayne, 1979.

Pearson, John (1613–1686) *nonfiction writer, poet*

John Pearson was the son of Robert Pearson, the rector of Great Snoring, Norfolk, England. He was educated at Eton College and King's College, Cambridge University, and served as rector of Thorington, Suffolk, from 1640 to 1646. Pearson's first writings were verses in Latin to commemorate Charles I's recovery from smallpox and verses upon the death of Edward King (1612–37), for whom John MILTON wrote *Lycidas.*

Pearson supported the king when the Puritan party rose up against him in the Civil War and during the period in which the monarchy was abolished and the puritan general Oliver Cromwell ran the country. He survived by preaching at St. Clements, Eastcheap. He subsequently published these sermons as *An Exposition of the Creed* (1659), which has become a standard work of English religious study. In this work, Pearson examines the Apostle's Creed, which he defines as "a brief comprehension of the objects of our Christian faith." He goes through each line of the creed, such as "I believe in the Holy Ghost" and "He Descended into Hell," explaining the reasons that the church believes what it does.

After the monarchy was reestablished in the Restoration, Pearson received several appointments, becoming the archdeacon of Surrey and a royal chaplain to Charles II. His scholarship was respected, and he was involved in amendments to the English BOOK OF COMMON PRAYER, a standard religious text. He also produced a Latin and Greek grammar for use in schools (1664).

Pearson became a professor of theology at Cambridge (1661) and produced theological treatises from his lectures. From 1662 to 1673 he was master of Trinity College, Cambridge, where he wrote *Vindiciæ Epistolarum S. Ignatii* (1672), (*A Vindication of the Letters of St. Ignatius*), his second important work. Pearson was made bishop of Chester in 1673, a position he held until his death.

Peele, George (1558–1596) *playwright*

George Peele was born in London to James Peele, a clerk at Christ's Hospital, and his wife, Anne. He entered Oxford University in 1571, receiving a B.A. in 1577 and an M.A. two years later. He then moved to London and became a member of the UNIVERSITY WITS, a group who, in Robert GREENE's words, "spent their wits in making plays." Peele spent the rest of his life following literary pursuits, mostly writing plays.

Five of Peele's dramas survive, the most famous of which is *The Arraignment of Paris* (staged perhaps in 1581 and printed 1584). *King David and Fair Bethsabe* (ca. 1588) was based on the biblical story. *The Battle of Alcazar* (1589) was a historical drama based on an actual battle that took place in 1578 in which the king of Portugal, Sebastian, was killed. *The Old Wives Tale* (ca. 1590), whose sources lie in folktales, concerns a princess who is kidnapped by a sorcerer; it is considered highly innovative for its complex plot. Peele's last play, *King Edward I* (ca. 1593), is a history play that tells the story of the English king Edward I's conquest of Scotland.

Peele's plots are often weak and his characters, as the critic Werner Senn observes, are not "developed and individualized strongly enough to dominate the action" of a play. Still, Peele helped establish the use of blank verse, or unrhymed lines of 10 syllables each, alternating unstressed and stressed syllables, in drama.

What is perhaps more important about Peele's dramas is the way they combine national folk traditions with classical mythology, an element of his playwriting that is evident from the very beginning of his career. His earliest known play, *The Arraignment of Paris,* was put on for ELIZABETH I. It was written with the tastes of the court in mind and therefore is more classical than popular. Indeed, its plot begins with the Greek myth about the origin of the Trojan War. According to the myth, Paris, a Trojan shepherd, is appointed to judge a beauty contest among the goddesses. He gives the golden apple to Venus, goddess of love, and is rewarded with Helen, the wife of Menelaus, the king of Sparta, who begins the Trojan War to retrieve his wife. In Peele's play, however, Paris's decision is not upheld. Instead, he is brought before Jupiter for choosing incorrectly. Diana, the goddess of chastity, is then appointed to award the prize, and she gives it not to one of the goddesses but to a nymph called Eliza, that is, Queen Elizabeth, who is superior to all. Diana explains:

> This peerless nymph, whom heaven and
>   earth belove,
> This paragon, this only, this is she
> In whom do meet so many gifts in one,
> On whom our country gods so often gaze,
> In honor of whose name the Muses sing:
> In state Queen Juno's peer, for power in
>   arms
> And virtues of the mind Minerva's mate,
> As fair and lovely as the Queen of Love,
> As chaste as Dian in her chaste desires.

Peele's appeal to the popular taste is also present in *The Arraignment of Paris.* In the play there is, as the scholar L. G. Salingar notes, a mixture of Latin and Italian songs and folk materials. In the first song between Paris and Oenone (a water nymph), for instance, Paris is described in terms similar to

those used to describe shepherds in English pastoral poems. He is "the fairest shepherd on our green . . . As fresh as bin the flowers in May." Moreover, "Oenone's song of complaint," Salingar continues, keeps some elements "of [an English] folk-song in spite of its classical allusions."

The final result is that the classical characters seem to inhabit an English country setting. Thus Salingar credits Peele with helping to increase "the range of national traditions which combined in the making of Shakespeare's theatre" and with helping to combine "the influence of courtly revels and folk pastime, which was later to culminate in the masques of Ben JONSON."

While his literary reputation has declined since the 16th century, Peele was a highly regarded figure in the 1580s. Thomas NASHE, for example, praised his "dexterity of wit, and manifold variety of invention" in a discussion of *The Arraignment of Paris* and asserted that Peele "goeth beyond all that write."

Other Works by George Peele
Works. 2 vols. Edited by A. H. Bullen. Port Washington, N.Y.: Kennikat Press, 1966.

Works about George Peele
Purcell, Sally. *George Peele.* Pin Farm: Fyfield Books, 1972.
Senn, Werner. *Studies in the Dramatic Construction of Robert Greene and George Peele.* Druck, Germany: Francke Verlag Bern, 1973.

Pembroke, Countess of
See SIDNEY, MARY.

Pepys, Samuel (1633–1703) *diarist*
Samuel Pepys achieved fame after his death by being an accidental historian. Pepys spent 10 years keeping a detailed journal that gives the modern reader a vivid picture of 17th-century life. The events of his life, from the most infinitesimal details of daily tasks to momentous historical events

like the Great Fire and the Plague, are perceptively recorded.

The scholar Hermione Lee sums up the size and scope of Pepys's *Diary*: "His famously candid, minute and inexhaustibly vigorous account of every detail of his daily life filled six leather-bound books written in shorthand."

Pepys was born in London, the son of a tailor, John Pepys. In 1650 he was awarded a scholarship to Trinity Hall, Cambridge University, but later transferred to Magdalene College. Two years after his graduation, Pepys married Elizabeth St. Michel, the 15-year-old dowryless daughter of a Huguenot (French Protestant) refugee.

In 1660, five years after his marriage, Pepys began writing his diary. He begins with the adventure of going to sea as secretary to a relative, Sir Edward Montagu. The object of the journey was to bring Charles Stuart back from Holland and restore him to the English throne. On the return voyage Pepys heard the king's stories of his flight from Cromwell's armies:

Upon the quarter-deck he [the king] fell in discourse of his escape from Worchester. Where it made me ready to weep to hear the stories that he told . . . As his travelling four days and three nights on foot, every step up to the knees in dirt . . . that made him so sore all over his feet he could scare stir.

In 1661 Pepys observed the coronation of Charles II. Although he had earlier been appointed justice of the peace for Middlesex, Essex, Kent, and Hamptonshire, his station in society was not such that he was allowed a coveted seat at the coronation, so he observed it from the chapel at Westminster Abbey. Pepys's description of this day is so detailed that he even includes the memory of desperately needing an outhouse and of sneaking into the banquet hall to get a bit of food from the tables. Pepys admits to drinking too much that night, or being "foxed," and vomiting as a result. He stayed with his friend William Sheply, telling his wife he could not find a coach to drive him home while in

actuality he was roaming the streets downing pots of ale.

Women are routinely mentioned in Pepys's journal, with scandalous enough selections that many passages were edited out of the early editions. To the modern reader, his enjoyment of "mighty pretty" women may even seem boyish and guileless. But in any age, his many infidelities are notable; he often wrote about them in a mix of English and other languages so as to record yet disguise his indiscretions.

Pepys's career was another focus of the *Diary*. He advanced through the ranks of the British navy by being a sharp observer, both of the people he worked with and what needed to be done. Thus, he was successful in doing the right thing without needing to be told, which impressed his superiors.

Pepys's meticulous journal-keeping may have given him skills that helped him do well professionally. He kept spotless records, which he was always able to locate immediately despite their impressive volume. He had an eye for history and could tell superior officers about things their grandfathers had accomplished. In 1662 he wrote of reform and improvement needed in the navy, which earned him a commendation for conduct.

By 1665, after being appointed treasurer for Tangier, Pepys was mainly responsible for supplying the navy. Charles II himself spoke with Pepys about the ships. Honored, Pepys wrote: "And this is the first time that ever the King did know me personally."

There was the occasional enemy at work, such as Sir William Warren, a "cunning" man and former friend who enjoyed making digs at Pepys, especially in regards to Warren's greater wealth. Warren himself kept questionable accounts and tried to shift the focus of Pepys's suspicion by making sly accusations against him.

In 1665 Pepys also recorded the events of the bubonic plague in London:

This day, much against my Will, I did in Drury-lane, see two or three houses marked with a red cross upon the doors, and 'Lord have mercy upon us' writ there; which was a sad sight to me . . . It put me into an ill conception of myself and my smell, so that I was forced to buy some roll-tobacco to smell and to chaw, which took away the apprehension.

Like many people who had the means to do so, Pepys and his wife Elizabeth left London during the worst time of the plague. They settled in Woolwich, but Pepys often ventured back into London to work in his office. One fourth of the population of London was killed by the plague; Pepys wrote: "every day sadder and sadder news."

The next year another tragedy struck London: the Great Fire. Strong easterly winds and a summer drought culminated in the worst destruction the city would see until the Blitz of 1941. Pepys's birthplace was destroyed, but his home and office were spared. He admits he was "much terrified in the nights . . ., with dreams of fire and falling down of houses." He even recalls the start of the fire. As fires were common in London, no one expected the massive destruction that would result. But Pepys reports that the Lord Mayor himself went from scorning that "[a] woman might piss it out" to bemoaning, "Lord, what can I do? I am spent!"

Once again Pepys and his wife fled to Woolwich. Pepys had saved the navy offices by ordering the buildings around them destroyed and worried about the fate of the thousands of homeless people facing the winter. When he returned to London, he found an outraged citizenry looking for someone to blame for the tragedy. He feared he would lose his job for ordering buildings destroyed, but he successfully faced a Parliamentary Committee of Navy Accounts.

In 1669 Pepys discontinued his diary because his eyesight was failing. His wife Elizabeth died of a fever the next year. In 1679 Pepys was accused of betraying the navy and spent a short time in the Tower of London before his name was cleared in 1670. In 1684 he was made president of the Royal Society. He is buried at St. Olave's Church in London.

Critical Analysis

While Pepys's journal contains a lively view of politics, art, and lifestyles of the 1660s, part of what makes his *Diary* famous is his eye for women. His inability to remain faithful to his wife was naturally a scandal, but his thoughts and observations have led some to label him a "ladies' man," although he was actually often rather timid in his approach.

Pepys may have been more talk than action, but he occasionally did act, and he kept honest records of both infidelities and rejections. This candid style is the reason for the success of the journal, and the more lurid sections recalling his dalliances with women have only helped the reputation of the *Diary* grow. The biographer Ivan E. Taylor commented, "The *Diary* is also famous because of Pepys' reputation—a bad one—with women."

Still Pepys's affairs do not alienate the reader, but, rather, allow Pepys be seen as a believable, real person. When he writes of his affair with his wife's maid, Deborah Willet, he frequently expresses feeling genuine love for her and refuses to call her a "whore" in a letter, even when his wife demanded it.

Pepys's dealings with women also reveal the role of class in 17th-century London society. In fact, as Taylor notes, "Under certain circumstances, when he was alone with a woman a notch of two beneath him in social rank, Pepys could be very successful with the ladies." But like a good, flawed hero, Pepys openly declares love to his wife, with fond and proud praise of her, such as when he writes, "the King and Duke of York minded me, and smiled upon me, at the handsome woman near me."

The same talent for storytelling that Pepys shows in the racy parts of his *Diary* extends to topics that could easily be rendered dull, such as day-to-day chores and navy work. As the author Philip Hensher writes, "Pepys was interested in everything, and everything in the *Diary* is interesting." The *Telegraph* reviewer and writer Christopher Howse describes Pepys as "full of life and curiosity, writing it all down, with no apparent filter of shame, pride or reinvention."

One of Pepys's most famous admirers was novelist Robert Louis Stevenson, who called the *Diary* "a work of art." Stevenson acutely notes that "Although not sentimental in the abstract, . . . Pepys he was sweetly sentimental about himself. His own past clung about his heart, an evergreen." Stevenson goes on to expound on the reasons for success of the *Diary*. It is Pepys's

> sincerity which makes . . . the *Diary* a miracle among human books. He was not unconscious of his errors—far from it; he was often startled into shame, often reformed, often made and broke his vows of change. But whether he did ill or well, he was still his own unequalled self; still that entrancing ego of whom alone he cared to write; and still sure of his own affectionate indulgence, when the parts should be changed, and the writer come to read what he had written. Whatever he did, or said, or thought, or suffered, it was still a trait of Pepys, a character of his career; and as, to himself, he was more interesting than Moses or than Alexander, so all should be faithfully set down.

Samuel Pepys is a writer whose life and personality are synonymous with the work he produced. Stevenson wrote of him: "He shows himself throughout a sterling humanist. Indeed, he who loves himself, not in idle vanity, but with a plenitude of knowledge, is the best equipped of all to love his neighbors." Pepys's friend John EVELYN described him as "universally beloved, hospitable, generous, learned in many things, skilled in music, a very great treasurer of learned men."

Works about Samuel Pepys
Coote, Stephen. *Samuel Pepys.* New York: Palgrave, 2001.
Taylor, Ivan E. *Samuel Pepys.* Boston: Twayne, 1989.

Petrarch, Francis (Francesco Petrarca) (1304–1374) *poet*

Francis Petrarch was born in Arezzo, Italy, to an exiled Florentine family. The family moved to Avignon, France, where the pope's court was temporarily in residence, when Petrarch was a boy, and he was educated in Montpellier, France, and later in Bologna, Italy. His father was a legal clerk who intended Francis to be a lawyer, but the boy disliked what he saw of the practice of law and spent as much time as he could reading literature. He discovered the work of the classical Roman orator Marcus Tullius Cicero (106–43 B.C.), which led to a lifelong passion for all the classics. Although he is mostly known today for his Italian works, he wrote more in Latin, which was considered a nobler language.

After his father's death in 1326, Petrarch abandoned his legal studies in Bologna, returned to Avignon, and began to study for the priesthood. On Good Friday 1327, Petrarch supposedly saw Laura, the woman who was to be the main inspiration behind much of his writing. Scholars argue about her true identity, but she was almost certainly married, and Petrarch probably never had any time alone with her—he may never even have had a conversation with her—but his distant love for her inspired almost 300 sonnets and other poems. These form part of his most famous work, the *Canzoniere* (ca. 1350) (*Song Book*), which is a collection of poems in various forms, written in Italian, most of them about love but some on moral subjects, others about Rome and his love for its history. Petrarch added to the *Canzoniere* and reorganized it over the years. Two of the most moving of the sonnets concern Laura's death in 1328 of plague. Despite Laura's demise, Patrarch continued writing sonnets to her for many years.

Petrarch's other great vernacular work is the *Trionfi* (*Triumphs,* 1470), written, like Dante's *Divine Comedy,* in the three-line stanzas of *terza rima.* It presents a procession of six allegorical figures: Love, Chastity, Death, Fame, Time, and Divinity. Each triumphs over its predecessor, until Divinity rises above them all, representing peace, everlasting life, and Petrarch's pure, eternal union with Laura.

In 1630 Petrarch took minor clerical orders and entered the service of Cardinal Colonna. He spent much of the rest of his life traveling, often on diplomatic missions for the church, but always finding time to explore libraries and add to his own collection of manuscripts. He especially sought out works of classical authors, and his infectious enthusiasm for the task, which inspired others, probably saved many older works from loss. Petrarch's efforts, with BOCCACCIO's, certainly contributed greatly to the RENAISSANCE revival of classical scholarship.

Petrarch's fame as a poet so grew rapidly that in 1341 he was honored by being crowned poet laureate of his beloved city of Rome. He was also a voluminous letter writer. Among his correspondents was his friend Boccaccio, with whom he exchanged ideas about the writer's craft. In one of his letters to Boccaccio, written in 1366, he discusses what it means to write in the vernacular rather than in Latin. In his youth, he says, he was drawn to writing in Italian, which, because it was still in the process of formation, offered stimulating opportunities for the writer to enrich and improve it. But he found that his short Italian works became so popular, recited and copied everywhere, that he ceased to have any control over them, and he turned to Latin for his more important works, confident that in Latin they could be read only by educated people who would respect their author's intentions.

In addition, Petrarch wrote letters addressed to classical authors, including two to his hero Cicero, and also a letter to posterity in which he describes his own personality and outlook with some intriguing details. Although careful to include information about some of his accomplishments and the honors he had received, he says, with striking modesty, "I have taken pride in others, never in myself, and however insignificant I may have been, I have always been still less important in my own judgment." Petrarch died in Arqua, near Padua, Italy, a day before his 70th birthday.

Petrarch did not invent the sonnet, but he perfected it. Throughout the Renaissance, which spread through Europe over the next 300 years, poets of different countries imitated his sonnets. Among them were, in France, Pierre de RONSARD and, in England, Geoffrey Chaucer; Thomas WYATT; Henry Howard, Earl of SURREY; Sir Philip SIDNEY; Edmund SPENSER; and William SHAKESPEARE. John MILTON was a later exponent of the Petrarchan sonnet. In fact, Petrarch's progeny in England may be greater than in Italy, partly because his English followers borrowed both form and content from the Italian poet's work, introducing into English new metrical schemes such as *terza rima*. As John HARINGTON commented in 1591, "In his sweet-mourning sonnets, the doleful Petrarch . . . seems to have comprehended all the passions that all men of that humour have felt."

Other Works by Francis Petrarch

Petrarch: The Canzionere, or Rerum Vulgarium Fragmenta. Translated by Mark Musa. Bloomington: Indiana University Press, 1999.

Petrarch's Lyric Poems. Translated by Robert Durling. Cambridge, Mass.: Harvard University Press, 1976.

Works about Francis Petrarch

Kennedy, William J. *Authorizing Petrarch.* Ithaca, N.Y.: Cornell University Press, 1994.

Mazzotta, Giuseppe. *The Worlds of Petrarch.* Durham, N.C.: Duke University Press, 1993.

Reeve, Henry. *Petrarch.* Honolulu, Hawaii: University Press of the Pacific, 2002.

Petrarchism

Petrarchism describes a type of poetry popular in England from about 1591 to 1620. The term comes from English writers' imitation of the Italian poet Francis PETRARCH, whose *Canzoniere* written to his beloved Laura was translated into English around 1527. Most of the poems in Petrarch's collection are sonnets, 14-line poems with a particular rhythmic and metrical pattern. The poems form a sequence that unveils the story of the poet's unrequited love for Laura.

In telling his story, Petrarch uses certain conventions that came to be repeated and recognized in other sonnet sequences written by English writers such as Thomas WYATT, Sir Philip SIDNEY, Edmund SPENSER, and William SHAKESPEARE. These conventions include descriptions of the beloved, or the sonnet lady, as beautiful with golden hair, eyes like the stars or the sun, red lips, white skin, and perfect teeth. Shakespeare parodies these conventions when he writes in his Sonnet 130, "My mistress' eyes are nothing like the sun; / Coral is far more red than her lips' red." However, Shakespeare often used the conventions in a straight manner both in his sonnets and in the speeches of lovers in his plays.

The speaker of the Petrarchan sonnets also portrays certain conventional attitudes. He is despairing, longs for the night, but has bad dreams; his heart alternately burns and freezes; when he sees his beloved, he's happy, then sad that she does not love him. Such depictions of opposites are common in Petrarchan poems. Other conventions include the exchange of hearts and the representations of love as Cupid, usually depicting him as either a mischievous child or a tyrannical god.

Eventually Petrarchism fell out of favor, partly because of the repetitious self-punishing nature of the verse. Many poets including Shakespeare, began to write anti-Petrarchan poetry that criticized or made fun of Petrarchism.

Works about Petrarchism

Evans, Maurice, ed. *Elizabethan Sonnets.* London: Everyman, 1996.

John, Lisle. *The Elizabethan Sonnet Sequences: Studies in Conventional Conceits.* New York: Columbia University Press, 1966.

Pettie, George (1548–1589) *prose writer, translator*

George Pettie was born to John and Mary Pettie in Oxfordshire, England. He attended Cambridge University from 1564 to 1569 and after graduating traveled extensively throughout Europe.

In 1576 Pettie published *A Petite Pallace of Pettie his Pleasure,* a collection of 12 intricately plotted romantic tales. Adapted from medieval legend and classical myth, the work was filled with moral maxims such as, "It is better to be alone than in ill company" and "Things most excellent are ever most envied."

Pettie had an elaborate style that would find further development in the work of John LYLY. Here is Pettie addressing his female readers: "Now I would wish you blazing stars which stand upon your chastity, to take light at this lot, to take heed by this harm." Of Pettie's work the writer Ernest Baker says, "Though his diction was full of artifice, he often clinched the moral in a pithy phrase that could not fail to stick: *The sea hath fish for every man.*"

At this time the educated classes felt that prose written in English was coarse and unrefined. Pettie set out to show that English was as good as French or Italian for prose fiction, as long as words that would enrich it were introduced.

In 1581 Pettie's translation from the Italian of the first three volumes of Stefano Guazzo's *The Civile Conversation,* a guide to proper conversational etiquette, was published. Pettie did not translate the fourth volume, feeling it too slight and unworthy of publication. The work was wildly popular, anticipating the Elizabethan craze for courtesy literature—works that illustrated refined and aristocratic manners and morals.

Pettie, like many writers of this period, was committed to education and the acquisition of knowledge. The critic Sir Edward Sullivan writes, "Pettie is wholeheartedly on the side of scholarship and study, urging his readers . . . not to be ashamed to show their learning . . ." As Pettie's writes in *Petite Palace,* "In divers thinges, nothing so good as learning."

Philips, Katherine (1631–1664) *poet, translator*

Katherine Philips (née Fowler) was born in London to Katherine Oxbridge and John Fowler, a merchant. She received her education at a boarding school for girls, where she likely developed the appreciation for close female friendship that would occupy a central place in her poetry. At 16 she married Colonel James Philips.

In 1651 Philips formed the Society of Friendship, a group of mostly women who corresponded and shared literary work. Philips circulated her early poetry in manuscript among the group. Her verse includes epitaphs, elegies, and poems on political themes. Yet it is her poems about female friendship that earned her the attention of her contemporaries and of later critics. Strong bonds between men were a common subject of English poetry of the period, but Philips was the first English poet to express the importance of female companionship. In "A Friend" (1664) she writes,

> If soules no sexes have, for Men t'exclude
> Women from Friendship's vast capacity,
> Is a Design injurious or rude,
> Onely maintain'd by partial tyranny.
> Love is allow'd to us, and Innocence,
> And noblest friendships doe proceed from
>   thence.

In this verse Philips argues that women should not be left out of friendship by male "tyranny." In the final two lines she announces that women, too, are capable of friendship. The phrase "soules no sexes have" refers to the notion of platonic love, an idealized, nonromantic form of love that was popularized by many lyric poets in mid-17th-century literature.

Philips draws upon the contemporary language of love poetry to describe the intimacy and emotions of friendship that occur in private. A clear influence upon her was the poet John DONNE, known for his elaborate conceits, or extended metaphors, describing the intimate withdrawal of lovers away from the world. Philips's poem "Friendship's Mysterys" (1664) evokes such a movement:

> To the dull, angry world let's prove
> There's a religion in our love.

Echoing Donne's "The Canonization" (1633), a poem comparing private lovers' devotion to religion, Philips describes love removed from the hostile outer world. As the critic Susanna Mintz comments, Philips's verse "explores the tension between female friendship and the social, political world, in conjunction with a steady focus inward, mapping out the psychological contours of the space of friendship."

Philips goes on to describe the inner, mental connection that grows between two friends:

> Here Mixture is Addition grown;
> We both diffuse, and both ingross [expand]:
> And we whose Minds are so much one
> Never, yet ever, are alone.

Describing the mental intimacy of friendship, the poem uses parallelism, or similarly structured phrases, in the line "both diffuse, and both engrosse" to emphasize the sameness and mutual absorption of friends.

Concerning the broader context of her work, Philips's verse is similar to CAVALIER POETRY, which was written by supporters of the king during the English Civil War. Cavalier poetry often turned to the imagery of pastoral, or rural, escape. Some of Philips's friendship poetry celebrating withdrawal from the world also includes political commentary, as in "A retir'd Friendship, to Ardelia" (1664):

> Here is no quarrelling for Crowns,
> Nor fear of changes in our fate;
> No trembling at the Great ones frowns,
> Nor any Slavery of State.

In this stanza, four negative comparisons are contrasted to the calm space of friendship. The final charge, "Slavery of State," is a shot at the rule of Oliver Cromwell, the Puritan who ruled England after the Civil War.

Philips composed her most openly politicized work upon the Restoration, the return of the monarchy under Charles II in 1660. She exhibits her Royalist views in verse such as "Upon the Double Murder of King Charles," a reference to the execution of Charles I during the Civil War. She also wrote verse in honor of the royal family, even sending her poems to court in order to boost her husband's reputation. Because of these poems, Philips became a court favorite.

Philips's early death at 33 from smallpox cut short a promising literary career. In addition to poetry, she translated two plays by French dramatist Corneille, *Horace* (1667) and *Pompey* (1663), both of which were well received. Her reputation was clearly appreciated by other contemporary poets. Abraham COWLEY wrote her epitaph, celebrating "A Sp'rit so rich, so noble, and so high." The romantic poet John Keats commended her "feminine modesty" and her "most delicate fancy." Philips also left an important legacy for women writers. According to the critic Bronwen Price, "[B]y the end of the century Philips acquired a number of imitators, establishing a new feminized poetics devoted to romantic female friendship."

Other Work by Katherine Philips

The Collected Works of Katherine Philips: The Matchless Orinda. Edited by Thomas Patrick. Stump Cross, U.K.: Stump Cross Books, 1990.

Works about Katherine Philips

Andreadis, Harriette. *Sappho in Early Modern England: Female Same-Sex Literary Erotics, 1550–1714.* Chicago: University of Chicago Press, 2001.

Barash, Carol. *Englishwomen's Poetry, 1649–1714: Politics, Community, and Linguistic Authority.* New York: Clarendon Press, 1996.

Pikeryng, John (John Pickering)

See PUCKERING, JOHN.

Pix, Mary (1666–1720) *playwright, novelist*

Mary Pix was the daughter of Roger Griffith, the rector of Padbury and master of the Royal Latin School in Buckingham. Her mother, Lucy Berriman, was a musician. She later married George Pix, a merchant tailor, and moved with him to Hawkhurst, Kent, and from there to London.

Her first published work was the novel *The Inhuman Cardinal, or: Innocence Betrayed* (1696),

which tells the story of a lustful cardinal's pursuit of the beautiful Melora. Between 1696 and 1706 Pix wrote 13 plays, many of them set in such faraway locales as Spain and Russia. Her first and best-known play, *Ibrahim, the Thirteenth Emperor of the Turks* (1696), is a historical tragedy about a wicked emperor and his harem. The emperor's misdeeds bring ruin upon his country: "The Mufti hates our Licentious Emperour; his late / Attempt upon the Relict of *Morat;* / His despising all his Queens when once enjoy'd." Pix also wrote comedies such as *The Spanish Wives* (1696), a farce about a Spanish governor and his unfaithful wife.

Pix was one of the three "female wits" satirized in the anonymous play *Female Wits, or, The Triumvirate of Poets at Rehearsal* (the other two were Catharine Trotter and Delariviere Manley). Pix was caricatured as Mrs. Wellfed, who drinks too much. Unlike Trotter and Manley, who portrayed strong women, Pix often portrayed her female characters as weak and unassertive and their friendships as inconstant and selfish.

Other Work by Mary Pix

The Plays of Mary Pix and Catherine Trotter. Edited by Edna L. Steeves. New York: Garland Press, 1982.

A Work about Mary Pix

Morgan, Fidelis. *The Female Wits: Women Playwrights on the London Stage 1660–1720.* London: Virago, 1989.

Pomfret, John (1667–1702) *poet*

John Pomfret was born in Luton, England, the son of a vicar. He went to school at Bedford and Queens' College in Cambridge. In Bedforshire he became the rector of two parishes after delivering a successful elegy on the death of Queen Mary II.

He published *Poems on Several Occasions* in 1699, but his most successful work would come the following year—the poem *The Choice.* This poem describes the ideal life of a gentleman and depicts his estate and way of life: "I'd have a Clear, and Competent Estate / That I might live Gentiely, but not Great." The poem embraces a genteel, charitable, and idealistic life. It recommends having plenty but not wasteful luxury: "A frugal plenty should my table spread, / With healthy, not luxurious dishes fed." At first it was published anonymously, and as its fame grew so did the curiosity surrounding its author. It eventually became the best-selling poem of 18th-century England. Despite the popularity of the poem, when Pomfret's authorship was revealed it hurt his career, because the bishop of London was displeased by the poem. He felt the line about Pomfret's desire to "have no wife" was a declaration of a desire to live in sin with a mistress. Pomfret continued to write but never came close to the success of *The Choice*.

Poquelin, Jean-Baptiste

See MOLIÈRE.

Preston, Thomas (1537–1598) *dramatist*

Thomas Preston was born at Simpson, Buckinghamshire, England, and educated at Eton and King's College, Cambridge University, receiving his doctorate in law in 1576. He was named master of Trinity Hall in 1584, and became vice chancellor of the university in 1589–90.

Preston is best known for his *Lamentable Tragedy mixed full of Mirth conteyning the Life of Cambises, King of Percia . . .* (1569), which is based on material from Herodotus, the Greek historian (ca. 480–ca. 425 B.C.). It tells the story of the fall of King Cambises and also contains a number of abstractions, such as Murder, Cruelty, and Vice, as characters. For this reason *Lamentable Tragedy* is considered an important transitional moment between the medieval morality play, which was made up of characters representing abstractions, and the RENAISSANCE historical chronicle, a play based on real people and events.

Although the play is historically significant, by today's standards it appears primitive and comical. The character Ambidexter, or Vice, is introduced in this manner:

> *Ha, my name, my name would you so fain*
> *[do you want to] knowe?*
> *Yea iwis shall ye [you will], and that with*
> *all speed:*
> *I have forgot it therefore I cannot showe,*
> *A, A, now I have it, I have it in deed.*
> *My name is Ambidexter . . .*

Ashley Thorndike included *Lamentable Tragedy* in his *Minor Elizabethan Drama* (1933) because, in spite of its crudeness, "it is increasingly being recognized as having great significance for English tragedy."

Primrose, Diana (fl. 1630) *poet*

Hardly anything is known of the life or origins of Diana Primrose, who published only one poem, *A Chaine of Pearl* (1630), in praise of Queen ELIZABETH I, who had died more than a quarter century earlier. Scholars believe that Primrose was probably married to a man with that surname, derived from a prominent Scottish family. Marion Wynne-Davies, who included Primrose's verse in her anthology *Women Poets of the Renaissance* (1999), suggests that her husband might have been Gilbert Primrose, a minister in the French Huguenot (Protestant) church who left France with his wife in 1622 or 1623, after French authorities imposed a ban on foreign clergy.

A Chaine of Pearl is dedicated "To All Noble Ladies and Gentlewomen." In the preface Primrose makes quite clear that the intended readers of the book are women, and she warns them, in contrast to the usual warnings about female deceit, against "men's siren-blandishments, / Which are attended with so foul events." At this period, a work written by a woman for women about a woman was somewhat unusual. Written in iambic pentameter, *A Chaine of Pearl* is an allegorical poem in which Primrose compares 12 virtues—among them, Religion, Chastity, Prudence, Science, Patience, and Bounty—said to be possessed by the queen to pearls on a strand. The poem opens:

The goodliest Pearl in fair Eliza's Chain
Is true religion, which did chiefly gain
A royal lustre to all the rest . . .

As source texts, Primrose used Edmund SPENSER's *The Faerie Queene* and William CAMDEN's *Annales*.

A Work about Diana Primrose

Wynn-Davies, Marion, ed. *Women Poets of the Renaissance*. New York: Routledge, 1999.

Protestant Reformation

See REFORMATION.

Prowse, Dering Anne

See LOCK, ANNE VAUGHAN.

Prynne, William (1600–1669) *nonfiction writer, pamphleteer*

William Prynne was born in Somerset, England, to Thomas Prynne, a gentleman farmer, and Marie Sherston Prynne, daughter of the mayor of Bath. He earned a B.A. from Cambridge University in 1621 and immediately enrolled at Lincoln's Inn to study law; he was called to the bar in 1628.

Although Prynne had devoted himself to the study of law, his interests began to lie more and more with religious reform, a subject he tackled in several pamphlets. In particular, he was opposed to the growing influence of Arminianism (the doctrine, put forth by the Dutch theologian Jacob Arminius [1560–1609], that God has given people the choice to accept or reject him) in the court of Charles I. Prynne was a Puritan, and as such he believed in the unyielding doctrines of predestination and original sin.

In 1627 Prynne published the controversial pamphlet *The Perpetuitie of a Regenerate Man's Estate*. In this work he harshly criticized the Arminian cause, and as a result he was summoned to court to defend the publication. Avoiding imprisonment, Prynne continued to produce pamphlets, such as *The Church of England's Old Antithesis to the New Armenianism*.

Prynne was not satisfied merely to criticize religious practices, and in 1628 he turned his attention to social behaviors of the day. In *The Unloveliness of Lovelocks* (1528) Prynne condemned his fellow Puritans for their elaborate dress and hairstyles. Particularly disturbing to Prynne was the growing tendency of men to grow their hair long and of women to sometimes cut their own hair short. He condemned these practices, citing scripture to illustrate the ungodliness of such acts.

Prynne also found fault with the theater. His most famous work, the 1632 *Histriomastix: Or, the Players Scourge and Actors Tragedy,* details his dissatisfaction with the stage and its players. General discontent with theatrical practices was, in itself, nothing new: Nearly 50 other such attacks had appeared in the years prior to Prynne's own scathing account. However, parts of Prynne's work were seen as blatant attacks on Charles I and his queen, Henrietta Maria, who loved good drama. When, for example, Prynne calls women who take part in dramatic performances such as court masques whores, he did not exempt Henrietta Maria, herself an actor in many court masques. He also objected to dancing, a favorite pastime at court, writing:

Dancing is for the most part attended with many amorous smiles, wanton compliments, unchaste kisses, scurrilous songs and sonnets, effeminate music, lust-provoking attire, ridiculous love pranks, all of which savour only of sensuality, of raging fleshly lusts. Therefore it is wholly to be abandoned of all good Christians. Dancing serves no necessary use, no profitable, laudable or pious end at all. It is used only from the inbred pravity, vanity, wantoness, incontinency, pride, profaneness or madness of men's depraved natures.

Prynne once more found himself on trial. Found guilty, he was sentenced to life imprisonment in the Tower of London, payment of a hefty fine, revocation of his law degree, and the loss of both of his ears. While this latter punishment was carried out, copies of *Histriomastix* were being burned. Because officials feared that he would produce more pamphlets in jail, he was denied pens, ink, and books while in prison. But when Parliament prevailed in its fight with Charles I (the English Civil War), Prynne was released. He went on to hold high positions in the parliamentary government and had the satisfaction of seeing the theater banned for the duration of the Commonwealth. Nevertheless, he was not a pliant government supporter: He opposed the 1649 execution of Charles I, and supported the Restoration of the monarchy under Charles II.

Prynne continued to write until his death. His works number over 200, though probably none of them are read today except in extracts. The scholar J. Dover Wilson remarked in *The Cambridge History of English and American Literature* of the 20th-century response to *Histriomastix:*

> To us, it seems half pathetic and half ridiculous, a gigantic monument of misplaced energy and zeal, a pyramid left gaunt and useless on the sands of time.

Puckering, John (John Pickering, John Pikeryng) (1544–1596) *dramatist*

Sir John Puckering was a native of Flamborough, County York, Ireland. He attended law school at Lincoln's Inn and was called to the bar in 1567. In the mid 1580s Puckering became the speaker of the House of Commons, where he presented a petition for the execution of Mary, Queen of Scots (*see* MARY STUART). He served as Lord Keeper of the Great Seal, the chief legal officer in the court of Queen ELIZABETH I, from 1592 to 1596.

It is very likely that Sir John Puckering is the same person as John Pikeryng, whose play *A New Interlude of Vice Containing, the History of Horestes with the cruel revengment of his Fathers death, upon his one natural Mother* appeared at the Red Lion Theatre in 1567 and was printed the same year. Interludes—plays of about 1,000 lines performed with music—were popular with students of the

Inns of Court (Elizabethan law schools), where John Puckering completed his legal training. In the original production, six actors played 27 roles.

Based on the ancient Greek *Oresteia*, a cycle of three tragedies by Aeschylus, *History of Horestes* is the first known British revenge tragedy. As in the source, the character Horestes (Orestes) revenges his father's death by killing his mother and taking his rightful place as ruler of the land. Unlike the *Oresteia*, *Horestes* uses elements of allegory, a story in poetry or prose in which characters, events, or settings represent abstract qualities. The play alternates between the revenge story line and commentary from the allegorical figure of Vice, who in an early scene encourages Horestes to kill his mother before he changes his mind: "Fall to it then and slack no time, for time once passed away / Doth cause repentance, but too late to come, old folks do say."

The 14-syllable lines alternating unstressed and stressed syllables and the rhyming couplet typify the verse style of *Horestes*. Later Elizabethan revenge tragedies like *The Spanish Tragedy* by Thomas KYD and William SHAKESPEARE's *Hamlet* echo the theme that a revenger has to act immediately, or else risk changing his mind about exacting revenge.

Purchas, Samuel (ca. 1577–1626) *nonfiction writer*

Samuel Purchas was born in Thaxted, Essex, England, and educated at St. John's College, Cambridge University. He became a clergyman and was vicar of Eastwood, in Essex on the Thames River, from 1604 to 1614. He was later promoted to rector of St. Martin's Church, London. He never traveled more than 200 miles from his birthplace, but he brought news of other people's travels to his generation and succeeding ones.

Purchas's first book, *Purchas, his Pilgrimage* (1613), was conceived as a survey of the peoples and religions of the world. It was so successful, and the interest in the accounts of voyages was so great, that he followed it with a compilation of travel literature: *Hakluyt's Posthumus: or, Purchas, his Pilgrimes* (four volumes, 1625), for which he used Richard HAKLUYT's manuscript collections as well as his own and the records of the East India Company. When he was at Eastwood, it is likely that he was able to interview returning mariners about their voyages by visiting the docks on the river.

Purchas also published *The King's Tower and Triumphal Arch of London* (1623) and *Microcosmus, or the History of Man* (1627), but it is his travel books for which he is remembered. They were one of the main sources through which English readers learned about the explorations of his time, and they continued to be read for many generations thereafter.

Among Purchas's readers was Samuel Taylor Coleridge (1772–1834). *Hakluyt's Posthumus* includes this passage:

In Xanadu did Cublai Can build a stately Palace, encompassing sixteen miles of plain ground with a wall, wherein are fertile meadows, pleasant springs, delightful streams, and all sorts of beasts of chase and game, and in the midst thereof a sumptuous house of pleasure.

Coleridge tells readers, in a note to his poem "Kubla Khan," that he was reading this passage when he fell asleep; the dream he had in that sleep inspired the poem, which begins:

In Xanadu did Kubla Khan
A stately pleasure dome decree . . .

A Work about Samuel Purchas

Pennington, Loren, ed. *The Purchas Handbook: Studies of the Life, Times, and Writings of Samuel Purchas.* London: Hakluyt Society, 1997.

Puttenham, George (ca. 1529–1591) *poet, nonfiction writer*

Born to the sister of Sir Thomas ELYOT, George Puttenham was an English gentleman about whose life few details are known. He enrolled at Cambridge University and studied law at the Inner Temple but also traveled abroad during his formative years. He married Lady Elizabeth Windsor in about 1560 and was sufficiently attached to the court of Queen ELIZABETH I that he wrote a collection of poems, *Partheniades* (1579), and probably at least one political treatise for the queen. His knowledge of the court also led him into trouble: He was imprisoned for a murder plot against a Calvinist bishop and for speaking out against Elizabeth's advisers.

Puttenham is best known as the author of *The Arte of English Poesie* (1589), which he also addressed to Queen Elizabeth. Because it was published anonymously, some scholars have attributed this work to George Puttenham's brother Richard, but literary historians generally agree that George was the author. This prose work belongs to the same genre—poetics, or literary theory—as the more famous *Defence of Poesie* (*Defense of Poetry*) by Puttenham's contemporary, Sir Philip SIDNEY.

The Arte of English Poesie has three parts. In the first, "Of Poets and Poesie," Puttenham defines poetry and discusses European and English poets. He asserts that poets are both "makers" and "imitators," defends poetry in the vernacular English, and describes suitable topics for and types of poetry. He ends a weighty discussion of the great English poets with typical courtier sycophancy: "But last in recitall and first in degree is the Queene our soueraigne Lady, whose learned, delicate, noble Muse, easily surmounteth all the rest that haue written before her time or since, for sence, sweetnesse and subtillitie. . . ."

The second part of *The Arte of English Poesie*, "Of Proportion Poetical," addresses prosody, or rhythm and accent in poetry. Here Puttenham explains various types of meter and stress, and he warns against their misuse: "Now there can not be in a maker a fowler fault, then to falsifie his accent to serue his cadence, or by vntrue orthographie to wrench his words to helpe his rime."

The third part of Puttenham's work, "Of Ornament," treats figurative language and style. Here his conclusion is that the best poetry has decorum and seems natural; too much ornamentation is unseemly.

The Arte of English Poesie provides a systematic statement of English RENAISSANCE poetic theory and a defense of poetry against the antipoetic Puritan impulses of the day. It also anticipates issues (ancient versus modern, Greco-Roman versus English) that would be more fully developed by John DRYDEN in the next century. As a literary work, it serves as an example of courtly language and 16th-century argumentation.

Quarles, Francis (1592–1644) *poet, pamphleteer*

Francis Quarles was born in Essex, England, to James Quarles, a minor official at the court of ELIZABETH I. He was educated at Cambridge University and went on to study law, although he never became a lawyer. When civil war broke out in 1642, he sided with the Royalists, publishing pamphlets in support of the king in 1644.

Quarles remains best known for his religious poetry, publishing his first verse collection, *A Feast for Worms,* in 1620. Thereafter he produced a large body of work, which includes, among other collections, *Sion's Elegies* (1624), *Sion's Sonnets* (1624), *Divine Fancies* (1632), and *Hieroglyphics of the Life of Man* (1638). *Argalus and Parthenia* (1629), one of his most popular works, is Quarles's only long poem not based on a religious source. Instead, it is a love story set in a mythical land of shepherds and maidens, which he describes as "That sweet Arcadia; which, in antique dayes, / Was wont to warble out her well-tun'd layes."

Quarles's best-known work is *Emblems,* a series of poems and symbolic illustrations. Each poem opens with a biblical passage, on which the verse comments. The poem ends with a passage from an early Christian theologian, such as Saint Augustine, and a four-line epigram, or terse and witty saying, that offers a moral. The poems of *Emblems* blend religious and political themes. The first poem of the volume, for example, begins with the biblical passage "Every man is tempted, when he is drawn away by his own lust, and enticed." The body of the verse then comments on the temptation of Adam and Eve in the Garden of Eden. It concludes with an epigram commenting on the Civil War:

> *Unlucky parliament! wherein, at last,*
> *Both houses are agreed, and firmly past*
> *An act of death confirm'd by higher pow'rs.*

Some scholars have criticized Quarles for his lack of subtlety and emotional intensity. He also supposedly lacks thematic variety. The critic Masoodul Hasan observes that Quarles's constant purpose in writing "was to glorify God." Although such moralizing poetry has fallen out of favor in modern times, Quarles is remembered as one of the better religious poets of the RENAISSANCE.

Racine, Jean (ca. 1639–1699) *poet, playwright*
Jean Racine was orphaned at a young age and
raised by his grandparents, who were members of
a Catholic sect known as Jansenists. Jansenists
maintained a very strict code of conduct, did not
believe in free will, and held that grace was necessary for salvation. Racine was educated at the
Jansenist school at Port Royal, where he studied
Latin and Greek classics, and the influence of the
austere members of this sect can easily be seen in
his later writing. At the age of 18 he was sent to
Paris to study law but turned instead to the theater.

Racine's plays were quite different from the
overblown tragedies full of pompous speeches that
were popular at the time he wrote. As he says in the
preface to *Britannicus*, "It would be very easy to
[satisfy my critics] . . . if I were willing to sacrifice
common sense. I need only disregard nature and
rush into the sensational." He preferred "a simple
action, not overladen, which, progressing steadily
to the catastrophe, is sustained by the interest, the
feelings, and the passions of the characters." His
topic is often doomed love and his style is quite
austere, much more like classical Greek drama
than what was popular at the time he wrote. His
plays are simple, intense, elegant, and always beautifully written. He wrote in alexandrines, or iambic
hexameter, a meter known for its stateliness.

Racine wrote his best works between 1664 and
1677, including the tragedies *Andromaque* (1667),
Britannicus (1669), and *Phèdre* (1677). *Andromaque* focuses on the aftermath of the Trojan War
and on Andromaque, the widow of the great hero
Hector, who is captured by King Pyrrhus. When
Pyrrhus abandons his betrothed, Hermione, for
Andromaque, Hermione convinces Orestes, who is
passionately in love with her, to kill Pyrrhus. *Britannicus* tells the story of the Roman emperor
Nero's youthful stepbrother, Britannicus, whom
the emperor poisons. *Phèdre* is Racine's masterpiece. Based on a Greek play by Euripides, it is the
story of the title character's doomed love for her
stepson, Hippolytus. Thinking her husband Theseus is dead, *Phèdre* declares her love for the boy
but learns that he loves another. But Theseus is not
dead, and when he returns, Phèdre, in a jealous
rage, allows him to believe that she was raped by
the innocent boy. Theseus banishes his son and
asks the god of the sea, Neptune, to destroy him.
Hippolytus is killed, and Phèdre kills herself in
grief. Although it is difficult to hear the beauty of
Racine's verse in translation, these lines, spoken by
Phèdre when she realizes Theseus is still alive, give
a sense of the passion and the dignity of the language. This is from Ted Hughes's translation. Phèdre says she is not among the women

Who manage their infidelity
With a polished smile and a stone heart.

The other great French playwright of the day was Pierre Corneille, whose supporters so disliked Racine that they bought a large quantity of tickets to *Phèdre* but did not attend, leaving seats conspicuously empty and ruining the performance. This so hurt Racine that he stopped writing. He returned to the theater 20 years later at the request of Madame de Maintenon, mistress of King Louis XIV, with the moral fables *Esther* (1689) and *Athalie* (1691). Both of these plays were biblical stories based on the Old Testament and were intended to be performed by the pupils of the convent of Saint-Cyr. *Esther* (1689) tells the story of Haman and the Jewish queen who risks her life to save her people from certain destruction. *Athalie* (1690) tells the story of an idol-worshipping queen who has a dream of her death after coming to power by murdering the royal family. Racine spent the remainder of his life editing his plays until his death from liver cancer in 1699. Racine influenced several British playwrights, and there were many English adaptations of his plays in the late 17th and early 18th centuries. Thomas OTWAY's *Titus and Berenice* (1676), for example, was based on Racine's *Bérénice* (1670). The character of the Widow Blackacre in William WYCHERLEY's *The Plain Dealer* (1676) is indebted to Racine's *Les Plaideurs* (1668). Ambrose Philips adapted Racine's *Andromaque* as *The Destrest Mother* (1712), and Edmund Smith wrote *Phaedra and Hippolitus* (1707) based on Racine's *Phèdre*.

A Work about Jean Racine

Tobin, Ronald W. *Jean Racine Revisited.* New York: Twayne, 1999.

Raleigh, Sir Walter (Sir Walter Ralegh)
(1552–1618) *poet, nonfiction writer*

Sir Walter Raleigh was born in Devonshire, England, the youngest child of Walter Raleigh and Katherine Champernowne. He studied at Oxford University and at the Middle Temple in London. At the London home of his older half brother Humphrey GILBERT he met John DEE, whose notions concerning England's calling to establish colonies in North America excited him.

In 1580 Raleigh went to Ireland to help suppress a rebellion against English rule; his service there brought him to the notice of Queen ELIZABETH I, and on his return he rose rapidly in her esteem, quickly becoming her principal favorite. Because the queen demanded his presence, instead of exploring he funded explorations, including the ill-fated colony at Roanoke Island in North Carolina, the first Virginia expedition, now known as "the lost colony." He also was a patron of poetry, for example supporting Edmund SPENSER and introducing him at court.

Much of Raleigh's own poetry was written as an element of his relationship with the queen. He was highly regarded as a poet by other poets of his time, but he did not publish any of his work and much of what he wrote has been lost. Most of the poets among Elizabeth's courtiers were content to produce variations on conventional themes, rarely showing a trace of personal involvement. Even during his most prosperous times, however, Raleigh had a sense of the hollowness of human achievement that finds a voice in his poems. Christopher MARLOWE's "The Passionate Shepherd to His Love" is a delightful idyll of pastoral life that opens with the famous lines:

Come live with me and be my love,
And we will all the pleasures prove
That valleys, groves, hills, and fields,
Woods, or steepy mountain yields.

Raleigh's response to Marlowe's poem, "The Nymph's Reply to the Shepherd," has all Marlowe's grace and musicality, but in the nymph's "if," melancholy reality intrudes:

If all the world and love were young
And truth in every shepherd's tongue,
These pretty pleasures might me move,
To live with thee, and be thy love.

Raleigh's luck changed in 1592, when, in disgrace with the queen for having secretly married one of Elizabeth's ladies-in-waiting, Elizabeth Throckmorton, he was confined to the Tower of London. He was released after a matter of months, and he and his bride were able to retire to one of the country estates the queen had given him, where a son, Wat, was born; but for several years following, Raleigh was not welcome at court.

Now free to travel, in 1595 Raleigh led an expedition to explore the area he called Guyana (in present-day Venezuela). His efforts to find gold there were unsuccessful, but the book he wrote about what he saw, *The Discovery of the Large, Rich and Beautiful Empire of Guyana* (1596), is recognized as one of the finest pieces of Elizabethan travel writing and was a popular success at the time of its publications. Unlike many writers on travel of the time, Raleigh was not interested in the religious aspect of exploration—bringing the true faith of Christianity to the heathen. He found the Native Americans he met full of dignity, and was disturbed by the harsh treatment they suffered at the hands of the Spaniards. One of the themes of his book is that if English power could replace the Spanish empire, those oppressed people would be "delivered from servitude."

Elizabeth I did not follow Raleigh's advice to launch a campaign against Spanish interests in Guyana, but she did turn to him for help against Spain in Europe, and in the last years of her life she readmitted him into her favor. Unfortunately, when Elizabeth died in 1603, the new king, JAMES I, chose to follow a course of peaceful relations with Spain and saw the queen's former favorite as a liability. Within months, Raleigh was convicted of treason and sentenced to be beheaded. A few days before the sentence was to be carried out, James commuted the sentence to life imprisonment.

Raleigh spent most of the next 15 years back in the Tower of London during which time he undertook a huge project: *The History of the World.* He only got as far as the Macedonian Wars (160 B.C.), but unfinished as it is the work is massive: The five volumes total about 2,700 pages. The first two volumes, which cover biblical events, tend to point up lessons about the futility of human purposes when compared with the plans of God:

> God derideth the wisdom of the worldly men,
> when forgetting the Lord of all power, they rely
> on the inventions of their own most feeble, and
> altogether darkened understanding.

The five completed volumes of the history were published in 1614 and became immensely popular, to the king's embarrassment.

In 1616 Raleigh managed to convince King James that, if he were released, he could lead an expedition to Guyana that was sure to bring back gold for the royal coffers. The expedition was a failure, however, and as soon as he landed at Plymouth, in western England, Raleigh was arrested. James revived the sentence he had suspended in 1603, and Raleigh was beheaded on October 29, 1618, displaying a remarkable dignity and courage at the scaffold. A poem he wrote on the flyleaf of his Bible, only three hours before his death according to one source, is actually a reworking of something he had written years before, but is no less moving for that:

> Even such is time, which takes in trust
> Our youth, our joys, and all we have,
> And pays us but with age and dust:
> Who in the dark and silent grave
> When we have wandered all our ways
> Shuts up the story of our days.
> And from which earth and grave and dust
> The Lord shall raise me up I trust.

The remarkable dignity of these lines is typical of this poet and adventurer.

Other Works by Sir Walter Raleigh

The Discoverie of the Large, Rich, and Bewtiful Empyre of Guiana. Edited by Neil L. Whitehead. Norman: University of Oklahoma Press, 1998.

The Poems of Sir Walter Raleigh. Edited by Michael Rudick. Ithaca, N.Y.: Cornell University Press, 2000.

Works about Sir Walter Raleigh

Greenblatt, Stephen Jay. *Sir Walter Raleigh: The Renaissance Man and His Roles.* New Haven, Conn.: Yale University Press, 1973.

May, Steven W. *Sir Walter Raleigh.* Boston: Twayne, 1989.

Ramus, Peter (Petrus Ramus, Pierre de la Ramée) (1515–1572) *philosopher*

Peter Ramus was born in the village of Cuts in France, the son of Jacques and Jeanne Charpentier de la Ramée. His family, though of noble descent, was poor, and his father worked as a laborer. When he was 12 years old, Ramus began his studies at the Collège de Navarre in Paris. His poverty was such that he had to work as a servant to other students in order to pay for his education. In 1536 he received his master's degree, completing a thesis whose translated English title is "all Aristotle's doctrines are false." This was a daring position to defend, since Aristotelian philosophy was the basis for nearly all learning in Europe at the time.

Ramus's *Criticisms of the Aristotelian Dialectic,* published in 1543, was harshly criticized by academics and eventually condemned by the French parliament, and he was forbidden to teach or write for a time. In 1547 Cardinal Charles de Lorraine successfully appealed to France's new king, Henry II, to allow Ramus to resume his teaching career, and in 1551 Ramus was appointed Regius professor of philosophy and eloquence at the Collège de France.

Ramus converted to Calvinism in 1562 and, in the same year, proposed reforms to the curriculum and teaching methods at the University of Paris. He advocated a return to the seven classical liberal arts (grammar, rhetoric, logic, music, arithmetic, astronomy, and geometry) and a concentration on applied learning. He also proposed and later endowed a chair of mathematics and opposed the imposition of student fees.

Ramus joined 3,000 Huguenots (Protestants) in Paris in 1572 to witness the marriage of Marguerite de Valois to Henry III of Navarre, a ceremony that was to symbolize a new era of tolerance for Protestants in France. But on the eve of the Feast of St. Bartholomew on August 24, French Catholic troops, on the order of the youthful King Charles II, attacked the crowd and continued murdering Protestants for more than a month, eventually killing at least 50,000 people (see SAINT BARTHOLOMEW'S DAY MASSACRE). Ramus was among those murdered in the first days of carnage. It is said that his hiding place was betrayed by a fellow faculty member who disagreed with his ideas.

Ramus's thinking had an important influence on the study of rhetoric down to the present day. He was intent on simplifying distinctions among various academic subjects and wanted no overlap between the various disciplines. Thus he declared that the art of rhetoric, which Aristotle said included arrangement, style, delivery, memory, and logic, actually encompassed only "style" and "delivery." Ramus placed "invention" and "arrangement" under logic. The result of this distinction was that rhetoric began to be viewed as primarily style as opposed to logical content, and elaborate, highly stylized writing began to emerge on the continent and in England, culminating in the elaborate prose of John LYLY.

Ramus also had a significant effect on American culture through his influence on Puritan divines. Ramist logic, according to Perry Miller, author of *The New England Mind* (1939), had a profound effect on how the Puritan settlers of New England wrote and thought. While Aristotelian logic was deductive, beginning with specifics and moving toward generalizations, Ramist logic was inductive, beginning with the premise that all creation was a reflection of God's plan. Thus the conclusion was presupposed, and logic was used to show the path to the proper conclusion. For example, when a snake entered the congregation of Reverend Allen in Braintree, Massachusetts, and was killed by one of the elders, this became the basis for a sermon. Through a series of logical oppositions, the preacher demonstrated that the snake was the devil who had recently tempted the congregation; his death was a sure sign of their faith and triumph over evil. Thus, the preacher knew the meaning of the natural event the moment it happened; his only task was to use logic to prove what he already knew. According to Samuel Logan in "The Hermeneutic of Jonathan Edwards," Ramus claimed that his logic actually corresponded to the exact way that things were both in the present temporal world and in the nontemporal eternal world. To grasp the idea was to grasp the thing.

Another of Ramus's greatest contributions was to conceptualize logic as available to everyone, not just to philosophers and academicians. His emphasis on the clear boundaries that defined academic subjects and the clarity of his logic affected Francis BACON and influenced subsequent scientific investigation.

Randolph, Thomas (1605–1635) *poet, playwright*

Thomas Randolph was born in Northamptonshire, England, the son of William Randolph, a steward or manager of an estate, and Elizabeth Smith Randolph. A promising student from his earliest years, Randolph became a king's scholar at Westminster School, then attended Trinity College, Cambridge University, from which he received a master's degree in 1628.

Noted for his facility with Latin and English poetry, Thomas came under the watchful eye of Ben JONSON, who served as a mentor to him and encouraged his writing. Randolph dedicated several poems during this period to Jonson. His finest poems are considered to be his "Ode to Master Anthony Stafford, to Hasten Him into the Country" and his "Eclogue to Master Jonson" (both 1638). In the former, Randolph praises a country life:

> Come spurre apay,
> I have no patience for a longer stay;
> But must goe downe,
> And leave the chargeable noise of this great
> Towne.

Randolph began writing plays while a student. Among the comedies he wrote during his college days are *Aristippus, or the Jovial Philosopher* (1625), which is set at Cambridge and pokes fun at scholars; and *The Drinking Academy* (ca. 1626), which is set at a boys' school. Randolph's dramas were noted for their wit and allusions to classical drama. *The Conceited Pedlar* (ca. 1630), a monologue by a traveling tradesman, again mocks intellectuals. *The Jealous Lovers* (1632), a romantic comedy, was one of Randolph's most popular works.

Around 1631 Randolph decided to abandon his academic career for the stage and went up to London as a manager/playwright for a theater company. His most successful play there was *Amyntas, or The Impossible Dowry* (published 1638), a pastoral comedy that included verses in both Latin and English and was performed at court. The plot revolves around three pairs of lovers who all achieve happiness:

> All Loves are happy, none with us there bee,
> Now sick of coynesse, or unconstancy.
> The wealthy summes of Kisses doe amount
> To greater scores than curious art can
> count!

Randolph is remembered today for his plays more than his poetry. He is considered one of the finest dramatists in the era of Jonson.

Reformation

The Reformation began in Germany in 1517 when the monk Martin LUTHER nailed a paper to a church door in Wittenberg that essentially argued for reform (thus the name of the movement) of the Catholic Church. Luther's act sparked an upheaval in religious thought that spread throughout much of Europe during the 15th and 16th centuries. Luther and other opponents of the church, among them John CALVIN in France, argued that the church had strayed too far from the original tenets of the faith, and that church leadership had grown too worldly and too corrupt. These protestors and reformers were called Protestants.

In England the Reformation came about because Henry VIII wanted a divorce from his wife,

Catherine of Aragon, who had not produced the son the English king so desperately wanted. Refused a divorce by the pope, Henry ended his marriage anyway and declared himself head of the CHURCH OF ENGLAND in 1534. The historian Lacey Baldwin Smith notes that in England, "Only after an act of state established the church did the floodgates open and a spiritual reformation begin."

In 1538 Henry declared that every church must have a copy of the Bible in English, not Latin as had been tradition. No longer was knowledge of the Bible's content restricted to those who could understand Latin. Each worshipper could be his or her own interpreter of the Bible. William TYNDALE's English translation of the Gospels had been an illegal enterprise for which Tyndale paid with his life; now Thomas CRANMER's translation was heard in the lessons read aloud every Sunday across the country. The BIBLE, KING JAMES VERSION (1616) was a culmination of the Reformation effort to bring scripture to everyone. In addition, Cranmer's BOOK OF COMMON PRAYER, first adopted in 1549, gave people who knew no Latin the opportunity to participate in religious services with understanding. Church attendance was required in the reign of ELIZABETH I, so almost the whole population was hearing and echoing the sonorous rhythms of Cranmer's language every week. Few writers can have escaped being influenced by this exposure.

The Reformation in England had setbacks, notably during the reign of the Queen Mary I ("Bloody Mary"), who tried to drag England back into the Catholic fold by decree and persecution. The terrors of Mary's reign were recorded graphically by John FOXE in his best-selling *Book of Martyrs*. Mary was succeeded by the Protestant Elizabeth I, but Protestantism was still not secure. Attempts by Catholic factions to recapture the throne, and real and threatened attacks by the Catholic king Philip of Spain, led to a sense of insecurity which probably contributed to the dominance of intrigue and violence in the dramas of the Elizabethan and Jacobean periods. Anti-Catholicism became identified with patriotism, as shown by the popularity of Thomas MIDDLETON's *A Game at Chess* (1624).

The Church of England was a government institution, with the monarch at its head. There were many Protestants who felt that it did not take Reformation far enough, and who refused to grant authority over their spiritual lives to a monarch or bishop. These dissenters, as they were called, were subject to discrimination for most of the 17th and 18th centuries, but they influenced the development of English literature in a number of ways. They produced devotional texts—for example, John BUNYAN's *The Pilgrim's Progress* (1678–84). They acquired political influence in varying degrees, and during the period after the English Civil Wars (1642–51) they had political ascendancy for the period of the Commonwealth (1649–53). A direct effect of this political dominance was that in 1642 they brought about the closing of the theaters, which did not open again until the RESTORATION of Charles II in 1660. During this time, a lively brand of literature was shut off, and writers turned to more private avenues of expression. The dissenting Protestant's intense relationship with his God found its most magnificent form in the grandeur of John MILTON's *Paradise Lost* (1667).

A Work about the Reformation
Haigh, Christopher. *English Reformations: Religion, Politics and Society under the Tudors.* Oxford, U.K.: Clarendon Press, 1993.

Renaissance

Renaissance, which means "rebirth" in French, is a term that has been used since the 19th century to describe the movements in art, literature, music, and philosophy that ended the Middle Ages and prefigured the modern world. Beginning and ending dates for the Renaissance vary, but most scholars accept that in Italy the period began in the late 14th century and ended in the early 16th century. In the rest of Europe, including England, the Renaissance began and ended at least 50 years later.

The term *Renaissance* was first used by Jakob Burckhardt in his book *The Civilization of the Renaissance in Italy* (1867). Burckhardt said that the distinguishing characteristic of the Renaissance was that people began to think of themselves not as part of a tribe, race, family, or other group but as individuals. This, he claimed, marked the beginning of modern culture. The primary motivating force behind the Renaissance was the revival of classical learning that began following the Fourth Crusade's conquest of Constantinople.

Classical learning led to the concept of HUMANISM—the philosophical idea of the importance of people as individuals. Humanism focuses on the individual's own abilities and accomplishments rather than his or her dependence on God; it focuses on the beauties and challenges of this life as well as on the hereafter. The Italian humanist Leon Battista Alberti summed up the spirit of humanism when he said, "Men can do all things if they will."

Thinkers and writers of the Renaissance rejected medieval ways of learning and knowing the world, and in particular they rejected the scholastic method of inquiry. In scholasticism, logic was subordinate to faith, and the use of reason was legitimate only to the extent that it served to deepen religious faith. Renaissance thinkers, on the other hand, placed a high value on reason as humanity's highest faculty, which led to a greater emphasis on independent inquiry, including scientific inquiry. This does not mean that humanists rejected faith; on the contrary, many of the greatest thinkers of the Renaissance were deeply religious. But they rejected faith based on church authority and asserted the right to think for themselves about religion.

In the visual arts, sculptors studied anatomy in order to be able to portray the human body realistically. Painting—the dominant art of the age—developed techniques to capture light and shadow and to give a sense of three-dimensionality. While the visual arts continued to focus on religious themes, more and more painters and sculptors honored wealthy patrons with portraits and statues. Stories from the Roman writer Ovid's *Meta-* *morphoses* inspired many works of art. Early Renaissance churches moved away from the verticality of Gothic cathedrals and created spaces that were more "to the measure of man," that did not dwarf people but allowed them to feel comfortable in a sacred space. Filippo Brunelleschi's Santo Spirito Church in Florence is a good example of the classical influence on Renaissance architecture. In the same way, writers of the Renaissance focused on realistic situations and human emotions that had little to do with religious awe and much to do with passion, grief, greed, and joy. The quintessential English writer of the English Renaissance is William SHAKESPEARE, whose plays explored the human condition and human psyche in a way that no other writer had done before.

Works about the Renaissance

Nauert, Charles G. *Humanism and the Culture of Renaissance Europe.* Edited by William Beik and C. W. Blanning. Cambridge, U.K.: Cambridge University Press, 1995.

Pater, Walter. *The Renaissance: Studies in Art and Poetry.* Edited by Adam Phillips. Oxford, U.K.: Oxford University Press, 1998.

Restoration period

The Restoration refers to the reinstatement of the English monarchy in May 1660. It was at this time that Charles II ascended to the throne that had been his father's 11 years earlier. The period between the monarchies, when the government was headed first by Oliver Cromwell and then by his son Richard, is called the interregnum, or period between kings.

The monarchy had been abolished as a result of the English Civil Wars of 1642–51. This conflict was sparked by sharp disagreement between the king and Parliament over religious issues and questions about the rights of the monarchy. With the defeat and execution of Charles I at the end of the war, Puritan member of Parliament Oliver Cromwell established the English Protectorate, during which time England was ruled by an Executive

Council of State and the Rump Parliament—that is, members of the original Parliament who were loyal to Cromwell. The Protectorate not only marked the end of the monarchy but also of the House of Lords and the Anglican Church, leading to years of religious turmoil. Dissenters, or those who dissented from the CHURCH OF ENGLAND, were given government positions and sometimes the estates of those who were loyal to the king. Uprisings across the land had to be quelled, and Cromwell's army ended up slaughtering huge numbers of Irish Catholics who would not convert. Scottish Presbyterians fought for the restoration of the Stuarts to the throne and were defeated. The Protectorate, however, did not long survive the death of Cromwell in 1658. His son, Richard, ruled for two years until Charles II was restored.

The Restoration lasted from 1660 to 1688. It was marked by renewed conflict between the king and Parliament and debates over religious toleration for both Protestant Dissenters and Catholics. The Restoration ended with the 1688 Glorious Revolution, in which James II, Charles's brother and successor, was driven from England and replaced by William of Orange and his wife, Mary. James's unpopularity stemmed in part from his conversion to Catholicism; William and Mary were Protestants.

In terms of British literature, the Restoration was characterized by an outpouring of philosophical writing, poetry, and drama. Theater, which had been forbidden by Cromwell's Puritan government, flourished, and the stage was filled with witty, sometimes bawdy, comedies by such writers as William WYCHERLEY, Richard Sheridan, William CONGREVE, and George Farquhar. Classical works of ancient Greece and Rome inspired much of the literature of this period, leading to England's Augustan Age. English writers compared the period of the Restoration to the Augustan Age of Rome, a period of about 50 years under the emperor Augustus. Many of the greatest of Rome's literary works, including Virgil's *Aeneid*, were written in this period. In Restoration England writers were deeply influenced by these ancient works, which they translated in great numbers and imitated. The most notable Restoration poets are Alexander Pope and John DRYDEN. Jonathan Swift's satires and the essays of Addison and Steele are among the finest prose works of the era.

Reynolds, Henry (ca. 1560s–ca. 1630s)
nonfiction writer, translator

Henry Reynolds was probably born in Holton, Suffolk, England, to Edward and Elizabeth Reynolds, prosperous landowners who had earned their wealth through the weaving trade. He first came to public attention in 1606 as the assistant to the master of ceremonies in the court of King JAMES I, where he helped arrange court entertainments and masques. He later served as the secretary to the Earl of Suffolk, after which he became a schoolmaster in London.

Reynolds is best remembered for his *Mythomystes: Wherein A Short Svrvay Is Taken Of The Natvre And Valve Of Trve Poesy And Depth Of The Ancients Above Ovr Moderne Poets, To which is annexed the Tale of Narcissues briefly mythologized* (1632). This book argued that the authors of the ancient classical texts were better than modern writers, not, as was usually argued, because they were better in their portrayals of human nature, but because they were heirs to a mystical tradition that concealed meaning in enigmatic language. Reynolds also translated into English the *Aminta*, a masterful pastoral drama by the Italian Renaissance poet Torquato TASSO.

A Work by Henry Reynolds

Tasso's Aminta and Other Poems. Edited by Glyn Pursglove. Lewiston, N.Y.: Edwin Mellen Press, 1991.

Rich, Barnabe (Barnabe Riche, Barnaby Richee) (1542–1617) *fiction writer, nonfiction writer, pamphleteer*

Born in Essex, England, Barnabe Rich was a speculator, informer, and captain in the English military.

A prolific writer of at least 22 books and pamphlets, Rich wrote military tracts, romances, satires, chronicles, and other pieces. His writings are valued most for their revealing insights into the social, political, and religious issues of the period. Much of his work was drawn from his years of military service in Ireland. In *A Path-way to Military Practice* (1587), dedicated to Queen ELIZABETH I, Rich stresses the importance of a well-prepared and properly organized army.

Rich's best-known work is *His Farewell to Military Profession* (1581), a collection of eight stories. Incorporating a number of literary genres—including the fabliau (a short, comic, earthy story) and the romance (a story of improbable adventures that stress the power of love)—the collection is written in conversational and sometimes lofty dialogue and is one of the finest English imitations of the Italian novella (a brief prose tale). The *Farewell* is also one source of William SHAKE-SPEARE's *Twelfth Night,* which is modeled on the volume's second tale. This story about a group of three lovers who engage in "amorous devices" seeks to discover "the ground . . . of reasonable love whereby the knot is knit of true and perfect friendship." As the scholar John Edward Price writes, Rich presents a "world-weary moralist and rascal . . . who simultaneously disapproves of and celebrates current follies and fashionable excess."

In his later years Rich turned from writing romances to writing pamphlets that criticized what he considered improper behavior. One pamphlet that currently receives much attention is *My Ladies Looking Glasse* (1616). Infused with Protestant morality and dedicated to the wife of the Lord Deputy of Ireland, the work condemns questionable behavior exhibited by women. A bad woman, argues Rich, exhibits shamelessness and impudence, and she is like "the serpent" because she is "hard to be found out." In *Excellency of Good Women* (1613) Rich praises women who lead virtuous lives that exhibit temperance and patience and who aspire to "the deep capacity of arts and sciences."

Given their depth and variety, Rich's writings cover a wide range of topics that reveal much of the multifaceted world of early modern England. As the critic Donald Beecher explains, Rich occupies a position of "great value and importance," and from him we can learn "a great deal of information about the age."

Rich, Mary (Countess of Warwick)
(1625–1678) *nonfiction writer*
Mary Rich (née Boyle) was born in Youghal, Ireland, to Richard Boyle, the Earl of Cork, a wealthy landowner, and his wife, Catherine. Rich's mother died when she was young, and she was raised by a nearby tenant of her father's. It is unlikely that she had much formal education beyond instruction in religion and needlework, although she did speak French and was well-read. In 1641, after rejecting another suitor, she married Charles Rich, son of the Earl of Warwick, and settled with him in Essex, England. She became Countess of Warwick in 1659 at the death of Charles's father.

In England, Rich converted to Puritanism, and it is her deep spirituality that is at the center of most of her writing. Her *Rules for Holy Living,* for example, is an account she sent to a friend of her daily religious exercises and mediations (published 1847). Other similar works are her *Occasional Mediations* (1847), and *Pious Reflections on Several Scriptures* (1848). Rich also kept a journal, from 1666 until her death, which reflects her pious and self-effacing nature. For example, when recounting the death of her son in 1664, she says, "I begane to consider what sines I had committed that should cause God to call them to remembrance and slay my sonn." The journals were unpublished in her lifetime.

Overall, Rich is remembered for her religious writings and convictions. Upon her death, her minister called her "the most illustrious Pattern of Sincere Piety, and Solid Goodness this Age hath produced."

A Work about Mary Rich

Mendelson, Stuart. *The Mental World of Stuart Women: Three Studies.* Amherst: The University of Massachusetts Press, 1987.

Richmond and Derby, Countess of

See BEAUFORT, MARGARET.

Rochester, John Wilmot, Earl of
(1647–1680) *poet*

John Wilmot, later to become the second Earl of Rochester, was born on April Fools' Day at Woodstock, Oxfordshire, England. His mother was Anne St. John, and his father, Henry Wilmot, was a Royalist general who helped the future Charles II escape capture during the English Civil War. The 14-year-old Rochester graduated Oxford with a master's in 1661, displaying talent in the fields of classical literature, science, and philosophy. Charles II did not forget the favor performed by Rochester's father, and he welcomed the young man into his court in 1664.

Rochester's early love poems, such as the pastoral *Dialogue between Strephon and Daphne* (ca. 1667) are largely conventional. Some of Rochester's best early poetry was written to Elizabeth Malet, who would become his wife. Rochester's poetry improved as it began to mirror his increasingly scandalous lifestyle. Indeed, some of his best poems remained out of print for years because of their obscene nature.

Rochester's "Fair Chloris in a Pigsty Lay" (ca. 1671) mocks the pastoral genre in which he had earlier written. As the swineherdess Chloris naps, she dreams of a "love-convicted swain" who lures her to a cave and ravishes her. She wakes "with her own thumb between her legs," both "innocent and pleased" with the dream.

Rochester's view of sexuality would grow darker, however, as evidenced in *A Ramble in St. James's Park* (ca. 1672). St. James's Park was a common meeting ground for lovers, and Rochester characterizes it as a place "consecrate[d] to prick and cunt," where mythological sperm fell on the ground causing trees like "mandrakes tall [to] rise / Whose lewd tops fucked the very skies." Upon seeing Corinna, a name taken from the pastoral tradition, pass him by, the speaker is disappointed to see her take up with three fashionable fops. The poem ends with a number of curses directed at Corinna—not for her rejection of the speaker, but for her choosing such unworthy fellows out of an affected desire for fashion.

The Imperfect Enjoyment (ca. 1672) has been called by the Rochester scholar Jeremy Treglown "the best poem ever written about premature ejaculation." Corinna is very willing to oblige in this poem, but as the speaker "prepare[s] to throw / The all-dissolving thunderbolt below," he "dissolve[s]" in "liquid raptures" and cannot continue their sexual tryst. "Ev'n her fair hand, which might bid heat return / To frozen age" has no effect on the speaker, who compares himself to a "trembling, confused, despairing, limber, dry . . . weak, unmoving lump."

Thinking that Charles would enjoy a poem called "Signor Dildo" (ca. 1673), which describes the excitement of several prominent ladies at the arrival of the new Italian invention in England, Rochester gave the king what he thought was a copy. Unluckily, he instead handed him *A Satyr on Charles II* (ca. 1673). The poem praises the king in unusual terms: "Peace is his aim, his gentleness is such, / And love he loves, for he loves fucking much." Thus far Rochester is safe with Charles, who had several mistresses. However, Rochester implies that the mistresses influence governmental policy in the following lines: "His scepter and his prick are of [equal] length; / And she may sway the one who plays with th' other." The king, the poem continues, would throw aside "safety, law, religion, life" for the sake of sex, leaving him "a merry monarch, scandalous and poor." These lines rang a little too true since Charles's excesses had left the treasury low and his illegitimate children would eventually cause political unrest. Consequently, Rochester was banished from the court for a time.

In later years Rochester's works took a darker turn, with less playful satire and celebration of sexuality and more inward-looking musings. Many scholars consider his *Satyr against Reason and Mankind* (ca. 1674) to be one of his greatest (and most pessimistic) works. Influenced by his reading of Thomas HOBBES, Rochester wrote, "I'd be a dog, monkey, or a bear, / Or anything but that vain animal / Who is so proud of being rational." One of Rochester's last poems, based on a passage from the ancient Roman Seneca, opens "After death nothing is, and nothing, death" (ca. 1680).

However, as Rochester's life of excess brought him near his end at age 33, long conversations with Anglican bishops including Gilbert BURNET prompted a deathbed religious experience that has been a source of interest and debate ever since. Pious interpreters see Rochester returning to the faith his Puritan mother taught him; others find reasons to disbelieve Burnet's painstaking narrative.

According to the editor David M. Vieth, Rochester's life is "so compelling that it constantly threatens to overwhelm his poetry." Still, Vieth writes, the poems retain a "perennial appeal to readers who care nothing about the seventeenth century and know little about their author."

A Work by John Wilmot, Earl of Rochester

The Complete Poems of John Wilmot, Earl of Rochester. Edited by David M. Vieth. New Haven, Conn.: Yale University Press, 1968.

Works about John Wilmot, Earl of Rochester

Greene, Graham. *Lord Rochester's Monkey Being the Life of John Wilmot, Second Earl of Rochester.* New York: Viking, 1974.
Combe, Kirk. *A Martyr for Sin: Rochester's Critique of Polity, Sexuality, and Society.* Newark: University of Delaware Press, 1998.

Ronsard, Pierre de (1524–1585) *poet, nonfiction writer*

Pierre de Ronsard was born at the Château de la Poissonnière in France, the youngest son of Loys and Jeanne de Ronsard. Both his parents came from well-connected noble families. Ronsard was sent to the Collège de Navarre in Paris when he was nine, but shortly afterward he was made a page to King François I's eldest son, the dauphin François. When, in 1536, the king's daughter Madeleine mar-

ried James V of Scotland, Ronsard was part of the retinue that accompanied her to her new home, and even though Madeleine died only seven weeks after she arrived in Edinburgh, Ronsard spent the next three years in Scotland and England, returning to France at the age of 16. He was subsequently appointed to diplomatic missions, traveling to Flanders and again to Scotland, but what looked like a promising career in diplomacy was cut short in 1540 by a severe fever that left him almost deaf.

Ronsard decided to make the most of the isolation his deafness forced on him by giving all his time to study. He took minor holy orders in 1543. In 1545, at age 20, Ronsard met 13-year-old Cassandre Salviati, the daughter of an Italian banker. It is likely that he never saw Cassandre again, but she served for Ronsard, who was already enthralled by the work of PETRARCH, as his Laura—his muse and inspiration, at least for the time being.

In 1547, still deep into his studies, Ronsard met Joachim du Bellay. The two friends joined with five fellow students to form a literary group that became known as the Pleiade (after the constellation the Pleiades, or Seven Stars). The Pleiade's first manifesto, *Défense et illustration de la langue française,* (1549) was written by du Bellay. It argues that French poets should refine their art by imitating classical Latin and Greek models and the sonnets of Petrarch, rather than confining themselves to French traditions established during the Middle Ages. Ronsard began to publish poetry that demonstrated the possibilities of this approach: the first four books of his *Odes* appeared in 1550, *Amours de Cassandre* (*Loves of Cassandra*) and the fifth book of *Odes,* in 1552.

In 1555 Ronsard's work took a different tack when he fell in love again, this time with a 15-year-old peasant from Anjou named Marie Dupin. For her he gave up the complicated images derived from Petrarch and aimed at clarity and simplicity. His work soon became the all rage at court, and he became known as the "Prince of Poets." He was especially favored by King Charles IX, who acceded to the French throne in 1560 and showered him with gifts.

Most of Ronsard's work is composed of brief lyrics, especially sonnets; in fact, he was the first French poet to perfect this form. He also experimented, with great success, with meters used by the Roman poet Horace (65–68 B.C.) in his odes. Encouraged by Charles IX, Ronsard also composed a patriotic epic. The first four books of the *Franciade* were published in August 1572, about two weeks after the SAINT BARTHOLOMEW'S DAY MASSACRE. In the tense atmosphere of the time, the poem was not popular, and Ronsard never finished it.

In 1578 Ronsard met another love: Hélène de Surgères, a lady-in-waiting to Catherine de Medici in mourning for a lover who had died in the French religious wars. She was the inspiration for some of Ronsard's most famous poems, collected in *Sonnets pour Hélène* (1578). This collection includes the sonnet beginning, "Quand tu sera bien vieille, au soir, à la chandelle . . .," which was unforgettably and masterfully translated by William Butler Yeats (1869–1939) as

> When you are old and grey and full of sleep,
> And nodding by the fire, take down this
>   book,
> And slowly read, and dream of the soft look
> Your eyes had once, and of their shadows
>   deep.

After 1580 Ronsard wrote no new poems but devoted himself to revising (and not always improving) his existing works. He was in Tours when he died, and he was buried there in the church of Saint-Cosme.

Ronsard's reputation went into eclipse in France soon after his death, and he was only rediscovered there by the romantic poets in the early 19th century. But he was greatly admired by Sir Philip SIDNEY and Edmund SPENSER, who imitated his work extensively, especially the sonnets, and through them he influenced English poetry for generations. Ronsard's odes in imitation of Horace may also have inspired the Horatian odes of 17th-century English poets such as Ben JONSON, Robert HERRICK, and Andrew MARVELL.

Other Works by Pierre de Ronsard

Selected Poems by Pierre De Ronsard. Translated by Malcolm Quainton and Elizabeth Vinestock. New York: Penguin, 2002.

Lyrics of the French Renaissance: Marot, Du Bellay, Ronsard. Edited by Norman R. Shapiro. New Haven, Conn.: Yale University Press, 2002.

Works about Pierre de Ronsard

Campo, Roberto E. *Ronsard's Contentious Sisters: The Paragone Between Poetry and Painting in the Works of Pierre De Ronsard.* Chapel Hill: University of North Carolina Press, 1999.

Perry, Kathleen A. *Another Reality: Metamorphosis and the Imagination in the Poetry of Ovid, Petrarch, and Ronsard.* New York: Peter Lang, 1990.

Sturm-Maddox, Sara. *Ronsard, Petrarch and the Amours.* Gainesville: University Press of Florida, 1999.

Roper, Margaret (1505–1544) *translator, letter writer*

Margaret Roper (née More) was the daughter of Sir Thomas MORE and Lady Jane More, who were among those who continued to practice Roman Catholicism after Henry VIII had declared himself head of the English church. Visitors to the powerful and prominent More family included the king; the German artist Hans Holbein the Younger, who painted a portrait of the family; writers Thomas ELYOT and John COLET; and the Dutch humanist Desiderius ERASMUS. William Roper joined the More household in 1518, perhaps as an apprentice to Sir Thomas. He and Margaret married three years later.

Margaret Roper, who showed that women could excel through classical studies, had impressed Erasmus. When he produced his Latin commentary on the Lord's Prayer (*Precatio Dominica*, 1523), Roper translated it into English as *A Devout Treatise Upon the Pater Noster* (1524). That same year Erasmus wrote and addressed her as "not least among the glories of your generation and your native England." The treatise meditates on the prayer and was popular enough to be reprinted three times. The scholar Rita M. Verbrugge has compared the Latin and English versions, concluding that Roper shows her opinions and personality by, among other things, "emphasizing the contrast between man's unworthiness and vileness against God's goodness . . . far more than the original work suggests." Verbrugge shows that, where Erasmus refers briefly to God as a shepherd, Margaret expands on Erasmus by describing the "wandering and straying sheep: thou curest and makest whole the sick and scabby sheep."

Among Roper's surviving works is her final correspondence with her father, who was executed for refusing to swear an oath denying the leadership of the pope and declaring Henry VIII the head of the church in England. The scholar R. W. Chambers has pointed out that one of Roper's letters to her stepsister Alice Alington is like Plato's *Crito*. One similarity is that Crito asks Socrates to avoid execution by doing as everyone else wishes, and Roper asks the same of More; another is that Socrates and More both win their arguments. However, when Roper says of her father, "My heart was full heavy for the peril of his person, for in faith, I fear not [for] his soul," she speaks as herself, not Crito.

Modern critics believe that Roper's success as a translator encouraged some important men of her time to support education for women. Roper furthered this tradition by teaching her own children. One daughter, MARY BASSETT, translated both Thomas More's *Treatise on the Passion* (1557) and the *Ecclesiastical History* by Eusebius Pamphilus, which was written sometime during the reign of the Emperor Constantine (306–327).

Roscommon, Earl of

See DILLON, WENTWORTH.

Rowlands, Samuel (ca. 1570–ca. 1630)
poet, prose writer

Samuel Rowlands was probably born in London, where it seems he remained for the rest of his life.

Who his parents were or what he did before 1598, when he published *The Betraying of Christ,* a book of sacred poems, is not known. Indeed, as Edmund Gosse, the editor of his *Complete Works* notes, "In no case has history been more persistent in silence than when summoned to give . . . news of Samuel Rowlands."

All that can really be said about Rowlands is that from 1598 to 1620 he generally wrote a book of prose or a collection of verse every year, though in some years he published as many as three. His first work, *The Betraying of Christ* (1598), was a collection of religious poems about the crucifixion.

Rowlands is better known for his satires (works that hold up human folly or vice for scorn or humor) than for his religious poetry. His best-known satire is *The Letting of Humor's Blood in the Head-Vein* (1600), which refers to the medical practice of treating patients by opening their veins and bleeding them. There is certainly a pun on "vain" since "vein" is written as "vaine" in the original title. In this poem Rowlands addresses his contemporaries in the introduction, attacking their frivolity:

> *Will you stand spending your invention's*
> *treasure*
> *To teach stage parrots speak for penny*
> *pleasure,*
> *While you yourself, like music sounding*
> *lutes*
> *Fretted and strange, gain them their silken*
> *suits?*

Rowlands here is attacking writers and audiences for wasting their time on literature that is written purely to entertain. First, he denounces those who waste their talents on writing plays and accuses players of playing them like lutes and growing rich. He goes on to denounce writers of erotic love poems:

> *Leave Cupid's cut, women's face-flattering*
> *praise,*

Love's subject grows too threadbare
nowadays.

Rowlands's intent is to cure his audience of its folly, and he draws them back into his own work by assuring his fellow writers that works such as the one before them have more merit and are financially more rewarding:

Change Venus' swans to write of Vulcan's
geese,
And you shall merit golden pens apiece.

The public will demonstrate its worth by showing its interest in such works as his.

Rowlands excelled at caricatures, or comically distorted portraits of RENAISSANCE social types. The character of the Curious Divine (a priest) from *Look to It, or I'll Stab You* (1604) is typical. Rowlands rails against "Divines, that are together by the ears, / Puffed up, high-minded, seedsmen of dissension"—that is, members of the clergy that attempt to create religious conflict.

Rowlands wrote prodigiously for many years, producing, besides his satires and religious poetry, poems about popular figures such as Guy, Earl of Warwick (1607). His productivity slackened in the 1620s. He produced only two works; his final, in that decade, was a satire called *Good News and Bad News* (1622) and a religious book of prose and verse entitled *Heavens' Glory, Seek It: Earth's Vanity, Fly It: Hell's Horror, Fear it* (1628).

Rowlands has remained in the background of literary studies. Edmund Gosse's description of him as "a poet of considerable talent without one spark or glimmer of genius" still rings true today.

Rowlandson, Mary (ca. 1637–ca. 1711)
nonfiction writer

Little is known about the early years of Mary Rowlandson. Her maiden name was White, and she was probably born in England. Her parents immigrated to America in 1639. In 1660 she married Joseph Rowland, a Puritan minister. The couple had four children, but one died in infancy.

Rowlandson gained a measure of fame because of a tragedy that befell her family in February 1676 during a series of raids carried out by the Wampanoag people. Their leader, Metacomet, was called King Philip by the English, so these raids eventually came to be called King Philip's War. Rowlandson's husband had gone to Boston to ask for protection from the raids. While he was gone a group of warriors attacked the small town of Lancaster, Massachusetts, where he and his wife lived. Many were killed in the attack, and Rowlandson and her three children were taken captive. Rowlandson and her daughter Sarah had been wounded by the same bullet in the attack. Although Rowlandson's wounds healed, her daughter died of blood loss during her first week of captivity. Rowlandson traveled with her captors for a total of 11 weeks, until she was ransomed by her husband for 20 English pounds. Some months later Rowlandson was reunited with her surviving children. Little is known about her later life, except that she died in 1710 or 1711.

Rowlandson originally wrote the story of her captivity, *The Sovereignty & Goodness of God, Together, with the Faithfullness of His Promises Displayed; Being a Narrative of the Captivity and Restauration of Mrs. Mary Rowlandson* (1682), for her children. Although other women had been captured, Rowlandson was the only one to write her own story. Cotton Mather, a Puritan clergyman, wrote the narrative of another notable female captive, Hannah Dustan. Rowlandson's narrative is still regarded as an especially fine example of this uniquely American genre. Her story went through four editions during her lifetime and 39 total editions.

Rowlandson's narrative shares many characteristics with other narratives that were written during the colonial period in America. These works often had a religious message, in that they portray captivities as God's way of testing the faith of those who went through the ordeals. Thus, Rowlandson says of the massacre that initiated her captivity, "yet the Lord by His almighty power preserved a number of us from death." The narratives also typically portray Native Americans as barbarians and devils. Rowlandson describes the horrors perpetrated by her attackers in great detail and ends her description with "Thus were we butchered by those merciless heathen, standing amazed, with the blood running down to our heels." But Rowlandson's narrative has an unselfconscious honesty that many of the other captivity narratives do not possess. For example, when one of Rowlandson's captors loses a child, Rowlandson is grateful because "there was more room." She also justifies taking a piece of meat from a child and eating it herself because it was too tough for the child to chew. It is this honest, even naïve, self-portraiture that makes Rowlandson's story so interesting to read even today. Her story is also interesting because so few women of the era wrote anything for publication. As Marylin Wesley notes in "The Travel Text in 'A Narrative of the Captivity and Restauration of Mrs. Mary Rowlandson,'" "Except for the reluctant publication of Anne Bradstreet's poetry, Mary Rowlandson's unprecedented account of women's travel is the only conspicuous breach of the Puritan ideology of female public silence and private passivity."

A Work about Mary Rowlandson

Faery, Rebecca Blevins. *Cartographies of Desire: Captivity, Race, and Sex in the Shaping of an American Nation.* Norman, Okla.: University of Oklahoma Press, 1999.

Rowley, Samuel (ca. 1570–1624) *playwright*

Samuel Rowley, a popular actor-playwright, first appeared on the stage in 1597. As a member of the ADMIRAL'S MEN, a theatrical company in Elizabethan and Jacobean England, Rowley performed in such plays as *Frederick and Basilea* (1597), *Fortune's Tennis,* and *The Battle of Alcazar* (1594), and in 1602 he became a shareholder in the company.

In addition to his role as an actor and shareholder in the Admiral's Men, Rowley wrote several plays for the company, including the biblical plays *Judas* and *Joshua,* written in 1601 and 1602, and the *Tragedy of Richard the Third, or the English Prophet, Hardshifte for Husbands or Bilboes the Best Blade,* and *A Match or no Match,* all written between 1623 and 1624. Rowley's only surviving work, however, is *When You See Me, You Know Me, Or the Famous Chronicle Historie of King Henry VIII* (1605). *The Noble Souldier* (1634) also remains, and, although the play is attributed to Rowley, the authorship of the play is not definitive; it is often believed to have been the work of Rowley as revised and reworked by Thomas DEKKER.

When You See Me, You Know Me is a history of King Henry VIII which has been described by the historian A. F. Pollard as "remarkably accurate, except in matters of date." This play is a likely source for Shakespeare's *Henry VIII* (1613), and it serves to display Rowley's comic style through the character of court fool Will Sommers. Also evident in the play are sentiments that reflect the religious upheaval in England during the time in which the play was written, as Rowley exhibits, according to the scholar F. P. Wilson, a "strong Protestant bias." This bias is evident when Sommers calls for "A halter and a rope, for him that would be pope, Against all right and reason."

Rowley is also credited with several additions to and revisions of other plays, including Christopher MARLOWE's *Doctor Faustus,* to which Rowley, along with William Bird, added several comic scenes. According to the scholar Lynn E. Burr, Rowley's comic talent is evident in *When You See Me, You Know Me* as well as in his revisions and collaborations, as his "handling of the clown figure surpasses that of many of his contemporaries."

Rowley, William (ca. 1585–1626) *playwright*

Little is known of the origins or early life of William Rowley, who first surfaced as a comic actor with some of the theater companies that thrived in Elizabethan and Jacobean London. Following a common practice during this period,

Rowley wrote several plays for his fellow actors and collaborated on others, notably with Thomas MIDDLETON but also with John Day, Thomas DEKKER, John FORD, and George Wilkins.

Rowley's first collaborative effort, with Day and Wilkins, was the script for *The Travails of the Three English Brothers* (1607). The first plays he wrote on his own were *A Shoemaker, A Gentleman with the Life and Death of the Cripple that Stole the Weathercock at Paules* (1608), *A New Wonder* (1610), and *A Woman Never Vexed* (1611). These and most of his other works were comedies, tragicomedies, or farces about love, lust, and loyalty, designed to entertain mass audiences but also notable for their ingenuity in plot, design, and expression. Other solo works include *Hymen's Holiday or Cupid's Vagaries* (1612) and *All's Lost by Lust* (1619), in which Rowley himself played the role of Jacques. Two of his successful works that have been lost to posterity are, *A Knave in Print* (1613) and *The Fool Without Book* (1613). Rowley drafted plots and apparently provided many of the comic scenes for his coauthors.

Around 1616 Rowley began a fruitful collaboration with Middleton, which yielded such joint efforts as *A Fair Quarrel* (1617); *The World Toss'd at Tennis* (1619), in which Rowley played the role of Simplicity; *The Changeling* (1622), considered a masterpiece of the era and their finest work together; and *The Spanish Gypsy* (1623). *The Changeling*, for which Rowley apparently wrote the opening and closing scenes, concerns cuckoldry involving an older man and his young wife, a familiar theme in dramas of the period. His most notable collaboration with Dekker and Ford was on *The Witch of Edmonton* (1622–24).

Roydon, Matthew (Hadrian Dorrell)
(1564–1622) *poet*

The most notable thing about Matthew Roydon was the company he kept, including fellow writers like George CHAPMAN, Christopher MARLOWE, and George PEELE. His most critically praised work was a commemorative poem about another friend. "An Elegie, or friends passion, for his Astrophill" (1586) eulogized the famed Sir Philip SIDNEY.

An Elegie was not Royden's only poem written for Sidney, but it was the only one that did not praise his family name and its nobility. Roydon himself was an impoverished, struggling poet lacking a patron. His *Elegie* focuses on love as Sidney's poetic inspiration, which was a double-edged sword. Some believed Sidney's passionate sonnet sequence *Astrophil and Stella* contained a hidden confession of infidelity. Roydon's poem is diplomatically ambiguous, as he never mentions marriage between the characters in question, yet he seems to approve of adultery, if that is what the relationship involved: "Sweet saints it is no sinne nor blame / To love a man of vertuous name."

The poem *Willobie His Avisa* was published under the name "Hadrian Dorrell," whom some believe was Matthew Roydon. Once again, Roydon's name is mentioned because of the fame of another: the poem is most significant because it opens with a preface mentioning William SHAKESPEARE's name for the first time in print.

Roydon was championed by George Chapman, who dedicated to Roydon two works with lengthy prefatory letters. Chapman was inspired by his friend's artistic purity and the fact that he was undaunted by poverty. Chapman valued one who pursued the arts over wealth and wrote letters to Roydon denigrating uninspired readers as well as writers. One encouraging letter to Roydon stated, "The profane multitudes I hate, & onelie consecrate my strange Poems to these serching spirits, whom learning hath made noble, and nobility sacred."

Matthew Roydon's famous friends brought him trouble in 1593 when Christopher Marlowe was arrested for his religious views after a statement given by the tortured Thomas KYD. Before he could be questioned, Roydon fled to Scotland.

A Work about Matthew Roydon

Huntington, John. *Ambition, Rank, and Poetry in 1590s England.* Urbana: University of Illinois Press, 2001.

Rubens, Peter Paul (1577–1640) *painter*

Peter Paul Rubens was born in Siegen, Westphalia, where his family was in exile because his father was a Calvinist. After the father's death in 1587, the family returned to their native Antwerp (in modern Belgium) and embraced the approved Catholic faith. Rubens was educated at a Jesuit school, and at 14 he began a series of apprenticeships to minor painters. In 1600, an established painter, he went to Italy, where he spent eight years in the service of the duke of Mantua. When he returned to Antwerp, he was quickly recognized as the city's foremost painter. Students flocked to him, including the young Anthony VAN DYCK.

Rubens traveled a good deal, executing commissions for the French and Spanish courts and also acting as a diplomat. For example, he was involved in the negotiations about a royal marriage between the Spanish and English royal families. About 1629 he went to England, where he became a court favorite. King Charles I knighted him, and he painted the *Allegory of War and Peace,* now in the National Gallery, London. He returned to Antwerp in 1630, but still worked on English commissions, including the grand paintings for the ceiling in the Banqueting House in the Palace of Whitehall, completed in 1635.

At 53, he married the beautiful 16-year-old Helen Fourment, who is the subject of many of his paintings. He died of gout at 63, at the height of his creative powers and reputation. Rubens was the foremost painter of his era and he is admired today not only for the exhuberance and beauty of his paintings but also for the sheer volume of his output. Rubens's landscapes profoundly influenced British paintings, including Gainsborough and Constable.

Works about Peter Paul Rubens

Belkin, Kristin Lohse. *Rubens.* New York: Phaidon Press, 1998.
Scribner, Charles. *Peter Paul Rubens.* New York: Harry N. Abrams, 1989.

Rymer, Thomas (1641–1713) *nonfiction writer*

Thomas Rymer was educated at Cambridge University and Gray's Inn to become an attorney, but his great interest was in literature, particularly drama. Although he wrote one play, *Edgar, or the English Monarch* (1678), it was never performed. Instead, Rymer is famous for taking the side of the ancients, or classical Greek and Roman writers (and particularly Aristotle), in the famous debate between the ancients and the moderns during the RESTORATION and early 18th century. Jonathan Swift, in his satire *The Battle of the Books,* imagines the books themselves conducting the debate in the form of a heroic battle in a library. At the same time he gives an excellent summary of the tone of the controversy. Before the fight begins,

> a solitary Ancient, squeezed up among a whole shelf of Moderns, offered fairly to dispute the case, and to prove by manifest reason that the priority was due to them from long possession, and in regard of their prudence, antiquity, and, above all, their great merits toward the Moderns. But these denied the premises. . . . As for any obligations [the Moderns] owed to the Ancients, they renounced them all. "It is true," said they, "we are informed some few of our party have been so mean as to borrow their subsistence from you, but the rest, infinitely the greater number (and especially we French and English), were so far from stooping to so base an example, that there never passed, till this very hour, six words between us."

In *The Tragedies of the Last Age* (1678) and *A Short View of Tragedy* (1693) Rymer denounced Elizabethan drama, including the work of Shakespeare, and favored French neoclassical ideas. He went so far as to characterize *Othello* as "a bloody farce without salt or savor." He coined the term *poetic justice,* which means that a literary outcome should be justified in an especially appropriate way by the action leading up to it. He also said that dramatic action needed to be probable and that characters needed to be either idealized or typical of their class and status. Rymer also wanted to return to the convention of the Greek chorus. John DRYDEN argued in favor of the moderns while carefully indicating his respect for Rymer's learning.

S

Sackville, Thomas (1536–1608) *poet, dramatist*

Thomas Sackville was born to Sir Richard Sackville, a member of the court of Henry VIII. He attended Oxford University briefly and then settled in London in 1553 to follow his father's footsteps in political service. His interest went beyond politics, however. He was also the chancellor of Oxford University, an architect, a musician, a poet, and a dramatist.

In 1561 Sackville wrote the play *Gorboduc* with Thomas NORTON. *Gorboduc* was the first English play to be written in blank verse, or unrhymed lines of 10 syllables with alternating stresses, the form in which much RENAISSANCE drama, including the plays of William SHAKESPEARE, was cast. It is based on the story of Gorbodugo in Geoffrey of Monmouth's history of England. Gorbodugo is an aging king who divides his land between two of his sons, with tragic results. Sackville also published two poems—the "Induction," or introduction, and "Buckingham's Complaint"—in *The Mirror for Magistrates* (1563), a collection of tragic poems in which historical figures narrate the story of their downfall.

"Induction" is a better piece of literature; along with the other poems in *The Mirror for Magistrates,* it modernizes a medieval theme, the turning of Fortune's wheel, or the belief that one's life is controlled by external forces and that, like a wheel turning, a person could be up one moment and down the next. Sackville and the other poets update this theme by blending it with an idea taken from classical thought and in particular the ancient Greek philosopher Aristotle. The narrator in each poem has a tragic flaw, that is, a flawed personality trait that leads to the character's tragic end. Each, therefore, is responsible for his own downfall.

The Mirror begins with Sackville's "Induction." He situates the tales in a physical setting that foreshadows their theme:

> And sorrowing I to see the summer flowers,
> The lively green, the lusty leas [leaves]
>   forlorn,
> The sturdy trees so shatter'd with the showers,
> The fields so fade that flourish'd so beforn,
> It taught me well all earthly things be born
> To die the death, for nought long time my
>   last;
> The summer's beauty yields to winter's
>   blast.

Just as the seasons cycle from summer to winter and back again, so the characters in *Mirror for*

Magistrates experience the highs and lows of fate. For this work and especially for *Gorboduc,* Sackville has earned his place as one of the major writers of the time and one of the key English dramatists before Shakespeare.

Saint Bartholomew's Day Massacre
(1572)

The entire 16th century was a time of struggle, throughout Europe, between supporters of the Roman Catholic Church and Protestant reformers. In France, the struggle came to the point of civil war three times during the 1560s—in 1562–63, 1567–68, and 1569–70—and reached a climax in the Saint Bartholomew's Day Massacre, which began on August 24, 1572, Saint Bartholomew's Day. The precipitating event was the August 18 marriage of Marguerite de Valois, daughter of France's Catholic king Charles IX, to Henri de Bourbon, the Protestant king of Navarre. Many of France's leading Catholic nobles feared that Henri's intimate connection with the royal family would make the Protestant faction dominant.

Jacques-Auguste de Thou (1553–1617), who witnessed some of the events, reported that at a meeting between Charles's mother, Catherine de' Medici, and some of her advisers it was agreed that the leader of the Protestant faction, Admiral Gaspard de Coligny, should be assassinated. An attempt was made on Coligny's life on August 22; it failed, but roused the Protestants' anger and the Catholics' fear of Protestant revenge. Urged by his mother, Charlex IX gave orders for the leading Protestant nobles, beginning with Coligny, to be systematically killed. The plan was carried out by Swiss mercenaries under the direction of Henri, duc de Guise. After Coligny had been killed, his body fell into the hands of a Catholic mob who mutilated it and went on to seek out other Protestants to kill and homes to loot. Estimates of the carnage vary, but it is likely that at least 2,000 people were killed in Paris in the three days after Coligny's death, and a further 3,000 in the rest of France in the ensuing weeks.

Among those who were killed was the philosopher Peter RAMUS.

In England, the events of Saint Bartholomew's Day became emblematic of the reasons for hating and fearing Catholics. They were dramatized by Christopher MARLOWE in his tragedy *The Massacre at Paris.* Marlowe's duke of Guise is one of the literature's more memorable villains. Sir Philip SIDNEY was visiting the French ambassador, Francis Walsingham, in Paris during the uprising. He rehearses the tragic events several times in *The Arcadia,* thereby influencing a host of English authors.

Works about the Saint Bartholomew's Day Massacre

Kingdon, Robert M. *Myths about the St. Bartholomew's Day Massacres, 1572–1576.* Cambridge, Mass.: Harvard University Press, 1988.
Knecht, Robert Jean. *The French Wars of Religion 1559–1598.* New York: Longman, 1996.

Sandys, George (1578–1664) *translator, nonfiction writer, poet*

George Sandys was born in Yorkshire, England, the youngest son of Edwin Sandys, archbishop of York, and went on to study at Oxford University. A poet and translator, he served as the treasurer of the English company for the colony of Virginia from 1621 to 1626.

Like many RENAISSANCE poets, Sandys took an interest in the Greek and Roman classics. He is best known for a verse translation of Ovid's *Metamorphoses* from Latin into English. In Sandys's 1626 translation, which was the first book written in America, the author not only preserves the literal meanings of the original Latin words but also maintains their melodious tempo. In the second edition of his translation, Sandys appended to the end of each book a series of interpretive commentaries.

Sandys also translated Book I of Virgil's *Aeneid* and published a journal of his travels in the Middle East, *Relation of a Journey* (1615).

Savile, Sir George, Marquis of Halifax
(1633–1695) *nonfiction writer*

George Savile was born in Thornhill, England, and educated at Shrewsbury School. He was married in 1656 to Dorothy, daughter of Henry Spenser, Earl of Sunderland.

A prominent English statesman throughout his life, George Savile supported a path of moderation that earned him the nickname "The Trimmer." The title, originally meant to be a derogatory term, was proudly taken up by Savile. A truly political man, Savile apparently had no literary aspirations but instead wrote as a way to express his opinions and to influence the politics of his day, which were in a particularly complicated state of unrest. He was involved in such important changes as the RESTORATION of King Charles II to the throne of England in 1660 and was a central figure in the decision to allow the Roman Catholic James, Duke of York, to succeed his brother, Charles. A member of the Privy Council, Savile's middle-of-the-road politics were not always popular, and he was at times demoted from positions of power, even by James II, whose position as sovereign he had helped secure. Yet he did not hold a grudge, for when William of Orange invaded England at the request of Parliament in 1688, he attempted to bring about a compromise between him and James II. When the attempt failed, however, he chose to support William, and his support was largely responsible for the acceptance of William and Mary as joint rulers of England by the Convention Parliament in 1689.

Perhaps Savile's most important literary work is *The Character of a Trimmer* (1684), in which Savile expresses his opinions on both domestic policy and world politics. For example, he opposes the laws that penalized Catholics for practicing their faith and prevented them from holding certain positions. He also describes the decline of British power in world politics and the growth of French power, lamenting the sight of "Roses blasted and discoloured while lilies triumph and grow insolent upon the comparison." (The Rose is the symbol of the English monarchy and the Lily that of

the French.) He also wrote *The Rough Draft of a New Model at Sea* (1694), in which he discusses the naval establishment. The work opens with a thoughtful question:

'What shell we do to be saved in this world?' There is no other answer but this, 'Look to your moat.' The first article of an Englishman's political creed must be that he believith in the sea.

Clear, persuasive, and elegant, these works are most relevant for their effect on his contemporary audiences, but can also be enjoyed today, especially as a guide for moderation.

Other Work by George Savile
The Works of George Savile Marquis of Halifax. 3 vols. Edited by Mark N. Brown. Oxford: Clarendon Press, 1989.

Savile, Sir Henry (1549–1622) *translator*

Henry Savile, the son of Henry and Elizabeth Savile, was born in Bradley, near Halifax, Yorkshire, England. He was educated at Brasenose College, Oxford University, and a teacher at Merton College. Part of Savile's education included the study of mathematics and Greek, which he also taught until 1578. In 1582 he became tutor in Greek to Queen ELIZABETH I. He married Margaret Gerrard, a widow, probably in 1592; was appointed provost of Eton College in 1596; and was knighted in 1604 by JAMES I OF ENGLAND.

Savile was the first to translate the Latin *Histories of Tacitus* into English, a work he published in four volumes in 1591. He also translated into Latin King James I's poem *Apology for the Oath of Allegiance* (1609), and was among the scholars who translated the King James Bible (1611; see BIBLE, KING JAMES VERSION). In particular, he translated the Evangelists, the Acts of the Apostles, and the Book of Revelations.

Savile's next great work was an eight-volume edition of *St. John Chrysostom* (1610–13). He had searched Europe to find the oldest manuscripts written by the saint, and then had these copied and translated. This was an expensive project, and Savile produced a luxurious book which did not sell well. However, according to the scholar Adam Nicolson a copy survives in the "Sansovino library in Venice . . . each volume bound in crimson satin."

Savile also produced an edition of Xenophon's *Cyropaedia* (1613), which is a romanticized biography of the Persian ruler Cyrus the Great; an edition of Thomas Bradwardine's *De Causa Dei contra Palagium,* which asserts that faith and theology are more important for salvation than reason and philosophy; a treatise on geometry; and letters.

Savile had worked with Thomas BODLEY on the foundation of the Bodleian Library, and when he died he left his manuscripts to the library, including his originals for *Chrysostom.* He also founded two chairs at Oxford, one in geometry and one in astronomy.

Scot, Reginald (Reginald Scott)
(ca. 1538–1599) *nonfiction writer*
Reginald Scot was born in Kent, England, to Richard Scot of an old Kentish family who had served as members of Parliament and sheriffs, and Mary Whetenall Scot, daughter of the sheriff of Kent. Although Scot did not inherit the right to fulfill such positions, being the younger son of a younger son, it is assumed that he studied law, for he did serve as a justice of the peace.

Scot's first book, *Perfect Platform of a Hop-Garden,* was the first guidebook published in England on the growing of hops, an important ingredient in beer. In 1584 he published the book for which he is remembered, *The Discovery of Witchcraft* (1584), in which he set out to demonstrate that witchcraft was not real, as many believed. For Scot, the scholar Jean Howard observes, witches "were simply . . . charlatans [fakes] who gained their power by tricks, illusions, and the artful leading on of their clients."

In his book Scot attempts to explain why some people imagine that others are witches. Those accused, Scot argues, are

women which be commonly old, lame, bleareyed, pale, foul, and full of wrinkles; poor, and sullen, superstitious . . . so as, what mischief, mischance, calamity, or slaughter is brought to pass, they are easily persuaded the same is done by themselves; imprinting in their minds an earnest and constant imagination hereof.

In other words, those accused of witchcraft were often outcasts who were mistreated. Additionally, Scot continues, they "curseth one [a person], and sometimes another. . . . Doubtless (at length [and by chance]) some of [them] die, or fall sick; or some of their children are visited with diseases that vex them strangely."

The more significant feature of Scot's *Discovery,* however, is the way it illustrates how charlatans use tricks to deceive naive people into believing they practice magic:

Their . . . [use of] strange names, their [use of] diffuse [miscellaneous] phrases . . ., their foolish words mingled with impiety . . ., their bargaining with fools, their cousening of the simple, their scope and drift for money doth bewray [betray] all their art to be counterfiet cousenage [kinship].

The scholar Stephen Greenblatt commends Scot for showing how magicians manipulated their audiences by playing on the popular belief in witchcraft. Although he wrote only two books, Scot remains of interest to scholars for the reason Greenblatt points out: his *Discovery of Witchcraft* is an important document in the movement away from medieval superstition during the RENAISSANCE.

A Work about Reginald Scot
West, Robert H. *Reginald Scot and Renaissance Writings on Witchcraft.* Boston: Twayne, 1984.

Sedley, Charles (1639–1701) *poet, dramatist*
The son of a baronet who died before he was born, Charles Sedley attended Oxford University but

never received a degree. His brother, William, died shortly after he enrolled, leaving Sedley with the title and the family estate. He wed Katherine Savage in 1657, and two years later the couple had a daughter who would eventually become the mistress of James II. Their marriage was not a happy one, however, since Katherine began to show evidence of mental illness and had to be taken care of in a convent. After the RESTORATION in 1660, Sedley became one of the wits who frequented the court of the king, Charles II. Like others in what was called at the time the "ministry of pleasure," few of Sedley's works were published in his lifetime. Rather, as was the accepted practice among men in his position, they were circulated in manuscript form.

Sedley authored several plays and a wide variety of verse, demonstrating skill in song, lyric, and epigram, or witty sayings in verse. In 1664 he helped translate Pierre Corneille's *Pompey the Great: A Tragedy,* but his first original effort was the comedy *The Mulberry Garden* (1668), based partly on MOLIÈRE's *The School for Husbands.* His most popular play was *Bellamira: Or the Mistress* (1687), a bawdy comedy in which the heroine is a thinly disguised representation of the Countess of Cleveland, the mistress of Charles II.

Sedley is best remembered today for his song "Phyllis Is My Only Joy," a witty take on the paradox of love:

> Though, alas! too late I find
> Nothing can her fancy fix,
> Yet the moment she is kind
> I forgive her all her tricks;
> Which, though I see,
> I can't get free;
> She deceiving,
> I believing;
> What need lovers wish for more?

Another of his love poems, "Love Still Has Something of the Sea," is an extended comparison. Both love and the sea

> are becalm'd in clearest days,
> And in rough weather tost;
> They wither under cold delays,
> Or are in tempests lost.

In his later years Sedley became increasingly involved in politics and penned many satiric epigrams. It is usually for his earlier lyrics, however, that he is most highly regarded.

Settle, Elkanah (1648–1724) *dramatist, poet*

Elkanah Settle was born at Dunstable, Bedfordshire, England, the son of Josias Settle. He studied at Trinity College, Oxford, but did not receive his degree. In the 1670s he was one of the young playwrights King Charles II hoped would lead a renaissance in English drama that would rival the accomplishments of the important French playwrights of the era.

Settle's most significant literary works were the dramas *Cambyses, Knight of Persia* (1667), about the mad Persian ruler of Egypt, and *The Empress of Morocco* (1673). The latter was written with the encouragement of the Earl of Rochester, who hoped Settle would become a rival to John DRYDEN. It was the first play in the RESTORATION period to have its climax in a musical scene, with its own score. It is also believed to have been the first play printed in England with engraved illustrations. Dryden responded by contributing to a pamphlet that harshly criticized the play, in which he describes Settle as

> an animal of a most deplored understanding, without conversation. His being is in a twilight of sense, and some glimmering of thought, which he can never fashion into wit or English. His stile is boisterous and rough-hewn, his rhyme incorrigibly lewd, and his numbers perpetually harsh and ill-sounding. The little talent which he has is fancy.

Dryden also cast Settle as Doeg, a character in his satirical poem *Absalom and Achitophel.* In it he bitterly criticizes Settle as one of "two fools that crutch their feeble sense on verse." Settle was also savaged by Alexander Pope in his *Dunciad*.

Something of an opportunist, Settle also wrote various political pamphlets, shifting his allegiances between Tories and Whigs during the controversy over the succession of the Catholic James II to the throne. He served for a time in James II's army, although Settle had earlier been an opponent of the king. In 1691 Settle forsook partisan politics and was appointed City Poet of London, a position for which he was expected to write noncontroversial pageants. He lived out his last days as a "poor brother" in the Carthusian Order and is reputed to have been a performer in street fairs, where he played the role of a dragon in a handmade green leather suit.

Shadwell, Thomas (1640 or 1641–1692)
dramatist, poet
Thomas Shadwell was born in Norfolk, England, to gentry, John and Sarah Shadwell. Shadwell attended Cambridge University and the Middle Temple, where he studied law.

Shadwell wrote 19 plays, the first of which was *The Sullen Lovers,* produced in 1668 with great success. The play features two couples who view the enjoyment of life differently. One couple seeks to shield themselves from the folly of everyday life, whereas the second, younger and happier couple seeks to enjoy the gaiety around them.

Shadwell's *Epsom Wells* (1672) features a rake, that handsome, sexually adventurous man already a mainstay of the RESTORATION stage. In an interesting twist, however, this rake is not single, nor married to a wife who suffers his infidelities patiently, but is married to a woman who is equally promiscuous. Many dramatists were to recognize the interesting possibilities of such a setup and follow Shadwell's pattern.

Shadwell was an accomplished musician and worked on operatic adaptations, including William SHAKESPEARE's *The Tempest* (1674). He also adapted Shakespeare's drama *Timon of Athens.* He wrote

various poems for special occasions after he became poet laureate in 1688.

Shadwell's next major drama was *The Libertine,* based on the story of the famous rake, or "libertine," Don Juan. In Shadwell's version Don John (as he calls him) exhibits superhuman levels of lust and violence and is dragged into hell at the end of the play. Termed a tragedy when published, the play can also be read as a satire of the familiar Restoration figure of the rake. Three later plays, *A True Widow* (1678), *The Woman-Captain* (1679), and *The Lancashire Witches* (1681), all feature women who, in the words of the biographer Michael W. Alssid, manage to "triumph in a world presumably dominated by the male." Among Shadwell's late comedies, *The Squire of Alsatia* (1688) enjoyed a long run. Alsatia is the name for a lawless district of London, where, in this play, a nobleman's son falls in with rogues and must be rescued from a life of colorful but shameful behavior.

Thomas Shadwell's work, and eventually his name, fell into obscurity shortly after his death, with one famous exception. John DRYDEN wrote a scathing poem, *MacFlecknoe,* that portrays Shadwell as utterly devoid of talent. Since Dryden's work is much more widely read than Shadwell's, Dryden's characterization of Shadwell's work as fit "relics of the bum," that is, suitable for use as toilet paper, is all that many ever learn of this notable dramatist. However, as the scholar Robert D. Hume notes, "Shadwell is always a bellweather"; he set many of the trends that were characteristic of Restoration drama.

Shakespeare, William (1564–1616)
playwright, poet
William Shakespeare was born in Stratford-on-Avon to John Shakespeare, a leatherworker who served on the town council and was also mayor for a short time, and Mary Arden Shakespeare. Although there is no record of his having gone to school, he likely went to a local grammar school, where he would have learned Latin, rhetoric (how to be persuasive and argue a case), and classical literature.

What Shakespeare did after leaving school and before going up to London sometime in the mid-1580s is not known, although it was reported that he taught Latin at a grammar school. Also unknown are his activities between 1585, the year Hamnet and Judith (his twin son and daughter) were born, and 1592, the year the dramatist and pamphlet writer Robert GREENE called him "an upstart crow" and plagiarist. Greene's reference and other records, such as the diary of Philip Henslowe, an independent proprietor, show that Shakespeare was achieving success as a dramatist in the early 1590s. Scholars therefore believe that Shakespeare's first play was written in the first years of that same decade. It is a commonly held belief that Shakespeare left his family and moved to London to pursue a career in the theater at this time.

It is likely that Shakespeare began his career in the theater as an actor. This was not uncommon at the time, as playwrights often took an active role in all aspects of their productions. Shakespeare most likely had a financial stake in his drama, considering his name does not appear in other business records of the time. He was a member of two well-known acting troupes of the time: the CHAMBERLAIN'S MEN (beginning in 1594, soon after their creation), and the KING'S MEN (founded in connection with King JAMES I's accession to the throne in 1603). The rise of the public theater—places where paying customers, and not just members in the royal circle, could watch these theatrical troupes—coincided with Shakespeare's early successes. Some theaters in London included the Rose, the BLACKFRIARS, and the GLOBE THEATRE. The frequency with which Shakespeare produced plays in the early 1590s hints that he must have had enough financial success to avoid working as an actor for long.

Shakespeare's first experiments in dramatic writing consisted mostly of comedies. Elizabethan comedies are typically works that focus on romantic relationships between characters and end in marriage, promising a positive future for the play's heroes. The early comedies *The Taming of the Shrew* and *The Comedy of Errors,* both of which are

on record as first being staged in 1594 (and whose dates of composition are uncertain), are less complex than the later masterpieces *As You Like It* (ca. 1599) and *Twelfth Night* (ca. 1600–01). But they still contain evidence of Shakespeare's genius—a complexity of language, unique characters, and interesting plots.

The first two plays are sometimes referred to as citizen comedies, or urban comedies, because they portray nonroyal figures in public settings such as marketplaces and town squares. The *Comedy of Errors* is a story of mistaken identity (a popular theme in English comedies), while the *Taming of the Shrew* explores issues of romance and female identity. The latter two plays mentioned are considered pastoral, because, like the Italian plays in whose tradition they follow, the story shifts from the city to the country. In *As You Like It,* the participants in the drama retreat to the forest of Arden (a real place near Stratford, where Shakespeare grew up) before returning home to the city, older and wiser as a result of their adventures.

The tragedies *King Lear* (ca. 1605) and *Macbeth* (ca. 1606) are mature examples of Shakespeare's turn toward the darker themes of murder and madness and how they relate to politics (both title characters are national leaders who lose their minds and lives). This shift invites us to wonder if Shakespeare was undergoing difficulties or depression in his personal life at this stage of his life. Certainly his drama did not suffer because of any such turmoil: *Othello* (ca. 1604), *Antony and Cleopatra* (ca. 1606–07) and, of course, *Hamlet* (ca. 1600) are considered to be among the greatest achievements in world literature. All of these plays depict the demise of military or royal figures, honorable men who are fatally flawed or self-destructive.

The final works of Shakespeare's career are best described as "problem plays" or tragicomedies—dramatic stories that combine elements of both tragedy and comedy while exploring the complexities of human existence. The plays *The Winter's Tale* (ca. 1610–11) and *The Tempest* (ca. 1611)—the last play we can be certain he wrote by himself—address a variety of issues, ranging from the personal (parenthood, friendship, ambition) to the social (politics, sexuality, slavery). It is particularly attractive to consider *The Tempest* to be Shakespeare's farewell to the theater because Prospero, the play's protagonist, or main character, uses magic (which represents artistic genius) to solve the problems of his family and friends on a remote island. Shakespeare thus begins his career as a writer interested in exploring the financial possibilities of the theater business through experimentation in form, language, and plot, and concludes it by demonstrating the power of the creative spirit.

All told, the playwright authored or coauthored at least 35 plays, not to mention a remarkable sonnet sequence and other short poems. The 154 sonnets (a specific type of poem in 14 lines invented by the Italian poet PETRARCH), which were first published in 1609, explore many of the same themes (such as love, duty, death, and divinity), making his body of work timeless and universal. The narrative poems (longer works that tell a story) *Venus and Adonis* (published in 1593) and *The Rape of Lucrece* (published in 1594) were the only pieces of writing he ever published in his lifetime.

The first "complete collection" of Shakespeare's plays was published in 1623. His words still seem fresh and exciting today to people across cultures. By the end of his career, Shakespeare had accumulated enough wealth to purchase properties in Stratford and London (he bought a portion of the Blackfriars theater in 1613) and was already considered by his peers to be one of the greatest writers in England. However, his stature as an artist at the time was not nearly as great as it is today: Only a modest grave and a sculpture in his liking exist to this day in the Holy Trinity Church of Stratford, where he was buried at the age of 52.

Critical Analysis

Shakespeare had an extraordinary career. He is one of the few RENAISSANCE playwrights to write both successful comedies and tragedies. Unlike comedies, tragedies are more difficult to define but are usually easily identified, in that they tell the story of a single character's downfall. They concentrate on an essentially good, yet importantly flawed, person so as to invite the audience to identify with his or her troubles (a classic Shakespearean example of this is *Hamlet*). Modern critics usually divide his plays into tragedies, comedies, and histories. Sometimes these same critics refer to Shakespeare's "romances" and "problem plays," which are works that combine elements of all three genres.

Other dramatists tried their hand at both genres but were generally successful in only one of them. Ben JONSON, for example, is known for comic masterpieces like *Volpone* (1606), but when he turned his attention to tragedy, he produced stilted failures like *Sejanus* (ca. 1603).

Shakespeare not only wrote successful comedies and tragedies, he also helped redefine each of these categories. "From first to last each play of Shakespeare's," the scholar Derek Traversi observes, "represents not only a development from what has gone before, but a new beginning, a fresh attack on problems involved in the very decision to write a particular kind of play." In *The Tragedy of Richard III* (ca. 1592–93), for instance, Shakespeare restructures actual events of English history so as to create a history play that follows a simpler story. He presents key episodes of Richard's reign in a more digestible form. This practice was not unique to Shakespeare, as the history play as a dramatic form was in fact gaining popularity by the year. It can, however, be said that Shakespeare was a key contributor to this movement in the culture and tradition of English drama.

Shakespeare was also an innovative poet. In his sonnet sequence (ca. 1592–96), for example, he often combined both Italian and English elements of the sonnet. For the rhyme scheme of his sonnets, Shakespeare followed the English tradition of constructing a four-part structure consisting of three quatrains—that is, four-line poetic units—and a final couplet (two concluding lines that end with rhyming words). From the Italian tradition, he borrowed a two-part argument-structure, a method that introduces a problem in the first eight lines and then resolves it in the last six lines. Such experimentation is evident in Sonnet 18, as the rhyme scheme and problem/solution formula follow in Shakespeare's innovative Anglo-Italian style:

> *Shall I compare thee to a summer's day? (A)*
> *Thou art more lovely and more temperate:*
> *   (B)*
> *Rough winds do shake the darling buds of*
> *   May, (A)*
> *And summer's lease hath all too short a*
> *   date: (B)*
>
> *Sometime too hot the eye of heaven shines,*
> *   (C)*
> *And often is his gold complexion dimm'd;*
> *   (D)*
> *And every fair from fair sometime declines,*
> *   (C)*
> *By chance or nature's changing course*
> *   untrimm'd; (D)*

In these first two quatrains—groups of four lines—the first line rhymes with the third line and the second rhymes with the fourth. This manner of rhyming is commonly referred to as the ABAB CDCD pattern, as the letters correspond to the way in which certain words rhyme. Also note that the theme of the poem is a problem: To what can Shakespeare compare the beauty of the person he describes? In the final six lines, in the aforementioned Italian fashion, Shakespeare proposes a possible solution in the third quatrain and final couplet.

> *But thy eternal summer shall not fade (E)*
> *Nor lose possession of that fair thou owest;*
> *   (F)*
> *Nor shall Death brag thou wander'st in his*
> *   shade, (E)*
> *When in eternal lines to time thou growest:*
> *   (F)*
>
> *So long as men can breathe or eyes can see,*
> *   (G)*
> *So long lives this and this gives life to thee.*
> *   (G)*

The third quatrain begins to resolve the problem of the first two, while the couplet (GG) provides a sense of closure. Shakespeare realizes that he does not need to worry about finding an object with which to compare his subject's beauty: Because it is something "eternal," the true beauty of his subject cannot die. The poet proposes that his poem will be a lasting testament to this beauty—That is, so long as his poetry is read, his subject's beauty will live forever, in the mind of the reader. Such a concept (along with the poetic structure) is typical of the Shakespearian sonnet in that it validates both the power of poetry and human beauty.

In the sonnets, Shakespeare's favorite topics or themes are physical beauty, love, suffering, death, and the power of the written word. Critics have long noticed that most of the sonnets fall into one of three categories concerning the subject of the poems. Shakespeare wrote a great deal about a dark-haired lady, a handsome young man, and a light-skinned mistress who failed to return the poet's love. Of particular interest are the poems about the young man; some critics insist that the homoerotic nature of the feelings expressed is proof of Shakespeare's uncertain sexuality. No matter what the exact nature of his preference was, the sonnets show that Shakespeare was motivated to write some of his most beautiful literature through the experience of eros, or love.

In his plays, Shakespeare developed what today has become recognized as a modern understanding of human character. The critic Joel Fineman credits Shakespeare with inventing the psychological view of the self that is assumed in modern thought. Scholar Harold Bloom, in a similar vein, has argued that Shakespeare is responsible for "the invention of the human."

Indeed, Shakespeare represents characters differently from earlier writers of fiction and nonfiction. The difference between his notion of selfhood and that of earlier writers can be illustrated by briefly comparing the view of the self illustrated in *Hamlet* and the view that is assumed in Stephen Gosson's *Plays Confuted in Five Actions* (1584), which is a condemnation of Elizabethan drama.

Gosson argues that drama corrupts its audiences by training them to perform—to act falsely—something that will lead, he fears, to social disorder. The ability to conceal one's true identity, after all, is what allows criminals to trick their victims and dupe them out of their money. In a population of people with the ability to play roles, one is unable to know with whom one is dealing, so Gosson asks his readers not to "seem to be, what they [are] not" for the good of the social order. For Gosson there is a simple connection between a person's inward being and his outward self, so all one has to do to be true to one's self is to avoid acting. He thereby assumes that people have an inward self that can either be revealed or concealed.

Shakespeare, by contrast, regards the relationship between a person's inward being and his outward appearance as a far more complicated matter. In *Hamlet,* Hamlet tells his mother, Queen Gertrude, that it is impossible for one to reveal one's true self. At the beginning of the second scene of Shakespeare's play, Gertrude attempts to convince her son that it is time to stop mourning for his dead father. Death is a common thing, she notes, and Hamlet agrees with her. "If it be, / Why seems it so particular with thee?" she then asks. In other words, Gertrude accuses her son of being unreasonable for *seeming* so sad for so long, since he knows death must come to all. "I know not 'seems,'" Hamlet replies:

> 'Tis not alone my inky cloak, good mother,
> Nor customary suits of solemn black, (. . .)
>
> That can denote me truly. These indeed seem,
> For they are actions that a man might play;
> But I have that within which passes show,
> These but the trappings and the suits of woe.

Hamlet begins this speech assuring his mother of the authenticity of his behavior. He does not seem to mourn; he truly mourns. But despite his assertion that he "knows not 'seems,'" he insists that he is unable to do anything but seem. His exterior, the way he dresses in mourning for his dead father, is not able to reveal his true inner self. This claim contradicts Gertrude's opinion that seeming is the same as being, that the "show" is real. The outward signs—such as sighs, tears, and dejected behavior—cannot truly represent that which is within: the human spirit, or individual identity.

Hamlet is following the advice of moralists like Gosson and refusing to act in a manner that hides his true self, yet he feels obliged to continue acting. An essential difference between the inner and outer man, Hamlet assumes, prevents one's inner self from emerging to the surface. Shakespeare, in short, assumes that the outward man can never be anything more than an inauthentic representation of the inward man.

Shakespeare did not begin his career with the notion of selfhood that he presents in *Hamlet,* nor did he develop it in a moment of sudden insight. The notion not only emerges slowly in his work, but it seems to result from his attempt to answer a particular question: How does being alienated from the social order affect the individual? Early in his career, Shakespeare explored the relationship between a character's alienation, his selfhood, and theatricality, or acting, in *Richard III,* a historical play about the deformed Richard of Gloucester's takeover of the English crown and his subsequent tyranny.

In this play Richard does not possess a "within which passes show." His role is to be an outrageous villain who is almost too evil to be believed. He is a master of deception, but his true feelings are also, especially at the beginning of the play, clear to the audience. As the play progresses, however, Richard distances himself from the audience. Thus, the scholar Alexander Leggatt argues, "Richard seems for a while to be not just alone, but alone with us [Shakespeare's audience]. But as we move more fully into the play we realize how deceptive this appearance is."

The audience's initial, if perhaps tentative, sympathy for Richard recedes, and it is forced to acknowledge that his physically deformed appearance is a sign of his morally deformed soul. Thus the scholar Jean Howard argues that the play displays "an anxiety about theatricality that ultimately finds its apogee [or peak] in the monstrous figure of Richard III."

The paradox, or the contradictory nature at the heart of Richard, is that he is never anything but himself, whether he is playing a role or not, and that the less the audience thinks it knows about his true feelings, the more it knows about his true self. Richard's ability to conceal his true self, in fact, is just another manifestation of his monstrousness.

The problem of character in *Richard III* is, however, not as simple as the above analysis makes it seem. The analogy between Richard's physical deformity and his spiritual deformity, after all, suggests that he was born evil and could not have become other than what he is. Shakespeare rejects such an explanation from the beginning. In the play's opening soliloquy, Richard proclaims:

> *I, that am curtail'd of this fair proportion,*
> *Cheated of feature by dissembling Nature,*
> *Deform'd, unfinish'd, sent before my*
> *   time...*
> *Have no delight to pass away the time,*
> *   (...)*
>
> *And therefore, since I cannot prove a*
> *   lover...*
> *I am determined to prove a villain.*

Alienated from the social world because people are repulsed by his appearance, Richard chooses to embrace evil. Once he makes his choice, however, he becomes evil. It comes, like his deformity, to define who he is. Indeed, since evil is something necessarily opposed to social norms, which were often represented as divinely ordained in the period, Richard III, it could be argued, has little choice but to choose as he does. The alienation to which his deformity gives rise shapes the personality that finds pleasure in monstrous behavior. He chooses monstrousness, and conversely monstrousness chooses him.

Alienation does not continue to function as something that produces evil characters in Shakespeare's work. It does, however, play an important role in the development of Shakespeare's view of the self. At the end of *Richard II* (1595), a play about Henry Bolingbroke's hostile takeover of the kingdom rightly ruled by Richard II, Shakespeare edges toward imagining the idea of the self that he articulates in *Hamlet*. Richard II is in this way an introduction or ancestor to the character of Hamlet: They are two men seemingly obsessed with their own complex personalities.

At the end of the play, as he is being deposed, Richard observes, "[M]y grief lies all within / And these external manners of lament / Are merely shadows to the unseen grief." Richard is commenting on the changes that the loss of his position as king obliges him to undergo. He is, in fact, not just losing his kingship, he is excluded from the social order altogether. There is no place for a former king in it, and for the rest of the play, confusion over how to categorize him remains. Characters such as the Duchess of York continue to regard him as King Richard, and Bolingbroke, now King Henry IV, is compelled to have him murdered to remove the confusion that Richard's presence causes, thus securing his own place.

Richard II suggests that alienation from the social order gives rise to an alienation from the self. When Hamlet comes upon the stage and announces that his true self is something "within which passes show," Shakespeare seems to be suggesting that he is an alienated figure. Hamlet, however, is at the center of his social world: He is, after all, a prince who will, King Claudius (Hamlet's uncle and his father's killer) announces, become the next king. Naturally he is disturbed by his father's sudden death and complains bitterly about his mother's quick marriage. But he is not, at least at this point in the play, aware of any foul play. (His father's ghost does not reveal that Claudius reached the throne by killing him until the next scene.) What Hamlet suggests in his "I-know-not-seems speech" is that alienation—a sense of confusion in the face of life's mysteries—is a fact of human experience, even for princes and kings.

Shakespeare thereby reflects something that most 16th-century thinkers and writers were unable to recognize: The traditional social order was disappearing. Perhaps the play that best represents Shakespeare's understanding of social change is *King Lear.* In this work about an elderly king who loses both his grasp on the throne and then his sense of self, the playwright describes how certain episodes of England's history—and the individual stories of its leaders—mirror the changes in government that were taking place during Elizabeth's reign. Lear's tragedy is in this way an English tragedy, a national problem. Because his kingdom is taken from him unlawfully (even his own daughters Regan and Goneril conspire with the bastard Edmund to overthrow the king), the process of becoming king (through inheritance within the family) is thrown into doubt.

Although Shakespeare was not the only playwright to write about this problem, his drama is unique because he is able to address social issues through stories about individual people, like Lear and Macbeth. The tragedy of Macbeth differs in that he is the one committing crimes and sins (with the help of his wife, Lady Macbeth, he kills King Duncan in his sleep) instead of the one being unlawfully removed from rule. What connects the plays is that the thirst for power corrupts men, it makes them break laws and codes of ethics. While Elizabeth in the final years of the 16th century was relatively safe from plots (compared to the uncertain years at the beginning of her reign in the 1560s and 1570s), members of the aristocracy (or the ruling class) were in constant fear for their power, their money, and their lives. Shakespeare suggests that these threats are more than just individual problems. Rather, they are at the heart of social unrest and damage the nation as a whole. When Lear loses his sense of reality (one might say that he resembles a lunatic when he walks around in rags and considers the weather to be attacking him personally), we are meant to question what happens when non-kings can gain power through evil deeds.

What differentiates Shakespeare's most memorable and lifelike characters from those of other Elizabethan and Jacobean dramatists is their self-awareness. The tragic figures of Hamlet, Richard III, Lear, and Macbeth are not the only characters in Shakespeare's drama that demonstrate the playwright's interest in human psychology. Harold Bloom considers Sir John Falstaff of the history plays *Henry IV,* Parts One and Two, *Henry V, Henry VI* Part One, and *The Merry Wives of Windsor,* to be, along with Hamlet, the most realistic of Shakespeare's characters. He is a larger-than-life figure, an overweight, over-the-hill knight whose main interests are alcohol, food, money, and bragging. What is so interesting about his character is that he is the childhood friend of Prince Hal (the boy who becomes King Henry V) and has a sensitive side that is occasionally visible. Falstaff understands that his existence is meaningless compared to his young friend; he recognizes that he is not a noble being. There is something pathetic and even touching in his sense of humor, which makes him someone who simultaneously laughs at others and is laughed at:

> Men of all sorts take a pride to gird at me. The brain of this foolish-compounded clay, man, is not able to invent any thing that intends to laughter more than I invent or is invented on me: I am not only witty in myself, but the cause that wit is in other men.

The word *invent* is important because it refers to man's ability to create himself, to play a role. This concept echoes Jaques's famous line about life as a drama from *As You Like It:* "All the world's a stage, / And all the men and women merely players."

The outlook that society is comprised of actors is not as pessimistic as it might seem to us as a modern audience. For Shakespeare the theater was a place of possibility and wonder. In a society that did not afford everyone the same opportunities to achieve happiness and personal growth, drama presented people with an image of the world that reflected life's joy and its pain, but mostly its beauty.

What Shakespeare ultimately suggests about human character is that there is always a difference between what people consider to be their authentic selves and how people reveal themselves to others. One is always obliged, in a sense, to act like, rather than to be, one's self. This idea is the same message that 20th-century novelists package as selfhood. Thus Shakespeare's greatest achievement, Bloom argues, is that he was able to demonstrate "how new modes of consciousness come into being."

Other Work by William Shakespeare

Complete Works. Edited by Richard Proudfoot, et al. New York: Arden, 2001.

Works about William Shakespeare

Bednarz, James P. *Shakespeare and the Poets' War.* New York: Columbia University Press, 2001.

Bevington, David. *Shakespeare.* Malden, Mass.: Blackwell Publishing, 2002.

Bloom, Allan. *Shakespeare on Love and Friendship.* Chicago: University of Chicago Press, 1993.

Bloom, Harold. *Hamlet: Poem Unlimited.* New York: Riverhead Books, 2003.

de Sousa, Geraldo U. *Shakespeare's Cross-Cultural Encounters.* New York: St. Martin's Press, 1999.

Goldberg, Jonathan. *Shakespeare's Hand.* Minneapolis: University of Minnesota Press, 2003.

Greenblatt, Stephen. *Hamlet in Purgatory.* Princeton, N.J.: Princeton University Press, 2001.

Honan, Park. *Shakespeare: A Life.* Oxford, U.K.: Oxford University Press, 1998.

Kamps, Ivo, ed. *Materialist Shakespeare: A History.* London: Verso, 1995.

McDonald, Russ. *The Bedford Companion to Shakespeare: An Introduction with Documents.* Boston: St. Martin's Press, 1996.

Sheffield, John (1648–1721) *poet, essayist*

John Sheffield, Earl of Mulgrave and first Duke of Buckingham and Normanby, was the son of Edmund, Earl of Mulgrave, who died when Sheffield was 10 years old. The boy dismissed his tutor when he was 12 and resolved to educate himself, a move described by Samuel Johnson in these words:

"Such a purpose, formed at such an age and successfully prosecuted, delights as it is strange, and instructs as it is real."

When war broke out with the Dutch, the 17-year-old Sheffield volunteered in the king's service and commanded a cavalry troop that was defending the English coastline. He later commanded his own ship, the *Katherine,* became colonel of a foot-regiment, and was rewarded with high civilian posts in Yorkshire and Hull, though he was later banished from court for his romantic entanglement with Princess Anne, the daughter of James II, later Queen Anne.

Sheffield's reputation as a writer rests on two poems, the *Essay on Satire* (1679) and the *Essay on Poetry* (1682). The first work was thought for a time to have been written by John DRYDEN and resulted in that poet's being beaten by the Earl of Rochester's men, who felt the earl had been insulted by the poem. Sheffield begins in praise of satire:

> SATIRE has always shin'd among the rest,
> And is the boldest Way, perhaps the best,
> To shew Men freely all their foulest Faults;
> To laugh at their vain Deeds, and vainer
>   Thoughts.

He then goes on to criticize various writers of the age for their bad poetry and worse morals. His *Essay on Poetry* Samuel Johnson calls "the great work" of his pen. He begins by declaring poetry the greatest of the arts:

> Of Things in which Mankind does most
>   excell,
> Nature's chief Master-piece is writing well;
> And of all sorts of Writing none there are
> That can the least with Poetry compare;

He goes on to criticize bad poetry and then discusses the contribution of the great poets:

> Read Homer once, and you can read no
>   more,

For all things else will seem so dull and
    poor,
You'l wish't unread; but oft upon him look,
And you will hardly need another book;

John Sheffield became Lord Chamberlain under King James II and supported the installation of King William III and Queen Mary II as joint sovereigns. Later, Queen Anne made him Lord Chamberlain and first Duke of Normanby and of Buckinghamshire. After the accession of the Hanoverian George I in 1714, Sheffield retired from public life.

Sherlock, William (1641–1707) *nonfiction writer*

William Sherlock was born in Southwark, England, and became rector at St. George's in London in 1669. His *The Case of Resistance of the Supreme Powers* was published in 1684, a treatise in which he discusses the "doctrine of passive obedience." This was a controversial topic at the time, having to do with the extent to which a person must obey the laws of the state if those laws contradict his or her religion.

In 1689 he published *A Practical Discourse Concerning Death.* The work advised its readers how to share in the joys of heaven, and was very popular. In 1690 he published *A Vindication of the Doctrine of the Trinity,* in opposition to Unitarian writers, who denied the existence of the Trinity of Father, Son, and Holy Spirit. He claimed to be able to make the mysterious doctrine of the Trinity as simple and clear as the belief in one God by saying that the Father, Son, and Holy Spirit are three individuals, as distinct as any three of the apostles. The Unitarians responded by accusing Sherlock of believing in three gods.

In 1691 Sherlock became dean of St. Paul's. His sermons were published in two volumes in 1755.

Shirley, James (1596–1666) *playwright, poet, nonfiction writer*

James Shirley was born in London and went to study at Oxford in 1612. The following year, he left the university and apprenticed with Thomas Frith, a scrivener (someone who makes handwritten copies of documents). Two years later Shirley entered Cambridge University, where he received a B.A. in 1617, the same year he became a priest in the CHURCH OF ENGLAND. Three or four years later, he converted to Catholicism.

In 1618 Shirley published a narrative poem based on classical mythology called *Eccho, or the Infortunate Lover.* No copies of the book have survived, but most critics believe that the poem was republished as *Narcissus, or The Self-Lover* in 1646.

With the success of Shirley's first play, *Love Tricks with Compliments* (1625), a romantic comedy, he became a full-time dramatist. Over the next 18 years, he turned out 37 plays. Turning to playwriting at the end of a period in which some of the greatest dramatists in English literature, including William SHAKESPEARE and Ben JONSON, were writing, Shirley inherited a wealth of material, which he freely included in his own work. Although he constructed his own plots, he borrowed characters and incidents from his predecessors.

Shirley's plays not only hark back to the drama of an earlier age but, as Shirley scholar Ira Clark notes, they also exhibit belief in a social hierarchy where males dominate females and the monarchy dominates its subjects. However, the monarchy was falling out of favor in those years before the English Civil War, in which the king was executed.

Shirley is best remembered for *The Lady of Pleasure* (1635) and *The Cardinal* (1641). The latter is a revenge tragedy, a play in which there is a murder followed by a search for revenge. Revenge, in turn, leads to a tragic conclusion. *The Cardinal* has secured the interest of scholars, as Ben Lucow points out, because of its commentary on public events. A group of characters, the "shorthaired men," represent the English Puritans who were critical of the Anglican Church and the monarchy.

The Lady of Pleasure is a comedy of manners, which is usually about young lovers from the upper class and in which the comic effect is chiefly produced by the characters' witty dialogue. It is more typical of Shirley's work in that it promotes the need for people to accommodate themselves to social norms or conventions. The play is built around a conflict between living properly or living for pleasure. This theme is announced in the opening scene, when Lady Aretina Bornwell arrives in London to exchange "a calm and retire[d] life [traditional country living] / For this wild town," where one spends one's life attending dinner parties and going to the theater or dances. As the play concludes, pleasure and propriety have been reconciled. Sir Thomas Bornwell, Aretina's husband, calls for music, observing "when our Ladies / Are tired with active motion, to give / Them rest in some new rapture to advance / Full mirth, our souls shall leap into a dance."

Shirley's adaptation of earlier plays and his belief in a social system with the monarch at the top have led some critics to define him as one of the last Elizabethan dramatists. However, he is not entirely steeped in the world order, much of which disappeared during his lifetime. In his comedies he achieves, as the scholar Norman Rabkin writes, a "bright comedy of manners and [a] vivid portrayal of London life."

When the Puritans took control of England in 1642 and closed the theaters, which were thought to be centers of immorality, Shirley returned to nondramatic poetry, publishing a collection, *Poems* (1646). He also published a grammar book for students, *The Rudiments of Grammar* (1656). Today, though, he is primarily remembered as a dramatist.

Other Works by James Shirley

A Critical, Modern-Spelling Edition of James Shirley's The Opportunity. Edited by Mary J. Mekemson. New York: Garland Press, 1991.

The Dukes Mistris: An Old-Spelling Edition. Edited by Kim Walker. New York: Garland Press, 1988.

A Work about James Shirley

Burner, Sandra. *James Shirley: A Study of Literary Coteries and Patronage in Seventeenth-Century England.* Stony Brook: State University of New York Press, 1988.

Sidney, Mary (Mary Herbert, Countess of Pembroke) (1561–1621) *poet, translator*

Mary Sidney was the daughter of Mary Dudley and Henry Sidney and the sister of Sir Philip SIDNEY. In 1577, at 15, she married Henry Herbert, second earl of Pembroke, becoming the Countess of Pembroke.

Sidney served as patron (*see* PATRONAGE) for numerous writers, including Edmund SPENSER, Samuel DANIEL and Michael DRAYTON. She was well educated, fluent in three languages, and eventually became not just a patron of writers but a writer herself. In her lifetime she published translations of *Discourse of Life and Death* by Philippe de Mornay and *Antonius, A Tragedie* by Robert Garnier. She probably helped edit Philip's *Arcadia* after his death in 1586, and she also published one original work, the pastoral "Dialogue in Praise of Astraea," a compliment to ELIZABETH I. She also dedicated her version of the Psalms to Elizabeth I in a dedicatory poem, "Even Now that Care."

Sidney completed the verse translation of the Psalms that her brother had begun. Although many original sources exist, one of Sidney's greatest achievements is her synthesis of all these sources rather than relying on any one. As a translator, Sidney did not merely replace a foreign word with an English one but reworked the original. Thus, the Psalms were paraphrases of the originals and contain many innovative techniques of form and style. Her translation influenced religious lyric poetry written by such writers as John DONNE, George HERBERT, Richard CRASHAW, and John MILTON.

When Sidney translated PETRARCH's *The Triumph of Death*, she followed the text more closely. However, she altered some aspects of the work enough to shift the focus from the male poet to the female beloved; for example, she does not use "I" where the original does. This often makes the action passive, so that some control shifts to Laura, Petrarch's beloved, as an actor.

Sidney's *Psalms* were influential, and her translation of *Antonie* was a key source for many of Shakespeare's Roman plays, especially *Antony and Cleopatra*. Indeed, many of Sidney's alterations to the original can be found in Shakespeare's version of that play.

Sidney thus contributed to the literary history of England through her influence on writers such as Donne and Shakespeare, through her use of many complex verse forms in her translations, and through her patronage of other writers. She also served as a model for later female writers such as Mary WROTH, her niece, and Amelia LANYER.

Other Work by Mary Sidney

The Collected Works of Mary Sidney Herbert, Countess of Pembroke. Edited by Margaret P. Hannay, Noel J. Kinnamon, and Michael G. Brennan. Oxford, U.K.: Clarendon Press, 1998.

Works about Mary Sidney

Burke, Mary, Jane Donawerth, Linda L. Dove, and Karen Nelson, eds. *Women, Writing and the Reproduction of Culture in Tudor and Stuart Britain.* Syracuse, N.Y.: Syracuse University Press, 2000.

Hannay, Margaret P. *Philip's Phoenix.* New York: Oxford University Press, 1990.

Sidney, Sir Philip (1554–1586) *prose writer, critic, poet, nonfiction writer*

Sir Philip Sidney was born in Penshurst, Kent, England, the son of Sir Henry Sidney and Lady Mary Dudley Sidney, who was the daughter of the Duke of Northumberland. The Sidneys were a prominent family with close ties to the court of Queen ELIZABETH I and other influential people in England and Europe. Philip's father served as president of the Council of Wales and as lord deputy of Ireland under Elizabeth; his uncle Robert Dudley, Earl of Leicester, was one of the queen's closest advisers.

As a youngster, Philip attended the Shrewsbury School, where he was a classmate of Fulke GREVILLE, whose biography of Sidney offers an early and intimate glimpse of this cultivated man of many talents (author, soldier, statesman, courtier), long depicted as the prototypical Elizabethan gentleman. After studying at Christ Church, Oxford University, Sidney traveled in Europe for three years, largely under the tutelage of Hubert Languet, a humanist scholar some 36 years his senior. In his biography, Greville described the relationship between Languet and Sidney as that of "an humble hearer to an excellent teacher." Under Languet's guidance, Sidney progressed in his knowledge of classical languages and literature.

Returning to England in 1576, Sidney was appointed to the honorary position of cupbearer to the queen and spent some time in Ireland assisting his father in the management of his estates. His first published work, a treatise called *Discourse on Irish Affairs* (1577), supported his father's harsh anti-Irish policies while Lord Deputy in that country. When Sidney went back to England the following year, he wrote *The Lady of May,* a pastoral entertainment in honor of Queen Elizabeth, whose court he frequented.

Taking an active interest in diplomatic affairs, Sidney began to write and advocate in support of the Protestant cause. His *Letter to Queen Elizabeth* (1579–80) was written to dissuade her from marrying the duke of Anjou, the Roman Catholic heir to the French throne, who was courting her at the time. Serving in Parliament in 1581 and again in 1584–85, Sidney became an avid supporter of the New World explorations of Sir Martin Frobisher and others, and he helped promote Sir Walter RALEIGH's plans to settle a colony in Virginia. Sidney maintained a rich correspondence with many artists and intellectuals of his day, many of whom sought his PATRONAGE or dedicated works to him, including the poet Abraham FRAUNCE, the dramatist Thomas LODGE, and the poet Edmund SPENSER.

In 1585 Sidney and his uncle, the Earl of Warwick, were appointed as joint masters of the ordnance, the agency in charge of England's military weaponry. The following year he volunteered in a campaign to thwart Spanish military maneuvers in Zutphen, Holland. Although mortally wounded, he continued his heroic charge, but he died in Arnhem at the age of 31. His funeral cortege to St. Paul's Cathedral, London, was one of the most elaborate ever seen there, and his death occasioned deep mourning throughout England.

Ever reluctant to have his work commercially exploited, Sidney steadfastly refused to allow his writings to be published during his lifetime, a stance that his survivors supported by their reluctance to bring his work into print. It was not until 1598, some 11 years after his death, that his sister, Mary SIDNEY Herbert, published his significant works in a collection called *The Countess of Pembroke's Arcadia.* Today, more than four centuries after his death, Sidney's works remain in print and are read in English and translation.

Critical Analysis

Sidney's most prolific period as a writer spanned the nine years from 1577, when he started writing his most acclaimed work, *The Arcadia,* until his death in 1586. *The Arcadia* was published in various "old" and "new" editions after his death, notably as *The Countess of Pembroke's Arcadia.* Although it remained only half completed after several editions, and some segments of it were not published until 1926, Sidney's *Arcadia* stands as the most important prose work in English literature of the period.

Probably completed in 1580, the earliest version of *The Arcadia* was an epic romance in five books whose muse was undoubtedly his sister Mary, of whom he wrote: "You desired me to do it, and your desire to my heart is an absolute commandment." In crafting this masterwork, Sidney drew on his considerable knowledge of chivalric romances in French and Italian as well as the Arthurian legends in English. Critics have also pointed out the influence of classical mythologies, including Apuleius's *Golden Ass* and Heliodorus's *Æthiopian Historie,* which had recently been translated into English. Replete with some of the stock characters and situations found in such works, such as damsels in distress, knights in shining armor, gender reversals, and sexual license, *The Arcadia* in many ways epitomizes the cult of courtly love and passion associated with medieval and RENAISSANCE England. It also draws heavily on the forms of pastoral poetry, making it reminiscent of Virgil's *Eclogues,* which used the voices of shepherds and other unschooled

characters to impart moral and ethical teachings. The beginning of the first book gives a sense of the idyllic setting of the work:

> ARCADIA amonge all the Provinces of *Grece* was ever had in singuler reputation, partly for the sweetnes of ye Aire and other naturall benefittes: But, principally, for the moderate & well tempered myndes of the people, who, (fynding howe true a Contentation ys gotten by following the Course of Nature, And howe the shyning Title of glory so muche affected by other Nacions, dothe in deede help litle to the happines of lyfe) were the onely people, w[hi]ch as by theire Justice and providence, gave neyther Cause nor hope to theyre Neighboures to annoy them, so were they not stirred with false prayse, to trouble others quyett.

Shakespeare drew on a section of *The Arcadia* for the Gloucester subplot in his drama *King Lear,* and many other writers were influenced by the work.

Sidney's sonnet sequence, *Astrophel and Stella* (1582), exalts the playful wit and passion of Elizabethan love poetry. The opening and closing sonnets provide a frame for the others, which portray the changes in the relationship of the lovers named in the title. Thus, the poem begins by declaring the poet's intention to woo his love through the words that portray his "woe":

> Luing in trueth, and fayne in verse my loue
> to show,
> That she, deare Shee, might take som
> pleasure of my paine,
> Pleasure might cause her reade, reading
> might make her know,
> Knowledge might pittie winne, and pity
> grace obtaine,
> I sought fit wordes to paint the blackest face
> of woe;
> Studying inuentions fine, her wits to
> entertaine,
> Oft turning others leaues, to see if thence
> would flow

> Some fresh and fruitful showers vpon my
>   sun-burnd brain.

Some of the poem's allusions can be traced to actual events and personages in the royal court during Elizabeth's reign.

His next work, *Defence of Poesie* (ca. 1580), was a seminal work of literary criticism that helped define the parameters against which Elizabethan literature has been judged ever since. Describing his literary calling as "my unelected vocation," Sidney writes that he has "just cause to make a painful defense of poor poetry, which from almost the highest estimation is fallen to be the laughing-stock of children."

Sidney also used his literary talents to express his Protestant piety when he undertook a new English rendition of the Old Testament Psalms of David, based not on the original Hebrew text or Latin translations but on more recent French metrical translations and the English psalter or book of psalms that accompanied the CHURCH OF ENGLAND's *BOOK OF COMMON PRAYER*. By the time of his death, he had completed only 43 of the 150 Psalms, each of which he wrote in a different metrical form. His sister Mary, continued the project; their version of Psalm 139 was included in *Songs of Praise* (1931), the so-called "Oxford Hymnal" compiled by Percy Dearmer. Its first stanza reads: "O Lord, in me there lieth nought / But to thy search revealèd lies; / For when I sit / Thou markest it, / Nor less thou notest when I rise; / The closest closet of my thought / Hath open windows to thine eyes."

For a man who lived such a short life, Sidney's accomplishments are staggering and the range of his talents amazing. According to biographer Allen Stewart, "Among the gilded youth of Elizabethan England, no one was more golden than Philip Sidney. Courtier, poet, soldier, diplomat—he was one of the most promising young men of his time."

Works about Sir Philip Sidney

Berry, Edward I. *The Making of Sir Philip Sidney*. Toronto: University of Toronto Press, 1998.
Stewart, Alan. *Philip Sidney: A Double Life*. London: Chatto & Windus, 2000.

Sidney's Circle

The term *Sidney's Circle* refers to a group of friends, many of them poets, who were influenced by Sir Philip SIDNEY. Sidney produced such noteworthy works as the sonnet sequence *Astrophel and Stella* (published 1591), the critical work *A Defence of Poesie* (written ca. 1580, published 1595), and the prose romance *Arcadia* (first version completed 1581). Among the circle's members were Samuel DANIEL, Fulke GREVILLE, Michael DRAYTON, Edmund SPENSER, and Richard STANIHURST.

The members of the circle benefited from Sidney's poetic examples and in some cases from his PATRONAGE (financial support). Sidney shaped his peers by circulating his innovative work among them privately. His sonnet sequence inspired a series of others by such members of his circle as Greville, Drayton, and Spenser, which in spite of their differences shared the characteristics of an ongoing dramatic story line and use of the conventions of PETRARCHISM. Sidney's *Astrophel and Stella* follows the vicissitudes of the ultimately unhappy relationship between the title characters. Greville's *Caelica* (published 1633) follows the speaker as he moves away from love and into involvement with political and religious ideas. Drayton's *Idea's Mirror* (1594, revised many times until 1619 when the name was simplified to *Idea*) illustrates the point made by Drayton in one of the sonnets, about the variability of a personality:

> My verse is the true image of my Mind,
> Ever in motion, still desiring change:
> And as thus, to variety inclined;
> So in all humours sportively I range . . .

The Sidney Circle was not limited to men. The Elizabethan era was a time when certain upper-class women were given the opportunity to achieve a high level of education, and though generally women who ventured into print were regarded with suspicion, women could write for private sharing. Sidney's younger sister, Mary SIDNEY Herbert, Countess of Pembroke, was impressively learned and translated several works. The first version of

Philip Sidney's *Arcadia* (1581) was written for her at her country house at Wilton, which was the center of much literary activity by the Sidney Circle. In his notes on Mary Sidney, John AUBREY reported, "In her time Wilton house was like a college, there were so many learned and ingenious persons."

Other women who were important in the group were Penelope Rich, who was probably the Stella of Sidney's *Astrophel and Stella;* Mary WROTH; and Katherine PHILIPS. Philip Sidney himself believed that the field of English readers should be widened to include more women. He began to make a place for women in literature with his many depictions, as in *Arcadia,* of female characters reading.

A Work about the Sidney Circle

Lamb, Mary Ellen. *Gender and Authorship in the Sidney Circle.* Madison: University of Wisconsin Press, 1990.

Skelton, John (ca. 1460–1529) *poet, playwright, translator*

Nothing is definitely known about John Skelton's early life other than that he was educated at both Cambridge and Oxford Universities, receiving degrees in rhetoric from both and also from the university at Louvain in Belgium. He was already well known as a translator and rhetorician when he entered the employment of King Henry VII, serving as tutor to the young prince, the future King Henry VIII, from 1496 to 1501. Desiderius ERASMUS, in a 1500 ode entitled *De Laudibus Britanniae (In Praise of Britain),* congratulated the prince on having such a fine teacher as Skelton, "a light of British letters."

In 1498 Skelton was ordained a priest in the Catholic Church. That year he wrote a satiric poem about court life, *The Bowge [reward] of Court.* The poem's narrator, in a dream, embarks on a ship, *The Bowge of Court,* which is guided by Fortune and on which he meets such unsavory court characters as Favell (flattery), Hervy Hafter (deceiver), Disdain, and Riot. Skelton was briefly imprisoned for debt in 1501, probably because of a court dispute. That same year he published a book about his educa-

tional principles, *Speculum Principis (The Mirror of Princes),* but it has not survived. He retired from court in 1503, to a parish church in Norfolk.

Skelton's poem *Philip Sparrow* written before 1508, may reflect Skelton's life in the country. It is addressed to a young lady whose pet sparrow has been killed by a cat. The bird is described at length, as is his mistress's grief at his loss, and all the birds are called to the funeral:

> To weepe with me look that ye come,
> All manner of birds in your kind;
> See none be left behind. . . .
> Some to sing, and some to say,
> Some to weep, and some to pray,
> Every bird in his lay.
> The goldfinch, the wagtail;
> The jangling jay to rail,
> The flecked pie to chatter
> Of this dolorous matter;
> And robin redbreast,
> He shall be the priest
> The requiem mass to sing,
> Softly warbling. . . .

The list of the different birds goes on at length, showing Skelton's lively awareness of the natural world, and the short lines with their simple rhymes convey grief in an unpretentious manner.

In 1512, when Henry VII died, Skelton wrote an elegy for him. The new king, Henry VIII, soon brought Skelton back to court, giving him the title Orator Regius (king's orator). Skelton's new job was to write poetry for the king, and he wrote several poems celebrating English victories in wars against the Scots and the French. He also wrote a play, *Magnyfycence,* in 1515–16; there were probably other plays, but this is the only one to survive. It is a morality play, an allegory with characters named Felicity, Counterfeit Countenance, Fancy, Liberty, Despair, and Magnificence (the word *magnificence* in Skelton's time meant the ostentatious display of wealth). The conclusion, spoken by the character named Perseverance, is that no mortal happiness can be relied upon:

Today it is well; tomorrow it is all amiss
Today in delight; tomorrow bare of bliss
Today a lord; tomorrow lie in the dust
Thus in this world there is no earthly
trust.

Court life was no less political under Henry VIII than under his father. Skelton feuded with Cardinal Wolsey, who was for a time the king's right hand and one of the most powerful people in the country. He wrote several poems attacking Wolsey for his worldly ways, including *Speak, Parrot* (ca. 1521) and *Colin Clout* (1522), a satire on bad priests; consequently, he spent some time in prison at Wolsey's behest. Skelton's autobiographical poem *The Garland of Laurel* (1523) contains an apology to Wolsey. Skelton died before the great upheavals of Henry VIII's court that led to the separation of the CHURCH OF ENGLAND from the Roman Catholic Church.

Edmund SPENSER used the name Colin Clout, presumably drawn from Skelton, for his narrator in *The Shepherd's Calendar*. The scholar Maurice Evans remarked in *English Poetry in the Sixteenth Century* that Skelton "is perhaps the most considerable poet between Chaucer and Spenser and comes at the point of intersection between the medieval and humanist traditions."

Other Works by John Skelton

The Book of the Laurel/John Skelton. Edited by F. W. Brownlow. Newark: University of Delaware Press, 1990.
John Skelton, the Complete English Poems. Edited by John Scattergood. New Haven, Conn.: Yale University Press, 1983.

Works about John Skelton

Evans, Maurice. "John Skelton and Early Tudor Poetry." In *English Poetry in the Sixteenth Century.* New York: W. W. Norton, 1967.
Kinney, Arthur F. *John Skelton, Priest as Poet: Seasons of Discovery.* Chapel Hill: University of North Carolina Press, 1987.

Smith, John (1580–1631) *nonfiction writer*

John Smith was born in Willoughby, Lincolnshire, England, to George Smith, a farmer, and Alice Rickard Smith. He was educated at grammar schools in Alford and Louth, where he picked up some Latin and learned to write.

In 1595 Smith was apprenticed to Thomas Sendall, a merchant, but in the following year he abandoned his apprenticeship and went to the Netherlands, where he joined the fight to free the Dutch from Spanish rule. By 1602 he was in Hungary fighting the Turkish army. There he was promoted to the rank of captain, but he was soon captured and sold as a slave. According to Smith's *True Travels* (1630), he was able to escape, because of the kindness of a woman to whom he was presented as a gift.

In 1606 Smith was chosen to be a member of the governing body of the Virginia colony, and he arrived in Jamestown, Virginia, the following year. His leadership abilities were soon recognized, and in 1608 he was elected president of the colony.

Smith returned to England in 1609, after suffering an injury caused by a gunpowder explosion, and never visited Virginia again. He spent many years trying to find backers for another expedition and did manage to find someone to fund his mapping of the coast of New England in 1614. This was to be his last voyage to America; he spent the rest of his life in England.

Smith wrote about his Virginia and New England experiences in *A True Relation of Such Occurrences and Accidents of Note as Happened in Virginia* (1608), about the first 13 months of the Jamestown Colony. *A Map of Virginia and The Proceedings of the English Colony in Virginia* (1612) provides the first useful map of the Chesapeake Bay and continues the story of the colony up until 1610. In *A Description of New England* (1616), written after his return to England, Smith coins the term *New England* as a label for the northeast coastal region of the present-day United States. *New England's Trials* (1620–22) likewise describes Smith's travels in New England and Virginia. He later revised and collected these works, along with other books on the New World, in *The General History of Virginia, New England and the Summer Isles* (1624). His was the earliest full-length historical account of the British colonies in North America.

Critical Analysis

Filled with drama, adventure, and detailed accounts of Native American customs and ceremonies, Smith's writings, the scholar J. A. Leo Lemay notes, are an important historical source: "He gave more detailed and exact information than any other early writer; his writings are more exciting than others . . . and his plain style is more readable."

The story of Smith's being surrounded by "at least seven hundred . . . well armed" Native Americans in 1608 or 1609 is typical of the stories to be found in Smith's narratives. While his companions were "dismayed with the thought of such a multitude," Smith remains calm. "I little cared were they as many more," he exhorts his friends, "if you dare do, but . . . we are sixteen, and they but seven hundred at most; and assure yourselves, God will assist us, that if you dare stand but to discharge your pieces [guns], the very smoke will be sufficient to affright them. Yet howsoever, let us fight like men."

Thereupon Smith grabs the tribe's chief, with whom he was discussing trade and sticks a pistol to his head. By this means Smith convinces the tribesmen to lay down their arms and trade peacefully with him.

The most famous of Smith's adventures is his capture by Powhatan, a Native American chief, and his escaping execution with the help of Pocahontas, the chief's daughter. This Smith story is uncharacteristic of his writing because there is little place in it for Smith to demonstrate his bravery. He narrates his adventures in the third person:

> The Queen of Appamatuck was appointed to bring [Smith] water to wash his hands, another brought him a bunch of feathers, instead of a towel to dry them: having feasted him after their best barbarous manner they could, a long consultation was held, but the conclusion was, two great stones were brought before Powhatan:

> then as many as could lay hands on him, dragged him to them [the stones], and thereon laid his head, and being ready with their clubs to beat out his brains, Pocahontas the King's dearest daughter, when no entreaty could prevail, got his head in her arms, and laid her own upon his to save him from death.

Although Smith may have exaggerated his bravery, he was also interested in promoting the colonies. His books were part of his campaign to encourage the financing of future colonial enterprises. As with other promotional books on the New World, Smith's contained descriptions of the country's resources and the money that could be made by selling these resources: "Virginia doth afford many excellent vegitables and living Creatures. . . . The wood that is most common is Oke and Walnut, many of their Okes are so tall and straight, that they will beare two foote and a half square of good timber."

Smith's writings also have something else: They are an early expression of the American Dream. The society into which Smith was born insisted that aristocrats were treated in superior way to commoners. He, by contrast, insisted that greatness could reside in common people. He promoted this idea both by narrating his own tales of heroism and by suggesting that the New World was a place in which commoners could improve their lot. "Who can desire more content, that hath small means; or only his merit to advance his fortune?" Smith asked. North America, in Smith's mind, was a place that allowed people to rise above their birth through merit. "Captain John Smith's history of Virginia" the scholar A. L. Rowse points out, "has deeply influenced the American conception of the country's earliest days and made an indelible impression upon American folklore and popular belief, not to mention history."

Other Work by John Smith

Captain John Smith: A Select Edition of His Writings. Edited by Karen Ordahl Kupperman. Chapel Hill: University of North Carolina Press, 1988.

Works about John Smith

Emerson, Everett. *Captain John Smith*. Rev. ed. New York: Twayne, 1993.

Lemay, J. A. Leo. *The American Dream of Captain John Smith*. Charlottesville: University of Virginia Press, 1991.

Vaughan, Alden T., and Oscar Handlin. *American Genesis: Captain John Smith and the Founding of Virginia*. New York: Harper Collins, 1995.

South, Robert (1634–1716) *nonfiction writer*

Robert South was educated at Westminster School and at Oxford University before taking holy orders in 1658. He became known as a successful orator, speaking out in favor of Calvinism, the Protestant religion founded by John CALVIN that emphasized the idea that people were predestined for either salvation or damnation.

South wrote during a period of profound political and philosophical change during which people began to question ideas, such as the divine right of kings and certain articles of religious faith, including the existence of the Trinity of Father, Son, and Holy Spirit. In 1693 he published *Animadversions* (criticisms) *on Dr. Sherlock's Vindication,* in which he refutes fellow clergyman William SHERLOCK's view on the doctrine of the Trinity. Sherlock, in attempting to defend the idea of the Trinity, actually did the cause harm when he said that the mystery of the Trinity was as simple as the idea of three individuals. This led other supporters of the Trinity, such as South, to point out that Sherlock's idea sounded like he advocated worshiping three gods. South argued that Sherlock was incorrect in claiming that self-consciousness is the same thing as individuation and against the notion that the Trinity was made up of three individuals.

A Work about Robert South

Reedy, Gerard. *Robert South (1634–1716): His Life and Sermons*. Oxford: Oxford University Press, 1992.

Southerne, Thomas (ca. 1660–1746) *dramatist*

Thomas Southerne was born in Dublin on February 12, 1659 or 1660, to Francis Southerne, founder of the Brewers' Corporation of Dublin, and his wife, Margaret. Southerne was the youngest of six children and received his early education at the Free School in Dublin. In 1676 he enrolled in Trinity College in Dublin but was not allowed to graduate because of misbehavior. In 1680 Southerne was admitted to London's Middle Temple as a law student.

Southerne is remembered primarily for two dramatic plays, *The Fatal Marriage* (1694), based on the novel *The Nun* by Aphra BEHN, and *Oroonoko* (1695), based on the novel of the same title also by Behn. The heroine of *The Fatal Marriage,* Isabella, was one of the most coveted female roles of the era. *Oroonoko* was the first English drama to deal with the issue of African slavery. The story follows the life of an African prince who is taken as a slave to the South American country of Suriname. He leads a rebellion against the slave owners and is killed. In the play Southerne writes of the betrayal and suffering that the slaves experience. "You do not know the heavy grievances, the toils, the labors, weary drudgeries which they impose; burdens more fit for beasts, for senseless beasts to bear than thinking men." According to the Southerne scholar Robert L. Root, Jr., the success that *Oroonoko* saw during Southerne's lifetime was "grounded in the power it had to move the emotions."

Works about Thomas Southerne

Jordan, Robert, and Harold Love. *Thomas Southerne*. Oxford: Clarendon Press, 1988.

Root, Robert L., Jr. *Thomas Southerne*. Boston: Twayne, 1981.

Southwell, Robert ca. 1561–1595) *poet, nonfiction writer, saint*

Robert Southwell was born in Horsham St. Faith's, Norfolk, England, to Richard Southwell, a gentleman, and Bridget Copley Southwell, daughter of Sir Roger Copley. He was sent, when still a child, to study at Roman Catholic schools in France and Italy. In 1580 he joined the Jesuits, a

Catholic religious order, and four years later he was ordained a priest. In 1586 he returned to England, and six years later he was arrested for practicing the Catholic faith in a Protestant country. Eventually he was hanged and quartered at Tyburn in London.

Southwell is best remembered for his religious poetry. According to the scholar Geoffrey Hill, in his poetry Southwell "employed all the resources of his wit to moderate between grace and peril in the most dangerous area of religious life." Thus, one of Southwell's most frequent themes was the conflict between's God's mercy and grace and the punishment meted out in hell for disobeying God's laws. His most famous poem, "The Burning Babe," is a meditation on the meaning of Christ's birth. The central image of the poem is a vision of the Christ-child burning:

> [His] faultless breast the furnace is . . .
> Love is the fire, and sighs the smoke, the
>   ashes shame and scorns;
> The fuel justice layeth on, and mercy blows
>   the coals,
> The metal in this furnace wrought are
>   men's defiled souls.

The critic F. R. Brownlow remarks that Southwell's metaphor of fire thus presents a vision of a humanity whose very injustice fuels the fire of salvation.

Another of Southwell's poems, "Christ's Sleeping Friends," discusses Jesus's disciples falling asleep the night before his death, even though "With milde rebuke he [Jesus] warned them to wake." The poet extracts a moral from this biblical story: "Awake ye slumbring wightes [people] lift up your eies." He uses the poem, thus, to urge readers to greater attention to religious duty.

Southwell also wrote prose tracts, such as *Mary Magdalen's Funeral Tears* and *Humble Supplication* (both published in 1591), in which he defended the Catholic cause in England. *Humble Supplication* refutes the charge that Catholic missionaries are more interested in wealth than religion:

> For to say we do [the alleged treasons] upon hope to be enriched with those possessions that others now enjoy hath but very small semblance of probability, considering how much likelier we are to inherit your racks [devices of torture] and possess your places of execution.

In passages such as this we see what Hill calls Southwell's "direct, unaffected eloquence." As both a poet and a prose writer, Southwell brought attention and eloquence to the Catholic cause in 16th-century England. He was canonized by the Catholic Church in 1970.

A Work about Robert Southwell

Brownlow, F. R. *Robert Southwell.* New York: Twayne, 1996.

Sowernam, Ester (fl. 1617) *pamphleteer*

Ester Sowernam, a pseudonym, was the name affixed to the 1617 pamphlet *Ester Hath Hang'd Haman.* Although the name Ester Sowernam is clearly feminine, the gender of the writer is questionable, for the pamphleteer cryptically declares that the writer is "neither Maide, Wife, nor Widdowe, yet really all, and therefore experienced to defend all." This statement may be a refusal to be categorized solely in relation to men and a claim for the universality of feminine experience. On the other hand, it may indicate that Sowernam was, in fact, a man.

The pamphlet is a response to Joseph SWETNAM's *The Arraignment of Lewd, Idle, Froward, and Unconstant Women* (1615). Indeed, "Sowernam" is a pun responding to "Swetnam" ("sour" vs. "sweet"), a barb in the battle of wits taking place in print over the question about the nature of women.

Both pamphlets are a part of the longstanding debate over the nature of women that began in the Middle Ages. Theologians and writers were intensely concerned with the question of whether women were inherently sinful or virtuous. Those who criticized women based their attacks in part on the biblical story of Adam and Eve. They claimed that woman caused the first sin, an act that should consequently condemn the entire gender.

These philosophical debates gained renewed intensity during the RENAISSANCE, partly because of the transition from Catholicism to Protestantism during the REFORMATION. Because Protestantism permitted the clergy to marry, it intensified discussions about the virtues and sins of women and what proper gender roles should be in marriage.

Swetnam's pamphlet took the position that women were sinful and that their company would corrupt any man who associated with them in marriage. Sowernam's defense offers counterexamples to Swetnam's corrupt women. For instance, the title *Ester Hath Hang'd Haman* refers to the biblical tale of Queen Esther, a heroine who delivered her country from Haman, an enemy of the Jews. In addition to Esther, the author finds many other virtuous biblical women, such as Rebecca, Elizabeth, and "that blessed mother and mirrour of al woman-hood, the Virgin *Marie*."

Sowernam furthers her argument by turning the tables on Swetnam and writes that never was woman guilty of lust "but that she was first solicited [enticed] by a man." The author charges men with being drunkards and spendthrifts who abuse their wives. As the critic Linda Woodbridge remarks, Sowernam "has the makings of a feminist." Witty, learned, and forceful, Sowernam joined the RENAISSANCE debate and offered a strong defense for women.

A Work about Ester Sowernam

Woodbridge, Linda. *Women and the English Renaissance: Literature and the Nature of Womenkind, 1540–1620.* Urbana: University of Illinois Press, 1984.

Speed, John (1552–1629) *nonfiction writer, cartographer*

John Speed was born at Farndon, Cheshire, England, and settled in London around 1582. While earning a living as a tailor, Speed developed a strong interest in history, particularly antiquities and genealogies. He also became interested in mapmaking. His first cartographical work, a wall map of Canaan in biblical times, was published in 1595. In 1600 Speed donated a number of maps to the Merchant Taylors Company, who noted his "very rare and ingenious capacitie in drawing and setting forth of mappes and genealogies and other very excellent inventions."

Speed is best known today for two atlases: *The Theatre of the Empire of Great Britaine,* published in 1611; and the *Prospect of the Most Famous Parts of the World,* published in 1627. Many cartographers consider his works to be the most important atlases of his day. Speed also wrote two works on religion: *Genealogies Recorded in Sacred Scripture* (1611) and *A Cloud of Witnesses . . . Confirming . . . God's Most Holy Word* (1616).

Speght, Rachel (ca. 1597–ca. 1630)
pamphleteer, poet
Rachel Speght was a well-educated woman from the middle class. She lived in London and is most famous for her contribution to the pamphlet debate about women that took place from about 1615 to 1620. Her pamphlet, *A Mouzell [muzzle] for Melastomus,* is a defense of women written in response to Joseph SWETNAM's published attacks.

Speght's tract differs from others in that it reveals the real name of the author, unlike Jane ANGER and Constantia MUNDA, authors whose names were pseudonyms. Additionally, Speght's work diverges from the others in that, rather than make use of simple rhetorical retorts, she mounts an emotional and original argument in defense of women. Her primary argument is based on reinterpretation of both the Bible and liturgy that includes a new reading of the creation story, the fall of man, and the "Homily on the State of Matrimony." Speght says, for example, that woman's creation by God means that she "can not chuse but be good, yea very good." She also emphasizes that both man and woman were created in God's image and are therefore equal. In arguing these positions, Speght attacks not just Swetnam but also the ideas presented on occasion every Sunday in church sermons.

Speght also wrote a long poem, *Mortalities Memorandum* (1621), with *A Dream,* a shorter allegorical poem, attached. *Mortalities Memorandum* is a meditation on death and is meant as a tribute to Speght's mother and godmother. The poem is not technically astute, but it offers insight into such things as Christian education, dispensation of property, and wills. The allegory of *A Dream* centers on the pursuit and benefits of education. This was an important topic for women, who were normally excluded from formal education at schools and universities. Speght's primary contribution to literary history is her willingness to "rethink the implications of the dominant biblical discourse in regard to women" and to "argue her own and all good women's worth and substantial equality."

Other Work by Rachel Speght
The Polemics and Poems of Rachel Speght. Edited by Barbara Kiefer Lewalski. New York: Oxford University Press, 1996.

A Work about Rachel Speght
Burke, Mary Elizabeth, et al., eds. *Women, Writing and the Reproduction of Culture in Tudor and Stuart Britain.* Syracuse, N.Y.: Syracuse University Press, 2000.

Spenser, Edmund (ca. 1552–1599) *poet, pamphleteer*
Born in London, the son of John Spenser, a cloth-maker, Edmund Spenser was brought up in humble circumstances. As a child, he attended the newly founded school of the Merchant Taylors, whose headmaster, Richard MULCASTER, encouraged him to write. Spenser went on to Cambridge University as a sizar, a scholarship student who was required to work for his tuition. He received his bachelor's degree from Cambridge in 1573 and his master's in 1576. Through a college friend, Gabriel HARVEY, Spenser obtained a position in the household of Robert Dudley, Earl of Leicester, where he began service in 1577, and where he met the poets Sir Philip SIDNEY, Edward DYER, and Fulke GREVILLE. Together with a few others these young men made up an informal intellectual society (*see* SIDNEY'S CIRCLE).

Spenser was appointed secretary to Arthur, Lord Grey, in 1580, the year Grey became lord deputy of Ireland and was sent to suppress one of many Irish rebellions against English rule. In 1582 Grey was called back to England, but Spenser remained in Ireland, except for two trips to London, for the next 19 years. He became friends with Sir Walter RALEIGH, whose Irish estate was not far from his, and who helped him bring the first three books of his romantic epic *The Faerie Queene* to the attention of Queen ELIZABETH I. In 1589 he became clerk to the council of Munster, one of the four provinces of Ireland, and took up residence in Kilcolman Castle, County Cork.

A sonnet sequence, *Amoretti* (Italian for *Little Loves*), commemorates Spenser's courtship of Elizabeth Boyle, whom he married in 1594; he celebrated their marriage in the beautiful and complex poem *Epithalamion,* which was published with *Amoretti* in 1595. Books IV to VI of *The Faerie Queene* were published in 1596. In 1598, during another Irish rebellion, Kilcolman Castle was burned down, and Spenser, now in financial difficulties, returned to England with his family. Ben JONSON reported that Spenser died for "lack of bread," which seems unlikely, but it is probable that he was distressed and harassed at the end of his life. He was honored after death by being buried near Geoffrey Chaucer (ca. 1343–1400), the poet he regarded as his master, in Westminster Abbey.

Living in Ireland, as one might expect, had some influence on Spenser's poetry, even though he avoided accepting elements of Irish culture. His relationship to Ireland, in fact, always remained that of the colonizer. This tendency of Spenser's thought is evident in *Colin Clouts Come Home Againe* (written 1591; published 1595), a pastoral poem—or a poem depicting an idealized view of country life—in which Spenser, using his poetic name Colin Clout, describes his visit to England in 1589. In this work, Spenser inserts, as the Spenserian scholar Hallet Smith notes, "a passage of 55 lines describing the marriage of two Irish rivers," using a motif that was popular among 16th-century English landscape poets. Transferring this motif of English landscape poetry into an Irish setting seems to have been a way for Spenser to imaginatively transform the Irish landscape into an English one, or to create a poetic image of England's colonization of Ireland.

In the mid-1590s Spenser considered more practical methods of transforming Ireland into an image of England when he wrote a pamphlet called *A View of the State of Ireland* (registered for publication in 1598 but left unpublished until 1633). This pamphlet proposed a plan—based on the plan Lord Grey had followed when he set out to suppress the Irish rebellion of the early 1580s—to impose English rule on the Irish. The proposal involved sending 10,000 foot soldiers and 1,000 cavalry into Ireland, dispersing them in garrisons, and giving the Irish 20 days to submit to English authorities before hunting resisters down and putting them to the sword. Spenser acknowledged the cruelty of his plan, but argued that there was no other way for the English to bring order to Ireland and rid it of what he regarded as the harmful influence of Catholicism.

Spenser's anti-Catholicism was such that he represented the faith as the monster Errour in the first canto of Book I of *The Faerie Queene* (1590, 1595). Errour, in the poem, vomits forth "bookes and papers," which represent the texts proliferated by the Catholic Church to defend its practices during the REFORMATION:

> Therewith she spewd out of her filthy maw
> A floud of poyson horrible and blacke. . . .
> Her vomit full of bookes and papers
>   was. . . .

The error of Catholicism is defeated in the poem when Red Crosse, the knight of holiness, slays the monster. Errour, however, is more than simply a figure of the Catholic Church. She is, perhaps more

significantly, a figure of disorder. Errour and the Irish rebels are, in Spenser's view, parallel figures, and his approval of their destruction is based on a tradition of thought that regarded violence as a justifiable tool in the eradication of disorder. Indeed, for Spenser it is not only justifiable for a society to use violence to maintain order, but it is also justifiable for an individual to use it to attain salvation. The scholar Stephen Greenblatt argues that "the rich complexities of Spenser's art, its exquisite ethical discriminations in pursuit of the divine in man, are not achieved in spite of what is for us a repellent political ideology—passionate worship of imperialism—but are inseparably linked to that ideology."

Spenser's poetry, however, is important for reasons other than the way in which it reflects his views of how the English should approach the resistance of the Irish to the rule of civilization. Unlike most poets of his era, who saw poetry as a means to gain advancement at court, Spenser aimed to become the greatest nondramatic poet of the Elizabethan age; a place at court was a secondary ambition. While Spenser failed to reach his political goals, receiving no more than a pension of £50 from Queen Elizabeth after he published the first three books of *The Faerie Queene* (a poem that was written, in part, to praise her), many of his contemporaries believed he had succeeded in his poetic goals. They called him, among other things, "our principal poet"; poets who came after him have agreed.

Spenser is often called the poet's poet, because his poems have had such an impact on English literature. His influence was essential in the development of John MILTON's poetic vision, and in the Romantic Age the Spenserian stanza—a nine-line stanza with an ABABBCBCC rhyme scheme that Spenser developed for *The Faerie Queene*—was used by John Keats in the *Eve of St. Agnes* (1820); by Percy Bysshe Shelley in his elegy to Keats, "Adonais" (1821); and by George Gordon, Lord Byron, in *Childe Harold's Pilgrimage* (1812, 1816, 1818). The scholars J. C. Smith and E. De Selincourt observe that Spenser "is among the very greatest of our poets, but the significance of his poetry in the history of our literature is even greater than its intrinsic value."

Critical Analysis

Today Spenser is best remembered for writing *The Faerie Queene,* a long allegorical poem—or a poem in which the characters, settings, and events stand for abstract ideas—which was left incomplete when he died. At one point Spenser scholars focused their attention almost exclusively on this poem, something which may not have done justice to his accomplishment but which had a certain Spenserian logic to it. In Spenser's mind, the completion of the 12 projected books of *The Faerie Queene* would have been the achievement of the poetic objective he set out to accomplish when he first began writing. His career was launched in 1579 with the publication of *The Shepheardes Calendar,* a book of 12 poems, each named after one of the months. These poems are characteristic of those Spenser would write for the rest of his life in two ways. First, they illustrate his habit of experimenting with poetic forms, for they contain 13 different types of poetic units, including three different types of couplet, three different types of four-line stanza, and a sestina (an intricate verse form of six six-line stanzas). Second, they were written, like his later poems, in an English that Spenser himself considered archaic, or outdated—a language that could best be described as an Elizabethan imitation of Chaucer's Middle English.

Spenser's decision to use the form of language he used has troubled readers from the start, even those who found value in what he was doing. "The *Shepheard's Calendar,*" Sir Philip Sidney writes in *A Defence of Poetry,* "hath much poetry in his eclogues, indeed worthy the reading, if I be not deceived. That same framing of his style to an old rustic language I dare not allow." Spenser foresaw such criticism, and to alleviate the difficulty of reading his language, E. K. (who has been identified as Spenser by some; as Edward Kirke, a friend from Spenser's Cambridge days, by others; and left unidentified by most) was employed to provide notes that defined difficult words and offered interpretations of certain passages in *The Shepheardes Calendar.*

E. K. also wrote an introduction in which he suggested that Spenser would follow the lead of poets like the great Roman Virgil (70–19 B.C.), who began his career writing pastoral poems and ended it writing the great epic poem *The Aeneid.* "In time [Spenser] shall be hable to keep wing with the best," E. K. boasts, promising that the poet we are about to read will one day achieve what the greatest poets in times past have achieved. For those in the RENAISSANCE, this meant writing a great epic, or a long poem relating the adventures of a hero. Spenser recalls this promise in the opening lines of *The Faerie Queene,* reminding us that he was "the man, whose Muse whilome did maske / . . . in lowly Shepheards weeds"—that is, he was formerly a pastoral poet. He goes on to announce that he is now taking on a greater task:

> And now enforst a far unfitter taske,
> For trumpets sterne to chaunge mine Oaten
>   reeds
> And sing of Knights and Ladies gentle
>   deeds.

The poem entitled "October" in *Calendar* also sets forth the proper pattern for a poet to follow. In this poem, the central character, Cuddie, laments the uselessness of his poems: "I have pyped erst so long with payne, / . . . Yet little good hath got, and much lesse gayne." His friend Piers advises Cuddie to "Lyft up [his] self out of the lowly dust: / And sing of bloody Mars, of wars, of giusts [jousts]." In other words, he should turn, like Virgil, to epic subjects. Cuddie objects that epic no longer attracts the respect it once did, and "vaunting Poets [are] found nought worth a pease"—that is, poets are thought to be worthless.

The position Spenser takes up in "October" is paradoxical in that he denounces his age as a time that is unfit for epic and yet announces his intention of writing one. The paradox may explain, in part, the reason Spenser wrote the type of epic that he did, for despite his referring to Virgil's example, Spenser did not write the type of epic that Virgil wrote—a poem glorifying the accomplishments of a single, heroic individual. Rather, he wrote a 12-book poem about the exploits of 12 knights. Furthermore, the knights are only to be understood as heroes on one level of the poem's meaning; on another level, each knight represents a particular virtue. The figures in the six books that Spenser finished represent Holiness, Temperance, Chastity, Friendship, Justice, and Courtesy.

The adventures of the heroes are thus allegorical representations of something else, and in its allegorical sense, the poem could be said to be about one figure, the ideal human. In fact, Spenser explains in a letter to Sir Walter RALEIGH, "The generall end of all the booke . . . is to fashion a gentleman or noble person in vertuous and gentle discipline." In other words, Spenser set out to write a poem that would help each of his readers to become heroic in a moral sense.

The Faerie Queene's representation of how the moral ideal is achieved illustrates the connection between the political views Spenser put forth in *A View of the State of Ireland* and his notions about one's quest for salvation. This is particularly evident in Book II, "The Legend of Sir Guyon, or Of Temperance." (Temperance in this case can be defined as self-control.) Sir Guyon resists a number of temptations as he travels toward the Bower of Bliss, the realm of Acrasia, an enchantress and the allegorical representation of intemperance, or overindulgence. Acrasia's realm, however attractive it may seem (even to Guyon), must be destroyed if Sir Guyon is to achieve his destiny. As the scholar Ernest B. Gilman puts it, "At the center of Acrasia's 'painted' world, Guyon must not simply face the temptation of the Bower but 'deface' it." This is exactly what Guyon does:

> But all those pleasant bowres and Pallace
> brave,
> Guyon broke downe, with rigour pittiless;
> Ne ought their goodly workmanship might
> save

> Them from the tempest of his
> wrathfulnesse,
> But that their blisse he turn'd to
> balefulnesse:
> Their groves he feld, their gardens did
> deface,
> Their arbers spoyle, their Cabinets
> suppresse,
> Their banket houses burne, their buildings
> race,
> And of the fairest late, now made the
> fowlest place.

Commenting on the significance of this moment in the poem, Gilman observes, "Whether in the psyche, in Ireland, or in the New World, civility is achieved," in Spenser's view, by the self's "imposing and indeed celebrating its control over that which attracts it and (as in the case of the Anglo-Irish) threatens it with absorption." The pleasure of the Bower and the rebelliousness of the Irish are different manifestations of the disorder that the civilized must eradicate to transform themselves into noble and virtuous people. But Spenser wanted to do more than inform his readers what one had to do to become civilized. He wanted the act of reading his poem to assist his readers in doing so. Thus, the scholar David Norbrook argues, "Learning to read Spenser's poem is not just a means towards the further end of moral and political education, it is part of the process."

Other Works by Edmund Spenser

Edmund Spenser's Poetry. Edited by Hugh MacLean and Anne Lake Prescott. New York: Norton, 1993.
Fierce Wars and Faithful Loves: Book One of Edmund Spenser's The Faerie Queene. Edited by Roy Maynard. Moscow, Idaho: Canon Press, 1999.

Works about Edmund Spenser

Hadfield, Andrew. *Edmund Spenser's Irish Experience: Wilde Fruit and Savage Soyl.* Oxford, U.K.: Clarendon Press, 1997.
Heale, Elizabeth. *The Faerie Queene: A Reader's Guide.* New York: Cambridge University Press, 1999.

Kaske, Carol V. *Spenser's Biblical Poetics.* Ithaca, N.Y.: Cornell University Press, 2000.

Mallette, Richard. *Spenser and the Discourses of Reformation England.* Lincoln: University of Nebraska Press, 1999.

Oram, William Allan. *Edmund Spenser.* Boston: Twayne, 1997.

Waller, Garry. *Edmund Spenser: A Literary Life.* New York: St. Martin's Press, 1994.

Sprat, Thomas (1635–1713) *poet, nonfiction writer*

Thomas Sprat was an English poet and historian who wrote during the period of the English RESTORATION. He was born at Beaminster, Dorset, England, and educated at Wadham College, Oxford. In 1669 he became canon of Westminster and in 1670 rector of Uffington, Lincolnshire. In 1676 he served as chaplain to Charles II, and in 1679 he became a lecturer at St. Margaret's, Westminster. He went on to be canon of Windsor in 1681, dean of Westminster in 1683, and bishop of Rochester in 1684.

Sprat's major contribution to British literature is the *History of the Royal Society* (1667), of which he was one of the first members. The Royal Society was an organization of scholars who met periodically to discuss philosophical and scientific questions. Although the origins of the society can be traced back to the 1640s, its official date of foundation is 1660. The first scientific journal in English, *Philosophical Transactions,* was issued by the society in 1665.

In his *History* Sprat writes something akin to a history of all the knowledge available in 18th-century England, and as such his work is an invaluable resource for historians. He also examines, among other things, the appropriate language (English or Latin) and style for scientific writing. He advocates a positive and natural method of expression and notes that the society's members must

> reject all amplifications, digressions, and swellings of style: to return back to the primitive purity, and shortness, when men deliver'd so many *things,* almost in an equal number of *words.* They have exacted from all their members, a close, naked, natural way of speaking; positive expressions; clear senses; a native easiness: bringing all things as near the Mathematical plainness, as they can: and preferring the language of Artizans, Countrymen, and Merchants, before that, of Wits, or Scholars.

To the modern reader the idea that scientific language ought to be clear, simple, and free of rhetorical embellishments may seem obvious, but the point was not so obvious at the time, and Sprat had a profound influence on the language of scientific journals. In addition to his commentary on language, Sprat advances his fellow Englishmen as the best scientific and philosophical thinkers in the world because of the English national character:

> If there can be a true character even of the Universal Temper of any Nation under Heaven: then certainly this must be ascribed to our Countrymen: that they have commonly an unaffected sincerity; that they love to deliver their minds with a sound simplicity; that they have the middle qualities, between the reserved subtle southern, and the rough unhewn northern people: that they are not extremely prone to speak: that they are most concerned, what others will think of the strength, than of the fineness of what they say: and that a universal modesty possesses them. These Qualities are so conspicuous, and proper to our Soil; that we often hear them objected to us, by some of our neighbour Satirists, in more disgraceful expressions.

Sprat is also known for his *Life and Writings of Cowley* (1668), a biography of the English poet. He also wrote a poem about COWLEY, "Upon the Poems of Abraham Cowley," in which he wonders about the origins of Cowley's talent:

> *Cowley! what God did fill thy breast,*
> *And taught thy hand t' indite?*

(For Gods a poet too,
He doth create, and so do you)
Or else at least
What angel sat upon thy pen when thou
*   didst write?*

Stanihurst, Richard (Richard Stanyhurst)
(1547–1618) *nonfiction writer, translator*

Richard Stanihurst was born in Dublin, Ireland, the son of James Stanihurst, speaker of the Irish House of Commons. He attended Kilkenny Grammar School, after which he attended University College, Oxford University, graduating in 1568 with a B.A. degree. At Oxford he came under the tutelage of the English Jesuit, later saint, Edmund Campion, whom he accompanied on a visit to Ireland in 1577, helping him to collect material for Campion's book *The History of Ireland.*

Stanihurst published his first work, a Latin commentary on the classical philosopher Porphyry's *Introduction,* in 1570. In the same year he became a member of Sir Philip SIDNEY's literary circle in England and began a lifelong friendship with the great poet. He went on to publish *Treatise containing a Plaine and Perfect Description of Ireland,* his own description of Ireland as an addition to Campion's history and which was published in *Holinshed's Chronicles* (1577). In 1584 he published *De Rebus in Hibernia Gestis,* a detailed narrative on the early history of Ireland. Stanihurst was later severely criticized by Irish historians for his hostile view and portrayal of Gaelic Ireland. For example, in describing the Irish he says that "the people are thus enclined, religious, franke, amorous, irefull, sufferable of infinite paynes, very glorious, many sorcerers, excellent horsemen, delight with wars, great almsgiver, passing hospitality." This was a common unflattering portrayal found throughout the book.

Stanihurst's translation of the first four books of Virgil's *Aeneid* into English heroic verse (1582) is a famous literary failure. The work was harshly criticized upon publication for its poor translation and mishandling of language. Stanihurst invented a series of onomatopoetic words, or words that imitate the sound of the thing they refer to, as when he says men's hearts are beating "with thwick thwack . . . thundering." He also invented other words, as when he describes a hatchet as "boucherous." And he sometimes has Virgil's characters speak in RENAISSANCE English slang. In trying to force English into hexameters, the meter used by Virgil, he distorts both the sound and the sense of the original work beyond recognition. Edward Arber, who edited the 1880 edition of Stanyhurst's Virgil, said: "One may say of him, that he, at any rate, had the courage of his convictions; that he, at least, had not the fear of man before his eyes, when he set to work to torture the English language."

Stanley, Thomas (1625–1678) *poet,*
translator, nonfiction writer

Thomas Stanley was born in Hertfordshire, England, the son of Sir Thomas Stanley (grandson of Edward Stanley, third Earl of Derby) and Mary Hammond Stanley (a cousin of Richard LOVELACE). As a child, he was tutored by William Fairfax, the son of Edward FAIRFAX, who was the translator of Torquato TASSO. Stanley was an outstanding classical scholar who also excelled in French, Italian and Spanish poetry. He attended both Cambridge and Oxford universities, graduating from Cambridge with an M.A. in 1641. Thereafter he traveled throughout Europe, returning in the 1640s to London, where he committed himself to his literary work, becoming a prolific translator and writer of verse.

In 1647 Stanley published his first volume of poems. He went on to publish several later volumes that included translations from Bion, Battista Guarini, Giambattista Marino, PETRARCH, and others. In 1651 he published a rendition of Anacreontic poems,—poems celebrating love and drinking—which also included his version of Pico della Mirandola's "A Platonick Discourse upon Love." This publication would become a Stanley classic.

In 1655 Stanley published his most famous and serious work, *The History of Philosophy.* This work, which appeared in three successive volumes between 1655 and 1661, took the form of a series of critical biographies of the philosophers. It became a standard in the history of classical philosophy throughout the later 17th century and early 18th century, being widely read and quoted by writers and philosophers such as John LOCKE. In 1663 Stanley published his edition of Aeschylus with a Latin translation and commentary.

Thomas Stanley serves as an interesting transitional figure in English literature, as the last of the metaphysical poets. He remains known as one of the most accomplished translators in English literature as well as gifted writer of verse.

Stationers' Company

The Stationers' Company was a professional association based on a guild that had been established in London in 1403. In medieval England most craftspeople organized themselves into guilds to set standards and prices, regulate the admission of apprentices to the field, protect themselves from competition, and take care of members and their families who fell on hard times. The Stationers' Guild included anyone involved in the book trade—the scriveners who copied the books, the limners who decorated and illustrated them, and the merchants who sold the books and the materials to make them. After the introduction of printing, the guild extended its membership to printers, and by the mid-16th century the printers and booksellers dominated it.

The guild had also become of more interest to the government, as the printing press was an obvious means by which antigovernment views could be spread. It was reestablished in 1556 as the Stationers' Company, with 97 original members, and given particular responsibility for regulating what came out of the printing presses. It was now illegal for anyone who was not a member of the Stationers' Company to print anything (unless a special government patent had been issued). Every member was obligated to enter in the Company Register the name of any work he wished to print. The

company's charter gave it the right to search all printers' and booksellers' premises and destroy any illegal publications. These regulations remained in force throughout the 17th century.

The Stationers' Company was established during the reign of the Catholic queen Mary I, and for the first three years of its existence it was used by her government to prevent the publication of any Protestant texts. After the accession of the Protestant ELIZABETH I in 1660, it was used to silence Catholics and anyone else Elizabeth was suspicious of. The company was expected to submit any religious, foreign, or political texts to a commission of bishops for authorization, which was often withheld.

Although it is not a complete list of everything printed in the period, because some works were published by special patent and many were printed illegally, the Stationers' Company Register is an invaluable resource for scholars seeking to establish facts about, for example, the chronology of a writer's works. The company's registration system was also important as a precursor of the copyright system. At this period there was no such thing as an author's copyright; an author would usually write a book or pamphlet for a fee, and any profit would accrue to the printer. But through the registration system and the company's methods of enforcement, the idea took hold that making unauthorized copies of a text was wrong. Only once this was established could the author's right come to seem important.

Works about the Stationers' Company

Halasz, Alexandra. *The Marketplace of Print: Pamphlets and the Public Sphere in Early Modern England.* New York: Cambridge University Press, 1997.

Myers, Robin, and Michael Harris. *The Stationers' Company and the Book Trade: 1550–1990.* New Castle, Del.: Oak Knoll, 1997.

Stow, John (ca. 1525–1605) *historian*

John Stow was born in London to a tallow chandler (a supplier of lamp oil and candles), Thomas

Stow, and his wife, Elizabeth. Stow became both a tailor and a historian whose works include *A Summary of English Chronicles* (1565), a condensation of previously published information on English history from Roman times to the 16th century; *The Chronicles of England* (1580), an expansion of his previous work; and *The Annals of England* (1592), another English history.

Stow's tailoring left him open to some light-hearted mockery. "It seems we are beholding to Mr. [John] SPEED [another tailor/historian] and Stow for *stitching* up for us our English history," a contemporary joked. Stow was, contrary to this impression, well respected for his knowledge, which was acquired not through formal schooling but through a self-directed course of reading and study. Other historians sought him out for both his fund of information and his collection of reference works.

Stow is best remembered as the author of *The Survey of London* (1598, 1603). Both a history and a guide to London, *The Survey* is organized as a walk through the city. The reader follows as Stow moves through the London streets, stopping at sites to lecture on their history. His facts are sewn together from material gathered from his extensive library, manuscripts owned by the city, and his memories. For example, Stow writes about how Sir Thomas Cromwell, a top adviser to Henry VIII, took for himself 22 feet of every man's land north of his estate. The author then recalls that "my father had a garden there, and a house standing close to the south pale; this house they loosed from the ground, and bare upon rollers into my father's garden twenty-two feet, ere my father heard thereof."

The odd mixture of history and biography in *The Survey* suggests that Londoners in Elizabethan England were able to integrate their life stories into the history of their city and vice versa. The route Stow follows through London contributes to this impression. "I will begin at the east," he writes, "and so proceed through the high and most principal street of the city to the west." This path, as the scholar Steven Mullaney points out, is the same one that ELIZABETH I followed on her way to be

crowned queen of England, and the path the queen has marked out is the path her subjects should follow. Stow's *Survey,* according to the scholar Barrett L. Beer, thereby "contributes to a broad and inclusive concept of nationhood and patriotism."

Stow also, Beer continues, "contributed significantly to [Edmund] SPENSER's 'kingdom of our own language.'" By writing a history of London in English, Stow helped to make English, rather than Latin, the principal literary language of England. While he is best remembered today for his guide to London, he is also, for his careful scholarship and attention to the details of previous historians, an important figure in the development of modern standards of historical accuracy.

Strype, John (1643–1737) *nonfiction writer*

A preacher by training and trade, John Strype was licensed by the bishop of London in 1674. While the church was his livelihood, his interests also turned to history and writing.

Strype's literary career consisted of writing biographies of famous figures in the church and also collecting, editing, and republishing works by other authors. His books are today considered not only good primary sources on the state of the church and city during the period but also good collections of other primary source writing that may have been lost or damaged.

The more important publications from Strype include *Memorials of Thomas Creamer, Archbishop of Canterbury* (1694), *Life of the Learned Sir Thomas Smith* (1698), *Annals of the Reformation in England* (1709), *of Matthew Parker, Archbishop of Canterbury* (1711), and *of John Whitgift, Archbishop of Canterbury* (1718).

One of Strype's texts, *An Accurate Edition of Stow's Survey of London* (1720), provides an account of how individuals located themselves in London both physically and psychologically during the RESTORATION. This history book includes illustrations, such as "exact maps of the city and suburbs, and of all the wards; and likewise of the out-parishes of London and Westminster: Together with many other fair draughts of the more eminent and publick edifices and monuments."

Stuart, Arbella (1575–1615) *letter writer*

Arbella Stuart was the daughter of Elizabeth Cavendish and Charles Stuart, Earl of Lennox. She was the niece of MARY STUART (Mary, Queen of Scots) and the cousin of JAMES I OF ENGLAND, as well as a potential heir to the throne. Orphaned at seven, Stuart was raised by Bess of Hardwick, one of the most powerful women in England. Her education included classical literature, languages, and rhetoric. After her cousin James became king, she enjoyed a position in the royal household and was considered one of the most learned women at court. However, when she married against James's wishes, she was imprisoned in the Tower of London, where she eventually died after several years of declining health.

Stuart left a legacy of highly crafted letters, to her husband, friends, and relatives dating from 1602 to 1611. Scholars consider the RENAISSANCE letter to be an important literary form that involves creativity and rhetorical language. Letters provide a particularly important record of women's writing in a day when women were discouraged from the public authorship that men pursued.

Stuart's earliest correspondence reveals a romantic imagination. She invents scandalous letters about an imaginary lover whose love she compares to "gold which hath binne so often purified that I cannot finde one fault." Here she adopts the popular language of love poetry, using a metaphor that compares love to riches. Stuart adopts various personas or character roles in her letters; as the critic Sara Jayne Steen notes, she "casts herself in two related literary roles, the beloved woman and the heroic victim." These letters, which are filled with passionate emotion, surely functioned as an outlet for Stuart's frustration and creativity.

Later correspondence spans Stuart's time at the royal court. She writes informal, entertaining letters to relatives and friends recounting court gossip and activities such as dancing at court masques (royal theatrical and musical productions). She also writes formal letters about official court matters, many concerning her own fate and marriage, in which she demonstrates her capacity for the highly structured rhetoric, or formal rules of writing, that was fashionable in the RENAISSANCE. Through Stuart's creative and formal letters, as Steen explains, "we can watch an intelligent and well-educated Renaissance woman fashion a self in prose."

A Work by Arbella Stuart

The Letters of Lady Arbella Stuart. Edited by Sara Jayne Steene. New York: Oxford UP, 1994.

A Work about Arbella Stuart

Lewalski, Barbara. *Writing Women in Jacobean England.* Cambridge, Mass.: Harvard University Press, 1994.

Stuart, Elizabeth (1596–1662) *letter writer*

Elizabeth Stuart was born to King James VI of Scotland and Anne of Denmark. In 1603, before Stuart had reached her 10th birthday, her father became JAMES I OF ENGLAND. By 12 she had mastered several languages and studied theology, history, geography, and music.

In 1613 Stuart married a German prince, Frederick V, Elector and Prince Palatine of the Rhine. The couple's engagement and marriage became the subject of poems and plays. John DONNE, for example, wrote "Epithalamium" for the occasion, and William SHAKESPEARE added a wedding masque to his play *The Tempest* (1611) in the couple's honor. In 1619 Frederick became king of Bohemia, but conflict forced the couple into exile from that country after less than a year. Sir Henry WOTTON was among the diplomats assigned to try to consolidate Frederick's hold on his throne, and his poem "On His Mistress, the queen of Bohemia," is about Stuart, who would come to be known as "The Winter Queen" because her rule in the Bohemian capital of Prague lasted only one season. Thereafter she lived mostly in the Netherlands.

Frederick died in 1632, and as the widow of an exiled king, Stuart endured humiliating poverty, especially after the English Civil War broke out (her brother, King Charles I, was executed by parliamentary forces in 1649). She maintained cheerfulness and courage throughout, and was a formidable presence in the lives of her many children, among them Princess Sophie, who married the Elector of Hanover and was the mother of King George I of England. In 1661, after the RESTORATION of her nephew, King Charles II, Stuart returned to England, where she died.

From an early age Stuart loved to write letters. Separated from family as she often was, she maintained her ties through constant correspondence, and her letters are an invaluable source on the history of the period, although historians are frustrated by the fact that she did not date them. One of the earliest letters, written when she was in her early teens, was to her beloved brother Prince Henry, and it poignantly though formally evokes her affection for him:

> . . . I will ever endeavor to equal you, esteeming that time happiest when I enjoyed your company, and desiring nothing more than the fruition of it again: that as nature has made us nearest in our love together, so accident may not separate us from living together.

Although Stuart's marriage was arranged for dynastic reasons, she was deeply attached to her husband, as her letter to Sir Thomas Roe describing her reaction to his death attests:

> . . . I shall grieve for as long as I live. Though I make a good show in company, yet can I never have any more contentment in this world. For God knows I had none but I took in his company. . . .

Stuart was nonetheless an irrepressibly lively personality, accepting any invitations that came her way and reporting to her many correspondents on any new thing she experienced. A letter from the 1650s describes a disaster that she traveled from her home in the Hague to see:

> I was at Delft to see the wrack that was made by the blowing up of the powder. It is a sad sight—whole streets quite razed, not one stone upon another. . . .

The letter breaks off in a mess of ink, below which she explains that her little dog, "with leaping into my lap, has made this blot."

A Work about Elizabeth Stuart

Ross, Josephine. *The Winter Queen: The Story of Elizabeth Stuart.* New York: Dorset, 1986.

Stuart, James

See JAMES I OF ENGLAND.

Stuart, Mary

See MARY STUART.

Stubbes, Philip (ca. 1555–ca. 1610)
nonfiction writer

Philip Stubbes is believed to have been born to genteel parents, but little is known about his upbringing. As a young man he attended Cambridge University but did not finish his degree. Instead he turned a restless disposition to traveling, and he later claimed to have spent seven years roving through England to observe the customs and morals of humans.

Stubbes clearly became dismayed at the England he saw, for his best-known work, *The Anatomie of Abuses* (1583), was a harsh account listing the widespread social ills of the day. The book proved popular, going through four editions in the 1580s and '90s.

A staunch Puritan man, Stubbes condemned idleness, gambling, dicing, swearing, dancing, and the wearing of fine clothing, among other social vices. Indeed, after his opening condemnation of "Pride" as the root of all sins, *The Anatomie* exemplifies the point by attacking the wearing of excessively fine apparel, which Stubbes calls "newfanglednesse." He was reacting to the recent availability and affordability of luxury goods, due in part to England's recent expansions in overseas trade. To Stubbes, finery was symbolic of greed and self-indulgence, and it bred social confusion. He complains, "[I]t is verie hard to knowe, who is noble, who is worshipfull, who is a gentleman, who is not." Widespread wearing of finery could confuse perceptions of social class, a very important concept to an English culture that believed one was born to one's social station and should remain there.

Like many other RENAISSANCE moralists, such as Stephen GOSSON and John Northbrook, Stubbes attacks the theater in *The Anatomie*. For him and for others, the public theater, a cultural institution growing in popularity and importance, had become a lightning rod for social controversy, much like today's entertainment industry. He believed theater was a vehicle for immorality, and in the crowds of commoners and aristocrats who gathered in the theater, Stubbes saw the class mingling he was so opposed to, in addition to the vices of idleness, impiety, and sexual license. Furthermore, he believed the theater drew Elizabethans away from their proper vocations or duties to idleness and sin. Voicing a strong distrust and contempt for the common man's capacity for discrimination, Stubbes charges the theater with representing the most base characters and acts of crime and sin. Plays portrayed

> Anger, Wrath, . . . Crueltie, Iniurie, Incest, Murther [murder] and . . . Flatterie, Whoredome, Adulterie . . . [and] Whores, . . . Knaves, . . . Lecherous old men, Amorous yong men, with suche like of infinite varietie. . . . For so often, as they goe to those houses where Plaiers [players] frequent, they goe to Venus Pallace . . . to worship Devilles, and betraie Christ Jesus.

Writing in his characteristically bombastic style, in which he piles on example after example and uses strong rhetoric, Stubbes compares going to the theater to sacrilege—going to "Venus['s] pallace," a pagan goddess of sexuality, and worshipping the devil.

In addition to attacking the theater, Stubbes directed his stringent criticism to broader Elizabethan tastes in literature and reading: "[B]ooks and pamphlets of scurilitie [vulgarity] and baudrie [licentiousness, obscenity] are better esteemed, and more venerable, than the godlyest and sages books that be." He thus entered into a heated late 16th-century debate about the capacity and function of literature to imitate life and to teach virtue. Condemnation of the theater—as well as other literary forms—as a distraction from religion, as a path to sin, and as a representation of false idols was a popular Puritan position.

Literature's defenders also had a strong voice, and Stubbes was mercilessly satirized for his strict views by the dramatist Thomas NASHE in *Anatomie of Absurditie* (1589). In Nashe's work, an attack on many enemies of art and bad authors of his day, he critiques "other men's fury, who make the press the dunghill whither they carry all the muck of their melancholy imaginations, pretending, forsooth, to anatomize abuses and stub up sin by the roots." He further charges Stubbes with being unlearned, unoriginal, and hypocritical in his condemnations of other men's sins. Some years after Nashe's publication, the playwright Thomas HEYWOOD wrote the *Apologie for Actors* (1612), a defense of the theater that was in part a reply to the continued popularity of Stubbes and his position.

Stubbes wrote other religiously inspired works, including *The Rosarie of Christian Praiers and Meditations* (1583), a guide to Christian worship; and *A Christal Glasse for Christian Women* (1591), a work in praise of his deceased wife as a model for proper and virtuous Christian womanhood. Stubbes's writing provides valuable insight on the debates over morality that occupied the literary world in the late 16th century.

Suckling, Sir John (1609–1642) *poet, playwright*

John Suckling was born near London to John and Martha Suckling. His father was the owner of extensive lands and had an appointment as comptroller of King JAMES I's household. Suckling enrolled at Cambridge University at age 14 and later studied law at Gray's Inn in London. His father's death in 1627 left him with a large fortune, and he promptly went abroad, studying briefly at the university at Leyden. In his biographical notes about various famous people John AUBREY reported of Suckling, "He returned to England an extraordinary accomplished Gent. [gentleman], grew famous at Court for his readie sparkling witt . . . most sparkling when most sett-upon and provoked."

In 1630 Suckling was knighted by Charles I, probably having purchased the honor. In 1631–32 he accompanied the diplomat Sir Henry Vane on an embassy to King Gustavus Adolphus of Sweden. His letters to Vane concerning this mission show personal ambition and serious concern with the great events of his day.

Suckling received an official appointment at court in 1638, by which time he had also written two plays. The first, *The Sad One* (probably written soon after his 1632 return to England), was never finished, but it provided practice and material for the second, *Aglaura,* a melodramatic concoction involving the love of the King (described in the list of characters as "lustfull and cruel") for Aglaura, who is in love with Thersames; in a subplot, the Queen is plotting with the King's brother to assassinate the King. The play was performed first at court in a lavish production in early 1638 and again later that year at the Cockpit Theater in London. Suckling rewrote the last act for the second production. The original version ended with all the major characters dead on the stage—Thersames accidentally, at the hand of Aglaura. The revised play allows the villains to repent without completing their evil schemes, and allows Aglaura, though she still stabs Thersames by mistake, to avoid any major organs. The play's strengths are the witty conversations and songs that run through it. The Queen and her lover, even as they scheme, take the time to discuss the transitory nature of beauty and the power of love to survive beauty's decay; a transition scene is filled with a discussion among minor characters about the place of lust in elegant society:

> Will you then place the happiness, but
>   there,
> Where the dull plow-man and the
>   plow-man's horse
> Can find it out? Shall souls refin'd, not
>   know
> How to preserve alive a noble flame,
> But let it die, burn out to appetite?

As the critic Joshua Scodel points out, the characters celebrate "coyness"—the deferring of sexual gratification—as a way for "refined" aristocrats to prolong sexual excitement.

Suckling followed *Aglaura* with two more plays. *The Goblins* (written sometime between 1637 and 1641) is a pastoral (set in the countryside, with idealized shepherds and shepherdesses as characters) that wishfully represents a society reconciling after a civil war. England itself was rapidly approaching an all-too-real split: the English Civil War (1642–51). *Brennoralt, or the Discontented Colonel* (1642) has a complicated plot which culminates in lovers discovering each other's love as they fall dead by each other's hands. The play is executed deftly, at high speed and with musical interludes. All three of Suckling's finished plays, artificial and mannered as they are, were revived during the Restoration to great acclaim.

Suckling is best known as a poet. His poems, like those of most of the CAVALIER POETS, were circulated in manuscript and set to music, but they were not published until five years after his death, in a book entitled *Fragmenta Aurea* (*Golden Fragments,* 1646). His verse had effortless-seeming lyrics, which though they often express a cynical view of love, have such a sweet musicality that the cynicism is muted.

Suckling's most famous poem is "Song (Why So Pale and Wan, Fond Lover)," which appeared as one of the musical numbers in *Aglaura,* and it shows his strengths as a poet:

Why so pale and wan fond Lover?
Prithee why so pale?
Will, when looking well can't move her
Looking ill prevail?
. . .
If of her selfe she will not Love,
Nothing can make her,
The Devill take her.

As Suckling biographer Charles Squier remarks, it "could have been written by a rakehell with a hangover, but a hungover rakehell with a poetic facility that comes only through artistic discipline and continued practice." No one disputes the artistic discipline, and more recently scholars such as Thomas Clayton have traced the seriousness that underlies the wit and sensuality of Suckling's verse.

Other Works by Sir John Suckling

The Cavalier Poets: An Anthology. Edited by Thomas Crofts. New York: Dover, 1995.
The Works of Sir John Suckling: The Plays. Edited by L. A. Beaurline. Oxford, U.K.: Oxford University Press, 1971.
The Works of Sir John Suckling: The Non-Dramatic Works. Edited by Thomas Clayton. Oxford, U.K.: Oxford University Press, 1971.

Works about Sir John Suckling

Clayton, Thomas. "'At Bottom a Criticism of Life': Suckling and the Poetry of Low Seriousness." In *Classic and Cavalier: Essays on Jonson and the Sons of Ben.* Pittsburgh, Pa.: University of Pittsburgh Press, 1982.
Corns, Thomas N., ed. *The Cambridge Companion to English Poetry, Donne to Marvell.* New York: Cambridge University Press, 1993.
Scodel, Joshua. "The Pleasures of Restraint: The Mean of Coyness in Cavalier Poetry." *Criticism* 38:2 (Spring 1996), p. 239ff.
Squier, Charles L. *Sir John Suckling.* Boston: Twayne, 1978.

Surrey, Henry Howard, Earl of
(1517–1547) *poet, translator*

Henry Howard, Earl of Surrey, was born at Kenninghall Palace, Norfolk, England, to Lord Thomas Howard and Elizabeth Stafford Howard, the daughter of the Duke of Buckingham and a descendant of King Edward III of England. He was given the title Earl of Surrey in 1524 when his father became Duke of Norfolk. Two of his cousins, Anne BOLEYN and Catherine Howard, were married to Henry VIII. Surrey's family connections provided him with a wealth of opportunities. Among other posts, he served as the king's welcomer and lieutenant general of the king on sea and land for all continental possessions of England—that is, a small portion of France controlled by the English.

Surrey had a fiery temper, which landed him in trouble a number of times. He was imprisoned for brawling in 1537 and 1542, for rioting in 1543, and finally for high treason in 1546. This last charge led to his beheading.

Surrey apparently began composing poetry while he was imprisoned at Windsor Castle in 1537. IIe remained, by necessity, an occasional poet, writing for the most part when he was not fulfilling some political office or following some military campaign.

Critical Analysis

Surrey made a valuable contribution to English literature when he translated Books II and IV of the Roman poet Virgil's *The Aeneid,* an epic or book-length poem telling of the end of the Trojan war and the founding of Rome. In his translation Surrey uses, for the first time in English, blank verse—unrhymed lines of iambic pentameter, or lines of 10 syllables alternating between unaccented and accented syllables. This poetic form has since come to seem like a natural part of the English language. Indeed, the rhythms of blank verse most closely resemble the rhythms of spoken English. Thus the Surrey scholar William A. Sessions observes that Thomas NORTON's and Thomas SACKVILLE's use of blank verse for spoken drama "merely reproduced Surrey's successful experiment with language."

Surrey's *Aeneid* also demonstrates his use of the paragraph to break up long sections of verse. By breaking a long poem into paragraphs, just as prose is divided, he was able to make a long, continuous section more readable and to construct smaller units of meaning.

Another of Surrey's great innovations was the development of the English sonnet (sometimes called Shakespearean after William SHAKESPEARE). The sonnet, a 14-line poem popularized by the Italian poet Francis PETRARCH, was introduced into England by Surrey and a poet with whom he is frequently linked, Thomas WYATT. Wyatt tended to use the Italian form, which is divided into two parts: an eight-line unit, known as the octave, and a six-line unit, the sextet. The octave and the sextet each consist of separate sets of rhyming lines. In other words, the lines of the octave rhyme and the lines of the sextet rhyme. The pattern established by the rhyme also establishes the pattern of the poem's argument: A problem is set forth in the octave and conclusion in the sextet.

The form that Surrey developed, by contrast, has three four-line units, known as quatrains, and a concluding two lines, the couplet. Surrey's rhyme scheme was ABAB CDCD EFEF GG. In this type of sonnet the poet poses a problem in the three quatrains, with each quatrain dealing with a separate, though related, aspect of the problem. The poet then presents a conclusion in the couplet.

In one of Surrey's characteristic sonnets, "Love, that liveth and reigneth in my thought," adapted from Petrarch's *Sonnetto in Vita* 91, Surrey writes of love as a military drama. In the first quatrain Love is characterized as a military figure who takes the field:

> *Love, that liveth and reigneth in my*
> *thought,*
> *That built his seat within my captive*
> *breast;*
> *Clad in the arms wherein with me he*
> *fought,*
> *Oft in my face he doth his banner rest.*

The Beloved's response is presented in the second quatrain:

> *She, that taught me to love, and suffer pain;*
> *My doubtful hope, and eke [also] my hot*
> *desire*
> *With shamefaced cloak to shadow and*
> *restrain,*
> *Her smiling grace converteth straight to ire.*

In the third quatrain Love retreats:

> *And coward Love then to the heart apace*
> *Taketh his flight; whereas he lurks, and*
> *plains*
> *His purpose lost, and dare not shew his*
> *face.*
> *For my Lord's guilt thus faultless bide I*
> *pains.*

In the couplet the speaker enters the drama, stating his intention to die on the field of battle in the pursuit of his love: "Yet from my Lord shall not my foot remove: Sweet is his death that takes his end by love."

In addition to developing blank verse and the English sonnet, Surrey was also among the earliest English poets to struggle for smooth metrical patterns in his lines. The meter, or rhythm, of very old English poetry is accentual, meaning that each line contains a certain number of stressed syllables but can have any number of syllables. Later poets used a syllabic-accentual meter, meaning that each line contains the same number of syllables and the same number of accented syllables. A line of iambic pentameter, for instance, always contains 10 syllables, five of which are stressed.

Prior to Surrey, English poets only loosely followed syllable counts in their lines. Surrey, however, learned from the Italians "the structural value of regularity, of keeping exact iambs," as Sessions notes, and he worked at making his lines' rhythms metrically correct. His verse is, consequently, smoother than the verse of his predecessors, and after his death, poets followed his example. His most recent editor, Dennis Keene, observes that Surrey, "having achieved a revolution in the rhythm and vocabulary of poetry . . . determined the nature of poetic vocabulary for the following two hundred years."

Other Works by Henry Howard, Earl of Surrey

Selected Poems. Edited by Dennis Keene. New York: Routledge, 2003.

Wyatt, Surrey, and Early Tudor Poetry. Edited by Elizabeth Heale. Boston: Addison-Wesley, 1998.

A Work about Henry Howard, Earl of Surrey

Sessions, W. A. *Henry Howard, the Poet Surrey: A Life.* New York: Oxford University Press, 1999.

Sutcliffe, Alice (fl. 1632) *prose writer, poet*

Alice Sutcliffe (née Woodhouse) was the daughter of a Luke Woodhouse from Norfolk, England; nothing more is known of her early life. By 1624 she had married John Sutcliffe, a man who held minor positions at the court of JAMES I OF ENGLAND and, later, at that of Charles I.

Sutcliffe is known for her *Meditations of Man's Mortality, or, A Way to True Blessedness* (1632). The volume begins with six prose meditations, each of which begins with quotations from the Bible and goes on to urge the readers to think about the spiritual dimensions of their lives. The meditations are followed by a long poem in six-line stanzas describing the tragedy of the fall of the man, the ingenuity of Satan, and ways in which humans have after all been redeemed by God. After a lengthy address to Eve, reproaching her for leading Adam into sin and all humankind into death and misery, Sutcliffe rallies:

> Yet courage woman, whose weak spirit's
> dead,
> GOD in his love a help for thee hath
> found . . .

But after only a few stanzas about Christ's redemption of man from sin, she begins to detail the traps Satan still sets:

> Old and crafty is our enemy grown.
> He knows all fish at one bait will not bite.
> He'll try a thousand ways to gain his own,
> He will not leave till he the mark hits right.
> Some with Drunkenness, Murders, Lust
> beside,
> Others with Idleness, excessive Pride.

Sutcliffe focuses on such daily sins as drunkenness and idleness more than on dramatic ones such as murder, stressing that one can become inured to a what seems a trivial fault:

> If man but yield a little unto evil,
> Sin will increase, though creeping like a
> Snail.
> And if unto a Custom it doth come,
> He feels it not, his soul is now grown numb.

Although Sutcliffe's religious devotion can hardly be questioned, *Meditations* appears to be more than a simple exercise in spirituality. The text was probably meant to aid the advancement of the author and her husband at the English court. The title page asserts the author's closeness to royalty, and the text is dedicated to two of the most important women as Charles I's court, the Duchess of Buckingham and the Countess of Denby. A further dedication to Philip, Earl of Pembroke, her husband's superior, and dedicatory poems from Ben JONSON, George WITHER, and others show both the author's high connections and her determination to make the volume into a major event at the court. It was enough of a success to warrant a second edition, published in 1634.

Like many woman writers of her time, Sutcliffe was virtually ignored by scholars until the late 20th century. A facsimile edition of *Meditations of Man's Mortality* was published in 1996, but further investigation is needed.

Swetnam, Joseph (Thomas Tell-Troth)

(fl. 1615) *nonfiction writer, pamphleteer*
Little is known of Joseph Swetnam before 1615. In 1617 he published a book on fencing titled *The*

Schole of the Noble and Worthy Science of Defence, which is still of interest to historians of the subject. It contains a certain amount of autobiographical information, including the disclaimer that he is "no scholar," having never been at Oxford or Cambridge except for brief visits; and a boast that he was fencing instructor to Prince Henry (the eldest son of JAMES I OF ENGLAND), who had died in 1612. The book also contains homey advice, much of it not about fencing but about the need to avoid such traps as drunkenness and laziness.

In 1615 Swetnam created a stir with the publication of a controversial pamphlet, *The Araignment of Lewde, idle, froward, and unconstant women.* Although this pamphlet appeared under the pseudonym Thomas Tell-Troth, it was soon ascribed to Swetnam.

The Araignment is a scornful tirade on the evils of women. Using biblical and historical references, for example the bad luck the Greek philosopher Socrates and the biblical King Solomon had with women, Swetnam details women's essential wickedness and warns his fellow men against involvement with them. Swetnam calls casually on men to ponder an ideal world in which men need not rely upon women for the continuance of the human race. He also suggests the need for physical abuse, as when he notes that "if thou go about to master a woman in hope to bring her to humility, there is no way to make her good with stripes [whipping] except thou beat her to death."

Swetnam's pamphlet was both scathing and hugely popular. By 1637 it had run through 10 editions, and it was reprinted numerous times during the 18th century. Nevertheless, much of the attention garnered by *The Araignment* was negative. Writers who disagreed with its basic anti-woman thesis were quick to respond in print. Three of the most famous were written from the woman's perspective by the authors Rachel SPEGHT, Esther SOWERNAM, and Constantia MUNDA; the latter two names were pseudonyms. These writers, whose pamphlets were all published in 1617, counter Swetnam's accusations that women are essentially evil, in large part by reinterpreting the creation story: They asserted that Eve's biblical temptation was a failure not only of woman but also of man.

In addition to the pamphlet wars that Swetnam's publication started, *The Araignment* also inspired an anonymous dramatic stage play, *Swetnam the Woman-hater* (1620). In this play Swetnam becomes "Misogynos," a man who tries to cause trouble for women through endless assaults on their characters. By the end of the play, however, Misogynos is cleverly outsmarted by the very women he attacks.

Swetnam is not known to have written anything else. His importance lies not so much in his works as in the controversy sparked by *The Araignment.*

Sylvester, Joshua (1563–1618) *poet, translator*

Joshua Sylvester was born in Kent, England, to Robert Sylvester, a well-to-do merchant. At 10 he was sent to study at a school in Southampton, where he likely learned French. His principal means of support as an adult was as a merchant.

Among the 16th-century poets writing sonnets, Sylvester wrote in a clearer style than many, something that can be observed in the following lines from "Love's Omnipresence" (1580):

> *Were I as base as is the lowly plain,*
> *And you, my Love, as high as heaven above,*
> *Yet should the thoughts of me, your humble*
>   *swain,*
> *Ascend to heaven in honor of my love.*

Here he compares himself to a plain and his lover to heaven, a very vivid and clear simile as opposed to the more complex metaphors of writers like William SHAKESPEARE.

Sylvester is best known for his translation of the French Protestant poet Guillaume du Bartas's *Divine Weeks* (1578–1603), an unfinished biblical epic that was intended to narrate the history of the world from the Creation to Judgment Day. *Divine Weeks* was very popular in early 17th-century England and influenced poets such as John MILTON, who wrote the greatest biblical epic in the English language, *Paradise Lost.*

Sylvester was, at least in part, responsible for du Bartas's popularity. Du Bartas's habit of creating words, using unusual compounds, and doubling the first syllable of existing words was distasteful to readers of the original French poem. Sylvester avoided these pitfalls as much as possible and refined du Bartas's language. His description of Eve's temptation, for example, is a model of clarity:

> *[Eve spoke to the serpent], "O know*
> *What e'er thou be (but thy kind care doth*
> *   show*
> *A gentle friend) that all the fruits and*
> *   flowers*
> *In this earth's heaven are in our hands and*
> *   powers*
> *Except alone that goodly fruit divine,*
> *Which in the midst of this green ground*
> *   doth shine;*
> *But all-good God (alas, I wot [know] not*
> *   why)*
> *Forbade us touch that tree on pain to die."*
> *She ceased: already brooding in her heart*
> *A curious wish that will her weal*
> *   [happiness] subvert.*

Sylvester is noteworthy for his simple, readable style in an era given to very complex wordings in poetry. He is a notable translator as well as an important sonnet-writer in the years following Thomas WYATT and Henry Howard, Earl of SURREY.

Tasso, Torquato (1544–1595) *poet, dramatist, critic*

Torquato Tasso was born at Sorrento, near Naples, Italy, to Bernardo Tasso, a nobleman and a writer, and Porzia de Rossi Tasso. He was educated at the court of the dukes of Urbino and later at the Universities of Bologna and Padua, where he studied philosophy and law. By the age of 18 he had composed a narrative poem set in the age of chivalry, *Rinaldo,* which made him famous. He found employment in the service of Cardinal Luigi d'Este in Ferrara and then as resident poet at the court of the cardinal's brother, Duke Alfonso II d'Este. He wrote a pastoral drama, *Aminta* (1573); some theoretical prose works about poetry; and his masterwork, the epic poem *Gerusalemme Liberata* (*Jerusalem liberated, or delivered*), the first version of which was completed in 1575.

Like Ludovico ARIOSTO's *Orlando Furioso, Gerusalemme Liberata* is set in the time of the Crusades. Its hero is the leader of the First Crusade, Godfrey of Boulogne, who goes under the name of Goffredo in Tasso's poem, and its focus is the capture of the holy city of Jerusalem from the Muslims by Christian forces. Ariosto was very highly regarded in Tasso's time, and Tasso seems to have reacted against Ariosto's example in writing his epic. His early writings on poetry criticize

Ariosto for the multiplicity of plots in his great work; in *Gerusalemme Liberata,* Tasso focuses closely on Goffredo's struggles to overcome in war and to win the love of his lady, Armida, by being the perfect Christian knight. Ariosto included a great variety of moods and styles in his work, but Tasso maintains in his a high level of seriousness and a constant awareness of religious experience and Christian doctrines.

In Tasso's time the Catholic Church was losing influence in many parts of Europe as Protestantism took hold. In reaction to this, the church was more sensitive than ever to threats to its authority and to suggestions of heresy. Tasso submitted his poem to church authorities for their approval and was asked to make significant changes. The task of revision proved extremely difficult and affected his life at court. By 1579 his emotional turmoil had become so severe that the duke had him committed to an insane asylum, where he spent seven years.

Tasso wrote several critical works during his confinement, and he was able to receive visitors, among them the French essayist Michel de MONTAIGNE. While he was there an unauthorized version of *Gerusalemme Liberata* was published by some of his friends. After his release from the asylum in 1586, Tasso lived for a time at Mantua under the protection of the Gonzagas, the city's ruling family, but he moved on hoping to find a better situation at another court. In these last years he finished a tragedy, *Il Re Torrismondo* (*King Torrismondo*), which he had begun years before, and wrote a poem about the creation, *Il Mondo Creato.* He also revised his epic; after six years it became *Gerusalemme Conquistata* (*Jerusalem Conquered*), which critics agree is an inferior work, but which was more acceptable to the religious authorities at the time. Tasso died in a monastery in Rome, where he had gone to be crowned poet laureate.

Edward FAIRFAX's English translation of *Jerusalem Delivered* was published in 1594, and it strongly influenced many English poets, especially Edmund SPENSER and John MILTON, who used Tasso's epic as a model for their own.

Other Works by Torquato Tasso

Aminta. In *Three Renaissance Pastorals: Tasso, Guarini, Daniel.* Edited by Elizabeth Story Donno. Binghamton, N.Y.: Medieval & Renaissance Texts & Studies, 1993.

Jerusalem Delivered: Gerusalemme Liberata. Translated by Anthony M. Esolen. Baltimore, Md.: Johns Hopkins University Press, 2000.

Works about Torquato Tasso

Fichter, Andrew. *Poets Historical: Dynastic Epic in the Renaissance.* New Haven, Conn.: Yale University Press, 1982.

Finucci, Valeria, ed. *Renaissance Transactions: Ariosto and Tasso.* Durham, N.C.: Duke University Press, 1999.

Kates, Judith A. *Tasso and Milton: The Problem of Christian Epic.* Lewisburg, Pa.: Bucknell University Press, 1984.

Rhu, Lawrence F. *The Genesis of Tasso's Narrative Poetry: English Translations of the Early Poetics and a Comparative Study of Their Significance.* Detroit, Mich.: Wayne State University Press, 1993.

Tate, Nahum (1652–1715) *poet, dramatist, translator, librettist*

Nahum Tate was born in Dublin to Faithful Teate, a clergyman. He graduated from Trinity College in 1672 and five years later published *Poems* (1677), his first volume of poetry.

Tate's credits included 102 poems and nine plays, many of which are translations or adaptations of other dramatists' works. *Poems* (1677) contains a number of verses about melancholy or depression. His first play, *Brutus of Alba,* is a historical drama about the mythical founder of Britain.

His adaptation of Shakespeare's *King Lear* (1681) was both celebrated and vilified for its alteration of the original plot, giving the tragedy a happy ending. Tate's version was preferred to Shakespeare's for the next 150 years.

In 1692 Tate became England's poet laureate, the official court poet. As laureate Tate wrote a number of official, occasional works, that is, verse that celebrated birthdays and anniversaries. His best known poem was "Panacea: A Poem upon Tea" (1700), which is a light verse praising tea: "'Tis Tea sustains, Tea only can inspire / The Poet's Flame, that feeds the Hero's Fire."

Many of Tate's contemporaries viewed his writing as undistinguished, unoriginal, and unbelievably dull. Alexander Pope perpetuated Tate's reputation in the *Dunciad* (1728, 1743). Modern scholars also see Tate's poetry as lackluster.

Despite these critical attacks, Tate secured an enduring place in music history because his verses lent themselves wonderfully well to being set to music. His most celebrated work was the libretto for Henry Purcell's opera *Dido and Aeneas* (1689), a tragic love story based on an episode from Virgil's *Aeneid.* With Nicholas Brady he produced *A New Version of the Psalms of David* (1696), a setting of the biblical psalms to music. Modern hymnals contain many of these texts, including Psalm 42 ("As Pants the Hart for Cooling Streams," arr. G. F. Handel), "Christ the Lord Is Risen Today," and Tate's beloved Christmas text, "While Shepherds Watched Their Flocks by Night."

Taylor, Edward (1642–1729) *theologian, poet*

Edward Taylor was born into a farming family in rural England. He received his early education in

England and for a time worked as a teacher. However, as Donald E. Stanford, who edited an edition of Taylor's poetry, points out, his Puritan convictions ultimately made it impossible for him to obtain the license needed to "preach, teach, or attend the universities of Cambridge or Oxford." In 1688 he sailed to New England, where, at the age of 29, he entered Harvard College. Thereafter he served as a minister in Westfield, Connecticut (now Massachusetts), married twice, and had 14 children.

Taylor wrote thousands of lines of poetry, only a few of which were published during his lifetime. It was not until the 1930s, when a manuscript containing almost 400 pages of verse was discovered, that the minister's significance to American literature became clear. The scholar Samuel Eliot Morison notes that in poems like "Huswifery," Taylor drew "similes from the humble occupations" of "spinning and weaving" as a way of imaginatively exploring the relationship between God and man.

Taylor's most sophisticated poems are contained in a collection entitled *Preparatory Meditations*. He used these poetic meditations (at least 217 of which have survived) to prepare his heart and soul for the sacred act of administering the Lord's Supper. These devotional poems provide insight into the way the early American literary imagination emerged out of the Puritans' theological beliefs and practices. The scholar Norman Grabo notes that the recovery of Taylor's poetry challenged the earlier tendency to "ignore the artistic side of colonial literature for its more attractive intellectual sister" and revealed the "influence of a vital emotional tradition on the thought and expression of American Puritans."

Other Work by Edward Taylor

The Poems of Edward Taylor. Edited by Donald E. Stanford. New Haven, Conn.: Yale University Press, 1960.

Works about Edward Taylor

Grabo, Norman. "The Veiled Vision: The Role of Aesthetics in Early American Intellectual History." *The William and Mary Quarterly.* 19 (1962): 493–510.

Morison, Samuel Eliot. *The Intellectual Life of Colonial New England.* New York: New York University Press, 1956.

Pearce, Roy Harvey. *The Continuity of American Poetry.* Princeton, N.J.: Princeton University Press, 1961.

Taylor, Jeremy (1613–1667) *nonfiction writer, theologian*

Jeremy Taylor was born in Cambridge, England, the son of Nathaniel Taylor, a barber, and Mary Taylor. He entered Caius College, Cambridge University, on a scholarship for poor youths and was ordained a priest at the age of 20. In 1634 the young cleric's sermons at St. Paul's Cathedral so impressed the archbishop of Canterbury, William Laud, that Taylor's rapid advance as a churchman was all but assured.

Taylor served as chaplain to the Stuart king Charles I, whose right to rule was vigorously opposed by antimonarchists; the Puritans eventually toppled the monarchy and established a Commonwealth government in which behavior was rigidly regulated. Taylor was imprisoned several times during these years and went to Ireland in 1658 to minister to the Anglicans (members of the CHURCH OF ENGLAND) there. During these difficult years, he penned several important theological works, including *The Rule and Exercises of Holy Living* (1650) and *The Rule and Exercises of Holy Dying* (1651), written to enhance the spiritual and devotional life of the believer. Both works are comprised primarily of prayers for particular occasions or for particular persons. For example, here is a prayer for parents to say with regard to their children: "Bless my children with healthful bodies, with good understandings, with the graces and gifts of thy Spirit, with sweet dispositions and holy habits; and sanctify them throughout in their bodies, and souls, and spirits, and keep them unblamable to the coming of the Lord Jesus."

Thus, Taylor's theological writings are more pastoral than intellectual; their author prefers to make his points by warmth and sensitivity than by cold logic or appeals to reason alone. The following prayer for the sick, from the BOOK OF COMMON PRAYER, was written by Taylor and gives a clear sense of the sensitivity of his nature:

> O God, whose days are without end, and whose mercies cannot be numbered; Make us, we beseech thee, deeply sensible of the shortness and uncertainty of human life; and let thy Holy Spirit lead us in holiness and righteousness all our days: that, when we shall have served thee in our generation, we may be gathered unto our fathers, having the testimony of a good conscience; in the communion of the . . . Church; in the confidence of a certain faith; in the comfort of a reasonable, religious, and holy hope; in favour with thee our God, and in perfect charity with the world. All which we ask through Jesus Christ our Lord.

Taylor also wrote a secular book, *A Discourse of the Nature, Offices and Measures of Friendship* (1657).

Works about Jeremy Taylor

Askew, Reginald. *Muskets and Altars: Jeremy Taylor and the Last of the Anglicans.* Herndon, Va.: Mowbray, 1997.
Carroll, Thomas K. *Wisdom and Wasteland: Jeremy Taylor in His Prose and Preaching Today.* Dublin: Four Courts, 2000.

Taylor, John (1580–1653) poet, nonfiction writer

John Taylor was a humorous poet and traveler who dubbed himself the "*Water-Poet*," since he was able to maintain a career as a poet and as a member of the waterman's guild, an organization of boat operators who transported passengers across the River Thames. Before being apprenticed as a waterman, he received a grammar school education and served in the English navy.

Taylor wrote numerous pamphlets that chronicled his travels, supporting himself by selling subscriptions to his pamphlets. His *The Pennyles Pilgrimage* (1618) was an account of his travels through Scotland with no money. In this work, Taylor proves to be an excellent observer of Scottish customs and dress. Here is an excerpt which is often cited in discussions of Scottish clothing of the era:

> Their habite is shooes with but one sole apiece; stockings (which they call short hose) made of a warm stuffe of diverse colours, which they call Tartane: as for breeches, many of them, nor their forefathers, never wore any, but a jerkin of the same stuffe that their hose is of, their garters being bands or wreathes of hay or straw, with a plead about their shoulders, which is a mantle of divers colours, much finer and lighter stuffe then their hose, with blue flat caps on their heads, a handkerchiefe knit with two knots about their necke; and thus are they attired.

Taylor is generally regarded as a minor English poet; however, he holds an important place in the social literary history of his time because of his use of satire as a way of observing and humorously criticizing human behavior. In his poem *The Arrant Thief*, for example, Taylor boasts tongue-in-cheek about England's many thieves, including Robin Hood who,

> *with little John agreed*
> *To rob the rich men, and the poore to feede.*
> *The Priests had here such small meanes for*
> *   their liuing,*
> *That many of them were enforc'd to*
> *   Thieuing.*
> *Once the fift Henry could rob ex'lent well,*
> *When he was Prince of Wales, as Stories tell.*
> *Then Fryer Tucke, a tall stout Thiefe*
> *   indeed,*
> *Could better rob and steale, then preach or*
> *   read.*

Most of Taylor's works are compiled in *All the Workes of John Taylor the Water-poet* (1630).

A Work about John Taylor

Capp, Bernard. *The World of John Taylor the Water-Poet.* Oxford, U.K.: Clarendon Press, 1994.

Tell-Troth, Thomas

See SWETNAM, JOSEPH.

Temple, William (1628–1699) *nonfiction writer*

William Temple was born in London to Sir John Temple, Master of the Rolls in Ireland. He was educated at Cambridge University but left without a degree. In 1655 he was married to Dorothy Osborne, whose collected love letters to him constitute an important historical document, as they were kept from marrying for seven years because Osborne's father was on the side of the king during the English Revolution and Civil Wars and Temple's on the side of Parliament.

Temple was a noted English statesman who was made a baronet in 1666. His accomplishments include serving as British ambassador to The Hague in the Netherlands and negotiating the historic marriage between William of Orange and Princess Mary of England, later William III and Mary II of England.

In 1681 Temple retired to his estate in Surrey and spent the next several years writing political works and essays. As a writer Temple is best remembered for his essay *Of Ancient and Modern Learning* (1690), which began the "ancient versus moderns" controversy, in which writers debated the relative merits of contemporary and ancient culture. Temple preferred the ancients. In discussing prose, for example, he praises Aesop as "the greatest Master in his kind" and notes that "all others of that Sort have been but Imitations of his Original" and the letters of Phalaris, which he says "have more Spirit, more Force of Wit and Genius than any others I have ever seen, either Ancient or Modern." This comment evoked commentary by a number of writers including Richard BENTLEY and William WOTTON, and Bentley asserted that Phalaris's letters were neither worthy of praise nor authentic. This assertion led to a number of counterattacks and led eventually to the publication of Jonathan Swift's *Battle of the Books,* in which Swift, who was at the time working for Temple, attacked Bentley. *Battle of the Books* is a mock-heroic poem in which the actual books themselves take up arms and hurl insults at one another. Bentley, however, was eventually proved correct in his belief that the letters were inauthentic.

Thimelby, Gertrude

See ASTON, GERTRUDE.

Thimelby, Katherine (Katherine Thimelby Aston) (ca. 1616–1658) *poet*

Katherine Thimelby was one of 14 children born to Richard and Mary Brookesby Thimelby of a prominent Catholic family in Irnham, Lincolnshire, England. Her best friend and future sister-in-law, Constance Aston FOWLER, facilitated the courtship between Thimelby and Herbert Aston, Constance's brother. After their marriage in 1638, Herbert and Katherine lived at Bellamour, an estate named by Aston for his wife. Katherine Thimelby Aston died after giving birth to her 10th child.

The Aston family regularly exchanged letters and poetry, and Thimelby's skill as a poet ensured her acceptance into her new family. Three of her poems appear in Constance Aston's handwritten collection of verses. In "A discourse of A dream," probably written before Thimelby's marriage in 1638, the poet regrets that the pleasure found in dreaming is false, especially compared to the "poverty" of real life. In the closing lines of the poem, she wishes that either she never knew the joys of dreaming or she did not know the "extremes" between dreams and reality: "Then let me wake, or ever have such dreams / And not by contradiction know th' extremes."

In a more lighthearted poem, also written before 1638, Thimelby replies to her friend Lady

Dorothy Shirley, who has accused her of being sad. As in the previous excerpt, she writes in iambic pentameter and rhyming couplets. "Madam you say I am sad I answer no / unless it be because you say I am so." The tone of the poem reflects the intimacy of female friendship and the informal role of poetry as a means of communication in the Aston-Thimelby circle.

Thimelby, Winefrid (Winefred Thimelby, Winifred Thimelby) (1618–1690) letter writer

Winefrid Thimelby was the 13th of 14 children born to Richard and Mary Brookesby Thimelby of Irnham, Lincolnshire, England. A member of a prominent Catholic family, she became a nun at the age of 16 and served as the abbess of St. Monica's Convent in Louvain, Belgium, for 23 years. Thimelby's sister-in-law Gertrude ASTON joined her at the convent after the death of Aston's husband (and Winefrid's brother), Henry Thimelby. Two nieces, daughters of Katherine THIMELBY and Herbert Aston, also took vows at Louvain.

Thimelby's correspondence survives in *Tixall Letters, or the Correspondence of the Aston Family, and their Friends, during the Seventeenth Century,* a two-volume set compiled by the scholar Arthur Clifford in 1815. Although she left her family as a teenager, Thimelby's letters reveal that they were never far from her thoughts. Furthermore, she did not allow her religious vocation to cut her off from the secular world. She wrote to her brother-in-law Herbert Aston, "Do not suppose me a well-mortified nun, dead to the world, for, alas! it is not so; I am alive, and as nearly concerned for those I love, as if I had never left them, and must share in all their fortunes, whether good or bad." Thimelby's love of life and her strong religious convictions come through in a letter to her sister Katherine: "I am one of the happiest persons living, though still, methinks, I should be happier dying." She also corresponded actively with her sister-in-law Constance ASTON.

Thornton, Alice (1627–1706) nonfiction writer

Alice Wandesford Thornton, the daughter of Sir Christopher Wandesford, married William Thornton in 1651. The couple had nine children, but six died before reaching adulthood. Thornton's husband died in the 1660s, and she survived him by many years.

Thornton was a member of a Royalist family, or family loyal to the king during the English Revolution and Civil Wars (1642–49), a period that culminated in the execution of King Charles I in 1649. During the Interregnum, or period between kings, Oliver Cromwell was lord protector of England from 1649 to his death in 1658, when he was succeeded by his son Richard. At this time the government regarded Royalists as enemies. The monarchy was restored with Charles II's accession to the throne in 1660.

Thornton wrote three volumes of an autobiography that she entitled *Book of Remembrances,* the first complete edition of which was not published until 2004. It covers the years of her life from 1629 to 1660. This autobiography provides excellent insights into what life was like for a woman in 17th-century England. The most compelling parts of the autobiography describe in graphic detail Thornton's pregnancies and childbirths—and highlight her deep religious faith. For example, she talks of traveling while pregnant and having to climb hills and walk on rough paths. After one trip she fell extremely ill:

> But truly, I found my heart still did cleave to my Maker that I never found myself more desirous of a change to be delivered from this wicked world and body of sin and death, desiring to be dissolved and to be with Christ. Therefore endured I all the rigors and extremity of my sickness with such a share of patience as my God gave me.

Thornton experienced a great deal of pain in her life, giving birth to nine children, six of whom died young, five within two years of their birth. As

Thornton says of the human condition, "We are so frail of nature that none can assure themselves health or life one day." Remarkably, Thornton survived all of her deliveries and outlived her husband, leaving behind a rich chronicle of her life.

A Work about Alice Thornton

Rose, Mary Beth. *Women in the Middle Ages and the Renaissance: Literary and Historical Perspectives.* Syracuse, N.Y.: Syracuse University Press, 1986.

Tillotson, John (1630–1694) *nonfiction writer*

John Tillotson was born to a Puritan clothier, Robert, and his wife, Mary Dobson, in Sowerby, Yorkshire, England. In 1647 he entered Cambridge University, graduating three years later. In 1661 Tillotson took holy orders and in the same year was present at the Savoy Conference, at which 12 CHURCH OF ENGLAND bishops and 12 Puritan ministers unsuccessfully attempted to revise the BOOK OF COMMON PRAYER so that both factions could use it. During the conference Tillotson represented the Presbyterian sect, but when the Act of Uniformity was passed in 1662 declaring the unrevised *Book of Common Prayer* the only legal book from which services could be conducted, Tillotson accepted that decision. In matters of religion, Tillotson was a latitudinarian, that is, one who believed in allowing individuals to practice whatever faith they chose.

By the mid-1660s Tillotson was revered as a preacher. In fact, he was the most popular preacher of the 1660s. His sermons attacked the frivolity he detected at the court of Charles II as well as atheism and Catholicism. In 1689 Tillotson was made Clerk of the Closet to the newly crowned king William III and his wife Mary II, and he was influential in persuading the monarchs to establish a commission to find a way to reconcile members of the Church of England with Dissenters, or those who did not adhere to the state religion. In 1691 Tillotson was appointed, somewhat reluctantly, archbishop of Canterbury. He served in this posi-

tion in a period of great religious turmoil among members of the Church of England, Dissenters, and a minority of Catholics. In his commonplace book Tillotson remarks upon the constant attacks that were leveled on him from all sides,

> It is surely an uneasy thing to sit always in a frame of mind and to be perpetually upon a man's guard; not to be able to speak a careless word, or to use a negligent posture, without observation and censure. Men are apt to think that they, who are in highest places, and the most power, have most liberty to say and do what they please. But it is quite otherwise; for they have the least liberty, because they are most observed.

Tillotson's sermons were collected and published after his death and were extraordinarily popular for a time. The poet John DRYDEN remarked that his own prose style was formed by his reading of Tillotson, and for many years Tillotson's sermons were considered models for all preachers. One of his sermons, "The Reasonableness of a Resurrection," provides an example of both his thought, which is clearly influenced by the Enlightenment preference for logic and reason over emotion, and his style, which is clear and simple. Tillotson begins, simply, "The resurrection of the dead is one of the great articles of the Christian faith; and yet so it hath happened that this great article of our religion hath been made one of the chief objections against it." He goes on to say, humorously, that there are some people who even feel that the more unbelievable an idea is, the "fitter [it is] to be believed." He adds that such absurdity may perhaps be an article of Catholic faith, but he expects a more reasonable approach from himself and his listeners. "I hope, by God's assistance, to make the possibility of the thing so plain as to leave no considerable scruple about it in any free and unprejudiced mind." In his argument Tillotson cites a question posed by St. Paul, "Why should it be thought a thing incredible . . . with you that God should raise the dead?" and he goes on to say that since God is the "author of nature" and more powerful than nature, it is not "incredible to natural reason" that God should be able to raise the dead.

Tillotson is certainly in keeping with the thought of his time in suggesting that human reason is the basis for religious faith. At the same time, however, he also invokes divine revelation to support his argument. "For as reason tells us it is not impossible, so the word of God hath assured us that it is certain." He ends his sermon by discussing the "practical inferences" one can make from the doctrine of the resurrection. "The first [is] for our support and comfort under the infirmities and miseries of this mortal life [and] the second [is] for the encouragement of obedience and a good life." This strategy, too, is typical of Tillotson's sermons, in that he takes a concept that seems mystical and brings it down to a level of practicality that his listeners can use in their own lives.

Toland, John (1670–1722) *nonfiction writer, poet*

John Toland was born in Londonderry, Ireland, and was rumored to be the illegitimate child of a Catholic priest. At 16 Toland rejected Catholicism and embraced Protestantism. He went to Scotland in 1687, receiving his master's degree from the University of Edinburgh three years later. From there he went to Holland to study at the University of Leiden. By 1693 he had moved to Oxford to work on an Irish language dictionary.

Toland's first and most famous work, *Christianity Not Mysterious* (1696), attempted to explain the principles of Christianity using reason. Whereas the Catholic Church asked its members to accept a great many implausibilities on faith, such as a virgin birth and resurrection from the dead, Toland attempts to rid Christianity of the mysteries of faith and explain its foundations in rational principles. As he explains in the conclusion, "Thus I have endeavour'd to shew others, what I'm fully convinc'd of my self, that there is no *MYSTERY* in *CHRISTIANITY,* or the most perfect *Religion;* and that by Consequence nothing *contradictory* or *inconceiv-*

able, however made an *Article of Faith,* can be contain'd in the *Gospel,* if it really be the Word of God."

Toland's deism, or rational exploration of Christian mystery, earned him both admirers and detractors. In his native Ireland his work was banned, and in England legal proceedings were brought against him. Toland went on to become a major writer for the Whig Party, an English political party that supported a strong Parliament and a weaker monarch, producing a wide range of works, including *Amyntor, or a Defence of Milton's Life* (1699), a biography of the Whig hero John MILTON. Toland also traveled a great deal, coming into contact with many of the major thinkers of the time, such as Gottfried Wilhelm Leibniz and Pierre Bayle.

Although Toland published dozens of works, his reputation rests on *Christianity Not Mysterious.* The editors of a modern edition call it "a scintillating deconstruction of mystery in religion and a stylish paean to reason."

Other Work by John Toland

Nazarenus. Edited by Justin Champion. Oxford, U.K.: Voltaire Foundation, 1999.

A Work about John Toland

Sullivan, Robert E. *John Toland and the Deist Controversy: A Study in Adaptations.* Cambridge, Mass.: Harvard University Press, 1982.

Tourneur, Cyril (ca. 1575–1626) *dramatist, poet*

Very little is known of Cyril Tourneur's life. A record of payment indicates that he spent time in the Netherlands in the service of the English government. He is known to have accompanied Sir Edward Cecil in 1626 on a failed raid against the Spanish fleet at Cadiz. As Cecil's fleet limped home after the defeat, several sick members of the expedition were set ashore at Kinsale, Ireland. Tourneur was among them, and he died there.

Tourneur's surviving works are few. His poems—a verse satire, *The Transformed Metamor-*

phosis (1600); *A Funeral Poem* on Sir Francis Vere, 1609; and an elegy on the death of JAMES I's much-admired eldest son, Prince Henry—are not distinguished. Tourneur's fame rests on his two plays: *The Revenger's Tragedy* (1607) and *The Atheist's Tragedy* (1611). Both belong to the tradition of revenge tragedy, which extends back to Thomas KYD's *Spanish Tragedy* (1586) and includes John WEBSTER's *White Devil* (1612) and William SHAKESPEARE's *Hamlet* (1601).

The Revenger's Tragedy, which is advertised on its title page as having been acted by the KING'S MEN (Shakespeare's company), is set at a corrupt Italian court. Its central character, Vindice (his name derives from the Italian word for revenge), is plotting how to get even with the Duke for having poisoned Vindice's beloved. With the encouragement of his brother and confidant, Hippolito, Vindice disguises himself and enters the service of the Duke's son, Lussurioso (the name, Italian for "luxurious," implies that its owner is a heartless playboy). The disguise permits Vindice to uncover hitherto unsuspected vileness everywhere, even in his own mother. The play's centerpiece is the grisly scene in which Vindice, who has managed to secure the skull of the Duke's dead mistress, covers it with poisoned makeup, attaches it to a body so that it looks alive, and sets the scene so that the Duke kisses it—only to fall dead. In the final moments of the play, the members of the Duke's family who are not directly killed by Vindice and Hippolito fall in a round robin of murder; Vindice himself is executed by the Duke's virtuous successor. In spite of the implausibility of the plot, the play's intense language and black humor have appealed to modern audiences as much as they did to the Jacobeans.

The Revenger's Tragedy was published anonymously; it was not attributed to Tourneur until later in the 17th century. In the 20th century some have questioned the attribution, and some argue, from internal evidence, that the play is the work of Thomas MIDDLETON.

The Atheist's Tragedy, on the other hand, was published in Tourneur's name. The central charac-

ter, D'Amville, is more thoroughly villainous than Vindice, since he is not given any clear motive for his malevolence. He introduces himself thus at the start of the play:

> *Let all men lose, so I increase my gain:*
> *I have no feeling of another's pain.*
> *(I.i.128–129)*

Through most of the play, D'Amville asserts and reasserts his conviction that there is no higher power than Nature, no good greater than material possessions, power, and sensual pleasure—the pursuit of which last leads him to attempt the rape of Castabella, his own daughter-in-law. But after he has murdered the guiltless Montferrers, he begins to be troubled by the dead man's ghost, and after the violent deaths of his own two sons, he has no recourse but suicide. He dies with these words:

> *. . . Nature is a fool. There is a power*
> *Above her that hath overthrown the pride*
> *Of all my projects and posterity . . .*
> *. . . yond power that struck me knew*
> *The judgment I deserv'd, and gave it. O,*
> *The lust of death commits a rape upon me,*
> *As I would ha' done on Castabella.*
> *(V.ii.257–268)*

A line from *The Revenger's Tragedy* is applicable to both Tourneur's plays: "When the bad bleed, then is the tragedy good." Still, it is not the bombast of his plots that distinguishes Tourneur; as C. E. Vaughan comments in *The Cambridge History of English and American Literature,* (1907–21) "It is as poet that Tourneur claims our attention: a poet whose imagination is poisoned by the sense of universal vanity and corruption, but who lights up this festering material with flashes of high genius."

A Work about Cyril Tourneur

White, Martin. *Middleton and Tourneur.* New York: St. Martin's Press, 1992.

Townshend, Aurelian (ca. 1583–ca. 1643)
poet, dramatist

Aurelian Townshend was probably born in West Dereham, Norfolk, England, the son of John and Anne Carlin Townshend. Little is known of his personal life, and there are long periods during which he seems to have vanished from public view.

In 1632 Townshend wrote *Albions Triumph,* a full-length masque intended for performance in the court of King Charles I. A masque is an allegorical play in which the parts are played by actors wearing masks. The famous architect Inigo Jones planned and designed the set for *Albions Triumph.* The prefix *albus* is Latin for "white," and *Albions Triumph* is set in Albipolis, the capital of the mythical kingdom of Albion (a poetic name for England), ruled by King Albanactus and Queen Alba (also the name for its protective goddess), "whose native Beauties have a great affinity with all Purity and Whitenesse."

Townshend intended his poetry to be set to music, and there are surviving arrangements for some of his poems by composers such as Henry Lawes and William Webb. The poet typically wrote in regular meter and used familiar stanzaic forms, as in "Victorious beauty, though your eyes / Are able to subdue an hoste, / And therefore are unlike to boast / The taking of a little prize, / Do not a single heart despise." Some of his songs exploited the wordplay and pastoral imagery popular in his day, such as "Thou Shepheard, whose intentive eye / On ev'ry Lamb is such a spy, / No wily Fox can make them lesse, / Where may I find my Shepheardess."

Other Work by Aurelian Townshend

The poems and masques of Aurelian Townshend, with music by Henry Lawes and William Webb. Edited by Cedric C. Brown. Reading, Berkshire, U.K.: Whiteknights Press, 1983.

Traherne, Thomas (1637–1674) *poet, nonfiction writer*

Thomas Traherne was born in Hereford, near the Welsh border of England, the son of a shoemaker.

After his parents' early death, he and his younger brother Philip were adopted by a wealthy relative who owned a tavern. Traherne went to Oxford University and was ordained an Anglican clergyman in 1660. He never married.

During Traherne's lifetime he published only one book, *Roman Forgeries* (1673), a polemical attack on Roman Catholicism that has little appeal today and less resemblance to the work for which he is now most known. In 1675, the year after his death, Traherne's *Christian Ethics* was published. This work is a description in verse of ethical Christian behavior. Traherne, for example, advises his readers:

> To act on obligations yet unknown,
> To act upon rewards as yet unshown,
> To keep commands whose beauty's yet
>   unseen,
> To cherish and retain a zeal between
> Sleeping and waking . . .

His brother, Philip Traherne, appears to have edited his poetry in preparation for publication, but the work was not completed. Indeed, most of Traherne's poetry and much of his prose remained unknown until 1896, when two of his manuscripts were found at a London bookstall. *Poetical Works* appeared in 1903, and *Centuries of Meditations,* a prose work, in 1908. A manuscript found in the British Museum was published in 1910 as Traherne's *Poems of Felicity.* Other manuscripts have been discovered but remain unpublished.

Centuries of Meditations appears to have been written as a comfort and devotional aid for Traherne's friend Susanna Hopton. It contains hints about Traherne's life and about a spiritual crisis he seems to have passed through while at Oxford:

> [I]n a lowering and sad evening, being alone in the field, when all things were dead and quiet, a certain want and horror fell upon me, beyond imagination. The unprofitableness and silence of the place dissatisfied me; its wideness terrified me; from the utmost ends of the earth

fears surrounded me. . . . I was a weak and little child, and had forgotten there was a man alive in the earth.

From this state of terror Traherne was able to reach an extraordinary degree of confidence in his relationship to God and the world. In *Centuries* he shares his process of discovery. There is little in his work about sin, nothing about God's anger. Rather, a famous passage reflects Traherne's characteristic theme of finding God's presence in everyday reality:

You never enjoy the world aright, till the Sea itself floweth in your veins, till you are clothed with the heavens, and crowned with the stars. . . . Till you can sing and rejoice and delight in God, as misers do in gold, and kings in sceptres, you never enjoy the world. Till your spirit filleth the whole world, and the stars are your jewels: till you are as familiar with the ways of God in all ages as with your walk and table: till you are intimately acquainted with that shady nothing out of which the world was made: till you love men so as to desire their happiness with a thirst equal to the zeal of your own: till you delight in God for being good to all: you never enjoy the world.

The richness of nature and its availability to everyone is a central theme in Traherne's poetry as well as in *Centuries*. In one of the *Poems of Felicity* entitled "The World" he writes:

For so when first I in the summer-fields
Saw golden corn
The earth adorn . . .
No rubies could more take mine eye;
Nor pearls of price . . .
More costly seem to me,
How rich so e'er they be
By men esteem'd.

Another characteristic theme of Traherne's is the rightness of the perceptions of childhood.

Traherne remembered how hard his elders had had to work to get him to understand the value of material possessions. In adulthood, as part of his spiritual work in relation to God, he felt that he had to unlearn that teaching, for as a child he had been right in the first place. His celebration of childhood, unprecedented in an age when religious writers tended to see children as the living proof of original sin, is exemplified in his poem "Wonder":

How like an angel came I down! . . .
A native health and innocence
Within my bones did grow,
And while my God did all his glories show,
I felt a vigour in my sense
That was all spirit . . .
I nothing but the world did know
But t'was Divine.

Other Work by Thomas Traherne
Select Meditations. Edited by Janet Smith. Manchester, U.K.: Carcanet Press, 1997.

Works about Thomas Traherne
Allchin, A. M., and Julia Smith. *Profitable Wonders: Aspects of Thomas Traherne.* Harrisburg, Pa.: Morehouse Publishers, 1989.
Day, Malcolm. *Thomas Traherne.* Boston: Twayne, 1982.
Dowell, Graham. *Enjoying the World: The Rediscovery of Thomas Traherne.* Harrisburg, Pa.: Morehouse Publishers, 1990.

Trapnel, Anna (ca. 1622–ca. 1680)
nonfiction writer
Anne Trapnel was born near London to shipwright William Trapnel. Very little is known about her early life other than the religious development she discusses in her work. She claimed that she experienced religious trances from an early age and that her mother prayed for her to receive the gift of prophecy.

While in her 20s Trapnel became active in a radical religious group called the Fifth Monarchists. During and following the English Civil War, a conflict between the king and Parliament over religious and political differences, many radical groups flourished that demanded freedom of religion and criticized the government. The Fifth Monarchists encouraged the fall of Oliver Cromwell, who ruled England for most of the period between the monarchies of Charles I and Charles II. The group also worked to establish the coming reign of Christ, which they believed to be imminent.

Trapnel came to public recognition in early 1654 during the trial of one of her fellow Fifth Monarchists. Falling into a trance that lasted 12 days, she uttered political and religious prophecies. Many flocked to her bedside to witness her words, which were then transcribed and published in two versions. *Strange and Wonderful Newes from Whitehall* (1654) was a short prose pamphlet account, and *The Cry of a Stone* (1654) was a longer work, consisting of a prose narrative as well as songs and verse. In an era when women were still commonly discouraged from speaking out in public, Trapnel adopted a passive position by speaking from a trance in which she was a vessel for the more "authoritative" voice of God.

In both works Trapnel uses biblical references to criticize the political state of England. Comparing Cromwell to Gideon, an Old Testament ruler, she attacks the failings of his government:

> And then oh Gideon, who art in the highest place, thou art not onely to do justice thy self, but thou art to see justice done in all Places, Courts, or councels, and Committees, that they may not feed upon the Poor. Thou art not onely to receive pleasures at home, but to establish Righteousness abroad.

In this passage Trapnel commands Cromwell's government to improve the treatment of the poor and to reform the injustices she sees in the courts.

Trapnel was later imprisoned for her outspokenness. As the critic Katherine Gillespie comments, this controversial and fascinating woman "sets forth a significant mid-seventeenth-century dynamic whereby dissenting women created alternative norms of femininity and piety."

A Work about Anna Trapnel

Hinds, Hillary. *God's Englishwoman: Seventeenth Century Radical Sectarian Writing and Feminist Criticism.* New York: Manchester University Press, 1996.

Tudor, Elizabeth
See ELIZABETH I.

Turberville, George (ca. 1540–ca. 1610)
poet, translator, nonfiction writer

George Turberville was born in Dorset, England, to Nicholas Turberville, a gentleman. He entered Oxford University in 1554 but left without taking a degree. In 1562 he began studying law in London, where he gained a reputation as a poet.

In 1567 Turberville published two books of translations—*The Heroical Epistles of Ovid* and *Eclogues of Mantuan,* both translations of ancient poetry—and one book of original poems—*Epitaphs, Epigrams, Songs and Sonnets.* On a trip to Russia the same year Turberville sent letters written in verse to friends, but few survive. He published a famous book on falconry (the art of training falcons), *The Book of Falconry or Hawking* (1575), and, 12 years later, another book of translations, *Tragical Tales* (1587), which are verse translations of the Italian writers Giovanni BOCCACCIO and Matteo Bandello.

Turberville often writes a singsong verse, that is, verse in which the rhythm remains very regular to the point of monotony. Such poetry was popular in the mid-16th century. In "Of a Fox that Would Eat no Grapes," from *Epitaphs, Epigrams, Songs, and Sonnets,* Turberville tells the story of a fox who spies a bunch of grapes hanging from a vine:

> *The fox would none because that he*
> *Perceived the highness of the tree.*

So men that foxly are
And long their lust to have
But cannot come thereby,
Make wise they would not crave.

Here the simplicity and regularity of the meter fits well with the simple subject and moral of the poem.

Turberville was recognized for his smooth, simple poetic style. Sir John Harington in his "In Commendation of George Turberville" writes, "When times were yet but rude, thy pen endeavored / To polish barbarism with purer style." Recently scholars have come to recognize the importance of Turberville's translations. Turberville, the critic Deborah S. Greenhut observes, brought "Ovid's *Heroides,* appropriately adapted, to the ear of the Tudor audience"—that is, he translated Ovid, the ancient Roman poet, so that English readers could read him as a contemporary.

Turner, Jane (fl. 1640–1660) nonfiction writer

The actual birthplace and birth date of Jane Turner are unknown, and she published only one work, a spiritual autobiography entitled *Choice Experiences of the Kind Dealings of God before, in, and after Conversion* (1653). The discourse traces her religious journey, beginning with her experiences in the Anglican and Presbyterian churches, to her short stint as a Quaker, and finally to her becoming a Baptist.

Choice Experiences contains numerous introductory prefaces, including one by Turner's husband, John, who had encouraged the book's publication. These "dedicatory epistles" praise her book as a legitimate and acceptable realization of feminine spirituality, the assumption being that the only acceptable written works by women were of the religious and spiritual variety. However, John Turner seems pleased by his wife's work for its originality, "having never seen anything written before in this method and manner."

Choice Experiences is actually one of many spiritual autobiographies written by women during the period. The books were seen as a legitimate channel through which women could publish their work.

Tusser, Thomas (ca. 1524–1580) poet

Thomas Tusser was born at Rivenhall, near Witham in Essex, England, to William and Isabella Tusser. As a boy he attended Eton College, where he studied under the playwright and schoolmaster Nicholas Udall. He then went to Cambridge University until sickness compelled him to leave. Eventually he settled on a farm in Suffolk.

In 1557 Tusser composed his *Hundreth good pointes of husbandrie,* which, by 1573, he had expanded to *Five hundreth pointes of good husbandry.* This work is a collection of maxims in rhymed couplets on farming, weather lore, forestry, agriculture, thrift, virtue, religion, and life in general. He is credited with writing famous proverbs including "Sweet April showers do spring May flowers" and "A rolling stone gathers no moss."

The scholars Emile Legouis and Louis Cazamian write, "Tusser's collection of practical counsels are completely prosaic, yet have some go and wit, and they are written in popular four-accented lines which seem to move at a gallop."

Tyler, Margaret (fl. 1578) translator

Margaret Tyler translated *The Mirror of Princely Deeds and Knighthood,* a romance by Diego Ortúñez de Calahorra, from Spanish to English in 1578. This is no small accomplishment: Prose romance was the most popular form of fiction in mid-16th-century Britain, and *The Mirror* is the first Spanish romance to be translated directly into English. This particular work proved popular enough to undergo two more editions before 1600.

Tyler, however, did more than simply translate an existing text. Her dedicatory letter stands on its own as an early document arguing for the rights of women to publish secular material. Identifying herself as both a woman and, as a servant to Lord Thomas Howard, a member of the upper class,

Tyler not only defends her own choice to translate the romance, she also contends that if men are allowed to write for a female audience, there is no reason why women should be forbidden from writing themselves. If women read men's works, they also deserve the opportunity to "wade in [ideas] to the search of a truth."

"[M]y persuasion has been thus: that it is all one for a woman to pen a story as for a man to address his story to a woman." Tyler thus deftly incorporates the common arguments that women should not write into her defense. In approaching her subject delicately, Tyler differs in rhetorical technique from other RENAISSANCE polemicists such as Jane ANGER who in *Her Protection for Women* (1589) employs more straightforward and direct criticism in her defense of the rights of women.

Tyndale, William (ca. 1494–1536)
translator, nonfiction writer

Born to a prosperous family, Tyndale completed his M.A. at Oxford University in 1515, was ordained, and taught at Cambridge, among humanists whose study of classic texts influenced him deeply. Fluent in seven languages, Tyndale wanted to translate the Bible into English. Although he died before he could complete the task, "no other Englishman—" argues biographer David Daniell, "not even Shakespeare—has reached so many" speakers of English.

In 1521, while tutoring for a merchant's family in Gloucestershire, Tyndale decided that Christians must be able to read the Bible in their own language. The Bible had already been translated into English, under the guidance of William Wyclif, but the 1408 Constitution of Oxford made it illegal to read an English Bible or to translate without church approval. Tyndale petitioned Bishop Tunstall of London for permission to translate. Tunstall, alarmed by the uproar surrounding Martin LUTHER's German Bible, advised against the project. Disappointed, Tyndale left England in 1524.

In Europe Tyndale lived, says Daniell, "a hand-to-mouth existence, dodging the Roman Catholic

authorities" who wanted to try him for heresy. In 1525 his New Testament, with a pastoral prologue, was being printed in Cologne when a priest bribed the printer's assistants to sabotage the print run and had the printer's work declared illegal. Tyndale fled to Worms, Germany, to complete the first printing. By 1526 about 18,000 copies of this New Testament had reached England, where Bishop Tunstall gave orders to have every copy seized and burned with "a ruthlessness that seems close to hysteria," reports Daniell. Only a dozen copies survive today.

Before his translation was burned, Tyndale had been quite mild in the defense of his work. After the burning of his New Testament, however, Tyndale published angry pamphlets attacking the church and its metaphorical interpretations of scripture. A literal reading of the Scriptures, Tyndale argued, should guide Christians' daily lives, and Tyndale's translations depended not on the Latin Vulgate, as had Wyclif's, but on original Greek texts. Tyndale alone, among native speakers of English, could read *all* the original Greek and Hebrew texts, as well as the Latin and German translations, and was uniquely qualified to translate them.

Tunstall next tried new ways to rein Tyndale in, offering him an important religious post in England. When Tyndale refused, Tunstall sent agents to Europe to force him back to England for trial. Tyndale worked in hiding in Antwerp, protected by the English Merchant Adventurers company.

In 1529 Tunstall instructed Sir Thomas MORE, then Henry VIII's chancellor, to study Tyndale's translations and expose their heresies. The two scholars argued in writing over the translations—for instance, debating whether a particular Greek word was best rendered as "priest" or "elder." This was no simple matter of taste but, rather, had ramifications for church structure and the roles of clergy. More, like Tyndale, was critical of the clergy but set aside his criticism to condemn Tyndale's use of "elder" for some church roles and "priest" for others. Tyndale explained his choices, which modern understanding of Greek supports. Daniell writes, "More was not listening. . . . He was objecting to the translation, but even more to the translator—a Lutheran, a heretic, incapable of right." More, on most subjects a brilliant thinker, feared heresy greatly; his attacks on Tyndale demonstrate the grave stakes of the matter.

In 1530 Tyndale's translation of Genesis was published. He continued to work at a furious pace, fearing betrayal and arrest. In 1534 Tyndale published his Pentateuch and a revised New Testament, his masterpiece. Working with translator Miles COVERDALE, he made over 4,000 changes to phrasing, and added cross-references and explanatory glosses.

On May 25, 1535, Tyndale was arrested near Brussels; he had been betrayed by an English spy, Henry Phillips. For 16 months priests tested Tyndale's beliefs. The English Merchants, Thomas Cromwell, and King Henry VIII himself petitioned authorities in Brussels for Tyndale's release, to no avail. Underfed, cold, and ill, Tyndale still wanted to work, requesting "a Hebrew Bible, a Hebrew grammar, and a Hebrew dictionary so that I might pass the time in study."

Tyndale was convicted of heresy in August 1536 and executed on October 6. Only months later, Henry VIII decreed that the English would have their own translation of the Bible.

Tyndale's ability to capture the cadence of Hebrew poetry and the clarity of classical Greek and render them in English was remarkable. He coined words for concepts once foreign to English, such as "peacemaker" and "scapegoat." His style is "swift, economical, clear, precise," Daniell writes. The biographer John Day agrees: Tyndale's translations "have shaped the religious language, and even the very phrasing of religious thought" for more than 400 years. Translators after Tyndale often copied chapters and even books of his translations, without acknowledgement. About 80 percent of the 1611 BIBLE, KING JAMES VERSION, which scholars place alongside Shakespeare's works for its impact on English prose, is Tyndale's translation.

Daniell calls Tyndale's New Testament the "first classic prose" of the English language, the work that moved Latin out of its preeminent position in an English-speaking nation. Tyndale "showed what the language could do. There is a direct line from Tyndale to the lucidity, suppleness and expressive range of the greatest English prose that followed: English, that is, rather than Latinised prose."

A Work by William Tyndale

New Testament. Translated from the Greek by William Tyndale in 1534. Edited and introduced by David Daniell. New Haven, Conn.: Yale University Press, 1989.

A Work about William Tyndale

Daniell, David. *William Tyndale: A Biography.* New Haven, Conn.: Yale University Press, 1994.

U

Udall, Nicholas (Nicholas Uvedale)
(1505–1556) *translator, playwright*

Nicholas Udall was born in Hampshire, England, and educated at Westminster School and Oxford University. He went on to teach Latin at Eton College, where he served as headmaster from about 1534 until 1541.

Udall published several translations and commentaries for the benefit of his students. In 1542 he published a translation of the third and fourth books of *Apophthegmes,* written by the Dutch humanist Desiderius ERASMUS, and from 1542 to 1545 he was engaged in the translation of Erasmus's *Paraphrase of the New Testament.*

Udall's most famous work is the play *Ralph Roister Doister,* which was written specifically for schoolboys to perform and is an adaptation of Latin comic plays. It is best categorized as a farce, a type of dramatic comedy that entertains the audience with unlikely and extravagant situations, mistaken identities, and crude verbal humor. Although a farce may contain a moral message, its primary intent is to entertain.

The title character of *Ralph Roister Doister* is an arrogant soldier-hero who thinks every woman he sees falls in love with him and who is finally shown to be a coward. Ralph is accompanied by Merrygreek, a parasite—or stock comic freeloader—who flatters Ralph. The scholars Emile Legouis and Louis Cazamian say, "Udall may have had a moral purpose—he may have desired to satirise glory—but his chief aim was to cause innocent laughter."

University Wits

The University Wits were six playwrights, graduates of Oxford and Cambridge Universities, who transformed English drama in the 1580s. Before the work of these playwrights, English drama consisted largely of educational plays, allegories, religious stories, and chronicles of history. The scholar F. E. Halliday writes that the University Wits "were in revolt" against this supposedly obscure, dry writing. They discarded classical rules and abandoned Aristotle's unities of place, action, and time. Their innovations inspired the criticism of many well-educated Englishmen, such as the poet Sir Philip SIDNEY, who complained of the wild plots and dissimilar settings, with "Asia on the one side [of the stage] and Affrick [Africa] on the other." The public, however, raved about this new, exciting kind of drama.

The first of the Wits to succeed on the London scene was John LYLY, whose complicated prose style influenced other writers. Lyly also pioneered charming diction; haunting songs; and in his many plays, such as *Endymion* (1591) and *Sapho and Phao* (1584), skillfully constructed plots. Thomas LODGE wrote pamphlets; prose fiction; and two plays, *The Wounds of War* and *A Looking Glass for London and England* (1594). His most famous work, *Rosalynde,* is the source for William SHAKESPEARE's *As You Like It.*

Lodge sometimes collaborated with Robert GREENE, who was famous for calling Shakespeare "an upstart Crow" and plagiarist in one of his pamphlets. These words give historians their first hint of Shakespeare's presence in London as an actor in 1592. Greene's *Pandosto* (1588) is the source for Shakespeare's *The Winter's Tale.*

Thomas NASHE, dramatist and pamphleteer, is distinguished among the Wits for wordplay, first imitating Lyly's ornate prose but later inventing words, as Shakespeare would soon do. Nashe collaborated with Christopher MARLOWE on *Dido Queen of Carthage* (1594) and wrote parts of *The Isle of Dogs* (1597).

Another member of the group was George PEELE, who wrote not only pastoral plays but city pageants and courtly masques as well. His comic plays and satires were well received but now seem wildly plotted. *The Arraignment of Paris* (1584), a pastoral, is often considered Peele's best work.

Of the six playwrights, Christopher Marlowe was the most influential. The debut of *Tamburlaine* in 1587 was, according to Halliday, "perhaps the most momentous performance in the history of the English theatre, for rejecting both the buffoonery of the native drama and the pedantry of pseudo-classical plays, Marlowe made a synthesis of the best elements of both, the vigour and action of the one, the form and structure of the other."

Few of the Wits' plays have survived, since scripts were often discarded after a run of performances ended. But the extant plays and the letters between and about the men make it clear that their defiant break with dramatic tradition prepared the ground for Shakespeare's innovative genius. As Halliday puts it, the University Wits provided "the explosive material" that awaited Shakespeare's "divine spark" to fire RENAISSANCE England's stage.

Urquhart, Sir Thomas (1611–1660)
novelist, translator

The Scottish writer Thomas Urquhart was educated at King's College in Aberdeen and traveled extensively in Europe as a young man until forced to return to Scotland to help save Cromarty, the family estate, which his father was mismanaging. During the civil strife that racked the British Isles during this period, Urquhart was a Royalist, siding with the Stuart king Charles I. He was forced to flee to London, where he was knighted for his services to the king.

Besieged by financial woes and a staunch Royalist supporter during the English Civil War, Urquhart is nonetheless remembered for his 1652 prose romance, *The Jewel,* considered to be one of the earliest Scottish novels. Its hero is based on the story of a real-life figure known as The Admirable Crichton, who in 1914 inspired a well-known drama by another Scotsman, James M. Barrie. Urquhart is most renowned, however, for his critically acclaimed translation from French to English of François Rabelais' epic comic masterpiece *Gargantua and Pantagruel.* He completed Books I and II, which were published in 1653, and part of Book III, which was published in 1693, more than a decade after his death.

Urquhart also published a number of minor works, including *Epigrams Divine and Moral* (1641); *Trissotetras* (1645), a work on trigonometry; and an eccentric genealogy, *Pantochronocanon, or a Peculiar Promptuary of Time* (1652), in which he purported to trace his ancestry to Adam and Eve. In his 1653 book *Logopandecteision,* he argued in favor of a universal language. In a 1774 reprint of some of his works, Urquhart was described as "a man of great learning and merit."

Works about Thomas Urquhart
Boston, Richard. *The Admirable Urquhart: Selected Writings.* London: Gordon Fraser, 1975.

Jack, R. D. S., and R. J. Lyall, eds. *The Jewel: Sir Thomas Urquhart.* Edinburgh: Scottish Academic Press, 1983.

Ussher, James (1581–1656) *theologian, nonfiction writer*

James Ussher was born in Dublin, Ireland, the son of well-to-do Anglo-Irish parents, and educated at Trinity College, Dublin. He was ordained a priest in 1601 and taught at Trinity from 1607 to 1621. Even with his Anglican identity, Ussher was sympathetic to Calvinistic thinking (adherence to the work of John CALVIN), and he became a supporter of Puritan causes. He was consecrated bishop of Meath in 1621, and in 1625 he became archbishop of Armagh and primate of Ireland.

Ussher is best known for his biblical chronologies that fixed the date of primeval events such as the Creation (October 23, 4004 B.C.), and the expulsion of Adam and Eve from the Garden (November 10, 4004 B.C.). He determined these dates not from geological evidence but by extrapolating them from references found in scripture and other ancient writings. Though his system was unscientific by modern standards, it was widely accepted as fact in many Christian churches through the 19th century and is still revered by many contemporary creationists who believe in a literal interpretation of scripture. His chronology was published as *The Annals of the World* (1650–54), a comprehensive work he claimed to be "deduced from the origin of time," with sweeping references to the histories of the Old and New Testaments and "also all the most memorable affairs of Asia and Egypt, and the rise of the empire of the Roman Caesars . . . [and c]ollected from all history, as well sacred, as prophane, and methodically digested."

Though Ussher's biblical chronologies are discredited outside of fundamentalist religious circles, his commentaries on the letters of the first-century St. Ignatius of Antioch are more highly esteemed. By studying ancient manuscripts, he was able to authenticate the text of seven letters by Ignatius. Ussher also published numerous works aimed at establishing the authenticity of the Christian religion and its connections with the world of the early church fathers. Among them are *Apostolic Fathers: SS. Patrum, qui Temporibus Apostolicis Floruerunt* (published 1724); and *A Briefe Declaration of the Vniversalitie Of The Chvrch of Christ, and the Vnitie of the Catholic Faith Professed Therein,* a sermon delivered before King JAMES I in 1624. Bishop James Ussher died in Reigate, England, on March 21, 1656.

Vanbrugh, John (1664–1726) *dramatist*

John Vanbrugh was born in London to Elizabeth and Giles Vanbrugh, a cloth merchant. The family then moved to Chester. Vanbrugh belonged to London's illustrious Kit-Kat Club, whose members included John DRYDEN, William CONGREVE, and Joseph Addison.

Vanbrugh's first play, *The Relapse* (1696), appeared in response to Colley Cibber's *Love's Last Shift*. In Cibber's play the immoral Loveless is reformed after being seduced by his own disguised wife, Amanda. In Vanbrugh's play Loveless and Amanda return to the city, where Loveless succumbs to temptation and seduces Amanda's cousin.

The Provok'd Wife (1697), Vanbrugh's most famous play, centers around Constant, who woos the wife of the loutish and abusive Lord Brute, and Constant's friend Heartfree, who flirts with Lady Brute's cousin, Bellinda. As the play ends Heartfree and Belinda marry, and Lady Brute continues to resist adultery, although the play suggests she may succumb eventually.

Both Vanbrugh plays were denounced as lewd in clergyman Jeremy COLLIER's influential *A Short View of the Immorality and Profaneness of the English Stage.* Vanbrugh's witty plays clearly expose corrupt behavior, such as the mistreatment of women, rather than merely presenting these acts for amusement. In fact, as the critic Robert Markley suggests, these comedies "search for ways to reinvest comedy with moral seriousness."

Most of Vanbrugh's later plays were adaptations. His most successful production, *The Confederacy* (1705), was a revision of the French *Les Bourgeoisies à la Mode.* In *The Confederacy* two friends conspire to extort money from their stingy husbands, while a young man masquerades as a colonel to court a woman whose marriage portion (money a husband received from his bride's family) he plans to use to pay his debts.

Late in his life Vanbrugh largely abandoned playwriting for a career as an architect. Some of his more renowned designs were for Blenheim Palace and Castle Howard. In 1714 he was knighted by George I. His final unfinished play was reworked by Colley Cibber as *The Provok'd Husband* (1728) after Vanbrugh's death. Alexander Pope once said that no English writer had "a freer, easier way for comedy" than Vanbrugh. As tastes changed, however, Vanbrugh's works largely ceased to be performed. Lost in the shift toward sentimental theater was, as the biographer Kerry Downes states, "the gusto and the vigour of the comic theater, the readiness to experiment, and [the] sense of the absurd" that characterized Vanbrugh's work.

A Work about John Vanbrugh

Bull, John. *Vanbrugh and Farquhar*. New York: St. Martin's Press, 1998.

Van Dyck, Sir Anthony (1599–1641)
painter

Anthony Van Dyck was born in Antwerp (now in Belgium), the son of a successful textile merchant. He enrolled as an apprentice to the painter Hendrik Van Balen at age 10; later he was the assistant to, then collaborator with, Peter Paul RUBENS, who became a surrogate father to him. In 1620, already well known, he was summoned to England by King JAMES I. The portrait he painted of James is lost, but two great paintings survive from his five-month stay: a portrait of the Earl of Arundel and a history painting called *The Continence of Scipio*. Van Dyck spent six years in Italy after that first visit to England, and then returned to Antwerp, where he was much in demand.

In 1632 King Charles I invited him back to England, where he remained for the rest of his life, except for short trips. He was showered with honors and commissions, and was knighted by the king. His many portraits of Charles were part of the Royalist romanticism that was also promoted by the CAVALIER POETS. As the art historian E. H. Gombrich says in *The Story of Art*, regarding one of Van Dyck's portraits of Charles, Van Dyck

> showed the Stuart monarch as he would have wished to live in history: a figure of matchless elegance, of unquestioned authority and high culture, the patron of the arts, and the upholder of the divine right of kings, a man who needed no outward trappings of power to enhance his natural dignity.

Van Dyck worked constantly, producing two or three full-scale portraits a month. He employed assistants to do the backgrounds and drapery, a method that allowed him to complete portraits relatively quickly. He lived in great luxury and kept several mistresses. In 1639 he married Lady Mary Ruthven, who gave birth to their daughter Justiniana in December 1641, a week before Van Dyck's death.

Works about Anthony Van Dyck

Brown, Christopher, ed. *Van Dyck: 1599–1641*. New York: Rizzoli, 1999.
Moir, Alfred. *Anthony Van Dyck*. New York: Harry N. Abrams, 1994.

Vaughan, Henry (1621–1695) *poet*

Henry Vaughan was born in Llansanffraid, near Brecon, Wales. His Welsh identity was important to him, and he signed himself "the Silurist" after the ancient Celtic tribe that inhabited the region. He and his twin brother, Thomas VAUGHAN, were the oldest children of Thomas Vaughan, a minor landowner, and Denise Morgan Vaughan. The twins were tutored privately and probably went together to Oxford University in 1638. Henry Vaughan seems to have gone to London in 1640 to study law, but he was soon back in Breconshire as secretary to a judge. Later he found his profession in the study and practice of medicine.

In 1646 Vaughan published *Poems with the Tenth Satire of Juvenal Englished*, a small collection of secular lyrics that are imitative in their choice of subject matter—lightly treated love and revelry among friends—of Ben JONSON and the CAVALIER POETS. *Silex Scintillans* (*The Flashing Flint*), a collection of religious poems, followed in 1650. The title refers to the flinty hardness of the human heart, from which divine love strikes fire. In the preface to a second, expanded edition of *Silex Scintillans*, published in 1655, Vaughan acknowledges his indebtedness to George HERBERT, to whose poetry he says he owes his spiritual awakening. Vaughan learned from Herbert the art of the intense opening passage, as in "The Retreat" ("Happy those early days, when I / Shin'd in my Angel-Infancy!") and "The World" ("I saw Eternity the other night, / Like a great ring of pure and endless light").

Vaughan also had learned the METAPHYSICAL POETS' habit of developing an image into an argument. In "The Timber," for example, the poet addresses a piece of wood holding up a house. Even in death, he says, the timber remembers the terrors of the storms that threatened the living tree, and that is why the house creaks when foul weather approaches. The poet evokes the tree's life with lively sympathy:

> Sure thou didst flourish once! and many
>   springs,
> Many bright mornings, much dew, many
>   showers
> Pass'd o'er thy head; many light hearts and
>   wings,
> Which now are dead, lodg'd in thy living
>   bowers.

But the timber is not what the poem is about. It is rather an image for the life of a person who has left the vanities of the world behind:

> He that hath left life's vain joys and vain
>   care,
> And truly hates to be detain'd on earth,
> Hath got an house where many mansions
>   are,
> And keeps his soul unto eternal mirth.

This person has become "dead unto the world" and yet still can be affected by "grief and old wounds":

> But though thus dead unto the world, and
>   ceas'd
> From sin, he walks a narrow, private way;
> Yet grief and old wounds make him sore
>   displeas'd
> And all his life a rainy, weeping day.

The argument develops that the pain the former sinner feels at these times and the tears he sheds are actually foreshadowings of the life-giving waters that flow in heaven after death.

In 1651 Vaughan published a collection of secular poetry and translations, *Olor Iscanus*. Named for the Usk River, which flowed by Vaughan's home, the book contains celebrations of the beauty of nature and friendship. Most of the poems were composed before those in *Silex Scintillans*. A few more collections followed, among them *Thalia rediviva* (1678; the Latin title translates as *Thalia Revived*—in Greek mythology, Thalia was the muse of comedy and pastoral poetry), which includes poems by Thomas Vaughan. None matches the poems in *Silex Scintillans*.

Critics have commented on the unevenness of Vaughan's poetry. The scholar Roger Sell remarks that Vaughan's general competence as a poet does not explain the "power to disconcert" found in his best work: "What lifts him to a more remarkable kind of writing is frankly a matter of psychic input. This varies, giving his best texts, whether poems of hope or poems of grief, a live, unplanned . . . flavour, which is actually reminiscent of informal communication."

Other Work by Henry Vaughan
Henry Vaughan: The Complete Poems. Edited by Alan Rudrum. New Haven, Conn.: Yale University Press, 1981.

Works about Henry Vaughan
Clements, Arthur L. *Poetry of Contemplation: John Donne, George Herbert, Henry Vaughan, and the Modern Period*. Albany: State University of New York Press, 1990.
Davies, Stevie. *Henry Vaughan*. Chester Springs, Pa.: Dufour Editions, 1996.
Rudrum, Alan, ed. *Essential Articles for the Study of Henry Vaughan*. Hamden, Conn.: Archon Books, 1987.

Vaughan, Thomas (1621–1666) *nonfiction writer, poet*
Thomas Vaughan, the twin brother of the poet Henry VAUGHAN, was born in Llansanffraid, near Brecon, Wales, to Thomas and Denise Morgan Vaughan, a wealthy and noble couple. He entered Oxford University in 1638 and received a B.A. degree in 1642. He eventually took up the study

of alchemy and published a number of tracts under his own name and the pseudonym Eugenius Philalethes. These include *Magia Adamica: Or, the Antiquity of Music* (1650), *Lumen de Lumine* (1651), and *The Man-Mouse Taken in a Trap* (1650).

Alchemy was a medieval pseudo-science that attempted to turn lesser metals into gold and sought the secrets of eternal life and a cure for all diseases, just as modern science was coming into existence. The view of the universe that had assumed the existence of an immortal soul, which formed the basis of alchemical thought, was on the way out. Vaughan, however, was not an eccentric: Alchemy was still a respectable field of study in the mid-17th century, and even Isaac NEWTON practiced it. "To its adherents," scholar Donald R. Dickson observes, "alchemy offered insights into and a method of exploring the fundamental processes and relationships of the universe." Alchemy was much more complex than mere attempts to turn metals like lead into gold, and Vaughan mocked those who were only interested in the pursuit of riches. His alchemical experiments were in fact similar to the experiments any chemist might conduct into the composition of metals and other substances. He was also interested in the spiritual element of alchemy, the attempt to achieve spiritual wisdom through study. The scholar Arthur Edward Waite has remarked on the "spiritual" side of Vaughan's work.

Like his brother, Vaughan also wrote poetry. He included poems within his alchemical treatises as well as writing dedicatory poems for editions of works by William CARTWRIGHT and Thomas Powell. But it is for his treatises, rather than his poetry, that Vaughan is remembered today.

Other Works by Thomas Vaughan

Aqua Vitae, Non Vitis. Edited and translated by Donald R. Dickson. Tempe: Arizona Center for Medieval and Renaissance Studies, 2001.

The Works of Thomas Vaughan. Edited by Alan Rudrum and Jennifer Drake-Brockman. Oxford, U.K.: Clarendon Press, 1984.

Vaux, Thomas (Baron of Vaux of Harrowden, Lord Vaux) (1510–1556) *poet*

Thomas Vaux was born in Harrowden, England, to Nicholas and Anne Green Vaux. His father, a statesman and soldier, was created the first Baron of Vaux of Harrowden and took a seat in the House of Lords in 1523, the same year he died and left the title to his son Thomas. Vaux was deeply involved in England's political affairs. In 1527 he traveled to France on a diplomatic mission. Five years later he served as an ambassador to France, and in 1533 he took his seat in the House of Lords in Parliament.

Little is known about when and why Vaux began writing poetry; 18 of his poems appeared in collections that were printed after his death, and the dates of their compositions are unknown. "The Aged Lover Renounceth Love" and "When Cupid Scaled First the Fort" appeared anonymously in *Tottel's Miscellany* (1557), perhaps the most influential anthology of poems ever printed. Thirteen more poems were published in *Paradise of Dainty Devices* (1576).

In general, Vaux's poems treated either love matters or moral issues. His most famous poem is "The Aged Lover Renounceth Love." The poem is about how old age renders love insignificant. It begins:

> *I loathe that I did love,*
> *In youth that I thought sweet,*

This poem was later set to music and is misquoted by the gravedigger in William SHAKESPEARE's *Hamlet* (1601). Where the gravedigger sings, "For Age with his stealing steps / Hath clawed me in his clutch," Vaux's original lines read, "For Age with stealing steps / Hath clawed me with his crutch." George PUTTENHAM commended Vaux for "the facility of his meter, and the aptness of his descriptions."

A Work by Thomas Vaux

The Poems of Lord Vaux. Edited by Larry P. Vonalt. Denver: A. Swallow, 1960.

Villiers, George

See BUCKINGHAM, GEORGE VILLIERS, SECOND DUKE OF.

W

Waller, Edmund (1606–1687) *poet*

Edmund Waller was born to a prosperous, politically connected family. At the age of 10, he inherited the family fortune. He later attended Eton College and Cambridge University. In 1631 he married heiress Anne Banks, offending Charles I, who had other plans for Anne's future. Waller, a charming man, convinced Charles to forgive him and give him control of Anne's wealth. He may have offered the king, who was always in need of ready cash, a financial incentive to get back in the royal graces.

When Anne died five years later, Waller composed his first poems. He wrote three kinds of poetry: love lyrics (his "Go, Lovely Rose" is best known today); private compliments to friends; and panegyrics, that is, poems praising rulers. Waller did not publish his poems at this time but, as was the practice, circulated manuscripts among his well-connected friends. "Go, Lovely Rose" is a "carpe diem" poem, one in which the poet urges his lover to "seize the day," to remember that life is too short to be coy about love. In his poem, Waller tells the rose to visit his love and demonstrate to her that she should not hide her beauties or wait for love. The poem, which begins lightly, ends on a slightly darker note:

> Small is the worth
> Of beauty from the light retired:
> Bid her come forth,
> Suffer herself to be desired,
> And not blush so to be admired.
>
> Then die—that she
> The common fate of all things rare
> May read in thee;
> How small a part of time they share
> That are so wondrous sweet and fair!

Waller's love lyrics are called the *Sacharissa* poems, Sacharissa ("sweet") being his name for Lady Dorothy Sidney, the great-niece of Sir Philip SIDNEY. To court a lady in verse was common at this time, and Waller may not have intended a serious relationship with Lady Dorothy. Rather, she became his muse, or inspiration. As he writes in "The Story of Phoebus and Daphne, Applied":

> Yet what he sung in his immortal strain,
> Though unsuccessful, was not sung in vain;
> All, but the nymph that should redress his
>   wrong,
> Attend his passion, and approve his song.

Thus, he says, even if the beloved does not appreciate the poetry, she inspires him to write, perhaps to public acclaim.

During the English Revolution and Civil Wars (1642–49), Waller, a member of Parliament, became involved in a plot to remove certain other members, called Roundheads, who were opposed to the monarchy. The plot was discovered, and Waller was brought before Parliament. He managed to escape death by selling his estates to pay bribes and was exiled, thus saving his life at the expense of his honor. The irony was that Waller had tried to steer a middle course in the conflict and not take sides, yet he became identified with the Royalist plot.

In exile in France, Waller began to publish his works, grudgingly, for he preferred the genteel practice of handing one's poems around among one's friends. Now, however, he needed to raise cash, so he surrendered his poetry to printers. In the end, getting his panegyrics into publication restored Waller's standing in England.

Waller lived fairly well in Paris with his second wife and their children. He traveled in Italy and Switzerland, biding his time until 1651, when the House of Commons revoked his sentence. Back in England, he wrote panegyrics praising Oliver Cromwell, England's lord protector and his distant relative. After Cromwell's death and the RESTORA-TION, Waller wrote *To the King, upon His Majesties happy return*, a panegyric for Charles II. In the poem Waller compares Charles with the sun bursting forth from the clouds:

> Your worth,
> Your youth, and all the splendour of your
>   state,
> (Wrapped up, till now, in clouds of adverse
>   fate!)
> With such a flood of light invade our eyes,
> And our spread hearts with so great joy
>   surprise,
> That if your grace incline that we should
>   live,
> You must not, sir! too hastily forgive.

Waller's conversational skills, gentlemanly behavior, and wit pleased Charles's court, and Waller was once again in favor with the royals.

Waller served again in Parliament, even into his 70s, mentoring younger members and urging religious tolerance and moderation. After his second wife's death in 1677, he retired from society. Collections of his poetry continued to be published, and he wrote panegyrics to James II and pious poetry until his death.

Admired by his contemporaries for his "even, sweet, and flowing" poetry, Waller lost ground quickly among the next generation of readers, who wanted something other than urbane, cool poetry. Still, Waller is considered one of the most important minor poets of the 17th century.

Wallis, John (1616–1703) *nonfiction writer*

John Wallis was born in Kent, England, the son of the Reverend John Wallis and his second wife, Joanna Wallis. Educated in Latin, Greek, Hebrew, arithmetic, and logic at an early age, Wallis attended Cambridge University in 1632, receiving his B.A. in 1637 and his M.A. in 1640. He had early showed signs of mathematical talent. As W. W. Rouse Ball describes in his *A Short Account of the History of Mathematics,* "[W]hen fifteen years old, [Wallis] happened to see a book of arithmetic in the hands of his brother; struck with curiosity at the odd signs and symbols in it he borrowed the book, and in a fortnight, with his brother's help, had mastered the subject."

Soon after graduating from Cambridge, Wallis was able to demonstrate his natural mathematical talents by deciphering a number of cryptic messages from Royalist partisans that had fallen into the hands of the parliamentarians, whom Wallis supported. He was rewarded for his work during the war with the appointment, in 1649, of Savilian professor of geometry at Oxford University. He would continue to be a driving force in the development of mathematics until his death, publishing a number of groundbreaking works.

Wallis was clearly an outstanding theoretician, but one of his most amazing abilities was doing mental calculations. Unable to sleep one night, he calculated in his head the square root of a 53-digit number. How he was able to accomplish this feat was so remarkable that it became the subject of a paper for England's Royal Society, which Wallis had helped to found (in 1685).

Wallis published *Arithmetica Infinitorum*, often considered his most important work, in 1655. The construction of the book was influenced by the research of the Italian physicist Evangelista Torricelli. In this work, Wallis develops the laws of quadrature (the process of constructing a square equal in area to any surface) by devising a method to include negative and fractional exponents. This procedure was instrumental in developing an entirely new approach to geometry by way of algebra. The work propelled Wallis to great fame as a leading English mathematician.

Isaac NEWTON, for example, stated that his own work on the binomial theorem and calculus stemmed from a thorough study of *Arithmetica Infinitorum* during his university years at Cambridge.

Wallis and the philosopher Thomas HOBBES carried on a 20-year-long argument over Hobbes's claim to have found a way to square a circle. Their dispute included some pointed barbs from one to the other. About Wallis, Hobbes wrote, "Of those who with me have written something about these matters, either I alone am mad, or I alone am not mad. No third option can be maintained, unless (as perchance it may seem to some) we are all mad." Wallis answered, "If he is mad, he is not likely to be convinced by reason; on the other hand, if [I am mad, I am] . . . in no position to attempt . . . [to convince him]."

In addition to his mathematical works, Wallis wrote on theology, logic, and philosophy, and he invented the first system for teaching deaf-mutes. He also contributed to the history of mathematics by translating ancient Greek works on science and mathematics by Ptolemy, Aristarchus, and Archimedes.

Walsh, William (1663–1709) *poet, nonfiction writer*

William Walsh, son of Joseph Walsh, was born in Worcestershire and at 15 entered Oxford University. He left college, however, before receiving his degree, choosing instead to pursue his studies at home.

Walsh's early works include *A Dialogue Concerning Women, Being a Defence of the Sex Written to Eugenia* (1691), for which John DRYDEN wrote the preface. This is an attack on an anonymous writer "Whose Mouth is fill'd with Fist instead of Sence." A year later he brought out *Letters and Poems, Amorous and Gallant* (1692), a collection of love poems.

The Golden Age Restored appeared in 1703 with the subtitle "An Imitation of the Fourth Eclogue of Virgil." An eclogue is a poem set in the country in which shepherds converse. Virgil's poem has a prophetic tone, and his topic is a little boy who will bring peace and harmony to the land. Walsh's poem is a similar prediction for England with political overtones:

> Now all our factions, all our fears shall
>   cease,
> And tories rule the promis'd land in peace.
> Malice shall die, and noxious poisons fail

Two years later Walsh wrote *Imitation of Horace* (1705), yet another poem with political overtones in which Walsh wishes for England the strength and security of Rome in its Golden Age:

> Yes, Britons, yes, with ardent zeal,
> I come, the wounded heart to heal,
> The wounded hand to bind:
> See tools of arbitrary sway,
> And priests, like locusts, scout away
> Before the western wind.
> Law shall again her force resume;
> Religion, clear'd from clouds of Rome,
> With brighter rays advance.
> The British fleet shall rule the deep,

The British youth as rous'd from sleep,
Strike terror into France.

That year also marked the beginning of Walsh's correspondence with Alexander Pope, who praised Walsh in his *Essay on Criticism* (1711). Walsh's last work was the posthumously published *Aesculapius, or the Hospital of Fools* (1714).

Walsh is perhaps best remembered today for the company he kept rather than his poetic merit. Samuel Johnson describes him as not so much a poet as "a man of fashion, and . . . ostentatiously splendid in his dress."

Walton, Izaak (1593–1683) *biographer, nonfiction writer*

Little is known of the early life of England's first literary biographer. Izaak Walton was born in Staffordshire, England, to Gervase Walton, an innkeeper who died when Walton was three. Walton's mother, Anne, remarried, and his stepfather became a town burgess. Walton had little formal education. Some time before 1618, he moved to London and lived with his sister Anne and her husband, Thomas Grinsell, a linen draper to whom he was apprenticed. In 1626 he married Rachel Floud, whose family was related to the family of Thomas CRANMER, archbishop of Canterbury. Walton's association with churchmen would shape his life in years to come. Indeed, through his business, his church positions, and his writing, he came to know many of the day's leading figures.

Walton prospered in his business and was active in his church, which is how he came to know John DONNE; he was in fact close enough to Donne to attend the poet at his deathbed in 1631. Walton's first literary work was a biography of Donne, written in 1640 to preface a collection of Donne's writing.

The year 1640 also saw the death of Walton's wife, Rachel. The couple had lost six of their seven children, and the seventh died shortly after Rachel. It was at about this time that Walton left London, retiring from commercial business to a farm. In 1646 he married Ann Ken; two children survived

from this union. The years of their marriage were productive for the businessman-turned-writer: In 1651 he published his first complete, freestanding biography, the *Life of Wotton* (Henry WOTTON); and in 1653 his enduring masterpiece, *The Compleat Angler,* first saw publication. In addition, Walton made extensive, careful revisions to his first literary endeavor, his biography of Donne, and published it as a whole in 1658.

In 1662 Walton lost his second wife. He moved to Winchester to serve as personal steward to his close friend George Morley. Living at some times in Winchester and at others with his daughter and son-in-law nearby, Walton continued to write biographies and to expand *The Compleat Angler,* which he revised for 23 years. The year 1665 saw the publication of his *Life of Hooker,* written at the request of Gilbert Sheldon. Thomas Hooker was a Puritan minister who founded what was to become the state of Connecticut. Hooker left England to escape trial for his nonconformist views by Bishop William Laud's High Commission. Sheldon wanted to rehabilitate Hooker's reputation and knew that Walton's sensitive approach to biography could achieve this goal.

Walton wrote two other biographies: *Life of Herbert* (1670) about the poet George HERBERT and *Life of Dr. Sanderson,* about Robert Sanderson, the bishop of Lincoln, completed when the author was 85 years old. This final biography was a labor of love for Walton, who had known Sanderson for 40 years.

Walton died in 1683, surrounded by his children, and is buried in Winchester Cathedral. In his will he left careful instructions for the disposal of his beloved library, having long thought that a person's library was, as biographer Sandra Naiman notes, "an index of his character." His own highly allusive writing attests to his wide reading.

Critical Analysis

Walton was most famous in his day for his *Lives,* the five biographies that were, after his death, published together. Though influenced by earlier biographies, especially those of Plutarch and the saints' lives in

John FOXE's *Book of Martyrs* (1523), Walton created a new kind of biography, a hybrid of the story of a life and the history of a time. The biographer P. G. Stanwood says that the biographer Walton is "an interpreter of what he knows and likes, a disseminator not so much of recorded affairs but of culture and belief." A conservative writer who supported the royals during the Civil Wars (though he took no active part), Walton wanted his biographies to serve as exemplars, models held up for readers to learn from and imitate. His *Lives* were cherished for a century after his death. William Wordsworth, in his sonnet praising the *Lives,* was moved to write these memorable lines:

> *There are no colours in the fairest sky*
> *So fair as these. The feather, whence the pen*
> *Was shaped that traced the lives of these*
> > *good men,*
> *Dropped from an Angel's wing.*

Despite the appreciation for Walton's *Lives,* his most enduring work is *The Compleat Angler, or, the Contemplative Man's Recreation. Being a Discourse of Rivers, Fishponds, Fish and Fishing not unworthy the Perusal of most Anglers.* This remarkable work, ostensibly a book about fishing, has comforted, educated, and charmed readers for four centuries and is said to be, in England, the most often reprinted work after the Bible and the BOOK OF COMMON PRAYER. Samuel Johnson named it among the books dearest to him, and allusions to it or uses of it occur in the novels, essays, and poems of several generations of English writers. Wordsworth wrote a sonnet on the flyleaf of his copy, beginning,

> *While flowing rivers yield a blameless sport,*
> *Shall live the name Walton: Sage*
> > *benign! . . .*
> *Meek, nobly versed in simple discipline—*
> *He found the longest summer day too*
> > *short . . .*

The Compleat Angler was published in its first form in 1653. By this date the monarchy had crumbled with the execution of Charles I, and his son Charles II had fled to France. The entire court was in exile, the Anglican clergy scattered, and Parliament alternately suspended or controlled by the Puritan government. In this time of loss and uncomfortable new ideas, *The Compleat Angler* soothed readers. P. G. Stanwood notes, "Walton is providing a general book of wisdom for hard times in the shape of a fishing manual."

The work is a mosaic of information and gentle entertainment, of witty sayings and cheering reminders. Walton justifies this approach early in the book:

> in writing of it I have made myself a recreation of a recreation; and that it might prove so to [the reader], and not read dull and tediously, I have in several places mixed, not any scurrility, but some innocent, harmless mirth.

In its final form, *The Compleat Angler* includes poems, songs (some with notation), quotes from authorities across centuries of time, weather chat, and recipes for cooking the day's catch. Instructions on where, when, and how to catch a certain fish jumble with complaints about fish-thieving otters and advice on being quiet. In fact, the book ends with a verse from the New Testament: "Study to be quiet."

The book is arranged as a conversation, primarily between Piscator (Latin for fisherman) and Venator (Latin for hunter). The two meet in the country and, as they are going the same way, walk along together. Venator argues that hunting is the nobler sport, and Piscator listens amiably to his points. Then Piscator, in a rambling conversation over several days, gradually convinces Venator that angling is nobler still. Some critics have wondered if Walton's use of the word *angling,* rather than *fishing,* is a sly reference to the Anglican church, and that Piscator's charming arguments support the reinstatement of the CHURCH OF ENGLAND in place of the Puritan church. Whether this meaning is implied or not, Piscator's inviting case for angling has surely driven many a reader to the nearest stream.

Piscator appeals to recent authorities, such as Michel de MONTAIGNE, and ancient authorities, such as the Old Testament, for praise of angling. He goes back further, in fact, to prove that the sport that takes place in the water is superior:

> The water is the eldest daughter of the creation, the element upon which the Spirit of God did first move, the element which God commanded to bring forth living creatures, abundantly. . . . Nay, the earth hath no fruitfulness without showers and dews.

Walton's overt purpose in *The Compleat Angler* is to convince Venator, and readers, that angling is an art, "and an art worth your learning. The question is rather, whether you be capable of learning it? for angling is somewhat like poetry, men are born to be so." All can learn something from angling, however, because it hones "an inquiring, searching, observing wit" and calls for "a large measure of hope and patience." Certainly wit, hope, and patience were required in a time of social upheaval, and this was Walton's covert message to dispossessed readers of his day.

Despite personal tragedies and uncertain times, Walton thrived during his long life, a friend to many who admired him and cherished his gifts of friendship and writing.

A Work about Izaak Walton

Stanwood, P. G. *Izaak Walton*. New York: Twayne, 1998.

Wanley, Nathaniel (1634–1680) *poet, nonfiction writer*

Nathaniel Wanley, the son of a merchant, was born at Leicester, England, and was educated at Trinity College, Cambridge, from which he graduated in 1653 and received a master of arts degree in 1657. In 1662 he replaced John Bryan as the vicar of the Holy Trinity Church at Coventry, a position that Wanley held until his death 18 years later. Wanley is best remembered (though much of this recog-

nition has only come within the last century) for his magnum opus, a folio entitled *The Wonders of the Little World, or a General History of Man* (1678), which is a collection of stories based on Wanley's extensive reading about odd people, primarily remembered for its great influence on poet Robert BROWNING. Here is an example of one of Wanley's anecdotes: "There have even been those who are allergic to pigs: A learned man told me . . . that he knew one in Antwerp, that would immediately swoon, as oft as a pig was set before him, upon any table where he was present." This was, however, a compilation that did not fully exemplify Wanley's literary abilities, as he explained in the preface that he was "not the Inventor, but the Reciter; not the Framer, but only the Collector."

While four of Wanley's poems appeared in *Seventeenth Century Poetry* (1835) and one, "The Invitation," was published in H. J. Massingham's *A Treasury of Seventeenth Century Poetry* (1919), the authorship of the poems was uncertain (often believed to have been written by Henry VAUGHAN, who indeed had a great influence on Wanley's poetry), and much of Wanley's poetry remained unseen until the scholar L. C. Martin's studies eventually led to the publication of 43 poems by Wanley in the 1920s. Among these poems are several lyric poems, primarily religious and moralistic in nature, including "Alphabet," "The Resurrection," "The Call," and "Sinne," two elegies ("Upon the Funerals of the Reverend Mr. John Angell Lecturer at Leicester" and "Upon the Funerals of Mrs. E.D."), and two narratives ("The Witch of Endor" and "Lazarus"). According to Martin, Wanley's poetic achievements are "far from negligible, and his work as a whole has . . . that transitional quality which gives a special historical value to much that was written in the second half of the seventeenth century."

Ward, Edward (Ned Ward) (1667–1731) *poet, nonfiction writer*

Edward Ward was born in Oxfordshire, England. Little is known about his early life except that he made a trip to the West Indies at some point during his youth. He returned to London in 1691 to become an innkeeper. Although Ward settled in London for much of the rest of his life, he continued to travel extensively and made these travels the center of several of his works. His first work, the 1698 *A Trip to Jamaica,* brought him some success. The book is an account of his journey to the island and not particularly complimentary. Ward insults the island itself, calling it, "As Sickly as a Hospital, as Dangerous as the Plague," and "as Hot as Hell." Despite his apparently unpleasant traveling experience in Jamaica, however, Ward wrote other travel books, including *A Trip to New England* (1699) and *A Trip to Germany* (1705).

Ward is known not only for his travel narratives but also for his other works of nonfiction and poetry. His writing is almost always witty and also at times bawdy. His most famous poem is *Hudibras Redivivus (Reborn)* (1705), a response to Samuel BUTLER's *Hubidras,* a satirical poem on Puritanism. In his preface he modestly acknowledges his source: "Tho' I have made bold, to borrow a Title from one of the best poems that ever was published in the English Tongue—yet I would not have the world expect me such a wizard as to conjure up the spirit of the inimitable Butler." In his version Ward attacks the Whigs and the queen, and he was later arrested for the sentiments he expressed. Of the Whigs he says:

> Thro' all their conscientious Cant
> A man of sense, with half an Eye,
> (Says he) may easily descry,
> What in reality they want;
> Which is, believe me, in a word,
> All that the Kingdom can afford.

Ward also put his wit to less controversial use in *The London Spy* (1698), an 18-part work full of descriptions of seamy London life. Throughout his life Ward devoted himself to any writing venture in which his wit and observational skills could earn him a living. He was overall a commercial writer and poet.

Ware, James (1594–1666) *editor*

James Ware, a Dublin antiquarian and historian, was responsible for the publication of Edmund SPENSER's treatise *A View of the Present State of Ireland,* which had been circulating in manuscript form since its completion in 1598 but did not appear in print until Ware included it in his collection of *Ancient Irish Chronicles* (1633). This pamphlet is in dialogue form, with "Irenius" speaking for Spenser, who supported England's oppressive rule over Ireland. He explains to his friend Eudoxus that the situation in Ireland is so bad that the only way to deal with it is "by the sworde; for all those evilles must first be cutt awaye with a stronge hande, before any good cann bee planted; like as the corrupt branches and unwholsome lawes are first to bee pruned, and the fowle mosse clensed or scraped awaye, before the tree cann bring forth any good fruicte." Thanks to Ware's publication, Spenser's political and social views on Ireland became widely known.

Ware did not hesitate to express his unhappiness with certain aspects of Spenser's text, commenting that "we may wish that in some passages it had bin tempered with more moderation." Andrew Hadfield and Willy Maley, who published a scholarly evaluation of Ware's work in 1997, declare that this edition is not an authorized version of Spenser's text, since Ware eliminated some of Spenser's "harsher judgments . . . in order to render the text of *A View* less offensive" Still, Ware's text is important in that it became the most widely known and influential edition of Spenser's work, one in which the spelling and punctuation were regularized.

Ware dedicated his edition to Sir Thomas Wentworth, the Earl of Stafford, who served as the Crown's deputy general in Ireland from 1633 to 1641 and was eventually impeached and executed for the harshness of his rule. In his introduction, Ware announces his intention of describing, through Spenser's words, the source of the "calamities" that had beset Ireland in "the former turbulent and tempestuous times."

Warner, William (ca. 1558–1609) poet, fiction writer

Little is known about the early years of William Warner, only that he was born in London, where he later worked as a lawyer and writer. His first known work is *Pan his Syrinx, or Pipe, compact of seven Reedes; including in one, seven Tragical and Comicall Arguments . . .* (1585; 1597). Warner explained that this title came from Ovid's legend of the nymph Syrinx who, pursued by the god Pan (half man, half goat), prayed to escape from him. She was turned into a "heap of reeds, which being stirred with a gentle blast, and *Pan* hearing them to yield a soft, melodious sound, with seven of the same reeds framed to himself the pipe after her name called *Syrinx*."

Each of Warner's reeds, or stories, is divided into chapters, and each story is related to the first.

Warner introduces the first story as follows: "*Sorares* and his company, in their sailing, are tempestuously driven into a sterile and harborless island; unto whom two forlorn and desolate men discover themselves." The second story tells that Sorares does not return, and so his sons, Atys and Abynados, set off to find him. Their adventures continue to the end of the book. As in BOCCACCIO's *Decameron*, the story of Sorares is a frame tale. The rest of the work is comprised of stories within the frame tale.

Albion's England. Or Historical Map of the same Island: prosecuted from the Lives and Acts and Labors of Saturne, Jupiter, Hercules, and Æneas . . . (1586) is Warner's most famous work. This is a partly mythical history of England in verse, which begins with Noah and extends through the Norman Conquest. A second edition updated the story to the time of Henry VII (1589), and the third edition included ELIZABETH I (1592). A final edition including the coronation of JAMES I OF ENGLAND (1609) appeared after Warner's death. Warner includes a number of fictitious episodes in his poem, the most famous of which is the story about the kings Edel and Adelbright, who shared a kingdom. As Adelbright dies, he asks Edel to protect his daughter and see to it that she inherits her father's kingdom when she is of age.

> But all that Edel understook, he afterward
>   denies.
> Yet well he fosters for a time the damsel,
>   that was grown
> The fairest lady under Heaven; whose
>   beauty being known,
> A many princes seek her love, but none
>   might her obtain
> For gripple ["grasping"] Edel to himself her
>   kingdom sought to gain,
> And for that cause from sight of such he did
>   his ward restrain.

Eventually Curan, the son of a Danish prince, sees the lovely Argentile and falls in love. He eventually kills Edel and weds Argentile.

Warner combines the decorative, euphuistic, style of John LYLY with Greek romance. His originality influenced some who followed him, such as Robert GREENE. His *Albion* was among the sources William SHAKESPEARE used for his great tragedy *King Lear*.

Watson, Thomas (1557–1592) poet, translator

Little is known about Thomas Watson's early life. He was born in London and studied at Oxford University, where he read Italian, English, and Greek literature and began writing Latin poetry. He translated the Greek tragedy *Antigone* by Sophocles into Latin and, in 1585, translated the Italian poet Torquato TASSO's pastoral drama *Aminta*.

Watson's best-known original work, *The Hecatompathia; or, Passionate Century of Love* (1582), is one of the earliest collections of sonnets in English. A sonnet is a 14-line poem that is usually divided into parts. The Petrarchan sonnet, named after the Italian RENAISSANCE poet Francis PETRARCH, is usually divided into two parts, one with eight lines, and one with six. The division in the lines indicates a change of some sort in the poem. Sometimes, for example, the poet may pose a question in the first lines and answer it in the second group. Most of Watson's poems are not strictly sonnets, however, because they have 18 lines rather than the traditional 14. Watson hoped that other poets would imitate his form, but this proved unfounded.

Hecatompathia comprises a sequence of sonnets about the sufferings of the poet, whose love is not returned. Sonnet V, for example, is a partial translation of Petrarch in which the lover laments:

> *If't be not love I feel, what is it then?*
> *If love it be, what kind a thing is love?*
> *If good, how chance he hurts so many men?*
> *If bad, how haps that none his hurts*
> * disprove?*
> *If willingly I burn, how chance I wail?*
> *If gainst my will, what sorrow will avail?*

Watson prefaces each poem with an introduction, sometimes naming his sources, which include Italian, French, and Latin works, and sometimes commenting on the work. In his introduction to Sonnet V, he says that all the lines but two are taken from Petrarch. He introduces his second sonnet with an explanation of the poem, "In this passion the Author describeth in how piteous a case the heart of a lover is, being (as he feigneth here) separated from his own body, and removed into a darksome and solitary wilderness of woes." The poem begins with the same paradox:

> *My heart is set him down twixt hope and*
> * fears*
> *Upon the stony bank of high desire,*
> *Two view his own made flood of blubbering*
> * tears*
> *Whose waves are bitter salt, and hot as fire:*

In 1593 Watson's collection of 60 sonnets, *The Tears of Fancie, or Love Disdained,* was published posthumously. These poems follow the sonnet form more closely in that they have 14 lines. Sonnet II begins with the poet saying that he does not want to fall in love:

> *Long time I fought, and fiercely waged*
> * warre,*

> *Against the God of amarous Desire*
> * [Cupid]:*
> *Who sets the senses mongst themselves at*
> * jarre,*
> *The harts inflaming with his lustful fire.*

Indeed, in this sonnet, he triumphs over Cupid. When he shoots his arrow, the poet says, "backe againe the idle shaft rebounded." But by Sonnet VII he is in love and by Sonnet VIII he is lamenting, "O what a life is it that Lovers joy, / Wherein both paine and pleasure shrouded is."

In his day Watson was regarded as the best among those who wrote in Latin, and his work was admired by no less a poet than Edmund SPENSER, who upon Watson's untimely death at the age of 35 wrote, "Amyntas quite is gone and lies full low / Having his Amaryllis left to moan." Watson was among the first to imitate Petrarch in English and as such certainly inspired William SHAKESPEARE's sonnets and his poem *Venus and Adonis.*

Weamys, Anna (Anne Weamys) (fl. 1651)
prose writer

Much of what is known about Anna Weamys is speculative, gathered from the front matter of her only known work, *A Continuation of Sir Philip Sidney's Arcadia* (1651), where the author's name appears as "Mistress A. W." Her father, Dr. Weamys, was probably a doctor of divinity in the CHURCH OF ENGLAND. Weamys was therefore probably part of an educated, but not aristocratic, family.

Weamys's *Continuation* is the second piece of original prose romance by an Englishwoman which continues Philip SIDNEY's *Arcadia* (1590). The first, Lady Mary WROTH's *The Countess of Montgomery's Urania* (1621), does not appear to have influenced Weamys; rather, her inspiration appears to come from Sidney's original. Her text blends the genres of the romance—a long, episodic, fictional story of heroes and extraordinary events—and the pastoral, a literary work that portrays country life in an idealized manner. The complicated plot and dizzying number of characters continue some of Sidney's narrative threads, but Weamys simplifies, rewrites, and omits some aspects of the original, emphasizing the love elements in the romance form. The prose typically consists of long, elliptical sentences: "Despise not Claius his complaints though he be afflicted with the infirmities of old age; youthful Strephon may seem more real and pleasing to the eye, yet Claius's heart, I am confident, is the firmest settled; youth is wavering, age is constant; youth admires novelties, age antiquities."

Sidney's *Arcadia* ends mid-sentence. In writing her *Continuation,* Anna Weamys participates in a lively literary tradition of her day, open to both men and women, of writing "answers" to Sidney.

Webster, John (ca. 1580–ca. 1634)
playwright

John Webster was born in London to John Webster, a wealthy coachmaker, and Elizabeth Coates Webster. He was educated in law at the Middle Temple, beginning in 1598. His knowledge of the law was to be important in his work because most of his best plays include a trial scene or display intimate legal knowledge.

Webster began his career writing comedies in collaboration with others. He and Thomas DEKKER wrote *Westward Ho!* (1604), a comedy that satirized the merchant class. The play was successful enough to motivate a rival company to write a play called *Eastward Ho!*. This sort of direct competition between companies was common, and Webster and Dekker promptly satirized the prodigal-son plot of *Eastward Ho!* in the witty *Northward Ho!* (1605).

Webster also wrote an introductory scene for a tragedy by John MARSTON called *The Malcontent* (1604). This was his first work for William SHAKE-SPEARE's company, the KING'S MEN. His next work was *The White Devil* (1612), based on events in the life of Vittoria Corombona, whose sensational story of adultery and murder had arrived from Italy some 25 years before. Vittoria's brother Flamineo, one of the central characters in the drama, helps facilitate the affair between her and the duke of Brachiano. He also arranges for the death of Vittoria's foolish husband, Camillo. Brachiano's wife, Isabella, meanwhile, is killed when she kisses a poisoned painting of her unfaithful husband. Isabella's brother Francisco de' Medici and his ally Cardinal Miticelso (who later becomes Pope Paul IV) eventually bring about the downfall of Vittoria and Brachiano.

Webster's best-known work is *The Duchess of Malfi* (1614), which enjoyed a successful run by the King's Men. Like *The White Devil, The Duchess of Malfi* is set in Italy and features an appealing if flawed heroine as the title character. The duchess, a young widow, has secretly married her servant Antonio, which enrages her twin brother Ferdinand and her older brother the Cardinal. The duchess is eventually killed, as are most of the main characters in this very bloody tragedy.

Among Webster's later plays, *The Devil's Law-Case* (ca. 1617) stands out. It is the story of a woman who attempts to disinherit her son by claiming he is illegitimate. In one of many odd coincidences in the play, however, the very man she says fathered the child out of wedlock is the judge before whom she argues her case.

Critical Analysis

The White Devil and *The Duchess of Malfi* are Webster's two masterpieces. In *The White Devil* he examines ideas of justice, both within and without the law. In a scene Webster titles "The Arraignment of Vittoria," the central character dismisses the accusations against her as "feigned shadows" and "painted devils" to "terrify babes." As long as the charges against her remain unproven, she tells her accusers, the accusations return to those who spoke them "as if a man should spit against the wind; the filth returns in's face." She is, however, found guilty and sentenced to confinement in "a house of penitent whores." In an example of poetic justice, Brachiano is killed by poison that is placed on the face cover of his war helmet. This death recalls both his wife's death and the filth returning to the face of the spitter.

Of note is Webster's characterization of Vittoria. Although she is the "white devil" of the title,

Webster is able to present her sympathetically by showing the folly of her husband and the hypocrisy of her enemies. Vittoria is smart and savvy, preserving her femininity even as she "personate[s] masculine virtue to the point." Francisco de' Medici even falls in love with Vittoria during the trial and asks her to escape to Florence with him. Vittoria comes across as a complete, rounded person, with her faults and failings balanced by her intelligence and self-assurance. Ironically, as the scholar Dena Goldberg points out, "Vittoria's failure to repress her natural self ultimately leads to her total destruction." Vittoria's characterization stands apart from the depictions of women during this period, except for those of Shakespeare.

The Duchess of Malfi has a very different feeling from its predecessor. It is the duchess's virtue and loyalty, not merely her sense of self, that define her character. For one thing the duchess is a mother who, moments before her death, gives instruction to her waiting woman, "I pray thee look thou givest my little boy some syrup for his cold, and let the girl say her prayers ere she sleep." Further, although the heroine's sexual life is important to the play, her situation involves a secret but legal marriage rather than adultery. A hint of sibling incest bubbles below the surface, as the duchess's brother Ferdinand shows rather too much interest in keeping his widowed sister unmarried and seems to go mad with desire for her. In contrast to Vittoria Corombona's constant railing against her enemies, the duchess remains calm throughout. When told of her impending death, she merely says, "I am the Duchess of Malfi still." Her defense is to affirm her identity, a trait which links her to Vittoria. The plot of *The Duchess of Malfi* is tighter than that of *The White Devil*, and its violent ending unforgettable.

Thomas MIDDLETON, William ROWLEY, and John FORD each wrote commendatory verses for the published version of *The Duchess of Malfi* showing their respect for their fellow dramatist's art. Rowley praises the characterization of *The Duchess*, saying that even the historical duchess "spoke never in her life so well" as in Webster's play. Ford proclaims Webster "a poet, whom nor Rome, nor Greece, Transcend in all theirs." The biographer Margaret Loftus Ranald characterizes *The Duchess of Malfi* as "even more frightening [than *The White Devil*] in its ineffable sadness, because it subverts morality by showing the destruction of what is good."

T. S. Eliot's verse description has become the most oft-quoted assessment of Webster's frequent depictions of lust and violence:

> *Webster was much possessed by death*
> *And saw the skull beneath the skin;*
> *And breastless creatures under ground*
> *Leaned backward with a lipless grin.*
> . . .
> *He knew that thought clings round dead*
>   *limbs*
> *Tightening its lusts and luxuries.*

These melodramatic qualities have perhaps helped secure Webster's lasting place in English theater. More subtle elements of his dramas are noted by the scholar Christina Luckyj, who notes Webster's skillful use of "juxtapositions, parallels and repetitions" in creating plays that "resist reduction to a single moral belief, yet need not lead to a chaotic vision of human experience."

The Duchess of Malfi and *The White Devil* still captivate readers with their complex title characters, their examinations of justice, and their depictions of evil. In one of the true tests of dramatic worth, these plays remain two of the most frequently produced of all non-Shakespearean RENAISSANCE tragedies.

Other Work by John Webster

The Selected Plays of John Webster. Edited by Jonathan Dollimore and Alan Sinfield. New York: Cambridge University Press, 1983.

Works about John Webster

Luckyj, Christina. *A Winter's Snake: Dramatic Form in the Tragedies of John Webster.* Athens: University of Georgia Press, 1989.
Ranald, Margaret Loftus. *John Webster.* Boston: Twayne, 1989.

Weever, John (1576–1632) *poet, antiquarian*

John Weever was born in Landshire, England. Little is known about his early life or his family, except that a wealthy uncle provided him with the money necessary for his education. He studied at Queen's College, Cambridge University, although it is not known if he actually received a degree.

After Cambridge, Weever moved to London, where he succeeded in making the acquaintance of many famous figures and becoming a prominent member of the literary scene. This scene and its figures became the subject for his earliest poem, *Epigrammes* (1599). The work, as its title suggests, is composed of dozens of epigrams (short poems that deal with only one thought) praising other poets. Those who earn Weever's acclaim in *Epigrammes* range from Robert Allott and Ben JONSON to William SHAKESPEARE. The work brought Weever both the friendship of some of those he praised and the scorn of others. Around the same time he published *Fanus and Melliflora* (1600), a poem that deals with the ecclesiastical ban on satirical books. The poem is, in some parts, erotic, and as a result it faced censorship.

In addition to being remembered as a poet, John Weever is also remembered as an antiquarian, or one who studies ancient manuscripts and artifacts. In 1631 he published his *Ancient Funeral Monuments,* a documentation of graveyard monuments throughout London. Although the book is largely a work of transcription and documentation, it does contain some comments by Weever himself, as well as a picture of the author. Underneath the picture, Weever describes himself in a way that downplays his own poetry but emphasizes his spirituality and interest in historical record, saying, "[H]is studies are of death. Of heaven his meditation."

A Work about John Weever

Honigmann, E. A. *John Weever.* New York: St. Martin's Press, 1987.

Wentworth, Anne (ca. 1630–ca. 1679)
nonfiction writer

In 17th-century England there were many apocalyptic prophets—that is, prophets who predicted doom. These individuals believed that they spoke with God or Christ and that they had information on the exact time of the Apocalypse, or the Last Judgment. The English people were very interested in these prophets and their messages, and the height of this interest is usually placed in the 1640s, during the English Revolution and Civil Wars. In *The World Turned Upside Down,* historian Christopher Hill posits that political unrest during this time caused a greater interest in apocalyptic thought and a general belief that the end of the world was near. Anne Wentworth, a commoner and writer, was a prophet in this tradition. However, as a female prophet, she had to overcome different obstacles than her male peers.

After many years in an unhappy marriage, Wentworth claimed that God had begun communicating with her about the Apocalypse. Her first publication, *A True Account,* was published in 1676. In her writing she emphasizes the truth of her prophetic voice; in writing to King Charles II, for example, she requests that he "Let me be but heard how and what and which way it will be and how I come to know, and then the thing will prove itself that I lie not." She also warns her readers that the Apocalypse is near, as in *The Revelation of Jesus Christ,* when she writes, "O England, the anger of the Lord is turned against thee!"

Unlike many of the self-appointed male prophets of the period, Wentworth did not provide a plan of action for Christians to take in order to prepare for the Last Judgment. Critics attribute this difference in prophecy and writing to gender. As Megan Matchinske argues in "Holy Hatred: Formations of the Gendered Subject in English Apocalyptic Writing, 1625–51," women had first to justify themselves as intelligent voices to the public. Thus, in only a limited sense, Anne Wentworth remains an important example of a female prophet from the period.

A Work about Anne Wentworth

Otten, Charlotte F., ed. *English Women's Voices, 1540–1700.* Miami: Florida International University Press, 1992.

Weston, Elizabeth Jane (Elizabeth Jane Westonia) (1581–1612) *poet*

Elizabeth Weston was born in England, but her stepfather, Edward Kelley, was court alchemist to Rudolf II of Prague, so she grew up in Bohemia. Kelley was somehow disgraced, and after his death Elizabeth attempted to earn money for the family by writing verse in Latin.

As a neo-Latin poet, Weston was well-received. In 1607 she published her largest volume of verse, *Parthenicon*. It was considered autobiographical, and future scholars were impressed that such a volume was published by a woman.

Upon her mother's death, Weston published "On the Death of the Noble and Gentle Woman, Lady Joanna Kelley . . .," also in Latin.

Weston scholars Donald Cheney and Brenda Hosington describe her work: "As many a contemporary poet observed, it was learned and inspired, written in the best tradition of Neo-Latin verse."

A Work by Elizabeth Jane Weston

Elizabeth Jane Weston: Collected Writings. Edited by Donald Cheney and Brenda Hosington. Toronto: University of Toronto Press, 2000.

Wharton, Anne (1659–1685) *poet*

Anne Wharton was born in Oxfordshire to wealthy landowners. Wharton was orphaned at birth, however, and was subsequently raised mostly by her grandmother. It is this grandmother who is responsible for instilling in Wharton the strong religious views that are evident throughout her writing. Wharton married at a young age but never had children, and she devoted her life mainly to poetry. She managed to establish literary connections with writers including Aphra BEHN and Robert Wosely, and they influenced and at times edited her work.

Wharton's works largely comprise religious poems. Despite the fact that she says in one, "Poems are seldom for the Authors writ / but for the readers," the poems remained unpublished until after her death. Once they were published, however, they established her as one of the most pious poets in England. Some of Wharton's poems are paraphrases of psalms, whereas others are written in a classical mode, such as her "translation" of a section of *The Ovid*, published in *Ovid's Epistles, Translated by Several Hands* (1712). Her writing style is simple and measured. Consider these lines from one of her psalm translations, "The Lord who always is to Peace inclin's, / Who suffers long, & bears with th'humble Mind. / Gentle and Mild, unwilling yet to chide; / Soon he forgives, long will his Anger hide." Although her verse may seem dry to the modern reader, several different collections of poetry that included her were published including *The Idea of Christian Love* (1688) and *A Collection of Poems by Several Hands Most of Them Written by Persons of Eminent Quality* (1693).

Wheathill, Anne (fl. 1584) *nonfiction writer*

Practically nothing is known about the life of Anne Wheathill except what derives from her single publication, *A Handful of Wholesome (though Homely) Herbs Gathered out of the Goodly Garden of God's most Holy Word* (1584), a book of 49 prayers addressed to "all religious ladies, gentlewomen, and others." In the work, Wheathill describes herself as an unmarried gentlewoman who has accepted the belief that her devotions, which she refers to as a small handful of gross herbs, will be as acceptable to God as the "fragrant flower" of the learned. In reflection on her own sins, she says: "I cannot but lament, mourn, and cry for help, as doth a woman whose time draweth near to be delivered of her child; for she can take no rest, till she be discharged of her burden." The work as a whole appears to be one of many prayer books written by English reformers in an attempt to revise the Roman Catholic devotion. Although the book is little known today, its prose is first rate and has become an important source for the study of the role of middle-class women of that time.

A Work about Anne Wheathill

Trill, Suzanne et al., eds. *Lay by Your Needles Ladies, Take the Pen: Writing Women in England 1500–1700.* London and New York: Edward Arnold and St. Martin's Press, 1997.

Whetstone, George (1550–1587)

dramatist, poet, prose writer, nonfiction writer

George Whetstone was one of several sons of Robert Whetstone, a wealthy London merchant, and Margaret Bernard Whetstone. His father died when he was still a boy; his mother's remarriage to a man who lived in Walcot, Northamptonshire, brought him into contact with the Cecil family, members of which were important advisers to Queen ELIZABETH I. The Cecils became supporters of Whetstone's literary career.

It is probable that Whetstone studied law at one of London's Inns of Court, where there was a strong literary tradition. He published his first book, *The Rock of Regard,* in 1576. It is a miscellany of narrative verse, prose fiction, and lyric poetry, loosely organized around moral themes.

In 1577, the same year he witnessed the death of his friend George GASCOIGNE, Whetstone published a biography in verse of Gascoigne, "A Remembrance of the Well Employed Life, and Godly End, of George Gascoigne, Esquire. . . ." This is important less for its literary merit than as a source of information about its subject, but it has been reprinted more often than any of Whetstone's other works.

Whetstone's two-part, 10-act verse drama *Promos and Cassandra,* based on a story in BOCCACCIO's *Decameron,* was published in 1578. The play, which was never produced on stage, is noted as the main source for William SHAKESPEARE's dark comedy *Measure for Measure.*

The same year, 1578, Whetstone sailed in the fleet led by Sir Humphrey GILBERT and accompanied by Gilbert's half brother Walter RALEIGH in search of unknown lands to claim for England. Evidence suggests that the ship Whetstone sailed in may have had to turn back before even leaving English waters. The expedition as a whole was a failure, but Whetstone was still eager for foreign adventure: In 1580 he made a journey to Italy, which provided material for all his subsequent works. *An Heptameron of Civil Discourses* (1582), though clearly modeled on Boccaccio's *Decameron,* is presented as an autobiographical account of a stay at a country mansion in Italy during Christmas week of 1580. The ladies and gentlemen present share stories, poems, and an ongoing discussion of the nature of marriage. One of the stories included is a prose version of the plot of *Promos and Cassandra.*

Most of Whetstone's subsequent publications were conceived as part of a grand work, *The English Mirror,* a sort of guide for different roles that were played in English life. *A Mirror for Magistrates of Cities* (1584) addresses the duties of civic leaders; *The Honorable Duty of a Soldier* (1585) is a conduct book for military men. These works, in spite of their moralizing tone, offer an interesting and lively view of the issues confronting Elizabethans in their daily lives. For example, Whetstone's recommendation in *A Mirror for Magistrates* of banning gambling is supported by this anecdote:

> I heard a distemperate dicer solemnly swear, that he faithfully believed, that dice were first made of the bones of a witch, and cards of her skin, in which there has ever since remained an enchantment, that whosoever once taketh delight in either, he shall never have power utterly to leave them, for quoth he, I a hundred times vowed to leave both, yet have not the grace to forsake either.

When Sir Philip SIDNEY died in the Netherlands of wounds suffered at the Battle of Zutphen, Whetstone's brother Bernard, who was also involved in the fighting there, was a witness. The two brothers collaborated on a verse elegy, celebrating the courtly soldier's courage in a detailed account of his last days that provides valuable biographical information. It was Whetstone's last work. The following year he joined the campaigns in the Netherlands himself, and died there in a duel with another English officer.

Whitney, Isabella (fl. 1567) *poet, letter writer*

Little is known about Isabella Whitney's life other than what she mentions in her poetry. Her published poetry includes a collection of verse letters, which scholars view as autobiographical. In these letters, addressed to a brother and three sisters, Whitney writes about her life and duties in London as a serving woman. She discusses losing her position and the threat of poverty that follows. If the information in this verse is true, Whitney is unique among female RENAISSANCE writers, most of whom came from aristocratic or privileged backgrounds with access to education and literary circles.

Whatever her background, Whitney was evidently well educated, for she employs references to classical works as well as to contemporary literature. She describes her own circumstances as a poet in a poem to a sister:

> But til some household cares mee tye,
> My bookes and Pen I wyll apply.

Scholars believe that these lines indicate she was unmarried and thus free to devote herself to poetry, although she is believed to have later had a husband and two children.

Whitney's first published work, which is also the first nonreligious poetry by a woman to appear in print in England, was *The Copy of a Letter* (1567). It includes four verse letters, two composed in the voice of a woman and two in that of a man. All recall ballads or popular verse, an indication that Whitney was aiming at a large audience.

With this collection Whitney also became the first woman to write poetry about women, a bold literary stance in a time when women were expected to be silent and submissive. Some male poets, such as Thomas WYATT and Henry Howard, Earl of SURREY, had on occasion written love poetry

from a woman's point of view. However, in general the voice in love poetry was male. According to the critic Paul A. Marquis, Whitney's "feminine . . . voice reveals an internal complexity that achieves a level of authenticity not found in the fictional feminine voices [written by men]."

Whitney's "The Copy of a letter, lately written in meeter, by a yonge Gentilwomen: to her unconstant Lover" is the complaint of a young woman treated unfairly in love. The narrator condemns a nameless young man for his mistreatment of her by comparing him to Aeneas, the hero of the ancient Roman Virgil's *The Aeneid* who abandons his lover Dido. As the speaker wrestles with reactions to her lover's misconduct, the verse reveals her contradictory emotions:

> And yet it [our love] is not so far past,
> But might agayne be wonne.

Thus, her love remains despite her suitor's deceit.

The poem later shifts tone again to display more conflicting feelings: "Wed whom you list, I am content / Your refuse for to be." The poem has moved from suggesting interest in getting back together to portraying the mistress as a passive sufferer. She is his refuse, or garbage. The poet wrestles with whether or not to express her anger and desire, thus refusing to adopt the more socially acceptable role of the patient, injured woman.

The themes of misconduct and disappointment in love are continued throughout Whitney's first collection. The other poem with a female voice is "An Admonition to al yong Gentilwomen, and to all other Mayds in general to beware of mennes flattery," which warns women of the dangers of men. The third and fourth letters are similar to the first two, except the speaker is male. In them a young man first addresses a fickle young woman and then follows with a general warning to men against women.

Whitney's second collection, *A Sweet Nosegay, or Pleasant Posy* (1573), brings together several types of verse. The "Nosegay" refers to 110 short poems on moral or philosophical subjects that comprise the bulk of the collection. In the opening poem the poet writes,

A slip I tooke to smell unto,
Which might be my defence.
In stynking streetes, or lothsome Lanes
which els might mee infect.

Here Whitney compares her verse to a nosegay, a bouquet of flowers traditionally intended to ward off disease or bad smells. The whole "Nosegay" becomes such a protective bouquet as it offers conventional and sometimes humorous advice about youth, education, aging, conduct, and love.

After a selection of verse letters to her friends and family, the collection closes with Whitney's "Will and Testament," in which she tells how she lost her position as a servant and was forced to leave London. She compares London to a cruel lover who has neglected her, adopting the voice of a wronged lover. Upon departing the city she whimsically creates a mock will, describing London's sites, sounds, and landmarks as the legacy she leaves to the city. This poem shows the uniqueness of Whitney's poetry in comparison to other poetry of her time. Unlike the aristocratic subjects of most period verse, she writes of the city's middle and lower classes, its prostitutes, its poor, and its hospitals and prisons. Whitney mastered the forms of popular poetry in creative ways, setting the trend for later women writers.

A Work about Isabella Whitney

Jones, Anne Rosalind. *The Currency of Eros: Women's Love Lyric in Europe, 1540–1620.* Bloomington: Indiana University Press, 1990.

Wight, Sarah (fl. 1647) nonfiction writer

Sarah Wight is most famous as the subject of Henry Jessey's 1647 *The Exceeding Riches of Grace Advanced . . . In an Empty, Nothing Creature, (viz.) Mris Sarah Wight.* Sarah Wight was an intense, troubled child who often tried to commit suicide. In 1647, at the age of 15, she attempted to kill her-

self by jumping from a roof but survived the fall, although suffering from a concussion and convulsions. This failed attempt was the beginning of her spiritual journey.

Henry Jessey, a minister, was responsible for recording Wight's experiences and words during her ordeal, but Sarah would also publish her own work, *A Wonderful, Pleasant and Profitable Letter* in 1656. After her fall, she was unable to stand and was deathly ill. According to *The Exceeding Riches,* she exclaimed, "My earthly Tabernacle is broken all to pieces, and what will the Lord do with me?" Shortly after, her hearing and sight failed, and she told Jessey, "If I should die the cruellest death . . . I have deserved it, I would still justify God . . . if he cast me to Hell." Then she fell into a trance for three days in which she claimed to have received inner guidance from God. In her *Letter* she wrote:

When the Lord is pleased to make bare his holy arm for the deliverance of his people out of troubles, he first . . . strips us naked and bare, and deprives us of all helps and props belowe, and that we may thereby learn to make the Lord alone our stay and trust.

When Wight came out of her trance, she began to fast, claiming that the Lord was nourishing her and to take food would make her sick. According to witnesses, her health did not decline despite her lack of food, and some thought this to be a miracle.

For many readers Sarah Wight's ordeal was symbolic of the death and rebirth of Christ. As she says, "He [God] did not only bring my soul to Hell, and brought it back again, but my body to the grave, that he might raise it up again, if he see it good." To increase the parallel with Christ, Wight finally asked for a piece of broiled fish (what Christ is recorded to have eaten after his resurrection). After eating the fish, she rose from her bed and dressed, although she had had "not a crumb of bread or . . . meat in 76 days."

During her ordeal, Sarah Wight's eyes were bandaged, and her hair was matted with blood, but to many women she spoke as a prophet, and they flocked to her for advice. Jessey noted in his *Exceeding Riches* that women of different Christian backgrounds come together in a time of religious conflict that convinced many of the coming of Armageddon.

Willobie, Henry (Henry Willoby)
(1574–1596) *poet*

The long, complex poetic work *Willobie His Avisa, or The true Picture of a modest Maid, and of a chast and constant wife* has been a somewhat perplexing riddle since it was first published in 1594. Filled with veiled references and bawdy undertones, the author of this composition, Henry Willobie, is just as mysterious as the characters he creates, and some scholars speculate that Matthew ROYDEN is the author. Little is known about the life of Willobie, and some even believe he is a fictitious personage. He was, however, supposedly born in Wiltshire, England (though there are no official records of the event), and received his education at St. John's College, Oxford University.

Consisting of 74 songs and a handful of other poems, *Willobie His Avisa* relates the tale of the unsuccessful wooing of Avisa by five different suitors. Various suggestions as to who the real-life model for Avisa and her suitors were have been proposed over the years. The most intriguing possibility comes from B. N. De Luna, who argues at length in *The Queen Declined: An Interpretation of Willobie His Avisa* (1910) that Willobie's work is based upon the various courtships of Queen ELIZABETH I. Nevertheless, modern interest in *Willobie His Avisa* is primarily based upon its possible connection with William SHAKESPEARE, who is mentioned by name in a prefatory poem: "Yet Tarquyne pluckt his glistering grape, And Shake-speare paints poore Lucrece rape." This verse is the earliest known reference to the famous playwright, who some scholars argue is also likely to be the real-life counterpart to "the old Player," a companion to one of the men pursuing Avisa, signified within the work only by the initials "W.S."

Wilmot, John
See ROCHESTER, JOHN WILMOT, EARL OF.

Wilson, John (1627–1696) *playwright*
John Wilson was born in London and educated at Exeter College, Oxford University. After completing his degree in 1644, he entered Lincoln's Inn to study the law, and in 1646 he was called to the bar.

Wilson was the author of four plays, the first of which was *The Cheats* (1662), a comedy about the con games of a quack astrologer. This play, which was quite popular in its day, is indebted to the comedy of Ben JONSON in its subject matter and tone. Jonson's *Volpone,* for example, is a realistic black comedy that deals with the acquisitiveness and greed of contemporary society. *The Cheats* not only portrays Mopus, the astrologer, but also Scruple, a Presbyterian minister who is convinced to convert to Anglicanism with a bribe. This role was famously played by the comic actor John Lacy.

Wilson's second play, *The Projectors* (1665), was another comedy about financial sharks (one of whom is named, famously, "Suckdry") who are out to dupe Sir Gudgeon Credulous. The source of this play is probably *Aulularia* (*Pot of Gold*) by the Roman writer Plautus.

Wilson also wrote a tragedy, *Andronicus Comnenius* (1664), and a tragicomedy, *Belphegor, or The Marriage of the Devli* (printed 1691). The former, a blank-verse tragedy, is based on the story of Byzantine emperor Andronicus Comnenus who murdered his cousin, Alexius II, in order to take over his throne. The play contains a scene between the usurper and the widow of his victim Alexius that follows very closely Shakespeare's treatment of a parallel situation in *Richard III* in which Richard woos the widow of one of his victims during her husband's funeral.

Wilson took the story for *Belphegor, or The Marriage of the Devil* from MACHIAVELLI. The play deals with the demon Belphegor, who is sent to earth to find out if there is such a thing as happiness in marriage.

Wilson's comedies are full of life and wonderful characters, and his more serious works are well-written and inventive.

Wilson, Robert (ca. 1550–1600) *playwright*

In addition to his career as a playwright, Robert Wilson appeared as a comic actor with the Earl of Leicester's Men (1572–81) and the Queen's Men (1583–ca. 1593). The classical allusions, blank verse, and Latin tags in his plays suggest he might have had some scholarly education. Wilson is one of only nine actor-authors of his day, including William SHAKESPEARE. He was buried at St. Giles's parish, Cripplegate, England, on November 20, 1600.

Wilson was a close friend of the noted actor Richard Tarlton, whose death he refers to in *The Three Lords and Three Ladies of London* (published in 1590 but probably written in 1588). That play is a companion and sequel to Wilson's 1584 work *The Three Ladies of London*. The texts of both plays combine verse and prose, with *The Three Lords* written mostly in blank verse, or unrhymed iambic pentameter. One of the lords asks, "O Sorrow when? when sorrow wilt thou cease / To blow the spark that burns my troubled soul." This character's apostrophe, or direct address, to Sorrow recalls the literature of the Middle Ages.

Both *The Three Ladies* and *The Three Lords* contain elements of medieval morality plays while anticipating the Elizabethan comedies and tragedies of the 1590s and beyond. In medieval style, the Three Ladies—Love, Lucre, and Conscience—are allegorical figures, characters that represent abstract ideas. Unlike a morality play, Wilson refers to contemporary people and events, like Tarlton's death, and incorporates human characters into the drama, including the only Jewish character to be portrayed sympathetically on the Elizabethan stage. At the end of *The Three Ladies*, Lucre, Love, and Conscience have been tried and condemned, and they face punishment without any hope of reform. In *The Three Lords*, Pomp, Pleasure, and Policy free and marry the Three Ladies, and good

triumphs over evil. This comedic resolution ties *The Three Lords* to the morality play tradition in which characters choose to mend their evil ways and get to live happily ever after.

Wilson, Thomas (ca. 1523–1581)

nonfiction writer

Thomas Wilson was the son of Anne and Thomas Wilson of Strubby, Lincolnshire. He was educated at Eton College and at King's College, Cambridge University, receiving his M.A. in 1549. He received doctorates in law from both Cambridge and Oxford. In 1579 he became secretary of state to ELIZABETH I.

In the 1550s Wilson served as tutor to Henry, Duke of Suffolk, and his brother Charles Brandon. After these nephews of Henry VIII died, Wilson and Walter Haddon produced a volume of verses entitled *Vita et Obitus Duorum Fratrum Suffolciensium, . . . (Life and Death of Two Brothers of Suffolk*, 1551).

Two years later, in 1552, Wilson also published *The Rule of Reason, conteinynge the Arte of Logique set forth in Englishe. . . .* In his dedication, Wilson explains his wish to provide a textbook for Englishmen who, not knowing Latin and Greek, "could otherwise not come to the knowledge of Logic."

The Arte of Rhetorique . . . sette forthe in Englishe . . . (1553) continued Wilson's purpose of providing textbooks in English. He says in his prologue to the 1660 edition that this book was considered heresy because he wrote in English rather than Latin, but he asks, "Now what [use is it] to speak when none can tell what the speaker means?" Although *The Arte of Rhetorique* was not original in terms of its content, it was much more complete and amusing than earlier works of rhetoric. Wilson is, however, original in his inclusion of humorous anecdotes and sample letters and speeches. A work such as Wilson's was much needed in RENAISSANCE England to combat problems resulting from the influx of foreign words into English, leading to ostentation and vulgarity in much writing and speech.

Following the model of the archbishop of Canterbury, Thomas CRANMER, who had translated church liturgy into English (1539), Wilson applied the same principle to textbooks in logic and rhetoric, so that they would be available in the vernacular. His works helped make education available in English and encouraged a style of English prose that was both simple and clear.

Winstanley, Gerrard (1609–1676)
pamphleteer

Gerrard Winstanley was born in Lancashire, England, to a Puritan cloth merchant, Edward Winstanley. He is known today as the leader of a radical political group called the Diggers. His involvement in this movement began after the second English Civil War in 1648, when he wrote his first pamphlet, an interpretation of the Fall of Man, entitled *The Mystery of God.* Although it was a religious work focusing on salvation and rebirth, the pamphlet contains many ideas that would shape Winstanley's political writings.

Winstanley wrote his first overtly political pamphlet, *The New Law of Righteousness,* in 1649. In it he states, "In the beginning of time God made the earth. Not one word was spoken at the beginning that one branch of mankind should rule over another, but selfish imaginations did set up one man to teach and rule over another." Inspired by, but also feeling somewhat betrayed by John LILBURNE and the Levellers—a radical party formed during the English Civil War that Winstanley felt had not carried out promises of social reform—he set forth philosophies in *The New Law of Righteousness* that would lead to his organization of an activist group known as the True Levellers, or the Diggers. The Diggers were Christian communists who advocated the abolition of private ownership of land, and whose beliefs were clearly defined in Winstanley's manifesto *The True Levellers Standard Advanced* (1649).

In *The True Levellers* Winstanley attempted to explain why, on April 16, 1649, a group of people began planting vegetables on St. George's Hill in Surrey. The "first reason" for their behavior, Winstanley says, is that "every one that is born in the land, may be fed by the Earth his Mother that brought him forth, according to the Reason that rules in the Creation." Winstanley and the Diggers were also reacting to the fact that landowners and land speculators were systematically driving peasants off the land, leaving them no way to make a living. Although the group was stopped by force, they continued to plant the land and tear down enclosures or fences in several other English counties. Many landowners were enraged, and the Digger communities were dispersed within a year.

In 1650 Winstanley wrote *A New-Yeers Gift for the Parliament and Army,* in which he asserted his renewed vigor and the Diggers' resolve: "Those diggers that remain are cheerful . . . rejoicing that they are counted worthy to suffer persecution for the sake of righteousness." In Winstanley's last pamphlet, *The Law of Freedom* (1652), he envisions an English commonwealth free of idleness, clergy, churches, lawyers, kingly law, and property. Although Winstanley lived for many more years, little is known of his life after 1652. The scholar Christopher Hill says that Winstanley's prose is so beautiful that we should read him "as we read a poet, as we read William Blake, as Winstanley himself read the Bible." These words, for example, from *The True Levellers Standard Advanced* have the power and simplicity of a biblical prophesy:

> And hereupon, The Earth . . . was hedged in to In-closures by the teachers and rulers, and the others were made Servants and Slaves: And that Earth that is within this Creation made a Common Store-house for all, is bought and sold, and kept in the hands of a few, whereby the great Creator is mightily dishonoured, as if he were a respector of persons, delighting in the comfortable Livelihoods of some, and rejoycing in the miserable povertie and straits of others. From the beginning it was not so.

A Work about Gerrard Winstanley
Schulman, George M. *Radicalism and Reverence: The Political Thought of Gerrard Winstanley.* Berkeley: University of California Press, 1989.

Wither, George (George Withers)
(1588–1667) *poet*

George Wither was born in Hampshire, England, and educated at Magdalen College, Oxford University, but left before earning his degree. He went on to study the law and, after a decade of publishing poetry, served as a general in the parliamentarian army during the English Civil Wars before devoting the later part of his life to writing for the Puritan cause.

Wither's *Abuses Stript and Whipt* (1613) is a two-volume collection of his satirical verse in which he criticizes the depraved behavior of humanity. In it, he says, "I will teach my rough satiric rimes, / To be as mad and idle as the times." He was imprisoned for publishing the book, but the reason for his imprisonment is unclear, since Wither, unlike some satirists, did not attack individuals but rather turned his attention to vices in general, such as Revenge, Ambition, and Lust.

While in prison, Wither wrote *The Shepherd's Hunting* (1615), five pastoral poems that celebrate the simplicity of rural life. In this work he also takes the opportunity to defend his earlier satires:

> *I have not sought to scandalise the State,*
> *Nor sown sedition, nor made public hate:*
> *I have not aim'd at any good man's fame,*
> *Nor taxt (directly) any one by name.*

In 1621 Wither published *Wither's Motto: nec habeo, nec careo, nec curo* ("Neither Have I, nor Want I, nor Care I"), a poem in which he celebrates his virtuous life. He says in an introduction, "My intent was to draw the picture of mine own heart. . . . But my principal intention was, by recording those thoughts, to confirm my own resolution and to prevent such alterations, as time and infirmities may work upon me." Again, mysteriously, his work offended, and he was again imprisoned.

In his book *English Satire and Satirists* (1965), Hugh Walker says the following of George Wither: "He writes pleasantly and leaves a pleasant impression of his own character . . . The moderation of his measured and sensible strictures makes his criticisms instructive, because we feel that they can be trusted."

Wood, Anthony à (Merton Wood)
(1632–1695) *nonfiction writer*

Anthony à Wood, the son of Thomas à Wood, was born in a stone house across from Merton College at Oxford University. He died in the same house some 63 years later, after devoting his entire professional life to compiling and writing historical and biographical works about that university.

Wood entered Oxford's Merton College when he was 19 and soon displayed a passionate interest in everything Oxonian, from the university's architecture and history to the "statelie bells" of Merton College that gave him such rapture. In fact, Wood wrote that the sound of church bells was "the music nighest bordering upon heaven." Somewhat eccentric and reclusive, he ventured beyond Oxford only a few times during his life. Few writers have abandoned themselves to a "sense of place" as much as this scholar, who was known as "Merton Wood" to his contemporaries. He did all his writing in a tiny garret to which none but his closest friends were admitted, and then only rarely. Even while he was living, some anonymous versifier composed a rhyme about him: "Merton Wood, with his Antiquitie / Will live to all Eternitie."

Wood's history of Oxford University and its colleges, *Historia et Antiquitates Universitatis Oxoniensis* (*History and Antiquities of the University of Oxford*) appeared in 1674. A later work, *Athenae Oxonienses* (1691–92) was a colossal biographical reference work about important scholars and clergy associated with Oxford. Wood wrote candidly of their lives and did not hesitate to be critical of those he disliked. In *Athenae* he went so far as to accuse Edward Hyde, first Earl of Clarendon, of corruption, which led to a libel suit and to Wood's expulsion from Oxford. Wood may have anticipated such a response, for in his preface he attempts to explain his "harsh expressions" and "severe reflections," saying "that faults ought no more to be conceal'd than virtues, and that, whatever it may be in a painter, it is no excellence in an historian to throw a veil on deformities."

Wood's *Diaries* (1657–95) give a detailed account of the life of this odd, grouchy recluse. But however strange he may have been, his love of Oxford redeems him, and his work is an invaluable legacy.

Woolley, Hannah (ca. 1623–ca. 1680)
nonfiction writer

Hannah Woolley was born in Essex, England, to a family of modest means. According to her own writings, she learned medical and surgical skills from her mother and sisters. By 17 she had served as a domestic servant in at least two noble households, where she was trained in cooking, cleaning, sewing, keeping accounts, and attending the lady of the house.

At 24 Woolley married Benjamin Woolley, a schoolteacher. In 1655 the couple moved to Hackney, near London, where they started a boarding school. Hannah helped supervise the school and used her skills in herbal and surgical medicine to take care of the boarders' health.

Benjamin Woolley died in 1661. That same year Hannah Woolley published her first book, *The Ladies Directory*. This work provided the reader with, among other things, elaborate instructions and recipes for preserving fruit. Other Woolley titles are *The Cook's Guide* (1664); *The Queen-like Closet, or, Rich Cabinet Stored with all Manner of Rare Receipts for Preserving, Candying, and Cookery* (1670); and *The Accomplisht Lady's Delight* (1672).

Woolley's 1675 *The Gentlewoman's Companion; Or, a Guide to the Female Sex* is the text for which she is best known. She explains in the preface her reasons for writing it:

> When I considered the great need of such a Book as might be a *Universal Companion and Guide to the Female Sex*, in all relations, Companies, Conditions, and states of Life even from Childhood down to Old age; and from the Lady at the Court, to the Cook-maid in the Country: I was at length prevailed upon to do it, and the rather because I knew not of any Book in any Language that hath done the like. Indeed many excellent Authors there be who have wrote excellent well of some particular Subjects herein treated of. But as there is not one of them hath written upon all of them; so there are some things treated of in this Book, that I have not met with in any Language, but are the Product of my Thirty years Observations and Experience.

There is a surprising sense of female solidarity transcending the bounds of class in her assumption that one book can be useful to any woman, "from the Lady at the Court, to the Cook-maid in the Country." The self-confidence with which she speaks of the knowledge she has gained from experience is also striking. A glance at the *Companion*'s table of contents reveals the wide range of advice that Woolley offers. To establish her authority, she begins with "A short account of the life and abilities of the Authoress of this Book." The largest section, some 70 pages, deals with etiquette and how to negotiate the class system, with headings such as "The duty of Children to their Parents"; "Of a Gentlewoman's Civil Behavior to all sorts of People in all places"; "Rules to be observed in walking with persons of honor, & how you ought to behave your self in congratulating and condoling them"; and "Of habit [clothing] and the neatness and propriety thereof; Of Fashions, and their ridiculous apish Imitation." There are sections of recipes, medicines, and particular advice for specific groups of servants—nursery maids, cook maids, and so on. The book concludes with a section of sample conversations, bringing the focus back to etiquette in a humorous vein. The dialogue "An impertinent and lying Travellers Discourse with his witty and Jocose Mistress" contains outrageous boasting on the part of a traveler and concludes with his lady saying, "Well, Sir, I see the difference between you and truth is so great, that there cannot be expected a reconcilement; wherefore I shall leave you."

Woolley's books can be distinguished from other household manuals of the time by the breadth of knowledge she displays. Not only is she able to divulge recipes and medicinal cures, but she also instructs women in the skills of accounting and mathematics. She sprinkles her texts with references to such authors as Philip SIDNEY, but she couches her knowledge in terms that make it applicable to the daily lives of average women.

Woolley shares with Aphra BEHN, in a completely different field, the distinction of being the first Englishwoman to make a living by writing. She did not write for literary recognition but to make money and to help other women learn the skills to do so as well. She became so well known in her time that her name itself was a selling point. (It is difficult to be sure which of the books ascribed to her are actually hers, because booksellers are known to have capitalized on her reputation by putting her name on works written by others.) Her books are a rich source of information about daily life in the 17th century, and they are entertaining reading as well.

Wotton, Sir Henry (1568–1639) *poet, letter writer, nonfiction writer*

Henry Wotton was born in Kent, England, and educated at Winchester College (a boarding school) and Oxford University. At Oxford he met John DONNE, who remained a close friend and wrote a number of poems addressed to Wotton.

In 1595 Wotton became a secretary to the Earl of Essex, a powerful favorite of Queen ELIZABETH I. Essex sent Wotton on several trips to the continent to gather intelligence. When the earl fell from grace for plotting against the queen (he was executed in 1601), Wotton quickly left England. He was in Florence in 1602 when the Grand Duke of Tuscany heard of a plot to murder James VI of Scotland. Wotton was entrusted with letters warning the king, and he traveled in disguise to Scotland by way of Norway. James welcomed him warmly, and Wotton remained at the Scottish court for three months before returning to Florence. In 1603, when James became King JAMES I OF ENGLAND, Wotton hastened to London; the king knighted him and appointed him ambassador to Venice, a job he held for most of the next two decades. There was, however, a period of unemployment beginning in 1612, after a German scholar published a book attacking James and included a quip that Wotton had written in a friend's album several years before: "An ambassador is an honest man sent to lie abroad for the good of his country." James was offended, and it was two years before he took Wotton back into favor.

In 1624 Wotton returned to England for good and secured the position of provost (principal) of Eton College. Here he passed his last 15 years in relative ease, frequently entertaining his friends. He often went fishing with Isaak WALTON, who later wrote his biography.

Wotton was a great letter writer, and his friends had high expectations of his literary career. But in spite of many projects, he wrote little for publication. The only major work he completed was *The Elements of Architecture* (1624), a translation of *Ten Books of Architecture* by the Roman author Marcus Vitruvius, which had some influence in bringing the ideals of classical architecture into currency in the 17th century. Wotton's summary of the aims of architecture is often quoted: "The end is to build well. Well-building hath three conditions: commodity, firmness and delight." Commodity, in Wotton's usage, meant the convenience of the client; firmness, the physical integrity of the building. Endearingly, Wotton remarked of himself in his preface to the book, "I am but a gatherer and disposer of other men's stuff."

Wotton had the idea of writing a history of Venice; a page of the manuscript has survived. King Charles I increased Wotton's stipend at Eton in 1630 on the understanding that he would write a history of England, but nothing of this seems to have been put on paper. Many of his letters and some poems were published in *Reliquiae Wottonianae* (1651, the year of Walton's biography). Only 15 of the poems can be securely attributed to him, and of these, two are among the most anthologized in the language. "On His Mistress, the Queen of

Bohemia," a tribute to Elizabeth STUART (queen of Bohemia), James I's daughter, is 20 lines of courtly graciousness. "The Character of a Happy Life" can be read as describing the life that Wotton achieved after his years of wandering and striving:

> *How happy is he born and taught*
> *That serveth not another's will;*
> *Whose armour is his honest thought*
> *And simple truth his utmost skill!*
> . . .
> *—This man is freed from servile bands*
> *Of hope to rise, or fear to fall;*
> *Lord of himself, though not of lands;*
> *And having nothing, yet hath all.*

Works about Sir Henry Wotton

Acton, Sir Harold. *Three Extraordinary Ambassadors.* London: Thames & Hudson, 1984.

Walton, Isaak. *Lives of Donne, Wotton, Hooker, Herbert and Sanderson, 1895.* Belle Fourche, S.D.: Kessinger, 2003.

Wroth, Mary (1587–1653) *fiction writer, poet, playwright*

Mary Wroth (nèe Sidney) was the eldest daughter of Sir Robert and Barbara Gamage Sidney and the niece of Sir Philip SIDNEY and Mary SIDNEY. During Wroth's childhood, she visited her aunt frequently and probably gained a knowledge and appreciation of literature from her. When she was 17 she married Robert Wroth, the son of a wealthy landowner. He died in 1614, and it is after this date that Wroth probably did most of her writing.

In 1621 Wroth published the first part of *The Countesse of Montgomerie's Urania,* a long prose romance with over 300 characters. The book is named for Susan Herbert, Countess of Montgomery and a friend of Wroth's. The title character, Urania, reflects many of the countess's characteristics. When the romance was published, it created a scandal because a prominent statesman, Edward, Baron of Waltham, believed Wroth had represented his family negatively in the text. The controversy caused Wroth to recall the book from booksellers and discontinue further printings.

Urania is a pastoral—that is, it is set in an idealized rural setting and has shepherds for many of its characters. The work focuses on the woman's point of view and depicts many kinds of romantic liaisons, from traditional arranged marriages to secret ones. The critic Josephine Roberts explains that Wroth questions "how, when, and even whether women should enter into exclusively monogamous relationships."

Although Wroth tends to depict arranged marriages negatively, she also seems to discourage marrying purely for love. For example, the main characters—the princess Pamphilia, whose name means all-loving, and Amphilanthus, the king of Naples—marry without parental consent, and the relationship turns out badly because of Amphilanthus's unfaithfulness. Despite his betrayal, Pamphilia remains faithful, explaining that by doing so she shows that she "loved him for himselfe, and would have loved him had hee not loved mee, and will love though hee dispise me." By maintaining her love for him, she says she maintains a "vertuous constancy."

At the end of the first volume, Pamphilia's faithfulness is rewarded when she is reunited with Amphilanthus and "is the Queene of all content." The reunion is a romantic one:

> she ranne unto him, forgiving, nay forgetting all injuries, he seeing her threw downe his helme [helmet], with open armes received her, and with all unfained [unfeigned/genuine] affection embraced her.

After this joyful reunion, Wroth ends the volume in mid-sentence; she continued the story of Pamphilia and Amphilanthus in volume two, which she never published.

Wroth explores the relationship between Pamphilia and Amphilanthus further in the sonnet sequence *Pamphilia to Amphilanthus.* Written from the viewpoint of Pamphilia, the poems probably represent the first sonnet sequence in English written by a woman. They explore Pamphilia's feelings for Amphilanthus and her decision to remain faithful even after his betrayal, repeating again and again the sadness and despair the princess feels over the absence of her beloved. Wroth creates innovative ways to show the speaker's sorrow. In one sonnet, for instance, she compares the speaker's grief to a tree's grief over the loss of its leaves: The trees have "leavles, naked bodies" as they "wither in theyr love." In the last two lines the poet makes the comparison explicit: "If trees, and leaves for absence, mourners bee / Noe mervaile that I grieve, who like want see." Like the trees and leaves, the speaker and her beloved are separated and mourn for each other.

Wroth wrote and privately circulated a play, *Love's Victory* (ca. 1620), which was probably performed by friends and family. Like her romance and sonnet sequence, the play focuses on love as it explores the relationships of several couples, who are at first thwarted in their efforts to win over their loves but who are ultimately united through the magic of Venus and Cupid.

The playwright and poet Ben JONSON praised Wroth's poetry in "A Sonnet, To the Noble Lady, Lady Mary Wroth," in which he says, "Since I exscribe [copy out] your sonnets, am become / A better lover, and much better poet." Other poets, such as William DRUMMOND OF HAWTHORNDEN and George CHAPMAN, also praised Wroth. Modern critics, however, have been slow to appreciate her work, although as new editions have appeared, more have begun to recognize her as an important woman writer. As the scholar Gary Waller writes, Wroth has "a distinctive voice, one that speaks powerfully to her age and beyond."

Other Work by Mary Wroth

The Poems of Lady Mary Wroth. Edited by Josephine Roberts. Baton Rouge: Louisiana State University Press, 1983.

Works about Mary Wroth

Miller, Naomi. *Changing the Subject: Mary Wroth and Figurations of Gender in Early Modern England.* Lexington: University of Kentucky Press, 1996.

Miller, Naomi, and Gary Waller, eds. *Reading Mary Wroth: Representing Alternatives in Early Modern England.* Knoxville: University of Tennessee Press, 1991.

Waller, Gary. *The Sidney Family Romance: Mary Wroth, William Herbert, and The Early Modern Construction of Gender.* Detroit: Wayne State University Press, 1993.

Wyatt, Thomas (1503–1542) *poet*

Thomas Wyatt was born in his family's castle in Kent, England, to Henry and Anne Skinner Wyatt. He entered Cambridge University in 1516; some biographers claim he received a B.A. in 1518 and an M.A. in 1520.

Wyatt held several positions under King Henry VIII. Among other assignments, he traveled to Rome on a diplomatic mission in 1527 and was high marshal of Calais, the sole remaining British possession in France from 1528 to 1532. Serving the king had its dangers, and in 1536 Wyatt was imprisoned for quarreling with the Duke of Suffolk and again imprisoned in 1541 for treason. The king pardoned him both times.

Wyatt wrote a great deal of poetry that circulated in manuscript. None of his work was published in his lifetime, and thus the dates of composition are unknown. He wrote in a variety of poetic forms and is best remembered for helping to modernize English poetry. He wrote, no doubt, to further his career at a time when those who attended court were required to display their cultured accomplishments in order to achieve advancement. It was Wyatt who introduced the sonnet, an extremely popular 14-line poetic form, to England, translating those of Francis PETRARCH and adapting the form for his own use. Some 40-odd years after Wyatt's death, the 16th-century critic George PUTTENHAM would remember him as a leader of the "company of courtly makers [that is, poets] who . . . having traveled in Italy and there tasted the sweet and stately measures and style of the Italian Poesy . . . greatly polished our rude and homely manner of vulgar Poesy, from that it had been before."

Critical Analysis

What is perhaps most interesting about Wyatt to modern readers is the quality of the poetic voice that he created. This feature of Wyatt's verse, and its relationship to his life as a courtier, comes across quite clearly in "Mine Own John Poins," a verse letter probably written after his release from the Tower of London in 1536 when he was forced to retire to his property in Kent. The poem attempts to explain his absence from the court, but it fails to mention the actual circumstances of his banishment. Wyatt claims that he has chosen retirement because he refuses to act in a way that is contrary to his principles:

> I cannot from me tune to feign [pretend],
> To cloak the truth for praise without desert
> Of them that list all vice for to retain . . .
> I cannot speak and look like a saint,
> Use wiles [deceitful means] for wit, and
>   make deceit a pleasure,
> And call craft counsel, for profit still to
>   paint.

By presenting his retreat as an escape from hypocrisy, Wyatt implies that retiring to his estate provides him with the leisure to be true to himself. He is, in effect, affirming his independence from and asserting his superiority over the corruption of his age.

Wyatt's position, however, is not that clear-cut, for although he claims that "In lusty leas [meadows] at liberty I walk," he acknowledges that "a clog doth hang yet at my heel. / No force for that, for it is ordered so, / That I may leap both hedge and dike full well." Because he is under house arrest, he is free to walk through his fields, but something is impeding his movement. What liberty he has is an effect of his submission to the power of the court.

The desire for independence coupled with the sense of entrapment in the previous poem can also be found elsewhere in his poetry, most notably in "They Flee From Me," a poem described by the scholar Stephen Merriam Foley as "a virtual stage set for the operation of the personal politics of the royal household." In this poem the speaker's private room functions much like the estate in "Mine Own John Poins." But rather than attempting to create a sense of independence by asserting moral superiority, the speaker of "They Flee From Me" seeks to establish his independence by gaining authority over others, particularly women. The poem is written in a moment of failure. The speaker is recalling a time when he had succeeded in achieving his goal:

> When her loose gown from her shoulders
>   did fall,
> And she me caught in her arms long and
>   small;
> Therewithall sweetly did me kiss
> And softly said, "dear heart, how like you
>   this?"

That was in the past. Now, however, "all is turned thorough my gentleness / Into a strange fashion of forsaking / And I have leave to go of her goodness."

Wyatt's most famous sonnet, "Who So List To Hunt," may be about his giving up his courtship of Anne BOLEYN because she had begun an affair with Henry VIII. The poem is an adaptation of Petrarch's "Rime 190." In translating Petrarch, Wyatt changes the sonnet into something completely new. In the original poem, the hind, or female deer, which represents woman, appears to the poet while he is alone in a meadow and belongs to an ideal realm. By contrast, the woman, symbolized by a deer about which Wyatt writes, inhabits the same political world that he does. She would thus seem to be attainable and has become the object of a hunt. But the poet is not finding success in this hunt. He is "of them that farthest cometh behind." Still, he is incapable of giving up the pursuit: "Yet may I by no means my wearied mind / Draw from the deer, but as she fleeth afore / Fainting I follow." The hunt, in fact, is a pointless effort for everyone involved:

> And graven with diamonds in letters plain
> There is written, her fair neck round about:

Noli me tangere, for Caesar's I am,
And wild for to hold, though I seem tame.

Wyatt's poems display the reality of the courtier's life in that they acknowledge the need to submit to authorities: the king in "Mine Own John Poins," the lover who has forsaken him in "They Flee from Me," and circumstance in "Who So List to Hunt." They also show the desire to fashion a self that is independent of the powers that limit one's freedom. The result is a poetry that is, in the words of the scholar Stephen Greenblatt, "at its best, distinctly more convincing, more deeply moving, than any written not only in [Wyatt's] own generation but in the proceeding century."

Other Works by Thomas Wyatt

Poems. Edited by Louise Cooper. Kidderminster: Joe's Press, 1994.
Selected Poems. Edited by Hardiman Scott. New York: Routledge, 2003.

Works about Thomas Wyatt

Heale, Elizabeth. *Wyatt, Surrey, and Early Tudor Poetry.* New York: Longman, 1998.
Szalay, Krisztina. *The Obstinate Muse of Freedom: On the Poetry of Sir Thomas Wyatt.* Budapest: Akadémia Kiado, 2000.

Wycherley, William (1641–1716) *dramatist*

William Wycherley was born in Clive, Shropshire, England, the son of Daniel Wycherley and Bertha Shrimpton. Daniel Wycherley was a self-made man who made a fortune both for his employer and himself as chief steward to the Marquis of Winchester. When he was 15, Wycherley's parents sent him to Angoulême, in southwestern France, for a more aristocratic education than was available in England at the time. This was the period of the Commonwealth, following the English Civil War (1649–53), when the monarchy had been overthrown and a kind of Puritan theocracy was in place. In Angoulême he was privileged to be invited to the salon of Madame de Montausier, the wife of the governor of the province, a charming and intelligent woman who is thought to have been a model for the heroines of Wycherley's plays. Her husband, Monsieur de Montausier, a principled man who refused to flatter King Louis XIV, may also have been a model for Wycherley for the character of Manly in *The Plain Dealer.*

After the RESTORATION of the monarchy in 1660 and the coronation of King Charles II, Wycherley returned to England. He spent a brief time in Oxford, which seemed unbearably stuffy to him after the sparkling society he had been used to in Angoulême, and then went to London, ostensibly to study law. His father would have been pleased to have him become a lawyer, but Wycherley was attracted to the life of Charles II's court, where his charm and wit made him sought after. He began to write; his first publication was a mock epic poem, *Hero and Leander in Burlesque* (1669). This was followed by his first play, *Love in a Wood, or St. James's Park* (1671), which was an instant success. The Duchess of Cleveland, who had until recently been the most important of the king's mistresses and was still a power at court, went to the play on two successive nights and took Wycherley as a lover for a time. He dedicated the publication of the play to her.

Wycherley became part of a group of court wits that included George ETHEREGE, Charles SEDLEY, and George Villiers, Duke of BUCKINGHAM. Through Buckingham's influence he secured a court post that involved little work, occasional attendance on the king, and an annual income, freeing him from dependence on his father and from the need to write for money. He went on to write three more plays: *The Gentleman Dancing-Master* (1672), *The Country-Wife* (1675), and *The Plain Dealer* (1677).

When Wycherley became severely ill in 1678 the king himself visited him at his lodgings and then gave him £500 to travel to the health resort of Montepellier, in France. Wycherley recovered, but it is thought that his fever caused permanent brain damage. His contemporaries noticed his forgetfulness, and he wrote nothing more of lasting quality after this illness. When Wycherley returned from France the following spring, the king appointed him tutor to the seven-year-old Duke of Richmond (one of his illegitimate sons), with a generous annual salary and the guarantee of a pension after the boy grew up. Wycherley, however, had the misfortune to fall in love with Laetitia Isabella, Countess of Drogheda. Their marriage in 1680 not only cost Wycherley the favor of the king and his position as tutor, but it also embroiled him in lawsuits over Lady Laetitia's debts. When Lady Laetitia died in 1681, the lawsuits continued, and in 1682 Wycherley, unable to keep up with his legal expenses, was imprisoned for debt. He remained in prison for four years.

In 1685 Charles II died and was succeeded by his brother, James II, who happened to see a production of *The Plain Dealer* that December. He enjoyed it immensely, particularly because he prided himself on his own plain dealing, and when he learned that the author was in debtor's prison saw to it that Wycherley was released. He also granted Wycherley a lifetime pension. The pension ceased when James II was driven from the throne in 1688, and Wycherley spent his last days in straitened circumstances, supported mainly by his father. He wrote only verse in his later years, publishing *Poetical Epistles to the King and Duke* (1683) and *Miscellany Poems* (1701), neither of which has been highly regarded in the centuries since his death. However, Wycherley was greatly respected by the new generation of writers, which included William CONGREVE and Alexander Pope, who sought out his company, and he had the gratification of knowing that his plays, constantly revived, continued to give pleasure.

Critical Analysis

By the time of *Love in a Wood,* the conventions of RESTORATION comedy had been established. The cast always includes one or more pairs of elegant lovers engaged in witty verbal sparring over their relationships; a pathetic older woman trying to catch a man while pretending to be a model of pious virtue; and a fop, a would-be fashionable male character whose efforts to be witty constantly come to grief. *Love in a Wood* uses all these conventions in the setting of the fashionable promenade of St. James's Park. The central character, Ranger, ignores the woman who loves him, Lydia, because he finds it more exciting to pursue someone who is less available—Christina, who is engaged to Valentine. Lydia's intelligence and spirit ultimately capture Ranger anyway. Meanwhile, the widowed Lady Flippant is casting a net for a husband. Lady Flippant ends up marrying the scheming Addleplot, who thinks she is rich, as she thinks he is—both have skillfully concealed their penniless condition. Although hardly original in conception, the play is lively and funny.

The Gentleman Dancing Master is a farce that focuses on a single situation, that of a young girl, Hippolita, whose father has kept her secluded from men and has arranged a marriage for her to a foolish man. It relates Hippolita's tricks to escape her father's scrutiny and marry a young man of her own choosing. It was written very quickly in the wake of the success of *Love in a Wood,* but it was not well received and lasted only six performances in its original production. It is still regarded today as the least successful of Wycherley's four plays. Although there is some amusing dialogue, there is not enough variety of material to carry an entire play.

Wycherley took more time over his next play. The poor success of *The Gentleman Dancing Master* still bothered him three years later, as can be seen in his referring to himself, in the prologue to *The Country-Wife,* as "The late so bafled Scribler." *The Country-Wife* goes back to the variety of plot Wycherley used in *Love in a Wood.* The central character is Horner, who has allowed a rumor to be spread that he is a eunuch, a castrated man. This allows him greater access to women than he would have if husbands believed him to be capable of seducing their wives. The wives are happy to keep up the pretence and enjoy Horner's sexual prowess without being suspected. The hypocrisy of the sexually rapacious aristocratic woman is satirized in the characters of Lady Fidget and

Mrs. Squeamish, especially when contrasted with the straightforward lustfulness of the "country wife," Margery Pinchwife, who wrecks the status quo by freely acknowledging the reason she enjoys Horner's company.

Wycherley does allow for a female ideal in the play: Alithea, whose growth in the play is shown in her breaking her engagement to a foolish man she was going to marry for reasons of convenience and accepting the love of Harcourt, someone she can love and respect. *The Country-Wife* has moments of broad, bawdy humor, many passages of amusing double entendre, but also a deeper sense of a moral ideal underlying the humor than is found in many Restoration comedies. It is the most frequently revived of all Wycherley's plays.

The Plain-Dealer focuses on the character of Manly, a sea captain who has just returned to London after displaying courage in a naval engagement. Manly is appalled by the hypocrisy and frivolity of London society. He rejects the friendship offered by Freeman, his lieutenant, because Freeman is not absolutely honest in social relationships. In the course of the play Manly learns the value of accepting and adapting to the foolishness around him, yet he is not a figure of fun; his angry speeches are given weight, and he may be seen to be speaking for the author's own frustrations with his social milieu.

As the scholar Katharine M. Rogers remarks, "Wycherley excelled his contemporary playwrights in his grappling with reality—real human nature, as distinct from the social surface; real moral issues, as distinct from delicate social nuances."

Works about William Wycherley

McCarthy, B. Eugene. *William Wycherley: A Biography*. Athens: Ohio University Press, 1979.

Rogers, Catharine M. *William Wycherley*. New York: Twayne, 1972.

SELECTED BIBLIOGRAPHY

Abrams, M. H. *A Glossary of Literary Terms.* 5th ed. New York: Harcourt, 1988.

Achinstein, Sharon. *Literature and Dissent in Milton's England.* Cambridge, U.K.: Cambridge University Press, 2003.

———. *Romance of the Spirit: Female Sexuality and Religious Desire in Early Modern England.* Baltimore: The Johns Hopkins University Press, 2002.

Aldrich-Watson, Deborah. *The Verse Miscellany of Constance Aston Fowler.* Tempe: Arizona Center for Medieval and Renaissance Studies in conjunction with Renaissance English Text Society, 2000.

———. *The Verse Miscellany of Constance Aston Fowler: A Diplomatic Edition.* Tempe, Ariz.: Renaissance English Text Society, 2000.

Alemán, Mateo. *The Rogue; or, The Life of Guzman de Alfarache.* Translated by James Mabbe. New York: A. A. Knopf, 1924.

Amours, R. J. *Scottish Alliterative Poems in Riming Stanzas.* Edinburgh, London: W. Blackwood and Sons, 1897.

Ariew, Roger, and Marjorie Grene. *Descartes and His Contemporaries.* Chicago: University of Chicago Press, 1995.

Armistead, J. M. *Nathaniel Lee.* Boston: Twayne, 1979.

Ascham, Roger. *The Scholemaster.* Edited by Lawrence V. Ryan. Ithaca, N.Y.: Cornell University Press, 1967.

Askew, Reginald. *Muskets and Altars: Jeremy Taylor and the Last of the Anglicans.* Herndon, Va.: Mowbray, 1997.

Auerbach, Erna. *Nicholas Hilliard.* London: Routledge & Kegan Paul, 1961.

Aughterson, Kate, ed. *Renaissance Women: Constructions of Femininity in England.* London: Routledge, 1995.

Augustijn, Cornelis. *Erasmus: His Life, Works, and Influence.* Toronto: University of Toronto Press, 1991.

Axton, Marie. *Three Tudor Classical Interludes.* Cambridge, U.K.: D.S. Brewer, 1982.

Axton, Richard, and Peter Happé, eds. *The Plays of John Heywood.* Cambridge, U.K.: D.S. Brewer, 1991.

Bacon, Francis. *Essays and New Atlantis.* New York: Black, 1942.

Bailey, Richard. *New Light on George Fox and Early Quakerism: The Making and Unmaking of a God.* San Francisco: Mellen Research University Press, 1992.

Baker, Ernest A. *History of the English Novel.* New York: Barnes & Noble, 1936.

Baker, James Rupert, ed. *Poems of Bishop Henry King.* Denver: Alan Swallow, 1960.

Bale, John. *Select Works of John Bale.* Edited by the Parker Society. Cambridge, U.K.: The University Press, 1849.

Barnes, Barnabe. *Parthenophil and Parthenophe.* Edited by Victor A. Doyno. Carbondale: Southern Illinois University Press, 1971.

Barrett, William Alexander. *English Church Composers.* London: Sampson, Low, Marston & Co., Ltd., 1925.

Baugh, Albert C. *A History of the English Language,* 2d ed. Englewood Cliffs, N.J.: Routledge and Kegan Paul, 1963.

———. *A Literary History of England.* New York: Appleton-Century-Crofts, 1948.

Beer, Barrett L. *Tudor England Observed: The World of John Stow.* Phoenix Mill, U.K.: Sutton Publishing, 1998.

Behn, Aphra. *Love-Letters Between a Nobleman and His Sister.* Maureen Duffy, ed. London: Virago, 1987.

———. *Oroonoko.* Joanna Lipking, ed. New York: Norton, 1997.

Beilin, Elaine V., ed. *The Examinations of Anne Askew.* New York: Oxford University Press, 1996.

Bell, Robin Graham, ed. *The Collected Poems of James Graham, First Marquis of Montrose.* New York: David Lewis, 1970.

Bennett, H. S. *Six Medieval Men and Women.* New York: Atheneum, 1968.

Benoit-Dusausoy, Annick, and Guy Fontaine. *History of European Literature.* Translated by Michael Wolff. London: Routledge, 2000.

Berlin, Norman. *Thomas Sackville.* New York: Twayne, 1974.

Berry, Edward I. *The Making of Sir Philip Sidney.* Toronto: University of Toronto Press, 1998.

Berthelot, Joseph A. *Michael Drayton.* New York: Twayne Publishers, 1967.

Best, Michael, ed. *The English Housewife.* Montreal: McGill-Queen's University Press, 1986.

Bevington, David, ed. *The Complete Works of Shakespeare,* 4th ed. New York: Longman/Addison-Wesley Educational Publishers, 1997.

Blain, Virginia, Patrician Clements, and Isobel Grundy, eds. *A Feminist Companion to Literature in English: Women Writers from the Middle Ages to the Present.* London: Blatsford, 1990.

Blank, Philip E. *Lyric Forms in the Sonnet Sequences of Barnabe Barnes.* The Hague: Mouton, 1974.

Boas, Frederick S., ed. *Giles and Phineas Fletcher: Poetical Works.* 1908. Reprint, Cambridge, U.K.: The University Press, 1969.

Bodin, Jean. *The Six Books of a Commonweale: A Facsimile Reprint of the English Translation of 1606.* Edited by Kenneth Douglas McRae. Cambridge, Mass.: Harvard University Press, 1962.

Booty, John E., David Siegenthaler, and John N. Wall, Jr., eds. *The Godly Kingdom of Tudor England.* Wilton, Conn.: Moreland-Barlow, 1981.

Bordinat, Philip, and Sophia B. Blaydes. *Sir William Davenant.* Boston: Twayne, 1981.

Bowen, Catherine Drinker. *Francis Bacon: The Temper of a Man.* Boston: Little, Brown, 1963.

Bradford, William. *Of Plymouth Plantation.* Edited by Samuel Eliot Morison. New York: Modern Library, 1967.

Brereton, Geoffrey. *Jean Racine: A Critical Biography.* London: Cassell, 1951.

Brown, Cedric C. *The Poems and Masques of Aurelian Townshend,* with music by Henry Lawes and William Webb. Reading, Berkshire, U.K.: Whiteknights Press, 1983.

Brown, Chris. *The Battle for Aberdeen, 1644.* Stroud, Gloucestershire, U.K.: Tempus, 2002.

Brown, Frank Clyde. *Elkanah Settle: His Life and Works.* Chicago: University of Chicago Press, 1910.

Brown, Stuart, trans. *Henry More (1614–1687): Tercentenary Studies.* Edited by Sarah Hutton. Boston: Kluwer Academic Publishers, 1990.

Brown, Sylvia, ed. *Women's Writing in Stuart England: The Mother's Legacies of Dorothy Leigh, Elizabeth Joscelin, and Elizabeth Richardson.* Thrupp, Stroud, Gloucester, U.K.: Sutton, 1999.

Browne, Thomas. *The Major Works.* Edited by C. A. Patrides. New York: Penguin, 1977.

Buchan, John. *Montrose: A History.* London: Hodder and Stoughton, 1938.

Bulgakov, Mikhail. *Monsieur de Molière.* New York: Funk & Wagnalls, 1970.

Bullough, Geoffrey. *Narrative and Dramatic Sources of Shakespeare.* New York: Columbia University Press, 1960.

Bunyan, John. *Pilgrim's Progress.* N. H. Keeble, ed. New York: Oxford University Press, 1984.

Burke, Mary E., et al., eds. *Women, Writing and the Reproduction of Culture in Tudor and Stuart Britain.* Syracuse, N.Y.: Syracuse University Press, 2000.

Burrage, Henry S. *Early English and French Voyages, Chiefly from Hakluyt,* 1534–1608. New York: Barnes & Noble, 1967.

Byrne, Muriel St. Clair, ed. *The Lisle Letters.* 6 vols. Chicago: University of Chicago Press, 1981.

Caldicott, C. *La Carriére de Moliére.* Amsterdam: Rodopi, 1998.

Canfield, Dorothea Frances. *Corneille and Racine in England: A Study of the English Translations of the Two Corneilles and Racine, with Especial Reference to Their Presentation on the English Stage.* New York: Macmillan, 1904.

Carey, Patrick W., and Joseph T. Lienhard, eds. *Biographical Dictionary of Christian Theologians.* Westport, Conn.: Greenwood Press, 2000.

Carroll, D. Allen, ed. *Skialetheia, or A Shadowe of Truth, in Certain Epigrams and Satyres.* Chapel Hill: University of North Carolina Press, 1974.

Carroll, Thomas K. *Wisdom and Wasteland: Jeremy Taylor in His Prose and Preaching Today.* Dublin: Four Courts, 2000.

Cascardi, Anthony J., ed. *The Cambridge Companion to Cervantes.* Cambridge, U.K.: Cambridge University Press, 2002.

Cassirer, Ernst. *The Platonic Renaissance in England.* Translated by James P. Pettegrove. Austin: University of Texas Press, 1953.

Castiglione, Baldesar. *The Courtier.* Translated by George Bull. London: Penguin, 1967.

Cawley, Robert Ralston, and George Yost, eds. *Studies in Sir Thomas Brown.* Eugene: University of Oregon Press, 1965.

Cecil, David, Lord. *Two Quiet Lives: Dorothy Osborne, Thomas Gray Century.* New York: Longman, 1992.

Cellier, Elizabeth. *Malice Defeated and The Matchless Rogue.* Intro. Anne Barbeau Gardiner. Los Angeles: William Andrews Clark Memorial Library, University of California, Los Angeles, 1988.

Cerasano, S. P., and Marion Wynne-Davies, eds. *Renaissance Drama by Women.* New York: Routledge, 1996.

Cervantes Saavedra, Miguel de. *The Adventures of Don Quixote.* Translated by J. M. Cohen. New York: Penguin, 1950.

———. *The Deceitful Marriage and Other Exemplary Novels.* Translated by Walter Starkie. New York: New American Library, 1963.

Chalmers, A., and D. P. French, eds. *Minor English Poets, 1660–1780.* Vol. 6. New York: Benjamin Blom, 1967.

Chamberlayne, William. *Loves' Victory; A Tragicomedy.* Edited by Charles M. Meschter. Bethlehem, Pa.: Bethlehem Printing, 1914.

———. *Pharonnida: An Heroic Poem in Five Books.* London: Pall Mall, 1820.

Chambers, E. K. *The Elizabethan Stage.* Oxford, U.K.: The Clarendon Press, 1967.

———, ed. *Aurelian Townshend's Poems and Masques.* Oxford, U.K.: Clarendon Press, 1912.

Chester, Allan G. *Hugh Latimer, Apostle to the English.* Philadelphia: University of Pennsylvania Press, 1954.

Chute, Marchette. *Shakespeare of London.* New York: Dutton, 1949.

Clark, John. *Bishop Gilbert Burnet as Educationist.* Aberdeen, Printed for the University, 1914.

Clark, Kenneth. *Leonardo Da Vinci: An Account of His Development as an Artist.* New York: The Macmillan Company, 1939.

Clarke, Danielle. *Isabella Whitney, Mary Sidney and Aemilia Lanyer: Renaissance Women Poets.* New York: Penguin Books, 2000.

Cleveland, John. *The Poems of John Cleveland.* Edited by Brian R. Morris and Eleanor Withington. Oxford, U.K.: Clarendon Press, 1967.

Colie, Rosalie. *Paradoxia Epidemica: The Renaissance Tradition of Paradox.* Princeton, N.J.: Princeton University Press, 1966.

Collinson, Patrick. *Godly People: Essays on English Protestantism and Puritanism.* London: Hambledon Press, 1983.

Conrad, Peter. *The Everyman History of Literature.* London: J. M. Dent, 1985.

Cook, Richard I. *Sir Samuel Garth*. Boston: Twayne, 1980.

Corgin, Peter, and Douglas Sedge, eds. *Three Jacobean Witchcraft Plays*, Wolfeboro, N.H.: Manchester University Press, 1986.

Cragg, Gerald R. *Freedom and Authority: A Study of English Thought in the Early Seventeenth Century*. London: Westminster Press, 1975.

Crandall, Coryl, ed. *Swetnam the Woman-hater: The Controversy and the Play*. Lafayette, Ind.: Purdue University Studies, 1969.

Cranfill, Thomas Mabry, and Dorothy Hart Bruce. *Barnaby Rich: A Short Biography*. Austin: University of Texas Press, 1953.

Cross, Wilbur L. *Development of the English Novel*. New York: The Macmillan Company, 1899.

Crum, Margaret, ed. *The Poems of Henry King*. Oxford, U.K.: The Clarendon Press, 1965.

Damrosch, Leopold, Jr. *God's Plot and Man's Stories: Studies in the Fictional Imagination from Milton to Fielding*. Chicago: University of Chicago Press, 1985.

Daniell, David. *William Tyndale: A Biography*. New Haven, Conn.: Yale University Press, 1994.

Darby, Harold S. *Hugh Latimer*. London: The Epworth Press, 1953.

Davis, Herbert, ed. *The Complete Plays of William Congreve*. Chicago: University of Chicago Press, 1967.

Day, Angel. *The English Secretary Or Methods of Writing Epistles and Letters with A Declaration of Such Tropes, Figures, and Schemes as either usually or for ornament sake are therein required*. Introduction by Robert O. Evans. 1599. Reprint, Gainesville, Fla.: Scholars' Facsimiles & Reprints, 1967.

Day, John. *The Blind Beggar of Bednall Green*. New York: AMS Press, 1970.

———. *The Isle of Gulls, a Critical Edition*. Edited by Raymond S. Burns. New York: Garland Publishing, 1980.

Delany, Veronica, ed. *The Poems of Patrick Cary*. New York: Clarendon Press, 1978.

DeMaus, Robert. *Hugh Latimer, A Biography*. London: The Religious Tract Society, 1881.

Denham, John. *The Poetical Works*. Edited by Theodore Howard Banks. Hamden, Conn.: Archon Books, 1969.

Descartes, René. *Discourse on Method and Meditations on First Philosophy*. Translated by Donald A. Cress. Indianapolis: Hackett Publishing Company, 1998.

De Sola Pinto, Vivian. *The English Renaissance, 1510–1688*. New York: Cresset Press, 1938.

———. *Sir Charles Sedley 1639–1701: A Study in the Life and Literature of the Restoration*. New York: Boni and Liverwright, 1927.

Dobin, Howard. *Merlin's Disciples*. Stanford, Calif.: Stanford University Press, 1990.

Docherty, Thomas. *John Donne, Undone*. New York: Methuen, 1986.

Dollimore, Jonathan. *Radical Tragedy*. 2d ed. Durham, N.C.: Duke University Press, 1993.

Doran, Susan, and Christopher Durston. *Princes, Pastors and People: The Church and Religion in England, 1529–1689*. London: Routledge, 1991.

Dryden, John. *Eighteenth-Century English Literature*. Edited by Geoffrey Tillotson et al. New York: Harcourt Brace Jovanovich, 1969.

Dryden, John. *John Dryden: The Oxford Authors*. Edited by Keith Walker. New York: Oxford University Press, 1987.

Dubinski, Roman R. *Alexander Brome: Poems*. Toronto: University of Toronto Press, 1982.

Dubrow, Heather. *Echoes of Desire: English Petrarchism and Its Counterdiscourses*. Ithaca, N.Y.: Cornell University Press, 1995.

Dugdale, Gilbert. *The True discourse of the Practices of Elizabeth Caldwell, Ma: Jeffrey Bownd, Isabell Hall widdow, and George Fernely, on the parson of Ma: Thomas Caldwell, in the county of Chester, to have murdered and poysoned him, with divers others*. London, 1604.

Duncan-Jones, Katherine, ed. *Sir Philip Sidney: A Critical Edition of the Major Works*. Oxford, U.K.: Oxford University Press, 1989.

Dunn, R. D., ed. *Remains Concerning Britain*. Toronto: University of Toronto Press, 1984.

Durant, Will. *The Story of Philosophy: The Lives and Opinions of the Great Philosophers of the Western World*. New York: Simon and Schuster, 1961.

Edmond, Mary. *Hilliard and Oliver: The Lives and Works of Two Great Miniaturists.* London: Robert Hale, 1983.

Eliot, T. S. *Selected Essays: 1917–1932.* New York: Harcourt, Brace and Company, 1932.

Elton, G. R. *Reform and Reformation: England, 1509–1558.* London: Edward Arnold, 1977.

Emerson, Everett. *Captain John Smith.* Rev. ed. New York: Twayne, 1993.

Espy, Willard R. *The Garden of Eloquence: A Rhetorical Bestiary.* New York: Harper & Row, 1983.

Evans, Maurice, ed. *Elizabethan Sonnets.* London: Everyman, 1996.

Evans, R. J. W. *The Making of the Hapsburg Monarchy, 1550–1700.* New York: Oxford University Press, 1979.

Eyre-Todd, George. *Scottish Poetry of the Sixteenth Century.* London: Sands & Company, 1892.

Fairfield, Leslie P. *John Bale, Mythmaker for the English Reformation West.* Lafayette, Ind.: Purdue University Press, 1976.

Felch, Susan M., ed. *The Collected Works of Anne Vaughan Lock.* Tempe: Arizona Center for Medieval and Renaissance Studies in Conjunction with Renaissance English Text Society, 1999.

Fellowes, Edmund H. *William Byrd.* 2d ed. London: Oxford University Press, 1948.

Fichter, Andrew. *Poets Historical: Dynastic Epic in the Renaissance.* New Haven, Conn.: Yale University Press, 1982.

Foxe, John. *The Acts and Monuments of the Church Containing the History and Sufferings of the Martyrs.* Edited by M. Hobart Seymour. New York: Robert Carter and Bros., 1855.

Fraser, Russell A., and Norman Rabkin, eds. *Drama of the English Renaissance.* Upper Saddle River, N.J.: Prentice Hall, 1976.

———. *Drama of the English Renaissance I: The Tudor Period.* New York: Macmillan, 1976.

Fyvie, John. *Noble Dames and Notable Men of the Gregorian Era.* New York: John Lane, 1911.

Gae, Holladay. *The Female Advocate: A Poem. Occasioned by Reading Mr. Duncome's Feminead.* Pasadena, Calif.: The Castle Press, 1984.

Gardiner, J. H. *The Bible as English Literature.* New York: C. Scribner's Sons, 1907.

Garnett, Richard, and Edmund Gosse. *English Literature: An Illustrated Record,* Vol. 2. New York: The Macmillan Company, 1904.

Gera, Deborah Levine. *Xenophon's Cyropaedia: Style, Genre, and Literary Technique.* Oxford, U.K.: Clarendon Press, 1993.

Gibbs, A. M., ed. *Sir William Davenant: The Shorter Poems, and Songs from the Plays and Masques.* Oxford, U.K.: Clarendon Press, 1972.

Gifford, Douglas, Sarah Dunnigan, and Alan MacGillivray, eds. *Scottish Literature.* Edinburgh: Edinburgh University Press, 2002.

Gilbert, Allan H. *Literary Criticism: Plato to Dryden.* Detroit: Wayne State University Press, 1962.

Godolphin, Sidney. *The Poems of Sidney Godolphin.* Edited by William Dighton. Oxford, U.K.: Clarendon Press, 1931.

Golding, Arthur. *The Fyrst Fower Bookes of P. Ouidius Nasos Worke, intitled Metamorphosis, translated oute of Latin into English meter.* London, 1565.

Golding, Louis Thorn. *An Elizabethan Puritan: Arthur Golding.* New York: R. R. Smith, 1937.

Googe, Barnabe. *Ecologues, Epitaphs and Sonnets.* Edited by Judith M. Kennedy. Toronto: University of Toronto Press, 1989.

———. *Selected Poems of Barnabe Googe.* Edited by Alan Stephens. Denver, Colo.: Books of the Renaissance Series, 1961.

Gorges, Arthur. *The Poems of Sir Arthur Gorges.* Edited by Helen Estabrook Sandison. Oxford, U.K.: Clarendon Press, 1953.

Gorst-Williams, Jessica. *Elizabeth, The Winter Queen.* London: Abelard, 1977.

Gosling, William Gilbert. *The Life of Sir Humphrey Gilbert: England's First Empire Builder.* London: Constable & Co., 1911.

Gosse, Edmund. *The Complete Works of Samuel Rowlands, 1598–1628.* Glasgow: Hunterian Club, 1880.

Gray, Charles Montgomery. *Hugh Latimer and the Sixteenth Century.* Cambridge, Mass.: Harvard University Press, 1950.

Greaves, Richard. *John Bunyan and English Nonconformity.* London: Hambledon Press, 1992.

Green, Ian M. *The Christian's ABC: Catechisms and Catechizing in England ca. 1530–1740.* Oxford, U.K.: Oxford University Press, 1996.

Greenblatt, Stephen. *Renaissance Self-Fashioning: From More to Shakespeare.* Chicago: University of Chicago Press, 1984.

———. *Shakespearean Negotiations.* Berkeley: University of California Press, 1988.

Greenblatt, Stephen J. *Sir Walter Ralegh: The Renaissance Man and His Roles.* New Haven, Conn.: Yale University Press, 1973.

Greene, Robert. *Greene's Groats-worth of Wit, Bought with a Million of Repentance.* Edited by D. Allen Carroll. Binghamton, N.Y.: Medieval and Renaissance Texts and Studies, 1994.

Greer, Germaine. *Kissing the Rod: An Anthology of Seventeenth-Century Women's Verse.* New York: Farrar, Straus & Giroux, 1988.

Gregory, Brad S. *Salvation at Stake: Christian Martyrdom in Early Modern Europe.* Cambridge, Mass.: Harvard University Press, 1999.

Grosholz, Emily R. *Cartesian Method and the Problem of Reduction.* Oxford, U.K.: Clarendon Press, 1991.

Grund, Gary R. *John Hoskyns, Elizabethan Rhetoric, and the Development of English Prose.* New York: Garland Publishing, Inc., 1987.

Guazzo, M. Stephan. *The Civile Conversation.* Translated by George Pettie. New York: AMS Press, 1967.

Gullans, Charles B., ed. *The English and Latin Poems of Sir Robert Ayton.* Edinburgh, London: William Blackwood & Sons, 1963.

Gurr, Andrew. *Playgoing in Shakespeare's London.* New York: Cambridge University Press, 1987.

Guy, John. *Thomas More.* London: Edward Arnold, 2000.

Hadfield, Andrew, ed. *Amazons, Savages, and Machiavels: Travel and Colonial Writing in English, 1550–1630: An Anthology.* New York: Oxford University Press, 2001.

Hadfield, Andrew, and Willy Maley, eds. *Edmund Spenser: A View of the State of Ireland from the First Pirated Edition.* 1633. Reprint, Malden, Mass.: Blackwell, 1997.

Haigh, Christopher. *English Reformations: Religion, Politics and Society under the Tudors.* Oxford, U.K.: Clarendon Press, 1993.

———. *Reformation and Resistance in Tudor Lancashire.* London: Cambridge University Press, 1975.

Halasz, Alexandra. *The Marketplace of Print: Pamphlets and the Public Sphere in Early Modern England.* Cambridge, U.K.: Cambridge University Press, 1997.

Halliday, F. E. *The Life of Shakespeare.* Baltimore, Md.: Penguin, 1961.

———. *A Shakespeare Companion: 1564–1964.* Baltimore, Md.: Penguin, 1964.

Hammond, Paul. *John Oldham and the Renewal of Classical Culture.* Cambridge, U.K.: Cambridge University Press, 1983.

Hammons, Pamela S. *Poetic Resistance: English Women Writers and the Early Modern Lyric.* Hampshire, U.K.: Ashgate Publishing Limited, 2002.

Hanning, Robert W. *Castiglione: The Ideal and the Real in Renaissance Culture.* New Haven, Conn.: Yale University Press, 1983.

Happe, Peter. *English Drama Before Shakespeare.* London, New York: Longman, 1999.

———. *John Bale.* New York: Twayne Publishers, 1996.

Happe, Peter, and John N. King, eds. *The Vocacyon of Johan Bale* Binghamton, N.Y.: Medieval and Renaissance Texts and Studies, 1990.

Hardin, Richard. *Michael Drayton and the Passing of Elizabethan England.* Lawrence: University of Kansas Press, 1973.

Harris, Jesse W. *John Bale: A Study in the Minor Literature of the Reformation.* West Lafayette, Ind.: Purdue University Press, 1976.

Harvey, Gabriel. *Elizabethan Critical Essays.* Edited by Gregory Smith. 1904. Reprint, Oxford, U.K.: Oxford University Press, 1937.

Hasan, Masoodul. *Francis Quarles, A Study of His Life and Poetry.* Aligarh, India: Aligarh Muslim University Press, 1966.

Hawcroft, Michael. *Word as Action; Racine, Rhetoric, and the Theatrical Language.* Oxford, U.K.: Oxford University Press, 1992.

Hayashi, Tetsumaro. *A Textual Study of Robert Greene's Orlando Furioso with an Elizabethan Text.* Muncie, Ind.: Ball State University Press, 1973.

Hayes, Wilson T. *Winstanley the Digger: A Literary Analysis of Radical Ideas in the English Revolution.* Cambridge, Mass.: Harvard University Press, 1979.

Head, Richard. *The English Rogue.* Boston: New Frontiers Press, 1961.

Hebel, J. William, and Hoyt H. Hudson, eds. *Poetry of the English Renaissance: 1509–1600.* New York: Appleton-Century-Croft, 1929.

Henderson, Katherine Usher, and Barbara F. McManus. *Half Humankind: Contexts and Texts of the Controversy about Women in England, 1540–1640.* Urbana: University of Illinois Press, 1985.

Herrick, James A. *The Radical Rhetoric of the English Deists: The Discourse of Skepticism, 1680–1750.* Columbia, S.C.: University of South Carolina Press, 1997.

Hill, Bridget. *The First English Feminist.* Aldershot, England: Gower Publishing, 1986.

Hill, Christopher. *The World Turned Upside Down: Radical Ideas During the English Revolution.* Middlesex, U.K.: Penguin Books, 1972.

Hill, W. Speed, ed. *New Ways of Looking at Old Texts, II: Papers of the Renaissance English Text Society, 1992–1996.* Tempe, Ariz.: Medieval & Renaissance Texts & Studies in conjunction with Renaissance English Text Society, 1998.

Hilliard, Nicholas. *A Treatise Concerning the Art of Limning.* Edited by R. K. R. Thornton and T. G. S. Cain. Manchester, U.K.: Carcanet Press, 1992.

Hind, Arthur. *Engraving in England in the Sixteenth & Seventeenth Centuries,* Vol. 2. Cambridge, U.K.: Cambridge University Press, 1955.

Hobbs, Mary, ed. *The Sermons of Henry King (1592–1669), Bishop of Chichester.* Rutherford, U.K.: Scolar Press, 1992.

Hoffman, Ann. *Lives of the Tudor Age, 1485–1603.* London: Osprey Press Ltd., 1977.

Hoffman, Arthur W. *John Dryden's Imagery.* Gainesville: University of Florida Press, 1962.

Hogrefe, Pearl. *Women of Action in Tudor England: Nine Biographical Sketches.* Ames: Iowa State University Press, 1977.

Holborn, Hajo. *A History of Modern Germany: The Reformation.* Princeton, N.J.: Princeton University Press, 1982.

Holinshed, Raphael. *Chronicles of England, Scotland and Ireland.* 6 vols. With new introduction by Vernon Shaw. 1807. Reprint, New York: AMS Press, 1976.

Holland, Richard. *The Buke of the Howlat.* Edited by David Laing. Edinburgh: James Ballantyne and Company, 1823.

Hollander, John, and Frank Kermode. *The Literature of Renaissance England.* New York: Oxford University Press, 1973.

Holman, Peter. *Dowland: Lachrimae.* 1604. Reprint, Cambridge, U.K.: Cambridge University Press, 1999.

Honigmann, E. A. J., ed. *Shakespeare and His Contemporaries: Essays in Comparison.* Manchester, U.K.: Manchester University Press, 1986.

Horne, Herbert, Havelock Ellis, Arthur Symons, and A. Wilson Verity, eds. *Nero and Other Plays.* The Mermaid Series. London: Vizetelly & Co., 1888.

Horwitz, Henry, ed. *The Parliamentary Diary of Narcissus Luttrell.* Oxford, U.K.: Clarendon Press, 1972.

Hosley, Richard. *Shakespeare's Holinshed: An Edition of Holinshed's Chronicles (1587).* New York: G.P. Putnam Sons, 1968.

Howarth, Jean. *The Stage and Social Struggle in Early Modern England.* New York: Routledge, 1994.

Howarth, W. D. *Molière, a Playwright and His Audience.* Cambridge, U.K.: Cambridge University Press, 1982.

Hoyles, John. *The Waning of the Renaissance 1640–1740: Studies in the Thought and Poetry of Henry More, John Norris and Isaac Watts.* International Archives of the History of Ideas. The Hague: Martinus Nijhoff, 1971.

Hubert, Judd. *Molière and The Comedy of Intellect.* Berkeley: University of California Press, 1962.

Hunt, Tristam. *The English Civil War: At First Hand.* London: Weidenfeld & Nicolson, 2002.

Hyland, Peter. *An Introduction to Shakespeare: The Dramatist in his Context.* New York: St. Martin's Press, 1996.

Ingrao, Charles. *The Hapsburg Monarchy, 1618–1815.* New York: Cambridge University Press, 1994.

Jack, Ian. *Augustan Satire: Intention and Idiom in English Poetry, 1660–1750.* Oxford, U.K.: Clarendon Press, 1952.

Jack, Ronald D. S. *Alexander Montgomerie.* Edinburgh: Scottish Academic Press, 1985.

Jacobus, Lee A. *John Cleveland.* Boston: Twayne Publishers, 1975.

Jardine, Lisa. *Wordly Goods: A New History of the Renaissance.* London: Macmillan, 1996.

Jesseph, D. M. *Squaring the Circle: The War between Hobbes and Wallis.* Chicago: University of Chicago Press, 1999.

John, Lisle Cecil. *The Elizabethan Sonnet Sequences: Studies in Conventional Conceits.* New York: Columbia University Press, 1966.

Johnson, Samuel. *Lives of the English Poets,* Vol. 1. Edited by L. Archer-Hind. London: Dent, 1964.

Jones, Michael K., and Malcolm G. Underwood. *The King's Mother: Lady Margaret Beaufort, Countess of Richmond and Derby.* Cambridge, U.K.: Cambridge University Press, 1992.

Jones, T. Canby, ed. *'The Power of the Lord Is Over All': The Pastoral Letters of George Fox.* Richmond, Ind.: Friends United Press, 1989.

Kaufmann, R. J. *Richard Brome: Caroline Playwright.* New York: Columbia University Press, 1961.

Kirby, Ethyn Williams. *William Prynne: A Study in Puritanism.* Cambridge, Mass.: Harvard University Press, 1931.

Kitchin, George. *A Survey of Burlesque and Parody in English.* Edinburgh: Oliver and Boyd, 1931.

Knott, John R. *Discourses of Martyrdom in English Literature, 1563–1694.* New York: Cambridge University Press, 1993.

Kolb, Robert. *For All the Saints: Changing Perceptions of Martyrdom and Sainthood in the Lutheran Reformation.* Macon, Ga.: Mercer University Press, 1987.

Kristeller, Paul Oscar. *Renaissance Concepts of Man and Other Essays.* New York: Harper & Row, 1972.
———. *Renaissance Thought.* New York: Harper Torchbooks, 1961.

Kunitz, Stanley J., and Howard Haycraft, eds. *British Authors Before 1800.* New York: H.W. Wilson Company, 1952.

Latham, Agnes. *Introduction to the Poems of Sir Walter Ralegh.* Cambridge, Mass.: Harvard University Press, 1951.

Latimer, Hugh. *Sermons and Remains George Elwes Corrie.* Cambridge, U.K.: Cambridge University Press, 1845.

Lea, Kathleen M. and T. M. Gang, eds. *Godfrey of Bulloigne: A Critical Edition of Edward Fairfax's Gerusalemme Liberata, Together with Fairfax's Original Poems.* Oxford, U.K.: Oxford University Press, 1981.

Lemay, J. A. Leo. *The American Dream of Captain John Smith.* Charlottesville: University of Virginia Press, 1991.

Leonardo Da Vinci. *The Mind of Leonardo Da Vinci.* Edited by Edward Mccurdy. New York: Dodd, Mead & Company, 1928.

Lewis, C. S. *English Literature in the Sixteenth Century, Excluding Drama.* New York: Oxford University Press, 1954.

Lindsey, Maurice. *History of Scottish Literature.* London: Robert Hale, Ltd., 1977.

Link, Frederick M. *Aphra Behn.* New York: Twayne, 1968.

Loftis, John, ed. *The Memoirs of Anne, Lady Halkett and Ann, Lady Fanshawe.* Oxford, U.K.: Clarendon Press, 1979.

Looney, J. Thomas, ed. *The Poems of Edward De Vere, Seventeenth Earl of Oxford.* London: C. Palmer, 1921.

Lord, George. *Complete Poetry of Andrew Marvell.* London: J. M. Dent & Sons, Ltd., 1984.

Ludlow, Edmund. *The Memoirs of Edmund Ludlow, Lieutenant-General of the Horse in the Army of the Commonwealth of England, 1625–1672.* Edited with Appendices of Letters and Illustrative

Documents by C. H. Firth. Oxford, U.K.: Clarendon Press, 1894.

Lyne, Raphael. *Ovid's Changing Worlds: English Metamorphoses, 1567–1632.* London: Oxford University Press, 2001.

MacQueen, John, ed. *Humanism in Renaissance Scotland.* Edinburgh: Edinburgh University Press, 1990.

Mair, G. H., ed. *Wilson's Arte of Rhetorique.* Oxford, U.K.: Oxford University Press, 1909.

Marlowe, Christopher. *The Complete Poems and Plays. By Christopher Marlowe.* Edited by E. D. Pendry, and J. C. Maxwell. London: J. M. Dent & Sons, 1976.

Martin, Randall, ed. *Women Writers in Renaissance England.* New York: Longman, 1997.

Marvell, Andrew. *The Complete Poems.* Edited by Elizabeth Donno. New York: Penguin, 1985.

McConica, James Kelsey. *English Humanists and Reformation Politics under Henry VIII and Edward VI.* Oxford, U.K.: The Clarendon Press, 1965.

McCrory, Donald. *No Ordinary Man: The Life and Times of Miguel de Cervantes.* London: P. Owen, 2002.

McCrum, Robert, William Cran, and Robert MacNeil. *The Story of English.* New York: Viking, 1986.

McDonald, Russ. *The Bedford Companion to Shakespeare.* New York: Bedford/St. Martin's, 1996.

McKisack, May. *Medieval History in the Tudor Age.* Oxford, U.K.: Clarendon Press, 1971.

McVeagh, John. *Thomas Durfey and Restoration Drama; The Work of a Forgotten Writer.* Burlington, Vt.: Ashgate, 2000.

Medine, Peter E. *Thomas Wilson.* Boston: Twayne Publishers, 1986.

Mendelson, Sara, and Patricia Crawford. *Women in Early Modern England 1550–1720.* Oxford, U.K.: Clarendon Press, 1998.

Meres, Francis. *From Palladis Tamia, Wit's Treasury in Elizabethan Critical Essays, Vol. 2.* Edited by Gregory Smith. Oxford, U.K.: Oxford University Press, 1937.

Merrill, L. R. *The Life and Poems of Nicholas Grimald.* New Haven, Conn.: Yale University Press, 1925.

Merritt, J. F., ed. *Imagining Early Modern London; Perception and Portrayals of the City from Stow to Strype, 1598–1720.* London: Cambridge University Press, 2001.

Middleton, Thomas. *A Game at Chess.* Edited by J. W. Harper. New York: Hill and Wang, 1967.

Miller, Naomi. *Changing the Subject: Mary Wroth and Figurations of Gender in Early Modern England.* Lexington: University of Kentucky Press, 1996.

Miller, Naomi, and Gary Waller, eds. *Reading Mary Wroth: Representing Alternatives in Early Modern England.* Knoxville: University of Tennessee Press, 1991.

Miller, Perry, ed. *The American Puritans, Their Prose and Poetry.* Garden City, N.Y.: Doubleday, 1956.

Miner, Earl. *The Cavalier Mode from Jonson to Cotton.* Princeton, N.J.: Princeton University Press, 1971.

———. *Dryden's Poetry.* Bloomington: Indiana University Press, 1967.

Mollineux, Mary. *Fruits of Retirement; or, Miscellaneous Poems, Moral and Divine.* Philadelphia: Samuel Keimes, 1729.

Montaigne, Michel de. *The Essays.* Translated by John Florio. Edited by Thomas Seccombe. London: Grant Richards, 1908.

———. *Selected Essays of Michel de Montaigne.* Translated by J. M. Cohen. New York: Penguin, 1958.

Montgomerie, Alexander. *Poems.* Edited by David J. Parkinson. Edinburgh: Scottish Text Society, 2000.

Moody, Joanna, ed. *The Private Life of an Elizabethan Lady: The Diary of Lady Margaret Hoby, 1599–1605.* Thrupp, U.K.: Sutton, 1998.

Morden, Robert. *The County Maps from William Camden's Britannia 1965 by Robert Morden; a Facsimile.* Newton Abbott, U.K.: J. David and Charles Reprints, 1972.

Morgan, Charlotte E. *The Rise of the Novel of Manners: A Study of English Prose Fiction Between 1600 and 1740.* New York: The Columbia University Press, 1911.

Morgan, Fidelis. *The Female Wits: Women Playwrights on the London Stage, 1660–1720.* London: Virago Press, 1989.

Morley, Thomas. *A Plain and Easy Introduction to Practical Music.* Edited by R. Alec Harman. London: J.M. Dent & Sons Ltd., 1952.

Motteux, Peter Anthony and John Eccles. *The Rape of Europa by Jupiter (1694) and Acis and Galatea (1701).* Introduction by Lucyle Hooke. Augustan Reprint Society: Los Angeles, 1981.

Mullaney, Steven. *The Place of the Stage: License, Play, and Power in Renaissance England.* Ann Arbor: University of Michigan Press, 1988.

Myers, Robin, and Michael Harris, eds. *The Stationers' Company and the Book Trade: 1550–1990.* New Castle, Del.: Oak Knoll, 1997.

Nash, Thomas. *Works.* Vol. 3. Edited by R. B. McKerrow. London: Sidgwick and Jackson, 1910.

Nashe, Thomas. "Strange News." In Prewitt, Kendrick W., and William Harvey. *The Circulation of The Blood and Other Writings.* Translated by Kenneth J. Franklin. Edited by Andrew Wear. London: Everyman, 1990.

Neil, Eric. *William Harvey and the Circulation of the Blood.* London: Priory Press, 1975.

Nenna, Giovanni Battista. *Nennio, or a Treatise of Nobility.* Translated by William Jones. Introduced by Alice Shalvi. 1595. Reprint, New York: Dodd, ca. 1880; Jerusalem: Israel University Press, 1967.

Nichols, John Gough, ed. *The Autobiography of Lady Anne Halkett.* Westminster: Nichols and Sons, 1876.

Nicolson, Adam. *God's Secretaries: The Making of the King James Bible.* New York: Harper Collins, 2003.

Nilsen, Don L. E. *Humor in British Literature, from the Middle Ages to the Restoration: A Reference Guide.* Westport, Conn.: Greenwood Press, 1997.

Norbrook, David. *Poetry and Politics in the English Renaissance.* Rev. ed. New York: Oxford University Press, 2002.

Norris, John. *An Account of Reason and Faith: In Relation to the Mysteries of Christianity.* London: S. Manship, 1697.

———. *Cursory Reflections on a Book Call'd, An Essay Concerning Human Understanding.* Los Angeles: University of California Press, 1961.

———. *Reflections Upon the Conduct of Human Life, With Reference to the Study of Learning and Knowledge.* London: S. Manship, 1691.

Novak, M. E. *William Congreve.* New York: Twayne, 1971.

O'Malley, Susan Gusheee, comp. and ed. *The Early Modern Englishwoman: A Facsimile Library of Essential Works.* Vol. 1, pt. 4. Aldershot, Hants, U.K.: Scolar Press, 1996.

Orr, John. *English Deism: Its Roots and its Fruits.* Grand Rapids, Mich.: Eerdmans, 1934.

Osborn, Louise Brown. *The Life, Letters, and Writings of John Hoskyns.* New Haven, Conn.: Yale University Press, 1937.

Osborne, Dorothy. *Letters to Sir William Temple.* Edited by Kenneth Parker. London, New York: Penguin Books, 1987.

———. *The Letters of Dorothy Osborne to Sir William Temple, 1652–1654.* Edited by Kingsley Hart. London: Folio Society, 1968.

Otis, William Bradley, and Morris H. Needleman. *A Survey-History of English Literature.* New York: Barnes & Noble Inc., 1938.

Otten, Charlotte F. *English Women's Voices 1540–1700.* Miami: Florida International University Press, 1992.

Palingenius, Marcellus. *The Zodiake of Life* (Zodiacus Vitae). Translated by Barnabe Googe. Edited by Rosemund Tuve. New York: Scholars Facsimiles and Reprints, 1947.

Parfitt, George. *English Poetry of the Seventeenth Century.* New York: Longman, 1992.

Parker, Patricia. *Shakespeare from the Margins: Language, Culture, Context.* Chicago: University of Chicago Press, 1996.

Parker, Tom W. N. *Proportional Form in the Sonnets of the Sidney Circle.* Oxford, U.K.: Clarendon, 1998.

Parkinson, John. *A Garden of Pleasant Flowers* (Paradisi in sole paradisus terrestris). New York: Dover, 1991.

Parr, Anthony, ed. *Three Renaissance Travel Plays.* New York: Revels Plays Companion Press, Manchester University Press, 1995.

Parsons, John Carmi, and Bonnie Wheeler, eds. *Medieval Mothering.* New York: Garland Press, 1996.

Patterson, Annabel. *Reading Holinshed's Chronicles.* Chicago: University of Chicago Press, 1994.

Pearce, Roy Harvey. *The Continuity of American Poetry.* Princeton, N.J.: Princeton University Press, 1961.

Pearl, Valerie. *London and the Outbreak of the Puritan Revolution: City Government and National Politics, 1625–43.* London: Oxford University Press, 1961.

Pebworth, Ted-Larry, and Claude J. Summers. *The Poems of Owen Felltham, 1604?–1668.* University Park, Pa.: University of Pennsylvania Press, 1973.

Peele, George. *Plays and Poems.* London: George Routledge and Sons, 1887.

Penninger, Frieda E. *William Caxton.* Boston: Twayne, 1979.

Perry, Henry Ten Eyck. *The Comic Spirit in Restoration Drama: Studies in the Comedy of Etherege, Wycherley, Congreve, Vanbrugh, and Farquhar.* New York: Russel & Russel, 1962.

Pliny, C. *The History of the World.* Translated by Philemon Holland. London: n.p., 1601.

Plumptre, D. D., E. H. *The Life of Thomas Ken, D. D. Bishop of Bath and Wells.* London: Wm. Isbuster, 1890.

Pocock, J. G. A. *The Ancient Constitution and the Feudal Law: A Study of English Historical Thought in the Seventeenth Century.* Cambridge, U.K.: Cambridge University Press, 1957.

Pooley, Roger. *English Prose of the 17th Century, 1590–1700.* New York: Longman, 1993.

Popkin, Richard H. *Great Thinkers of the Western World.* New York: HarperCollins, 1992.

Porter, Roy. *English Society in the Eighteenth Century.* London: Penguin, 1990.

Powicke, Frederick J. *The Cambridge Platonists: A Study.* Cambridge, Mass.: Harvard University Press, 1927.

Powys, Llewelyn. *The Life and Times of Anthony à Wood.* Edited by Andrew Clark. Oxford, U.K.: Clarendon Press, 1900.

Prouty, Charles T. *George Gascoigne: Elizabethan Courtier, Soldier, and Poet.* New York: Columbia University Press, 1942.

Purcell, Sally. *George Peele.* Manchester, U.K.: Carcanet Press, 1972.

Purkiss, Diane. *Three Tragedies by Renaissance Women.* London, New York: Penguin, 1998.

Puttenham, George. *The Arte of English Poesie in Elizabethan Critical Essays.* Edited by Gregory Smith. Oxford, U.K.: Oxford University Press, 1937.

Rackin, Phyllis. *The Stages of History: Shakespeare's English Chronicles.* Ithaca, N.Y.: Cornell University Press, 1990.

Randolph, Thomas. *Poetical and Dramatic Works.* Edited by W. C. Hazlitt. London: Reeves and Turner, 1875.

Rees, Joan. *Fulke Greville, Lord Brooke, 1554–1628.* Berkeley: University of California Press, 1971.

Reynolds, Henry. *Mythomystes: Wherein A Short Survay Is Taken Of The Natvre And Valve Of Trve Poesy And Depth Of The Ancients Above Ovr Moderne Poets, To which is annexed the Tale of Narcissues briefly mythologized.* London: Henry Seyle, 1632.

———. *Tasso's Aminta and Other Poems.* Edited by Glyn Pursglove. Lewiston, N.Y.: Edwin Mellen Press, 1991.

Rhu, Lawrence F. *The Genesis of Tasso's Narrative Poetry: English Translations of the Early Poetics and a Comparative Study of Their Significance.* Detroit: Wayne State University Press, 1993.

Rhys, Ernest, ed. *Holinshed Chronicle as Used in Shakespeare's Plays.* New York: E.P. Dutton, 1927.

Riche, Barnabe, *Barnabe Richee: His Farewell to Military Profession.* Edited by Donald Beecher. Ottawa, Canada: Dovehouse, 1992.

———. *The Excellency of Good Women.* London: Thomas Dawson, 1613.

———. *My Ladies Looking Glasse.* London: John Legat for Thomas Adams, 1616.

———. *A Path-way to Military Practice.* London: John Charlewood for Robert Walley, 1587.

Riley, E. C. *Cervantes's Theory of the Novel.* Newark, Del.: Juan de la Cuesta, 1992.

Roberts, Josephine. *The Countess of Montgomerie's Urania.* Binghamton, N.Y.: Center for Medieval and Early Renaissance Studies, 1995.

———. *The Poems of Lady Mary Wroth.* Baton Rouge: Louisiana State University Press, 1983.

Rogers, John. *The Matter of Revolution: Science, Poetry, and Politics in the Age of Milton.* Ithaca, N.Y.: Cornell University Press, 1996.

Rojas, Fernando de. *Celestina.* Edited by James Mabbe. 1631. Reprint, Warminster, Wiltshire, U.K.: Aris & Phillips, 1987.

Rosenblum, Joseph, ed. *MacGill's Choice: Shakespeare.* Pasadena, Calif.: Salem Press, 1998.

Ross, Josephine. *The Winter Queen: The Story of Elizabeth Stuart.* New York: St. Martin's Press, 1979.

Rowlands, Samuel. *Uncollected Poems, 1604–1617.* Gainesville, Fla.: Scholar Reprints, 1970.

Rowley, Samuel. *When You See Me, You Know Me.* Edited by F. P. Wilson. London: Malone Society, 1952.

Rump, Eric S., ed. *The Comedies of William Congreve, 1670–1729.* New York: Penguin, 1985.

Ruoff, James E. *Crowell's Handbook of Elizabethan and Stuart Literature.* New York: Thomas Y. Crowell Company, 1975.

Ryan, Lawrence V. *Roger Ascham.* Stanford, Calif.: Stanford University Press, 1963.

Saffar, Ruth El., ed. *Critical Essays on Cervantes.* Boston: G.K. Hall & Company, 1986.

Sage, Lorna. *The Cambridge Guide to Women's Writing in English.* New York: Cambridge University Press, 1999.

St. Clair, William, and Irngard Maassen, eds. *Conduct Literature for Women, 1640–1710.* London: Pickering, 2002.

Saintsbury, George. *A History of Elizabethan Literature.* London: Macmillan, 1887.

Salzman, Paul. *English Prose Fiction, 1558–1700: A Critical History.* New York: Oxford University Press, 1984.

Savage, E. James, ed. *The Conceited Newes of Sir Thomas Overbury And His Friends: A Facsimile Reproduction of the Ninth Impression of 1616 of Sir Thomas Overbury His Wife.* Gainesville, Fla.: Scholar Reprints, 1968.

Savile, George. *The Works of George Savile, Marquis of Halifax.* 3 vols. Edited by Mark N. Brown. Oxford, U.K.: Clarendon Press, 1989.

Sawday, Jonathan. *The Body Emblazoned.* London: Routledge, 1995.

Schelling, Felix E. *Elizabethan Drama, 1558–1642.* New York: Russell & Russell, Inc., 1959.

Schilling, Bernard N. *Dryden: A Collection of Critical Essays.* Englewood Cliffs, N.J.: Prentice-Hall, 1963.

Schoeck, Richard J. *The Achievement of Thomas More: Aspects of his Life and Works.* Victoria, B.C.: English Literary Studies, University of Victoria, 1976.

Schofield, Mary Anne, and Cecilia MacHeski. *Fetter'd or Free: British Women Novelists, 1670–1815.* Athens: Ohio University Press, 1986.

Scholes, Percy A. *The Life and Activities of Sir John Hawkins: Musician, Magistrate, and Friend of Johnson.* New York: DaCapo Press, 1953.

Schulman, George M. *Radicalism and Reverence: The Political Thought of Gerrard Winstanley.* Berkeley: University of California Press, 1989.

Scot, Reginald. *The Discovery of Witchcraft.* Carbondale: Southern Illinois University Press, 1964.

Scott, George Walton. *Robert Herrick: The Life of a Poet, 1591–1674.* New York: St. Martin's Press, 1974.

Scott, Virginia. *Molière.* Cambridge, U.K.: Cambridge University Press, 2000.

Sedley, Charles. *The Poetical and Dramatic Works of Sir Charles Sedley.* Edited by V. Sola de Pinto. London: Constable and Company, 1928.

Sena, Joseph F. *The Best-Natured Man: Sir Samuel Garth, Physician and Poet.* New York: AMS Press, 1986.

Seng, Peter J. *The Vocal Songs in the Plays of Shakespeare.* Cambridge, Mass.: Harvard University Press, 1967.

Senn, Werner. *Studies in the Dramatic Construction of Robert Greene and George Peele.* Bern: Francke, 1973.

Shakespeare, William. *Hamlet Prince of Denmark.* Edited by William Farnman. Baltimore, Md.: Penguin Books, 1971.

———. *King Henry IV Part I.* Edited by A. R. Humphreys. London: Routledge, 1989.

———. *Macbeth.* Edited by Alfred Harbage. Baltimore, Md.: 1971.

———. *Much Ado About Nothing.* Edited by Peter Holland. New York: Penguin Putnam, 1999.

————. *Twelfth Night.* Cambridge, U.K.: Cambridge University Press, 1985.

Sheidley, William E. *Barnabe Googe.* Boston: G.K. Hall & Co., 1981.

Sherman, William H. *John Dee: The Politics of Reading and Writing in the English Renaissance.* Amherst: University of Massachusetts Press, 1995.

Sidney, Mary. *The Collected Works by Mary Sidney Herbert, Countess of Pembroke.* Edited by Margaret P. Hannay, Noel J. Kinnamon, and Michael G. Brennan. Oxford, U.K.: Clarendon Press, 1998.

Silvete, Herbert. *Catalogue of the Works of Philemon Holland of Coventry, Doctor of Physick, 1600–1940.* Charlottesville, Va.: University of Virginia Press, J. S. Peters, 1940.

Simon, Linda. *Of Virtue Rare: Margaret Beaufort, Matriarch of the House of Tudor.* Boston: Houghton Mifflin, 1982.

Smith, Barbara, and Ursula Appelt, eds. *Write or Be Written: Early Modern Women Poets and Cultural Constraints.* Burlington, Vt.: Ashgate, 2001.

Smith, John. *The General History of Virginia, New England, and the Summer Isles.* Introduction by A. L. Rowse. Cleveland, Ohio: The World Publishing Company, 1966.

Smith, Lacey Baldwin. *Fools, Martyrs, Traitors: The Story of Martyrdom in the Western World.* New York: Knopf, 1997.

Smith, Robinson. *The Life of Cervantes.* London: George Routledge & Sons Limited, 1914.

Sorley, W. R. *A History of English Philosophy.* Cambridge, U.K.: Cambridge University Press, 1920.

Spedding, J. *Works of Francis Bacon.* London: Longman, 1858–74.

Speght, Rachel. *The Polemics and Poems of Rachel Speght.* Edited by Barbara Kiefer. New York: Oxford University Press, 1996.

Spellman, W. M. *John Locke and the Problem of Depravity.* Oxford, U.K.: Oxford University Press, 1988.

Spencer, Jane. *The Rise of the Woman Novelist; From Aphra Behn to Jane Austen.* Oxford, U.K.: Basil Blackwell, 1986.

Sprague, Richard S., ed. *The Rule of Reason Conteinyng the Arte of Logique.* Northridge, Calif.: San Fernando Valley State College, 1972.

Squier, Charles L. *Sir John Suckling.* Boston: Twayne, 1978.

Stanwood, P. G. *Izaak Walton.* New York: Twayne, 1998.

Steeves, Edna L., ed. *The Plays of Mary Pix and Catherine Trotter.* New York: Garland, 1982.

Stevenson, Jane, and Peter Davidson, eds. *Early Modern Women Poets: An Anthology.* New York: Oxford University Press, 2001.

Stewart, Alan. *Philip Sidney: A Double Life.* London: Chatto & Windus, 2000.

Stewart, Stanley. *George Herbert.* Boston: Twayne, 1986.

Stone, Lawrence. *The Family, Sex and Marriage in England, 1500–1800.* New York: Harper and Row, 1977.

Stow, John. *An Accurate Edition of Stow's Survey of London.* John Strype, ed. London: n.p., 1720.

————. *The Survey of London.* Edited by Henry B. Wheatley. London: J. M. Dent & Sons, 1929.

Strype, John. *Life and Times of John Aylmer, Lord Bishop of London.* London: n.p., 1701.

Sykes, Henry Dugdale. *The Authorship of "The Taming of a Shrew," "The Famous Victories of Henry V," and the Additions to Marlowe's "Faustus."* London: Chatto and Windus, 1920.

Taaffe, James G. *Abraham Cowley.* New York: Twayne Publishers, 1972.

Tasso, Torquato. *Aminta, Englisht. The Henry Reynolds Translation.* Edited by Clifford Davidson. Fennimore, Wis.: John Westburg & Associates, 1972.

Taufer, Alison. *Holinshed's Chronicles.* New York: Twayne Publishers, 1999.

Taylor, Edward. *The Poems of Edward Taylor.* Edited by Donald E. Stanford. New Haven, Conn.: Yale University Press, 1960.

Taylor, Gary. *Reinventing Shakespeare: A Cultural History from the Restoration to the Present.* Oxford, U.K.: Oxford University Press, 1989.

Teague, Frances, ed. *Bathsua Makin, Woman of Learning.* Lewisburg, Pa.: Bucknell University Press, 1998.

———. *The Early Modern Englishwoman: A Facsimile Library of Essential Works.* Aldershot, U.K.: Ashgate, 2001.

Thompson, Elbert N. S. *Literary Bypaths of the Renaissance.* New York: Books for Libraries Press, Inc., 1968.

Thorndike, Ashley, ed. *Minor Elizabethan Drama.* London: Dent, 1958.

Tilley, Morris Palmer. *Elizabethan Proverb Lore in Lyly's Euphues and in Pettie's Petite Pallace.* New York: McMillan, 1926.

Todd, Janet, ed. *British Women Writers: A Critical Reference Guide.* New York: Continuum Publishing, 1989.

———. *The Sign of Anglica: Women, Writing and Fiction, 1660–1800.* New York: Columbia University Press, 1989.

Toland, John. *John Toland's Christianity Not Mysterious: Text, Associated Works and Critical Essays.* Edited by Philip McGuinness, Alan Harrison, and Richard Kearney. Dublin: Lilliput Press, 1997.

Travitsky, Betty S., ed. *The Paradise of Women Writings by Englishwomen of the Renaissance.* Westport, Conn.: Greenwood Press, 1981.

Travitsky, Betty S., and Patrick Cullen, eds. *The Early Modern Englishwoman: A Facsimile Library of Essential Works; Series 1, Printed Writings 1500–1640: Part 2; Volume 10.* Ashgate, Hants, U.K., and Burlington, Vt.: Aldershot, 2001.

Travitsky, Betty S., and Anne Lake Prescott, eds. *Female and Male Voices in Early Modern England: An Anthology of Renaissance Writing.* New York: Columbia University Press, 2000.

Trevor-Roper, H. R. *Queen Elizabeth's First Historian: William Camden and the Beginnings of English 'Civil History.'* London: Cape, 1971.

Tupper, Frederick and James W. Tupper. *Representative English Drama from Dryden to Sheridan.* New York: Oxford University Press, 1914.

Turner, Celeste. *Anthony Mundy: An Elizabethan Man of Letters.* Berkeley: University of California Press, 1928.

Tuve, Rosemond. *Elizabethan and Metaphysical Imagery.* Chicago: The University of Chicago Press, 1947.

Tydeman, William, ed. *Two Tudor Tragedies.* New York: Penguin Books, 1992.

Tyler, Moses Coit. *A History of American Literature, 1607–1765.* Ithaca, N.Y.: Cornell University Press, 1949.

Uhler, John Earle. *Morley's Canzonets for Three Voices.* Baton Rouge: Louisiana State University Press, 1957.

Untermeyer, Louis. *Lives of the Poets: The Story of One Thousand Years of English and American Poetry.* New York: Simon & Schuster, 1959.

Vitkus, Daniel J., ed. *Three Turk Plays from Early Modern England:* Selimus, A Christian Turned Turk, *and* The Renegado. New York: Columbia University Press, 2000.

Vonalt, Larry P., ed. *The Poems of Lord Vaux.* Denver, Colo.: A Swallow, 1960.

Wagner, John A. *Historical Dictionary of the Elizabethan World: Britain, Ireland, Europe, and America.* Phoenix, Ariz.: Oryx Press, 1999.

Wain, John, ed. *The Oxford Anthology of English Poetry.* Vol. 1. Oxford, U.K.: Oxford University Press, 1990.

Waite, Arthur Edward. *The Magical Writings of Thomas Vaughan.* London: G. Redway, 1888.

Walker, Hallam. *Molière.* Boston: Twayne, 1990.

Walker, Hugh. *English Satire and Satirists.* London: J.M. Dent & Sons Ltd., 1925.

Walker, Kim. *Women Writers of the English Renaissance.* New York: Twayne, 1996.

Wall, Wendy. *Staging Domesticity: Household Work and English Identity in Early Modern Drama.* Cambridge, U.K.: Cambridge University Press, 2002.

Waller, Gary, ed. *The Early Modern Englishwoman: A Facsimile Library of Essential Works,* Vol. 6. Aldershot, Hants, U.K.: Scolar Press, 1996.

Walton, Izaak. *The Compleat Angler, or, the Contemplative Man's Recreation.* Modern Library Paperback, Charles Colton, ed. New York: Modern Library, 1998.

Wanley, Nathaniel. *The Poems of Nathaniel Wanley.* Edited by L. C. Martin. Oxford, U.K.: Clarendon Press, 1928.

Ward, Richard. *The Life of Henry More.* Edited by Cecil Courtney, et. al. Boston: Kluwer Academic, 2000.

Ware, James. *The Antiquities and History of Ireland, by the Right Honourable Sir James Ware, knt. Now First Published in One Volume in English; and the Life of Sir James Ware Prefixed.* Dublin: A. Crook, 1705.

———. *The Historie of Ireland, Collected by Three Learned Authors viz. Meredith Hanmer . . . Edmund Campion . . . and Edmund Spenser.* Dublin: The Societie of Stationers, 1630.

Warnicke, Retha M. *The Rise and Fall of Anne Boleyn: Family Politics at the Court of Henry VIII.* New York: Cambridge University Press, 1989.

Wasserman, George. *John Dryden (1631–1700).* New York: Twayne, 1964.

Weamys, Anna. *A Continuation of Sir Philip Sidney's Arcadia.* Edited by Patrick Colborn Cullen. New York: Oxford University Press, 1994.

Wedgwood, C. V. *Montrose.* New York: St. Martin's Press, 1995.

Weiger, John G. *The Substance of Cervantes.* Cambridge, U.K.: Cambridge University Press, 1985.

Wentworth, Anne. "Anne Wentworth to the King." Letter in Calendar of State Papers Domestic. 31 July 1677. Edited by F. H. Blackburne Daniell. London: His Majesty's Stationery Office, 1911. 279.

———. *The Revelation of Jesus Christ.* London, 1679.

White, Helen C. *The Metaphysical Poets.* New York: Collier, 1936.

Whitlock, Baird W. *John Hoskyns, Serjeant-at-Law.* Washington, D.C.: University Press of America, 1982.

Williams, George Walton, ed. *Thomas Middleton and William Rowley.* Lincoln: University of Nebraska Press, 1966.

Williams, William Proctor. *Jeremy Taylor, 1700–1976: An Annotated Checklist.* New York: Garland Press, 1979.

Wilson, Derek. *In The Lion's Court: Power, Ambition and Sudden Death in the Court of Henry VIII.* London: Hutchinson, 2001.

———. *A Tudor Tapestry: Men, Women and Society in Reformation England.* Pittsburgh, Pa.: University of Pittsburgh Press, 1972.

Wolfe, Heather, ed. *Elizabeth Cary, Lady Falkland: Life and Letters.* Cambridge, U.K.: RTM Publications, 2001.

Woods, Susanne, and Margaret P. Hannay, eds. *Teaching Tudor and Stuart Women Writers.* New York: The Modern Language Association, 2000.

Woolf, Virginia. *The Common Reader.* London: The Hogarth Press, 1986.

Wright, C. J. *Sir Robert Cotton as Collector: Essays on an Early Stuart Courtier and His Legacy.* Cambridge, U.K.: Cambridge University Press, 1997.

Wright, Herbert G. *Boccaccio in England, from Chaucer to Tennyson.* Fair Lawn, N.J.: Essential Books, 1957.

Wynne-Davies, Marion, ed. *Women Poets of the Renaissance.* New York: Routledge, 1999.

Young, Alan R. *Henry Peacham.* Boston: Twayne, 1979.

INDEX

Boldface page numbers denote main entries in the encyclopedia.

A

Abdelazer (Behn) 29
Abell, William 26
About Famous Women (Boccaccio) 37
About the Fortunes of Illustrious Men (Boccaccio) 37
Abrams, M. H. 99
Absalom and Achitophel (Dryden) 54, 127, 128, 349–350
Abuses Stript and Whipt (Wither) 430
The Accomplisht Lady's Delight (Woolley) 431
An Account of Reason and Faith (Norris) 296
An Accurate Edition of Stow's Survey of London (Strype) 376–377
Achinstein, Sharon 280, 281
Act(s) of Supremacy (1534, 1559) viii, 85
Act(s) of Uniformity (1559, 1662) 85, 393
actors and actresses 6, 34, 82, 152, 171–172, 203, 229, 230, 278–280, 309, 341–342, 351, 428. See also The Admiral's Men; The Chamberlain's Men; Earl of Leicester's Men; The King's Men; Prince Henry's Men; The Queen's Men
Acts and Monuments (Foxe) 9, 161–162, 265
Acts of Conference in Religion (Fenton, trans.) 151
Adagia (Erasmus) 139
Adams, Martin 36
Addison, Joseph 92, 334, 407
The Admiral's Men 1, 82, 258, 273, 310, 341
"An Admonition to al yong Gentilwomen" (Whitney) 425
"Adonais" (Shelley) 370
The Adoration of the Magi (Leonardo da Vinci) 239

Advancement of Learning (Bacon) 17
The Adventures of Master F. J. (Gascoigne) 166–167
The Aeneid (Virgil) xi, 96, 121–122, 334, 346, 371, 374, 381–382, 388, 425
Aerius Redivivus (Heylyn) 202
Aeschylus 322
Aesculapius (Walsh) 414
Aesop 77, 240, 391
Aethiopica (Heliodorus) 81
Æthiopian Historie (Heliodorus) 361
The Affectionate Shepherd (Barnfield) 24
"Against Flauius" (Davies) 108
"Against the Thievis of Lissidall" (Maitland) 255
"The Aged Lover Renounceth Love" (Vaux) 410
Aglaura (Suckling) 380
Agreement of the People (1647) 241
Aiton, Robert. See Ayto(u)n, Sir Robert
Alabaster, William 1–2
Alaham (Greville) 178
An Alarm to the Unconverted (Alleine) 3
Alba (Burton) 57
Alberti, Leon Battista 333
Albion's England (Warner) 418
Albions Triumph (Townshend) 396
The Alchemist (Jonson) 223, 224
Alcibiades (Otway) 300
Aldrich-Watson, Deborah 160
Alemán, Mateo 253
Alençon, duc d' See Charles III (duc d' Alençon)
Alexander VI (pope) 23
Alexander, William 2–3, 13
"Alexandreis" (Killigrew) 227–228
Alfonso I (duke of Ferrara) 5
Alfonso II (duke d'Este) 387
Alington, Alice 339

Allegory of War and Peace (Rubens) 343
Alleine, Joseph 3
Alleine, Theodosia 3
Allen, Thomas 116
Alleyn, Edward 1, 310
All for Love (Dryden) 127
"All in a garden green" (Howell) 215
Allot, Robert 183
Allott, Kenneth 183
Allott, Robert 422
All's Lost by Lust (Rowley) 342
All's Well That Ends Well (Shakespeare) 37, 305
All the Workes of John Taylor (Taylor) 390
"Alphabet" (Wanley) 416
Alphonsus of Aragon (Greene) 177
Alssid, Michael W. 350
"The Altar" (Herbert) 198–199
Amadis of Gaul (Rodriguez de Montalvo) 289
Amendments of Mr. Collier's False and Imperfect Citations (Congreve) 91
Amends for Ladies (Field) 152
Ames, Russell A. 286
Aminta (Tasso) 334, 387, 418
Amores (Ovid) 117
Amoretti (Spenser) 369
Amours de Cassandre (Ronsard) 337
Amphion Anglicus (Blow) 36
Amusements Serious and Comical (Brown) 49
Amyntas (Randolph) 331
Amyntor (Toland) 394
Amyot, Jacques 110, 297
Angluera, Peitro d' 134
An Answer to the First Part of a Certain Conference (Hayward) 195
Anatomical Exercises (Harvey) 192–193
Anatomie of Absurditie (Nashe) 379
The Anatomie of Abuses (Stubbes) 378–379
The Anatomy of Fair Writing (Davies) 109